THE ITV
ENCYCLOPEDIA
OF ADVENTURE

DAVE ROGERS

THE ITV ENCYCLOPEDIA OF ADVENTURE

DAVE ROGERS

TV Times

First published in 1988 by Boxtree Limited
© Dave Rogers 1988

ISBN   1 85283 205 3 hb
        1 85283 217 7 pb

Designed by Groom and Pickerill
Typeset by York House Typographic
Printed and bound in Great Britain by
Butler & Tanner Ltd, Frome and London
for Boxtree Limited
36 Tavistock Street
London
WC2E 7PB

Published in association with
Independent Television Publications Ltd

CONTENTS

Acknowledgements

Without the help and interest of the people and organisations named, this attempt to rectify the dearth of published material relating to popular television productions (both ancient and modern) would have been doomed to failure. The task of cross–referencing each entry was made much simpler by their cordial (and invaluable) help. To all, the author expresses his sincere thanks.

INDIVIDUALS
Graham P. Williams, who single–handedly solved many of the production 'location' venues. Pauline and Geoff Barlow (Queensland, Australia) for their documentation relating to 'archive' material. Sue Copeland. Carl Brookes. Roger and Karen Langley. The 'Five Musketeers': Neil Alsop, Andrew Pixley, Tony McKay, Michael Richardson and Tony Mechele, who came to the aid of the party with unselfish support. The Brookes family (Josie, Lewis and Carl) for the B/B (and putting up with the reams of paperwork). Stephen and Joy Curry, for their unfailing support.

ORGANISATIONS
Colin Bayley, of 'The Place', Wolverhampton. Kath and Bob Smart, of 'Fantasy World', Hanley. Martin Bigham, John Herron, Ray Jenkins, Vicky Hillard, and Jim Tong of the Weintraub Entertainment Group. Peter Bell, Rosane Chapman and Desi Maxim of Thames TV. Jonathan Masters, Trevor Poppell, John D. Hamilton and Julie Burnell of LWT TV. Don Mead, Roger Caton and Shelia Morgan of ITC. The Press Office staff of HTV West, and in particular, Richard Everitt, Michael Cox, Howard Baker, Derek Bennett and Kate Raphael of Granada TV.

For the photographs I wish to thank: Jack Breckon of Thames TV. Sue Godbert and Brassett of LWT TV. Joan Riley of Granada TV. Mike Lane of HTV. Tony Nutley of TVS TV. Don Mead of ITC. The *TV Times*.

Sources of research: TV Times. Time Screen Magazine. Number Six (The Prisoner Society). *The Avengers, The Avengers Anew, The Complete Professionals* (by guess who?)

Finally, I wish to express my warmest thanks to my wife Celia, daughter Leah and mum Annie, for putting up with my long bouts of absence during the initial research period and constant clatter of the typewriter keys during the months spent preparing the typescript. A special vote of thanks is due to my publisher for having faith in the product.

This volume is respectfully dedicated to the memory of my late friend, Bud Payton. Without his guidance and fortitude, none of this would have proved possible.

PREFACE

Ever since that 'little black box in the corner' first entered our lives and made such a resounding impact on the popular entertainments industry by providing each of us with an escape route from our humdrum nine–to–five workaday existence, 'heroes', be they of the special agent, private eye, undercover spy or medieval knight variety, have always shared an all–embracing love affair with the television viewer.

A glance at the television ratings chart will confirm that they also make their presence felt with a top–five placing. Some, like *The Prisoner* and *The Avengers,* have passed into television's Hall of Fame as classics of the genre, while others, *The Adventures of Robin Hood, The Saint* (to name but two of many) and the strings–attached antics of the Gerry Anderson puppet creations, continue to delight millions of viewers across the world decades *after* they were first transmitted.

That said, the question begs why?

The answer isn't really that surprising. Throughout history, heroes have always provided a source of entertainment to the popular masses. Whether their origins lay on the printed page, were beamed to millions of listeners on radio, or entranced us on the cinema screen, special agents, private eyes and so on, came to symbolise what each of us would like to be: the dashing knight in shining armour who rides his white charger into enemy–held territory to rescue the damsel in distress, then rides off into the sunset and romance; the super cool (sometimes superhuman) undercover agent who never loses a battle against some evil mastermind who had plotted an outlandish scheme to enslave mankind; the outer space hero who dares to go 'where no man has gone before'. Who among us *hasn't* wished to share their adventures at sometime in our lives?

The entry material in this book will provide you with the opportunity to recapture those never–to–be–forgotten moments and relive once again the adventures of your favourite hero. Included in these pages, is a comprehensive reference to every thriller, cops and robbers, private eye, secret agent, spy and science–fiction hero ever to grace the ITV network since the Independent channel made its debut on Thursday, 22 September 1955 – the majority of which have never previously been obtainable in one handy volume.

What you *won't* find are programmes screened by the BBC (perhaps that will come later?) or programmes of foreign origin. The sole purpose of this volume is to pay a long–overdue tribute to the wealth of popular television material that was produced *exclusively* in Britain which has long since convinced the American programme buyers that the quality of material produced in the UK is equal to, and indeed, in some cases, surpasses the standard of those made in the USA. (Anyone wishing to pursue their interest in imported series can easily do so by purchasing a copy of any number of excellent books published on the subject).

Researching material for a book of this nature wasn't, of course, without its drawbacks. Many of the programmes covered were produced during the days when independent television was in its infancy and few or, in some cases, no production documents remain available for perusal. It follows, therefore, that a few entries are incomplete, though these are in the minority and are conspicuous by their scarcity! In every case, the entries given are based on information supplied directly from the companies responsible for producing the programme under review and can therefore be taken as historically correct. Preparing this volume left me entirely dependent on the good nature of such people. Fortunately, of those I contacted for aid, the majority came through with flying colours and were delighted to help ensure that the entries reflected a true picture of their products' historical position in the chronology of British television. In the light of those who couldn't help, my own jottings and reference material, written and amassed over years of my own (ongoing) love affair with television, proved more than sufficient to fill the missing gaps.

All comments contained in the entry format are my own and should be viewed in that light. The purpose of this volume is *not* to award brickbats or bouquets, but to celebrate what many believe to be the best television in the world, and in particular, those programmes made during the 'golden years' of British television, 1958 – 1973.

My work is done. The results of my labours here to see. Yours is just beginning. Happy reading.

Dave Rogers
December 1987

ENTRY FORMAT

To facilitate easy reference, each entry spans *one programme in its entirety*
as denoted in the following example:
Programme Title: THE AVENGERS
Followed by a format appraisal and resident cast list:
[*John Steed played by* **Patrick Macnee**
Emma Peel ... **Diana Rigg**]

Season One
26 monochrome 60–minute episodes

Total number of episodes that made up *one complete transmission run.*
Produced in monochrome or colour. Duration of story (based upon
a commercial network one–hour/30–minute time slot.)
Where applicable, this is preceded by *Season One*
to denote the number of seasons spanned by each entry.

Episode title and author:

Hot Snow
w **Ray Rigby**
followed by a story synopsis and supporting cast.
(Whenever a semi–regular character appeared in more than one story,
I've noted their appearance: for example:
One–Ten ... **Douglas Muir**
Director: **Don Leaver**
Designer (where known): **Alpho O'Reilly**
(Note: every episode ever transmitted, and some that were not,
are listed in chronological order of transmission reading
downwards through left then right hand entries.)
Immediately after the final entry for each series
you'll find the production credits:
THE AVENGERS
Producer, Associate and Executive Producer
Music Composer (Where known)
Story Editor (Where known)
Production company:
An ABC Television Production
plus (where known) the production venue.
The total number of episodes that made up the *entire* series,
plus the first and last date of *first* transmission run.
(Each set of dates refers to one complete season, based upon
the ATV, later Central region.)

[USA]
Where known, I've given the dates of transmission in the USA.
(Unless noted otherwise, dates given are for *first*
transmission run only.)

ACE OF WANDS

Billed as 'The adventures of Tarot, Ace of Wands and renowned illusionist – a twentieth-century Robin Hood, with a pinch of Merlin and a dash of Houdini' – this children's television series depicted the exploits of Tarot, a young stage magician and escapologist who liked to solve mysteries and crimes of a magical nature in his off-duty hours. An enigma to the outside world, his boyish looks camouflaged a highly-efficient and mentally resourceful operator who, according to the production press release, 'could defend himself with the grace of a matador'. Of independent means, Tarot lived in a luxurious penthouse apartment from which he and his companions, Lulli and Sam, sallied forth to pursue their fight against injustice.

During the first two seasons, Tarot's companions were Lillian Palmer – known throughout by her nickname, Lulli – and Sam Maxstead, the magician's stage manager. Having (literally) bumped into Lulli when he and Sam were involved in a traffic accident during the first story, and discovering that the girl shared a telepathic link with him which enabled them to communicate over great distances, Tarot invited her to become his stage assistant and Lulli, an orphan, accepted. By this time, Sam, a reformed convict discovered by Tarot down on his luck, was already the magician's regular companion and shared Tarot's apartment where he could often be found devising new and intricate escape props for the magician's stage act.

Other regulars in the cast were: Mr Sweet, an antiquarian bookseller whose remarkable knowledge and international reputation as a lepidopterist and entomologist frequently pointed to a solution to Tarot's investigations. An eccentric character who dressed entirely in tweed and rode a motorcycle, the character appeared in all but one of the first 26 stories. Completing the team was Ozymandias, a Malayan fishing owl! Obviously a non-speaking role, Ozzie's sole purpose was to sit on his perch and adorn Tarot's apartment.

When, due to prior commitments, the actors playing Lulli and Sam found themselves unable to continue their roles, two new characters were introduced for the third season stories: Mikki, a young female journalist, and her brother Chas, a photographer, who lived in a studio overlooking a London street market. To facilitate the continued use of the magical elements from the previous series, a contrivance was found whereby Tarot discovered that Mikki also shared a telepathic link with him and the two newcomers quickly assumed their status as determined champions of Tarot's cause. Still around were Mr Sweet, who was now based at a university, and the inscrutable Ozymandias.

REGULAR CAST

Tarot Michael Mackenzie   *Sam* Tony Selby   *Lulli* Judy Loe
Mikki Petra Markham   *Chas* Roy Holder   *Ozymandias* Fred Owl

Season One

13 colour 30-minute episodes

One and One and One are Four

w Trevor Preston   *(A 3-part story)*
Hot on the trail of a device stolen from a
research laboratory – a cure for paralysis
which, in the wrong hands, could be used as
a devastating weapon – Tarot and his friends
meet the evil villainess Madame Midnight,
and her accomplice Teddy Talk.
Madame Midnight Hildegard Neil
Prof. Ekdorf Frederick Peisley
Teddy Talk Michael Standing
Kal Dave Prowse

Director: John Russell
Designer: Tony Borer

The Mind Robbers

w William Emms   *(A 4-part story)*
When Tarot discovers that an old adversary,
Senor Zandor, is involved in the
disappearance of two government ministers,
he and his companions follow a trail which
leads them to a mysterious house – and a
dangerous encounter with the Fat Boy and
Zandor's bizarre menagerie of strange
creatures.
Zandor Vernon Dobtcheff
Miss Jelicoe Sheelah Wilcox
Fat Boy Michael Wynne
Sir William Geoffrey Lumsden

Director: Michael Currer-Briggs
Designer: Bernard Spencer

Now You See It, Now You Don't

w Don Houghton   *(A 2-part story)*
A daring bank robbery leads Tarot, Lulli
and Sam to Falk, a villain with delusions of
grandeur, who occupies a houseboat filled
with computers and staffed by a new Nazi
regime.

Falk Christopher Benjamin
Cashier Tim Curry
Macready Ray Barron
Guard Billy Cornelius

Director: John Russell
Designer: Colin Andrews

The Smile

w Trevor Preston   *(A 4-part story)*
Tun-Ju, a master art thief, and his
accomplice Mrs Kite embark on an
audacious plot to steal the Mona Lisa. Tarot
and his friends meet them head on – but a
doublecross and loss of memory hampers
their progress.
Tun-Ju Willoughby Goddard
Digger Reg Lye
Mrs Kite Dorothy Reynolds
Sir Patrick Patrick McAlinney

Director: Michael Currer-Briggs
Designer: Frank Gillman

Season Two

13 colour 30-minute episodes

Seven Serpents, Sulphur and Salt

w Trevor Preston   *(A 3-part story)*
Aided by the bizarre and beautiful Polandi
and his servant Luko, Mr Stabs, an evil
magician, sets out to steal the missing
segment of the Secret Seven Serpents, which
are in Tarot's possession. Several people have
already died for possessing it, and Tarot is
the next victim on Stabs' hit list.
Mr Stabs Russell Hunter
Polandi Harriet Harper
Luko Ian Trigger
Charlie Postle Jack Woolgar

Director: Pamela Lonsdale
Designer: Tony Borer

Joker

w P. J. Hammond   *(A 3-part story)*
Investigating why normally well-behaved
children suddenly go beserk and wreck their
school classrooms, Tarot and his companions
find themselves up against the fiendish
Uncle Harry and his strange troupe of
travelling entertainers.
Uncle Harry **Dermot Tuohy**
The Queen **Carmen Munroe**
The Jack **Roy Holder**
The King **Walter Sparrow**

Director: **John Russell**
Designer: **Bernard Spencer**

Nightmare Gas

w Don Houghton   *(A 3-part story)*
The theft of a deadly hallucinatory gas,
H23, by the deadly Thalia and her brother
Dalbiac, plunges Tarot and his friends into a
nightmare adventure. Contact with the gas
induces deep sleep and nightmares so real
that the victim dies from shock after 23
minutes: captured and exposed to the gas,
Tarot has only minutes to live . . .
Thalia **Isobel Black**
Dr Winthrop **Laurence Carter**
Dalbiac **Jonathan Newth**
Police sergeant **Lewis Wilson**

Director: **Ronald Marriot**
Designer: **Harry Clark**

The Eye of Ra

w Michael Winder   *(A 4-part story)*
The Eye of Ra, a diamond reputed to have
the power to turn people into chalk, is high
on eccentric chessmaster Ceribraun's
shopping list. Believing that the diamond
has turned Mr Sweet into a chalk statuette,
Tarot decides to act. He soon finds himself a
prisoner of Ceribraun's talking computer,
and in danger of being crushed to death
between giant robotic chess pieces.
Ceribraun **Oscar Quitak**
Mr Quince **Edward Jewesbury**
Fredericks **Nicholas Smith**
Computer **Charles Morgan**

Director: **John Russell**
Designer: **Bernard Spencer**

Season Three
20 colour 30-minute episodes

The Meddlers

w P. J. Hammond   *(A 3-part story)*
With his new companions, Nikki and Chas,
Tarot investigates a strange curse which has
frightened the stallholders away from a
London street market. Mr Dove, who
watches from a nearby tower block through
his binoculars, and Mockers, the local
'prophet of doom' are determined to hamper
his progress.
Dove **Paul Dawkins**
Spoon **Michael Standing**
Mockers **Barry Linehan**
Drum **Stephen Kalipah**

Director: **John Russell**
Designer: **Bill Palmer**

The Power of Atep

w Victor Pemberton   *(A 4-part story)*
Simultaneous dreams shared by Tarot and
Mikki, and a meeting with medium John
Pentacle, lead Tarot and his companions to
Egypt where, in Atep's tomb, the magician
encounters a high priest and Quabel –
Tarot's former double and stage partner.
John Pentacle **Sebastian Graham-Jones**
Tramp **Michael Rose**
High priest **Michael Mulcaster**
Fergus Wilson **Joe Dunlop**

Director: **Nicholas Ferguson**
Designer: **Harry Clark**

Peacock Pie

w P. J. Hammond   *(A 3-part story)*
Tarot meets Mr Peacock, a man with the
power of suggestion. In Peacock's hands,
torn strips of newspaper become bank notes;
people book holidays to places they don't
want to visit – and Tarot's stage act becomes
a shambles.
Mr Peacock **Brian Wilde**
Young Mrs Macfadyean **Jenny McCracken**
Mrs Macfadyean **Dorothy Frere**
Manageress **Valarie Van Ost**

Director: **John Russell**
Designer: **Gordon Toms**

Mama Doc

w Maggie Allen   *(A 3-part story)*
When one of Mr Sweet's university
colleagues, Professor Dorian, disappears,
Tarot and his companions follow a trail
which leads them to a bizarre doll's hospital
run by the eccentric Mama Doc. With her
accomplice Bobby, the woman turns real
people into dolls!
Mama Doc Pat Nye
Prof. Dorian Robert Grange
Bobby Michael Mundell
Posy Peagram Wendy Hamilton

Director: Nicholas Ferguson
Designer: Philip Blowers

Sisters Deadly

w Victor Pemberton   *(A 3-part story)*
When Chas returns from a photographic
assignment with no memory of the event or
what happened after it – or the fact that he
robbed the village post office shortly
afterwards – Tarot uncovers the bizarre
events behind a plot to kidnap a NATO
Commander-in-Chief.
Mathilda Edgington Henrietta Rudkin
Postmaster Bartlett Mullins
Letty Edgington Sylvia Coleridge
The Major James Bree

Director: Darrol Blake
Designer: Andrew Drummond

The Beautiful People

w P. J. Hammond   *(A 4-part story)*
When Mikki is refused entry to a small
town fete run by two astonishing beautiful
girls, Dee and Emm, Tarot investigates. He
uncovers a complicated plot organised by a
group of extra terrestrials – beautiful people
with very special powers.
Dee Susan Glanville
Jay Edward Hammond
Emm Vivien Heilbron
Elderly woman Kathleen Sainsbury

Director: Vic Hughes
Designer: Eric Shedden

ACE OF WANDS
Series created by: Trevor Preston
Producer: Pamela Lonsdale
[Seasons 1 and 2]
John Russell [Season 3]
Music by: Andrew Bown
Magical adviser: Ali Bongo
A Thames TV Network Production
Filmed at Teddington Studios
46 colour 30-minute episodes
29 July – 21 October 1970
21 July – 13 October 1971
19 July – 29 November 1972

ADVENTURER

Continuing the exploits of Jack Vincent, first seen in the
popular *Smuggler* series. This time around we join Vincent on
board the prison ship HMS *Success,* presumably being transported
to a prison colony as a result of being found guilty of murdering
Arrow [see final story of *Smuggler*], but this is never fully
explained.

Sadly, this series failed to recapture the production values of
the earlier series and the programme was less than successful.

REGULAR CAST

Jack Vincent Oliver Tobias   *Lt Anderson* Paul Gittins
Cassidy Peter Hambleton   *Mason* Marshall Napier

Episode 1

w Richard Carpenter

As HMS *Success* nears its destination, Jack Vincent finds himself facing a struggle for his sanity against two old enemies, one of whom has him totally at his mercy — and swears to make Vincent's life a living hell.

Episode 2

w Richard Carpenter

Having overpowered his enemy, Vincent casts Anderson adrift — only to find himself and his makeshift crew at the mercy of a violent storm. Shipwrecked, they find themselves marooned.

Episode 3

w Richard Carpenter

Marooned on a coral island, Vincent and the other castaways find themselves befriended by a tribe of Maori natives. But are they as friendly as they first appear?

Episode 4

w Richard Carpenter

A strange ship docks at the island and Vincent and his crew see their chance to escape — but they must first overcome the villainous Captain Campbell and free their newly-found ally, Maru, from captivity.

Maru **Temeura Morrison**
Captain Campbell **John Mellor**
Towers **Peter Bland**

Episode 5

w Richard Carpenter

Having overpowered the crew of the *Sea Wolf,* Vincent enters the captain's cabin and discovers Campbell's log — together with a pouchful of pearls, and a new enemy.

Li **Peter Chin**
Tahuru **Whatanui Skipwith**

Episode 6

w Chris Greene

Vincent and Maru formulate a plan to get the pearls . . . but find more than they bargained for. Vincent is captured and left to face his enemy Anderson.

Episode 7

w Chris Greene

Having escaped Anderson's clutches, Vincent and his friends made their bid for freedom. Out at sea they discover a capsized boat: on board, a wounded man and a woman.

Sovay Banks **Alison Bruce**
Grindall **Peter Brunt**

Episode 8

w Richard Carpenter

With Anderson hot on his trail, Vincent leads the convicts in a mutiny. Anderson and his crew are cast adrift. Vincent and Maru go in search of the pearls.

De Witt **Jeffrey Thomas**
Makiwi **Rolley Manihera**

Episode 9

w Charles Crichton

Returning without the pearls, Vincent and his followers sail to a strange island. They find themselves in a tricky situation — and Vincent becomes obsessed when he drinks a strange brew.

Tohunga **Colin Welsh**
Waireka **Pania Lassey·**

Episode 10

w Charles Crichton

Still under the influence of Malachi's 'grog', Vincent unwittingly betrays his friends. All hell breaks loose and Vincent and Mason escape — only to find further troubles.

Malachi **Peter Green**
Tressler **Matthew Evans**

Episode 11

w Richard Carpenter

Having regained possession of his ship, Anderson swears to see Vincent swing from the gallows. Meanwhile Vincent's friends light a rescue beacon, but run into further jeopardy.

Becket **Desmond Kelly**
Tohu **Shane Dawson**

Episode 12

w Richard Carpenter

Having challenged his tribal leader for leadership, Maru loses the fight and pleads with Vincent to fight for him. Should he lose the penalty is death. But Vincent has other worries: Anderson is closing in for his funal confrontation with his enemy.

Haukino Paki Cherrington
Mahue Pere Pomana

ADVENTURER
Created by: Richard Carpenter, Paul Knight and Sidney Cole
Producer: Sidney Cole
Executive Producer: John McRae
Associate Producer: Bryan H. Estate
Music by: Matthew Brown
Director: Chris Bailey
Production Designer: Duncan Young
A Thames TV International Production in association with Gatetarn Ltd. & TV New Zealand
12 colour 30-minute episodes
(Twice-weekly)
23 July – 28 August 1987

THE ADVENTURER

A glossy but nevertheless cheap attempt to inject new life into a much overused theme. Not a million miles removed from the thirty-minute *Danger Man* format, its star, Gene Barry, had neither the finesse nor the acting ability to inject credibility into the jaded and frequently ridiculously inept scripts.

Barry played Gene Bradley, a US Government espionage agent working undercover in the guise of a globetrotting film star and tycoon. Billed as 'everybody's pin-up . . . nobody's fool', the actor had a tough time proving either statement.

To add insult to injury, the producers squandered the talent of actor Barry Morse. Injected into the series as Mr Parminter, Bradley's secret service contact posing as the film star's business manager-cum-producer, he was given little to do beyond carry a look of total disbelief at the entire proceedings.

REGULAR CAST

Gene Bradley Gene Barry   *Mr Parminter* Barry Morse
Diane (Bradley's agency contact) Catherine Schell
Gavin Jones (Bradley's companion – also an agent) Garrick Hagon
Vince Stuart Damon

Miss Me Once, Miss Me Twice and Miss Me Once Again

w Marty Roth

An agent expects to put his life on the line. But why should Parminter ask Bradley to play the most dangerous role of his career – as a stand in for a potential murder victim?

Wayne Ed Bishop
Vladimir Horvic John Barrie
Gregory Varna Alex Scott
Zentner Bernard Kay

Director: Cyril Frankel

Poor Little Rich Girl

w Donald James
With a little help from Bradley and Diane,
a spoiled heiress learns the hard way how to
live with her millions.
Suzy Dolman Judy Geeson
Consul John Savident
Zavar Maurice Browning
Kanarek Mark Suber

Director: Cyril Frankel

Thrust and Counter Thrust

w Frank Telford
A consulate party in Nice has some
unexpected guests – and gives Bradley's
romantic interlude with Countess Marie a
touch of intrigue and danger.
Countess Marie Eunice Gayson
Nicholas Wensley Pithey
Baron Drovotkin Clifford Evans
Colonel Simon Lack

Director: Paul Dickson

The Bradley Way

w Gerald Kelsey
Bradley plays on a husband's jealousy to
help save an elderly general from foreign
agents, who are forcibly keeping the man
drugged.
Werner von Beck Richard Marner
Gerda Hoffman Joanna Dunham
Virginia Douglas Janet Key
Kerston Anthony Ainley

Director: Val Guest

Return to Sender

w Marty Roth
Requested by Mr Parminter 'to be ready for
action' while visiting the French Riviera,
Bradley's holiday plans take on sinister
implications when he discovers a dead girl
in his hotel room.
Fleming Patrick Mower
Gorman Donald Churchill
Valerie Green Sharon Gurney
Michele Pamela Salem

Director: Cyril Frankel

Counterstrike

w Tony Williamson
When scientist Andrei Korony tries to
defect to the West, but makes a
navigational error and lands in Central
Europe, Bradley hatches a clever plot to
engineer his escape.
Kolony Stephan Kulik
Karen Voriska Kara Wilson
Lanik George Mikell
Prokov Martin Wyldeck

Director: Paul Dickson

Love Always, Magda

w Philip Broadley
When he receives a cable from his friend
Don Fleming, saying that he has met
Magda, the girl whom Bradley loved, but
who walked out on him suddenly, the
Adventurer flies to Beirut to learn the truth
about her departure.
Magda Cyd Hayman
Nessim Kieron Moore
Fleming Paul Maxwell
Maurice Stephan Kalipha

Director: Cyril Frankel

Nearly the End of the Picture

w Philip Broadley
Two lovely girls and a beautiful painting
involve Bradley in an adventure which leads
him into danger and intrigue in the South
of France.
Dorinda Angela Scoular
Brandon Dennis Price
Clarissa Fiona Lewis
Martin David Buck

Director: Cyril Frankel

Deadlock

w Donald James
Bradley's friendship with scientist Franz
Kolmar leads him into danger when
Kolmar's plans for a new project are stolen.
The ransom for their return? One million
dollars to be paid in cash to a mysterious
man in Istanbul.

Kolmar Mervyn Johns
Kay Masterson Jennie Linden
Sakuma Wolfe Morris
Johnny Morrison Burt Kwouk

Director: Val Guest

Has Anyone Here Seen Kelly?

w Tony Williamson
When his good friend, Mike Kelly, fails to keep an appointment in Switzerland, Bradley visits Mike's office in Geneva. He finds that Mike hasn't been seen for several weeks . . . and his apartment has a new occupant – a beautiful young girl.
Milena Corri Anouska Hempel
Mike Kelly Rio Fanning
Gerard Laroche Sandor Eles
Luigi Eric Pohlmann

Director: Val Guest

Skeleton in the Cupboard

w Donald James
The Adventurer finds himself involved in a bizarre mystery. Why should a respected university professor turn thief, fake his own death and place his whole future in jeopardy?
John Ballard Basil Dignam
Sir Richard Richard Vernon
Karen Ballard Syvia Syms
Marks Roy Kinnear

Director: Cyril Frankel

Target!

w Philip Broadley
Realising that he is too well known not to be recognised when claiming to be an illegal arms dealer, Bradley, anxious to expose Dutch dealer Mosselman, dons the disguise of Mr Cotton.
Willet Mosselman Guy Deghy
Astrid Astrid Frank
Venner George Sewell
Police Insp. Alan Downer

Director: Cyril Frankel

Action!

w Brian Clemens
Why should Bradley deliberately avoid a group of his fans when arriving in Scotland? Why should the film star also miss an important appointment with General McCready, whose life is in danger? The answer spells death for someone. Bradley has been 'programmed' to kill.
John Campbell John Collin
General McCready Cec Linder
Ann Somerby Natasha Pyne
Lola Wells Alexandra Bastedo

Director: Barry Morse

Full Fathom Five

w Donald James
A modern-day bunch of brigands give Bradley and his friend, Father Antonius, a run for their money when they try to retrieve some priceless stained glass windows.
Father Antonius Andre Morell
Ryman Peter Jeffrey
Maria Gustave Prunella Ransome
Sir Richard Michael Wynne

Director: Val Guest

I'll Get There Sometime

w Tony Williamson
When Bradley goes to the aid of a man being attacked in an hotel room he finds himself in more trouble than he bargained for. Meanwhile Mr Parminter plays the role of knight errant to help a damsel in distress.
Ryker Patrick Jordan
Werner Frank Barrie
Karen Dorran Pippa Steel
Tony John Levene

Director: Val Guest

To the Lowest Bidder

w Donald James
The Adventurer finds himself taking sides when a crooked business combine makes the competing bids for a new highway a contract – or death – issue.

Sarah Cookson **Jane Asher**
Forrester **Carl Rigg**
Samuel Cookson **Anthony Nicholls**
Laura **Sheila Gish**

Director: **Val Guest**

Going, Going . . .

w **Gerald Kelsey**
When a foreign scientist, given asylum in
Britain, disappears, Mr Parminter suspects
Bradley of playing a double game. Can
Bradley prove his innocence in time to allay
further suspicion and arrest?
Taiho **Burt Kwouk**
Brooks **Norman Bird**
Eisen **Arnold Diamond**
Yvette **Bridget Armstrong**

Director: **Val Guest**

The Not-So-Merry Widow

w **Marty Roth**
When a beautiful woman claims to be his
girlfriend, Bradley has every reason to be
confused – he's never seen her before! What
is she up to? The Adventurer digs deeper –
and lands himself in a cartload of trouble.
Lady Diana **Barbara Murray**
Insp. Chilton **Charles Kay**
Brandon **Dennis Price**
Vanessa **Angela Douglas**

Director: **Cyril Frankel**

Mr Calloway is a Very Cautious Man

w **Donald James**
Bradley deliberately allows himself to be
arrested and face a jail sentence to learn the
truth behind the mysterious case of a dead
man who appears to be very much alive.
Calloway **Freddie Jones**
Insp. Tribe **Victor Lucas**
Stopford **Paul Daneman**
Ingrid **Toby Robins**

Director: **Barry Morse**

Double Exposure

w **Marty Roth**
When Mr Parminter hears that Bradley's
friend, multi-millionaire industrialist Jan de
Groote, has been replaced by an impostor,
the Adventurer is sent to Amsterdam to
investigate who is behind the attempt to
take over de Groote's industrial empire.
Jan de Groote **Donald Houston**
Elayna **Ingrid Pritt**
Colonel Kazan **Carl Duering**
Rostov **George Little**

Director: **Cyril Frankel**

The Case of the Poisoned Pawn

w **Philip Broadley**
The stakes are high when Bradley faces
Brian Hamilton, a young gambler, across
the gambling table. Parminter has ordered
Bradley to thrash Hamilton in the hope that
he will then divulge the secret source of his
money.
Hamilton **Stuart Wilson**
Asteri **Martin Benson**
Lady Anne **Dawn Addams**
Julia Franklin **Jenny Handley**

Director: **Cyril Frankel**

The Solid Gold Hearse

w **Tony Williamson**
Mr Parminter has a problem on his hands:
how to prevent a huge amount of gold
bullion leaving the country. Bradley cannot
help. He's busy making a Western – but he
can offer a solution to Parminter's dilemma.
Wyvern **Sydney Tafler**
Riener **Janos Kurucz**
Miesner **Kevin Stoney**
Fairley **David Weston**

Director: **Val Guest**

Make it a Million

w **Tony Williamson**
Returning from location work in India,
Bradley discovers that he is being
impersonated as part of a clever confidence
trick. The answer appears simple: he'll beat
his double at his own game – but there are
difficulties when you impersonate yourself.
Charlesworth **Paul Eddington**
Julia **Joanna Jones**
Hilverston **Ronald Radd**
Newbury **George Pravda**

Director: **Barry Morse**

Icons Are Forever

w Tony Williamson

Gene Bradley has personal reasons for helping a lovely young Contessa to elope – and for discovering what secret lies behind the closely-guarded Russian icon in an Italian castle.

Contessa Stephanie Beacham
Darron Alfred Marks
Holvera Noel Willman
Carlo Alan Lake

Director: Cyril Frankel

Somebody Doesn't Like Me

w Donald James

Someone clearly doesn't like Gene Bradley: a big reward is offered to whoever kills him. Mr Parminter believes that 'con' girl Krista Magnus is behind the plot, but the Adventurer isn't so sure. Then his private jet is sabotaged . . .

Krista Penelope Horner
Sorenson Reginald Marsh
Roberts Peter Vaughan
Buckley Robin Hawdon

Director: Cyril Frankel

The Good Book

w Lou Shaw

Sowing the seeds of distrust is easy for the jet-setting espionage agent, Gene Bradley. But sometimes things have a tendency to backfire in your face. Has Bradley overplayed his hand this time? Parminter believes he has – and sets out to prove it.

Nita Adrienne Corri
Pierre Ben Kingsley
Marian Gabrielle Drake
Armand John Moffat

Director: Cyril Frankel

THE ADVENTURER
Producer: Monty Berman
Executive story consultant: Dennis Spooner
Music by: John Barry
An ITC Production
Filmed on location in England and the South of France
26 colour 30-minute episodes
29 September 1972 – 30 March 1973
[USA: Syndicated 1972]

THE ADVENTURES OF AGGIE

The misadventures of Aggie (Aasgard Agnette Anderson), a fashion expert for a large London fashion house, whose selling technique was an unorthodox as her creations. Aggie's job took her to many exotic locations around the world, but wherever she travelled, the accident-prone heroine was liable to end up in a humorous – or dangerous – situation. When Aggie was around, things had a tendency to go disastrously wrong: simple business transactions became contracts of murder. Displaying an original creation led to industrial espionage; and importing fashions brought Aggie into contact with unscrupulous international smuggling rings, and so on.

A super-quickie cheapo, notable only for the presence of several luminaries from the film and television world – today major names, then comparative newcomers. A young actor named Patrick Mc Goohan appeared in the stories 'Spanish Sauce' and 'Cock & Bull'. Christopher Lee played a Police Inspector in the story entitled 'Cut Glass'. Anthony Valentine played a page boy in 'London Story' and world-famous film director John Schlesinger appeared as a ski instructor in 'Swiss Stakes'.

REGULAR CAST
Aggie Joan Shawlee

Top Secret
Hypertension*
Snap Judgement
Tail Pigeon
Death of the Party*
Grip of Danger
Cobalt Blue*
Tangier*
The Chiseller*
Monk's Prior*
Spanish Sauce*
Peace and Quiet*
Wedding in Corsica*

Tarboosh
Cut Glass*
Haivah*
London Story
The Man Who Forgot*
Something Rotten in Denmark
Diamonds in the Rough
Swiss Stakes
Cock and Bull
Fortune's Cookie
Berlin Story
Festival of Fear*
Hi-Ho Silver

THE ADVENTURES OF AGGIE
Series produced by Michael Sadler [ME Films]
Associate producer: Ted Holiday
Director: John Guillermin [denoted by asterisk], John Gilling, Henry Kaplan, Desmond Davis
Writer: Ernest Borneman, Martin Stern
26 monochrome 30-minute episodes
17 September 1956–18 March 1957

THE ADVENTURES OF DON QUICK

Loosely based on the Don Quixote legend, this short-lived satirical series portrayed the hilarious adventures of Captain Don Quick (Quixote) and his companion, Sergeant Sam Czopanser (Sancho Panza). As an astronaut and member of the International Maintenance Squad, Quick's only concern should have been the 'nuts and bolts' department in which he and Czopanser were employed. But the Captain was never content with this servile role and, together with his companion, he roamed the universe in his space capsule seeking out new worlds on which, more likely than not, Quick's aspiration to become the roving ambassador of Earth, combined with his passion for leadership (interference?), frequently upset the delicate balance of humanity.

For the period, a technically-impressive series. (The production team constructed a huge, 30-foot space ship in the studio.) It nevertheless failed to attract an audience and after three episodes were transmitted in a prime time slot, the series was relegated to a late-evening 'sleeper' spot and vanished without trace.

REGULAR CAST
Captain Don Quick Ian Hendry   *Sergeant Sam Czopanser* Ronald Lacey

The Benefits of Earth

w Peter Wildeblood
Landing on a planet shared by two races, one technically advanced though addicted to warfare and human sacrifice, the other living in a dream world of peace and sensitivity, Quick regards them as ideal material for reform.
Bekuchuk Kevin Stoney
Marvana Anouska Hempel
Chief dreamer Thorley Walters

Director: Mike Newell
Designer: Bryan Bagge

People isn't Everything

w Kenneth Hill
It doesn't pay to leave your spaceship in the care of the first friendly face you meet. Don and Sam discover this the hard way when, landing on the planet Ophiuchus, they find more than they bargained for: the face belongs to a castaway robot who also likes a drink!
Skip Tony Bateman
Peleen Kate O'Mara
Rebel Colin Baker

Director: Quentin Lawrence
Designer: Bryan Bagge

The Higher the Fewer

w Peter Wildeblood
Planet Melkion 5 is a planet with a difference. Its inhabitants have all taken refuge in 2000-storey skyscrapers, the top floors of which are reserved for the top people, while the lower classes occupy the lower floors. Don, as usual, can't leave well alone and starts turning everything upside down.
Hendenno James Hayter
Mrs Arborel Hildegard Neil
Arborel Derek Francis

Director: Cliff Owen
Designer: Rodney Cammish

The Love Reflector

w Keith Miles
A planet populated entirely by beautiful girls holds hidden dangers for Don and Sam. Anyone succumbing to their charms pays a high price: an astronaut Don encounters succumbed a generation ago – and he is now only 6 inches tall!
Angeline Liz Bamber
Leonie Madeline Smith
Queen Bee Faith Brook

Director: Cyril Coke
Designer: John Emery

The Quick and the Dead

w Keith Miles

When Don and Sam accidentally land their space capsule in a live volcano crater, Sam is convinced that he's dead. He panics further when the astronauts discover that the volcano houses a strange assortment of gods.

Aphrodite Patricia Haines
Hera Pauline Jameson
Zeus Graham Crowden

Director: Bob Hird
Designer: Rodney Cammish

THE ADVENTURES OF DON QUICK
Exec. producer: Peter Wildeblood
*A London Weekend Television Production
filmed at LWT Wembley Studios*
6 colour 60-minutes episodes
30 October – 4 December 1970

Paradise Destruct

w Charlotte and Dennis Plimmer

A planet where all the girls are beautiful, the vegetation lush and night and winter have been abolished. Paradise? It would be – to anyone but Don Quick, who cannot leave anything alone and sets out to change the odd thing or two.

Jonquil Kara Wilson
Willow Lorna Heilbron
Sycamore Roy Marsden

Director: Bill Turner
Designer: John Emery

THE ADVENTURES OF ROBIN HOOD

When King Richard I of England departed on his Crusade to the Holy Land, he left his son, Arthur, in the care of his brother, Prince John, a man who schemed to rid himself of the young Prince and thus declare himself heir to the throne. To help him achieve this aim, Prince John gathered around him the powerful Norman lords and placed the shire of Nottingham under the 'protection' of his friend, the Sheriff. It wasn't long before the poor people of England were reeling under the harsh taxes imposed by the Prince. But there was one young nobleman who remained faithful to King Richard – Robin of Locksley, who, as leader of a band of freedom fighters, outlawed by Prince John, robbed the rich and gave to the poor. Robin and his men became a constant thorn in the Sheriff's side and an unwelcome threat to Prince John's plans.

The adventures of England's legendary hero were brought vividly to life in this popular fifties series which, primarily aimed at the younger viewer, quickly established itself as a firm favourite with viewers of all ages. It went on to become one of the longest-running television shows of all time and made its stars among the best known faces on television.

Robin, played throughout by Richard Greene, cut a dashing figure as he and his men thwarted the Sheriff's plans at every turn, helped, more often than not, by the lovely Lady Marian Fitzwalter (although she did not appear in every story). Known to Robin and his men as Maid Marian, two actresses became associated with the role: Bernadette O'Farrell and Patricia Driscoll. A childhood friend of the outlaw leader, she helped Robin and his men in every way possible to defeat the plotting and intrigue of their common enemy. One fact frequently overlooked by television historians is that although Archie Duncan is credited as playing Robin's second-in-command, the gentle giant, Little John, the role was actually shared by two actors: Duncan broke his leg during the production while attempting to halt a bolting horse which threatened to trample two child actors underfoot – a feat which earned him the Queen's Medal for Bravery – and in ten of the stories he was replaced by actor Rufus Cruikshank. Other notable roles shared by two or more actors were: Prince John, played on various occasions by Donald Pleasance, Hubert Gregg and, in one story, Brian Haines. Will Scarlett, a travelling minstrel who was 'adopted' by Robin's men, was played on two occasions by actor Ronald Howard, before the part was taken over permanently by Paul Eddington for the final season. Young Prince Arthur was portrayed by three actors: Peter Asher, Richard O' Sullivan and Jonathan Bailey.

The series holds a second claim to fame: it spawned a million-selling signature tune which entered the top twenty in January 1956, and remained there for a lengthy stay. Written and recorded by Dick James, the song became one of the most successful television themes of all time. Few of us could resist the temptation to sing along when the opening bars informed us that:

Robin Hood, Robin Hood, is riding through the glen;
Robin Hood, Robin Hood, with his band of men.
Feared by the bad, loved by the good,
Robin Hood, Robin Hood, Robin Hood.

A technicolor cinema version of the legend, Sword of *Sherwood Forest,* was filmed in 1969. Produced by Hammer Films, in conjunction with Columbia Productions, this lacked the appeal of the television series. Though Richard Greene reprised his role as Robin, his outlaws – faces we'd come to know so well on television – were played by new actors. The film wasn't a success, and it would be twenty years before Robin Hood and his men reappeared on the television series – though the title character in that series would be far removed from the green-garbed, dashing hero portrayed by Greene. (See Robin of *Sherwood)*

REGULAR CAST

Robin Hood **Richard Greene**   *Maid Marian* **Bernadette O'Farrell, Patricia Driscoll**
Little John **Archie Duncan, Rufus Cruikshank**   *Friar Tuck* **Alexander Gauge**
Will Scarlett **Ronald Howard, Paul Eddington**   *Derwent* **Victor Woolf**
Alan-a-Dale **Richard Coleman**   *Prince John* **Hubert Gregg, Brian Haines,
Donald Pleasance**   *Sheriff* **Alan Wheatley**
Deputy Sheriff **John Arnatt**
Joan (a village girl & frequent visitor to the outlaw camp) **Simone Lovell**

Season One

39 monochrome 30-minute episodes

The Coming of Robin Hood

w Ralph Smart and Eric Heath
After several years fighting in the Holy Land
with King Richard, young Robin of
Locksley returns to England to find that his
estates have been seized by a Norman
knight, Roger de Lisle. Unable to gain
justice at the court of the newly-elected
Sheriff of Nottingham, Robin is forced to
turn outlaw.
Roger de Lisle **Leo McKern**
Count de Serverne **Gerald Heinz**
Edgar **Alfie Bass**

Director: **Ralph Smart**

The Moneylender

w Eric Heath
Forced to retreat to Sherwood Forest, Robin
joins Scatlock's outlaw band. To prove his
worth, he is sent to deal with an
unscrupulous moneylender who is charging
100 per cent interest on money he has lent
to the poor. Robin's handling of the affair
leads to conflict with Scatlock, who sees the
newcomer as a threat to his leadership.
Scatlock **Bruce Seton**
Herbert **Leo McKern**
Lord Fitzwilliam **John Drake**

Director: **Ralph Smart**

Dead or Alive

w Ralph Smart and Anne Rodney
Little John, a serf at Rutland Court, is
ordered by his master to capture Robin
Hood. Discovering the outlaw's camp, and
finding sympathy with Robin's cause, Little
John joins the band of outlaws and is
appointed Robin's second-in-command.
Little John **Archie Duncan (Intro.)**
Countess **Agnes Bernelle**
Earl of Rutland **John Rutland**
Joan **Simone Lovell (Intro.)**

Director: **Ralph Smart**

Friar Tuck

w Ralph Smart
Disguised as a monk, Robin visits Friar
Tuck, a jovial, fat, holy man, and together
they organise the escape of Mildred from the
clutches of the evil Lord Germaine and the
Sheriff. Though his church is in
Nottingham, the friar becomes a close ally
of the outlaw and begins to pay frequent
visits to Sherwood.
Friar Tuck **Alexander Gauge (Intro.)**
Lord Germaine **Douglas Wilmer**
Mildred **Faith Bailey**

Director: **Ralph Smart**

Maid Marian

w Ralph Smart
Having ambushed the Sheriff's courier,
Robin's life is placed in peril: he is arrested
by the Sheriff and Lady Marian Fitzwalter,
his childhood companion, is accused of
being in league with the outlaws
Maid Marian **Bernadette O' Farrell (Intro.)**
Ned **John Drake**
Much **Willoughby Grey**
Edgar **Shaun Noble**

Director: **Ralph Smart**

The Inquisitor

w Anne Rodney

When Friar Tuck is arrested by the Abbot of a nearby abbey, Robin and Little John secretly enter the abbey in wine barrels. Overhearing their friend confess to crimes he did not commit, Robin overpowers Tuck's inquisitor and, in disguise, pleads the friar's innocence to the Archbishop.
Archbishop Carl Bernard
Abbot Lloyd Pearson
Inquisitor Willoughby Grey

Director: Ralph Smart

The Knight Who Came To Dinner

w Eric Heath

The outlaws lend Sir Richard of the Lea, a penniless knight, the money he needs to pay off his debts. To ensure that the debts are repaid, Robin sends Friar Tuck along disguised as Sir Richard's squire – the friar and the knight soon find themselves up to their necks in trouble.
Sir Richard Ian Hunter (Intro.)
Sir Bertram Robin Bailey
The Abbot Frank Royd

Director: Ralph Smart

The Challenge

w Eric Heath

Believing that one of his troops can outshoot anyone in England with the longbow, the Sheriff organises an archery contest. Sir Richard of the Lea, a gambler at heart, enters Robin's name for the contest.
Sir Richard Ian Hunter
Lady Leonia Patricia Burke
Simon John Drake

Director: Ralph Smart

Queen Eleanor

w Eric Heath

When the Queen Mother, Eleanor of Aquitaine, departs from Nottingham castle with a large donation she has collected for King Richard's campaign, the Sheriff arranges to have her entourage ambushed and steal her gold – but he has reckoned without Robin Hood.

Queen Eleanor Jill Esmond (Intro.)
Count de Waldern Ballard Berkley
Bruno Gerald Cross

Director: Dan Birt

Checkmate

w Ralph Smart

Hearing that the Count de Waldern is planning to conscript 3,000 recruits to terrorise the community, Robin hatches a plan to thwart the Count's evil scheme.
Count de Waldern Leslie Philips
Cedric Victor Woolf
Major Domo Willoughby Grey
Joan Simone Lovell

Director: Ralph Smart

A Guest for the Gallows

w Eric Heath

For obvious reasons, Robin and the Sheriff are sworn enemies. Why then should the Sheriff seek the outlaw's help? With no love lost between them, Robin is on his guard for treachery.
Will Stukely Robert Desmond
Young Girl Jan Miller
Butcher Dennis Shaw
Derwent Victor Woolf

Director: Ralph Smart

The Ordeal

w Eric Heath

When Edgar, a member of Robin's band, is falsely accused by the Sheriff of murdering Jack the Waggoner and is ordered to submit to trial by ordeal – plucking an iron bar from a boiling cauldron – Robin decides to intervene.
Edgar Alfie Bass
Alvin John Drake
Matilda Dorothy Alison
Derwent Victor Woolf

Director: Dan Birt

Husband for Marian

w John Dyson

When Marian's hand is promised in marriage to an unpleasant and

untrustworthy knight, Robin, disguised as a German knight, needs all his powers of persuasion to halt the wedding ceremony.
Little John **Rufus Cruikshank (Intro.)**
Sir Hubert **Brian Worth**
Ada **Thora Hird**
Uncle George **A. J. Brown**

Director: **Bernard Knowles**

The Highlander

w **Eric Heath**
Duncan, a highland visitor to the outlaw camp, is viewed with suspicion by Little John. Robin, however, pays no heed to his friend's observation – until one morning Duncan is discovered trying to burgle the outlaws' treasure cave.
Little John **Rufus Cruikshank**
Otto **Willoughby Grey**
Duncan **Hugh Mc Dermott**
Derwent **Victor Woolf**

Director: **Bernard Knowles**

The Youngest Outlaw

w **John Dyson**
While out hunting, Robin and Little John find a boy who claims he has run away from Waldern Castle, to join Robin's outlaws. Unknown to them the lad is really Prince Arthur, son of King Richard – and Prince John has issued orders to have the boy killed.
Little John **Rufus Cruikshank**
Lord Torrence **Bruce Seton**
Arthur **Peter Asher**
Lady Torrence **Patricia Burke**

Director: **Bernard Knowles**

The Betrothal

w **Paul Symonds**
Once again Sir Richard of the Lea has financial troubles due to his heavy gambling. Robin has a solution to the knight's problem: Sir Richard's son should marry the daughter of a wealthy knight. But will Sir Richard agree to Robin's proposition?

Little John **Rufus Cruikshank**
Gladys **Jennifer Jayne**
Sir Richard **Ian Hunter**
Sir Claude **Philip Guard**

Director: **Ralph Smart**

The Alchemist

w **Eric Heath**
When a village woman is accused of dabbling in witchcraft and is sentenced to be burned at the stake, Robin must find a way of postponing the sentence until he can prove her innocence.
Little John **Rufus Cruikshank**
The Earl **Anthony Sharp**
Milicent **Joyce Blair**
The Countess **Harriet Johns**

Director: **Ralph Smart**

The Jongleur

w **John Dyson**
A travelling minstrel finds out the hard way that it doesn't pay to take the Sheriff's word on trust. Having led Robin and Little John into a well-prepared trap devised by the Sheriff, the vagabond soon finds himself singing a different tune.
Little John **Rufus Cruikshank**
Count de Waldern **Willoughby Grey**
Bartholomew **Peter Hammond**
Physician **John Dearth**

Director: **Bernard Knowles**

The Brothers

w **Eric Heath**
Robin has his work cut out when trying to decide which of two brothers, rescued by the outlaws when fleeing from the Sheriff, wishes to take his vows as a priest. Is it David or Guy? Robin seeks the help of an Abbot – who provides a startling solution.
David/Guy **Michael Brill**
Stationarius **Willoughby Grey**
Abbot **A. J. Brown**
Derwent **Victor Woolf**

Director: **Bernard Knowles**

The Intruders

w Paul Symonds

Robin and Little John come to the aid of two pilgrims who have been robbed as they strolled through Sherwood Forest. Their story intrigues the outlaws – the robbers called themselves Robin Hood's men.
Little John Rufus Cruikshank
The Abbot John Longden
Jules Michael Mc Keag
Godric Ian Whittaker

Director: Ralph Smart

The Sheriff's Boots

w James Aldridge

The Sheriff is well known for priding himself on being well dressed, but when he orders a new pair of boots, what would he say if he knew the ones he'd received were outlaw boots – supplied by his arch enemy, Robin Hood!
Little John Rufus Cruikshank
Master Higgins John Dearth
Nell Joan Sims
Blackbeard Charles Stampley

Director: Ralph Smart

Errand of Mercy

w John Dyson

Nottingham village is stricken with a disease called St Anthony's Fire. Robin and his outlaws give their services to the local apothecary to find herbs to combat the outbreak, but trouble of a different kind plagues the outlaws when Robin is recognised by a beggar.
Little John Rufus Cruikshank
Beggar John Dearth
Anselem Hal Osmond
Master Giles Willoughby Grey

Director: Ralph Smart

The Vandals

w C. Douglas Phipps

A village is pillaged and Robin's men get the blame. Then a dead man is found with an arrow in his back – an arrow supposedly fired by Robin. The outlaw leader must act swiftly if he is to bring the perpetrator to justice and clear his name.

Little John Rufus Cruikshank
Charles the Hunter Charles Stapley
Baron Hubert John Dearth
Lady Irena Ingeborg Wells

Director: Arthur Crabtree

Richard the Lionheart

w Paul Symonds

Everyone knows that Robin Hood is one of King Richard's most faithful subjects. Why then should Robin have so much trouble proving his loyalty to Peregrinus, a heavily hooded visitor to the outlaw camp?
Peregrinus Patrick Barr
De Belvoir John Dearth
Lady Coulchard Muriel Young
Hubert Willoughby Grey

Director: Bernard Knowles

Ladies of Sherwood

w Paul Dudley and Ralph Smart

Arthur of Tetsbury, an ally of the outlaws, is sentenced to be hanged for supposedly holding back money meant for King Richard's Crusade. Aware that Robin will try to rescue his friend, the Sheriff lays a trap – but women's clothes can hide many things, including outlaws.
Arthur of Tetsbury Willoughby Grey
The Judge Walter Hill
Joan Simone Lovell
Derwent Victor Woolf

Director: Ralph Smart

Will Scarlet

w John Dyson

Will Scarlet's eye for the ladies, and his habit of trusting everyone readily, leads Robin and his men into a load of trouble between two lovely ladies and the Sheriff.
Will Scarlet Ronald Howard (Intro.)
Olivia Jennifer Jayne
Joan Simone Lovell
Captain Lash John Dearth

Director: Ralph Smart

The Deserted Castle

w Neil R. Collins

When the Sheriff leads an attack on a deserted castle in which 'something is going on', what he finds there only increases his hatred for Robin Hood. To add insult to injury, it also severely dents his pride in front of his men-at-arms.

Will Scarlet Ronald Howard
Pinot John Stuart
Queen Eleanor Jill Esmond
Sir Galliard Charles Stapley

Director: Bernard Knowles

The Miser

w Ralph Smart

Robin's nature is such that he trusts everyone – until they give him cause to think otherwise. It follows, then, that a miser stands little chance of gaining the outlaw's friendship – and this leads to complications of a very strange variety.

Sir William Larry Naismith
Lady de Courcier Pat Marmont
Seneschal Charles Stapley
Hodge Willoughby Grey

Director: Bernard Knowles

Trial By Battle

w Arthur Baer

The Sheriff's vendetta against Robin Hood erupts into his most villainous scheme yet. Lady Marian is arrested and sent for trial, suspected of murder. To prove her innocence, two men must battle for her life – and only if her defender wins is she proved innocent.

Sir Gyles of Wren John Longden
Sir Hubert Barry Shawzin
Sir Walter Nicholas Parsons
Joan Simone Lovell

Director: Terence Fisher

Children of the Greenwood

w John Cousins

Arthur A'Bland stands accused of a murder he didn't commit. Overpowering his guard, he flees to Sherwood, leaving his children behind. They in turn are held as hostages,

unless A'Bland gives himself up – and Robin feels obliged to rescue them.

Arthur A'Bland Arthur Skinner
Alice Jane Asher
Oswald Peter Asher
Walter FitzUrse John Longden

Director: Ralph Smart

The May Queen

w Ralph Smart

It is the May Queen's prerogative to signal the start of the May Day tournament. Robin and his men use this to their advantage: it is difficult to see exactly who is contesting what under thick tournament armour – as the Sheriff finds out to his cost.

Genevieve Gillian Sterrett
Rolf Paul Hansard
Sir Walter Ian Bannen
Lady Dorrington Dulcie Bowman

Director: Bernard Knowles

The Wanderer

w Albert G. Ruben

When Joseph, a healer, cures Sir Walter by unconventional means, it annoys the other Nottingham healers – and Joseph's flight into Sherwood brings an annoyance that the outlaws find hard to dismiss.

Joseph Karel Stepanek
First healer Willoughby Grey
Walter de Lys John Longden
Second healer John Dearth

Director: Bernard Knowles

The Byzantine Treasure

w Paul Symonds

Discovering that two gold plates taken from an entourage travelling through Sherwood belong to the Queen Mother, Robin asks Sir Richard of the Lea to return them: such treasures could prove 'too hot to handle' – but can Sir Richard be trusted?

Sir Richard Ian Hunter
Archbishop John Longden
Lady Leonia Patricia Burke
Vef William Squires

Director: Bernard Knowles

The Secret Mission

w Ralph Smart and Paul Symonds
Peregrinus returns to the Greenwood.
Having displayed his prowess with the bow
and sword, he continues to cast doubts on
Robin's allegiance to King Richard. What's
his motive? And why is the stranger so
protective of his identity?
Peregrinus Patrick Barr
Innkeeper Paul Connell
Wulfric John Longden
Derwent Victor Woolf

Director Lindsay Anderson

Table's Turned

w Anne Rodney
Derwent and Much are conned into
accepting some loot they believe to be gold.
When it turns out that the prize is two
young children, who prove to be a thorn in
the outlaws' side, Robin must find a way of
turning the tables on the con men.
Derwent Victor Woolf
Suzette Anne Davy
Much Paul Hansard
Francois Andrew de la Matte

Director: Bernard Knowles

The Traitor

w Norma Shannon and Ralph Smart
Robin must find out which one of the three
men entrusted with carrying the ransom
money for King Richard's release is a
traitor. All three men have taken a knight's
oath of innocence, and Robin must discover
the libertine.
Westmorland High Latimer
High Constable Willoughby Grey
Exeter Charles Stapley
Faversham John Dearth

Director: Terence Fisher

The Thorkill Ghost

w Arthur Baer
Harold, its tenant, believes that Thorkill
Castle is haunted. Robin doesn't, so he sets
out to lay the spectre of a long-dead knight
once and for all — but before you can

exorcise a spirit, you must first of all find it
and that, as Robin discovers, isn't the
easiest of tasks.
Harold Ian Whittaker
Derwent Victor Woolf
Edmund Charles Stapley
Quentin Arthur Skinner

Director: Terence Fisher

The Wager

w Warren Howard
Betting Friar Tuck that he can collect more
by begging than the friar can by prayer, the
two men separate, each determined to win
the bet — and each to their own troubles,
which arrive very quickly indeed.
Blind Beggar Geoffrey Keen
Lame Beggar John Watson
Dumb Beggar Leonard Sharp
Feeble Beggar John Dearth

Director: Bernard Knowles

The Prisoner

w Anne Rodney
Robin believes that a courier sent by Prince
John to the Sheriff bears news that is of
importance to the outlaws. Rumour has it
that the messenger brings news of King
Richard's death, but Robin refuses to
believe this and sets out to find the truth.
Prince John Donald Pleasance
Archbishop Jack Melford
Jacques Donald Bradley
Blondel Willoughby Grey

Director: Bernard Knowles

Season Two

39 monochrome 30-minute episodes

A Village Wooing

w Neil R. Collins
No one really needs a reason to join Robin's
band. They just ask. But Wat Longfellow's
request is most unusual: he loves the
Widow Winifred, and asks Robin and
Marian to play the role of Cupid on his
behalf.

Wat Longfellow Leslie Phillips
Bailiff Baldwin Donald Pleasance
Widow Winifred Betty Impey
Derwent Victor Woolf

Director: Bernard Knowles

The Scientist

w Neil R. Collins

Anxious to lay his hands on a new discovery
from Albertus, the scientist, Prince John
forces Albertus to retreat to Sherwood
where, deep in the dense foliage, the
scientist seeks refuge to continue to work to
aid King Richard.
Albertus Miles Malleson
Gervaise Paul Handard
Abbot Charles Lloyd Pack
Roger of Danby Willoughby Grey

Director: Terry Bishop

Blackmail

w Paul Symonds

When a stranger overhears a conversation
between Marian and the outlaw leader, it
spells trouble for Robin: he is soon the
victim of a blackmail attempt. But a
pendulum swings two ways, and Robin has
a stroke of good fortune.
Lucas Anthony Dawson
Ulf Edward Mulhare
Lady Leonia Patricia Burke
Joan Simone Lovell

Director: Bernard Knowles

A Year and a Day

w Neil R. Collins

Surgeon Calend, a runaway serf, is being
pursued by the Sheriff's men when Robin
and his men find him. If the runaway can
stay at large for a year and a day, the law
states that he will be declared a freeman.
Robin decides that there is no better place
to hide than Sherwood Forest.
Surgeon Calend Shaun O'Riordan
Lawyer Peter Bennett
Lord Quincey Martin Lane
Constable Paul Hansard

Director: Bernard Knowles

The Goldmaker

w Paul Symonds

Easily led astray by any moneymaking
opportunity, Sir Richard of the Lea turns to
Robin for help when Lepidus, an alchemist
who says he can turn pewter into gold,
offers to do so to Sir Richard's family plate.
Lepidus Alfie Bass
Lady Leonia Patricia Burke
Sir Richard Ian Hunter
Mercier Peter Bennett

Director: Terry Bishop

The Impostors

w Norman Best

Robin must devise a plan to test his theory
that Lady Pomfret has found a way around
the law which states that, after an absence of
seven years, a person is deemed to be dead
and his property forfeit: Robin believes
Lady Pomfret's husband is very much alive.
Lady Pomfret Brenda De Banzie
Prival Nigel Greene
Lord Pomfret Jack Melford
LeBlond Edward Mulhare

Director: Lindsay Anderson

Ransom

w John Dyson

The poor and ill-used villagers of
Nottingham are ordered to pay 500 crowns
each in taxes. But where can such a price be
found among the needy? Robin provides the
answer – much to the Sheriff's annoyance.
Sir Guy Paul Daneman
Senechal Martin Lane
Count Beaumont Robert Raglen
Joan Simone Lovell

Director: Terence Fisher

Isabella

w Neil R. Collins

A girlhood friend of Marian's, Avice, now
the wife of Prince John, calls on Marian to
ask her to enlist Robin's help: her husband
is planning to divorce her so that he can
marry Isabella, a French princess, thus

getting the support of France. Robin's dilemma – can the woman be trusted?
Isabella Zena Walker
Prince John Donald Pleasance
Princess Avice Helen Cherry
Pembroke Alan Edwards

Director: Lindsay Anderson

The Hero

w John Dyson
Mark, a cunning vagrant, is acclaimed a hero when he kills the Sheriff's brother. But when he retreats to Sherwood for safety from the Sheriff's men, his 'heroics' lead the outlaws into a greater danger than they've thus far experienced.
Mark Bill Owen
Head villager Paul Eddington
Montfichet Ralph Michael
Sorel John Dearth

Director: Terence Fisher

The Haunted Mill

w Paul Symonds
Sir William is trying to buy an old mill so that he can charge whatever he wishes for grading flour. To strengthen his claim, he lets it be known that the mill is haunted but Robin, who doesn't believe in ghosts, sets out to frustrate Sir William's plans.
Sir William Laurence Hardy
Hale John Schlesinger
Tom the Miller James Hayter
Baron Mornay Edward Mulhare

Director: Lindsay Anderson

Outlaw Money

w John Dyson
To help the overtaxed villagers of Lotham, Robin asks Master Henry, a silversmith, to melt down tableware into coin. Unknown to the outlaw, Henry, suspected of being sympathetic to King Richard, is being watched by the Sheriff's men.
Master Henry Sidney James
Count William Paul Eddington
Minter Leonard Sachs
Rufus Richard Pascoe

Director: Terry Bishop

The Black Patch

w John Dyson
Sir Duncan, a guest of Lady Marian, discloses to her his vow to the Sheriff to wear a black eye patch until he has captured Robin Hood and claimed the reward. On her way to deliver this news to Robin, Marian falls victim to a well-laid trap.
Sir Duncan Duncan Lamont
Agnes Gwenda Williams
Fitzherbert Colin Croft
Joan Simone Lovell

Director: Terry Bishop

The Friar's Pilgrimage

w Peter Kay
When Friar Tuck decides to visit Canterbury to learn bee-keeping, Robin decides to join him. The friar is soon glad he did so: their adventure is less straightforward than expected and the holy man learns more than he bargained for.
Lady Margaret Greta Gynt
Constable Patrick Troughton
Count Duprez Paul Eddington
Edward Shaun O'Riordan

Director: Arthur Crabtree

The Trap

w Charles Early
The Sheriff's feud with the outlaws takes on a new turn when he asks Sir Simon, a trusted ally to Prince John, to capture Robin Hood. Simon advises a clever scheme and, posing as a cobbler, he is admitted into the outlaw band.
Sir Simon Alfred Burke
Tom O'Gaunt Andrew Downie
Eldred Peter Bennett
Monk Alister Hunter

Director: Terry Bishop

Hubert

w Ralph Smart and Anne Rodney
Forced into marrying a man she does not love, Rowena is imprisoned in her husband's castle. When her true love, Sir Hubert, is captured while trying to free her, the task of saving the lovers falls to Robin and his men.

Rowena Dorothy Bromily
Thomas William Mervyn
Sir Hubert William Greene
Derwent Victor Woolf

Director: Terence Fisher

The Dream

w Anne Rodney
When Lady Marian's cousin, Sir William, arrives at the outlaw camp bearing a message from the Queen Mother asking for help, Robin instantly agrees to do so. But his plans are soon changed when Marian dreams that the outlaw is walking into a trap.
Sir William Patrick Troughton
Sailor Shaun O'Riordan
Nanny Marie Burke

Director: Terence Fisher

The Blackbird

w Francis Nesbitt
When Little John storms off into the forest, after losing his temper during a friendly game with the outlaws, he is immediately captured by the Sheriff – who then offers a handsome reward to anyone willing to hang the outlaw.
Seneschal Patrick Troughton
Derwent Victor Woolf
Bishop Walter Horsbrugh
Joan Simone Lovell

Director: Terence Fisher

The Shell Game

w Anne Rodney
Annoyed when their leader gives shelter to Pick, a confidence trickster, Robin's men become even more alarmed when he asks Pick to steal some jewels for King Richard's campaign. Robin believes the man is trustworthy – his men do not.
Pick Sam Kydd
Sad Simon Paul Eddington
Polly Irene Handl
Traveller Patrick Troughton

Director: Terry Bishop

The Final Tax

w Paul Symonds
Friar Tuck plans to thwart a rascally bailiff who intends to collect taxes from Tom Joyner, a dying man. Though the bailiff is legally entitled to do so, with Robin's help, the friar has other ideas.
Bailiff Dennis Edwards
Tom Joyner Fred Goddard
Sir Charles Paul Eddington
Simon Barry Fennell

Director: Terry Bishop

The Ambush

w Ralph Smart and Ernest Borneman
To pave the way for his own ambitions, Prince John orders the Sheriff to kill Prince Arthur and leave evidence which will lay the boy's assassination at Robin's door. When the outlaw gets whim of the Sheriff's plans, he decides to ambush the ambushers.
Prince John Donald Pleasance
Constance Dorothy Alison
Prince Arthur Peter Asher
Derwent Victor Woolf

Director: Lindsay Anderson

The Secret Pool

w John Dyson
Robin and Marian are fishing in a pool that lies on Sir Cedric's estate – although it appears that the knight is unaware of its existence. When Robin shares dinner with Cedric that evening, the outlaw has an unusual tale to impart.
Sir Cedric George Benson
Howard Alan Edwards
Henry Paul Eddington
Warden Victor Woolf

Director: Don Chaffey

The Bandit of Brittany

w Milton S. Schlesinger
While escorting Prince Arthur to the safety of France, Robin and Friar Tuck discover there is a French 'Robin Hood' – Jacques – who captures them and refuses to release the

friar until Robin embarks on a special
mission for him.
Jacques Harold Kasket
Raoul Patrick Troughton
Prince Arthur Peter Asher
French robber Paul Hansard

Director: Terry Bishop

The Goldmaker's Return

w Alan Moreland
Lepidus the alchemist returns to
Nottingham – and immediately falls foul of
the Sheriff, who sentences him to be hanged
unless he produces gold within a week.
Feeling responsible for the man's plight,
Robin decides to rescue the goldmaker.
Lepidus Alfie Bass
Sir Paul Paul Eddington
Sir Peter Bryan Coleman
Derwent Victor Woolf

Director: Terry Bishop

Flight From France

w Milton S. Schlesinger
While waiting for a boat to take them back
to England, Robin and Friar Tuck see Sir
Roderick, an emissary of Prince John,
collecting gold for his master.
Overpowering Sir Roderick, Robin decides
to impersonate him and claim the gold for
the outlaws.
Sir Roderick Alan Edwards
Duc de Mirancy Alec Mango
Emile Michael Barrington
Duc de Guise Paul Eddington

Director: Terry Bishop

The Path of True Love

w Alan Moreland and Basil Dawson   (USA:
Locksley Hall)
When Robin and Marian decide to visit
Locksley Hall – a place which holds
sentimental attachments for both of them –
neither is prepared for the reception they
receive from its present owner, Sir Charles.

Sir Charles Lionel Jeffries
Hereward Ronald Hines
Ricardo Hal Osmond
Serf John Dearth

Director: Terence Fisher

Fair Play

w Sidney Wells
'The Flying Four', a troupe of travelling
acrobats, are waylaid by Robin's men as
they pass through Sherwood. They plead for
mercy, but Robin's men mean them no
harm – in fact their arrival is very fortuitous
indeed.
Herr Mielke Thomas Gallagher
Tom Paul Eddington
Owen Colin Broadley
The Flying Four The Volants

Director: Terry Bishop

The Dowry

w Neil R. Collins
A prosperous London merchant and his
daughter Bess are on their way to
Nottingham with a dowry of 1,000 gold
crowns. Garth, a recent recruit to Robin's
band, decides to relieve them of the money
– a crime which incurs the Sheriff's wrath
and spells further trouble for outlaws.
Garth David Cameron
Judd William Mervyn
Alan-a-Dale John Schlesinger
Bess Jeanette Hutchinson

Director: Anthony Squire

The York Treasure

w Clare Thorne
When Robin hears that someone is plotting
to steal gold meant for refugees, he and
Little John set out to waylay the brigands
and return the money to its intended
recipients – but danger of a different kind
marks their every move.
Joseph of Cordoba Karel Stepanek
Malbete Allan Cuthbertson
Esther Helena de Crespo
Fisherman Wilfred Brambell

Director: Terry Bishop

The Borrowed Baby

w Aileen Hamilton
Suspecting that Lady Marian is an
accomplice of the outlaws, the Count de
Severne devises a plan to expose her.
Though an unwilling pawn in the game, the
Sheriff agrees to the plan – providing Robin
Hood is brought in for 'questioning'.
Count de Severne Guy Verney
Giles Graham Stewart
Kate Dorothy Gordon
Derwent Victor Woolf

Director: Don Chaffey

Food For Thought

w Sidney Wells
Count Oliver's tenants are starving. He has
instructed his tax officer to take the food
ration and place it in storage. Robin's
dilemma? How to steal the food and return
it to the villagers without the Count's
knowledge.
Count Oliver John Sharplin
Ludlow Meredith Edwards
Seneschal Patrick Troughton
Barker Duncan Lamont

Director: Terry Bishop

Too Many Earls

w Milton S. Schlesinger
Marian's uncle, the Earl of Rochdale, begins
quarrelling with the Earl of Northgate. The
outcome is stalemate, so Marian suggests
that they settle their differences with an
archery contest. But who is the mysterious
archer chosen by the Sheriff to shoot for
Northgate?
Earl of Rochdale Brian Worth
Lord Lawrence Nigel Davenport
Earl of Northgate Andrew Downie
Derwent Victor Woolf

Director: Robert Day

Highland Fling

w Leighton Reynolds
Robin and Friar Tuck are on a mission for
King Richard: they are to visit Scotland and
collect 500 gold crowns owed to Richard by
King William of Scotland – but why should
the Scottish King be so reluctant to hand
over the gold?
King William Duncan McIntyre
Duncan Hugh McDermott
Davy Andrew Faulds
Baron Mornay Paul Eddington

Director: Terry Bishop

The Mystery of Ireland's Eye

w James Carhart and Nicolas Winter
Suspecting that her uncle is being held
prisoner on an island off the Irish coast,
Marian, together with Robin and Friar
Tuck, hire a boat to take them there. Their
arrival is greeted with alarm – and Marian
receives the fright of her life.
Rolf Eddie Byrne
Bridgid Concepta Fennell
Sir Edward A. J. Brown
Seaman Ronald Hines

Director: Terry Bishop

The Little People

w James Carhart and Nicolas Winter
Escorting Marian back home from Ireland
after rescuing her uncle, Robin and Friar
Tuck hear the legend of the little people.
Robin scoffs at the tale, but Tuck is not so
sceptical.
Pat Nolan Barry Keegan
Brian Colin Broadley
Maeve Nolan Peggy Marshall
Hermit John Dearth

Director: Don Chaffey

The Infidel

w John Dyson and Basil Dawson
Sir James devises a plot to inherit his uncle's
fortune. Blame for the crime will point at
an innocent man – Ali ben Azra – and the
Sheriff has been informed. Can Robin teach
Sir James a lesson in sportsmanship – and
clip the Sheriff's wings at the same time?
Ali Francis Matthews
Lucas Alex Scott
Sir James Nigel Davenport
Baron Mark Noel Coleman

Director: Terence Fisher

The Frightened Tailor

w Michael Connor

When a list of people loyal to King Richard comes into the Sheriff's possession, Robin, with a little help from his friend the tailor, retrieves the list before his enemy can put it to wrongful use.

The Tailor Hugh Burden
Seneschal Michael Peake
Waldo Graham Stewart
Ned Ronald Hines

Director: Anthony Squire

The Black Five

w Michael Connor

When the Sheriff receives threats to his life, what could be more natural than to send for his 'friend' Robin Hood! Robin's interest is aroused by his enemy's change of tune, but what has caused this reversal of thought? And who or what are 'The Black Five'?

Earl de Moreville Patrick Cargill
Sheriff's seneschal Manning Wilson
Seneschal Dennis Edwards
Guard Duncan Moore

Director: Anthony Squire

The Road in the Air

w Paul Symonds

Robin must think of a way to cross the land approaching Tom's mill: Sir William, Tom's landlord, has imposed an import duty on grain taken from the mill and his guards are gathered to repel intruders. An ingenious device provides Robin with the answer.

Tom the Miller James Hayter
Claude Nigel Davenport
Sir William Laurence Hardy
Derwent Victor Woolf

Director: Robert Day

Carlotta

w Michael Connor and Basil Dawson

Robin and his band have set a date to steal a gold shipment planned for Prince John's coffers, but Little John is nowhere to be found. Has the gentle giant finally been smitten by the love of a fair lady?

Carlotta Jennifer Jayne
Derwent Victor Woolf
Joan Simone Lovell
Outlaw Ronald Hines

Director: Anthony Squire

Season Three

39 monochrome 30-minute episodes

The Salt King

w Carey Wilbur

Certain lords are maintaining a monopoly on essential goods: one such commodity is salt, and Lord Guthrie has formed an alliance with the Sheriff to hold back supplies. Robin gets to hear of this, and things get very spicy indeed.

Maid Marian Patricia Driscoll (Intro.)
Captain Tony Thornton
Lord Guthrie Manning Wilson
Wilfred Paul Eddington

Director: Don Chaffey

A Tuck In Time

w James Carhart

Edgar, Tuck's brother, returns home from overseas. With him, he's brought a deadly machine and he's prepared to sell it to the highest bidder – Prince John. Tuck must attempt to lead his brother back into the fold before the deal is completed.

Edgar John Forest
Sir Reginald Paul Eddington
Prince John Hubert Gregg (Intro.)
Jeremy Wilfred Downing

Director: Terry Bishop

Pepper

w Michael Connor

Robin and his men become involved in the affairs of a Byzantine Princess, Irene, who is being held hostage by Prince John. Their dilemma? How does one enter a heavily guarded castle without being seen?

Princess Irene Monica Stevenson
Ambassador Peter Welch
Prince John Hubert Gregg
Guard Carlo Brookes

Director: Robert Day

The Charter

w John Dyson

The only person who knows the hiding place of a charter which will limit Prince John's power should he become King is Lord Greenwald, who is seriously ill. Marian discovers where the charter is hidden, but can Robin retrieve it before the Sheriff?

Sir Bascomb Harry H. Corbett
Squire Sean Lynch
Sir Eustace Paul Eddington
Hulm Philip Ray

Director: Terry Bishop

A Change of Heart

w Basil Dawson

Having heard that Lord Humphrey intends to expel the Celts from the Forest of Dean, Friar Tuck seeks Robin's advice and together they force the knight to rethink his motives.

Lord Humphrey Eddie Byrne
Meg Sally Travers
Brack Michael Ripper
Alan-a-Dale Richard Coleman

Director: Terry Bishop

Brother Battle

w Ralph Smart

When Brother Wootan starts a school in Sherwood, much to the outlaws' amusement, Little John becomes a somewhat unwilling pupil. What are his motives? The answer sets the Greenwood alive with laughter.

Brother Wootan Francis De Wolff
Howard Paul Eddington
Mark Claude Kingston
Derwent Victor Woolf

Director: Robert Day

My Brother's Keeper

w Leslie Poynton

Still banished to the Greenwood by the Sheriff for teaching the children of serfs to read, Brother Wootan engages Robin's help to further his cause. But the outcome isn't exactly to the outlaw leader's liking.

Brother Wootan Francis De Wolff
Derwent Victor Woolf
Mark Claude Kingston
Alan-a-Dale Richard Coleman

Director: Robert Day

An Apple For the Archer

w James Aldridge

Ordered by her father's will to marry the finest bowman in England, Mary Quartermain must choose between family loyalty and her love for Pierre of Bordeaux. Robin pulls a few strings to help her dilemma.

Mary Quartermain Ann Firbank
Timothy Kenneth Cope
Pierre of Bordeaux Paul Eddington
Derwent Victor Woolf

Director: Terry Bishop

The Angry Village

w Shirl Westbury

A drought hits Sherwood, and Robin and Little John have to leave the safety of the forest to search for water. During their travels, they meet some villagers hiding grain to avoid paying their taxes. The next day, the grain disappears and suspicion falls on the strangers.

Jason Harry H. Corbett
Cal Geoffrey Bayldon
Hogarth Rowland Bartrop
Woodsman Clive Forest

Director: Terry Bishop

The Mark

w Robert Newman

Sir Blaise, a Norman lord, plans to build a fortress on his land. To dupe the community, he lets it be known that the new building is to be a church in honour of St Barnaby. Enter Robin Hood and Friar Tuck, and the knight is soon given a very heavy cross to bear.

Sir Blaise Charles Gray
Dickon Kenneth Cope
Walter Philip Ray
Derwent Victor Woolf

Director: Robert Day

The Bride of Robin Hood

w Oliver Skene

To escape a forced marriage to Walter, Brenda runs away from home. Having proved herself a gallant archer by saving Robin's life, in return she asks a favour – she wishes to become Robin's wife!

Brenda Billie Whitelaw
Derwent Victor Woolf
Walter Ronald Allen
Joan Simone Lovell

Director: Anthony Squire

To Be A Student

w Sidney Wells

When Prince John tries to recruit young children for troops, Peter Larkin flees to the Greenwood to join Robin and his outlaws. But his arrival is a portent of doom for Robin's men, and they soon have reason to regret his presence.

Peter Derek Waring
Belmont Hugh Moxley
Agnes Maureen Davis
Alan-a-Dale Richard Coleman

Director: Robert Day

The Christmas Goose

w Oliver Skene

Davy, an 11-year-old boy caught stealing mistletoe on Sir Leon's estate, is sentenced to be flogged. Robin, however, gives the boy his own kind of Christmas present – one which helps to cook the bailiff's goose.

Davy John Whitely
Sir Leon Jack Watling
Bailiff Paul Eddington
Derwent Victor Woolf

Director: Don Chaffey

Challenge of the Black Knight

w Leon Griffiths

As a special birthday treat to his son, Will, Ned Dale, an outlaw, takes him hunting with Little John. But things go terribly wrong when they are challenged by a knight dressed entirely in black armour, and Will decides to prove his manhood.

Will Richard O'Sullivan
Sir Roger John Arnatt
Ned Dervis Ward
Squire Roger Walker

Director: Anthony Squire

The Rivals

w Leslie Poynton

When ordered to increase the taxes, the Sheriff's lieutenant proposes an alternative plan to raise money – one which will benefit both men. Why not form a rival gang of outlaws and steal from the rich like Robin Hood!

Dick Banks Carl Bernard
Edwin Michael Ashwin
Seneschal Paul Eddington
Joan Simone Lovell

Director: Robert Day

The Profiteer

w Samuel B. West

When the Lord of the Manor refuses to help the people of Lothan village after their crops have failed, Robin Hood comes to their rescue by sending Andrew, a serf, to buy food from London. But the Sheriff gets wind of Robin's plan and hatches a scheme of his own.

Andrew Gordon Jackson
Margaret Barbara Archer
Hodges John Longden
Rypon Paul Eddington

Director: Terry Bishop

Knight Errant

w Michael Connor

Engrossed in his archery practice, Robin ignores Marian's pleas to speak with him on a matter of urgency. Furious, she storms off alone, and that's when the trouble starts – for Marian, Robin and Sir Jack of Southwork.

Sir Jack William Lucas
Derwent Victor Woolf
Captain Paul Eddington
Joan Simone Lovell

Director: Anthony Squire

The Healing Hand

w Leon Griffiths

Viewed by his friends as large of frame and small of mind, Little John is the ideal victim for Oswald of the Healing Hand, a 'quack' doctor, who finds it an easy task to dupe the outlaw – but things have a way of turning out for the best.

Oswald Michael Ripper
Thin Man James Ellis
Baron Barclay Bryan Coleman
Joan Simone Lovell

Director: Bernard Knowles

One Man's Meat

w George and Gertrude Fass

Squire Woodstock has discovered a new kind of bran which he dubs his 'universal food'. Believing that it will replace all other food, he arranges for Robin and Friar Tuck to taste the 'wonder' bran, with comical results.

Squire Woodstock Robin Bailey
Henry Gary Raymond
Thadeus Kevin Stoney
Derwent Victor Woolf

Director: Don Chaffey

Too Many Robins

w John Dyson

One Robin in Sherwood is one too many for the Sheriff – now there are two! Tom the Thatcher is impersonating the outlaw to impress his girlfriend, Alma. But as Tom soon discovers, playing outlaw has its serious side.

Tom the Thatcher Derek Waring
Bart Jack Lambert
Alma Susan Stephen
Joan Simone Lovell

Director: Robert Day

The Crusaders

w Samuel B. West

Robin, keeping a rendezvous with four knights with whom he fought in the Crusades, does not know he's walking into a trap hatched by the Sheriff. Can his enemy win this time? Or has Robin an ace up his sleeve?

Beaumont Bryan Coleman
Sir Hugh Paul Eddington
Lieutenant Roy Purcell
Derwent Victor Woolf

Director: Gerry Bryant

Castle In the Air

w Oliver Skene

Once again on the losing end of a gambling game, Sir Richard of the Lea turns to Robin for help. His opponent in the game is Sir Adrian, a man who believes in winning at any cost – and Robin suspects the game was crooked.

Sir Richard Ian Hunter
Lady Leonia Patricia Burke
Sir Adrian David Oxley
Lieutenant Ronald Hines

Director: Peter Maxwell

The Double

w Basil Dawson

When Bolbec, sworn enemy of Robin Hood, arrives at Nottingham Castle, he bears news of interest to the Sheriff. He has a foolproof plan to rid the forest of the outlaw. He then introduces his hooded guest – Robin's double.

Luke Tanner Richard Greene
Prince Arthur Richard O' Sullivan
Bolbec John Gabriel
Joan Simone Lovell

Director: Gerry Bryant

Roman Gold

w Basil Dawson

Out hunting, Robin and his men unearth some ancient Roman gold, which the outlaw leader plans to distribute to the needy. The Sheriff, however, content that his need is the greatest, lays claim to the treasure in the crown's name.

Dr Quince George A. Cooper
Derwent Victor Woolf
Tybalt Ballard Berkley
Lieutenant Paul Hansard

Director: Peter Maxwell

The Ghost that Failed

w Leon Griffiths

Believing that the land belonging to Simon Dexter is haunted, local farmers seek advice from Friar Tuck. He is sceptical but agrees to accompany Robin to Dexter's estate. What they find astonishes both men.
Simon Dexter Rupert Davies
Ralph Kevin Stoney
Jenny Barbara Lott
Yeoman John Barrie

Director: Peter Maxwell

At the Sign of the Blue Boar

w Sidney Wells

Master Blount, a miserly tailor, is jealous of Ulrich, the landlord of the Blue Boar Inn which Robin and his men frequent. To implicate the innkeeper, Blount informs the Sheriff, who employs the tailor to spy for him.
Blount Geoffrey Chater
Saunders Harold Goodwin
Ulrich Martin Wyldeck
Derwent Victor Woolf

Director: Ernest Borneman

The Quickness of the Hand

w R. W. Bogany

The tournament over, three knights decide to earn some money by claiming the reward for Robin's capture. Disguised as strolling players, they enter the outlaws' camp and await their opportunity to strike.
Sir Laurence Richard Pasco
Sir Ralph Richard Caldicot
Sir John Brian Oulton
Lieutenant John Dearth

Director: Robert Day

The Elixir of Youth

w Samuel B. West

In desperate need of money, Sir Boland has promised the hand of his ward, Melissa, to Sir Louis, an elderly Norman. When Tuck, a friend of the girl's, hears this news, he and Robin make arrangements of their own.
Sir Boland Patrick Troughton
Sir Louis Reginald Beckwith
Melissa Angela Beckworth
Derwent Victor Woolf

Director: Terry Bishop

The Genius

w Oliver Skene

Nicodemus, a master mathematician, seeks entrance to the Abbey of Southwall to escape Prince John – who is anxious to use the scholar's genius to construct a deadly weapon. Refused entrance, Nicodemus seeks refuge in Sherwood.
Nicodemus Harry H. Corbett
Abbot Charles Lloyd Pack
Count de Severne Geoffrey Bayldon
Joan Simone Lovell

Director: Peter Seabourne

The Youthful Menace

w Arthur Dales

Edwin, Marian's nephew, is scornful of her claims about Robin's allegiance to King Richard. To confirm her knowledge, Marian takes him to the outlaw camp. A mistake: Edwin's presence there becomes a threat to the outlaws' freedom.
Edwin Peter Kerr
Derwent Victor Woolf
Peasant John Gantrell
Bowman John Dearth

Director: Robert Day

The Minstrel

w Leslie Poynton

A minstrel's song can prove very handy, particularly when it helps Robin and his outlaws foil a dastardly plot by Prince John, who is conspiring to form an alliance with the Prince of Aragon.

Roland Francis Matthews
Ambassador Roger Delgado
Prince John Brian Haines
Derwent Victor Woolf

Director: Peter Seabourne

The Doctor

w Leslie Poynton
When Little John breaks his leg while
escaping from the Sheriff, Robin and Friar
Tuck take him to the home of Sir George
Woodley, a specialist in broken limbs.
While the doctor attends Little John, his
servant reports their visit to the Sheriff!
Sir George John Harvey
Howard Paul Eddington
Benvolio Henry Vidon
Alma Susan Stevens

Director: Peter Seabourne

The Lottery

w Peter Yeldham
The Sheriff plans to raise some money for
Prince John by using a clever variation on
an old theme. His plan seems foolproof –
but as always, he has reckoned without
Robin's intervention.
Will Sharpe Alfred Burke
Cook Edmund Warwick
Frisby Ian Whittaker
Derwent Victor Woolf

Director: Peter Seabourne

The Fire

w Philip Bolsover
Having cornered Little John and Derwent in
a cave, the Sheriff orders his men to smoke
them out. From the flames of defeat appears
new hope – and the Sheriff will eventually
have to seek Robin's help.
Forester Neil Hallett
Lieutenant Paul Eddington
Derwent Victor Woolf
Sergeant John Dearth

Director: Robert Day

Lincoln Green

w Neil R. Collins
Forewarned that Robin Hood and Maid
Marian will visit Nottingham Fair to buy
new supplies of Lincoln Green cloth, the
Sheriff stations his men-at-arms in the town
square – but a tailor's scissors provide Robin
with an unusual escape route.
Shanks Charles Houston
Weaver Leonard Sharp
David Geoffrey Chater
Joan Simone Lovell

Director: Terry Bishop

Women's War

w Philip Bolsover
After she has been rescued from the Sheriff's
men, Robin agrees to allow two of his men
to escort Ann de Brisac, a noblewoman, to a
place where she claims to have hidden gold:
after their departure, Marian arrives with
news that the woman is a spy.
Ann de Brisac Zena Walker
Derwent Victor Woolf
Midivel Neil Hallett
Sheriff's man Arthur Dales

Director: Peter Seabourne

Little Mother

w Philip Bolsover
Seeing an elderly woman being abused by
two of the Sheriff's men-at-arms, Marian
and Little John intervene: to his surprise,
Robin's second-in-command discovers that
the man is his mother!
Little Mother Renee Houston
Two Fingers Desmond Llewellyn
Duke Charles Houston
Derwent Victor Woolf

Director: Terry Bishop

Marian's Prize

w Philip Bolsover
Robin's name has been entered for an
archery contest. The problem is, he's away
visiting friends. Can Marian, selected in his
absence, fool the Sheriff and win the
shooting tournament?

Lord Northcleave Jack Melford
Will Brian Alexis
Prince John Donald Pleasance
Derwent Victor Woolf

Director: Peter Seabourne

Farewell to Tuck

w Arthur Dales
When the Archbishop of Canterbury visits
Nottingham, the Sheriff sees a way of
depleting Robin's band by one: he'll get rid
of the troublesome Friar Tuck once and for
all. As usual, the outlaws have the last
laugh.
Archbishop Carl Bernard
Deputy Sheriff John Arnatt (Intro.)
Alison Anne Reid
Page boy Peter Haines

Director: Terry Bishop

Season Four
26 monochrome 30-minute episodes

Goodbye to Little John

w Raymond Bowers
Little John is concerned that Will Scarlett
has taken his place – in all but name – as
Robin's lieutenant. Robin denies this is
true, but his friend angrily storms out of
Sherwood, swearing never to return.
Will Scarlett Paul Eddington (Intro.)
Derwent Victor Woolf
Bault Graham Stuart
Deputy Sheriff John Arnatt

Director: Robert Day

The Oath

w Arthur Dales
It doesn't pay to underestimate Friar Tuck –
as the Deputy Sheriff finds out when he
hatches a plot to have the Friar take an oath
that he doesn't consort with the outlaws.
Archbishop Carl Bernard
Courier Roy Purcell
Deputy Sheriff John Arnatt
Joan Simone Lovell

Director: Compton Bennett

A Race Against Time

w Arthur Dales
The Duchess of Britanny is taking Prince
Arthur to safety in the North, and Robin is
asked to provide an escort. The outlaw
leader offers to lead the entourage himself –
and finds some surprising adventures along
the way.
Duchess Patricia Marmont
Wilfred Michael Ripper
Prince Arthur Jonathan Bailey
Sir Hartley David Davies

Director: Terry Bishop

The Edge and the Point

w Raymond Bowers
Former Crusader M'Boland decides to make
some money by capturing the outlaw leader,
and demanding payment from the Sheriff.
He soon discovers that you must first
capture your prey – and Robin has ideas of
his own.
M'Boland Michael Gough
Sergeant Terry York
Deputy Sheriff John Arnatt
Will Scarlett Paul Eddington

Director: Gordon Parry

The Champion

w Leon Griffiths
When Marian tells Robin that, following
the death of her father, her estate is to be
taken over by Sir Quentin, Robin has other
ideas – particularly when he suspects the
Sheriff is behind the scheme.
Sir Quentin Jack Allen
Will Scarlett Paul Eddington
Sir Guy John Horsely
Surveyor Keith Rawlings

Director: Gordon Parry

The Debt

w Leon Griffiths
Posing as one of Robin's outlaws, a
foreigner attacks and robs several people as
they wander through Sherwood. The man's
capture brings Robin a dilemma: seven years
earlier, the man had saved his life in the
Crusades.

Deputy Sheriff John Arnatt
Will Scarlett Paul Eddington
Martin Brian Rawlinson
John Dale Terry York

Director: Anthony Squire

The Parting Quest

w Louis Marks

Duncan, a wild Highland clansman, is hardly a welcome guest in Robin's camp – particularly when his interest apears to be solely in the Lady Marian. A worried outlaw leader seeks Friar Tuck's advice.
Duncan Hugh McDermott
Alan-a-Dale Richard Coleman
Jessie Ellen McIntosh
Will Scarlett Paul Eddington

Director: Terry Bishop

The Bagpiper

w Jan Read

Duncan, the wild Highland clansman, returns to the outlaw camp and reeks havoc among Robin's men. This time he has a plan to overthrow the Sheriff. Robin's dilemma? How to oppose the clansman without incurring his wrath.
Duncan Hugh McDermott
Will Scarlett Paul Eddington
Sir Falke Patrick Troughton
Tam Andrew Downie

Director: Terry Bishop

The Pharoah Stones

w William Templeton

Little John is given three dice-stones by a pedlar, which he claims once belonged to the Ancient Egyptian Kings. Truth or not, the stones bring more than their fair share of trouble to the Greenwood.
Pedlar Carl Bernard
Will Scarlett Paul Eddington
Edgar John Forest
Derwent Victor Woolf

Director: Gordon Parry

A Touch of Fever

w Leon Griffiths

Difficulties arise for Marian when she recognises one of three knights captured by the outlaws as her cousin. Before she can beg for his release, she must first of all discover why he is in the company of rogues.
Sir Nigel John Carson
Sir Gerald Humphrey Lestocq
Sir John Ronald Hines
Will Scarlett Paul Eddington

Director: Peter Seabourne

Six Strings To His Bow

w Richard Bowers

Unaware that he is wanted for murder by Prince John, Alan-a-Dale returns to Sherwood. His arrival serves to increase the already tension-filled feud between Robin and the Sheriff, who is hot on the minstrel's trail.
Alan-a-Dale Richard Coleman
Sheriff's lieutenant Martin Lowry
Sheriff Alan Wheatly
Joan Simone Lovell

Director: Terry Bishop

The Devil You Don't Know

w Owen Holder

When Robin and Will Scarlett are out searching for Alan-a-Dale, who has failed to return to camp, they see a group of soldiers escorting a man shackled in irons. Their intervention on the man's behalf leads to surprising results.
Will Scarlett Paul Eddington
Alan-a-Dale Richard Coleman
Ralph John Arnatt
Bault Keith Rawlins

Director Peter Seabourne

The Lady Killer

w Jan Read

Robin and Derwent, out hunting, are recalled to their camp on a matter of great urgency: Will Scarlett has been arrested for poaching! Their plan to rescue him from the

Sheriff's clutches has a most unusual outcome.
Deputy Sheriff John Arnatt
Derwent Victor Woolf
Will Scarlett Paul Eddington
Joan Simone Lovell

Director: Terry Bishop

A Bushel of Apples

w Jan Read
When he hears that Sir Watkyn's men-at-arms have extorted livestock and wages from the peasants, Friar Tuck turns to the church for help. Sir Watkyn has denied the charge, but Father Ignatius – abetted by Robin – has a solution to the problem.
Sir Watkyn Harry H. Corbett
Deputy Sheriff John Arnatt
Father Ignatius Philip Latham
Will Scarlett Paul Eddington

Director: Terry Bishop

Tuck's Love Day

w Alan Hackney
Always in trouble with his Abbot, Friar Tuck is unusually concerned when he is unable to collect his share of the church money. In despair, he turns to the outlaws – and Robin finds a very unusual cure for his friend's ailment.
Abbot Walter Horsbrugh
Will Scarlett Paul Eddington
Sir Geoffrey Basil Dignam
Derwent Victor Woolf

Director: Terry Bishop

The Loaf

w Philip Bolsover
If there is money to be made, the Sheriff seldom worries about the plight of others. However, when he decides to make a fat profit by selling off flour grain belonging to the villagers, Robin teaches him some table manners.
Sheriff Alan Wheatley
Derwent Victor Woolf
Lord Giles Anthony Jacobs
Alan-a-Dale Richard Coleman

Director: Peter Seabourne

Sybella

w Michael Connor
A nobleman is attacked while on his way to join King Richard in the Holy Land. His murderer, Baron Onslow, changes clothes with the dead man and rides to Nottingham Castle in his place. But will his disguise fool Robin Hood?
Sybella Soraya Rafat
Ralph Geoffrey Taylor
Baron Onslow David Davies
Derwent Victor Woolf

Director: Terry Bishop

The Flying Sorcerer

w Palmer Thompson
Lord Giles of Richmond, in Nottingham to collect taxes, sees an opportunity to misuse his position by robbing the needy. With Friar Tuck's help, Robin teaches him a lesson.
Lord Giles Anthony Jacobs
Harold Gordon Whiting
Lord Eilmar Arthur Howard
Dickon Anthony James

Director: Bernard Knowles

Bride for an Outlaw

w Louis Marks
Sir Bligh, a wealthy merchant, learns that his daughter's suitor plans to visit her. Robin, escaping from the Sheriff's men, enters the house and is mistaken for the man – an event which leads the outlaw leader into treachery.
Sir Bligh John Horsley
Sir Peter Nigel Davenport
Judith Mary Manson
Squire Charles Houston

Director: Gordon Parry

Double Trouble

w Louis Marks
Edgar, Friar Tuck's identical twin brother, arrives in Nottingham and brings mayhem in his wake: he has agreed to lead the Sheriff to the outlaw camp – little realising that by doing so, he places his brother's life in peril.

Edgar Alexander Gauge
Will Scarlett Paul Eddington
Deputy Sheriff John Arnatt
Derwent Victor Woolf

Director: Terry Bishop

The Truce

w Leon Griffiths
The Deputy Sheriff, usually hostile to Robin
Hood, sends a message to Sherwood
declaring a truce. Out of necessity, he
requires the outlaws' help. Robin,
suspecting treachery, formulates a plan of
campaign.
Deputy Sheriff John Arnatt
Will Scarlett Paul Eddington
Sir Crispin Derek Tansley
Lord Repton Richard Caldicot

Director: Gordon Perry

The Charm Pedlar

w Alan Hackney
To Robin, a man willing to trust his fellow
man in most things, Issac, the charm pedlar
recently arrived in Sherwood, appears to be
a harmless quack. So why should Tuck be so
suspicious of the newcomer?
Issac Ballard Berkley
Will Scarlett Paul Eddington
Woodsman Clive Hepton
Derwent Victor Woolf

Director: Peter Seabourne

The Reluctant Rebel

w Leon Griffiths
In order to gather first-hand knowledge of
life in the Greenwood, Sir Geoffrey, a
writer, and his manservant, Herbert, pose as
outlaws and join Robin's band. What they
discover – if they live long enough to write
about it – would fill a book.
Sir Geoffrey John Carson
Will Scarlett Paul Eddington
Herbert Leslie Phillips
Jim Stark Hugh Cross

Director: Peter Seabourne

Hostage For a Hangman

w Arthur Dales
No stranger to trouble, Robin faces the
Sheriff's latest threat with grave concern: his
enemy has threatened to hang one serf a day
until the outlaw gives himself up.
Lord Orford Humphrey Lestocq
Alan-a-Dale Richard Coleman
Lord Beaumont Jack Melford
Derwent Victor Woolf

Director: Peter Seabourne

Hue and Cry

w Alan Hackney
Set upon and robbed of his chain of office by
a masked man, the Deputy Sheriff wrongly
suspects the outlaws of the crime. What
follows places Robin's life under threat –
and provides unwanted troubles for Little
John and Maid Marian.
Jenny Geraldine Hagen
Will Scarlett Paul Eddington
Dick Ronald Hines
Blacksmith Kevin Stoney

Director: Compton Bennett

Trapped

w Wilton Schiller
Sir Marmot, a Norman knight, seizes
travellers and then places them on trial on
trumped up charges. If they refuse to pay
the fine he imposes, he sentences them to
work on his estate. One of his victims is
Little John – which proves to be a very
costly mistake!
Sir Marmot Laurence Hardy
Peter Ronald Hines
William Maurice Kaufmann
Will Scarlett Paul Eddington

Director: Terry Bishop

THE ADVENTURES OF ROBIN HOOD
Produced by: Sapphire Film Productions for
ITC
Executive producer: Hannah Weinstein
Associate producer: Sidney Cole
Filmed at Nettlefold Studios, Walton-on-Thames
143 monochrome 30-minute episodes
17 February 1956 – 12 November 1960
[USA: Syndicated. CBS September 1955 –
September 1958]

THE ADVENTURES OF SHERLOCK HOLMES

see: *The Return of Sherlock Holmes*

THE ADVENTURES OF SIR LANCELOT

The classic deeds of King Arthur and his Knights of the Round Table, as depicted by the adventures of Sir Lancelot du Lac, a chivalrous, devil-may-care knight and the brightest star at King Arthur's court. The stories concerned themselves mainly with Lancelot's calling as the Queen's Champion to stave off threats to the throne by marauding invaders. Though seen, Excalibur, Arthur's legendary sword, was almost entirely forgotten. Not so the powers of Merlin, the court magician, whose 'spells' and 'potions' were treated with reverence – by all save the youngest member of the court.

An animated and thoroughly enjoyable – though sometimes unintentionally amusing – version of the Camelot legend. The series is best remembered for its spirited action sequences and the performance of its star, William Russell.

Now listen to my story, listen while I sing. Of days of old in England when Arthur was the King.

Of Merlin the Magician and Guinevere the Queen and Lancelot, the bravest knight the world has ever seen.

In days of old, when knights were bold, the story's told of Lancelot.

He rode the wilds of England, adventures for to seek. To rescue maidens in distress and help the poor and weak.

If anyone oppressed you, he'd be your champion; he fought a million battles and never lost a one.

In days of old, when knights were bold, the story's told of Lancelot.

REGULAR CAST

Sir Lancelot William Russell   *King Arthur* Bruce Seton (Eps 1 to 3 only)
Ronald Leigh-Hunt   *Queen Guinevere* Jane Hylton   *Merlin* Cyril Smith
Brian Robert Scroggins

The Knight of the Red Plume

w Leslie Poynton and Ralph Smart

Riding to Camelot to join King Arthur's knights, Sir Lancelot du Lac is challenged by three armed knights. Having defeated them, he proceeds to Camelot where, after proving his worth in a duel, he is appointed Champion to Queen Guinevere.
Sir Kay Brian Worth
Sir Gervaine Andrew Crawford
Leonides Peter Bennett

Director: Ralph Smart

Ferocious Fathers

w Leighton Raynolds

His master's castle under siege, Brian, a kitchen boy for Sir Ugan, races to Camelot to seek King Arthur's help. Sir Lancelot is given the task of helping Sir Ugan, and in return, the knight allows young Brian to serve as Lancelot's squire.
Sir Ugan Ballard Berkley
Brian Robert Scroggins (Intro.)
Helen Norah Gorsen

Director: Ralph Smart

The Queen's Knight

w Leslie Poynton

When Queen Guinevere is abducted by King Arthur's cousin, Sir Modred, who wishes to exchange her for Arthur's kingdom of Northumbria. Disguised as a cartier, Lancelot endeavours to rescue her – but is captured and thrown into a dungeon.
Sir Modred Brian Worth
Sir Tor Edwin Richfield
King Pell John Dearth

Director: Ralph Smart

The Outcast

w Leslie Poynton

When Brian takes up training to become a knight, the other boys show resentment.

One of them, Osbert, accuses Brian of stealing the Queen's ring, and it takes the combined efforts of Sir Lancelot and Mary, the Queen's ward, to clear his name.
Sir Glavin Patrick McGoohan
Sir Kay David Morrell
Mary Simone McQueen

Director: Bernard Knowles

Winged Victory

w John Ridgely

Prince Boudwin's castle is besieged by King Mark and his men. Lancelot, leading a party of King Arthur's knights to repel the invaders, is captured. The wily old Merlin has a rescue plan – involving his pet pigeons!
King Mark Nigel Greene
Prince Boudwin Douglas Argent
Queen Isoult Mary Wood

Director: Arthur Crabtree

Sir Bliant

w John Ridgely

When Sir Bliant's three sons kidnap the three daughters of their neighbour, Sir Rolf, the distressed knight seeks King Arthur's help. Merlin's magic is called for – and Sir Bliant receives 'double' retribution from 'himself'.
Sir Bliant William Russell
Sir Rolf Frederick Treves
Breuse Derry Nesbitt

Director: Bernard Knowles

The Pirates

w Leslie Poynton

When a pirate ship beaches near Camelot and King Arthur receives news that the pirates intend to rob the tomb of his father, Uther Pendragon, Sir Lancelot and his knights are faced with the task of guarding Pendragon's vault.

Llian Noel Purcell
Sir Lionel Paul Williamson
Mac Kevin Derry Nesbitt

Director: Bernard Knowles

The Magic Sword

w Leighton Reynolds
When he announces that Sir Lancelot's sword has magical powers, Merlin courts trouble of his own making. Sir Bernard puts the magician's claim to the test – with surprising results for both Lancelot and Merlin.
Sir Bernard Dan Cunningham
Lydia Nora Cheyney
Sir Hugh Douglas Argent

Director: Arthur Crabtree

Lancelot's Banishment

w Peggy Philips
Learning that King Marhaus, an ambitious foreigner, plans to kill King Arthur during a 'friendly' jousting tournament, Lancelot informs his sovereign. Unwilling to accept his friend's guilt, the King banishes Lancelot from his court!
King Marhaus Derek Aylward
Lady Angela Zena Walker
Firth Derry Nesbitt

Director: Anthony Squire

The Roman Wall

w Harold Kent
At the invitation of King Boltan, who tells them that his daughter, Iolta, has been abducted by ghostly warriors dressed in Roman attire, Lancelot and Brian scale a high boundary wall and discover a sign which says 'Rome – 1,200 miles'!
Lady Iolta Yvonne Warren
Trullus Gerald Cross
Probus Nigel Green

Director: Arthur Crabtree

Caledon

w Leighton Reynolds
On a lone mission of friendship to a distant Northern ally, and carrying a priceless gift from his King, Sir Lancelot is attacked, robbed and left for dead by brigands. Help arrives in a strange form – a wonder horse named Caledon.
Jaggyd George Murcell
Farmer Nigel Green
Sir Kay David Morrell

Director: Bernard Knowles

Theft of Excalibur

w H. H. Burns and Peggy Philips
A knight is held for ransom. The price for his release – King Arthur's sword, Excalibur. With Merlin's help, Lancelot and Brian engage the kidnappers in battle in order to retrieve the sword before it can be used for misdeeds.
Barny Brandygore Alfie Bass
Michael David Bough
Tristram Derry Nesbitt

Director: Bernard Knowles

The Black Castle

w Leslie Poynton
Torwald, a knight, holds Lord Trebizond to ransom in the Black Castle. Lorraine, Trebizond's daughter, rides to Camelot to seek the help of her betrothed, Sir Cedric. Meanwhile, Lancelot and Brian find themselves outside Torwald's castle.
Torwald Peter Coke
Trebizond Douglas Argent
Lorraine Michael Blakeman

Director: Bernard Knowles

Shepherds' War

w Leslie Poynton
Hearing that friendly shepherds are under attack by plundering knights, Sir Lancelot volunteers to help. But first he must teach the shepherds the importance of self-defence – a task complicated by their loathing of combat.
Elsa Jennifer Jayne
Chad Derry Nesbitt
Adrian Meadows White

Director: Bernard Knowles

The Magic Book

w Peggy Phillips

Fearing that the Danes will attack Tyning Abbey and steal valuable documents, King Arthur sends Lancelot and Merlin to defend the Abbot. But how can two men stave off an attack by many? Merlin provides the answer.

Father Till Eddie Malin
Father Telford John Cazabon
Telmah Norman Mitchell

Director: Terry Bishop

The Ruby of Radnor

w H. H. Burns

King Arthur has a dilemma. Despite providing extra guards, the crown jewels have been stolen from Radnor Abbey. Lancelot and his knights must recover them within 24 hours – but they must first discover who stole them!

Everard Colin Tapley
Garth Edward Judd
Sir Robert Eric Corrie

Director: Laurence Huntington

The Lesser Breed

w Peggy Phillips

When Lancelot and Brian set forth to dispel the rumour of a three-headed sea monster terrorising the district, they find more than they at first bargained for: a stunningly beautiful girl, and a very dangerous situation.

Sella Ann Stephens
Eck Gerald Heinz
Fisherman Wilfred Brambell

Director: Bernard Knowles

Witches' Brew

w Peggy Phillips

News reaches Camelot that King Rolf has imprisoned his own son for treason. Disturbed by such unlikely behaviour from his peace-loving ally, King Arthur sends Sir Lancelot to investigate.

King Rolf Leonard Sachs
Eunice Maxine Audley
Hendrick Richard Hearne

Director: Terry Bishop

Sir Crustabread

w Leslie Poynton

A visit from the Lady Lynette plunges Sir Lancelot into a danger-fraught mission. Disguised as a disreputable baker, he must save her daughter from a bigamous marriage to Baron Braynor.

Lady Lynette Virginia Vernon
Baron Hector Ross
Sir Grinamore Alan Edwardes

Director: Bernard Knowles

Maid of Somerset

w Selwyn Jepson

When the Maid of Somerset arrives at Camelot seeking King Arthur's help against an oppressor of her village, the King nominates Sir Lancelot to handle the affair. During their journey to Somerset, the knight and his ward are attacked and taken prisoner.

Ellen Patricia Kneale
John Brian Derby
King Meliot Duncan Lewis

Director: Bernard Knowles

Knight Errant

w Peggy Phillips and Selwyn Jepson

Helen and Bragwaine have inherited their father's kingdom, but their wicked guardian, Kafan, is determined to marry Helen off to an aged King. When she refuses to agree to his request, Sir Lancelot and Sir Kay are sent to her aid.

Helen Margaret Anderson
Bragwaine Hazel Penwarden
Kafan Julian Somers

Director: Bernard Knowles

Double Identity

w Harold Kent

Sir Richard, on his way to Taunton to be married, is kidnapped by his cousin, Alfred, who takes his place. Attending the wedding ceremony, Sir Lancelot sees through Alfred's disguise and lays a plot to unmask the impostor.

Sir Richard/Sir Alfred Howard Pays
Lady Margaret Diana Fairfax
Sir John John Bailey

Director: Laurence Huntington

The Lady Lilith

w Leslie Poynton

When Sir Liones's claim to an inheritance is disputed by the Lady Lilith, King Arthur must find a way to end the dispute without offending either party. Requested to help, Sir Lancelot offers a novel solution to the King's dilemma.
Lilith Shirley Cooklin
Sir Liones Richard Leech
Sir Ivor Edward Judd

Director: Laurence Huntington

The Bridge

w Peter Key

By an ancient treaty, the bridge connecting the village of Pontifax with the kingdom of King Marhaus must be kept free of taxes. When Arthur's enemy threatens to close the bridge, the King sends two of his knights to help the villagers.
King Marhaus Derek Aylward
Lady Angela Zena Walker
Sir Grint Edward Judd

Director: Peter Maxwell

The Ugly Duckling

w Leslie Poynton

Sir Lancelot and Brian try to help a young girl who has put her life in danger to attract attention to herself. Having been rejected by her suitors, they find the girl suspicious of their motives – until Brian has a bright idea.
Sybil Carol Marsh
Gault Ian Whittaker
Sir Christopher Edward Judd

Director: George More O'Farrell

Knights' Choice

w Peggy Phillips

There is a vacant seat at the Round Table, and King Arthur decides to hold a contest to find the bravest knight in England. Morgan le Fay enters – but she's a woman . . . isn't she?
Morgan le Fay Alison Leggatt
Sir Rupert Robert Hardy
Balin Derek Waring

Director: Peter Maxwell

The Missing Princess

w Leslie Poynton

What has happened to Princess Anne? That's the dilemma facing Sir Lancelot when King Arthur pleads with him to find her – but sometimes people have no wish to be found, and who should question their motives?
Princess Anne Mary Steele
Marta Linda Grey
Athelred John Horsley

Director: Desmond Davis

The Mortaise Fair

w Leslie Poynton

The Madras Pearl, given to Queen Guinevere by the Rajah of Kaipur, is lost during a fire. Aware that its loss could jeopardise relations between King Arthur and his ally, Lancelot swears to find it.
Baron Mortaise William Franklyn
Rajah Richard Hearne
Hassim Martin Benson

Director: Laurence Huntington

The Thieves

w H. H. Burns

Attempting to show King Arthur how difficult it is to get honest employment once a man has been branded a thief, Lancelot persuades the King to join him in the streets. Disguised as robbers, they enter a den of thieves – and find trouble in abundance!
Lord Vanton Colin Tapley
King's man Edward Judd
Norrin Jack Melford

Director: Bernard Knowles

The Prince of Limerick

w Leslie Poynton

In Ireland, on a mission for their king, Lancelot and Brian find that the Emerald Isle holds a special fascination of its own – particularly if you're a friend of the Prince of Limerick.

Prince Jerome Willis
Baron Wicklow Thomas Duggan
Princess Lyne Furlong

Director: Laurence Huntington

THE ADVENTURES OF SIR LANCELOT
Producer: Sidney Cole, Dallas Bower and Bernard Knowles
Executive producer: Hannah Weinstein
Music by: Edwin Astley
A Sapphire Films Production for ITC
Filmed at Nettleford Studios, Walton-on-Thames
30 colour 30-minute episodes
15 September 1956 – 20 April 1957
[USA: Syndicated. NBC September 1955 – June 1957. ABC October 1957 – September 1958]

THE ADVENTURES OF WILLIAM TELL

In the fourteenth century, the small town of Altdorf in Switzerland was conquered by the Austrians, who ruled the community with a rod of iron wielded by the dreaded Landburgher Gessler, an obese and thoroughly evil tyrant who imposed heavy tax on his Swiss subjects and had his soldiers slay anyone who refused to pay. Only one man, a resident of the nearby village of Berglan, dared to oppose the Austrian governor – William Tell. With courage and cunning, Tell and his small band of followers fought for freedom and justice. Like England's Robin Hood, Tell robbed the rich to feed the poor, and his name became a symbol of hope for the downtrodden Swiss villagers.

The first episode adapted the original story by Johann von Schiller: Tell, captured by Gessler's troops, was forced to display his renowned marksmanship with the crossbow by shooting an apple off his own son's head. With unfailing accuracy he did so but, as a precaution against Gessler's treachery, the archer secreted a second arrow upon his person with which he would have killed the Austrian governor if his marksmanship had failed him. Discovering this ruse, Gessler issued orders for Tell's arrest and the bowman was forced to retreat to a mountain hideaway where, outlawed to a cave with his wife, Hedda, and their son, Walter, he gathered around him a small group of followers who banded together in their attempt to free the Swiss people from Austrian oppression.

REGULAR CAST

William Tell Conrad Phillips   *Hedda* Jennifer Jayne   *Walter* Richard Rogers
Gessler Willoughby Goddard   *Fertog (The Bear)* Nigel Greene

The Emperor's Hat

w Rene Wilde and Leslie Arliss
Overrun by Austrians, and ruled by the evil
tyrant, Landburgher Gessler, Switzerland
soon forms a resistance movement. One such
band is led by William Tell.
Frederick Norman Mitchell
Sentry Derren Nesbitt
Villager Charles Houston

Director: Ralph Smart

The Hostages

w Doreen Montgomery and Ralph Smart
Annoyed by Tell's activities, Gessler issues
orders to have the archer arrested – but Tell
has disappeared. Not to be outdone, Gessler
seizes six villagers as hostages: each of them
will die – unless Tell returns within 12
hours.
Hofmanstahl Peter Hammond
Fritz Roy Purcell
Franz James Booth

Director: Peter Maxwell

The Secret Death

w Doreen Montgomery and Ralph Smart
When his wife is captured by Gessler's
troops and sentenced to death, Tell offers
himself in exchange – a dangerous move?
Not when you have the loyalty of several
trustworthy supporters.
Judge Furst Jack Lambert
Schmidt Howard Lang
Schaffer Sidney James

Director: Peter Maxwell

The Gauntlet of St Gerhardt

w Doreen Montgomery
A religious relic, the Gauntlet of St
Gerhardt, appears to inspire the Swiss to
feats of valour. Gessler makes plans to steal
it by having the Abbot who guards it
killed. Tell, however, has other plans.
Captain Werner Derren Nesbitt
Trooper Edward Judd
Abbot Ian Wallace

Director: Peter Maxwell

The Prisoner

w John Kruse
On his way to deliver a message to William
Tell, a resistance man is captured and taken
to a secluded fortress. It appears Tell will
never learn his secret – but the resistance
leader has other plans.
Bullinger Bruce Seton
Pettitpiere Jerry Verno
Max Michael Caine

Director: Peter Maxwell

Voice in the Night

w Ralph Smart
After a disagreement with Gessler, Judge
Furst is thrown into a dungeon. His clerk –
a secret Austrian collaborator – is appointed
Judge in his place, but Tell plans to expose
him.
Frederick Derren Nesbitt
Gunther Ronald Leigh-Hunt
Judge Furst Jack Lambert

Director: Terry Bishop

The Assassins

w Rene Wilde and Ralph Smart
Two Swiss collaborators, arrested by Gessler
for murdering Prince Karl, are given a
chance to save their necks from the
hangman's noose. They must discover Tell's
hiding place and kill him!
Maddeaux Edwin Richfield
Bolf Alfred Burke
Captain Willoughby Grey

Director: Terry Bishop

The Baroness

w John Kruse and Ralph Smart
When her husband is invited to visit the
castle of a beautiful baroness who says she is
being blackmailed, Hedda, suspecting the
woman of working for Gessler, follows Tell
and uncovers a devious plot.
Baroness Delphi Lawrence
Bullinger Bruce Seton
Maria Norma Purcell

Director: Peter Maxwell

The Elixir

w Lindsay Galloway (from a story by Ralph Smart)

A local monastery, run by Italian monks, is making a delicious brew, then donating the proceeds to founding a school for Swiss children. Never one to pass up an opportunity to swell his coffers, Gessler arrests the holy men.

Ferdinand Jack Watling
Jules John McCarthy
Innkeeper Hamlyn Benson

Director: Terry Bishop

The Suspect

w Doreen Montgomery and Larry Forester

Tell must prove a young girl innocent of the charge of giving information to the Austrians about secret arms shipments to the resistance workers. If he doesn't, the girl will be hanged by the townspeople.

Josephine Sheila Raynor
Gruner Peter Bennett
Officer Edward Judd

Director: Quentin Lawrence

The Cuckoo

w Ralph Smart

Early every morning, Gessler is awakened by a cuckoo. At his wits' end, his problem is compounded further when he receives a message from the Emperor demanding taxes Gessler hasn't yet collected!

Hofmanstahl Peter Hammond
Ferdinand Jack Watling
Sergeant-at-arms David Davenport

Director: Peter Maxwell

The Bear

w Doreen Montgomery (from a story by Michael Connor)

When his son joins Tell's group, and refuses to return home, the Bear, a robber, swears to seek revenge on Tell and his followers. As events turn out, the two men form an uneasy but beneficial alliance.

The Bear Nigel Greene (Intro.)
Bruno John Howard Davies
Burgomaster Meadows White

Director: Ernest Morris

The Magic Powder

w Martin Worth (from a story by Ralph Smart)

Doctor Klein, a scientist working for Gessler, invents an explosive powder for use in road-making. When his employer decides to use the invention for warfare, Klein seeks refuge with William Tell – who has greater need of such a discovery.

Doctor Klein Henry Oscar
Ludwig Gerald Cross
Soldier Anthony Parker

Director: Peter Maxwell

The Golden Wheel

w Michael Connor

Having discovered where the resistance hides its funds, Gessler makes plans to stop further money reaching them. As always, he has reckoned without William Tell's interference – and the Landburgher's coffers suffer as a result.

Wolfgang Derek Godfrey
Hunzler Patrick Troughton
Fritz Charles Ross

Director: Peter Maxwell

The Bride

w Doreen Montgomery (from a story by John Kruse)

Maddelenna is being forcibly taken to Altdorf Castle as a bride for Gessler. Tell sees this as an opportunity to teach their enemy a lesson, but his wife Hedda is not so sure.

Maddelenna Nadja Regin
Anton Glyn Owen
Master-at-arms Derren Nesbitt

Director: Quentin Lawrence

Boy Slaves

w John Kruse

Can Tell trust the word of his enemy? He must, if he is to obtain the release of several young boys whom Gessler is holding as slaves in a labour camp. Alone and unarmed he may be – but Tell has an ace up his sleeve.

Carl Frazer Hines
Aunt Maria Majorie Rhodes
Schulenberg Derren Nesbitt

Director: Terry Bishop

The Young Widow

w Paul Christie
Having escaped from Gessler's troops, Tell and his wife are given refuge by the beautiful Countess von Marheim. Recognising her guests, Paul, her servant, threatens to inform Gessler of their whereabouts – unless the Countess agrees to marry him.

Countess Melissa Stribling
Paul Charles Houston
Kurt Julian Somers

Director: Peter Maxwell

Landslide

w John Kruse
Tell comes face to face with his exact double – an Austrian imported by Gessler to impersonate the resistance leader and rob Swiss peasants. But which of the look-alikes is which? Gessler's attempts to find out cost him dearly.

Herr Speckler Charles Lloyd Pack
Josef Wilfred Brambell
Weber Charles Houston

Director: Quentin Lawrence

The Trap

w Doreen Montgomery and Max Savage
By using a traitor planted in Tell's camp, Gessler plans to smash the resistance movement in one swoop. But even the best-laid schemes are prone to failure – as the Landburgher soon discovers.

Ingrid Colette Wilde
Peter Robert Shaw
The Bear Nigel Greene

Director: Quentin Lawrence

The Shrew

w Max Savage
Hedda, lured away by a message that her sister is ill, finds herself an unwilling pawn in Gessler's latest plot to squash the resistance. Confident that this time Tell will be taken, the Austrian is in for a surprise.

Gertrude Harriet Jones
Karl Roy Godfrey
Gretel Joanna Dunham

Director: Peter Maxwell

Manhunt

w Doreen Montgomery (from a story by Ralph Smart)
Trapped on an island owned by Prince Erik, a man who enjoys hunting human prey, Tell's career appears to be at an end – but help arrives from a most unexpected quarter, and the resistance leader finds a new ally.

Prince Erik Christopher Lee
Heinrich Kevin Stoney
Count Hegel Leslie Perrins

Director: Peter Maxwell

The Killer

w Lindsay Holloway
Accused of murdering a partisan helper and stealing his gold, Tell must find a way to prove his innocence – and that's not so easy when you suspect one of your accusers of being the real killer.

Frau Anna Monica Grey
Frau Strauss Sally Travers
Merchant Richard Vernon

Director: Peter Maxwell

The Surgeon

w Doreen Montgomery
Seriously wounded, Tell is taken to the home of a Swiss surgeon. To throw Gessler off their trail, Tell's followers pretend their leader is stricken with the plague. Will their ruse work? Tell's life depends on the outcome.

Kramer Derek Aylward
Apothecary Stanley van Beers
Heinburgher Frank Thornton

Director: Peter Maxwell

The Ensign

w Max Savage and Leslie Arliss

When faced with conflict between duty and conscience, Fritz, a young Austrian soldier, unexpectedly turns not to Gessler, but to William Tell for help – a move which places the resistance leader's life in great peril.
Fritz John Carson
Hoffman Edward Evans
Hugo Julian Somers

Director: Quentin Lawrence

The Unwelcome Stranger

w Paul Christie

Investigating why people from the swordmaking village of Linzon have stopped sending arms to his headquarters, Tell's visit to the community is treated with an air of suspicion. What's more, the villagers are anxious to get rid of him. Why?
Karl David de Keyser
Martin Derren Nesbitt
Dina Susan Travers

Director: Peter Maxwell

The Avenger

w Lindsay Galloway

When Tell investigates why two envoys disappeared while on their way to him to discuss a treaty of friendship, he uncovers a far greater mystery – one that threatens to engulf his family and will ultimately test the loyalty of his followers.
Duke of Burgundy John Le Mesurier
Louis Derek Waring
Anna Diane Lambert

Director: Anthony Squire

The Bandit

w Lindsay Galloway (from a story by Ralph Smart)

When one of his men fails to return from a mission to Rinaldo, a rival resistance leader, Tell suspects treachery. Unknown to him, a bandit is in the area, under orders from Gessler, seeking to cast doubt on Tell's activities.
Rinaldo Brian Rawlinson
Carl Maurice Kauffman
Marco Kenneth Cope

Director: Anthony Squire

Gessler's Daughter

w Lindsay Galloway

With his daughter Anna kidnapped and held for ransom, Gessler knows of only one man who can help him obtain her release – his arch enemy, William Tell. But can he swallow his pride long enough to meet Tell on neutral ground?
Anna Gessler Pelita Nelson
Muller Michael Golden
Frau Muller Catherine Finn

Director: Ernest Morris

The Raid

w Leslie Arliss and Rene Wilde

Disguised as Austrian soldiers, Tell and Hans enter the fortress at Schwartzburg. Their mission is to seize arms needed by the resistance – but disaster strikes when Tell is recognised by a guard.
Hans Michael Brennan
Fritz Tony Thawnton
Guard Terence Cooper

Director: Leslie Arliss

The General's Daughter

w Ian Stuart Black

While collecting provisions from a Swiss patriot, the Bear is captured and flung into Gessler's dungeons. Tell must devise an ingenious method of engineering his friend's release.
The Bear Nigel Greene
General Bruce Seton
Sergeant Wiener Michael Caine

Director: Peter Maxwell

Castle of Fear

w Roger Marshall (from a story by Max Savage)

Visiting Werner Castle to track down the murderer of a resistance leader, Tell finds himself involved in a deadly game of fear and intrigue – with his own life offered to the victor.

Gustaf Fergy Mayne
Eric Edwin Richfield
Hans Keith Rawlins

Director: Peter Maxwell

The Black Brothers

w Arnold Abbot

Stealing arms intended for the Swiss resistance movement is crime enough, but when three Italian rogues compound their crime by attempting to sell the weapons to William Tell, they have cause for concern indeed.

Luigi Roger Delgado
Pietro Paul Stassino
Carlo Warren Mitchell

Director: Quentin Lawrence

The Lost Letter

w Michael Connor

So anxious is he to read a letter from Judge Furst informing William Tell of the location of a large arms shipment, Gessler fails to realise that the missive is in the sole of his own boot. When finding it, the hapless Austrian really puts his foot into it!

Judge Fursk Jack Lambert
Franz Alex Scott
Frederick Derren Nesbitt

Director: Terry Bishop

The Secret Weapon

w Doreen Montgomery

The resistance leader and the Bear set out to investigate reports that Gessler is erecting new fortifications along the Swiss coastline. Should the rumour be confirmed, it will effectively cut off the resistance group's escape route.

Jacques John Horsley
Captain Jack Watling
Hans Derek Sherwin

Director: Ernest Morris

The Master Spy

w Doreen Montgomery

Armed with a new 'secret weapon' – Mara, a beautiful, but highly dangerous spy known only as the Shadow – Gessler lures Tell and his followers into a trap. Could this spell the end of Tell's fight for freedom?

Mara Adrienne Corri
Anton Glyn Owen
Heinz Harvey Hall

Director: Ernest Morris

The Traitor

w Roger Marshall and Leslie Arliss

Certain that no one knows their whereabouts, Tell and his wife visit a friendly resistance leader's camp. During their journey home, they are attacked by a gang of rogues.

Kramer William Lucas
Bullinger Bruce Seton
Rothman Neil Hallett

Director: Peter Maxwell

The Spider

w Ralph Smart and Roger Marshall

Hearing that a ruthless Austrian commander, nicknamed the Spider, has captured two of his men and threatens to torture them unless they divulge the location of Tell's camp, the resistance leader infiltrates the Spider's ranks.

The Spider Donald Pleasance
Johann Howard Pays
Gerda Sheila Wilcock

Director: Ernest Morris

The Mountain People

w Doreen Montgomery (from a story by John Kruse)

A beautiful young girl, rescued by Tell from a troop of Austrian soldiers, leads him into a situation from which the resistance leader barely escapes with his life – and reputation – intact.

Eve Maureen Davis
Johann Lee Montague
Josef James Booth

Director: Quentin Lawrence

Undercover

w Lindsay Galloway

Hearing that a close friend, an agent to the Emperor, has died, Tell enters enemy territory disguised as a trader. He intends to rescue Magda, the Emperor's daughter – but things go disastrously wrong.

Magda Jill Browne
Emperor Derek Bond
Michaelis Ian Colin

Director: Ernest Morris

THE ADVENTURES OF WILLIAM TELL
Producer: Leslie Arliss
Executive producer: Ralph Smart
An ITC Production
Filmed at the National Studios
39 monochrome 30-minute episodes
15 September 1958 – 15 June 1959
[USA: Syndicated 1957]

AFRICAN PATROL

The adventures of Patrol Inspector Paul Derek, a law officer whose beat was the African jungle. Armed with only his wits, his gun and his knowledge of the dense arid veldt, Britain's answer to Jungle Jim pursued criminals and injustice across an environment in which a 'concrete jungle' policeman would have found a trail impossible to follow – and bored the pants off everyone in the process!

REGULAR CAST
Inspector Derek John Bentley

Episodes denoted with asterisk rescued from boredom by the presence of Honor Blackman.

The Baboon Laughed	The Abduction
The Hunt	The Silver Story
Lost	Black Ivory
Murder is Spelled L.O.V.E.	Robbery
The Bad Samaritan	No Place To Hide
Hooded Death	The Mortimer Touch
Shooting Star	Shadowed Light
No Science	Ghost Country
Heart of Gold	The Sickness*
Counterfeit	Snake in the Grass
Mombasa	The Speculator
Tycoon	The Trek
Hashish	Hell Hath No Fury
Knife of Aesculapius	Knave of Diamonds
Killer From the Forest	Witness to Murder*
Breakout	Deadly Twenty Minutes

The Girl
Missing Doctor
Dead Shot

The Accident
Bodango Gold
The Duel
Man and Beast

AFRICAN PATROL
Series produced by: Michael Sadler for M.E.
Productions
Associate producer: Ted Holliday
Music by: Phil Green
Script supervisor: Lynn Cariddi
*Filmed entirely on location in East Africa
by Kenya Productions Ltd*
39 monochrome 30-minute episodes
5 April 1958 – 6 February 1959
[USA: Syndicated 1957]

AIRLINE

Set in the period between summer 1946 and autumn 1948, this series depicted the trials and tribulations of an ex-wartime pilot down on his luck. Recently demobbed, with a £70 gratuity and little else beyond his ambition to continue flying, Jack Ruskin, unable to get a job with a civilian airline, buys an old plane and sets up Ruskin Air Services in partnership with his ex-RAF colleague, Peter Witney – a 'golden opportunity' which promptly turns sour.

A superb production, with breathtaking aerial sequences and top drawer production values.

REGULAR CAST

Jack Ruskin Roy Marsden   *Peter Witney* Richard Heffer
McEvoy (Ruskin's engineer) Sean Scanlan
Jennie Shaw (Ruskin's fiancee) Polly Hemingway   *Ernie Cade* Terence Rigby

Look After Number One

w Wilfred Greatorex
Flt-Sgt Jack Ruskin spends the final hours of his wartime flying career bringing demob-hungry servicemen home from India. Meanwhile, Sqd-Ldr Dickie Marlowe, stationed in Germany, is intent on making his fortune by black market activities.

Dickie Marlowe Anthony Valentine
Wing Commander Walter Gotell
Gray Graham Rees

Director: Michael Ferguson
Designer: Richard Jarvis/David Crozier

Brave New World

w Wilfred Greatorex

Civvy street, and Jack Ruskin's battle for survival begins. The anticipated hero's welcome fails to materialise, and Ruskin must get to grips with the realities of post-war life.

Chairman Ronald Leigh-Hunt
Frank Shaw Peter Schofield
Mrs Shaw Jeanne Watts

Director: Michael Ferguson
Designer: Richard Jarvis/David Crozier

Conscience

w Wilfred Greatorex

July. Ruskin Air Services gets off to a flying start – until what appears to be an attractive business deal in Palestine turns sour, and almost costs Ruskin and his partner their lives.

Alan Shaw Nicholas Owen
Sanders Paul Foulds
Glover Stewart Bevan

Director: Michael Ferguson
Designer: Richard Jarvis/David Crozier

Touch and Go

w Wilfred Greatorex

February. Ruskin Air Services is grounded: locked in the icy grip of winter. Enter Ernie Cade, with a proposition the men find hard to refuse. Had they known what they were letting themselves in for, they would have remained earthbound.

Harrison Michael Browning
Dr Hadfield Roger Hammond
Kellett Michael Wisher

Director: Roger Cheveley
Designer: Richard Jarvis/David Crozier

Fool's Errands

w Nick McCarty

March 1947. Ruskin is broke. His plane is badly damaged and Cade is putting the screws on. Hardly the time to expand, one would think. But Ruskin's determination to succeed knows no bounds.

Alby Clarke Christopher Gray
Kellett Michael Wisher
Maynard Ralph Arliss

Director: Roger Cheveley
Designer: David Crozier/Richard Jarvis

Captain Clarke Plus One

w Ray Jenkins

Spring 1947. With the forces of bureaucracy massing against him in England, Ruskin finds himself in Malta, with no fuel, no cooperation and no way out. All seems lost until the winds of fortune change – for the worse!

Air Cmdre Rupert Kenneth Watson
Enquiry chairman Laurence Payne
Snell Anthony Schaeffer

Director: Michael Ferguson
Designer: Richard Jarvis

Not Much of a Life

w Jane Franklin

Stripped of his pilot's licence and no airline to run, Ruskin, undaunted, embarks on a new 'money earner' – and that's where he comes unstuck: military training hasn't exactly prepared his crew for carrying passengers.

Kellett Michael Wisher
Alby Clarke Christopher Gray
Dr Hadfield Roger Hammond

Director: Peter Duguid/Roger Cheveley
Designer: Richard Jarvis/David Crozier

Officers and Gentlemen

w Nick McCarty

Spring 1948. Dark clouds are gathering over Jennie and Jack's wedding plans. The airline is in deep – and deadly – trouble. Ruskin must make a decision which will affect the lives of everyone around him. But will he make the right choice?

Starmer Neil Dickson
Kellett Michael Wisher
Alby Clarke Christopher Gray

Director: Roger Cheveley
Designer David Crozier/Richard Jarvis

Too Many Problems

w Michael Russell

Autumn 1948. With high financial rewards to be made from the Berlin airlift, independent operator Ruskin has nothing to operate. He has lost his licence, one of his planes and most of his crew. Can he save himself from disaster?

Malton Dudley Jones
Kellett Michael Wisher
Seymour Roger Llewellyn

Director: Michael Ferguson
Designer: Richard Jarvis/David Crozier

AIRLINE
Created by: Wilfred Greatorex
Producer: Michael Ferguson
Executive producer: David Cunliffe
Music by: Tony Hatch
Aviation adviser: Dick Millward
A Yorkshire TV Network Production
9 colour 60-minute episodes
3 January–28 February 1982

ARTHUR OF THE BRITONS

'Arthur as he must have been', proclaimed the studio press release. 'No Guineveres, Lancelots, Galahads or Merlins. No armour, no romance. Just grime!' Given the premise that the legend of King Arthur of England, ruler of Camelot, was just that, a romantic myth, and that in reality the historical Arthur was a *Welshman* and never crowned King of England, this series set out to sever the last link between the legends and placed Arthur firmly in the forests of Britain in the Dark Ages – a time when 'armies' of 20 men waged petty little battles. Chivalry, a vital ingredient in previous productions, went out the window.

In this series, Arthur was portrayed as a sixth-century warlord who virtually single-handedly held off the invasion by the English barbarians. His aim: to unite the kingdoms under one military command. To this end, he and his companions, Llud the Silver Hand, a pagan, and Kai, a Saxon foundling, made daily sorties against English-held territories and wreaked havoc among their enemies.

Peppered with lusty sword fights and a liberal helping of ambitiously-staged, rugged (and often violent) hand-to-hand combat scenes, the series provided ample thrills for the viewer and elevated Oliver Tobias to star status.

REGULAR CAST

Arthur Oliver Tobias   *Kai* Michael Gothard   *Llud* Jack Watson
Mark of Cornwall (Arthur's rival) Brian Blessed   *Cerdig* Rupert Davies

Arthur is Dead

w Terence Feely

Though the message says Arthur is dead, it is in fact a plan by Arthur to unite his warring Celtic fellow-chieftains against their common Saxon enemy – who, finding their plans to take over Arthur's territory thwarted, serve out harsh retribution.
Mark of Cornwall Brian Blessed
Cerdig Rupert Davies
Dirk Donald Burton

Director: Peter Sasdy

The Gift of Life

w Terence Feely

When a Saxon raiding party attacks and burns Arthur's village, the warlord expects a further onslaught. But 'trouble' of a very different kind arrives – two Saxon children discovered floating in a river.
Horgen Stephen Chase
Hildred Heather Wright
Ulrich Dennis Banda

Director: Pat Jackson

The Challenge

w Terence Feely

Appointed leaders of two villages to the north, cousins Garet and Gawain give Arthur more trouble than he'd bargained for. But trouble of a different variety threatens to place his life in dire peril.
Garet Nicky Henson
Gawain Ken Hutchinson
Saxon leader Terry York

Director: Sidney Hayers

The Penitent Invader

w Terence Feely

Rolf's conversion to Christianity does not put an end to his savage looting of his fellow Celts. But Arthur, faced with an impending attack by invading Picts, sees a way of 'converting' Rolf's thinking to his own.
Rolf Clive Revill
The Abbot Hedley Goodall
Hereward Michael Graham Fox

Director: Patrick Dromgoole

People of the Plough

w Bob Blake and Dave Martin

On a mission for Arthur, Kai befriends an attractive Saxon girl named Freya, who is fending for herself in an isolated homestead. Their meeting portends grave problems for the Celtic warlord.
Freya Valerie Ost
Rulf Mark Edwards
Mordant Mike Pratt

Director: Sidney Hayers

The Duel

w Terence Feely

Having persuaded Mark of Cornwall to join them, Arthur and his companions set off on their journey to give aid to a village under attack by the Saxons. During the journey, one of Mark's men is killed. Though accidental, Mark accuses Llud – and challenges him to trial by combat.
Mark Brian Blessed
Luke Max Faulkner
Mahon Terry York

Director: Pat Jackson

The Pupil

w Terence Feely

Returning to his village, Arthur is attacked by Corin, a young boy. Having disarmed him, the warlord listens with interest when the boy tells him that he wants to be a warrior and only attacked Arthur to prove his worth.
Corin Peter Firth
Llud's wife Trisha Mortimer
Mordor Gerry Wain

Director: Sidney Hayers

Rolf the Preacher

w Terence Feely

Cured of his warrior ways and converted to Christianity, Rolf returns to Arthur's kingdom – and becomes an even greater threat than before! His arrival threatens to reopen old wounds and place Arthur's life in danger.

Rolf Clive Revill
Mark Brian Blessed
Maeren Mel Davies

Director: Sidney Hayers

Enemies and Lovers

w Scott Forbes

Mistaken for Saxon spies, Arthur and Kai are captured by Morcant, the would-be successor to King Athel. Their saviour is King Athel himself who, recognising a clasp worn by Arthur, introduces the two men to his daughter Goda – a girl whom Morcant plans to have for himself.
Morcant Mark Eden
Athel Esmond Knight
Goda Hilary Dwyer

Director: Sidney Hayers

The Slave

w Robert Banks Stewart

Arthur and Kai must devise a plan to free villagers being used as slaves. So pitiful are their conditions of imprisonment that, should Arthur need men for his army, many will die unless they are rescued soon.
Rodolph Anthony Bailey
Col David Prowse
Thana Deborah Watling

Director: Pat Jackson

The Wood People

w David Osborne

Two gypsy children are held hostage by the Saxons. The ransom is Arthur's life, and the gypsies themselves will be his executioners. But when Arthur is brought before them, the Saxons are in for an unwelcome surprise.
Saxon leader Bernard Bresslaw
Yan Christopher Douglas
Elder Daphne Heard

Director: Sidney Hayers

The Prize

w Robert Banks Stewart

After a daring escape from captivity, Arthur travels to Cornwall to seek Mark's help in plundering a vast hoard of treasure from the Saxons. Unknown to the warlord, his plans will place the lives of his friends in jeopardy.
Mark Brian Blessed
Hoxel Tim Condren
Galt Richard Duerden

Director: Pat Jackson

The Swordsman

w Terence Feely

Arthur falls foul of King Mordred's cunning and hatred. Forced into facing a deadly swordsman in mortal combat, the warlord needs all his cunning to stay alive.
Karn the Swordsman Martin Jarvis
Trader Alfie Bass
Elsa Elsa Smith

Director: Sidney Hayers

Rowena

w Robert Banks Stewart

Victims of a surprise attack, Arthur and Kai escape and go to look for fresh horses. To get them, they have to strike a strange bargain with Yorath – in payment, they must deliver his daughter, Rowena, to her bridegroom.
Yorath George Marishka
Rowena Gila von Weiterhausen
Fenred Sidney Johnson

Director: Patrick Dromgoole

The Prisoner

w Robert Banks Stewart

When his childhood friend, Roland, a Saxon, enters Arthur's camp, Kai's allegiance to Arthur is put to the test. Can the Celts' friendship prove strong enough to overcome this latest threat to Arthur's life?
Mark Brian Blessed
Roland Michael Gambon
Leini Sally James

Director: Pat Jackson

Some Saxon Women

w David Osborne

Five Saxon women – daughters of the enemy – for a barrel of wine. That's the bargain

Yorath strikes with a Greek trader – a bargain that gives Arthur and his companions a major headache.
Yorath George Marishka
Rowena Gila von Weiterhausen
Trader Ferdy Mayne

Director: Patrick Dromgoole

Go Warily

w Jonathan Crown
A nightmare, in which he sees himself pursued, captured and tortured by a giant warrior, strikes terror into Llud's heart. Meanwhile, Arthur forms a treaty with Brandreth – a man who has a twin brother who has sworn to kill the warlord.
Brandreth/Gavron Tom Baker
Kellas Colin Rix
Brosk David Prowse

Director: Sidney Hayers

The Marriage Feast

w Terence Feely
Arthur is filled with anguish: Rowena, the girl he loves, has promised to marry Mark of Cornwall. The warlord has one chance to prevent this happening – but it means exposing Mark's true character and facing his wrath when the truth is known!
Mark Brian Blessed
Rowena Gila von Weiterhausen
Yorath George Marishka

Director: Sidney Hayers

In Common Cause

w Michael J. Bird
When a plague hits Saxon wildstock, Arthur's men see reason to rejoice. But the wily warlord, realising that the same pestilence could affect his own herds, proposes a truce to fight a common cause – a solution which horrifies his followers.
Cerdig Rupert Davies
Amlodd Peter Stephens
Ulm Kenneth Ives

Director: Patrick Dromgoole

Six Measures of Silver

w Robert Banks Stewart
Kurk, the Saxon, is a charming but dangerous rogue. So when the cattle he sells to Rowena turn out to be stolen, Arthur proposes that Llud teaches Kurk a painful – and important – lesson in chivalry.
Kurk Michael Craig
Berthold Peter Copely
Hurn David Brierley

Director: Pat Jackson

Daughter of the King

w David Pursall and Jack Seddon
Arthur, confident that he has discovered a way to force Bavick to stop murdering his fellow Celts – he intends to use Bavick's daughter Eithna as hostage – fails to take into account Bavick's cunning.
Bavick Iain Cuthbertson
Eithna Madeline Hinde
Tugram Tony Steedman

Director: Peter Sasdy

The Games

w David Osborne
When Arthur holds inter-tribal games, he discovers that more is at stake than simply proving one's worth as a warrior. Herrick and Barth are planning to use the games for their own evil ends.
Herrick Drew Henley
Barth Christopher Mitchell
Erwith Rollo Gamble

Director: Sidney Hayers

The Treaty

w Terence Feely
A truce with Cerdig appears to realise Arthur's dream of a peaceful land. But suspicion runs high when one of Cerdig's followers proposes a 'friendly' get together in enemy territory.
Cerdig Rupert Davies
Voden Ray Witch
Yorath George Marishka

Director: Patrick Dromgoole

The Girl from Rome

w Terence Feely

When a beautiful but haughty Roman princess seeks refuge in Arthur's camp, but refuses to return home when her father arrives, Arthur's vision of a peaceful land receives a setback that severely tests his leadership skill.

Princess Catherine Schell
Nestor Noel Trevarthen
Mark Brian Blessed

Director: Sidney Hayers

ARTHUR OF THE BRITONS
Producer: Peter Miller
Executive producer: Patrick Dromgoole
An HTV Network Production
Filmed on location at Stroud, Gloucestershire
24 colour 30-minute episodes
6 December 1972 – 28 November 1973

THE AVENGERS

The adventures of John Steed, a tough, cynical, yet incomparable undercover agent working for the British Secret Service who, with his beautiful and vivacious femal sidekicks, protects England's shores from all manner of dastardly villains and diabolic masterminds.

This hugely successful tongue-in-cheek adventure series actually began life as standard cops 'n' robbers fare. Starring Ian Hendry as a doctor turned amateur sleuth when he found himself co-opted into the dangerous world of crime-busting by Patrick Macnee's cynical professional undercover man, John Steed, the first season ran for one year until an actors' strike brought the production to an abrupt halt – an event which heralded the introduction of the first of Steed's dynamic female colleagues.

The second season introduced us to Mrs Catherine Gale, an icy-cool blonde with a PhD in anthropology, a passion for wearing black leather fighting suits, and a leaning towards dishing out her own brand of rough justice with skilful displays of judo. As played by Honor Blackman, Mrs Gale became a 1960s version of Shaw's emancipated young woman providing the conscience in combat with Steed's contemporary Chocolate Soldier. It was this series – the first to be sold abroad (it was seen in Canada, Australia and Italy, though not, at this juncture, in America) – that placed John Steed and his partners into their permanent position at the top of the television popularity stakes and its future was guaranteed, until, after completing 52 episodes in the role, Honor Blackman dropped a bombshell in the producers' laps and said she wouldn't be staying with the show for the projected fourth season of filmed episodes (the previous 78 stories had been produced on videotape).

The rest, of course, is history. Diana Rigg was introduced as Mrs Emma Peel, and the show was set to take the television world by storm. Like her predecessor, Catherine Gale, Emma Peel — by far and away the most popular of Steed's female colleagues — was portrayed as the one-jump-ahead jet-set female with the same propensity for wearing ultra-modern leather clothes and dealing with thugs. As before, Steed continued to handle underlings with high-handed nonchalance, but his character too had undergone a slight change. Always an eccentric character, he now drove a vintage Bentley convertible and fought with a swordstick, rolled umbrella or any other handy implement, as opposed to his fists or the guns he'd preferred in the previous series.

Diana Rigg's sojourn on the show endured through two seasons until, in 1968, the final series of adventures were filmed starring newcomer Linda Thorson as Tara King. The youngest of Steed's partners, Tara brought glamour and femininity to the show. Unlike her predecessors, she had no specialised fighting technique. Instead, she would rely more on feminine guile than muscular skill and would dispose of her assailants with a straight right hander, her handbag, or whatever weapon was at hand. Although this season featured some of the best ever Avengers stories, the series was fast running out of steam and this would prove to be the swansong of the original Avengers team. However, true to the maxim that you can't keep a good man down, it wasn't the last we'd see of agent extraordinaire, John Steed. The super-cool spy-smasher would return barely seven years later with two new partners and television viewers worldwide would start the ball rolling all over again. (See *The New Avengers*.)

REGULAR CAST

John Steed Patrick Macnee   *Dr David Keel* Ian Hendry
Catherine Gale Honor Blackman
Venus Smith (Steed's partner in six stories during the Blackman era) Julie Stevens
Dr Martin King (Steed's partner in three stories during the Blackman era)
Jon Rollason   *Emma Peel* Diana Rigg   *Tara King* Linda Thorson
Steed's superiors:
One-Ten (Hendry and Blackman first season stories(Douglas Muir
Charles (two stories in Blackman second season) Paul Whitsun-Jones
Quilpie (one story in Blackman second season) Ronald Radd
Mother (throughout Thorson era) Patrick Newell
Other regulars
Carol Wilson (Dr Keel's receptionist) Ingrid Hafner
One-Twelve (Steed's superior and second-in-command to One-Ten) Arthur Hewlett

Season One

26 monochrome videotaped episodes
Starring Ian Hendry and Patrick Macnee

Hot Snow

w Ray Rigby
Swearing to avenge the death of his fiancée –
gunned down in a London street – Dr David
Keel meets undercover agent John Steed.
Coopted into helping Steed fight crime, the
two men set off on a series of adventures.
Dr Tredding Phillip Stone
Peggy Catherine Woodville
Spicer Godfrey Quigley

Director: Don Leaver
Designer: Alpho O'Reilly

Brought to Book

w Brian Clemens
Keel and Steed continue their search for the
gang who murdered the Doctor's fiancée –
little knowing that Vance, the man
responsible for Peggy's death, has ordered
gang-member Spicer to kill the undercover
man.
Vance Robert James
Spicer Godfrey Quigley
Det. Supt Wilson Alister Williamson

Director: Peter Hammond
Designer: Robert Fuest

Square Root of Evil

w Richard Harris
Assigned to impersonate a convicted forger,
Riordan, who is due to be released from
prison, Steed gains entry to a gang. Its
leader, Hooper, accepts the fake gaol-bird,
but his second-in-command, 'The Cardinal',
does not – and sets out to expose Steed.
Hooper George Murcell
The Cardinal Alex Scott
Carol Ingrid Hafner

Director: Don Leaver
Designer: Patrick Downing

Nightmare

w Terence Feely
An eerie phone call from one of his patients,
Faith Browntree, leads Dr Keel to

investigate her husband's disappearance
from a top secret research establishment. He
is attacked and taken to hospital – then
Steed asks him to impersonate the missing
man!
Faith Browntree Helen Lindsay
Carol Ingrid Hafner
Commander Michael Logan

Director: Peter Hammond
Designer: Robert Fuest

Crescent Moon

w Geoffrey Bellman and John Whitney
Sent to a Caribbean island to investigate the
kidnapping of a young girl, Carmelite
Mendozza, Steed discovers that her father is
playing dirty tricks in a bid to bring his
own political party to power.
Carmelite Mendozza Bandana Das Gupta
Vasco Roger Delgado
Senora Mendozza Patience Collier

Director: John Knight
Designer: Alpho O'Reilly

Girl On the Trapeze

w Dennis Spooner
A young girl's drowned body recovered from
the Thames leads Dr Keel and Carol to
investigate the goings-on behind the facade
of the Radeck State Circus – a not-so-
entertaining establishment which acts as a
cover for international espionage.
Carol Wilson Ingrid Hafner
Zibbo the Clown Kenneth J. Warren
Anna Danilov Naja Regin

Director: Don Leaver
Designer: Paul Bernard

Diamond Cut Diamond

w Max Marquis
Hunting down a gang of diamond thieves,
Dr Keel and Steed find problems of their
own: the former in the shape of a vicious
escaped criminal, the latter in the shape of
two beautiful women.
One-Ten (Intro) Douglas Muir
Fiona Sandra Dorne
Stella Joy Webster

Director: Peter Hammond
Designer: Robert Fuest

The Radioactive Man

w Fred Edge

Marko, an immigrant working as a cleaner at a medical research laboratory, picks up and takes away a radioactive capsule – unaware that it will kill him in a few hours and seriously injure anyone touching him. Steed and Keel must find him before such an event takes place!

Marko George Pravda
Carol Ingrid Hafner
Mary Sommers Christine Pollon

Director: Robert Tronson
Designer: Alpho O'Reilly

Ashes of Roses

w Peter Ling and Sheilah Ward

Convinced that a warehouse fire was started deliberately – and that it ties in with other cases of suspected arson – Steed sends Carol to a hairdressing salon, unaware that he is placing her life in danger.

Olive Beronne Olga Lowe
Jacques Beronne Mark Eden
Carol Ingrid Hafner

Director: Don Leaver
Designer Patrick Downing

Hunt the Man Down

w Richard Harris

Assigned to follow Preston, an ex-prisoner, and discover where he has hidden the proceeds of a robbery, Steed and Dr Keel find themselves pursuing the man through the London sewers – with themselves the prey of two killers.

Paul Stacey Maurice Good
Stella Preston Melissa Stribling
Nurse Wyatt Susan Castle

Director: Peter Hammond
Designer: Robert Fuest

Please Don't Feed the Animals

w Dennis Spooner

When Felgate, a minor Whitehall civil servant dealing with secret cyphers, is suspected of being blackmailed, Steed and Keel follow him to a private zoo – but are too late to stop him handing over a package to a very unusual contact: a monkey!

Felgate Tenniel Evans
Christine Carole Boyer
Kollakis Harry Ross

Director: Dennis Vance
Designer: Patrick Downing

Dance With Death

w Peter Ling and Sheilah Ward

When someone tries to murder Elaine Bateman, the owner of a dancing school, Dr Keel places her under his care and investigates the circumstances surrounding the murder attempt. Soon afterwards, he is arrested and charged with murder.

Elaine Bateman Caroline Blakiston
Beth Wilson Angela Douglas
Philip Anthony Geoffrey Palmer

Director: Don Leaver
Designer: James Goddard

One For the Mortuary

w Brian Clemens

Unaware that Steed has placed an important new medical formula, reduced to microdot form, on a document he is carrying, Dr Keel heads for Geneva – and soon finds himself up to his neck in trouble.

Scott Ronald Wilson
Pallaine Dennis Edwards
Dubois Frank Gatliff

Director: Peter Hammond
Designer: Robert Fuest

The Springers

w John Whitney and Geoffrey Bellman

Asked by his colleague to impersonate a convict whom Steed suspects will shortly be helped to escape from prison, Dr Keel has himself arrested and ends up in the man's cell. That is only teh beginning of his headache!

Pheeney David Webb
Straker Charles Farrell
One-Ten Douglas Muir

Director: Don Leaver
Designer: Alpho O'Reilly

The Frighteners

w Berkley Mather

On the trail of a gang who order the beating up of suspects for money, Steed and Dr Keel trick one of the gang into leading them to his leader – a vicious thug, known as the Deacon.
The Deacon Willoughby Goddard
Sir Thomas Stratford Johns
Nigel David Andrews

Director: Peter Hammond
Designer: Robert Fuest

The Yellow Needle

w Patrick Campbell

When an attempt is made on the life of Sir Wilberforce Lungi, an African leader visiting London, Steed asks Dr Keel, an old friend of Lungi's, to investigate. Steed meanwhile flies to Tenebra to meet Lungi's arch rival, Shebro.
Lungi Andre Dakar
Shebro Bari Johnson
Ali Wolfe Morris

Director: Don Leaver
Designer: Alpho O'Reilly

Death On the Slipway

w James Mitchell

Masquerading as a metallurgist, Steed visits a secret dockyard where submarines are being built. A member of Steed's department has already been killed there by a foreign spy – a man whose identity is unknown to Steed, but who knows the British agent by sight.
Kolchek Peter Arne
Sir William Frank Thornton
One-Ten Douglas Muir

Director: Peter Hammond
Designer: Robert Fuest

Double Danger

w Gerald Verner

On the trail of a fortune in diamonds, stolen from Hatton Garden, Steed's interest is aroused when one of Dr Keel's patients – dying from gunshot wounds – whispers the words 'Hot Ice'.

Crawford Charles Hodgson
Dew Robert Mill
Brady Peter Reynolds

Director: Roger Jenkins
Designer: James Goddard

Toy Trap

w Bill Strutton

Steed and Keel are asked to lay their lives on the line to exterminate a call-girl racket. Steed uses himself as a decoy, while Dr Keel enters the criminals' domain to flush out the gangleader.
Mrs McCabe Ann Tirade
Freddie Brandon Brady
Bunty Sally Smith

Director: Don Leaver
Designer: Douglas James

The Tunnel of Fear

w John Kruse

When Black, an escaped convict, appears at Dr Keel's surgery bearing injuries caused by broken glass, Steed and his colleague find themselves visiting a mysterious funfair to discover who is handing over top-secret documents to the enemy.
Maxie Lardner Stanley Platt
Harry Black Murray Mayne
One-Ten Douglas Muir

Director: Guy Verney
Designer: James Goddard

The Far Distant Dead

w John Lucarotti

Returning home from Chile, Dr Keel stops over in Mexico to offer his help to the victims of a cyclone disaster. En route, he meets the beautiful Dr Sandoval – a meeting that portends danger and death.
Dr Sandoval Katherine Blake
Zeebrugge Francis de Wolff
Rayner Tom Adams

Director: Peter Hammond
Designer: Robert Fuest

Kill the King

w James Mitchell

Assigned to protect a visiting monarch who is in London to sign an oil treaty, Steed discovers that the enemies of royalty are every bit as deadly as the criminals he's used to dealing with on his home ground.
King Tenuphon Burt Kwouk
Prince Serrakit James Goei
General Tuke Patrick Allan

Director: Roger Jenkins
Designer: Paul Bernard

Dead of Winter

w Eric Paice

When the body of Schneider, a wanted war criminal, turns up in a deep-frozen consignment of meat unloaded at the London docks, Steed and Dr Keel uncover a fiendish plot to reestablish a Fascist Party in England.
Schneider Carl Duering
Weber Neil Hallet
Margaritta Zorenah Osborne

Director: Don Leaver
Designer: Robert Fuest

The Deadly Air

w Lester Powell

When Dr Heneger, a scientist working on top-secret experiments to provide a vaccine for a serious disease, is attacked and the vaccine stolen, Steed and Dr Keel volunteer to be guinea pigs during his next test – and all hell breaks loose.
Dr Heneger Keith Anderson
Dr Chalk Allan Cuthbertson
One-Ten Douglas Muir

Director: John Knight
Designer: Robert Macgowan

A Change of Bait

w Lewis Davidson

A shipment of bananas and a strike-bound dockyard provide Steed and Dr Keel with an unusual case of murder and deception – one which almost costs Steed his life, and places Dr Keel's practice in jeopardy.

Duncan Victor Platt
Barker Gary Hope
Carol Ingrid Hafner

Director: Don Leaver
Designer: James Goddard

Dragonsfield

w Terence Feely

On a solo mission to investigate why a scientist has been exposed to radiation while working to produce a new material to protect space travellers from nuclear leakage, Steed, acting as a guinea-pig in the experiment, almost loses his life.
Saunders Alfred Burke
Redington Ronald Leigh-Hunt
Susan Summers Barbara Shelley

Director: Peter Hammond
Designer: Voytek

Season Two

26 monochrome videotaped episodes
Starring Patrick Macnee, Honor Blackman
Julie Stevens and Jon Rollason

Mr Teddy Bear

w Martin Woodhouse

Suspecting that an outbreak of diabolically clever murders are the work of Mr Teddy Bear, a professional assassin, Steed sends Catherine Gale to investigate – little realising that he is signing his own death warrant.
Mr Teddy Bear Bernard Goldman
Henry Michael Robbins
One-Ten Douglas Muir

Director: Richmond Harding
Designer: Terry Green

Propellant 23

w John Manchip White

Ordered to meet a passenger en route from Tripoli who is carrying a sample of a new liquid rocket fuel, Steed and Mrs Gale find their contact dead, and the sample missing. Thus begins a tension-filled race against time to recover the fuel before the enemy.

Manning Geoffrey Palmer
Laura Catherine Woodville
Siebel John Dearth

Director: Jonathan Alwyn
Designer: Paul Bernard

The Decapod

w Eric Paice
Assigned to ensure the safety of Borb, a
foreign President visiting London, Steed and
his colleague, Venus Smith, find themselves
up against the Decapod, a wrestler who
squeezes the very life from his victims.
Borb Paul Stassino
Stepan Philip Madoc
Ito Wolfe Morris

Director: Don Leaver
Designer: Terry Green

Bullseye

w Eric Paice
Steed arranges for Mrs Gale to join the
board of Anderson's Small Arms Limited – a
firm whose chairman has been killed, and
which is suspected of smuggling weapons to
trouble spots abroad.
Brigadier Charles Carson
Young Felix Deebank
Karl Bernard Kay

Director: Peter Hammond
Designer: Robert Macgowran

Mission To Montreal

w Lester Powell
Taking advantage of the fact that his friend
Dr King needs a holiday, Steed assigns
himself aboard a luxury liner as a steward
and books passage for his colleague as
private doctor to a film actress. The voyage
takes on sinister implications when a secret
microfilm is stolen.
Carla Berotti Patricia English
Peggy Pamela Ann Davy
Budge Gerald Sim

Director: Don Leaver
Designer: Terry Green

The Removal Men

w Roger Marshall and Jeremy Scott
Steed flies to the Riviera on the trail of a
gang which kills for money. Together with
Venus Smith, appearing there at a
nightclub, he uncovers far more than he
bargained for – and places both their lives in
peril.
Dragna Reed de Rouen
Siegel Edwin Richfield
One-Ten Douglas Muir

Director: Don Leaver
Designer: Patrick Downing

The Mauritius Penny

w Malcolm Hulke and Terence Dicks
When the Mauritius Penny, a very rare
stamp, is offered for sale at a price well
below its real value, Steed and Mrs Gale
uncover a plot which threatens British
security: an extremist group calling
themselves New Rule plan to take over the
country by force of arms.
Lord Matterly Richard Vernon
Goodchild Philip Guard
Shelley David Langton

Director: Richmond Harding
Designer: Philip Harrison

Death of a Great Dane

w Roger Marshall and Jeremy Scott
Informed that a man badly injured in a road
accident is carrying a fortune in diamonds in
his stomach, Steed and Mrs Gale soon find
themselves hot on the trail of a gang of
smugglers, led by Getz, a blackmailer.
Getz Frederick Jaeger
Gregory Leslie French
Sir James John Laurie

Director: Peter Hammond
Designer: Patrick Downing

The Sell-Out

w Anthony Terpiloff and Brandon Brady
When assassination attempts are made on
the life of M. Roland, a United Nations
official, Steed asks Dr King to keep an eye
on Harvey, a ministry associate he suspects
of being in the pay of the enemy.

M. Roland Carleton Hobbs
Harvey Frank Gatliff
One-Twelve Arthur Hewlett

Director: Don Leaver
Designer: Terry Green

Death On the Rocks

w Eric Paice
Hearing that vast amounts of illegal stones
are swamping Hatton Garden, Steed and
Mrs Gale enter the diamond business to
expose the gang behind the smuggling
activities – a move that endangers Mrs
Gale's life.
Max Daniels Hamilton Dyce
Mrs Daniels Naomi Chance
Van Berg Richard Clarke

Director: Jonathan Alwyn
Designer: James Goddard

Traitor In Zebra

w John Gilbert
Someone at HMS *Zebra* – a naval shore
establishment – is passing secrets to the
enemy. Steed joins the unit as a
psychiatrist, and Mrs Gale goes undercover
as a control room assistant, to expose the
traitor.
Franks Richard Leech
Graham William Gaunt
Rankin John Sharpe

Director: Richmond Harding
Designer: Terry Green

The Big Thinker

w Martin Woodhouse
Plato, the largest and most advanced
computer ever built, is being sabotaged.
Steed and Mrs Gale must discover who is
behind the sabotage attempts – a task
complicated by the fact that the computer
itself holds the answer to their problem –
and Plato is out of commission.
Dr Clemens Walter Hudd
Prof. Farrow David Garth
Dr Hurst Tenniel Evans

Director: Kim Mills
Designer: James Goddard

Death Dispatch

w Leonard Freeman
When a British courier is murdered in
Jamaica, but manages to prevent his
diplomatic bag from being stolen, Steed and
Mrs Gale are confused – the bag contained
only routine documents. An attempt on
Steed's life convinces them to inspect its
contents more closely.
Miguel Rosas Richard Warner
Muller David Cargill
Anna Rosas Valerie Sarruf

Director: Jonathan Alwyn
Designer: Anne Spavin

Dead On Course

w Eric Paice
Investigating a suspicious plane crash on the
Irish coast, Steed and Dr King find
themselves involved in a clever bank fraud –
one that involves a nearby convent and its
not too friendly Mother Superior
Mother Superior Peggy Marshall
Deidre Elizabeth Murray
Margot Margo Jenkins

Director: Richmond Harding
Designer: Robert Fuest

Intercrime

w Terence Dicks and Malcolm Hulke
Acting on a tip-off, Steed has Hilda Stern, a
member of Intercrime – an international
crime organisation – arrested, and Mrs Gale
takes her place. All goes well until Stern
escapes from prison and confronts her
'double' at the gang's headquarters.
Hilda Stern Julia Arnall
Moss Alan Browning
Fielder Kenneth J. Warren

Director: Jonathan Alwyn
Designer: Richard Harrison

Immortal Clay

w James Mitchell
One-Ten assigns Steed to check on claims
made by Alan Marling that he has created
an unbreakable ceramic. Accompanied by
Mrs Gale, Steed sets off for the Potteries –
and immediately walks into danger.

Alan Marling Gary Watson
Richard Marling Paul Eddington
One-Ten Douglas Muir

Director: Richard Harding
Designer: James Goddard

Box of Tricks

w Peter Ling and Edward Rhodes
NATO secrets are being leaked and Steed is
convinced that this is tied up with the death
of a magician's girl assistant at a nightclub
where Venus Smith is working. The
undercover agents discover that a magician's
box of tricks contains many surprises – some
of which are deadly!
General Sutherland Maurice Hedley
Dr Gilham Edgar Wreford
Denise April Olrich

Director: Kim Mills
Designer: Anne Spavin

Warlock

w Doreen Montgomery
When Neville, a scientist who has perfected
a new fuel formula, is found in a coma,
Steed must ask the question: can black
magic be the cause? Sceptical, he
nevertheless seeks Mrs Gale's help to
uncover the truth – and she too falls victim
to magic of a surprising variety.
Gallion Peter Arne
Markel John Hollis
One-Ten Douglas Muir

Director: Peter Hammond
Designer: Douglas James

The Golden Eggs

w Martin Woodhouse
Steed and Mrs Gale are hot on the trail of a
gang of crooks who have stolen two gold-
plated-eggs – one of which contains a new
strain of virus which could prove deadly if
released into the atmosphere.
Dr Ashe Donald Eccles
De Leon Gordon Whiting
Elisabeth Bayle Pauline Delaney

Director: Peter Hammond
Designer: Douglas James

School For Traitors

w James Mitchell
When a university tutor who has been
working on important research is found
dead, Steed, suspecting murder, arranges for
Venus Smith to give a concert at the
establishment. Venus soon finds herself
singing for her supper – and her life.
East John Standing
Claire Melissa Stribling
Higby Reginald Marsh

Director: Jonathan Alwyn
Designer: Maurice Pelling

The White Dwarf

w Malcolm Hulke
Steed informs Mrs Gale that Professor
Richter, murdered while observing a star
called the White Dwarf, left notes stating
that the star will destroy Earth, and asks her
to visit the observatory, to investigate the
dead man's claims.
Cartwright Philip Latham
Maxwell Barker George A. Cooper
Minister Daniel Thorndyke

Director: Richmond Harding
Designer: Terry Green

Man In the Mirror

w Geoffrey Orme and Anthony Terpiloff
Photographs taken by Venus Smith at a
funfair, and Steed's investigations into the
suicide of a cypher clerk, provide the basis
for believing the man was actually a murder
victim. But can Steed prove his suspicions
in time to save his colleagues' life?
Strong Ray Barrett
Betty Daphne Anderson
Brown Julian Somers

Director: Kim Mills
Designer: Anne Spavin

Conspiracy of Silence

w Roger Marshall
Steed and Mrs Gale place their lives on the
line to help a circus clown escape from Sica,
a member of the Mafia, whose smuggling
operation is under threat from the clown.

But first they must discover whose face lies beneath the clown's make-up.
Carlo Robert Rietty
Sica Alec Mango
Rickie Sandra Dorne

Director: Peter Hammond
Designer: Stephen Doncaster

A Chorus of Frogs

w Martin Woodhouse
Holidaying in Greece, Steed is asked to investigate the mysterious death of a deep-sea diver. Clues point to a luxury yacht owned by Mason, a wealthy industrialist, so Steed stows away on board – and bumps into Venus Smith, who has been invited to entertain Mason's guests.
Mason Eric Pohlmann
Pitt Norton Frank Gatliff
Ariston John Carson

Director: Raymond Menmuir
Designer: James Goddard

Six Hands Across a Table

w Reed de Rouen
Invited to a house party given by an old school friend, Rosalind Waldner, Mrs Gale is looking forward to a peaceful weekend. But with Steed never far away, plans have a way of going disastrously wrong – as she soon discovers.
Oliver Waldner Guy Doleman
Brian Collier Edward De Souza
George Stanley Campbell Singer

Director: Richmond Harding
Designer: Paul Bernard

Killerwhale

w John Lucarotti
When Mrs Gale introduces Steed to a young boxer named Joey Frazer, neither of them suspect that the young man will lead them into a dangerous adventure involving an extortion racket and murder.
Joey Kenneth Farrington
Pancho Driver Patrick Magee
Fernand John Bailey

Director: Kim Mills
Designer: Douglas James

Season Three
26 monochrome videotaped episodes
Starring Patrick Macnee and Honor Blackman

Brief For Murder

w Brian Clemens
In order to obtain evidence to convict two solicitors, brothers Jasper and Miles Larkin, who carefully arrange for people to be murdered and then obtain the killer's acquittal, Steed has himself arrested for the 'murder' of Mrs Catherine Gale.
Miles Larkin Harold Scott
Jasper Larkin John Laurie
Wescott Alec Ross

Director: Peter Hammond
Designer: James Goddard

The Undertakers

w Malcolm Hulke
Steed is disturbed when he hears that Professor Sayer – a man with whom Steed was going to promote a new invention – has gone into meditation at a rest home. Suspicious, he asks Mrs Gale to investigate the claim – and she uncovers a cleverly devised scheme to defraud the government of death duties.
Madden Patrick Holt
Lomax Lee Patterson
Paula Jan Holden

Director: Bill Bain
Designer: David Marshall

The Man With Two Shadows

w James Mitchell
Ordered by his superior, Charles, to investigate claims that top agents have been replaced by doubles, Steed has no inkling that he, too, will soon suffer the same fate – or that Mrs Gale will see 'double'.
Charles Paul Whitsun-Jones
De Terence Geoffrey Palmer
Cummings Philip Anthony

Director: Don Leaver
Designer: Paul Bernard

The Nutshell

w Philip Chambers

With Steed suspected of being a double
agent, Mrs Gale must persuade him to tell
the truth about the accusation that he
copied Big Ben, a secret file listing double
agents. But Steed refuses to do so – and
attacks his partner! Why?

Disco (Director of Operations) John Cater
Venner Charles Tingwell
Elin Edina Ronay

Director: Raymond Menmuir
Designer: Philip Harrison

Death of a Batman

w Roger Marshall

How could Wrightson, Steed's one-time
batman, have amassed such a large fortune?
The undercover man asks Mrs Gale to
investigate, and she uncovers a clever
scheme to defraud the Stock Exchange by
issuing forged currency documents.

John Wrightson David Burke
Van Doren Philip Madoc
Lord Teale Andre Morrell

Director: Kim Mills
Designer: Paul Bernard

November Five

w Eric Paice

In order to expose a major security scandal,
Steed coopts Mrs Gale into standing as a
candidate in a by-election. But things go
disastrously wrong, and Mrs Gale must use
all her ingenuity to escape from a bomb
threat on the House of Commons.

Major Swinburne David Langton
Michael Dyter Gary Hope
Fiona Iris Russell

Director: Bill Bain
Designer: Douglas James

The Gilded Cage

w Roger Marshall

On the trail of Spagge, a millionaire
suspected of being the mastermind behind
several recent gold robberies, Steed coopts
Mrs Gale to help him to bait a trap that the
bullion robber will find hard to ignore.

Spagge Patrick Magee
Benham Edric Connor
Fleming Norman Chappell

Director: Bill Bain
Designer: Robert Macgowan

Second Sight

w Martin Woodhouse

Informed that Halvarssen, a blind
millionaire, intends to use two cornea grafts
from a live donor to regain his sight, Steed
sends Mrs Gale along to attend the
operation, but she finds the patient's room
empty – save for an unfinished portrait.

Anstice Peter Bowles
Dr Vilner Steven Scott
Dr Spender Ronald Adam

Director: Peter Hammond
Designer: Terry Green

The Medicine Men

w Malcolm Hulke

While he checks out a pharmaceutical
company, Steed ask Mrs Gale to investigate
the death of a Chinese girl. Discovering a
link between the two events, the two agents
soon find themselves up against a deadly
plot to overthrow Arab countries.

Geoffrey Willis Peter Barkworth
John Willis Newton Black
Miss Dowell Joy Wood

Director: Kim Mills
Designer: Paul Bernard

The Grandeur That Was Rome

w Rex Edwards

When he receives reports of crop failures,
unknown diseases in animals and outbreaks
of illness in all parts of the world, Steed and
Mrs Gale follow a trail which leads them to
a gang preparing to take over the world by
spreading bubonic plague.

Bruno Hugh Burden
Marcus John Flint
Octavia Colette Wilde

Director: Kim Mills
Designer: Terry Green

The Golden Fleece

w Roger Marshall and Phyllis Norman
Having obtained a lead to a gang which
sells stolen Army weapons, then uses the
proceeds to support deserving ex-colleagues,
Mrs Gale goes undercover at the depot to
await further developments.
Captain Jason Warren Mitchell
Sgt Major Barry Lineham
Mr Lo Robert Kee

Director: Peter Hammond
Designer: Anne Spavin

Don't Look Behind You

w Brian Clemens
Mrs Gale, invited to spend the weekend at
the home of Sir Cavalier Resagne, finds the
house deserted save for Ola, a housemaid,
who leaves shortly afterwards. That's when
Cathy's nightmares begin.
Ola Janine Gray
Young man Kenneth Colley
Man Maurice Good

Director: Peter Hammond
Designer: Paul Bernard

Death A La Carte

w John Lucarotti
Assigned to organise the visit of Emir
Akaba, who is visiting London for his
annual medical check-up, Mrs Gale,
suspecting an attempt will be made to
assassinate the visitor, asks Steed to keep an
eye on security.
Emir Henry Soskin
Dr Spencer Paul Dawkins
Umberto David Nettheim

Director: Kim Mills
Designer: Unknown

Dressed to Kill

w Brian Clemens
When a World War Three early-warning
station is activated and the threat is found
to be a false alarm, Steed's sojourn at a New
Year's Eve fancy-dress party aboard a train
turns into an assembly of death.

Sheriff John Junkin
Robin Hood Leonard Rossiter
Pussy Cat Aneke Wills

Director: Bill Bain
Designer: Richard Harrison

The White Elephant

w John Lucarotti
When Snowy, a white elephant, is stolen
from a zoo, Mrs Gale joins the staff as a big
Game hunter Steed, meanwhile, finding
traces of ivory dust at a gun shop, decides to
join his partner – and finds her locked in a
tiger's cage!
Lawrence Edwin Richfield
Noah Marshall Geoffrey Quigley
Brenda Judy Parfitt

Director: Laurence Bourne
Designer: Unknown

The Little Wonders

w Eric Paice
Steed and Mrs Gale find themselves up
against a criminal organisation called
Bibliotek. When Steed's identity is exposed,
both he and Mrs Gale face harsh retribution
from Sister Johnson and Beardmore, the
gang's leader.
Sister Johnson Lois Maxwell
Beardmore Tony Steedman
Bishop David Bauer

Director: Laurence Bourne
Designer: Anne Spavin

The Wringer

w Martin Woodhouse
Told by his superior, Charles, that fellow
agent Anderson has not returned from his
last mission, Steed's enquiries lead him to
Scotland – and a plot to sabotage the Service
by creating suspicion and mistrust among
its members.
The Wringer Terence Lodge
Bethune Neil Robinson
Charles Paul Whitsun-Jones

Director: Don Lever
Designer: David Marshall

Mandrake

w Roger Marshall

Steed and Mrs Gale uncover a plot to kill off millionaires for their money, then bury their arsenic-filled bodies in a remote Cornish cemetery – but their enquiries are impeded when Cathy is taken prisoner by a not-so-friendly Reverend.

Rev. Wyper George Benson
Benson Robert Morris
Dr Macrombie John Le Mesurier

Director: Bill Bain
Designer: Unknown

The Secrets Broker

w Ludovic Peters

When one of Steed's associates is murdered, the agent has only two clues – a wine list, and a reference to a research establishment. Steed visits the wine shop, while Mrs Gale, working undercover, is sent to the research station – and danger.

Waller Jack May
Paignton Ronald Allen
Julia Wilson Jennifer Wood

Director: Jonathan Alwyn
Designer: Richard Harrison

The Trojan Horse

w Malcolm Hulke

Asked by the Foreign Office to keep his eye on a wealthy Shah's racehorse, Steed coopts Mrs Gale's assistance to expose a betting syndicate which preys on unsuspecting racehorse owners.

Heuston T. P. McKenna
Johnson Derek Newark
Ann Meadows Lucinda Curtis

Director: Laurence Bourne
Designer: Unknown

Build a Better Mousetrap

w Brian Clemens

Mrs Gale joins a motorcycle gang to help Steed solve the mysterious jamming of all electrical and mechanical devices in a small village. Two elderly sisters, Cynthia and Ermintrude, appear responsible, but Steed has other ideas.

Cynthia Athene Seyler
Ermintrude Nora Nicholson
Wesker John Tate

Director: Peter Hammond
Designer: Douglas James

The Outside-In Man

w Philip Chambers

Assigned by Head of Operations, Quilpie, to take charge of the security arrangements for a trade conference, Steed coopts Mrs Gale to supervise the security arrangements. Neither agent can foresee the trouble ahead.

Mark Charter James Maxwell
Sharp Philip Anthony
Quilpie Ronald Radd

Director: Jonathan Alwyn
Designer: David Marshall

The Charmers

w Brian Clemens

Believing that the 'opposition' are purging ministry personnel, Steed suggests a truce so that both sides can work together to expose a common enemy. As an act of good faith, each side should supply an hostage: Steed receives attractive Kim Lawrence – and hands Mrs Gale over in return.

Keller Warren Mitchell
Kim Lawrence Fenella Fielding
Mr Edgar Brian Oulton

Director: Bill Bain
Designer: Richard Harrison

Concerto

w Terence Dicks and Malcolm Hulke

Entrusted with the safety of Veliko, a brilliant Russian pianist, Steed puts Mrs Gale in charge of security for important trade talks. Cathy discovers discord among the conference members – and murder amid the Russian's piano recital.

Zelenko Nigel Stock
Veliko Sandor Eles
Peterson Bernard Brown

Director: Kim Mills
Designer: Douglas James

Esprit De Corps

w Eric Paice

Captain Trench, of the Highland Guards, is seeking support for Operation Claymore – a scheme to place London under military rule. On Steed's orders, Mrs Gale offers her 'support' – and discovers that she is the rightful heir to the Scottish throne!

Captain Trench John Thaw
Stewart-Bollinger Duncan Macrae
Pte Jessop Roy Kinnear

Director: Don Leaver
Designer: David Marshall

Lobster Quadrille

w Richard Lucas

Having discovered the body of an agent among the ashes of a burnt-out fishing hut, Steed and Mrs Gale follow a trail which leads them to a dope-smuggling ring. Working alone, Mrs Gale is captured and left to die in a blazing inferno!

Quentin Corin Redgrave
Bush Gary Watson
Mason Burk Kwouk

Director: Kim Mills
Designer: Richard Harrison

Season Four

26 monochrome filmed episodes
Starring Patrick Macnee and Diana Rigg

The Town of No Return

w Brian Clemens

Together with his new partner, Mrs Emma Peel, Steed embarks on a journey which will lead them to Bazeley-by-the-Sea, a remote Norfolk village, from which several agents have vanished without trace.

Brandon Alan MacNaughton
Jill Manson Juliet Harmer
Vicar Jeremy Burnham

Director: Roy Baker

The Gravediggers

w Malcolm Hulke

Steed and Emma travel to Pringby, a village lying in the path of a recent radar block which developed a fault in the nation's early-warning system. What they uncover leads to Emma playing the part of a damsel in distress – tied to railway lines.

Johnson Paul Massie
Sir Horace Ronald Fraser
Miss Thirwell Caroline Blakiston

Director: Quentin Lawrence

The Cybernauts

w Philip Levene

Investigating the violent deaths of several executives, Steed and Mrs Peel meet Dr Armstrong, a cripple confined to an elaborately-automated wheelchair, from which he controls his empire of deadly robots – the Cybernauts.

Dr Armstrong Michael Gough
Benson Frederick Jaeger
Jephcott Bernard Horsfall

Director: Sidney Hayers

Death at Bargain Prices

w Brian Clemens

What secret lies behind the facade of Pinter's Department Store? To find out the truth, Mrs Peel goes undercover as a sales girl while Steed, posing as an efficiency expert, uncovers a plot to hold all England to ransom under threat of an atomic bomb!

Wentworth T. P. McKenna
Farthingale Allan Cuthbertson
Horatio Kane Andre Morrell

Director: Charles Crichton

Castle De'ath

w John Lucarotti

When Ian, the 35th Laird of Castle De'ath, receives a visit from Emma Peel, posing as a member of Aborcashata (Advisory Bureau on Refurbishing Castles and Stately Homes) and author John McSteed, his problems start in earnest – with murder!

Ian Gordon Jackson
Angus Robert Urquhart
McNab Jack Lambert

Director: James Hill

The Masterminds

w Robert Banks Stewart

Steed and Emma Peel encounter the members of Ransack, a club for intellectuals whose establishment hides a clever plot to indoctrinate its members into committing acts of murder and sabotage.

Holly Trent Patricia Haines
Dr Campbell Ian McNaughton
Davina Todd Georgina Ward

Director: Peter Graham Scott

The Murder Market

w Tony Williamson

What criminal activity is going on behind the doors of the Togetherness Marriage Bureau? Steed goes looking for a wife to find out – and is given orders to kill Emma Peel as an act of good faith.

Mr Lovejoy Patrick Cargill
Jessica Stone Naomi Chance
Dinsford Peter Bayliss

Director: Peter Graham Scott

A Surfeit of H₂O

w Colin Finbow

Freak rainstorms, and a village poacher drowned in the middle of a field! Can this really portend the return of the Great Flood? To find the answer, Steed and Mrs Peel gain admission to a very unusual factory – and land up to their necks in trouble.

Dr Sturm Albert Lieven
Joyce Jason Sue Lloyd
Jonah Bernard Noel Purcell

Director: Sidney Hayers

The Hour That Never Was

w Roger Marshall

Invited to the closing-down party of RAF Camp Hamelin, a camp at which Steed saw service during the war, the undercover man and Mrs Peel discover more than their fair share of bodies. Nevertheless, they exit laughing.

Leas Dudley Foster
Ridsdale Gerald Harper
Hickey Roy Kinnear

Director: Gerry O'Hara

Dial A Deadly Number

w Roger Marshall

When sudden death strikes big business, Steed and Mrs Peel decide to play the stock market. Their investigations almost get Steed killed by a deadly remote controlled device – and lead Emma into deadly peril.

Jago Anthony Newlands
Ruth Jan Holden
Fitch John Carson

Director: Don Leaver

The Man-Eater of Surrey Green

w Philip Levene

When her friend, Laura Burford, goes missing, together with several other eminent horticulturists, Mrs Peel and Steed follow up rumours of a giant man-eating plant which is terrorising the Surrey community – a mission which tests their abilities to the full.

Sir Lyle Peterson Derek Farr
Dr Sheldon Athene Seyler
Laura Gillian Lewis

Director: Sidney Hayers

Two's A Crowd

w Philip Levene

When four agents, known to have worked for foreign spy Colonel Psev, establish themselves at their Embassy in England, Steed gets shot at by a toy submarine, and Mrs Peel sees double.

Brodny Warren Mitchell
Pudeshkin Wolfe Morris
Vogel Julian Glover

Director: Roy Baker

Too Many Christmas Trees

w Tony Williamson

When Steed is plagued by recurring nightmares, Mrs Peel invites him to accompany her to a Christmas party given by publisher Brandon Storey, to cheer him up. But their arrival at Storey's home adds further tension to Steed's already confused state of mind.

Brandon Storey Mervyn Johns
Dr Teasel Edwin Richfield
Janice Crane Jeanette Sterke

Director: Roy Baker

Silent Dust

w Roger Marshall
Investigating an area of desolation at
Manderley which is under War Department
control, Steed and Emma place their lives
on the line to defeat a ruthless gang who are
planning to destroy Britain county by
county unless they receive a £40,000,000
ransom.
Omerod William Franklyn
Juggins Jack Watson
Mellors Conrad Phillips

Director: Roy Baker

Room Without A View

w Roger Marshall
The sudden reappearance of scientist John
Wadkin, after two years' unexplained
absence, places Steed in an execution squad's
firing line and Mrs Peel in an interrogating
camp cell.
Chessman Paul Whitsun-Jones
Varnals Peter Jeffrey
Dr Wadkin Peter Madden

Director: Roy Baker

Small Game For Big Hunters

w Philip Levene
Called in to investigate a strange outbreak
of sleeping sickness, Steed and Mrs Peel
uncover a plot to desolate the state of Kalaya
with a deadly strain of tsetse fly immune to
all known insecticides – but not, as the
villains discover, to Steed's intervention.
Simon Trent James Villiers
Colonel Rawlins Bill Fraser
Fleming Peter Burton

Director: Gerry O'Hara

The Girl From Auntie

w Roger Marshall
Returning from a holiday, Steed finds a
shapely blonde, Georgie Price-Jones,

impersonating Emma Peel. His attempts to
discover what has happened to his real
partner lead him to a very unusual Knitting
Circle – and a girl in a gilded cage.
Georgie Price-Jones Liz Frazer
Gregorio Auntie Alfred Burke
Arkwright Bernard Cribbins

Director: Roy Baker

The 13th Hole

w Tony Williamson
Murder investigations lead Steed and Mrs
Peel to the Cranleigh Golf Club – and a
gang of ruthless men with world
domination on their minds. Emma is struck
down in her prime, and Steed has cause to
shout 'fore'.
Reed Patrick Allen
Colonel Watson Hugh Manning
Collins Francis Matthews

Director: Roy Baker

The Quick-Quick-Slow Death

w Robert Banks Stewart
Hidden behind the Terpsichorean Training
Technique dancing school lies deadly
danger. Steed and Mrs Peel enrol as dancing
partners – and find themselves dancing to a
tune of death.
Lucille Banks Eunice Gayson
Ivor Bracewell Maurice Kaufmann
Peever James Bellchamber

Director: James Hill

The Danger Makers

w Roger Marshall
When two important VIPs are killed while
taking part in a chicken-run, Steed and Mrs
Peel are assigned to find out what's going
on. Their investigations lead them to a
society called The Danger Makers – an
association of murderers.
Major Robertson Nigel Davenport
Dar Long Douglas Wilmer
Col Adams Fabia Drake

Director: Charles Crichton

A Touch of Brimstone

w Brian Clemens
A twentieth-century Hellfire Club, whose members intend to assassinate three important government ministers, spells death and danger for Steed and Mrs Peel: the former becomes a Toff, while Emma becomes the Queen of Sin!
John Cartney Peter Wyngarde
Lord Darcy Colin Jeavons
Willy Frant Jeremy Young

Director: James Hill

What the Butler Saw

w Roger Marshall
Someone is selling secret defence plans and Steed and his partner must discover the guilty party. Steed enlists as a student in the Gentleman's Gentlemen Association, and Emma enrols as an unwilling victim in Operation Fascination – a ploy to trap a traitor.
Benson John Le Mesurier
Sgt Morgan Ewan Hooper
Capt Miles Dennis Quilley

Director: Bill Bain

The House That Jack Built

w Brian Clemens
Lured to a secluded country house on the pretence that her Uncle Jack has died and left her his estate, Mrs Peel finds herself prisoner in a house run by a deadly computer – a machine with orders to kill her!
Prof. Keller Michael Goodliffe
Burton Griffith Davies
Withers Michael Wynne

Director: Don Leaver

A Sense of History

w Martin Woodhouse
When Bloom, the author of the visionary Europa Plan to eliminate world poverty, is found dead with an arrow in his back, Steed and Mrs Peel enter a university to find his killer – but intrigue and death await their arrival.

Grindley John Glyn-Jones
Carlyon Nigel Stock
Duboys Patrick Mower

Director: Peter Graham Scott

How To Succeed At Murder

w Brian Clemens
To discover who is murdering top executives, Steed dons a millionaire's cap and Emma enrols in a keep-fit class at a school which is a cover for modern-day suffragettes – intent on the total elimination of men!
Henry Throgbottom Artho Morris
Josuha Rudge Jerome Willis
Sara Penny Angela Browne

Director: Don Leaver

Honey For the Prince

w Brian Clemens
When the fantasies created by the Quite Quite Fantastic Company turn into reality and its clients begin to die, Steed finds himself protecting a Bahrainian Prince and his entourage, and Emma sheds her inhibitions to perform the dance of the Seven Veils.
Prince Ali Zia Mohyeddin
Ponsonby-Hopkirk Ron Moody
Arkadi George Pastell

Director: James Hill

Season Five

25 colour filmed episodes
Starring Patrick Macnee and Diana Rigg

From Venus With Love

w Philip Levene
When several people are found dead, their hair bleached white as snow, Steed and Mrs Peel join the British Venusian Society to find a killer who uses laser power to rub out his enemies.
Venus Barbara Shelley
Primble Philip Locke
Brigadier Whitehead Jon Pertwee

Director: Robert Day
Designer: Wilfred Shingleton

The Fear Merchants

w Philip Levene
Steed and Mrs Peel enrol in the Business Efficiency Bureau, a firm which uses criminal methods to eliminate its rivals by subjecting them to things they fear. Steed fears nothing – until Emma faces torture by operation.
Pemberton Patrick Cargill
Dr Voss Annette Carell
Gilbert Garfield Morgan

Director: Gordon Flemyng
Designer: Wilfred Shingleton

Escape In Time

w Philip Levene
When several agents disappear and turn up dead shortly afterwards, Steed and Emma Peel unearth a perfect escape route for criminals – a time machine. Steed books a one-way trip to the past, while Emma faces a masked executioner.
Thyssen Peter Bowles
Vesta Judy Parfitt
Clapham Geoffrey Bayldon

Director: John Krish
Designer: Wilfred Shingleton

The See-Through Man

w Philip Levene
Steed and Mrs Peel renew their acquaintance with Brodny, the Russian Ambassador, and Vazin, an 'invisible' man. Both men lead the agents on a merry chase before an unseen Steed plays his own version of 'Now you see me, now you don't.'
Brodny Warren Mitchell
Quilby Roy Kinnear
Elena Moira Lister

Director: Robert Asher
Designer: Wilfred Shingleton

The Bird Who Knew too Much

w Brian Clemens
Captain Crusoe, a parrot, leads Steed and Mrs Peel on a merry cross-country chase after a group of criminals selling off Government secrets. The bird has a remarkable memory and Steed wants it to talk – but Crusoe disappears!
Jordan Ron Moody
Cunliffe Anthony Valentine
Twitter John Wood

Director: Roy Rossotti
Designer: Wilfred Shingleton

The Winged Avenger

w Richard Harris
When strange claw marks are found on the body of publishing tycoon Roberts, Steed and Emma find themselves confronting the Winged Avenger – a large bird like creature who is rubbing out top publishing executives.
Sir Lexius Cray Nigel Green
Arnie Packer Neil Hallett
Professor Poole Jack McGowran

Director: Gordon Flemyng
Designer: Wilfred Shingleton

The Living Dead

w Brian Clemens
The Avengers find themselves investigating the strange goings on at the Duke of Benedict's estate – rumoured to be haunted. They are joined by Mandy McKay of FOG (Friends of Ghosts), and Spencer, of SMOG (Scientific Measurement of Ghosts) – two very odd characters.
Mandy McKay Pamela Ann Davy
Spencer Vernon Dobtcheff
Masgard Julian Glover

Director: John Krish
Designer: Robert Jones

The Hidden Tiger

w Philip Levene
A medallion found next to the body of a big-game hunter leads Steed and Mrs Peel to PURRR, the Philanthropic Union for Rescue, Relief and Recuperation of Cats, an organisation giving shelter to our feline friends. At least, that's what they'd have you believe.

Cheshire Ronnie Barker
Manx Lyndon Brook
Angora Gabrielle Drake

Director: Sidney Hayers
Designer: Robert Jones

The Correct Way to Kill

w Brian Clemens
Two top enemy agents are found dead and
suspicion falls on Steed and Emma Peel. To
prove themselves innocent, they decide to
join forces with the opposition, Steed
working with Olga, Emma with Ivan –
until he disappears!
Olga Anna Quayle
Nutski Michael Gough
Ponsonby Terence Alexander

Director: Charles Crichton
Designer: Robert Jones

Never, Never Say Die

w Philip Levene
When a corpse walks out of a mortuary,
Steed and Mrs Peel find themselves facing a
deadly new threat to their careers –
duplicates, computerised doubles capable of
thinking for themselves and armed with the
strength of a dozen men!
Professor Stone Christopher Lee
Dr Penrose Jeremy Young
Dr James Patricia English

Director: Robert Day
Designer: Robert Jones

Epic

w Brian Clemens
Kidnapped, Mrs Peel is forced to star in a
film depicting her own life – and death! Its
producers – director Z. Z. Schnerk and
over-the-hill actors Stewart Kirby and
Damita Syn – see the film as restoring their
lost glory. Steed has other ideas.
Kirby Peter Wyngarde
Von Schnerk Kenneth J. Warren
Damita Syn Isa Miranda

Director: James Hill
Designer: Robert Jones

The Superlative Seven

w Brian Clemens
Marooned on an isolated island with several
other guests, Steed needs all his cunning if
he is to defeat his 'unbeatable' opponents at
their own game. With Mrs Peel back in
England, the odds are definitely not in his
favour.
Jessel Donald Sutherland
Wade James Maxwell
Hana Charlotte Rampling

Director: Sidney Hayers
Designer: Robert Jones

A Funny Thing Happened On The Way To The Station

w Roger Marshall
Believing that someone is passing on top
secret information to the enemy, Steed and
Mrs Peel join the passengers on the 8.10 to
Norborough – and unknowingly become
part of a plot to assassinate the Prime
Minister of England!
Ticket collector James Hayter
Crewe John Laurie
Bride Isla Blair

Director: John Krish
Designer: Robert Jones

Something Nasty in the Nursery

w Philip Levene
Aware that vital defence secrets, stolen by
the enemy, had been entrusted to only three
men, all of them from the noblest of British
families, Steed asks Mrs Peel to check out
GONN – the Guild of Noble Nannies –
whom he suspects are mixed up in the
affair.
Mr Goat Dudley Foster
Miss Lister Yootha Joyce
General Wilmot Geoffrey Sumner

Director: James Hill
Designer: Robert Jones

The Joker

w Brian Clemens
Emma is invited to spend the weekend at
the country home of Sir Cavalier Rousicana.
Arriving at his Devonshire home, she is

greeted by Ola, a maid. No other guests are in attendance – but someone makes several attempts on Emma's life.
Prendergast Peter Jeffrey
Ola Sally Nesbitt
Stranger Ronald Lacey

Director: Sidney Hayers
Designer: Robert Jones

Who's Who?

w Philip Levene
Steed and Mrs Peel must discover who is killing off agents serving under Major B, a green-fingered flower expert, who codenames his agents after flowers. There's just one problem: Steed and his colleague have been replaced by doubles, and neither agent can be sure if their partner is the real thing!
Basil Freddie Jones
Lola Patricia Haines
Major B Campbell Singer

Director: John Moxey
Designer: Robert Jones

The Return of the Cybernauts

w Philip Levene
Steed and Emma renew an acquaintance with their old adversaries – the Cybernauts, death-wielding killing machines. But this time, the Avengers themselves appear to be their main prey – why? And who is controlling the robots?
Beresford Peter Cushing
Benson Frederick Jaeger
Dr Neville Charles Tingwell

Director: Robert Day
Designer: Robert Jones

Death's Door

w Philip Levene
Assigned to organise the security for a peace conference, Steed and Mrs Peel find they must first overcome the sudden terror which strikes fear into the heart of the conference Chairman. Not an easy task – as the agents soon discover.

Boyd Clifford Evans
Stapley William Lucas
Lord Melford Allan Cuthbertson

Director: Sidney Hayers
Designer: Robert Jones

The £50,000 Breakfast

w Roger Marshall
A ventriloquist's dummy leads Steed and Emma Peel to expose a remarkably clever plot to smuggle a fortune in diamonds out of the country by using a 'dead' man as courier.
Glover Cecil Parker
Miss Peagram Yolande Turner
Sir James David Langton

Director: Robert Day
Designer: Robert Jones

Dead Man's Treasure

w Michael Winder
Steed and Mrs Peel join a cross-country treasure hunt – pursued by several villains who are determined to lay their hands on a small metal despatch box containing vital government secrets.
Mike Norman Bowler
Benstead Arthur Lowe
Bates Ivor Dean

Director: Sidney Hayers
Designer: Robert Jones

You Have Just Been Murdered

w Philip Levene
When two attempts are made on the life of millionaire, Jarvis, but each time his handsome blonde assailant does not kill him, Steed and Mrs Peel become involved in the schemes of an evil mastermind known only as Needle.
Needle George Murcell
Unwin Barrie Ingham
Maxstead Robert Flemyng

Director: Robert Asher
Designer: Robert Jones

The Positive-Negative Man

w Tony Williamson

Someone is literally frying electronics experts to a crisp. Steed and Emma, hot on the trail of the culprit at Risley Dale, a research establishment, receive their fair share of shocks along the way.

Cresswell Ray McAnally
Haworth Michael Latimer
Cynthia Wentworth-Howe Caroline Blakiston

Director: Robert Day
Designer: Robert Jones

Murdersville

w Brian Clemens

When Emma Peel insists on driving her childhood friend, Paul, to his newly-bought home in Little Storping-in-the-Swuff, it sets in motion a train of events which lead her into a dangerous situation – with Steed as her knight in shining armour.

Hubert John Ronane
Dr Haynes Ronald Hines
Prewitt John Sharp

Director: Robert Asher
Designer: Robert Jones

Mission . . . Highly Improbable

w Philip Levene

A miniaturised John Steed, and an equally small Emma Peel, clear up the mystery of the missing military vehicles which vanished without trace while being demonstrated to prospective buyers.

Chivers Francis Matthews
Shaffer Ronald Radd
Susan Jane Merrow

Director: Robert Day
Designer: Robert Jones

The Forget-Me-Knot

w Brian Clemens

Agents from Steed's department are suffering from memory loss. So too are Steed and Emma – each of whom have been hit by memory-killing darts. It is left up to trainee agent, Tara King, to restore the status quo and rescue her fellow agents – before taking over as Steed's permanent new sidekick.

Mother Patrick Newell (Intro.)
Tara King Linda Thorson (Intro.)
Sean Mortimer Patrick Kavanagh

Director: James Hill
Designer: Robert Jones

Season Six

32 colour episodes
Starring Patrick Macnee and Linda Thorson

Game

w Richard Harris

Tara King is kidnapped. Steed investigating her disappearance, finds himself faced with playing a deadly game of 'Super Agent' to obtain her freedom. Should he fail to beat the obstacle course, Tara will suffocate to death in a giant hour-glass.

Bristow Peter Jeffrey
Manservant Garfield Morgan
Wishforth-Brown Anthony Newlands

Director: Robert Fuest
Designer: Robert Jones

The Super-Secret Cypher Snatch

w Tony Williamson

Mother assigns Steed to find missing agent Jarrett. His enquiries lead him to establish a connection with Classy Glass Cleaners, a company who have found a foolproof method of stealing secret material – foolproof, that is, until Steed and Tara get on their trail.

Maskin Simon Oates
Lather Nicolas Smith
Ferrett Ivor Dean

Director: John Hough
Designer: Robert Jones

You'll Catch Your Death

w Jeremy Burnham

When several top ear, nose and throat specialists sneeze themselves to death, Steed and Tara visit the Institute of Allergic Diseases for clues to the men's deaths. They uncover a lethal serum which kills by inhalation.

Colonel Timothy Ronald Culver
Glover Fulton Mackay
Dexter Dudley Sutton

Director: Paul Dickson
Designer: Robert Jones

Split

w Brian Clemens
The stringent security of the Ministry of
Top Secret Information is badly shaken
when an agent is murdered in the rest area.
Investigating the death, Steed and Tara
meet a 'dead' man, who plans to use Tara's
head as a carrier for his brain!
Lord Barnes Nigel Davenport
Dr Constantine Bernard Archard
Rooke Julian Glover

Director: Roy Baker
Designer: Robert Jones

Whoever Shot Poor George Oblique Stroke XR40?

w Tony Williamson
Steed and Tara are assigned to find out why
George XR40, a computer, suddenly goes
wrong. Together with Dr Ardmore, a
cybernetic surgeon, they oversee an
'operation' on the computer – until Tara is
taken hostage and left to die in a blazing
inferno.
Tobin Frank Windsor
Jason Dennis Price
Pelley Clifford Evans

Director: Cyril Frankel
Designer: Robert Jones

False Witness

w Jeremy Burnham
Why should agents deny all knowledge of
their treachery when faced with unshakeable
proof of their guilt? When Tara succumbs to
'memory-loss', Steed must find the answer
quickly, if he is to save her life.
Lord Edgefield William Job
Sykes John Bennett
Sloman Dan Meaden

Director: Charles Crichton
Designer: Robert Jones

All Done With Mirrors

w Leigh Vance
With Steed under house arrest at Mother's
headquarters, Tara teams up with trainee
agent, Watney, and drives to the Carmadoc
Research Establishment to investigate
reports that one of the staff is leaking secrets
to the enemy.
Watney Dinsdale Landen
Barlow Edwin Richfield
Sparshott Peter Copely

Director: Ray Austin
Designer: Robert Jones

Legacy of Death

w Terry Nation
Steed is given a gift – an ornate dagger –
but no other information save that it is a
legacy. Priceless it may be, but he soon
discovers that it has already cost several men
their lives – and Tara looks set to become its
next victim!
Sidney Stratford Johns
Humbert Ronald Lacey
Farrer Richard Hurndall

Director: Don Chaffey
Designer: Robert Jones

Noon-Doomsday

w Terry Nation
Recovering from injuries received in a recent
case, Steed is recuperating at a secret
convalescent home for agents. Tara,
meanwhile, discovering that two of Steed's
old enemies are on their way to kill him,
races to offer him assistance.
Grant T. P. McKenna
Farrington Ray Brooks
Kafta Peter Bromilow

Director: Peter Sykes
Designer: Unknown

Look (Stop Me If You've Heard This One) But There Were These Two Fellers

w Dennis Spooner
Steed and Tara come face to face with two
vicious killers, Maxie Martin and Jennings –
vaudeville clowns whose antics leave a trail

of dead bodies in their wake. Steed's dilemma: which face hides a killer?
Maxie Martin Jimmy Jewel
Jennings Julian Chagrin
Marcus Pugman John Cleese

Director: James Hill
Designer: Robert Jones

Have Guns . . . Will Haggle

w Donald James
Steed becomes an arms dealer to expose a gang bidding for the top secret FN FF70 rifle. His bid must be the highest, otherwise Tara, held hostage by the gang, will be used as the bull's-eye on the target range.
Colonel Nsonga Johnny Sekka
Adriana Nicola Pagett
Conrad Jonathan Burn

Director: Ray Austin
Designer: Robert Jones

They Keep Killing Steed

w Brian Clemens
Believing that Steed is dead, Tara coopts Baron Von Court to help her track down a gang who intend to infiltrate a peace conference with a bomb. But then Steed reappears—followed by another Steed . . . and another . . . and another . . .
Arcos Ray McAnally
Baron Ian Ogilvy
Zerson Norman Jones

Director: Robert Fuest
Designer: Robert Jones.

The Interrogators

w Richard Harris and Brian Clemens
Steed and Tara face the interrogators, a group of ruthless agents who have conceived a brilliant scheme to extract secret information from Steed's department colleagues. Unaware she has been duped, Tara willingly undergoes the interrogation course.
Colonel Mannering Christopher Lee
Minnow David Sumner
Caspar Philip Bond

Director: Charles Crichton
Designer: Robert Jones

The Rotters

w Dave Freeman
When several important ministers die in mysterious circumstances, Steed and Tara find themselves facing the Rotters, a gang who dissolve woodwork. Hot on their trail, Tara takes refuse in a wooden hut – which suddenly dissolves around her!
Kenneth Gerald Sim
George Jerome Willis
Pym Eric Barker

Director: Robert Fuest
Designer: Robert Jones

Invasion of the Earthmen

w Terry Nation
What dark secret hides behind the closed doors of the Alpha Academy, a school for astronauts? Steed and Tara, posing as parents interested in sending their son to the school, investigate – and find themselves in very strange surroundings.
Brett William Lucas
Huxton Christian Roberts
Emily Lucy Fleming

Director: Don Sharp
Designers: Wilfred Shingleton and Robert Jones

Killer

w Tony Williamson
With Tara on holiday, Steed coopts trainee agent, Lady Diana Forbes-Blakeney, to help him defeat the threat of REMAK (Remote Electro-Matic Agent Killer) – a machine programmed to kill secret agents, which is depleting the ranks of Steed's fellow agents.
Lady Diana Jennifer Croxton
Brinstead William Franklyn
Merridon Grant Taylor

Director: Cliff Owen
Designer: Robert Jones

The Morning After

w Brian Clemens
Merlin, one of the most dangerous and charming spies ever to cross Steed's path, involves Tara and her colleague in a chase through the London streets, to thwart the

plans of Brigadier Hansing, the mastermind behind a scheme to hold all England ransom under the threat of an atomic bomb.
Merlin Peter Barkworth
Brigadier Hansing Joss Ackland
Sgt Hearn Brian Blessed

Director: John Hough
Designer: Robert Jones

The Curious Case of the Countless Clues

w Philip Levene
Ministry sleuth, Sir Arthur Doyle, has picked up all the carefully-laid clues at a murder scene, and reached the conclusion that Steed committed the crime. Tara must act swiftly if she is to prove her colleague's innocence.
Doyle Peter Jones
Stanley Tony Selby
Gardiner Kenneth Cope

Director: Don Sharp
Designer: Wilfred Shingleton

Wish You Were Here

w Tony Williamson
A postcard from her uncle leads Tara to a hotel-cum-prison from which there is no escape. Suspicious of her absence, Mother sends his nephew, trainee agent Latimer, after her. Both find themselves held captive by a gang who will stop at nothing to achieve their aims.
Maxwell Robert Urquhart
Latimer Brook Williams
Parker Dudley Foster

Director: Don Chaffey
Designer: Robert Jones

Stay Tuned

w Tony Williamson
Unaware that he has been hypnotised, Steed packs his luggage to leave for a holiday – the problem is he's only recently returned from a three-week Continental break! Worse still, the agent has been conditioned to kill Mother – and only Tara can stop him!

Lisa Kate O'Mara
Wilks Duncan Lamont
Proctor Gary Bond

Director: Don Chaffey
Designer: Robert Jones

Take Me To Your Leader

w Terry Nation
Assigned to follow an ingenious device – an attaché case that talks, which is being used by the enemy to transport stolen secrets – Steed and Tara have their work cut out traversing the deadly obstacle course laid by their opponents.
Stonehouse Patrick Barr
Captain Tim John Ronane
Cavell Michael Robbins

Director: Robert Fuest
Designer: Robert Jones

Fog

w Jeremy Burnham
Steed and Tara face a modern-day Jack the Ripper – the Gaslight Ghoul, a man hell bent on wiping out foreign delegates attending a disarmament conference. Like his predecessor, he too vanishes in the dense London fog.
President Nigel Green
Traveers Guy Rolfe
Carstairs Terence Brady

Director: John Hough
Designer: Robert Jones

Homicide and Old Lace

w Malcolm Hulke and Terence Dicks
To celebrate his birthday, Mother visits his two ageing aunts, Harriet and Georgina. Being ardent fans, they beg him to tell them a story about his feats of daring. He embarks on a story to end all stories – the case of the Great, Great Britain Crime!
Harriet Joyce Carey
Georgina Mary Merrall
Col Dorf Gerald Harper

Director: John Hough
Designer: Wilfred Shingleton and Robert Jones

Love All

w Jeremy Burnham

Before Steed can solve the murder of four important civil servants, he must first break the strange affair of Tara's romantic involvement: his colleague has fallen madly in love, and is prepared to go to any lengths to prove her devotion – including suicide!

Martha Veronica Strong
Bromfield Terence Alexander
Sir Rodney Robert Harris

Director: Peter Sykes
Designer: Robert Jones

Get-a-Way

w Philip Levene

When three foreign agents are caught and confined in a tightly-guarded monastery – but nevertheless manage to disappear without trace – Steed and Tara face one of their toughest cases.

Ezdorf Peter Bowles
Magnus Barry Lineman
Col James Andrew Keir

Director: Don Sharp
Designers: Wilfred Shingleton and Robert Jones

Thingumajig

w Terry Nation

A case with a difference for the Avengers – a lethal black box which subjects its victims to a white-hot discharge of electrical energy. Steed and Tara experience more than a few shocks before they defeat 'It' – one of the most deadly killers they've ever encountered.

Professor Truman Willoughby Goddard
Kruger Iain Cuthbertson
Stenson Vernon Dobtcheff

Director: Leslie Norman
Designer: Robert Jones

Pandora

w Brian Clemens

Kidnapped and brainwashed into believing that she is Pandora, the girl who jilted Gregory Lasindall in his youth, Tara King lies helpless in the clutches of the Lasindall

brothers. Steed, meanwhile, receives news that Tara has been killed in a car accident.

Rupert Lasindall Julian Glover
Henry Lasindall James Cossins
Gregory Lasindall Peter Madden

Director: Robert Fuest
Designer: Robert Jones

Requiem

w Brian Clemens

The inscription on the wreath reads: 'In loving memory of our dear Mother. Died suddenly – explosively – RIP'. Steed's department is at its lowest ebb. Tara, both legs in plaster, is confined to a wheelchair and Steed has disappeared!

Firth John Cairney
Barrett Mike Lewin
Miranda Angela Douglas

Director: Don Chaffey
Designer: Robert Jones

Take-over

w Terry Nation

Steed's annual visit to his friend Bill Bassett places the agent's life in danger. Bassett and his wife are being held hostage by a group of criminals intent on bombing a peace conference – but they have reckoned without another unwelcome visitor – Tara King.

Grenville Tom Adams
Circe Hilary Pritchard
Lomax Keith Buckley

Director: Robert Fuest
Designer: Robert Jones

Who Was That Man I Saw You With?

w Jeremy Burnham

Suspecting that Tara is selling secrets to the enemy, Mother reduces her security rating to zero minus and Steed is given 24 hours to prove her innocence. Events take a decidedly suspicious turn when Steed believes his colleague is guilty of murder.

Dangerfield Alan Wheatley
Zaroff Alan Browning
Fairfax William Marlowe

Director: Don Chaffey
Designer: Robert Jones

My Wildest Dream

w Philip Levene

When members of the Acme Precision Combine Limited are found dead, Steed and Tara King find themselves investigating an enemy who conditions people to eliminate his rivals. Unknown to the agents, Steed's name is next on the madman's hit list!

Jaeger Peter Vaughan
Nurse Owen Susan Travers
Chilcott Edward Fox

Director: Robert Fuest
Designer: Robert Jones

Bizarre

w Brian Clemens

The Avengers bow out with an adventure in which 'dead' men walk, and Steed goes underground to expose the antics of the Master – a man who arranges for businessmen to disappear in the not-so-hallowed plots of the Happy Meadows cemetery.

The Master Fulton Mackay
Bagpipes Happychap Roy Kinnear
Jupp John Sharp

Director: Leslie Norman
Designer: Robert Jones

THE AVENGERS
Season One
Producer: Leonard White
Music by: Johnny Dankworth
An ABC Television Production
Videotaped at Teddington Studios
7 January–30 December 1961

Season Two
Producer: Leonard White and John Bryce
Music by: Johnny Dankworth
Story editors: John Bryce and Richard Bates
An ABC Television Production
Videotaped at Teddington Studios
29 September 1962–23 March 1963

Season Three
Producer: John Bryce
Music by: Johnny Dankworth
Story editor: Richard Bates
An ABC Television Production
Videotaped at Teddington Studios
29 September 1963-21 March 1964

Season Four
Executive producer: Albert Fennel
Associate producer and story editor: Brian Clemens
Music by: Laurie Johnson
An ABC Television Production
Filmed at Elstree Studios
2 October 1965–26 March 1966

Season Five
Producers: Albert Fennell and Brian Clemens
Executive producer: Julian Wintle
Music by: Laurie Johnson
An ABC Television Production
Filmed at Elstree Studios
15 January–18 November 1967

Season Six
Producers: Albert Fennell and Brian Clemens
Executive producer: Gordon L.T. Scott
Music by: Laurie Johnson
Story consultant: Philip Levene
Script editor: Terry Nation
An ABC Television Production
Filmed at Elstree Studios
3 October 1968–25 March 1969

[USA: Season Four: ABC 28 March–8 September 1966
Season Five: ABC 20 January–1 September 1967
Season Six: ABC 10 January 1968–15 September 1969 Syndicated]
[The videotaped series was never screened in the USA]

THE AWFUL MR GOODALL

A short-lived though immensely enjoyable spy-cum-thriller series, which depicted the career of Jack Goodall, an ex-military gent working for an undesignated department of British Intelligence.

Though retired, the 55-year-old widower seldom found time to enjoy the quiet life. An ex-spycatcher, with over 15 years service as a Lieutenant-Colonel in the British Intelligence department MI5 and DI5 under his belt, Goodall found that the past had a way of catching up. His problem was that he had a 'sixth' sense; one which, having proved invaluable during his time spent sorting out double-agents, delicate international negotiations and secrets concerning his country's security, the 'department' could ill afford to be without. So, with regular monotony, Goodall found himself departing his lavishly-furnished Eastbourne flat, to heed the latest call from Millbrook, Head of Section at MI, and once again enmeshed in the seedy security problems he wished to leave behind forever.

REGULAR CAST

Mr Goodall Robert Urquhart   *Millbrook* Donald Churchill
Alexandra Winfield Isobel Dean

A Good English Breakfast

w Roger Marshall
Attending a reunion dinner with his ex-Army colleagues, Mr Goodall finds himself investigating a threat to Britain's security — an event which, if allowed to continue, could bring down HM's government.
Carrick John Ringman
Major Ripley John Franklyn-Robbins
Dr Moffatt Eleanor Bron

Director: John Reardon
Designer: Roger Hall

Indiscretion

w Trevor Preston
Mr Goodall must find the answers to the intriguing puzzles of a strange phone call in the night . . . a man in a hospital bed . . . a wife who refuses to tell the truth . . . and a party without guests.

Seddon Peter Jeffrey
Anne Seddon Diana Fairfax
Doctor Stephen Greif

Director: Jim Goddard
Designer: Frank Nerini

Clara

w Roger Marshall
A girl called Clara leads Mr Goodall into a web of intrigue surrounding the murder of a British agent working abroad. As he soon discovers, pretty girls and murder often walk hand in hand.
Ruth Carrick Margaret Ashcroft
Madame Clement Jacqueline Pearce
Historian Leon Eagles

Director: Jim Goddard
Designer: Andrew Drummond

Loyalty in My Honour

w Paul Wheeler

When a member of the Foreign Office is arrested, Mr Goodall finds himself faced with a race against time in his efforts to save both the man's career and honour.

Henry Mullard Ian McCulloch
Amanda Mullard Jennifer Daniel
Baines Llewellyn Rees

Director: Jim Goddard
Designer: Roger Hall

A Day to Remember

w Roy Russell

When Goodall takes Alex to lunch at the country home of his ex-Army friend, James Connelly, he finds himself torn between loyalty and friendship. To his astonishment, Alex expresses her dislike of Connelly – a turn of events that reopens old wounds.

Connelly David Waller

Director: John Reardon
Designer: Frank Nerini

The Good Samaritan

w Roger Marshall

When an attentive travel agent discovers a lost passport, Goodall finds himself investigating a mystery on his own doorstep: Eastbourne, it appears, is the main link in a puzzling smuggling racket.

Captain Stearns Benjamin Whitrow
Mrs Stearns Patricia Garwood
Mr Forbes Norman Claridge

Director: John Reardon
Designer: Michael Yates

THE AWFUL MR GOODALL
Producer: Richard Bates
Music by: Albert Elms
A London Weekend Television Network Production
6 colour 60-minute episodes
5 April–10 May 1974

THE BARON

Inspired by the character created by John Creasey (writing as Anthony Morton), whose novels described the Baron as a gentleman jewel thief until love changed his ways and he became a reformed character and Scotland Yard confidant, readers of the books would have had a tough time recognising the hero of this ITC-produced series as Creasey's lovable rogue. In the hands of producer Monty Berman, the character was translated into that of London-based American antiques dealer, John Mannering, a trouble-shooter for the antiques industry. Better known as the Baron – a nickname he'd acquired because the cattle on his American ranch sported the Baron brand – the stories depicted his investigations into crimes associated with the art world and his attempts to recover stolen art treasures, or expose the perpetrators behind a cleverly-excuted art swindle.

Aware that such material had limited dramatic appeal, Berman introduced several other new factors into the proceedings by making Mannering, a man with exclusive antiques shops in London, Paris and Washington, a character who was not above using these establishments as a front for undercover activities. On several occasions during the series, the hero found himself working for the head concho of British Intelligence – John Templeton-Green. To assist Mannering during these adventures, Berman introduced another character you'd be hard-pressed to find on the printed page – Cordelia Winfield, a bubbly, attractive agent working for the Special Branch Diplomatic Service. She swiftly became Mannering's full-time assistant, and appeared in virtually every story. Also featured in several adventures was David Marlowe, the Baron's business associate.

When likened to Simon Templar (aka The Saint) – the Baron's nearest contemporary – the series fared favourably in the action department, although it suffered somewhat from pedestrian scripts. It nevertheless proved popular with the public, and though the series was originally scheduled for 26 episodes, 30 were produced.

REGULAR CAST

The Baron **Steve Forrest**   *Cordelia* **Sue Lloyd**
Templeton-Green **Colin Gordon**   *David Marlowe* **Paul Ferris**

Diplomatic Immunity

w Dennis Spooner
Victim of a series of large-scale art robberies, the Baron and Cordelia go behind the Iron Curtain to recover the stolen loot. But they have reckoned without international diplomacy which, as they discover, can present unseen problems.
Cordelia Winfield **Sue Lloyd** (Intro.)
Templeton-Green **Colin Gordon** (Intro.)
David Marlowe **Paul Ferris** (Intro.)

Director: Leslie Norman

Epitaph for a Hero

w Terry Nation
Though it means betraying the trust of a man who saved his life, the Baron takes part in a well-organised jewel robbery. But as the thieves soon discover, even the best-laid plans are prone to Murphy's Law.
Helga Patricia Haines
Jim Carey Paul Maxwell
Charlie Nosher Powell

Director: John Moxey

Something for a Rainy Day

w Terry Nation
The Baron has to ask himself: is a jewel thief entitled to the rewards of his crime after he has served a long prison sentence? The insurance company says no, but Mannering has other ideas.
Max Holder Patrick Allen
Mark Seldon Michael Gwynn
Charlotte Russell Lois Maxwell

Director: Cyril Frankel

Red Horse, Red Rider

w Terry Nation
The Baron puts his life and reputation on the line to help a patriot sell a million-dollar antique to raise funds for a rebel cause. When intrigue and murder enter the picture, Mannering must plan his next move with caution.
Savannah Jane Merrow
Miros Frank Wolff
David Marlow Paul Ferris

Director: John Moxey

Enemy of the State

w Dennis Spooner

When Cordelia, standing in for him at an appointment behind the Iron Curtain, is arrested by State Security, Mannering instigates a daring plan to obtain her release – a plan which involves placing himself in the firing line.

Szoblik Anton Diffring
Col Bucholz Joseph Furst
Templeton-Green Colin Gordon

Director: Jeremy Summers

Masquerade
Part One 'Masquerade'

w Terry Nation and Dennis Spooner

An audacious scheme to murder the Baron and replace him with a double, helped by plastic surgery, places the lives of Mannering and Cordelia in great danger. Their dilemma is increased when Mannering 'disappears', and Cordelia sees double.

Masquerade
Part Two 'The Killing'

w Terry Nation and Dennis Spooner

The Baron faces the greatest test of his career – how to foil a plan to steal the Crown Jewels, and lay the blame at Mannering's door? His life depends on his ability to impersonate himself.

Morgan Travis Bernard Lee
Selina Travis Yvonne Furneaux
Revell John Carson

Director: Cyril Frankel

The Persuaders

w Dennis Spooner

In an effort to persuade the Baron to act as their front man in a major art swindle, a gang of ruthless art thieves kidnap his assistant, David Marlowe, and hold him hostage under the threat of his life.

Verity Montand Georgina Ward
Harrington James Villiers
Templeton-Green Colin Gordon

Director: Leslie Norman

And Suddenly You're Dead

w Terry Nation and Dennis Spooner

The Baron and Cordelia find themselves faced with a terrifying enemy – a group of people will stop at nothing to achieve their aims . . . including the threat to open up new horrors in germ warfare!

Ingar Sorenson Kay Walsh
Holmes Alan MacNaughton
Templeton-Green Colin Gordon

Director: Cyril Frankel

The Legions of Ammak

w Michael Cramoy

When the Baron transacts a deal for an eccentric millionaire who wishes to purchase a fabulous treasure from a foreign king, he uncovers a fantastic plot to swindle a foreign President of his country's art treasures.

King Ibrahim/Noyes Peter Wyngarde
Cossackian George Murcell
David Marlowe Paul Ferris

Director: John Moxey

Samurai West

w Brian Degas

When he buys a valuable Samurai sword from a Japanese dealer, the Baron incurs the wrath of several people seeking to bring the Japanese gentleman – a former commandant of a prisoner-of-war camp – to justice.

Asano Lee Montague
Norman Stirling Raymond Huntley
Tom Stirling Colin Jeavons

Director: John Moxey

The Maze

w Tony O'Grady (a.k.a. Brian Clemens)

The Baron 'loses' 24 hours of his life. Tracing back the path of events for that missing day brings him into contact with a deadly enemy – and leads him through a maze of remarkable events.

Gaydon Alan MacNaughton
Det Insp Walsh Glynn Edwards
Det Sgt Miller David Morrell

Director: Jeremy Summers

Portrait of Louisa

w Terry Nation

When a woman asks him to buy her some valuable miniatures, the Baron is drawn into a web of blackmail and murder – with himself as the fall guy of the plot.

Louisa Moira Redmond
Jane Benson Jo Rowbottom
Nigel Brockhurst Terence Alexander

Director: John Moxey

There's Someone Close Behind You

w Terry Nation and Dennis Spooner

Mannering's nose for trouble sniffs out a big-scale robbery attempt – which leads to the smell of death when a gang boss orders the Baron to be eliminated.

Gregg Wilde Richard Wyler
Frank Oddy Philip Madoc
Sheldon Mike Pratt

Director: Roy Baker

Storm Warning
Part 1 'Storm Warning'

w Terry Nation

When Cordelia witnesses a murder on board a cruise liner, Mannering finds himself victim of an unusual hijack attempt.

Storm Warning Part 2 'The Island'

w Terry Nation

Victims of a gang of hijackers, the Baron and Cordelia must find a way of defeating a fantastic plot to steal a manned space capsule.

Brian Carlton Dudley Sutton
Captain Brenner Reginald Marsh
Baggio Derek Newark

Director: Gordon Flemyng

Time To Kill

w Dennis Spooner

The Baron has to decide whether the curse on a valuable cameo is mere superstition. Several people have already given their lives

to possess it, and the trail of tragedy looks like continuing when Mannering is asked to buy it.

Vitale Hamilton Dyce
Mendez Peter Bowles
Christina Geraldine Moffatt

Director: Robert Asher

A Memory of Evil

w Terry Nation and Dennis Spooner

When Nazi art treasures appear on the British antiques market, Mannering finds himself making a trip overseas – to find murder and treachery in a mountain retreat.

Hoffman Robert Hardy
Nikki Holtz Ann Bell
Heller Edwin Richfield

Director: Don Chaffey

You Can't Win Them All

w Dennis Spooner

Mannering stakes his life to expose a big-time gambler he knows to be a ruthless killer. Though the odds are stacked against him, the Baron has an ace up his sleeve.

Sefton Folkard Sam Wanamaker
Forbes Reginald Marsh
David Marlowe Paul Ferris

Director: Don Chaffey

The High Terrace

w Dennis Spooner

A phoney religious order and a trail of treachery lead the Baron to suspect that the mystery surrounding the disappearance of two wealthy women bears closer investigation.

Sara Knight Jan Holden
Phyllis Thornton Veronica Hurst
The Chosen One Max Adrian

Director: Robert Asher

The Seven Eyes of Night

w Terry Nation

A valuable necklace, bought from a beautiful French widow, leads Mannering into an ingenious plot to steal a valuable art treasure.

Jeff Walker Jeremy Brett
Madame Devereaux Patricia English
Nancy Cummings Hilary Tindall

Director: Robert Asher

Night of the Hunter

w Terry Nation

Aware that money raised by him from the sale of antiques belonging to the wife of a foreign President will be used to finance a revolution, the Baron decides to deliver the money himself – and finds himself face to face with a ruthless dictator.
Madame Nicharos Katharine Blake
The General Derek Godfrey
Paeblo John Richards

Director: Roy Baker

The Edge of Fear

w Dennis Spooner

When a painting is stolen from the Louvre in Paris, the criminal fraternity ask the question: is it the Mona Lisa? To confirm their suspicions, they consult the one man who can confirm its authenticity – the Baron.
Kent Jordon William Franklyn
Colbert Willoughby Goddard
David Marlowe Paul Ferris

Director: Quentin Lawrence

Long Ago and Far Away

w Dennis Spooner

Two young girls lead the Baron and Cordelia into a web of intrigue, murder and revenge. Mannering must find out what lies behind the shuttered windows of a mysterious country house.
Frank Ashton George Baker
Dr Thornton John Franklyn-Robbins
Joyce Grant Gillian Lewis

Director: Robert Tronson

So Dark the Night

w Terry Nation and Dennis Spooner

Two young girls lead the Baron and Cordelia into a web of intrigue, murder and revenge. Mannering must find out what lies behind the shuttered windows of a mysterious country house.
Frank Ashton George Baker
Dr Thornton John Franklyn-Robbins
Joyce Grant Gillian Lewis

Director: Robert Tronson

The Long, Long Day

w Tony O'Grady (a.k.a. Brian Clemens)

While visiting a friend in Italy, the Baron finds himself protecting a murder witness – a young girl who can expose the leader behind a spate of killings. Mannering's dilemma: the Mafia boss knows their whereabouts, and is closing in for the kill.
Maria Dallia Penn
Navini Peter Arne
Murphy Eddie Byrne

Director: Roy Baker

Roundabout

w Terry Nation

Informed that his own Paris office is being used as a cover for a dope-smuggling racket, the Baron sets out to trace the leader of the gang – a vicious mobster who will let nothing stand in the way of get-rich schemes.
Delair Edwin Richfield
Jeanne Varda June Ritchie
Samantha Ballard Annette Andre

Director: Robert Tronson

The Man Outside

w Terry Nation

The loss of a valuable ring leads Mannering to Scotland where, together with Cordelia, he uncovers an astonishing plan to wreck Britain's economy. It isn't long before he and his colleague find themselves up to their necks in trouble.
Bruno Orsini David Bauer
Dino Rossi Paul Maxwell
Vince Florio Michael Coles

Director: Roy Baker

Countdown

w Terry Nation

Unaware of the reason why they have been asked to keep a rendezvous with a stranger, Mannering and Cordelia arrive at the designated meeting point – and find themselves facing a countdown to death.

Logan Michael Wynne
Compton Philip Locke
White Harold Lang

Director: Robert Asher

Farewell to Yesterday

w Harry H. Junkin

Working undercover, the Baron investigates claims that a dead airline steward had been working for one of the largest art smuggling rings of the century. His enquiries bring startling results.

Cathy Dorne Sylvia Syms
Nick William Sylvester
Templeton-Green Colin Gordon

Director: Leslie Norman

THE BARON
Producer: Monty Berman
Music by: Edwin Astley
Script editor: Terry Nation
An ITC Production
Filmed at Elstree Studios and on location
30 colour 60-minute episodes
28 September 1966–19 April 1967
[USA: ABC 20 January–14 July 1966 26 episodes. Syndicated]

BIG BREADWINNER HOG

An ambitious attempt to portray the criminal fraternity in realistic terms – as vicious underworld thugs who'd stop at nothing to achieve their aims – this thriller series raised a public outcry when it was screened towards the end of the 'Swinging Sixties'.

The 'hero' of the piece was Hog, a young, handsome, but ruthlessly ambitious thief who'd set his sights on taking over London's crime-ridden streets and becoming number one – the undisputed leader of the underworld, the Big Boss. No one and nothing would stand in the way of his goal. Cross Hog and he'd melt your face with acid. Threaten his independence and he'd ensure that you spent several weeks in an intensive-care hospital unit waiting for your broken limbs to mend. Hog had over 500 ways of making you believe he was for real – all of them nasty, many of them permanent. For Hog, it was all or nothing. There were no halfway measures. But his climb to the top was a thorny one: the older generation of villains saw his anarchistic methods as as big a threat to their existence as law and order, and they retaliated – violently . . . and therein lay the problem. As it transpired, the viewing public – reared on a diet of imported pseudo-gangster series that depicted 'violence' Hollywood-style (simulated killings and tomato-ketchup blood) – were not yet ready to accept the realistic mayhem provided by the series. Barely minutes after the first episode was transmitted, the Granada switchboard was inundated with phone calls from viewers registering their abhorrence of the deliberately unrestrained violent scenes which permeated the first story. So numerous were the complaints that the production company were forced to precede the second story with an apology for the previous week's episode. This failed to placate the viewers: the company was forced to tone down the tougher aspects of the series, and the series format suffered accordingly.

REGULAR CAST

Hog Peter Egan   *Ackerman* Donald Churchill   *Edgeworth* Rosemary McHale
Grange David Leland   *Lennox* Timothy West   *Raspery* Peter Thomas
Singleton Tony Steedman   *Izzard* Alan Browning   *Ryan* Godfrey Quigley

BIG BREADWINNER HOG
Producer: Robin Chapman
Music by: Derek Hilton
Directors: Mike Newell and Michael Apted
Designer: Michael Grimes

A Granada Television Network Production
7 colour 60-minute episodes
11 April–30 May 1969

BIGGLES

Twenty-six years before the cinema brought us the first big-screen adventure of Captain W.E. Johns' celebrated flying hero, Granada television produced this – the first and to date only small screen adventures based on the character.

Primarily aimed at the younger viewer and faithful to the printed page, the weekly (untitled) adventures certainly delivered the goods. Each story has an abundance of action-packed situations that propelled Biggles – now a Detective Air Inspector, attached to Scotland Yard – and his faithful companions, Ginger and Bertie, into a series of thrill-filled adventures in which they faced danger at every turn. Larger-than-life villains devised ingenious traps and devices which tested the trio's escape abilities. Each story contained at least one authentic (studio reproduced) flying sequence, and every episode ended in cliff-hanger fashion, with an on-screen announcement advising viewers to 'tune in again next week, for more daring adventures of . . .'

REGULAR CAST

Biggles **Neville Whiting**   *Ginger* **John Leyton**   *Bertie* **David Drummond**
Von Stalheim **Carl Duering**

BIGGLES
Producer: Harry Eldon and Kitty Black
Directors: Stuart Latham, Chris McMaster,
Douglas Hurn, Derek Bennet, Eric Price
Stories adapted by: H.V. Kershaw, Alick
Hayes, Rex Howard, Tony Warren

A Granada Television Network Production
24 monochrome 30-minute episodes
1 April–9 September 1960

THE BILL

This gritty, down-to-earth police series – in the words of its producer Michael Chapman 'an attempt to show the police being policemen rather than investigators in someone else's story' – came as a breath of spring to an audience reared on imported cops 'n' robbers thrillers.

Set in the busy Sun Hill police station, situated in London's East End, it depicted the routine (and not so routine) tours of duty of officers of the law collectively know as The Bill, whose patch covered a radius of two miles surrounding their 'nick' (codename 'Uniform Oscar').

The shining light of the department was Detective Inspector Dave Galloway, head of the station's CID squad. Having worked his way up through the ranks to become the youngest DI in the division, Galloway, a tough and relentless task-master, had few close friends in (or out of) the department. Hot-headed and fearless of authority, he always got the job done and was never afraid to 'bend the rule book' – if it brought the 'right result'.

Sharing a crusty, but mutually respectful relationship with Galloway was Police Sergeant Bob Cryer, the station officer. Viewed as a father figure by his young patrolmen, Cryer – frequently at odds with Galloway and his methods – knew that his fifteen years service gave him enough weight to take on senior management whenever he got whiff that his 'boys' were getting a raw deal. Boys like PC 'Taffy' Edwards, the youngest member of the team, or his patrol partner 'probationer' PC Jimmy Carver, a sensitive newcomer looking to better himself by seeking advice from time-served PC Dave Litton, an ambitious copper with his eyes set on promotion to the CID. (By season three, it was PC Carver who inherited that post.) Other members of Cryer's 'woodentops' (CID slang for the boys in blue) were WPCs June

Ackland and Martella, two women doing a man's job – and proving themselves every bit as capable as their male colleagues. Rounding up the team were Galloway's CID assistants, Detective Constable Dashwood and Detective Sergeant Roach, the hothead of the squad who was constantly in trouble with his superiors. New arrivals in season three were Inspector Kite, a no-nonsense, time-served policeman, Sergeant Peters and PCs Shaw and Melvin.

'Woodentop', a prototype for the series, was transmitted in 1983 in the Thames TV *Storyteller* series.

REGULAR CAST

Det Insp Dave Galloway John Salthouse   *Sgt Bob Cryer* Eric Richard
PC Edwards Colin Blumenau   *PC Carver* Mark Wingett   *PC Litten* Gary Olsen
WPC Ackland Trudie Goodwin   *WPC Martella* Nula Conwell
Det Sgt Roach Tony Scannell   *PC Hollis* Jeffrey Stewart   *PC Smith* Robert Hudson
PC Frank Ashley Gunstock   *Chief Supt Brownlow* Peter Ellis
PC Lyttleton Ronny Cush   *PC Muswell* Ralph Brown   *Sgt Penny* roger Leach
Insp Kite Simon Slater   *Sgt Peters* Larry Dann   *PC Shaw* Chris Walker
PC Melvin Mark Powley   *PC Patel* Sonesh Sira

Season One

11 colour 60-minute episodes

Funny Ol' Business — Cops and Robbers

w Geoff McQueen

The Sun Hill police force seldom find time to relax. Today is no exception: Sergeant Cryer briefs his team to look out for a crew of pickpockets and car thieves – while DI Galloway instructs them: 'Don't touch a thing. Stay on the scene till *my* team arrive . . .'

Sgt Burnside Christopher Ellison
Sgt Penny Roger Leach
Lennie Colin Higgins

Director: Peter Cregeen
Designer: Philip Blowers

A Friend in Need

w Barry Appleton

Three bomb hoax telephone calls. The Home Office breathing down the Commissioner's neck. Galloway instructed to clear things up – any way he can. So Galloway has a £10 bet with Cryer that he will crack this one. Things can't get worse – can they?

Matty Davis Peter Fenwick
Frankie Davis Tony London
Derek Higgins Jeffrey Stewart

Director: Peter Cregeen
Designer: Philip Blowers

Clutching at Straws

w Geoff McQueen

An indecent assault on three young girls aged between 7 and 12. Young Billy Marsh beaten up by three youths in the lift of a block of flats and a youth club that has been closed for some time. Three incidents under investigation by Cryer's boys.

Simon Doleman Anthony Ingram
Mrs Doleman June Brown
Billy Marsh Adam Armstrong

Director: Christopher Hodson
Designer: Philip Blowers

Long Odds

w Geoff McQueen

Every policeman shares the same nightmare: finding himself looking down the barrel of a gun. Today it's Detective Sergeant Roach's turn.

Det Chf Insp Kirk Ray Armstrong
Det Insp Wheeler Michael N. Harbour
WPC Picton Tessa Bell-Briggs

Director: John Michael Philips
Designer: Philip Blowers

It's Not Such a Bad Job After All

w Barry Appleton
A young girl seeking glamour in the
London streets leads the Sun Hill policemen
on a not-so-merry chase which culminates in
disaster – and a reprimand for Sun Hill's
finest.
Rachel Dymock Sadie Hamilton
Video shop owner John Savident
Film director Edward Brayshaw

Director: John Woods
Designers: John Plant and Phillip Blowers

The Drugs Raid

w Barry Appleton
When the tenants of a housing estate
request a meeting with Superintendent
Brownlow to discuss the alarming increase
in heroin abuse on their estate, the chief
super sees a chance to get to grips with the
problem in a military style operation.
Tomo Robertson Norman Beaton
Harry Decker Paul Newney
Maggie Liz Smith

Director: John Wood
Designer: Philip Blowers

A Dangerous Breed

w Barry Appleton
Anxious to impress Galloway, PC Litten, on
temporary secondment to the CID, has the
misfortune to meet a potentially dangerous
enemy – an informant, who has information
regarding the whereabouts of a valuable
necklace stolen from Lord Barstow-Smythe.
Lord Barstow-Smythe Osmund Bullock
Informant Trevor Martin
Sadie Cheryl Hall

Director: Christopher Hodson
Designer: Philip Blowers

Rough in the Afternoon

w John Kershaw
The officers at Sun Hill Police Station must
overcome their natural reluctance to get
involved in a 'domestic' crisis. A small
child, made a Ward of Court by his mother,
has 'disappeared' with his father.
Brownlow's advice: 'Keep the Press out of
it.'
Sid Leather Bernard Kay
Alan Ferne Tip Tipping
Joyce Ferne Katharine Levy

Director: Christopher Hodson
Designer: Philip Blowers

Burning the Books

w Barry Appleton
Finding himself up against an old adversary,
who has proved very slippery in the past,
Galloway swears he'll settle for nothing less
than a 'cop' – and sets out to challenge
Cohen, the man behind the distribution of
pornographic magazines.
Cohen John Blythe
Sharman James Faulkner
Bernie Brian Croucher

Director: Peter Cregeen
Designer: Philip Blowers

Death of a Cracksman

w Barry Appleton
When three would-be thieves break into a
factory and find a safe they can't open, they
seek the expertise of safe cracksman Alfie
Mullins, who doesn't want to know. Before
long, the Sun Hill boys are searching for a
missing safe – and a dead man.
Alfie Mullins Paddy Joyce
Eddie Lawrence Lambert
Andy Alan Polonsky

Director: Christopher Hodson
Designer: Philip Blowers

The Sweet Smell of Failure

w Barry Appleton
PC Carver and WPC Aukland have more
than enough on their place trudging

through their manor. Now they've become involved in the sordid affairs of an elderly pair of sticky-fingered thieves.
Bloomfield Lionel Haft
Lily Anthean Holloway
Fred Charles Lamb

Director: John Michael Philips
Designer: Philip Biowers

Season Two
12 colour 60–minute episodes

Snouts and Red Herrings

w Geoff McQueen
When PC Lyttleton, a coloured PC, joins the Sun Hill ranks, a clash of personalities adds further tension to the already strained relationship between the CID and Cryer's boys – to say nothing of the hassle on the streets.
PC Lyttleton Ronny Cush (Intro.)
PC Muswell Ralph Brown (Intro.)
Foreman electrician Charles Cork

Director: Peter Cregeen
Designer: Robin Parker

Suspects

w Barry Appleton
A £50,000 wages robbery. An American tourist robbed at a London Dock. A cigarette factory whose profits are going up in smoke. Put all three under Galloway's nose – and the outcome surprises everyone.
Chalky White John Burgess
Mrs White Edna Dore
Miss Marsh Imogen Claire

Director: Michael Ferguson
Designer: Robin Parker

Lost

w Ginnie Hole
For the officers of Sun Hill a missing child means heartache and hard work. Eight-year-old Samantha has gone missing on her way to school. But who cares, when there's a good result – *if* there's a good result.

School headmaster Ivor Roberts
Mrs Welch Patti Love
Miss Horrocks Annie Wensak

Director: Christopher Hodson
Designer: Robin Parker

Home Beat

w Christopher Russell
Eager to get a Neighbourhood Watch scheme off the ground on the Dairy Street Estate, Chief Superintendent Brownlow must ask himself: can a community police itself or will it always require men like Sergeant Cryer to do the dirty work?
Terry Mitchell Nick Stringer
Maizie Stannard Maggie Flint
Mr Ahmed Badi Uzzaman

Director: John Michael Philips
Designer: Robin Parker

Hostage

w Barry Appleton
With all leave cancelled, a man on the run and armed with a sawn-off shotgun, the prospects of the Sun Hill boys setting out on their annual fishing trip looks bleak. When they do take their outing, they hook a catch that no one wants.
Russel Archer Ian Gentle
Hooky Hoskins Mike Felix
Sadie Cheryl Hall

Director: Michael Ferguson
Designer: Robin Parker

This Little Pig

w Christopher Russell
Two pigs, 'Plonk' and 'Pickle'. Three animal rights demonstrators, shouting loudly in their cells. A wardrobe used as a cover for burglary and a bridegroom arrested as he leaves the church. Bedlam rules at Sun Hill Police Station.
Roger Philpot Tim Stern
Larry John Dair
Ricky Vassalo Gerard Horan

Director: John Woods
Designer: Robin Parker

Ringer

w Barry Appleton

When a Porche involved in a fatal road accident shows signs of being tampered with and the number plates have been changed, the Sun Hill boys become acutely aware that, though accidents can happen, they are not always what they seem.

Mrs Lockett **Heather Tobias**
DS Rigby **Andy Rashleigh**
Helen Crisp **Lavinia Bertram**

Director: **John Woods**
Designer: **Robin Parker**

Public and Confidential

w Lionel Goldstein

An unpaid roofer who decides to take the law into his own hands. A Polish seaman requesting political asylum and a cry for help from Sgt Penny's wife, who says her husband is beating her up. As usual Sun Hill is as quiet as a rugby scrum.

Roofer **Dean Harris**
Witos **Tomas Bork**
Mrs Penny **Janette Legge**

Director: **Christopher Hudson**
Designer: **Robin Parker**

Loan Shark

w Tim Aspinall

When a woman caught shopping in a supermarket tells Sgt Cryer that Aunty Peg and her son Freezer Bob are holding her pension book, the Sun Hill boys find themselves hot on the trail of illegal money-lenders who wish to collect more than their fair share of interest.

Aunty Peg **Antonia Pemberton**
Freezer Bob **Duncan Preston**
Mrs Taylor **Pamela Sholton**

Director: **John Michael Philips**
Designer: **Robin Parker**

With Friends Like That . . . ?

w Barry Appleton

When young Debbie Lindfield arrives at Sun Hill and says she has been raped after a disco, Galloway and his team are kind and sympathetic to the girl but find her friend Sandra difficult. Why? Hindered by Sandra, Galloway tries to bring a man to justice.

Debbie **Sara Moore**
Sandra **Wendy Nottingham**
Chris Jarbett **Glen Murphy**

Director: **Christopher Hudson**
Designer: **Robin Parker**

Whose Side Are You On?

w Jim Hill

It's the annual five-a-side football match between Sun Hill and the local youth club. The Superintendent expects all his personnel to attend, if not as players, as spectators. But a replacement has to be found for PC Carver – and someone suggests that WPC Martella is good with her feet.

Mrs Wilmore **Elizabeth Bradley**
Mr Boone **Stanley Page**
Mr Butler **Raymond Brody**

Director: **Peter Cregeen**
Designer: **Robin Parker**

The Chief Super's Party

w Barry Appleton

Chief Superintendent Brownlow throws a retirement party for his Clerk. All officers are to let their hair down. The drink flows and DS Roach leaves to drive home drunk – and the troubles really begin.

Sgt Burnside **Christopher Ellison**
Larry **John Dair**
Sadie **Cheryl Hall**

Director: **Peter Cregeen**
Designer: **Robin Parker Philip Blowers**

Season Three
12 colour 60-minute episodes

The New Order of Things

w Geoff McQueen

Despite changes at Sun Hill station, policing remains the same. PC Carver and DS Roach 'lose' a JCB excavating machine, a council tenant threatens to jump from the balcony of her sixth floor flat, and

Hardcastle, a visitor to the manor, has old debts to settle. Galloway, meanwhile, faces charges of 'cutting corners' to obtain a confession.
Hardcastle Tom Price
Peggy Chambers Carole Walker
Security guard Terence Mountain

Director: Michael Ferguson
Designer: Robin Parker

Some You Win, Some You Lose

w Barry Appleton
A drugs raid that turns sour. The riot that follows. This is only the beginning of Sun Hill's problems. What follows is a day of bedlam and anxiety for Sergeant Cryer's boys – and troubles galore for Galloway.
Det Con Sanders Neil Conrich
PC Patel Sonesh Sira
PC Stamp Graham Cole

Director: Peter Cregeen
Designer: Robin Parker

Brownie Points

w Christopher Russell
A child at risk. A tour of inspection by the Deputy Assistant Commissioner. A routine roundup of streetwalkers, and a visit to Sun Hill by a pack of Brownies. A day in the life of Sun Hill. A day to remember.
Det Ass Com Wainwright Jonathan Newth
Tara Winston Valerie Buchanan
Caroline Blake Catherine Hall

Director: Mary McMurray
Designer: Robin Parker

Missing, Presumed Dead

w Barry Appleton
With evidence of murder, but no body, the problem facing Galloway and his team is one of identifying the victim. Meanwhile, the Sun Hill constables have problems of their own to contend with. Life at Sun Hill continues at its hectic pace.
Det Con Sanders Neil Conrich
Det Sgt Lewis Dafydd Hywel
Chief Insp Crocker Berwick Kaler

Director: Michael Ferguson
Designer: Robin Parker

Domestics

w Edwin Pearce
Bob Cryer has a run-in with Councillor Gordon. The subject: a refuge for battered wives – a place that has proved unpopular with the Sun Hill police. PC Edwards, meanwhile, finds time to introduce his colleauges to his fiancé – and ends up showing them a great deal more than he bargained for!
Cllr Gordon Karen Archer
Mr Bradwell Jeffrey Gear
Mrs Bradwell Philomena McDonagh

Director: Peter Cregeen
Designer: Robin Parker

What Are Little Boys Made Of?

w Christopher Russell
A trio of young boys, two of whom say they have scooped a package of forged stamps from a canal, the third, who wishes to become a policeman, but has parent trouble, test the resolve of Cryer's team. CS Brownlow, meanwhile, attempts to find out who placed a hoax ad in the police magazine – one that advertised his car for sale!
Richard Fielding David Allister
Graham Driscoll Jonathan Lacey
Dr Marion Siddall Annie Leon

Director: Peter Duguid
Designer: Robin Parker

Blind Alleys, Clogged Roads

w Lionel Goldstein
Having arrested a taxi driver into whose cab his car crashed during a chase, Galloway finds himself in the throes of a cabbie war . . . a protest by the man's colleagues at his mistreatment. WPC's Ackland and Martella, meanwhile, decide to give PC Hollis the 'works'.
Gilbert Frank Lee
Reader Nick Burnell
Seaton Steve Wilsher

Director: Graham Theakston
Designer: Robin Parker

Double Trouble

w Barry Appleton

When a member of the public makes a complaint against the Sun Hill force and DI Galloway finds it difficult to organise an identification parade, life at the nick becomes intolerable. To add further misery, officers from the Complaints Investigation Bureau arrive to turn on the heat.

Daniel Briley Jim Beresford
Janet Weeks Veronica Roberts
Det Chf Supt Fairfax Julian Holloway

Director: Michael Ferguson
Designer: Robin Parker

Sun Hill Karma

w Christopher Russell

With a 'bear' on the loose and the late arrival of the bus to take offenders to court, Sgt Bob Cryer's tour of duty as Custody Sergeant starts with a whimper – but ends with a bang. Galloway's team investigate a break-in, and WPC Martella applies for a contract with the Bermuda police.

Mr Agni Rashid Karapiet
Fred Baer Joe Grossi
Riordan Paddy Ward

Director: Mary McMurray
Designer: Robin Parker

Skipper

w Chrisopher Russell

As part of the police force's friendly new community image, Sun Hill's finest get back on their bikes. CID, meanwhile find themselves with a slippery customer on their hands – a naked raider who has been robbing the tills of local petrol stations. Further smiles are raised when Inspector Kite decides to roll up his trousers and collect mud samples from the river Thames!

Richard Hambly Gary Brown
Sturgis Tim Kirby
Mr Polland Charles Simon

Director: Richard Bramall
Designer: Robin Parker

Overnight Stay

w Barry Appleton

Ordered to guard a murder trial jury who are staying at a London hotel while they reach a verdict, Sun Hill's officers find trouble galore. Before the night is over, WPC Ackland will take solace in a double gin – and sweat it out in a sauna, DC Dashwood and PC Carver take a ducking, and DI Galloway finds himself with a 'bomb' on his hands.

Miss Hines Pamela Collins
Gibbon Steve Swinscoe
Mr Holland Richard Durden

Director: Graham Theakston
Designer: Robin Parker

Not Without Cause

w Barry Appleton

While Galloway, Carver and Bob Cryer run to ground the man believed responsible for contaminating supermarket chocolate bars, Sun Hill's desk sergeant has to decide whether or not to take a young girl's claim that her pet tortoise is missing. Meanwhile, Sergeant Penny has disappeared without trace. Wounded and bleeding in a derelict house occupied by Alice, a strange old woman, he lies inches from death!

Alice Ruby Head
Mercer Paul Brennan
Mrs Penny Janette Legge

Director: Peter Cregeen
Designer: Robin Parker

THE BILL
Devised by: Geoff McQueen
Producers: Michael Chapman (Season 1)
Peter Cregeen (Season 2 and 3)
Executive Producer: Lloyd Shirley
Series' Script Editor: John Kershaw
A Thames Television Network Production
35 colour 60-minute episodes
16 October 1984 – 22 January 1985
11 November 1985 – 10 February 1986
21 September – 7 December 1987

BOGNOR

A short-lived series based on the novels by Tim Heald, which portrayed the adventures of Bognor, a crisis-prone investigator for the Department of Trade – Special Investigations Branch. Played mainly for laughs, it wasn't so much a case of *who*dunnit, but why they (the production company) bothered.

REGULAR CAST

Bognor David Horovitch   *Monica* Joanna McCallum
Parkinson [Head of S/I] Ewan Roberts

Unbecoming Habits

w Adapted by T. R. Bowen   *(a 6-part story)*
When trade secrets for the manufacture of a special brand of honey are handed over to Middle Eastern rivals, Parkinson, Head of the Special Investigations Branch of the Department of Trade, assigns agent Colingdale to find out who is selling the formula. When Colingdale dies, Bognor is assigned to the case.
Anselm James Maxwell
Sir Erris Beg Geoffrey Chater
Xavier Patrick Troughton

Director: Robert Tronson
Designer: Rod Stratford

Deadline

w Adapted by T. R. Bowen   *(a 6-part story)*
When a newspaper gossip columnist is found murdered, the paper's proprietor asks Parkinson to assign a discreet specialist to the case. With no one else on duty, the department head sends Bognor along – and not for the first time, the agent puts his life on the line to bring a murderer to justice.
Sir John Derby Glyn Jones
Milburn Port Peter Jeffrey
Lord Wharfdale Richard Vernon

Director: Carol Wiseman
Designer: Desmond Crowe

Let Sleeping Dogs Die

w Adapted by Carey Harrison   *(a 6-part story)*
Bognor and Monica are assigned to investigate shady goings-on at a world famous dog show. Clues point to show judge Percy Pocklington being somehow implicated in the mystery, but Bognor believes that the beautiful Coriander Cordingley, who paints dog portraits, is the more likely suspect. Whatever, whenever Bognor is around, things have a tendency to turn nasty.
Percy Pocklington Robin Bailey
Coriander Cordingley Kate Fahy
Cecil Handyside Andrew Ray

Director: Neville Green
Designer: Rod Stratford

BOGNOR
Producer: Bernard Krichefski
Executive producer: John Frankau
Music by: Mike Steer
A Thames Television Network Production
18 colour 30-minute episodes
[Shown twice-weekly]
10 Feburary–9 April 1981

Boon

A comedy/drama series, depicting the off-beat adventure of Ken Boon, a man prepared to handle any task – provided it was legal.

An ex-fireman, forced into accepting early retirement from the service because his lungs were damaged in an heroic rescue attempt, Boon had made several abortive attempts to adjust to his enforced drudgery. When the last of these – a plan to build a house in the country and open a market garden – turned sour and left him facing financial ruin, he turned in desperation to people seeking a freelance troubleshooter – a move which found him entrusted with an assortment of odd tasks (not all of which were to his liking, but 'any port in a storm'), and brought him into contact with an ever stranger assortment of people's problems. One week Boon would find himself hired as a childminder. A week later he'd be thwarting a kidnap attempt. At various times he was hired in an 'investigative' capacity. On other occasions he'd be hired as a courier, or asked to deliver an urgent message up North ('White Lightning', his motorcycle, came in handy here). Whatever the job, Boon took it in his stride and swiftly built up a reputation for commitment to the job in hand.

With the eminently watchable Michael Elphick as its star, the series' success was guaranteed.

A fourth season is now in production.

REGULAR CAST

Ken Boon **Michael Elphick**. *Harry Crawford* **David Dakar**
Season One
Doreen Evans **Rachel Davies**. *Ethel Allard* **Joan Scott**.
Nick **Bill Gavin**. (Eps 1 to 4)
Season Two
Rocky Cassidy **Neil Morrissey**. *Debbie Yates* **Lesley-Anne Sharpe**

Season One

13 colour 60-minute episodes

Box 13.

w Jim Hill & Bill Stair
Finding himself in debt, Boon turns to his old mate, Harry Crawford for advice. The result of their reunion is an advertisement in the local paper: 'ex-fireman seeks interesting work – ANYTHING LEGAL CONSIDERED' . . . and Boon is on his way as a freelance troubleshooter.

Harry Crawford **David Dakar** (Intro)
Doreen Evans **Rachel Davies** (Intro)
Ethel Allard **Joan Scott** (Intro)

Director: **Laurence Moody**

Fools Rush In.

w Jim Hill & Bill Stair
A dishevelled Irishman, who has difficulty in remembering his name, gives Boon plenty to worry about. He's apparently lost his memory, and has no inkling of where

the large bundle of cash he has on his person came from.

Frank Warren **Stephen Rea**
Tom Mc Geary **Gregor Fisher**
Peter Brandon **Jack Klaff**

Director: **Ian Knox**

Answers To the Name of Watson

w Francis Megahy

A large surprise awaits our hero when, asked by Arturo and Elena Sadini to recover their stolen cat, the freelance troubleshooter does so and discovers that Watson is no ordinary pet – but a lion!

Arturo **Frederick Warder**
Elena **Shirin Taylor**
Wadsworth **Terence Harvey**

Director: **Laurence Moody**

Grass Widows

w Anthony Minghella

Boon's fondness for gardening brings him added misfortune when, asked to chase up an unpaid hotel bill, he discovers that it's more than just a distraught widow's garden that is out of control!

Meg Lucie **Barbara Ewing**
Lionel Blakey **John Landry**
Hanif Kurtha **Gordon Warnecke (Intro)**

Director: **Ian Knox**

Unto Us Four a Son

w Guy Meredith

It's hardly a glamorous job, especially when the child you're minding is Daniel, the difficult son of a rock star. But when Boon is attacked outside the boy's school and Ken realises the real target is Daniel, things soon hot up.

Daniel **Nicholas Simpson**
Geoff Greenaway **Warren Clarke**
Laurie Langley **Linda Marlowe**

Director: **Laurence Moody**

Glasshouse People

w Paul Wheeler

Hired to discover who is behind a protection racket gang who have smashed mirrors and

crockery at Harry Crawford's hotel, Boon decides to take the battle to the enemy – with surprising results for all concerned.

Sidney Garbutt **Richard Griffiths**
Mather **Robert Gary**
Wiggins **Nick Stringer**

Director: **Ian Knox**

Northwest Passage to Ackocks Green

w Douglas Watkinson

A request to sail a barge from Hemel Hempstead to Birmingham appears to offer Boon an opportunity to spend an idyllic weekend with Doreen. The outcome is not what he'd planned.

Errol MacLaverty **T.P. McKenna**
Alan Prendergast **Larry Lamb**
Walter Prendergast **Ralph Nossek**

Director: **Laurence Moody**

Something Old, Something New

w John Flanagan and Andrew McCulloch

When Harry suggests a job shifting antiques for a London dealer, Boon is not particularly keen. His market-garden business has finally taken root, and he has no wish to tempt providence again – but a job is a job.

Georgina Pemberton **Michelle Newell**
Philip Banks **Richard Heffer**
Murdoch Jonstone **Andrew Keir**

Director: **Graham Theakston**

For Whom the Chimes Toll

w Geoff McQueen

Seeking further finance, Boon takes on a baby-sitting job with a difference – 'minding' a collection of antique clocks! What's more, Major Hopkinson, who owns them, appears to have some very unpleasant acquaintances.

Major Hopkinson **Maurice Denham**
Jack Evans **Donald Sumpter**
Van Kessel **Carl Duering**

Director: **Brian Morgan**

Jack of All Tradesmen

w Jim Hill and Bill Stair

Reluctant at first to track down the Mahoney brothers for a bookie, Boon soon changes his mind when the man offers him a substantial cash payment. But he's buying himself trouble galore when the roles are reversed and the brothers decide to find Boon!

Niall Mahoney Charles Lawson
Sean Mahoney Sean Lawlor
Brook Michael O'Hagen

Director: Graham Theakston

Billy the Kid

w Peter Barwood

When Harry Crawford signs Billy 'The Kid' Buchan as the main attraction at the Fireman's Charity football match, Boon, hired as Billy's 'minder', barely has time to catch his breath before the trouble starts.

Billy Buchan Malcolm Jamieson
Wally Patterson Malcolm Terris
Rhona Buchan Lindy Whiteford

Director: Brian Morgan

Grand Expectations

w Frances Galleymore

With 'White Lightning' off the road, its suspension broken in an accident, Boon seeks help from a local bike dealer. A mistake. Before long he will find himself racing off on a borrowed bike – with a young Sikh girl riding pillion.

Surinder Kaur Sneh Gupta
Ranjit Singh Tanveer Ghani
Balbir Singh Omar Salimi

Director: Graham Theakston

Full Circle

w Guy Meredith

Boon's market-garden is desolated. Meanwhile, Harry goes from strength to strength. On the verge of buying a new hotel, Harry over-reaches himself – with tragic results for all concerned.

Leon Karadia Alan Tilvern
Laura Karadia Hilary Townley
Det Insp Pierce Norman Jones

Director: Laurence Moody

Season Two

7 colour 60-minute episodes

Texas Rangers

w Guy Meredith

All change. Harry moves into a new hotel but has difficulty finding a celebrity to speak at the gala opening. Ken has problems of his own. He has discovered that his new motorcycle despatch business, 'The Texas Rangers', is fraught with Hazards – but help arrives, in the shape of Debbie.

Debbie Lesley-Anne Sharpe (Intro)
Rocky Neil Morrissey (Intro)
Emlyn Ronald Lacey

Director: Christopher King

Special Delivery

w Paul Wheeler

Threatened with eviction when Harry plans to expand the Coaching Inn, Boon finds himself helping Councillor Petherbridge, a man framed, to clear his name – and ends up in a shady strip club and a TV studio.

Petherbridge Simon Rouse
Linda West Diane Keen
Mrs Sefton Christina Greatrex

Director: Bren Simpson

The Day of the Yokel

w Dougie Watkinson

Philip Lainchbury wants to sell his sawmill but his elderly aunt Iris resists pressure from developers to move out. Enter Boon, who soon finds himself at the centre of the trouble – and pursued around Birmingham for his pains.

Iris Mablethorpe Phyllis Calvert
Philip Lainchbury Tom Chadbon
Rathbone Anthony Head

Director: Alex Kirby

Smokey and the Band

w Jim Hill

When Harry books a Country and Western band to play in his hotel, it gets him into trouble with agent Frankie Bass. Ken, meanwhile, becomes involved with Bebe, the band's singer —and the exercise costs Ken and Harry dear.
Bebe McLintock Fiona Hendley
Bronco Billy Alun Lewis
Frankie Bass Tricia George

Director: Bob Tronson

Taken For a Ride

w John Fletcher

Ken finds himself caught in a dirty takeover bid for control of Albion Fire-trucks. When faced with losing Texas Rangers or the loss of 3,000 Albion jobs, it's no contest — so Ken takes some advice from a page three girl!
Quinn Malcolm Storry
Sir Freddie Blackton Michael Medwin
Shandy Tremblett Camille Coduri

Director: Robert Tronson

Wheels of Fortune

w Anthony Horowitz

When renowned clairvoyant Phylis Nichols books into the Coaching Inn and warns Ken not to ride his motorcycle as she has a vision of impending danger, Ken finds himself with no option but to do so — someone has stolen Rocky's bike.
Phylis Nichols Sheila Allen
Mr Beamish Roy Kinnear
Dr Harnill Shaheen Khan

Director: Geoff Husson

A Ride On The Wild Side

w Billy Hamon

Boon finds himself involved with DC Margaret Daly and a sordid nightclub owner when Debbie's sister, Lindy, arrives at the hotel — then disappears. But that's only part of Ken's troubles: he finds himself arrested and accused of buying porno magazines.

DC Margaret Daly Amanda Burton
Barry Drinkwater Peter Blake
Lindy Yates Tricia Penrose

Director: Moira Armstrong

Season Three

6 colour 60-minute episodes
(Author's note: The following six stories were filmed back to back as part of Season Two, but transmitted as one complete season.)

Credit Where It's Due

w Roy Mitchell

Maurice, a visitor at the hotel, arouses Ken's suspicions. The newcomer turns Debbie's head — and she announces their forthcoming marriage! Harry, meanwhile, has his hands full keeping one eye open for forged credit cards, and the other on the beautiful Davida, a hotel guest.
Davida Duff Pamela Salem
Maurice Jeff Rawle
Barry Peter Caffrey

Director: Alex Kirby

Trudy's Grit

w Matthew Bardsley

When a firm of solicitors plot to repossess Lord Alderley's stately home, Trudy, his daughter, sets her sights on solicitor Nigel Brown. A meeting with Rocky leads her into accepting a job with the Texas Rangers, much to Debbie's chagrin, who sees the new girl as a threat. Ere long, both Brown and Boon will find Trudy a girl to be reckoned with.
Trudy Kirsten Hughes
Lord Alderley Llewellyn Rees
Nigel Brown Timothy Roland

Director: Sarah Hellings

A Fistful of Pesetas

w Gerald G. More

Why should Harry's ex-wife, Alison, fly into Birmingham airport with a suitcase full of Spanish banknotes? Is she out to wangle extra alimony out of her ex? Ken and Rocky, at the airport to collect a statue that no one appears to want, foresee trouble

ahead. Harry, meanwhile, can't see the wood for the trees.
Alison Georgina Hale
Teddy Rawlingston Christopher Benjamin
Luis Perez Tony Slattery

Director: Baz Taylor

Paper Mafia

w Tony McHale
While Boon races around delivering secret parcels for a lonely widower, Rocky, delivering orders for a pizza parlour, falls for the charms of the Pizza owner's daughter, Maxine. Harry, planning his holiday of a lifetime in Las Vegas, has unwanted problems with Franklyn, an hotel guest who has his own plans for Harry's spare plane ticket – ones that don't include Ken!
Giovanni John Bennett
Maxine Adrienne Posta
Franklyn David Simeon

Director: Ken Hannam

Fiddler Under the Roof

w Dougie Watkinson
With Harry rubbing his hands in glee at the prospect of a large wedding function being held at the Coaching Inn, fat profits look assured. But when the expected 100 or so guests turn out to be *400* unruly travelling tinkers, and the bridegroom has a secret he can only share with Ken, the wedding day festivities take on a decidedly unwanted aspect.

Sean Jones Shaun Scott
James McGillivray James Ellis
Brenda McGillivray Joanna Bartholomew

Director: Sarah Hellings

A Once Fluid Man

w Billy Hamon
Attending an aerobics class, Ken and Harry meet Margaret Daly, Ken's old flame. Pulses racing, Ken pursues his quarry while Harry searches for his perfect partner, via a lonely hearts ad in the local paper. Unexpectedly, their paths cross, and Harry is forced to contemplate selling his beloved hotel. Enter Terry Brent, a one-time fire service colleague of Ken and Harry's, to lower Harry's morale to new depths – at gunpoint. Ken will shortly leave the hotel on a stretcher!
Margaret Daly Amanda Burton
Terry Brent Anthony May
Mr Pucklebridge Ellis Dale

Director: Ken Hannam

BOON
Created by: Jim Hill and Bill Stair
Producer: Kenny McBain (Season 1)
Esta Charkham (Seasons 2 and 3)
Executive Producer: Ted Childs
Associate Producer: Laurie Greenwood
Music by: Dean Friedman
A Central Independent Network Production
26 colour 60-minute episodes
14 January – 8 April 1986
17 February – 31 March 1987
27 October – 1 December 1987

BOYD QC

This series, Britain's answer to Perry Mason, reflected all the tragedy and melodrama of an English law court as seen through the cases of barrister, Richard Boyd, Queen's Counsel, a respected and highly professional man-about-the-courts. Boyd took on all manner of clients and his practice brought him into contact with a wide variety of criminal procedure. Usually hired as counsel for the defence, he could equally well find himself appearing for the prosecution. His credibility as a defence lawyer was unsurpassed but, unlike his American counterpart Mason, Boyd didn't always win his cases.

A semi-documentary format which depicted the procedures and processes of English law, the series found instant success and ran for over eight years. Commendable in that every single one of its 75-plus stories were written by one man — a real-life assize court official, Jack Roffey.

REGULAR CAST
Richard Boyd, QC **Michael Denison**   *Jack (his clerk)* **Charles Leno**

BOYD QC
Producer: Caryl Doncaster
Directors: Michael Currer-Briggs, Ronald
Merrick, Jonathan Alwyn, Cliff Owen,
Geoffrey Hughes, Pat Baker, Richard
Gilbert, Raymond Menmuir
An Associated Rediffusion Network Production
Approx. 78 monochrome 30-minute
episodes
24 December 1956–23 September 1964

THE BUCCANEERS

Promoted as 'television's first ever pirate series', this swashbuckling adventure series presented the exploits of Captain Dan Tempest, a pardoned ex-pirate turned King's man, and his friendly rival Lieutenant Beamish, the newly-appointed deputy governor of New Providence — a Caribbean pirate stronghold, which had recently been taken back from the buccaneers.

Prior to the arrival of the King's men, Tempest had virtually ruled the island with his followers — a hearty crew of lovable rogues who, if the occasion demanded, would have followed their leader to the ends of the Earth. The arrival of the King's troops changed all that, and Tempest and his men became 'good guys' — their swords and allegiance sworn to the King, the rivalry with the new governor forgotten as side by side with Beamish they faced their common enemies, the Spaniards: sea-going rogues who refused to bow to the new authority and were the scourge of all free men.

Breaking with tradition, the producers used the first two

stories to record the events surrounding the purging of the pirates from the colony and Tempest – the series' lead character – didn't appear until the third episode.

REGULAR CAST

Dan Tempest **Robert Shaw**   *Lieutenant Beamish* **Peter Hammond**
Governor Woodes Rogers **Alec Clunes**   *Blackbeard* **Terence Cooper**
Tempest's crew
Benjy **Hugh David**   *Armando* **Edwin Richfield**   *Alfie* **Paul Hansard**

Blackbeard

w Thomas A. Stockwell
Woodes Rogers arrives at New Providence and takes up his position as Governor. His first task: free the island from buccaneers, and offer a pardon to those who swear allegiance to the King.
Blackbeard **George Margo**
Woodes Rogers **Alec Clune**
Morgan **Patrick Jordan**

Director: **Ralph Smart**

The Raiders

w Terence Moore
Worried that New Providence will be left undefended when he sets out to chase a pirate ship which has attacked the island, Governor Rogers leaves Lieutenant Beamish in command of the garrison.
Van Brugh **Alec Mango**
Charles Vane **Brian Worth**
Sikes **Peter Bennett**

Director: **Ralph Smart**

Captain Dan Tempest

w Terence Moore
Governor Rogers continues to offer free pardons to those pirates who reform. His main target is Dan Tempest – a man previously looked upon as uncrowned leader of New Providence. To convert him would be a triumph indeed.
Dan Tempest **Robert Shaw (Intro.)**
appearance)
Lolita **Judith Wyler**
Armando **Edwin Richfield**

Director: **Ralph Smart**

Dan Tempest's War With Spain

w Zacary Weiss
Displeased because Lolita, his girlfriend, has deserted him, Tempest is distracted by more important matters – the Spaniards have launched an attack on the island.
Lieut Beamish **Peter Hammond**
Gaff **Brian Rawlinson**
Costalleaux **Terence Cooper**

Director: **Ralph Smart**

The Wasp

w Peter C. Hodgking
Young Dickon, a stowaway aboard Tempest's ship, *The Sultana*, provides the captain and his crew with a major headache. But trouble of a different kind is brewing out at sea – Blackbeard is organising a campaign of attack.
Blackbeard **Terence Cooper**
Dickon **Wilfred Downing**
Pop **Willoughby Gray**

Director: **Terry Bishop**

Whale Gold

w Zacary Weiss
When ambergris – a valuable substance found in the sperm whale, and used in expensive perfume – is found by Pat, a colonist, it spells trouble for Tempest and his crew. Men have been known to kill for it – and it appears tht someone has plans to do just that.
Pat **Noel Purcell**
Grimes **Terence Cooper**
Taffy **Paul Hansard**

Director: **Leslie Arliss**

The Slave Ship

w John Cousins

A deserted galleon and three escaped prisoners lead Tempest and his crew into mayhem and intrigue. The buccaneer faces a race against time to rescue the three fugitives from their own foolhardiness.
Deacon Eymon Evans
Sam Earl Cameron
Captain Scobie Tony Thawnton

Director: Terry Bishop

Gunpowder Plot

w Terence Moore

When Blackbeard steals the garrison's gunpowder supply, Tempest is faced with finding a new supplier. But the naval authorities refuse to condone his departure – so the wily ex-pirate resorts to his former ways to cut through the red tape.
Governor Andre Morrell
Governor's daughter Pamela Wright
Governor's wife Noel Hood

Director: Leslie Arliss

Hand of the Hawk

w Peter C. Hodgking

If Tempest is to avert tragedy for himself and his crew, he must find a way of converting certain defeat into victory. His chance to do just that arrives from a very unexpected source.
Captain Flesk Anthony Dawson
Chantey Jack Sidney James
Armando Edwin Richfield

Director: Robert Day

The Articles of War

w Peggy Philips and Alan Moreland

Witnessing the slow starvation of several families, Tempest must find a way to ignore the Articles of War – which state that only children of the sick and needy may have meat.
Hernandez Eric Pohlmann
Count Pedro Dennis Lacey
Sailor Rupert Evans

Director: Leslie Arliss

Gentleman Jack and the Lady

w Zacary Weiss

When his plans to board a Spanish warship are thwarted by a French galleon, Tempest encounters trouble of a very strange variety indeed – Gentleman Jack, the French ship's captain, wears skirts . . . but is certainly no lady.
Anne (Gentleman Jack) Hazel Court
William John Gatrell
Bassett Neil Hallett

Director: Leslie Arliss

Mr Beamish and the Hangman's Noose

w Terence Moore

Lieutenant Beamish rarely makes mistakes. But this time Tempest feels he has gone to far. When the buccaneer receives word that Beamish has ordered his men to hang two lawbreakers, Tempest decides to oppose his ally.
Lieut Beamish Peter Hammond
Sergeant-at-arms Terence Cooper
Armando Edwin Richfield

Director: Pennington Richards

The Ladies

w Roger McDougall

Hearing that *The Caroline* carries a very precious cargo – women – Blackbeard makes plans to board the vessel under a flag of 'truce'. Tempest, however, has other plans.
Christine Petra Davies
Juanita Dalia Penn
Blackbeard Terence Cooper

Director: Pennington Richards

Before the Mast

w Roger McDougall

Tempest and his crew leave New Providence at daybreak. Their mission: to upset the carefully laid plans of El Supremo – a Spaniard who is waging war on Beamish's supply ships.
El Supremo Ferdy Mayne
Rodrigues Roger Snowdon
One Eye Sal Stewart

Director: Ralph Smart

Dan Tempest and the Amazons

w Zacary Weiss

A new kind of trouble plagues Tempest and his crew – women. Their arrival has placed the swashbuckler's life in jeopardy. With the Spaniards hot on his trail, the buccaneer seems doomed – but help is at hand.

Abigail Joan Sims
Captain Delacourt Roy Purcell
Costalleaux Terence Cooper

Director: Pennington Richards

Marooned

w Peter C. Hodgking

While everyone is attending the Queen's birthday festivities, someone breaks into the garrison's armoury and steals a powder magazine. Dan Tempest has his work cut out finding the guilty party.

West Bill Owen
Phineas Bunch Willoughby Goddard
Macarty Terence Cooper

Director: Leslie Arliss

The Surgeon of Sangra Rojo

w Thomas A. Stockwell

An epidemic sweeps the province. Tempest, assigned to bring the only surgeon available to administer aid, must run the gauntlet of Spanish guns waiting for any ship daring to leave New Providence island.

Francisco Dino Galvani
Van Brugh Alec Mango
Armando Edwin Richfield

Director: Pennington Richards

Cutlass Wedding

w Thomas A. Stockwell

Tempest and his crew are making preparations for Taffy's wedding to Emily – the first marriage to be performed in New Providence. But someone appears to bear the sweethearts a grudge – and the couple turn to Tempest for help.

Taffy Paul Hansard
Emily Maureen Davis
Abigail Joan Sims

Director: Robert Day.

Pride of Andalusia

w Basil Dawson and Zacary Weiss

Out to capture a large consignment of gold being transported by a Spanish galleon, Tempest comes face to face with a new enemy – the Marquesa, an opponent the buccaneer is hard pressed to ignore.

Marquesa Jean Cadell
Sebastian Conrad Phillips
Gomez Bruno Barnabe

Director: Peter Maxwell

The Decoy

w Alec G. Ruben

A young girl's story provides Tempest and his crew with plenty of surprises – all of them bad. She claims to have escaped from pirates, who took her husband prisoner. But is the girl telling the truth?

Rebecca Virginia Maskell
Turk Marne Maitland
George Derek Waring

Director: Pennington Richards

Instruments of War

w Peter Rossano

With *The Sultana* anchored off the Carolina coastline, Tempest – on a secret mission to Andrewsville, where a number of Scots are unjustly imprisoned – must plan his rescue attempt carefully. Should he fail, it could cost the lives of everyone aboard.

Laird Andrew Keir
Marsh Alfred Burke
Gaff Brian Rawlinson

Director: Bernard Knowles

Pirate's Honour

w Marion Myers

Though Tempest has resolved to sidestep any trouble while visiting Savannah, when he comes across a young boy being ill-treated his resolution is put severely to the test. His change of mind comes swiftly – and causes trouble for all concerned.

Edwin Michael Caridia
Black Bart Alex Scott
Woman Ilona Terence

Director: Peter Maxwell

Printer's Devil

w Terence Moore

When Tempest arranges the rescue of Josiah Parkerhouse – a man arrested for printing a series of articles criticising the state – his troubles are only just beginning, and his friendship with the man will be put under severe pressure.

Parkerhouse Miles Malleson
Sir James Noel Coleman
Sharp Maxwell Shaw

Director: Bernard Knowles

Dead Man's Rock

w Peter C. Hodgking

With *The Sultana* being overhauled, Tempest can offer no resistance when Lieutenant Beamish surrenders New Providence to the Spaniards, and is taken prisoner to the fortress known as El Morre – Dead Man's Rock.

Lieut Beamish Peter Hammond
Rodriguez Richard Pasco
Armando Edwin Richfield

Director: Pennington Richards

Blood Will Tell

w Zacary Weiss

Tempest is faced with a mission of the utmost urgency: he must locate the real owner of Gresham Island. Unless he does so, the island will be made a free port – one that will offer a safe stronghold for the Spanish fleet.

Piggot Dawson French
Bellows John Dearth
Serge Pearl Prescott

Director: Pennington Richards

Dangerous Cargo

w Zacary Weiss

Keeping a secret rendezvous with British warship captain, Steele, offers no threat to Tempest's peace of mind. But the sealed orders Steele is carrying will prove to be a nightmare for the buccaneer – even when they involve a beautiful woman.

Lady Hilary Sarah Lawson
Captain Steele Ivan Craig
Mendoza Roger Delgado

Director: Leslie Arliss

The Return of Calico Jack

w Zacary Weiss and Basil Dawson

With Tempest away on a mission, Calico Jack's arrival on New Providence is given a less than enthusiastic welcome. The newcomer appears unmovable – until Dan's crew come up with a foolproof method of defence.

Calico Jack Brian Worth
Groggins Meadows White
Raquel Jan Miller

Director: Pennington Richards

Ghost Ship

w Peter C. Hodgking

Becalmed in the Sargasso Sea, *The Sultana* has not moved for three days. The crew are growing restless and the situation worsens by the hour. Then Tempest sees a ship which apparently has no one on board – and all hell breaks loose.

De Groot Colin Douglas
Mate Alfred Burke
Jenkins Eddie Mallen

Director: Pennington Richards

Conquistador

w Terence Moore and Basil Dawson

Why should *The Sultana* leave New Providence sporting the Jolly Roger? Has Tempest reverted to his old ways? The answer surprises everyone, including Dan's crew – and an astonished Lieutenant Beamish.

Estaban Roger Delgado
Juan Roger Gage
Charlie Larry Hoodroff

Director: Robert Day

Mother Doughty's Crew

w Zacary Weiss

When Mother Doughty and her daughter, Betsy, announce the latter's forthcoming

marriage to Gaff, no one is more surprised than Gaff himself – who knows nothing of the affair! Engaged to be married to another girl, Gaff pleads with Tempest to help.
Mother Doughty Ena Burill
Betsy Ann Warmsley
Gaff Brian Rawlinson

Director: Pennington Richards

Conquest of New Providence

w Terence Moore
Returning from a mission abroad, Tempest and his crew find that New Providence has been taken over by Estaban. The Spanish flag is flying over the fortress, and Beamish and his troops are kicking their heels in a dungeon.
Estaban Roger Delgado
Maria Gillian Owen
Betty Diane Potter

Director: Robert Day

Hurricane

w Terence Moore and Peggy Philips
The hurricane which is sweeping across New Providence blows good fortune in its wake. Tempest hears that a Spanish pirate ship is grounded on the rocks – an opportunity too good to miss.
Spanish lieutenant Derek Sydney
Chief Frank Singuin
Spanish Admiral Ewan Solon

Director: Leslie Arliss

The Aztec Treasure

w Terence Moore
Martin, a man rescued by Tempest during a brawl in Port Royal, proposes a business proposition in thanks. If Tempest will finance the journey, Martin will lead him to the hiding place of a fabulous treasure. Tempest's dilemma – can the stranger be trusted?
Martin Thomas Duggan
Tazco Michael Ritterman
Quetzl Frederick Treves

Director: Pennington Richards

Mistress Higgins' Treasure

w Thomas A. Stockwell
It's the old treasure story again – and Tempest and his crew are always interested in buried treasure, no matter how strange the source of information. But can they believe the story circulated by Mistress Higgins – a school teacher?
Mistress Higgins Adrienne Corri
Pennington Howard Pays
Mingo Roy Purcell

Director: Pennington Richards

Dan Tempest Holds an Auction

w Alan Moreland
In South Carolina to sell cargo for the Governor, Sir Charles Johnson, Tempest, content that he's acquired the best deal possible, is taken aback when he discovers that he's been duped. Somehow he must find a way of repaying such treachery.
Sir Charles Robert Perceval
Paula Jane Griffiths
Knox John Harvey

Director: Peter Maxwell

Spy Aboard

w Neil R. Collins
Everyone knows that Captain Tempest trusts his fellow men, but lately, odd things have been happening. When it becomes apparent that one of his crew is spying for the enemy, the buccaneer's confidence reaches an all-time low.
Pegley Richard Johnson
Raikes Jack Hedley
Old Man Wilfred Brambell

Director: Robert Day

Flip and Jenny

w Neil R. Collins
Stowaways are trouble at any time. But when Tempest and his crew discover two young children hidden below decks, they have no inkling of the troubles that will beset them – or their ally, Lord Hatch.
Flip Peter Soule
Jenny Jane Asher
Lord Hatch Robert Hardy

Director: Peter Hammond

Ace of Wands Tarot (Michael Mackenzie) and Ozymandias.

The Adventures of Don Quick Sgt Sam Czopanser and Capt. Don Quick.

The Adventures of Robin Hood Robin Hood and Maid Marian.

The Adventures of Sir Lancelot Sir Lancelot (William Russell).

The Adventures of William Tell William Tell (Conrad Phillips) and his wife Hedda.

Arthur of the Britons (Oliver Tobias).

The Avengers Patrick Macnee as John Steed with partners: Honor Blackman (top left); Linda Thorson (top right); Diana Rigg (below).

The Bill Sgt Bob Cryer (far right) and his 'woodentops'.

Budgie (Adam Faith).

Bulman (Don Henderson).   **Callan** (Edward Woodward).

Callan Ten years on. Lonely (Russell Hunter) and Callan in a scene from 'Wet Job'.

C.A.T.S. Eyes Team one: Fred Smith, Maggie Forbes, Pru Standfast.

The Champions Left to right, Craig Sterling, Sharron Macready, Commander Tremayne and Richard Barrett.

(Left) Crane (Patrick Allen).
The Corridor People Syrie Van Epp.

(Below) Cribb Left to right, Con.
Thackeray, Insp. Jowett and Sgt Cribb.

The Indian Fighter

w Neil R. Collins

If Perkins, said to be a great Indian fighter, is as brave as he makes out, why should he run to Tempest for help when confronted by two police constables on the occasion of his triumphant return to New Providence?

Perkins Ronan O'Casey
Paula Jane Griffiths
Sir Charles Roger Perceval

Director: Peter Maxwell

To The Rescue

w Phillis Miller

On an errand of mercy to the port of Savannah, Tempest finds that several traders have been swindled. Never one to condone trickery or deceipt, the buccaneer decides to turn the tables on the thieves by employing some trickery of his own making.

Major Percy Ewan Solon
Louis Brion Andre Charisse
Sarah Brion Norma Parnell

Director: Peter Maxwell

THE BUCCANEERS
Producer: Sidney Cole, Ralph Smart and Pennington Richards
Executive producer: Hannah Weinstein
Music by: Edwin Astley, Albert Elms and Kenneth V. Jones
A Sapphire Films Production for ITC
Filmed at Nettlefold Studios, Walton-on-Thames
39 monochrome 30-minute episodes
19 September 1956–15 May 1957
[USA: CBS 22 September 1956–14
September 1957. Syndicated under the title:
Dan Tempest

BUDGIE

The fortunes and misfortunes of Budgie Bird, a young delinquent who clung to the fringes of bent society in London's Soho. With an eye to easy money, pretentions to the big time and a cornered market in failure, Budgie was the all-time eternal optimist – a loser whose lofty ideas seldom got beyond the starting post. Nevertheless, he continued to drift through life believing that something would always turn up: easy street was only a block away; the big money earner was just around the corner.

A memorable and much-loved series that became a cult classic.

REGULAR CAST

Budgie Adam Faith   *Hazel (his girlfriend)* Lynn Dalby
Jean (his wife) Georgina Hale   *Charlie Endell* Iain Cuthbertson
Mrs Endell June Lewis
Jack Bird (Budgie's dad) George Tovey

Season One

13 monochrome/colour episodes
(Eps 1 to 4 b/w)

Out

w Keith Waterhouse and Willis Hall
Budgie opens his account and has his first
meeting with local villain Charles Endell – a
man viewed by the young thief as 'Mr Big'.
Will Budgie's high-fallutin' ideas impress
Endell . . . ?
Charlie Endell Iain Cuthbertson (Intro.)
Hazel Lynn Dalby (Intro.)
Eddie Henderson Allan McClelland

Director: James Goddard
Designer: John Emery

Some Mothers' Sons

w KW and WH
With a flat right in the centre of Soho all to
himself for six weeks, Budgie seems to have
landed on his feet. What can go wrong?
When you're Budgie Bird – everything!
Mrs Endell June Lewis (Intro.)
Big Tony Mike Horsborough
PC Michael Stainton

Director: Michael Lindsay-Hogg
Designer: Frank Nerini

Brains

w KW and WH
Providing he can 'settle accounts' with Jean,
his ex-missus, Budgie's return to his home
ground could lead to 'something big'. He's
sure of a welcome there – or is he?
Jean Georgina Hale (Intro.)
Mr Grace Arthur Pentelow
Mr Drummond Bernard Kay

Director: Michael Hindsay-Hogg
Designer: Frank Nerini

Grandee Hotel

w KW and WH
Dressed appropriately, Budgie attends a
'luxury' evening. All he has to do is clinch
an important business deal – but being
Budgie, that's not always a simple task.

Jeff Staines Anthony Valentine
Peter Olliphant Peter Sallis
Benskin Jack Woolgar

Director: James Goddard
Designer: John Emery

In Deep

w KW and WH
Budgie in the money! It's unheard of, but
it's true. How did he get it . . . and more
importantly, how long can he hang on to it?
Maurice Kahn Terence Mountain
1st detective Ronald Hackett
2nd detective Michael Earl

Director: Michael Lindsay-Hogg
Designer: Frank Nerini

Could Do Better

w KW and WH
Hazel's problem starts off a sequence of
events that leads Budgie back to his old
school – and trouble. Budgie's position at
Charlie Endell's bookshop looks set to
become another dead end idea.
Marcus Lake John Frankly-Robbins
PC Warburton Ian Sterling
Det Sgt Oxley David Swift

Director: James Goddard
Designer: John Emery

Best Mates

w KW and WH
'A man's best mate is his best mate.' That's
what they say – so why should Budgie's
friend Maguire lead him into trouble . . .
and still more trouble?
Maguire Joe Gladwin
Mrs Fletcher Stella Tanner
Douglas Hardisty William Hoyland

Director: Mike Newell
Designer: Colin Pigott

Everybody Loves a Baby

w KW and WH
Another of Budgie's hapless ideas – a plan
to 'farm out' babies – goes disastrously
wrong, and sees our hero up to his neck in
trouble – but then Budgie is used to dealing
with that.

Helga **Anouska Hempel**
Hedda **Judith Arthy**
Leopold King **Johnny Shannon**

Director: **James Goddard**
Designer: **Frank Nerini**

A Pair of Charlies

w KW and WH (based on an idea by Jack Trevor Story)
Life for Budgie Bird is an unending conveyor belt of mishap and misfortune, but even our hapless hero revolts when someone tries to blow him up – and his 'friends' let him down.
Jumbo Stevens **George Innes**
Insp Upton **Norman Bird**
Constable Donnelly **Jack Shepherd**

Director: **Mike Newell**
Designer: **John Emery**

Fiddler on the Hoof Part 1

w Douglas Livingstone
All sons should share their parents' domestic problems, so when Budgie's dad seeks his help, what could be easier than to accede to his request – even if it means more trouble?

Fiddler on the Hoof Part 2

w Douglas Livingstone
Budgie's sister, Vi, wants to marry Tony. Budgie says he'll fix it – but he's reckoned without lady luck . . .
Jack Bird **George Tovey**
Violet Bird **Anne Carroll**
Tony Pringle **Donald Douglas**

Director: **Michael Lindsay-Hogg**
Designer: **Frank Nerini/John Emery**

Sunset Mansions (or Whatever Happened to Janey Baib?)

w KW and WH
Budgie meets Janey and Denzil, and joins the throbbing world of show business – with none-too-surprising results for everyone concerned.

Janey Baib **Brenda Bruce**
Denzil Davies **John Thaw**
Det. Con. Singleman **Richard Owens**

Director: **Mike Newell**
Designer: **John Newton Clarke**

And In Again

w KW and WH
When Budgie gives Charlie Endell a birthday present, Charlie shows his gratitude in a rather peculiar way – and Budgie finds himself back in the company of old friends.
Inchbeck **Tenniel Evans**
Det. Insp. Bryant **Derek Newark**
Det. Con. McKay **John Peel**

Director: **Michael Lindsay-Hogg**
Designer: **Frank Nerini**

Season Two
13 colour episodes

Dreaming of Thee

w KW and WH
Providing he behaves, Budgie is due to be released from prison in three weeks' time. It looks as though his luck has changed – but anyone who knows our hero can be certain that 'waiting' will prove a bit of a strain.
Prison governor **Kenneth Watson**
Dutchie Holland **Bill Dean**
Wossname **James Bolam**

Director: **Michael Lindsay-Hogg**

And the Lord Taketh Away

w KW and WH
Alive and well, and back home in Watford with his wife Jean, it isn't long before Budgie gets an itch to visit his old Soho haunts. What he finds there is not what he expected.
Wossname **James Bòlam**
Soapy Simon **Gordon Jackson**
Holy Mackerel **Frank Wylie**

Director: **Michael Lindsay-Hogg**

Louie the Ring Is Dead and Buried in Kensal Green Cemetery

w KW and WH

Old venues, some old faces – and some new. After a surprise meeting with his ex-girlfriend Hazel, Budgie decides it is high time to make some quick money. It isn't long before he's back to his old tricks again.
Louie's widow Pamela Manson
Sheila Diane Keen
Det. Con. Lilywhite Bernard Jackson

Director: Michael Lindsay-Hogg

The Jump-Up Boys

w KW and WH

When Budgie dons a white coat and takes a job, his friends are amazed. Could it be that he has started on the straight and narrow at last? Even Charlie Endell shows surprise – but then he's privy to 'secret' information.
Det. Insp. Bryant Derek Newark
Det. Con. Gunn James Warrior
Grogan Rio Fanning

Director: Mike Newell

Our Story So Far

w KW and WH

Budgie is on the run again. This time both the police and Charlie Endell are after his blood. It's just a question of who catches him first – and which is the lesser of the two evils.
Det. Insp. Bryant Derek Newark
Det. Con. Gunn James Warrior
Grogan Rio Fanning

Director: Mike Newell

Do Me a Favour

w KW and WH

When Hazel asks Budgie to take her cousin Herbert on a guided tour of London, she has no idea of the trouble her request will cause – most of it on her own doorstep.
Herbert Fletcher Derek Jacobi
Alfie Apple Roy Hanlon
Dickey Tin Car Ken Wynne

Director: Moira Armstrong

Glory of Fulham

w KW and WH

Our tactless hero does it again. Having arrived home very late one night, to face Hazel's wrath, he compounds the issue by telling her he has a friend waiting outside – one whom he's invited to stay the night.
Walnut McGuiness Joe Zaranoff
Twitchy Fred Kevin Moran
Mrs Inglewood Kathleen Heath

Director: Michael Lindsay-Hogg

Twenty Four Thousand Ball Point Pens

w KW and WH

When he meets Inky Ballentine, and gets involved in a new money-making racket – capital investment – Budgie believes he's struck it rich. He's thought that before – but look where it got him last time.
Inky Ballentine Kenneth Cranham
Dickie Silver Alfie Bass
Claude Christopher Benjamin

Director: Alan Gibson

King For a Day

w KW and WH

When Charlie Endell clothes him in a new suit and makes him his 'chief associate', Budgie is confident that Charlie has finally recognised his true potential – but Hazel isn't so sure . . .
Laughing Spam Fritter John Rhys-Davis
King Jorgenson David Bauer
Careless John J Carney

Director: Moira Armstrong

The Outside Man

w KW and WH

When Budgie asks Charlie Endell for a job reference, it appears that the lad has finally taken the decision to go straight. But in Budgie's world, things are seldom what they appear to be.
Det. Insp. Shepherd George A. Cooper
Det. Con. Leadbetter Jack Shepherd
Major Hawkins James Grout

Director: Michael Lindsay-Hogg

The Man Outside

w KW and WH

A chance meeting between Budgie and his old friend Inga the Stripper on a railway station sets in motion a chain of events which places our hero well and truly in the firing line – and leads to a final showdown.
Inga Margaret Nolan
Laughing Spam Fritter John Rhys-Davies
Det. Insp. Shepherd George A. Cooper

Director: Michaell Lindsay-Hogg

Brief Encounter

w K.W. and W.H.

A chance meeting between Budgie and his old friend Inga the Stripper on a railway station sets in motion a chain of events which places our hero well and truly in the firing line – and leads to a final showdown.
Inga Margaret Nolan
Laughing Spam Fritter John Rhys-Davies
Det Insp Shepherd George A. Cooper

Director: Michael Lindsay-Hogg

Run Rabbit, Run Rabbit, Run, Run, Run

w KW and WH

Budgie's blown it! Charlie Endell is after his blood, and this time he means business. Budgie's friends have gone to ground, and with the heavies looking for him all over London, he needs somewhere to hide. Where?
Laughing Spam Fritter John Rhys-Davies
Inga Margaret Nolan
Carrie Gretchen Franklin

Director: Mike Newell

BUDGIE
Producer: Verity Lambert
Executive producer: Rex Firkin
A London Weekend Television Network Production
26 colour 60-minute episodes
9 April–2 July 1971
21 April–14 July 1972

BULMAN

The return of Detective Chief Inspector George Bulman, the unconventional, classics-quoting policeman from the Inner City Squad. (See *Strangers*).

Having resigned from his police career after a four-year tour of duty with the ICS, Bulman was now the proprietor of a small antiques-cum-clock-repairing business. However, it wasn't long before he found himself taking on private enquiry work in the company of Lucy McGinty, the daughter of an ex-colleague and a university drop-out turned criminologist. ('You wrote the book on detection in this City, George. You were born to be a detective . . . not a clock mender.')

Having perfected the character through countless episodes of Bulman's earlier adventures, actor Don Henderson continued to build on the quirky details which made Bulman so appealing – and one of television's longest surving crimebusters. Bulman's grey woollen gloves – so much a part of the character's make-up – were retained, although he now wore them only when he was on a case. The plastic carrier bag, the nasal inhaler and the gold-rimmed 'Edwardian' reading glasses also survived into the new series.

As with *Strangers*, the series gained wide acclaim from the media and viewing public alike.

REGULAR CAST

George Bulman Don Henderson   *Lucy McGinty* Siobhan Redmond
William Dugdale Thorley Walters

Season One

13 colour 60-minute episodes

Winds of Change

w Murray Smith

Life in the 'clock hospital' is far from quiet when Bulman receives a surprise visit from two old police colleagues – Detective Chief Superintendent Lambie and Detective Sergeant Willis – and young Lucy McGinty, a girl who will change his life.
Det. Chf Supt Lambie Mark McManus
Det. Sgt Willis Dennis Blanch
Lucy McGinty Siobhan Redmond (Intro.)

Director: William Brayne
Designer: James Weatherup

The Daughter Was a Dancer

w Murray Smith

Asked to guard a trendy businessman, Bulman and Lucy have to do some fancy footwork to extricate themselves from an unusual predicament. They also find themselves involved in a spot of burglary.
Det. Chf Supt Lambie Mark McManus
Murdo McPherson Henry Stamper
Det. Insp. Snow Paul Angelis

Director: Ken Grieve
Designer: Chris Wilkinson

Pandora's Many Boxes

w Murray Smith

When Dylan Chadwick fails a security clearance for an executive post, he hires Bulman to clear his name. Bulman's enquiries unearth more than Chadwick bargained for, and the executive could well live to regret employing our hero.

Dylan Chadwick Clive Francis
Det. Sgt Willis Dennis Blanch
Lord Breconbury Basil Henson

Director: Christopher King
Designer: James Weatherup

Death of a Hit Man

w Murray Smith

When an underground 'godmother' hires Bulman to uncover the truth about her son's death, Bulman and Lucy find themselves involved with both the KGB and the British Secret Service.
William Dugdale Thorley Walters
Det. Sgt Figg Alun Armstrong
Ma Gurney Phillada Sewell

Director: Bill Gilmour
Designer: Stephen Fineren

The Name of the Game

w Murray Smith

Life is never quiet when Bulman is around, but when he and Lucy become entangled in a young widow's campaign of revenge on the policeman who killed her husband, they have more than cause for alarm.
Harry Scroop George Sewell
Elias Greenstein David Healy
Karen Tait Lesley Manville

Director: William Brayne
Designer: Chris Wilkinson

One of Our Pigeons Is Missing

w Murray Smith

To solve the murder of an old 'dosser', Bulman dons the disguise of a tramp. He discovers an intriguing plot involving pigeons being used to pass secrets over to

the Iron Curtain – and almost gets himself killed.
William Dugdale Thorley Walters
Dr Beasley Ursula Howells
Jack Sprat Murray Melvin

Director: Charlie Nairn
Designer: Taff Batley

Sins of Omission

w Murray Smith
While Bulman's back is turned, Lucy is recruited into British Intelligence – as bait for a beautiful KGB assassin who kills with bullets made of ice! Discovering the truth, Bulman sallies forth to rescue his partner.
William Dugdale Thorley Walters
Pushkin George Pravda
Irenya Konstantinovnia Katia Tchenko

Director: Roger Tucker
Designer: Christopher George

Another Part of the Jungle

w Henry Livings
Bulman's trip to a peaceful Yorkshire village brings death in its wake – there is a professional killer on the prowl, and Bulman must find him before any further murders are committed.
Victor Garforth Freddie Jones
The Face Peter Kelly
Dizzie Bowden Godfrey James

Director: Christopher King
Designer: Colin Rees

Born Into the Purple

w Paul Wheeler
Bulman and Lucy are asked to investigate a series of thefts from an aristocratic family. What they discover gives them cause for concern, and places a dark shadow over family loyalties.
Lady Springfield Pauline Jameson
Williams Alan David
Jan Veronica Smart

Director: Bill Gilmour
Designer: Taff Bately

A Cup For the Winner

w Murray Smith
An American diplomat hires Bulman to trace a family heirloom. There's only one snag – the priceless object, a piece of precious eighteenth-century metal, was stolen in 1761.
Wilbur C. McLeod Bruce Boa
Det. Sgt Reid Anthony May
Samuel Lane Richard Caldicot

Director: David Carson
Designer: David Buxton

I Met A Man Who Wasn't There

w Henry Livings
Employed to follow Gallio, a deported villain who has returned from exile to settle on old debt, Bulman and Lucy find themselves plodding through the seedy world of strippers and peep shows.
Gallio Peter Wyngarde
Kate Sheila Hancock
Dando David Foxxe

Director: Ken Grieve
Designer: Chris Wilkinson

A Moveable Feast

w Paul Wheeler
Bulman and Lucy take an interest in the take-away food trade when they are hired by a young couple to find out who is behind threats of sabotage. The wily ex-copper discovers that not all meat is as tasty as it looks.
Lisa Carolyn Pickles
Tim Simon Chandler
John Fistolarli Tony Anholt

Director: Bill Gilmour
Designer: Stephen Fineren

A Man of Conviction

w Murray Smith
Bulman faces one of the toughest cases of his career. In prison to trap a gang of armed robbers who make daring raids from the 'security' of their cells, his identity is blown and his life threatened. Lucy meanwhile, seeks help from Dugdale.

William Dugdale Thorley Walters
Joe Revell Alfred Lynch
Det. Chf Supt Lambie Mark McManus

Director: Tom Cotter
Designer: Taff Batley

Season Two
7 colour Sixty-minute episodes

Chinese Whispers

w Murray Smith
To forestall the contract placed on his life by
arch criminal Joe Revell, Bulman and Lucy
have spent eighteen months in exile in
China. Deciding that he must return to
England and confront Revell, he and Lucy
part company. Several attempts are made on
Bulman's life until the wily old detective
shows Revell that he is far from being the
dummy Revell believed him to be. Lucy is
reunited with her colleague and STG is back
in business.
Joe Revell Alfred Lynch
Commander McHeath David Horovitch
Edwin Gilbert John Forgeham

Director: William Brayne
Designers: Margaret Coombes and
Michael Grimes

Death By Misadventure

w Murray Smith
When Desmond Geraldine, an ace crime
reporter is killed at the races and there
appears to be no motive for his murder,
Viscount Fairfax, a friend of Bulman's, seeks
STG's help. Prior to his death, Geraldine
had been seen with an exotic looking lady.
Lucy and George must find her.
Geraldine Iain Cuthbertson
Fairfax Robert Hardy
Diana White Jane Cox

Director: David Carson
Designers: Margaret Combes and Michael
Grimes

White Lies

w Murray Smith
Bulman believes it's an honour: an
invitation by Commander Morrison, Head
of C-13, to visit Scotland Yard. Lucy is not
so sure, particularly when they are handed a
'delicate' mission – one that leads Bulman
into declaring his own private war.

Commander Morrison Emrys James
DC Danny Keech Stephen Dillon
Cassandra Stanley Amanda Hillwood

Director: Gareth Morgan
Designer: Margaret Coombes

Chicken of the Baskervilles

w Murray Smith
Installed in a country house, disguised as
Lord Kilmartin's butler, Bulman
investigates the disappearance of the butler
Chivers and the housekeeper. When Lucy
discovers that there is no registration of
death for the couple, Bulman takes to the
skies as a rare breed of bird.
Lord Kilmartin Tony Mathews
Art Mason John McGlynn
Laura Ingrid Pitt

Director: William Brayne
Designer: Michael Grimes

Thin Ice

w Murray Smith
Why should Russian GRU officer,
Ragozhkin, be interested in meeting
Bulman? Why does Willie Dugdale seek
Bulman's help on a security mater? When
Dugdale's body is dragged from the bottom
of a life shaft, the STG investigators unearth
dirty work in British Security.
Willie Dugdale Thorley Walters
Sir Michael Wallace Graham Crowden
Ragozhkin Jack Shepherd

Director: Bruce Macdonald
Designer: Alan Price

W.C. Fields Was Right

w Murray Smith
A surprise visitor from Bulman's past leads
the investigator to take stock of his life, and
two children and a stolen dog lead Bulman
and Lucy to uncover a murder plot. All this
and a visit by the VAT man. Bulman and
his colleague are in for an unwelcome
surprise.
Harry Malin Tony Doyle
Steven Richards Albert Welling
Peter Malin Kieran O'Brien

Director: Sarah Harding
Designer: Ken Wheatley

Ministry of Accidents

w Murray Smith

Bulman and Lucy find themselves being used as pawns in a game where the stakes are high. So high that Willie Dugdale returns from the 'dead' to seek their help. Asked to place their lives on the line, the investigators step into the firing line for one last mission together. George Bulman loses everything he loved and things will never be the same.

Willie Dugdale **Thorley Walters**
Czinner **Shaughan Seymour**
Dobson **Terry Gilligan**

Director: **Brian Mills**
Designer: **Alan Pickford**

BULMAN
Based on chracters created by: Kenneth Royce
Producer: Steve Hawes [Season 1]
Sita Williams [Season 2]
Executive Producer: Richard Everitt [Seasons 1 & 2]
Music by: Dick Walter
A Granada Television Network Production
20 colour 60-minute episodes
5 June – 28 August 1985
20 June – 8 August 1987

THE BULLSHITTERS

Roll Out the Gunbarrel

A down-to-earth, fast moving and hysterically funny parody of The Professionals (and just about every other cop-cum-superspies-cum-buddies television series), this gave us the opportunity to share one-off adventure with less-than-super-cool agents, Bonehead and Foyle, two ex-D15 undercover men who had been dismissed from the service one year earlier because of their involvement in a Russian Gay Serum plot!

Commander Jackson, Head of D15, concerned that his daughter, Jane, had been kidnapped by a ruthless hit squad, is forced to swallow his pride and reinstate the agents – two of the most unlikely contenders for the title 'macho-men' it had been his misfortune to employ.

CAST

Bonehead **Keith Allen**   *Foyle* **Peter Richardson**
Commander Jackson **Robbie Coltrane**

THE BULLSHITTERS
Created by: Keith Allen and Peter Richardson
Producer: Elaine Taylor
Director: Stephen Frears
A Michael White/Dinky Doo Production for Channel Four
50 minutes–colour
3 November 1984

CALLAN

A series of tough, uncompromising counter-epionage adventures, starring Edward Woodward as British agent, David Callan.

Originally created as a character in a one-off television play, *A Magnum for Schneider,* Callan was the agent who refused to lie down when the play had ended. The public liked what they'd seen and expressed a wish to learn more about him. His creator, author James Mitchell, duly obliged by writing six new adventures, and the Callan saga was underway.

In a nutshell, Callan was employed by a top secret department of British Secret Intelligence, set up to watch (and if necessary eliminate) dangerous enemies of the state. That's where Callan came in. As the section's top assassin, he alone was given the task of ensuring the enemy's silence, by any means possible to him – including intimidation or death! A killer, yes. But Callan had a conscience. He tended to ask too many questions, and he needed his own reasons for eliminating 'dangerous' men. On several occasions this brought him into direct conflict with his superior, Hunter: a code name given to all Heads of Section. (Highlights of each story were the scenes of heated disagreement between the agent and a succession of superiors.)

Other notable characters included Tony Meres, Callan's fellow agent – and rival. Meres, a nasty piece of work who shot first and asked questions later, resented Callan's position, and set his sights on becoming 'Number One'. Like Meres, Cross (a latecomer to the series, introduced at the start of the third season) was also envious of the department legend that had sprung up around Callan – who retained his position as the section's top agent against all competition.

If every series has its 'stooge' – a character brought in to give a touch of humour to the proceedings – in Callan's case it was a cringing, smelly little thief, known as Lonely (a nickname he'd acquired because, when nervous, he 'stunk like a skunk'). Callan first met Lonely, a petty burglar, while serving a two-year prison sentence in Wormwood Scrubs for robbery. Lonely served the agent by acting as a lookout or supplying him with 'untraceable' guns and suchlike. (The hapless thief believed 'Mr Callan' to be a successful criminal, before the realisation dawned that he was a government agent.) Though Callan frequently treated Lonely with contempt, he guarded him like a brother. Lonely himself was later recruited into the department to drive the section's 'mobile communications wagon' – a London taxi cab equipped with the latest communications technology.

The series spawned a feature film, *Callan,* in 1974, and the legend continued. Featuring the same plot as *A Magnum for Schneider,* the main characters were played by the TV cast, with the exception of Hunter (played by Eric Porter) and Meres (Peter Egan).

Seven years later, the ATV network in the Midlands commissioned a 90-minute television play by Mitchell, in which Callan – now retired and a dealer in militaria from a shop jointly owned by himself and a woman friend – is recalled to the service for one final dangerous mission. Slightly over-the-top (Lonely had gone straight and was running a company called 'Fresh and Fragrant Bathroom Installations'!), the story nevertheless rounded Callan's career out with a bang not a whimper.

REGULAR CAST

Callan Edward Woodward   *Lonely* Russell Hunter   *Hunter Mk 1* Ronald Radd
Hunter Mk 2 Michael Goodliffe   *Hunter Mk 3* Derek Bond
Hunter Mk 4 William Squire *Hunter Mk 5 (Wet Job)* Hugh Walters
Meres (TV play) Peter Bowles   *Meres Mk 2* Anthony Valentine
Cross Patrick Mower   *Hunter's secretary* Lisa Langdon

A Magnum For Schneider

w James Mitchell   (an Armchair Theatre production)
Callan, one time top agent in a secret British Intelligence 'hit' department, but now in disgrace due to his rebellious attitude, is given the opportunity to redeem himself. His mission, to snuff out gunrunner Rudolph Schneider. Unknown to Callan, the 'test' is a trap and Colonel Hunter, head of the section, has ordered Meres to frame Callan for Schneider's death.
Meres Peter Bowles
Colonel Hunter Ronald Radd
Schneider Joseph Furst

Director: Bill Bain
Designer: David Marshall

Season One
6 monochrome 60-minute episodes

The Good Guys Are All Dead

w James Mitchell
Callan, still smarting from Hunter's plan to frame him, is loath to accept another assignment for the department. It appears he has no choice. Strong-armed back into

the section, Hunter threatens to have him destroyed.
Hunter Ronald Radd
Meres Anthony Valentine (Intro.)
Lonely Russell Hunter

Director: Toby Robertson
Designer: Malcolm Goulding

Goodbye, Nobby Clarke

w Robert Banks Stewart
Callan finds himself up against his former mentor, Nobby Clarke, now turned vicious mercenary. 'You shouldn't have come here, Callan. I was always too good for you. I taught you, remember.'
Nobby Clarke Michael Robbins
Rena Fionnula Flanagan
Kanaro Denis Alaba Peters

Director: Peter Duguid
Designer: Bryan Graves

The Death of Robert E. Lee

w James Mitchell
Facing up to Hunter is one thing – Callan's used to that. But facing up to Hunter and oriental villain Robert E. Lee, is too much for one agent to handle. Or is it?

Robert E. Lee Burt Kwouk
Jenny Francesca Tu
Curtis Dale George Roubicek

Director: Robert Tronson
Designer: David Marshall

Goodness Burns Too Bright

w James Mitchell
Injured when out in the field, Callan must undergo a complete medical check-up. But what happens if someone wants you 'out of the way' for a few days – and is prepared to go to any lengths to achieve that aim?
Dr Schulz Gladys Cooper
Bauer Robert Lang
Maitland Jeremy Lloyd

Director: Bill Bain
Designer: Peter Le Page

But He's a Lord, Mr Callan

w James Mitchell
Ordered to dispose of a member of the aristocracy, Callan, working outside the protection of the agency ('should anything go wrong, we don't know you') finds his mission hampered by Lonely's reluctance to help him.
Captain Miller Gerald Flood
Lord Lindale Donald Hewlett
Caroline Fielding Ann Bell

Director: Guy Verney
Designer: Darrell Lass

You Should Have Been Here Sooner

w James Mitchell
Times are difficult for Callan. Hunter wants his blood, he's disowned by the department, and he's confronted with a witness to a crime who is unable (or unwilling) to reveal what he knows.
Loder Derek Newark
Pollock Jon Laurimore
Sue Lyall Pinkie Johnstone

Director: Piers Haggard
Designer: Darrell Lass

Season Two
15 monochrome 60-minute episodes

Red Knight, White Knight

w James Mitchell
Callan's motto is one of self-preservation: get the other guy before he gets you. A good maxim for a man who trades in death on a daily basis. But what happens when someone doesn't want to play by those rules? Who becomes the pawn? Who plays the knight?
Hunter Michael Goodliffe (intro.)
Bunin Duncan Lamont
Hanson John Savident

Director: Peter Duguid
Designer: Neville Green

The Most Promising Girl of Her Year

w James Mitchell
Love among scientists is always suspect. But when the girl is English and the boy is German, Callan has his work cut out delving through the piles of red tape – and treachery – or foreign 'diplomacy'.
Sonia Prescott Joan Crane
Horst Peter Blythe
Snell Clifford Rose

Director: Peter Duguid
Designer: Peter Le Page

You're Under Starter's Orders

w Robert Banks Stewart
When Callan is accused of taking files from Head Office and planning to flee the country, Hunter suspects that his number one agent has 'gone over'. Callan, however, is playing a very dangerous game – one that could cost him his life.
Millett Harold Innocent
Hannah Kathleen Byron
Nixon Morris Perry

Director: Mike Vardy
Designer: Terry Gough

The Little Bits and Pieces of Love

w James Mitchell
Callan attempts to persuade the wife of a distinguished scientist now working in East

Germany to act as bait in order to lure her husband home. The government want him back in London – but for what purpose?

Mrs Rule Pauline Jameson
Dr Rule Laurence Hardy
Mere's assistant David Rose

Director: Peter Sasdy
Designer: Stan Woodward

Let's Kill Everybody

w Ray Jenkins
An unknown enemy is systematically eliminating agents in Callan's department. Meres and Callan are dealt a losing hand, and Callan alone can save the day – providing he can find the Joker in the pack.

Gould Henry Knowles
Jenny Hilary Dwyer
Walker Kenneth Gilbert

Director: Robert Tronson
Designer: John Kershaw

Heir Apparent

w Hugh D'Allenger
Hunter is dead, long live the new Hunter. Callan is detailed to bring the new head of his department safely to England. There's just one problem: the new man is behind the Iron Curtain – and foreign agents are hot on his tail.

Hunter Derek Bond (Intro.)
Sir Michael Harvey John Wentworth
Jenkins Peter Cellier

Director: Peter Duguid
Designer: Peter Le Page

Land of Light and Peace

w James Mitchell
Callan must dabble in the occult to find the truth behind a seemingly innocent spiritualist organisation 'The League of Light'. Is it a bona fide society, or do its unearthly manifestations hide more sinister activities?

Jane Ellis Avril Elgar
Markinch Ian Cooper
Det. Insp. Charwood Wensley Pithey

Director: Piers Haggard
Designer: David Marshall

Blackmailers Should Be Discouraged

w James Mitchell
When an anonymous letter throws suspicion on Sir Gerald Naylor's past, Callan is asked to investigate. Naylor is due to take up a senior position with the Canadian Atomic Corporation, and the authorities seek Hunter's help.

Sir Gerald Nicholas Selby
Lady Naylor Karin MacCarthy
Todd Barry Andrews

Director: James Goddard
Designer: David Marshall

Death of a Friend

w Ray Jenkins
When a French intelligence officer is killed in a mysterious car crash in England, the French authorities send over their own agent to investigate. Callan finds that the man is an old friend – but is the OAS out to settle an old score?

Jean Coquet Geoffrey Cheshire
Messmer John Devaut
Lambert Barry Stanton

Director: Peter Duguid
Designer: Vic Symonds

Jack-on-Top

w Trevor Preston
When the KGB – Russian Secret Service – network in London is detected, the authorities move in for the kill. The head Russian slips through the net, and Callan is ordered to capture him.

Selby Anthony Blackshaw
Wilson Conrad Phillips
Holbrook Richard Matthews

Director: Mike Vardy
Designer: Tony Borer

Once a Big Man, Always a Big Man

w Ray Jenkins
Hunter sends Callan to retrieve a vital document which has been found in the safe of a ship that sank during the war. But other people are interested in the discovery

– people who are prepared to kill to obtain its secrets.
Watt Bernard Archard
Eva Jacqueline Pearce
Clive Michael Forest

Director: Bill Bain
Designer: Roger Allen

The Running Dog

w William Emms
When the leader of a Chinese Delegation says that he would consider no sacrifice too great for Chairman Mao, Callan has his hands full trying to protect the man from a Neo-Fascist party with unpleasant plans in mind.
Holder Terence Rigby
Felice Renny Lister
Tao Tsung Burt Kwouk

Director: James Goddard
Designer: Peter Le Page

The Worst Soldier I Ever Saw

w James Mitchell
Callan takes on a new role – as one of the domestic staff of an ex-Brigadier suspected of being chosen to lead a mercenary army against an emergent African nation. The agent needs his wits about him if he is to foil the Brigadier's plans.
Brigadier Pringle Allan Cuthbertson
Sarah Pringle Tessa Wyatt
Colonel Leslie Ronald Radd

Director: Robert Tronson
Designer: Terry Gough

Nice People Die at Home

w Robert Banks Stewart
Under the orders of Colonel Leslie, Hunter's temporary replacement, Callan is assigned to infiltrate a Russian spy network and bring in the head man – a difficult job, when the Russian is due to be replaced at any moment.
Belakov Frederick Jaeger
Chelenko Jonathan Burn
Colonel Leslie Ronald Radd

Director: Peter Duguid
Designer: Roger Allen

Death of a Hunter

w Michael Winder
Captured by the KGB, Callan is drugged, brainwashed and released – with instructions to kill Hunter. He obeys – but who actually dies? Hunter? Meres? Or Callan? Who gets shot in the process?
Koralin Norman Wooland
Andrews Michael Meacham
Suzanne Barbara Leigh-Hunt

Director: Reginald Collin
Designer: Neville Green
(Uncertain that the series would continue, producer Reg Collin filmed two different endings for this story. One showed Callan dying in Tony Meres' arms. The other left the way open for more stories. Following public demand, the latter ending was transmitted.)

Season Three
8 colour 60-minute episodes

Where Else Could I Go

w James Mitchell
Having recovered from his wounds, Callan is reinstated in the section. But during his absence things have changed. Hunter has a new face. Meres has been posted to Washington, and a new boy sits at his desk.
Hunter William Squire (Intro.)
Cross Patrick Mower (Intro.)
Judd Harry Towb

Director: James Goddard
Designer: Mike Hall

Summoned To Appear

w Trevor Preston
Callan and Cross are chasing an assassin. In the confusion, Cross kills an innocent man. He escapes, but Callan is detained as a witness. Under oath, he claims the man committed suicide – but another witness says it was murder!
Mr Karas George Pravda
Mrs Karas Hana-Maria Pravda
Insp. Kyle Norman Henry

Director: Voytek
Designer: David Marshall

The Same Trick Twice

w Bill Craig

Why should the Russians agree to a trade-off of captured agents? Hunter smells a trap. Callan has his own ideas – and sets out to teach Cross a thing or two about the spy business.

Bishop Geoffrey Chater (Intro.)
Mallory Patrick Connell
Surtees Richard Hurdnall

Director: Peter Duguid
Designer: David Marshall

A Village Called G

w James Mitchell

Liz, Hunter's secretary, is missing. Callan discovers that she had a date with Cross the night before she disappeared. Is there any connection? And why didn't she tell someone like Callan where she was going?

Liz Liz Langdon
Judd Harry Towb
Sabovski Joseph Furst

Director: Mike Vardy
Designer: Stan Woodward

Suddenly – At Home

w James Mitchell

Janet Lewis needs protection. Callan and Cross become her bodyguards, but the former becomes emotionally involved and finds that emotion is a dangerous enemy – and a kiss brings the taste of death.

Janet Lewis Zena Walker
Liz Liza Langdon
Rene Joinville Tony Beckley

Director: Piers Haggard
Designer: Stan Woodward

Act of Kindness

w Michael Winder

Assigned to prevent a courier's cover from being blown, Callan resorts to an old trick or two from the past. But playing war games with a blackmailer doesn't prepare one for the real thing – or the threat of sudden death.

Heathcote Land Anthony Nicholls
Donovan Prescott Ray Smith
Janice Land Jacqueline Maude

Director: Mike Vardy
Designer: Fred Pusey

God Help Your Friends

w William Emms

In Callan's hands, a bunch of flowers can be deadlier than a gun – especially when he's ordered to kill off a romance between Beth Lampton and a suspected spy. It's the thought that counts – particularly when state defence is at stake.

Beth Lampton Stephanie Beacham
Mark Tedder Michael Jayston
Senor Andarez Oliver Cotton

Director: Peter Duguid
Designer: Neville Green

Breakout

w James Mitchell

For Callan it's a date with destiny. Hunter is after his blood and Lubin, a foreign spy, has surrendered to the police. Callan and Cross must engineer his release – then kill him. Someone will have to give. Will it be Callan or Hunter?

Lubin Garfield Morgan
Judge Ernest Hare
Bonnington Robert Cartland

Director: Reginald Collin
Designer: Neville Green

Amos Green Must Live

w Ray Jenkins

A body dragged from the river. Threats against the life of Amos Green, a prospective parliamentary candidate with strong anti-immigration views. Callan must discover the link. His only clue – a box of matches.

Amos Green Corin Redgrave
May Coswood Annette Crosbie
Rutter Al Garcia

Director: James Goddard
Designer: Peter Le Page

Season Four
13 colour 60-minute episodes

That'll Be the Day

w James Mitchell

Callan is dead! He must be – Lonely threw ashes on his grave! So how come Callan resides in a KGB interrogation cell? He's back in the fold – and the storm clouds are gathering once again.
Bishop Geoffrey Chater
Richmond T. P. McKenna (Intro.)
Snell Clifford Rose

Director: Mike Vardy
Designer: Terry Pritchard

Call Me Sir!

w Bill Craig

Lonely is put in a red file. This means he's totally expendable. Can someone be using him as bait to trap Callan? If so, they're in for a nasty surprise.
Bishop Geoffrey Chater
Flo Mayhew Sarah Lawson
Trowbridge Glynn Edwards

Director: Mike Vardy
Designer: Stan Woodward

First Refusal

w Bill Craig

A list of 10 British agents leads Callan into a double double-cross from which he must extricate himself by whatever means available to him – including taking on the role of 'hunter'.
Meres Anthony Valentine (return)
Bishop Geoffrey Chater
Kitzlinger Martin Wyldeck

Director: James Goddard
Designer: David Marshall

Rules of the Game

w Ray Jenkins

Now acting as Hunter, Callan is drawn into a deadly game of tit-for-tat – a situation made infinitely more dangerous when Bishop decides to withold vital information from him.

Bishop Geoffrey Chater
Medov Mike Pratt
Alevtina Virginia Stride

Director: Voytek
Designer: Bernard Spence

If He Can, So Could I

w Ray Jenkins

Callan must decide what to do about Cross. His instability under fire has reached grave proportions, and only Callan can decide his future. But suddenly fate takes a hand – and the department undergoes a change.
Cross Patrick Mower (last story)
Bishop Geoffrey Chater
Snell Clifford Rose

Director: Peter Duguid
Designer: Mike Hall

None of Your Business

w Trevor Preston

Even Callan has difficulty getting a forged passport. So why should wanted agents continue to slip through the net? Investigating the problem, Callan finds he has also uncovered a novel way of getting enemy agents out of the country.
Bishop Geoffrey Chater
Hunter William Squire (return)
Reeves Brian Murphy

Director: Voytek
Designer: Stan Woodward

Charles Says It's Goodbye

w James Mitchell

Callan in love? It appears that the agent has finally succumbed to the inevitable. But has he? Is he as serious about romance as he is about his work? These two pluses produce a negative result in Hunter's eyes.
James Palliser Dennis Price
Susan Morris Beth Harris
Trent Richard Morant

Director: Peter Duguid
Designer: David Marshall

I Never Wanted the Job

w John Kershaw

Lonely witnesses a murder, and finds himself on the run from the police – and a gang of killers. Will Callan be able to find his friend? And if he does, what protection can he offer?

Dollar Val Musetti
Albert Ron Pember
Det Sgt Frank Coda

Director: James Goddard
Designer: Peter Le Page

The Carrier

w Peter Hill

Out in the cold again, Callan decides to seek a warmer climate. He discovers that going abroad is sometimes easier for the other side – until he works out the secret of their success.

Chief Supt Brown Windsor Davies
Peter Rose Peter Copley
Sir Charles Jeffrey Segal

Director: Jonathan Alwyn
Designer: Neville Green

The Contract

w Bill Craig

Callan is assigned to stop an assassination plot. Posing as a hired gunman, he enters new territory – and finds himself faced with a tough decision between loyalty and duty.

Major Harcourt Robert Urquhart
Lafage Michael Pennington
Kristina Jane Lapotaire

Director: Reginald Collin
Designer: Neville Green

Call Me Enemy
(The Richmond File 1)

w George Markstein

When the two top agents of the East and West – perhaps of the world – come face to face, like a game of chess, each move is considered and thought out. But someone must become the outright winner . . .

Richmond T. P. McKenna
Jarrow Brian Croucher
Bishop Geoffrey Chater

Director: Bill Bain
Designer: David Marshall

Do You Recognise The Woman?
(The Richmond File 2)

w Bill Craig

On the run from the section, Richmond fulfils his grim assignment and once again eludes Callan. Ordered to bring him back alive, Callan embarks on a dangerous journey.

Richmond T. P. McKenna
Bishop Geoffrey Chater
Flo Mayhew Sarah Lawson

Director: Peter Duguid
Designer: Mike Hall

A Man Like Me
(The Richmond File 3)

w James Mitchell

Callan corners his prey and, in direct contravention of Hunter's orders, kills Richmond. Confronted by Hunter – who declares that Callan's career with the section is now at an end – the agent walks away unrepentant.

Richmond T. P. McKenna
Bishop Geoffrey Chater
Snell Clifford Rose

Director: Reginald Collin
Designer: Bill Palmer

Wet Job

w James Mitchell

It's ten years since Callan 'retired' from the Secret Service. He now has a new name – David Tucker – and a new business – a shop called The Old Brigade, which sells militaria. Life has few of the drawbacks which beset his former occupation. But the past has a habit of catching up. The department prises him out of retirement to handle one last mission and he once again finds himself coping with danger at every turn.

Lonely Russell Hunter
Hunter Hugh Walters
Haggerty George Sewell
Dobrovsky Milos Kerek

Director: Shaun O'Riordan
Designer: David Chandler

CALLAN
A Magnum For Schneider
Producer: Leonard White
Story editor: Terence Feely
An ABC Weekend Network Production
60 minutes – monochrome
4 February 1967

Season One
Executive producer: Lloyd Shirley
Associate producer: Terence Feely
An ABC Weekend Network Production
6 monochrome 60-minute episodes
8 July – 12 August 1967

Season Two
Producer: Reginald Collin
Associate producer: John Kershaw
A Thames Television Network Production
15 monochrome 60-minute episodes
8 January–16 April 1969

Season Three
Producer: Reginald Collin
Music by: Jack Trombey
Story editor: George Markstein
A Thames Television Network Production
9 colour 60-minutes episodes
8 April–10 June 1970

Season Four
Producer: Reginald Collin
Music by: Jack Trombey
Story editor: George Markstein
A Thames Television Network Production
13 colour 60-minute episodes
1 March–24 May 1972

Wet Job
Producer: Shaun O'Riordan
An ATV Network Production
90 minutes–colour
2 September 1981

THE CAMPBELLS

A top-notch, colourful and immensely watchable series set in the uncharted territory of Canada in the 1830s.

Like dozens of other Scottish families, the Campbells, widower James Campbell, his daughter and two sons, left their homeland to face the challenge of starting a new life overseas. Before them lay many exciting adventures and hardships. Like so many other settlers in the new country, they gradually learned to adapt to their new environment. Life was tough, but determined to overcome anything, they gradually helped to mould the foundation of Canada.

CAST

Dr James Campbell Malcolm Stoddard   *Emma (his daughter)* Amber Lea Weston
Neil (his eldest son) John Wildman   *John (his son)* Eric Richards
Captain Sims (a neighbour) Cedric Smith   *Rebecca Sims* Wendy Lyon
Gabriel Leger Julien Poulin

THE CAMPBELLS
Producer: Leonard White (Eps 1 & 2) John
Delmage
Directors: Leonard White, George
Bloomfield, Joseph Scanlon,
Don Haldene, Tim Bond
Writers: Allan Prior, Kerry Sim, Ann
MacNaughton, Glenn Norman, Suzette
Coutre, D. A. Nathan, Michael Mercer,
Marc Strange, Matthew Segal, Peter Such,
Martin Lager, Ken Gross, Charles Lazer
A *Scottish Television Production*
Filmed on location in Scotland and Ontario,
Canada
22 colour 30-minute episodes
27 April–28 September 1986

CAPTAIN SCARLET AND THE MYSTERONS

A lavishly-mounted action-packed offering from the Gerry Anderson 'Supermarionation' stable, this came close to being the definitive Anderson product – almost, but not quite.

Set in the year 2068, the first story told how, during a Mars exploration mission, Captain Black, an agent of Spectrum (a world security network organisation whose agents were named after the colours in the spectrum) misinterpreted the intentions of the Martian inhabitants, the Mysterons, as hostile, and annihilated their city – leaving the Mysterons to retaliate by waging a war of attrition on Earth. Using their ability to recreate any object or person which has been destroyed, the Mysterons took control of Captain Black and used him to act as their agent on Earth. They later decide to kill and restore Spectrum agent, Captain Scarlet, by the same process, but their plan backfires and Scarlet becomes their indestructible enemy. Thereafter, the episodes depicted Spectrum's battle against the Mysterons and their attempts to discover a way of detecting their presence. (The Mysterons themselves were never seen.)

CHARACTER VOICES

Captain Scarlet Francis Matthews   *Colonel White* Donald Gray
Captain Blue Ed Bishop   *Captain Grey* Paul Maxwell
Captain Magenta Gary Files   *Lieutenant Green* Cy Grant
Dr Fawn Charles Tingwell   *Melody Angel* Sylvia Anderson
Rhapsody Angel Liz Morgan   *Voice of Mysterons* Donald Gray

Pilot Story (no on-screen title)

w Gerry and Sylvia Anderson
The inhabitants of an alien city on Mars turn their cameras on the human explorers. Captain Black, mistaking these for weapons, destroys the alien city. The Mysterons swear revenge, and the war of nerves begins.
Director: Desmond Saunders

Winged Assassin

w Tony Barwick
Captain Scarlet – now indestructible after his fatal fall – is sent to protect the General of the United Asian Republic, who is believed to be the Mysterons' next target.
Director: David Lane

Big Ben Strikes Again

w Tony Barwick
Pursuing the latest Mysteron threat – a plan to destroy London with a nuclear device – Captains Scarlet and Blue become interested when they hear from a transport driver that he heard Big Ben strike thirteen before he was knocked out.
Director: Brian Burgess

Manhunt

w Tony Barwick
When a break-in at an Atomic Research Centre goes wrong and video film is developed which shows that Captain Black is a Mysteron agent, Captain Scarlet is sent to hunt him down.
Director: Alan Perry

Avalanche

w Shane Rimmer
A Mysteron agent, posing as a truck driver, pumps liquid oxygen from his tanker into the control domes of the Outer Space defence system. Captain Scarlet and Lieutenant Green attempt to stop him.
Director: Brian Burgess

White As Snow

w Peter Curran and David Williams
Having threatened to destroy Colonel White, the Mysterons use their powers to recreate the man ordered to protect him – a steward on board a submarine in which Colonel White takes refuge.
Director: Robert Lynn

The Trap

w Alan Pattillo
When the Mysterons plan to clip the Angels' wings, by destroying the World Air Conference, Captain Scarlet and Symphony Angel are assigned to repel the attack.
Director: Alan Perry

Operation Time

w Richard Conway and Stephen Mattick
When Captain Magenta solves the latest Mysteron riddle – 'kill time' – and Spectrum reach the conclusion that it points to an attempt being made on the life of General Tiempo, a man about to undergo surgery, the operation venue is changed. But is it too late?
Director: Ken Turner

Spectrum Strikes Back

w Tony Barwick
Spectrum demonstrate their latest devices in their war against the enemy: an X-ray machine to detect the aliens, and a gun to destroy them. As they do so, the Mysterons attack.
Director: Ken Turner

Special Assignment

w Tony Barwick
In debt after gambling on roulette, Captain Scarlet resigns his post. He is then approached by two strangers who promise to clear his debts if he steals a Spectrum Pursuit Vehicle – for Captain Black.
Director: Bob Lynn

The Heart of New York

w Tony Barwick
When the Mysterons threaten to destroy Manhattan and Spectrum has the city evacuated, three crooks seize their opportunity to rob the Second National Bank – but Captain Black locks them in a vault.
Director: Alan Perry

Lunarville 7

w Tony Barwick

Receiving a message that the Controller of Lunarville 7, the Moon's largest colony, claims to have made peace with the Mysterons, Captains Scarlet and Blue are sent to investigate.
Director: Bob Lynn

Point 783

w Peter Curran and David Williams

Discovering that Commander of Supreme Headquarters Earth Forces (SHEF) is to be the Mysterons' next target, Colonel White sends agents Scarlet and Blue to protect him – and guard SHEF's ultimate new weapon, the Unitron.
Director: Bob Lynn

Model Spy

w Bill Hedley

André Verdain, a fashion designer, is marked for death by the Mysterons. Though agents Destiny, Symphony, Scarlet and Blue are sent to protect him, they must first overcome another Mysteron threat.
Director: Ken Turner

Seek and Destroy

w Peter Curran and David Williams

Scarlet and Blue go to the rescue of Destiny Angel when an attempt is made on her life whilst on holiday in Paris. Meanwhile the Mysterons announce that they will destroy the newly-built Angel Interceptors.
Director: Alan Perry

The Traitor

w Tony Barwick

When Spectrum Hovercrafts start crashing in Australia without reason, agents Scarlet and Blue investigate – but Scarlet finds himself held responsible for the accidents.
Director: Alan Perry

Renegade Rocket

w Ralph Hart

After undergoing the Mysteron recreation treatment, a rocket technician launches a rocket at Spectrum HQ. Scarlet and Blue must decipher the destruct code before the rocket hits its target.
Director: Brian Burgess

Crater 101

w Tony Barwick

When Scarlet, Blue and Green are sent to the Moon to destroy a Mysteron city, they have no way of knowing that the driver of the lunar tank bringing them an atomic device to do this is an agent for their enemy.
Director: Ken Turner

The Shadow of Fear

w Tony Barwick

Spectrum plan to observe the Mysteron city on Mars by planting a camera satellite on Phobos. Scarlet and Blue are given the task of guarding the astronomers – one of whom is a Mysteron agent.
Director: Bob Lynn

Dangerous Rendezvous

w Tony Barwick

Returning to Cloudbase with the pulsator device taken from the Mysteron city on the Moon – which has been adapted to allow Colonel White to speak to the aliens – Captain Scarlet is suspicious when the enemy agrees to meet for peace talks.
Director: Brian Burgess

Fire at Rig 15

w Bryan Cooper

Smith, a drilling expert, is attacked and given the 'treatment' by the Mysterons while capping a bore at Rig 15. Under Captain Black's orders, he sets out to destroy Spectrum's fuel supply complex.
Director: Ken Turner

Treble Cross

w Tony Barwick

The Mysterons plan to destroy Futura City by replacing Air Force Major Gravener with an alien double. Unaware that he's walking into a trap, Captain Scarlet enters the scene.
Director: Alan Perry

Flight 104

w Tony Barwick

Agents Blue and Scarlet are assigned to escort a leading astrophysicist by plane to a conference in Geneva. During their flight, the plane comes under the control of the Mysterons – and crashdives into the sea.
Director: Bob Lynn

Place of Angels

w Leo Eaton

When the Mysterons threaten to destroy 'the place of Angels', they take over research biochemist Judy Chapman – who then takes a deadly culture to contaminate the Los Angeles water supply.
Director: Leo Eaton

Noose of Ice

w Tony Barwick

Captain Scarlet and agent Blue go to a North Pole Tritonium mine, where the walls of ice are held back by elements powered by a generator substation – an establishment now under Mysteron control.
Director: Ken Turner

Expo 2068

w Shane Rimmer

The Mysterons threaten to destroy the North Atlantic Sea Board with a nuclear device stolen by Captain Black. Agents Scarlet and Blue are sent to intervene.
Director: Leo Eaton

The Launching

w Peter Curran and David Williams

When a newspaper reporter is killed on his way to visit President Roberts, the Mysterons' next target, and his body undergoes the alien recreation treatment, it spells trouble for Spectrum agent Captain Scarlet.
Director: Brian Burgess

Codename Europa

w David Lee

Mysteron agent Captain Black shoots electronics expert Carney, then sets out to destroy the Congress of Europe by killing its three main members.
Director: Alan Perry

Inferno

w Shane Rimmer and Tony Barwick

After it has been destroyed by asteroids, the Mysterons plan to use an SKR4 Space Recovery Ship to destroy a desalinisation plant in South America. Spectrum agents are sent to thwart their plans.
Director: Alan Perry

Flight to Atlantica

w Tony Barwick

When the Mysterons announce their plans to destroy the Atlantica World Navy complex, Colonel White sends agents Ochre and Blue to protect the base. But the two men suddenly begin to attack Atlantica – why?
Director: Leo Eaton

Attack on Cloudbase

w Tony Barwick

The Mysterons continue to mount raids against Spectrum-held strongholds. During an attack by alien flying saucers, the Angels are launched but Destiny is killed. In the ensuing chaos, Captain Scarlet loses his powers of indestructibility!
Director: Ken Turner

The Inquisition

w Tony Barwick

When Captain Blue is knocked out after a meal with agent Scarlet and regains consciousness on Cloudbase, deserted but for Colgan, a security agent who suspects Blue of being a traitor, Blue finds himself in a very tense situation – one that could have far-reaching consequences for the entire Spectrum network.
Director: Ken Turner

CAPTAIN SCARLET AND THE
MYSTERONS
Created by: Gerry and Sylvia Anderson
Producer: Reg Hill
Associate producer: John Read
Executive producer: Gerry Anderson
Music by: Barry Gray
Script editor: Tony Barwick
Visual effects supervisor: Desmond Saunders
An ITC/Century 21 Television Production
32 colour 30-minute episodes
29 September 1967–14 May 1968
(USA: Syndicated 1967
26 episodes)

C.A.T.S. EYES

An all action drama series in the *Charlie's Angels* mould, about an all-woman detective outfit called the Eyes Enquiry Agency. Outwardly the type of establishment which handled mundane enquiry cases, the agency was in fact a cover for a high-powered Home Office security operation from which the trio of troubleshooters tracked down everything from Russian spies to drug pushers and extortion gangs (C.A.T.S. stood for Covert Activities Thames Section).

Leader of the team was Pru Standfast. A tall, leggy ex-Oxford University graduate (president of the Students' Union), her tough no-nonsense organisational ability, flair for leadership and War Office background made her a natural for the post. (She was selected to lead the unit on the direct recommendation of a British Ambassador.) Equally at home among the hotbed of intelligence work handled by the team was ex-detective Maggie Forbes. With 18 years police experience to draw on (5 of them spent with the CID – see entry *The Gentle Touch*), she was a welcome addition to the unit. Her instinct for sniffing out villainy and investigative police-trained toughness, were qualities well suited to the role.

The third member of the team (the youngest – but made of the same stuff as her colleagues) was Frederica 'Fred' Smith. Recruited to operate the sophisticated computer hardware used by the unit (she'd begun writing programs at an early age, and was snapped up by the Ministry of Defence after her Civil Service file logged her expertise at the subject), her ability to drive cars hard and fast was put to good use whenever the trio were out on field assignments.

Aiding them in their investigations was Nigel Beaumont ('the man from the Ministry'). Assigned to keep tabs on the troubleshooters, he acted as linkman with the powers that be.

For a second series of adventures, Pru Standfast was replaced by a new girl, Tessa Robinson, and Maggie Forbes was elevated to leader. (No explanation was given as to why Pru had left the team – or why the producers deemed it necessary to replace her with a run-of-the-mill character.)

The stories continued as before, but somehow lacked the zip and pace of the previous series. Nevertheless, the programme was streets ahead of its nearest rival and the Eyes team will be sorely missed by their legion of fans.

One notable point: series one was accompanied by a stunning theme tune composed by John Kongos – so good, in fact, that it became a contender for my choice of all-time favourite TV theme (an honour held by Laurie Johnson's theme from *The Avengers*). This, too, was replaced by an instantly forgettable title theme.

REGULAR CAST

Pru Standfast **Rosalyn Landor**   *Maggie Forbes* **Jill Gascoine**
Fred Smith **Leslie Ash**   *Nigel Beaumont* **Don Warrington**
Tessa Robinson **Tracy-Louise Ward**

Season One

12 colour 60-minute episodes
+ a 90-minute pilot episode

Goodbye Jenny Wren

w Terence Feely   *(a 90-minute introductory story)*
Maggie Forbes arrives to join the new unit on the day that Jenny Kenwright, a member of the team, is killed while investigating a Russian trawler anchored in the Estuary. While Fred avenges Jenny's death in a cat and mouse game with the Russians, Maggie makes a mess of her first assignment – a run-of-the-mill adultery case.
Jenny Kenwright **Catherine Rabett**
Andrei Andreyev **Michael Petrovitch**
Sir Thomas **Christopher Goodwin**

Director: **William Brayne**
Designer: **Leo Austin**

The Black Magic Man

w Ray Jenkins
When a cat burglar known as The Black Magic Man breaks into a Special Branch

'safe house' where two illegal immigrants are being held for questioning, Maggie finds herself on his trail – but has to solve more than one mystery.
Reed **Nigel Gregory**
Det. Insp. Turnbull **Bernard Holley**
Teal **Matthew Aldrige**

Director: **James Hill**
Designer: **Leo Austin**

The Double Dutch Deal

w Martin Worth
Acting as 'best man' at a friend's registry office wedding, Fred stumbles across a marriage racket run by an unscrupulous organisation for Asian girls seeking EEC citizenship – she becomes even more alarmed when her Dutch 'boyfriend' is murdered.
Pieter **Steven Pinder**
Al Jarvis **Philip Jackson**
Samantha **Nula Conwell**

Director: **Ian Toynton**
Designer: **Ken Wheatley**

Frightmare

w Don Houghton

When Fred is assigned to guard the priceless Strathmar pendant, awaiting the arrival of a rich client, the jewel turns out to be a red herring – and before the case is over, Fred begins to doubt her sanity!

Mark Richard Austin
George Havant Patrick Newell
Doctor Rosemary Williams

Director: James Hill
Designer: Judy Steele

Love Byte

w Ben Steed

A wealthy client asks the Eyes team to follow an ex-con with whom his daughter has become involved. Fred is assigned to follow her, and unmasks a blackmail operation based on clients' personal information stored into a computer.

Charlie Hammond George Sewell
Kate Hammond Sally Jane Jackson
Det. Insp. Michael Troughton

Director: James Hill
Designer: Philip Murphy

Fingers

w Anthony Skene

Pru is asked to discover who stole an old Debussy manuscript from an exclusive piano emporium. She snares a young music buff – a member of a family of thieves who are not all as harmless as he is.

Billy Truscott T. P. McKenna
Dev Truscott Michael Thomas
Jessica Truscott Phyilida Law

Director: Robert Fuest
Designer: John Newton-Clarke

With Vinegar and Brown Paper

w Ray Jenkins

A death on a motorway leads Maggie and the Eyes team to a man on the run, in fear of his life – and a devious plot involving the Chinese and forged bearer bonds.

Maguire Malcolm Tierney
Steven Two Legs J. G. Devlin
Sir James Holloway James Horsley

Director: Robert Fuest
Designer: Leo Austin

Under Plain Cover

w Jeremy Burnham

Investigating the mysterious death of a man found floating in the river, Pru finds that an official 'block' has been put on the case. Despite this, she exposes a secret CIA deal – and discovers who her friends are.

Gerry Saunders Ed Devereaux
McNeill James Cosmo
Sir Patrick Swinnerton John Ringham

Director: William Brayne
Designer: Leo Austin

Something Nasty Down Below

w Terence Feely

Is Flo's long dead husband still alive? Flo thinks she has just seen him, but he was supposed to have perished in a submarine accident, forty years ago. Maggie is put on the case – and learns the hard way that old killers never die.

Flo Hawkins Julia McCarthy
Charlie Hawkins Hugh Lloyd
Amos Fraser George A. Cooper

Director: Ian Toynton
Designer: Philip Murphy

Cross My Palm With Silver

w Jeremy Burnham

Clairvoyant Madame Crystal asks Pru to find the location of a 'vision' – a place where she is convinced she is going to die. Pru discovers that other people are searching for it – and that sometimes there really is a pot of gold at the rainbow's end.

Madame Crystal Cherith Mellor
Quigley Ronald Lacey
Woodbridge Peter Vaughan

Director: Robert Fuest
Designer: Judy Steele

My Father Knew Lloyd Mbotu

w Terence Feely

President Mbotu, a newly-elected African leader, has a score to settle with General Standfast, Pru's father. Pru is sent to protect him, and her father learns for the first time of her real job. Meanwhile, Maggie exposes an insurance fraud.

Major General Standfast Frederick Treves
Mike Leapman Donald Churchill
Anne Standfast Faith Brook

Director: William Brayne
Designer John Newton-Clarke

Blue For Danger

w Jeremy Burnham

When a woman client asks the Eyes team to follow her husband, it seems a perfectly straightforward assignment. But it leads Maggie, Pru and Fred into dark and dangerous waters – and a case of murder

Driscoll George Innes
Mrs Driscoll Bridget Turner
Det. Insp. Rathbone Benny Young

Director: Tom Clegg
Designer: Philip Murphy

Sweet Toothed Barracuda

When a black businessman finds some cocaine among a consignment of sugar he has imported from the Caribbean, it leads Maggie to a secret society from the island, whose voodoo magic becomes a threat to her life.

(Note: No production details were available for this episode beyond those given. It was never transmitted on the ITV network.)

Season Two

11 colour 60-minute episodes

One Away

w Paul Wheeler

The Eyes team are assigned to stop escaped spy Edward Stone reaching a submarine which will take him out of the country. He continually eludes them – how? Is he receiving 'inside' help?

Edward Stone Neil Cunningham
Geoff Ray Winstone
Davies Nicolas Selby

Director: Dennis Abbey

Powerline

w Terence Feely and Gerry O'Hara

On the trail of a killer, Tessa and Fred infiltrate a group of travellers assembled for a ritual involving prehistoric stones. Maggie suspects the culprits could be Hell's Angels – until a sudden violent event changes her mind.

Lucy Leslie Nightingale
'Baby' Isabella Nightingale
Quist Gavin Richards

Director: Ian Sharp

Hit List

w Gerry O'Hara

A gang war between the Mafia and the Triads – with the Eyes team smack in the middle! Maggie, Fred and Tessa face extinction – unless they can crack down on the war barons.

Fitzgeorge John Golightly
Sir Giles Tim Wylton
Jacques Dubois Peter Harlow

Director: Raymond Menmuir

Good As New

w Paul Wheeler

When a mischievous young girl – who has cried wolf too often – claims that she was locked in a dungeon, her teachers suspect she is protecting a prankster. Nigel is not so sure – and sends the girls to investigate.

Sara Joanne Dukes
Angela Lane Penelope Wilton
Stefan Johns Oliver Cotton

Director: Carol Wiseman

Rough Trip

w Gerry O'Hara

On the trail of a woman believed to be a terrorist infiltrator, the Eyes team have their hands full discovering what she's up to –

until the woman displays the brutal purpose behind her smile.
Shafi Aziz Sneh Gupta
Sir Wallace Oxley Angus Mackay
Simon Maxstead Daniel Meader

Director: William Brayne

Passage Hawk

w Barry Appleton
A British criminal serving a prison sentence for a bank robbery in South Africa is released, terminally ill, and flown back to Britain. The normally compassionate Nigel suspects the man's claims. Why?
Hutchins John McEnery
Kerber Ian McNeice
Doctor Peter Burton

Director: Anthony Simmons

Freezeheat

w Terence Feely
When Nigel assigns the Eyes team to a new case, he has no idea of the trouble he's letting them in for. By the time the girls wrap up their enquiry, all three will have just cause to examine their lives.
Roker Morgan Shepherd
Jimbo Robert Gary
Denby Harris Tony Doyle

Director: Terry Marcel

Fit

w Reg Ford
A gruelling refresher course at a top secret spy school develops into a tense situation for Fred and Tessa, while Maggie, with a fortuitous ankle sprain, vets the establishment for trouble. It arrives – sooner than she expects.
Sir Jack Fenn Charles Gray
Greaves Joe Robinson
Jimmy Barron Michael Howe

Director: Terry Marcel

Honeytrap

w Terence Feely
Maggie, assigned to smoke out a KGB gigolo who is compromising Whitehall

spinsters, finds herself captured and held to ransom. Meanwhile, Fred and Tessa have problems of their own.
Yuri David Sumner
Zhukov Alan Downer
Sir Frederick Brian Hawksley

Director: Robert Fuest

Crack-Up

w Paul Wheeler
When a stake-out goes wrong and throws Maggie – in charge of the brief – into a personal crisis that threatens to put an end to her career, Nigel seeks Fred and Tessa's help to pull her back from the brink.
Miles Bennett Michael Jayston
Fox Brian Croucher
Simon Geoffrey Greenhill

Director: Edward Bennett

Tranmere Dan and Tokyo Joe

w Jenny McDade
What connection do an accident prone minister with bizarre tastes, a Japanese car boss with millions to invest and an ex-POW with a long memory have in common with the case being investigated by Nigel? The team must find the answer – before a major calamity takes place.
Nakimoto Yoshio Kawahara
Simmons David Saville
Edna Avril Angers

Director: Dennis Abey

Season Three
7 colour 60-minute episodes

Twelve Bar Blues

w Andy De La Tour and Gerry O'Hara
Who is behind a series of arms raids at military establishments? To find out, Tessa goes undercover as a barmaid, Fred poses as an innocent young lady and Maggie finds herself singing the blues to impress Jethro Blackstock, a man suspected of arms smuggling.
Jethro Blackstock Tony Selby
Derek Moore Ray Jewers
Marek Graham Weston

Director: Gerry Mill

Carrier Pigeon

w Paul Wheeler

Visiting Amsterdam for a few days' break, Fred recognises Sara, an old school chum. They arrange to meet, but their reunion is cut short when Sara is arrested for smuggling drugs through British customs. Convinced that her friend is innocent, Fred puts her own life at risk to prove it.

Sara Claire Toeman
Rawlings Leon Eagles
Evans David Gooderson

Director: J. B. Wood

Country Weekend

w Paul Wheeler

Tessa's plans to spend a quiet weekend at her mother's home accompanied by Fred take on nightmare proportions when three men arrive and hold them hostage. With Maggie back at the office, the girls must handle the crisis alone.

Charlie Geoffrey Hinsliff
Jim Temple Shaun Gascoine
Col Hackforth-Gray Richard Bebb

Director: Raymond Menmuir

The Big Burn

w Terence Feely

The discovery of electronic listening 'bugs' on some valuable antiques stolen from a country house leads the Eyes team into the world of espionage. The bugs are 'foreign' in design, but why have they been placed in the home of jailed forger McCrewer?

Joe McCrewer Neil McCaul
Henry Donald Churchill
Zhukov Alan Downer

Director: Alan Bell

A Naval Affair

w Francis Megahy

When ship designer Alan Moss's house burns down and all his work on a revolutionary design concept for warships is destroyed, the Eyes team find themselves assigned to prevent further attempts on his life. Then a bomb explodes in Maggie's flat.

Alan Moss John Fortune
Hutchins Timothy Carlton
Stark John Challis

Director: Claude Whatham

Family Tradition

w Paul Wheeler

Following an annual lunch with close friend Sir Edward Jordan – who recruited Nigel – the Eyes team are asked to investigate Sir Edward's son Howard, a civil servant with access to secrets, who is 'acting strangely'. When Howard tries to take his own life, Maggie discovers more than she, or Nigel, bargained for.

Sir Edward Jordan Alan MacNaughton
Howard Jordan Michael Elwyn
Wendy Jordan Patricia Garwood

Director: Raymond Menmuir

Backlash

w Terence Feely

Ordered to take a fortnight's holiday, Maggie looks up an old schoolfriend. Within hours they both narrowly escape two attempts on their lives. When her friend Penny is shot, a guilty Maggie leaves no stone unturned to find who is responsible.

Penny Osmond Isla Blair
Jack Brand Stephen Greif
Grogan Jonathan Kydd

Director: Francis Megahy

C.A.T.S EYES
Created by: Terence Feely
Producer: Dickie Bamber, Frank Cox (Season 1)
Raymond Menmuir (Seasons 2,3)
Executive producer: Rex Firkin (Seasons 1 to 2)
Music by: John Kongos (Season 1)
Barbara Thompson (Seasons 2,3)
Executive story editor: Gerry O'Hara (Seasons 2,3)
A TVS Network Production
1 colour 90-minute pilot story
30 colour 60-minute episodes
12 April – 26 June 1985
5 April – 14 June 1986
25 April – 6 June 1987

CATWEAZLE

Created by writer/actor Richard Carpenter, this witty children's fantasy series told the story of Catweazle – an eccentric eleventh-century wizard, trapped in the twentieth century.

In an attempt to discover the secret of flight, the wizard used his magical powers to (accidentally) leap through time into twentieth-century England – and found himself totally bemused by the succession of 'incredible flying machines' and 'amazing contraptions' that modern-day people took for granted.

Bewildered by the technical advances made by man, the wizard became totally engrossed by his new environment – but never lost sight of his prime objective, to return to his own time. (A mission he accomplished by the thirteenth episode.)

When the series returned one year later, Catweazle had returned to the present day (by accident, of course) and found himself searching for the 'thirteenth' sign of the Zodiac, which would enable him to fly back to his own time.

A winner in every department (the programme took the coveted Writers Guild of Great Britain 1971 award for Best TV Children's Drama Script), the series is best remembered for the excellent performance of Geoffrey Bayldon in the title role.

REGULAR CAST

Catweazle **Geoffrey Bayldon**
Carrot (a young boy who shared his adventures in Season One) **Robin Davis**
Mr Bennett (the boy's father) **Charles Tingwell**   Sam (a farmhand) **Neil McCarthy**
Cedric (Catweazle's friend in Season Two) **Gary Warren**
Lord Collingford **Moray Watson**   Lady Collingford **Elspet Gray**
Groome **Peter Butterworth**

Season One
13 colour 30-minute episodes

The Sun in a Bottle

w Richard Carpenter
Determined to discover the secret of flight, Catweazle zips through time and begins his unusual adventures. Confused by the technology he encounters, he's fortunate enough to meet Carrot, a boy who will share his adventures.
Director: Quentin Lawrence

Castle Saburac

w Richard Carpenter
Catweazle becomes further bemused by twentieth-century hardware, and Carrot becomes even further bemused by his new friend's antics.
Director: Quentin Lawrence

The Curse of Rapkyn

w Richard Carpenter
Believing that there is a curse on the farm that only Catweazle can banish, Carrot asks his friend to cast a spell, or two. He does so – with hilarious results.
Director: Quentin Lawrence

The Witching Hour

w Richard Carpenter

Affluent Miss Bonnington has designs on his father, so Carrot seeks Catweazle's help to cast a spell on her. The outcome surprises all concerned.

Director: Quentin Lawrence

The Eye of Time

w Richard Carpenter

When the evil Madame Rosa gives Sam racing tips, Catweazle intervenes – and sets in motion a chain of events that end in laughter.

Director: Quentin Lawrence

The Magic Face

w Richard Carpenter

Trouble for Catweazle. An American photographer arrives to photograph the wizard – and Catweazle thinks he is under the power of a sorcerer.

Director: Quentin Lawrence

The Telling Bone

w Richard Carpenter

More trouble for the eccentric wizard. Catweazle causes uproar and laughter with the local vicar and a telephone.

Director: Quentin Lawrence

The Power of Adamcos

w Richard Carpenter

Believing he has travelled back in time, Catweazle is distressed when he appears to have lost his magical knife.

Director: Quentin Lawrence

The Demi Devil

w Richard Carpenter

Because he refuses to teach Catweazle the secret of 'electrickery', the wizard turns Carrot into a strange creature – with even stranger habits.

Director: Quentin Lawrence.

The House of the Sorcerer

w Richard Carpenter

Tired of farming, Sam hands in his notice to Mr Bennett. Catweazle, suspicious of his

friend's new job, decides to investigate further.

Director: Quentin Lawrence

The Flying Broomsticks

w Richard Carpenter

Mr Bennett finds himself under interrogation by Sergeant Bottle, who suspects him of being mixed up with the disappearance of several broomsticks. Catweazle – the real culprit – has no idea of the trouble he's caused.

Director: Quentin Lawrence

The Wisdom of Solomon

w Richard Carpenter

A new addition to the Bennett household upsets Carrot, so Catweazle casts a spell to banish the 'invader'.

Director: Quentin Lawrence

The Trickery Lantern

w Richard Carpenter

Carrot bids Catweazle a sad farewell as the wizard discovers a way to return to his own time – but even a 'short hop' through time can raise a few problems.

Director: Quentin Lawrence

Season Two

13 colour 30-minute episodes

The Magic Riddle

w Richard Carpenter

Catweazle's return to the twentieth-century spells trouble, especially for Cedric, the young son of Lord and Lady Collingford, who arrives home to find the wizard hiding in his bedroom.

Director: David Reed

Duck Halt

w Richard Carpenter

Now that Catweazle has been introduced to life in King's Farthing, he needs somewhere to live, so that he can work on his perennial problem – learning how to fly.

Director: David Lane

The Heavenly Twins

w Richard Carpenter
'Magic is magic.' So says Catweazle in one of his more profound moments. But even he becomes confused when he meets a modern-day magician at a children's party.
Director: David Reed

The Sign of the Crab

w Richard Carpenter
When thieves raid King's Farthing, and their haul falls into Catweazle's hands, it is a day that they, and the community, will never forget.
Director: David Lane

The Black Wheels

w Richard Carpenter
Catweazle's attempts to 'find' Groome's lost voice reduce the residents of King's Farthing to near hysteria. Groome himself is not amused.
Director: David Reed

The Wogle Stone

w Richard Carpenter
Hearing that Lord Collingford is tempted to sell King's Farthing – and thereby Duck Halt – to a property tycoon, Catweazle intervenes, with unexpected results.
Director: David Lane

The Enchanted King

w Richard Carpenter
It's laughter all the way when a local sculptor is mistaken by Catweazle for a demon who 'turns people into stone'!
Director: David Reed

The Familiar Spirit

w Richard Carpenter
Two identical twins, both toad experts, give Catweazle cause for concern when they discover that Touchwood, the wizard's pet toad, is over 900 years old!
Director: David Lane

The Ghost Hunters

w Richard Carpenter
When she hears 'things that go bump in the night', Lady Collingford calls in two ghost hunters, much to the consternation of the real noisemaker – Catweazle.
Director: David Reed

The Walking Trees

w Richard Carpenter
Is Catweazle a spy? The Army think he is, and not even Cedric can save his friend from military interrogation – or can he?

Director: David Lane

The Battle of the Giants

w Richard Carpenter
When Catweazle decides to enter the local flower show with his giant marrow, it brings near chaos to King's Farthing.

Director: David Reed

The Magic Circle

w Richard Carpenter
Believing that he is seeing things, Groome consults a London doctor, who finds Catweazle a much more intriguing case than his patient.
Director: David Reed

The Thirteenth Sign

w Richard Carpenter
Having collected all twelve signs of the Zodiac, Catweazle must discover the thirteenth before he can fly back to his own time. Cedric helps him do so – and bids a fond farewell to his friend.
Director: David Lane

CATWEAZLE
Created by: Richard Carpenter
Producer: Quentin Lawrence (Series 1)
Carl Mannin (Series 2)
Executive producer: Joy Whitby (Series 1)
Associate producer: Carl Mannin (Series 1)
An LWT Television Production
26 colour 30-minute episodes
1 March–7 June 1970
2 March–7 June 1971

THE CHAMPIONS

Craig Sterling, Sharron Macready and Richard Barrett – The Champions – were agents for Nemesis, a Geneva-based crimefighting agency formed to combat situations that could have ended in international tension and destroyed the delicate balance of power between the great nations. The spy trio were agents with a difference – they were superhuman.

The background of how they acquired their powers was told in the first story. Assigned by Commander Tremayne, head of Nemesis, to locate and destroy deadly bacteria specimens possessed by ruthless Chinese scientists in Tibet, the agents achieved their mission, but were 'killed' when their escape plane crashed into the Himalayas while escaping from the enemy. Their bodies were found by a strange old man from a lost Tibetan civilisation who, in return for their sworn silence about the existence of the secret city, endowed them with amazing new powers. With their senses and minds adapted to a fantastic level (all three now had the capability of extra-sensory perception, extraordinary sight, smell and hearing – their combined 'mental and physical powers tuned to computer efficiency') the agents returned to the modern world to use their newly-acquired powers to combat world crime and become, in the words of the programme's introduction: 'Champions of law, order and justice'.

Though superhuman, the agents were not immortal. They could be killed. The greater the risks they took, the greater the danger to themselves. They made mistakes, but quickly learned to use their powers to the benefit of mankind, and their amazing secret became a bond between them.

One of the most popular Monty Berman/Dennis Spooner collaborations, this became a firm favourite with fans of the genre.

REGULAR CAST

Craig Sterling **Stuart Damon**   *Sharron Macready* **Alexandra Bastedo**
Richard Barrett **William Gaunt**   *Tremayne* **Anthony Nicholls**

The Beginning

w Dennis Spooner

When Nemesis agents Sterling, Macready and Barrett set out on a dangerous mission to Tibet, they have no idea that death awaits their arrival – or that they will be reborn and return to their base as superhumans.

Tibetan Priest **Felix Aylmer**
Whittaker **Kenneth J Warren**
Chislenkan **Joseph Furst**

Director: **Cyril Frankel**

The Invisible Man

w Donald James

Tipped off that the proceeds from a large bank robbery are to be placed in a Swiss bank, the Nemesis agents must find out from which bank the money is to be stolen. Somewhat surprisingly, noises in Craig's head reveal the answer.

Hallam Peter Wyngard
Sir Frederick Basil Dignam
Van Velden Aubrey Morris

Director: Cyril Frankel

Reply Box: 666

w Philip Broadley

Sent to the Caribbean to investigate a mysterious ad placed in a newspaper's personal column – 'Wanted, a parrot that speaks German' – the Champions find themselves facing a dangerous enemy who specialises in explosives.

Semenkin George Roubicek
Jules Anton Rodgers
Cleo Imogen Hassall

Director: Cyril Frankel

The Experiment

w Tony Williamson

A scientist tries to create superhumans to equal the Nemesis team. Sharron Macready is tricked into taking part in the experiment, and Craig Sterling and Richard Barrett are faced with their toughest opponents yet.

Cranmore Allan Cuthbertson
Marianne Grant Caroline Blakiston
Chrissie Madelena Nichol

Director: Cyril Frankel

Happening

w Brian Clemens

When three men find themselves isolated in an atom test area with a bomb due to go off at any moment, Champion Richard Barrett, one of the trio, must face deadly peril by trying to disarm the device.

Joss Michael Gough
Banner Jack MacGowran
Winters Grant Taylor

Director: Cyril Frankel

Operation Deep-freeze

w Gerald Kelsey

The leader of a small country attempts to force the United Nations to recognise his despotic power by establishing a secret missile base in Antarctica. The outcome has The Champions undergoing the deep-freeze treatment.

General Gomez Patrick Wymark
Hemmings Robert Urquhart
Margoli Peter Arne

Director: Paul Dickson

The Survivors

w Donald James

What lies behind the murder of three students in the Austrian Alps? The Champions are assigned to discover what or who is behind several killings in the same lakeside vicinity.

Franz/Colonel Reitz Clifford Evans
Richter Donald Houston
Emil Bernard Kay

Director: Cyril Frankel

To Trap a Rat

w Ralph Smart

Tainted drugs are being offered for sale in London, and drug addicts are becoming victims. The Champions are asked to find the suppliers behind the lethal consignments before any further damage is done.

Walter Pelham Guy Rolf
Jane Purcell Kate O'Mara
Sandra Edina Ronay

Director: Sam Wanamaker

The Iron Man

w Philip Broadley

When asked to protect the life of a former dictator, the superhumans take on a very unusual role – as domestic staff at his home.

Before long, domestic duties give way to far more dangerous considerations.

El Caudillo George Murcell
Pedraza Patrick Magee
Carlos Stephen Berkoff

Director: John Moxey

The Ghost Plane

w Donald James

Asked to investigate the movements of Dr Newman, a man whose plans for a revolutionary new aircraft have been shelved, the Champions find themselves hot on the trail of a secret's broker.

Dr Newman Andrew Kerr
Coates Michael Wynne
Hardwick Tony Steedman

Director: John Gilling

The Dark Island

w Tony Williamson

When three agents fail to return from a tropical island, The Champions are sent to investigate. Richard lands by parachute, Sharron and Craig arrive posing as husband and wife. All three face instant danger.

Kellor Vladek Sheybal
Admiral Alan Gifford
Perango Benito Carruthers

Director: Cyril Frankel

The Fanatics

w Terry Nation

Assigned to infiltrate a group of fanatical assassins, Richard Barret joins the gang – and learns that Tremayne is to be their next victim. But can one man stop a determined group of killers – perhaps, when you're superhuman.

Croft Gerald Harper
Anderson Julian Glover
Colonel Banks Donald Pickering

Director: John Gilling

Twelve Hours

w Donald James

Having seen a visiting president safely aboard a waiting submarine, the Nemesis agents believe their troubles to be over. But an unknown assassination attempt waits around the corner, and they'll soon require their special powers.

Drobnic Henry Gilbert
Raven Mike Pratt
Admiral Peter Howell

Director: Paul Dickson

The Search

w Dennis Spooner

When an atomic submarine, loaded with four nuclear weapons, is stolen by a new Nazi regime, The Champions find themselves racing against time to thwart the enemy plans: the Nazi group threaten to hold London hostage under nuclear threat!

Kruger John Woodvine
Dr Mueller Joseph Furst
Schultz Reginald Marsh

Director: Leslie Norman

The Gilded Cage

w Philip Broadley

When intruders break into Nemesis headquarters and steal Richard Barrett's file, Tremayne is worried that someone will attempt to wipe out Nemesis agents. To investigate further, Barrett allows himself to be kidnapped by the thieves.

Symond John Carson
Samantha Jennie Linden
Lovegrove Clinton Greyn

Director: Cyril Frankel

Shadow of the Panther

w Tony Williamson

Is the death of a Nemesis doctor the result of voodoo magic – or something more easily explained? The Champions' investigations lead them into danger against a throbbing background of voodoo drums.

Prengo Zia Mohyeddin
Crayley Donald Sutherland
Charters Hedger Wallace

Director: Freddie Francis

A Case of Lemmings

w Philip Broadley

When several Interpol agents take their own lives, Nemesis agents Barrett, Sterling and Macready go to Italy to investigate. What they discover leads them to a daring plot to infiltrate the entire Interpol network.

Umberto John Bailey
Claudine Jeanne Roland
Del Marco Edward Brayshaw

Director: Paul Dickson

The Interrogation

w Dennis Spooner

Agents Barrett and Macready are worried that their partner hasn't returned after his latest mission. Sensing that he is in trouble, they seek Tremayne's help – but he appears unconcerned. Meanwhile, Craig is in deadly danger.

The Interrogator Colin Blakely

Director: Cyril Frankel

The Mission

w Donald James

Craig and Sharon pose as a Mafiosa gangster and his girlfriend in an attempt to infiltrate an organisation which provides escape routes for criminals, who have had their faces altered by plastic surgery. Sharron finds herself booked for a facelift!

Dr Pederson Anthony Bate
Hogan Dermot Kelly
George Harry Towb

Director: Robert Asher

The Silent Enemy

w Donald James

Assigned to reconstruct the voyage of a nuclear submarine which has been found with all its crew dead, The Champions find themselves on a macabre voyage – which results in terrifying consequences.

Captain Baxter Paul Maxwell
Admiral Parker Warren Stanhope
Minoes Marne Maitland

Director: Robert Asher

The Bodysnatchers

w Terry Nation

What hidden meaning is contained in a letter received from a journalist in Wales? The trio of Nemesis agents find themselves involved in a macabre espionage plot in their attempt to find out.

Squires Bernard Lee
Yeats Philip Locke
Inge Ann Lynn

Director: Paul Dickson

Get Me Out Of Here!

w Ralph Smart

Sent to a Caribbean island to rescue Anna Maria Martes, a world famous doctor being held against her will, The Champions need all their combined powers to stave off the unwanted attention they attract on their arrival.

Martes Frances Cuka
Commandante Ronald Radd
Angel Martes Philip Madoc

Director: Cyril Frankel

The Night People

w Donald James

Unaware that she is heading into danger, Sharron Macready travels to Cornwall for a few days' well-earned rest. After receiving a phone call from her, Craig Sterling and Richard Barrett go to join her – but find that she has disappeared.

Douglas Trennick Terence Alexander
Mrs Trennick Adrienne Corri
Porth David Lodge

Director: Robert Asher

Project Zero

w Tony Williamson

The murder of Travis, a scientist, culminates in a series of strange disappearances among people working on a top secret experiment. The Champions, masquerading as boffins, set out to solve the case – and end up in deadly danger.

Voss Rupert Davies
Antrobus Peter Copley
Grayson Reginald Jessup

Director: Don Sharp

Desert Journey

w Ian Stuart Black
Attempting to escort a reluctant Bey to his strife-torn North African state, the Nemesis agents face a dangerous journey through the desert – a place where danger lies hidden among the swirling sand dunes.
The Bey Jeremy Brett
Yussef Roger Delgado
Sheikh Peter Madden

Director: Paul Dickson

Full Circle

w Donald James
Craig Sterling poses as a prisoner to plug a clever escape route. He and a fellow inmate make good their freedom, but the Nemesis agent finds more than he bargained for at their journey's end.
Westerman Patrick Allen
Garcian Martin Benson
Sara Gabrielle Drake

Director: John Gilling

Nutcracker

w Philip Broadley
After attempts are made to break into a vault containing top secret NATO documents, The Champions are assigned to test if the vault really is impregnable. Their mission is a dangerous one – the vault's safety device is programmed to kill any intruder!
Duncan William Squire
Mauncey David Langton
Warre John Franklyn-Robbins

Director: Roy Ward Baker

The Final Countdown

w Gerald Kelsey
What at first appears a simple task to three people endowed with unusual powers – locating an unexploded bomb – culminates

in a mission fraught with danger for the Nemesis agents.
Kruger Derek Newark
Splitz Alan MacNaughton
Neinmann Wolf Frees

Director: John Gilling

The Gun-runners

w Dennis Spooner
Assigned to track down a gang of ruthless gun-runners, the Nemesis agents find themselves faced with intrigue and murder in a Burmese jungle. Their opponents will stop at nothing to prevent them, and their lives are in deadly peril.
Hartington William Franklyn
Selvameni Paul Stassino
Filmer David Lodge

Director: Robert Asher

Autokill

w Brian Clemens
The Champions find themselves facing an unbeatable enemy – themselves! Someone has programmed one of the team to kill his colleagues, and the Nemesis agents face danger from all sides as they try to discover their real enemy.
Barkar Eric Pohlmann
Klein Paul Eddington
Doctor Amis Harold Innocent

Director: Roy Ward Baker

THE CHAMPIONS
Created by: Monty Berman and Dennis Spooner
Producer: Monty Berman
Music by: Edwin Astley
(Theme tune by: Tony Hatch)
Script supervisor: Dennis Spooner
An ITC Production
Filmed on location and at Elstree Studios
30 colour 60-minute episodes
25 September 1968–30 April 1969
(USA: NBC 11 July–12 September 1967 Syndicated.)

CHARLES ENDELL ESQUIRE

Featuring the return of the streetwise spiv first introduced in the popular BUDGIE series. (See entry *BUDGIE*)

Released from prison after serving a seven-year sentence, the one-time Soho 'Mr Big' (motto 'London belongs to me'), returned to his old haunts intending to take up where he left off. But things had changed during his absence and he found himself a forgotten man. Undeterred, Endell decided to set up shop in his home town of Glasgow — and that's when his troubles really began!

A short-lived attempt to recapture the succesful format of the earlier series — but lightning didn't strike twice.

REGULAR CAST

Charlie Endell Iain Cuthbertson   *Dixie* Annie Ross   *Alastair Vint* Rikki Fulton
Hamish MacIntyre Jr Tony Osba   *Det Sgt Dickson* Phil McCall
Janet Julie Ann Fullarton   *Kate Moncrieff* Rohan McCullock

Glasgow Belongs to Me

w Robert Banks Stewart
Out of jail after a seven-year sentence, Charlie Endell returns to his old haunts in Soho. Having failed to impress the new breed of villain who has taken over his territory, he returns home to Glasgow, convinced that the city belongs to him. He's in for a big surprise . . .
Bowie Jonathan Carr
Archibald Telfer Bernard Archard
Fiona Croall Gillian Gillespie

Director: Gerry Mill
Designer: Pip Gardner

As One Door Closes, Another Slams in Your Face

w Bill Craig
Charlie begins his search for the mysterious Archibald Telfer — a man who owes him far more than he can repay. He finds an ally in Major Forbes-Forbes — and an old enemy in Kenny 'King' Croall.

Forbes-Forbes Bernard Gallagher
'King' Croall Bill Denniston
Fiona Croall Gillian Gillespie

Director: Gerry Mill
Designer: Peter Alexander

Slaughter on Piano Street

w Robert Banks Stewart
Sunday should be a day of peace, but Charlie is shaken from his slumbers by thundering rock music. Only Charlie Endell could espy a way of turning this to his own advantage — and other people's loss.
Logan Boyd Nelson
Davie Freddie Boardley
Prison officer Neil Connery

Director: David Andrews
Designer: Geoff Nixon

The Moon Shines Bright on Charlie Endell

w Terence Feely
Charlie, strong on organisational ability, spots a chance to make a few quid when an old friend tells him a story. It's amazing

what can develop from a few drinks in a local bar.

'King' Croall Bill Denniston
Fiona Croall Gillian Gillespie
Jack Leakey Russell Hunter

Director: David Andrews
Designer: Neil Parkinson

Stuff Me a Flamingo

w Alistair Bell

When underworld boss 'King' Croall has to go into prison for a few weeks, he puts his affairs in order and asks his 'friend' Charlie to look after his daughter Linda's welfare. A mistake!

Linda Croall Patricia Denys
Sammy McPhee Jimmy Logan
Det. Sgt. Sterling Alec Monteath

Director: Gerry Mill
Designer: Pip Gardner

If You Can't Join 'Em, Beat 'Em

w Robert Banks Stewart

For once, Charlie gets it right. Having decided that sport needs further development, he enters into the spirit of things – then sits back to watch the money roll in.

Sandy Murdoch Jack McKenzie
Geordie Donald McMaster
Carradine Patrick Newell

Director: David Andrews
Designer: Neil Parkinson

CHARLES ENDELL ESQUIRE
Devised by: Robert Banks Stewart
Producer: Rex Firkin
Executive producer: Bryan Izzard
A Scottish Television Production
6 colour 30-minute episodes
28 July – 1 September 1979

CHARLIE

A tightly-drawn, but overlong, one-off adventure in the career of private detective, Charlie Alexander.

Charlie's troubles began when he found his name in a dead man's address book – a man he'd never seen before! The discovery led the detective to investigate the man's past – and Alexander found himself investigating not just one, but several murders before the case was concluded.

A star-studded cast and an inventive script, did nothing to further Alexander's career – this was the detective's sole television outing.

CAST

Charlie Alexander David Warner   *Harry Ainsworth* Frank Windsor
Paul Tucker Michael Aldridge   *Ella Peace* Maggie Steed
Susan Alexander Marion Bailey   *Saul* Patrick Malahide
Dave Abbott Geoffrey Hutchings

CHARLIE
Written by: Nigel Williams
Producer: Graham Benson
Director: Martin Campbell
A Central Television Production
Transmitted in 4 colour 60-minute parts
26–28 March, 2–4 April 1984

CHARLIE MUFFIN

A splendid one-off made-for-television film which told how Charlie Muffin, a scruffy, middle-aged, 'over-the-hill' British agent, put one over on the entire British and Russian spy networks.

The story told how, having captured Alexei Berenkov, head of the Soviet spy network in Europe, the British Intelligence Service needed evidence to convict him. They decide to hand the investigation over to Charlie – a man despised by his fellow colleagues. The 'dimwit' duly walks away both with the evidence they require – and the million dollar exchange fee requested by KGB Chief Kalenin for his defection!

Wonderful stuff, that deserves to be aired time and again.

CAST

Charlie Muffin **David Hemmings** *Ruttgers* **Sam Wanamaker** *Edith* **Jennie Linden**
Sir Archibald **Ralph Richardson** *Berenkov* **Clive Revill** *Kalenin* **Pinkas Braun**
Wilcox **Frederick Treves**

CHARLIE MUFFIN
Written by: Keith Waterhouse
(From a novel by: Brian Freemantle)
Production: Ted Childs
Ex. Producer: Verity Lambert
Director: Jack Gold
A Euston Films Production
120 minutes – colour
11 December 1979

THE CHEATERS

A boring drama series revolving around John Hunter, a claims investigator for the Eastern Insurance Company. Dedicated to the task of defeating fraudulent claims and protecting genuine policy-holders' interests, Hunter came across as a kind of male 'Avon-calling' agent, ringing an endless succession of doorbells in his pursuit of the bad guys. Awful!

REGULAR CAST
John Hunter **John Ireland**   *Walter (his assistant)* **Robert Ayres**

THE CHEATERS
Producers: the Danzigers
Directors: Max Varnell, John Moxey
Godfrey Grayson, Frank Marshall
A Danziger Production
39 monochrome 30-minute episodes
10 December 1960 – 23 June 1962
(USA: Syndicated 1960)

CHESSGAME

Based on the novels by Anthony Price, this short-lived (but nevertheless excellent) series about a team of counter-intelligence security agents led by David Audley, of the Defence Intelligence Staff, was stirring stuff – but failed to attract viewers and ran only to one season. With excellent performances from Terence Stamp and Michael Culver, scripts from the prolific Murray Smith, and high production values, it's difficult to understand why.

REGULAR CAST
David Audley **Terence Stamp**   *Faith Steerforth* **Carmen Du Sautoy**
Nick Hannah **Michael Culver**   *High Roskill* **Robin Sachs**

Flying Blind

w Murray Smith
The wreckage of a plane, which crashed 27 years ago, is discovered when a lake is being drained and when the Russians show their interest David Audley receives a priority call to investigate the wreckage.
Nick Hannah **Michael Culver** (Intro.)
Faith **Carmen Du Sautoy** (Intro.)
Hugh Roskill **Robin Sachs** (Intro.)

Director: **William Brayne**
Designer: **James Weatherup**

Cold Wargame

w Murray Smith
What secret is held by the wrecked plane being investigated by Audley and his team?

The agent has discovered only one thing – the Russians are prepared to kill to keep their secret safe.
Sir Alec Russell **John Horsley**
Theo Friesler **Oscar Quitak**
Igor Panin **George Pravda**

Director: **William Brayne**
Designer: **James Weatherup**

Enter Hasan

w Murray Smith
While planting a listening device under the car of a senior Foreign Office official, one of David Audley's colleagues is killed when the booby-trapped car blows up.

Guy Llewellyn **John Rowe**
Theo Friesler **Oscar Quitak**
Mary Jenkins **Rosalie Crutchley**

Director: **Ken Grieve**
Designer: **Taff Batley**

The Alamut Ambush

w Murray Smith
A high-ranking Foreign Office official is
shot while attending the funeral of Audley's
technician. This angers Audley, who
suspects the enemy are behind the death of
his colleague and the latest shooting
incident.
Sir Alec Russell **John Horsley**
Jack Soutar **Paul McDowell**
Gilbert Jones **Tony Steedman**

Director: **Ken Grieve**
Designer: **Taff Batley**

The Roman Connection

w John Brason
Certain that a young student's death is the
start of a communist conspiracy, a
university professor seeks Audley's help.

Sir Geoffrey Hobson **Willoughby Gray**
Handforth Jones **Richard Pearson**
Charles Epton **Seymour Green**

Director: **Roger Tucker**
Designer: **James Weatherup**

Digging Up the Future

w John Brason
At the request of a university professor,
David Audley and his team of counter-
intelligence agents investigate the
backgrounds of two students — one of whom
has died in mysterious circumstances.
Richardson **Paul Jaynes**
Gopal Aziz **Art Malik**
Handforth Jones **Richard Pearson**

Director: **Roger Tucker**
Designer: **James Weatherup**

CHESSGAME
Producer: Richard Everitt
A Granada Television Network Production
6 colour 60-minute episodes
23 November – 28 December 1983

CHOCKY

Adapted from the books by John Wyndham, this children's
fantasy/science fiction series, portrayed the adventures of
Matthew Gore, a young schoolboy who formed a friendship with
a female alien lifeform named Chocky. Invisible to everyone but
Matthew (and then only when 'she' decided to make herself
visible to him — at which time she appeared as a swirling vortex
of mist), Chocky's presence in the boy's mind caused much
consternation to his parents, who believed the boy was 'talking
to himself' — until they, too, became enmeshed in their son's
strange adventures.

Originally intended as a one-off adventure, the series'
popularity led to two further stories being made, *Chocky's
Children* and *Chocky's Challenge* (See following entries.)

REGULAR CAST

Matthew **Andrew Ellams** *Mary (his mother)* **Carol Drinkwater**
David (his father) **James Hazeldine**

Chocky

w **Anthony Read** *(A 6-part story)*
Matthew, a 12-year-old schoolboy, suddenly
starts to talk to himself. At first his parents
think it is just a passing phase, but when
the boy begins to act strangely and his
mother finds strange drawings in his
bedroom, trouble lies ahead for the Gore
family – who are unaware that Matthew has
formed a friendship with a being from
another galaxy.
Colin **Devin Stanfield**
Mr Trimble **James Greene**
Polly **Zoe Hart**
Chocky's voice **Glynis Brooks**

Directors: **Chris Hodson and Vic Hughes**
Designer: **David Richens**

Chocky's Children

w **Anthony Read** *(a 6-part story)*
It is almost a year since Chocky said
goodbye to Matthew, and life returned to
normal in the Gore household. But further
troubles are in store when they find
mysterious men eavesdropping on their
telephone calls. Matthew is sent on holiday
to his Aunt Cissie, and the boy is somehow
drawn to a young girl, Albertine. When it
transpires that Chocky has returned and is
seeking their help, Matthew and Albertine
find themselves on the run from the police
and a sinister doctor named Deacon, who
wishes to know their secret – leaving the
way open for 'Chocky's children' (his friends
from all over the world) to come to their
rescue.
Deacon **Ed Bishop**
Aunt Cissie **Angela Galbraith**
Albertine **Anabel Worrell**
Chocky's voice **Glynis Brooks**

Directors: **Peter Duguid, Vic Hughes**
Designer: **David Richens**

Chocky's Challenge

w **Anthony Read** *(A 6-part story)*
Matthew and Albertine continue their
studies, and Chocky feels she can now tell
them about her plans to solve the earth's
energy problem. Under Chocky's
supervision, Albertine is to build the
world's first cosmic energy-collector, but she
will need some help, so Chocky brings in
four other children to help her build the
anti-gravity screens designed by her – but
can their work be kept secret? And who is
the mysterious Mrs Gibson, who wishes to
finance the project? When Mrs Gibson traps
the children inside the cosmic power-pack,
who is left to help them?
Professor Wade **Kristine Howarth**
Mrs Gibson **Joan Blackham**
Professor Ferris **Richard Wordsworth**
Chocky's voice **Glynis Brooks**

Director: **Bob Blagden**
Designer: **Peter Elliot**

CHOCKY
Producer: Vic Hughes
Executive producer: Pamela Lonsdale
9 January – 13 February 1984

CHOCKY'S CHILDREN
Producer: Vic Hughes
Executive producer: Pamela Lonsdale
7 January – 11 Febrary 1985

CHOCKY'S CHALLENGE
Producer: Richard Bates
Executive producer: Brian Walcroft
29 September – 16 October 1986
(Screened twice-weekly)
18 colour 30-minute episodes
A Thames Television Network Production
(All series)

COLONEL MARCH OF SCOTLAND YARD

Derived from the novels of John Dickson Carr, this 'murder in a locked room' mystery series – one of the first filmed series to appear on ITV – depicted cases of a bizarre nature investigated by Colonel March, a one-eyed chief investigator from Scotland Yard's Department of Queer Complaints. With a talent for solving the 'unsolvable', ('murders' committed by ghosts during a seance, 'supernatural' happenings at an Oxford college, murder in a tightly sealed compression chamber and, on one occasion, 'The Abominable Snowman') March was a character who should have made for compulsive viewing – but didn't . The plots were as thin as the cardboard-constructed sets, and its star was the series' only redeeming feature. (The programme was nevertheless hugely successful and became a big international money earner!)

REGULAR CAST

Colonel March **Boris Karloff**   *Inspector Ames* **Ewan Williams**

Passage of Arms
The Sorcerer
The Abominable Snowman
Present Tense
At Night All Cats Are Grey
The Invisible Knife
The Case of the Kidnapped
  Poodle
The Headless Hat
The Missing Link
The Second Mona Lisa
The Case of the Misguided
  Missal
Death in Inner Space

The Talking Head
The Deadly Gift
The Case of the Lively Ghost
The Devil Sells His Soul
Murder is Permanent
The Silent Vow
Death and the Other Monkey
Strange Event at Roman Fall
The Stolen Crime
The Silver Curtain
Error at Daybreak
Hot Money
The New Invisible Man
Death in the Dressing Room

(Two of the stories were edited together and released in cinema form in 1964 under the title *Colonel March Investigates*)

COLONEL MARCH OF SCOTLAND YARD
Producer: Hannah Weinstein
A Sapphire Films Production
26 monochrome 30-minute episodes
22 February 1956 – 11 April 1957

THE CORRIDOR PEOPLE

Described by its producer, Richard Everitt, as 'an eccentric surrealistic thriller', (the scenario took in 'The State', governed by a Head of Internal Security who kept an eye on everything – and everyone – and frequently became involved in the lives of the main characters), this series was populated by two of the most outlandish charcters ever to appear on television. Named Scrotty and Krock, both were 'cops' – but as different as chalk and cheese.

The former was a private detective who sat in his office between cases staring at a huge framed photograph of Humphrey Bogart mounted on the wall behind his desk. (Scrotty thought Bogart was the greatest and dubbed him 'founder of the firm'.) Krock, on the other hand, was the archetypal cigar-smoking, no-nonsense CID man with a passion for doing things by the book – though how he ever managed to achieve this when lumbered with two of the most dim-witted colleagues it had ever been the department's misfortune to employ, was a miracle in itself. (Oh yes, as you would expect, they too shared oddball names – Inspector Blood and Sergeant Hound!!)

The villainess of the piece, Syrie Van Epp, was a seductive international adventuress who'd set her sights on making life as hazardous as possible for her opponents. (She also had two offbeat helpers: a talking computer and Nonesuch – a dwarf.)

Sadly, although the series promised to be exhilarating viewing, it ended almost as soon as it began. (At the time there was a great deal of interest – particularly among fans of *The Avengers* – to see how Elizabeth Shepherd, the girl who barely twelve months earlier had been chosen for the part of Emma Peel – but lost the role to Diana Rigg – would shape up. This series gave them a glimpse of how she may have looked as the female Avenger: she wore lots of way-out provocative clothes – and looked devastating!)

REGULAR CAST

Phil Scrotty Gary Cockrell *Kronk* John Sharp *Syrie Van Epp* Elizabeth Shepherd
Insp. Blood Alan Curtis *Sgt Hound* William Maxwell *Nonesuch* William Trigger

Victim as Birdwatcher

w Edward Boyd

Christopher Vaughan, a millionaire and birdwatcher, holds the casting-vote share in a large cosmetic company which has developed a means to make a perfume which deprives people of their senses for 24 hours at a time. Villainess Syrie Van Epp wants the secret – so she kidnaps the millionaire. Vaughan's uncle, Sir Wilfred Templar, hires Scrotty to find his nephew, but things go wrong and Vaughan is sentenced to death.

Chris *Vaughan* Tim Barret
Sir Wilfred Clive Morton
Sullivan Windsor Davies

Director: David Boisseau

Victim as Whitebait

w Edward Boyd

When six bodies mysteriously disappear from their coffins, Syrie Van Epp holds the key. She is financing a scientist who can bring people back to life. The man manages to resurrect a man called Whitebait – but Scotty does a bit of double-dealing with the wife of the reborn man. This dents Syrie's plans, and costs Whitebait his life – for good, this time.
Whitebait Kevin Brennan
Abigail Whitebait Ingrid Hafner
Nonesuch William Trigger

Director: David Boisseau

Victim as Red

w Edward Boyd

Asked to find Colonel Lemming by one of his regular customers, Scotty discovers that he has been kidnapped by Syrie Van Epp. But why? Lemming was believed to have defected to the Communists seven years earlier and his life could be in danger if he has outlived their usefulness to them. Surely Syrie has no wish to mix it with the Russians – even for two million pounds!
Colonel Lemming John Woodnut
Beryl Kempsford Betty McDowell
Blinky Ivor Salter

Director: David Boisseau

Victim as Black

w Edward Boyd

Villains are black, heroes are white. So the story goes. But when Scotty is asked to trace the son of eccentric Queen Helen, monarch of a mythical country, and unearths a plot whereby Queen Helen's country would become a world centre for black domination, he finds himself asking who are the good guys, and who are the bad? And why has Pearl, a black girl, been eliminated?
Queen Helen Barbara Couper
Ferdinand Roger Hammond
Pearl Nina Baden-Semper

Director: David Boisseau

THE CORRIDOR PEOPLE
Created by Edward Boyd
Producer: Richard Everitt
A Granada Television Production
4 monochrome 60-minute episodes
26 August – 16 September 1966

THE COUNT OF MONTE CRISTO

Loosely (very!) based on the classic Alexandre Dumas adventure story, this low-budget swashbuckler retold how Edmund Dantes was falsely convicted of crimes against the state and sentenced to life imprisonment in the dreaded Château d'If. Having learned of the existence of a fabulous treasure from a dying prisoner, Dantes escaped to the island of Monte Cristo, found the lost treasure and spent the next 38 adventures prancing around in period costume like a fifth-rate Errol Flynn. Its star, George Dolenz (father of

'Monkee' Mickey) had more buckle than swash, while his co-star,
Nick Cravat, simply repeated the role he'd played in the cinema
release, *The Flame and the Arrow*.

REGULAR CAST

Edmund Dantes (The Count of Monte Cristo) George Dolenz
Jacopo Nick Cravat   *Rico* Robert Cawdron

The Affair of the Three
   Napoleons (aka The Plot)
The Pen and the Sword
The De Berry Affair
The Black Death
Affair of Honour
First Train to Paris
The Sardinia Affair
A Toy for the Infanta
Marseilles
The Talleyrand Affair
The Texas Affair
The Luxembourg Affair
The Mazzini Affair
The Carbonari
The Devil's Emissary
Bordeaux
Return to the Château D'If
The Golden Blade
Andorra
The Duel

Victor Hugo
Flight to Calais
Naples
Albania
The Act of Terror
The Experiment
Mecklenburg
The Portuguese Affair
Lichtenburg
Burgundy
Majorca
Monaco
Sicily
A Matter of Justice
Point Counter Point
The Island
Athens
The Barefoot Princess
The Grecian Gift (aka The
   Brothers)

(Eposides 1 to 8 and episodes 17 to 21 were
told in serialised format)

THE COUNT OF MONTE CRISTO
Producers: Sidney Marshall, Dennis Vance
Directors: Charles Bennett, Dennis Vance
David MacDonald, Sidney Salkow
An ITC Production
39 monochrome 30-minute episodes
5 March – 16 November 1956

COVER HER FACE

(An Adam Dalgliesh Adventure)
See: *Dalgliesh, Adam*

CRANE

An adventure series which revolved around Richard Crane, a successful city business man, who tired of the big city rat race and headed for the sun-drenched shores of Morocco. Investing his savings in a beachside café and a boat, Crane settled down to wait for excitement to happen – and it did, often. Having let it be known that his services were available for 'import–export' assignments, he soon found himself involved in minor smuggling activities (illicit cigarettes and liquor – no drugs) – a move which frequently brought him into conflict with the local Chief of Police, Colonel Mahmoud. Developing a healthy respect for each other, there were occasions when the two men set aside their differences to join forces against a common enemy – before retreating to their respective opposing positions when such situations had been resolved.

Crane obviously had to choose his friends carefully, and he only had one close friend – Orlando O'Connor, an ex-Foreign Legionnaire, who became his trusted confidant. Glamour was brought to the series in the shape of Halina, a young Arab girl Crane employed to run the bar in his café

Originally created to run for a one-season, 13 episode, mid-summer 'filler', the programme proved so popular that the series was extended to 26 shows, and extended again to 39. It also spawned a long-running children's adventure series. (See entry *Orlando*)

REGULAR CAST

Crane **Patrick Allen**   *Orlando* **Sam Kydd**   *Colonel Mahmoud* **Gerald Flood**
Halina **Laya Raki**

Season One
13 monochrome episodes

A Death of No Importance

w Terence Feely
Crane relentlessly hunts a killer through the streets of Casablanca. He has good reason to find the man: the murderer was responsible for killing Crane's friend.
Jennings **Michael Robbins**
Margot **Jennifer Brown**
Primo **Guy Deghy**

Director: **Raymond Menmuir**

Bad Company

w Eric Allan
Orlando's favourite saying 'Pick up a strange woman and you pick up trouble', becomes a terrifying reality when he and Crane offer a lift to a young hitch-hiker.
Sonia **Katharine Blake**
Albert Ringwood **Charles Tingwell**
Insp. Slimene **Desmond Jordan**

Director: **Peter Moffat**

The Canabi Syndicate

w Ludovic Peters
Crane and Colonel Mahmoud find themselves up against a murder-for-sale

syndicate – a mysterious organisation which threatens to end both their careers unless they strike first.
Austin Crispin Peter Reynolds
Osman Derek Benfield
Sharif David Grinham

Director: Richard Doubleday

My Deadly Friend

w Patrick Alexander
It appears that someone is overly anxious to have Crane arrested on false charges. Who is behind the threats? Determined to find out, Crane receives a nasty surprise.
Insp. Larki Bruce Montague
Gil Anthony Steele
Rosamaria Thalia Kouri

Director: Christopher Hodson

The Executioners

w James Brabazon and Patrick Alexander
When Crane and Orlando give assistance to a wounded man, being hunted in Casablanca, they find themselves facing a new and deadly threat to their careers.
David Alexander Davion
Dorfmann Warren Mitchell
Malachi Bryan Woolfe

Director: Christopher Hodson

Yesterday's Woman

w Bruno Christian
Someone is trying to murder the beautiful Madeleine. The plan is an ingenious one. So ingenious that Crane has his work cut out trying to find the culprit. But he must – before an innocent man is convicted of the crime.
Madeleine Madi Hedd
Latour Donald Morley
Sgt Fazil Rex Garner

Director: Geoffrey Hughes

The Price of Friendship

w Max Marquis
When Haufmann's boat docks at Casablanca, Mahmoud – and Crane – show

interest. Both are looking for a gang of thieves – one of whom could be a ruthless killer.
Haufmann Dermot Walsh
Jacqueline Sally Nesbitt
Roberts Desmond Newling

Director: Peter Moffat

Three Days To Die

w Max Marquis
Though all the evidence points to the man being guilty of murder, Crane believes otherwise, and sets out to prove the man's innocence. There's just one snag – he has only three days in which to do so.
Nikkolai Peter Bowles
Insp. Misrai Reginal Barratt
Maitre Zem Margot Vanderburgh

Director: Christopher Hodson

My Brother's Keeper

w Max Marquis
A callous murderer is hiding in Casablanca. Mahmoud, faced with the traditional loyalties to the Foreign Legion, is helpless to arrest him. The policeman seeks Crane's help.
Szabo Barry Keegan
Dr Ahbib Alec Mango
Priest Maitland Ross

Director: Richard Doubleday

The Unwanted

w Phylis and Robert White
When Crane decides to take in a homeless, hungry orphan, he has no idea of the trouble he will cause – or that he is placing the lives of himself and his friends in great danger.
Abba Peter Newton
Krasses Steve Plytas
Hamid John Hollis

Director: Geoffrey Hughes

Return of a Hero

w Alan Plater
Having rescued a man being pursued through the dark streets of Morocco, Crane

finds himself faced with an intriguing mystery – one which somehow includes a yellow rabbit.
Matthews Edgar Wreford
Mickey the Crook John Rumney
Colonel Arthur Hewlett

Director: Peter Moffat

The Golden Attraction

w David Canning
When a corpse is discovered in a newly-dug grave, Crane has his own reasons for not getting involved. But fate has a way of changing one's mind – and that's when his troubles begin.
Alison Harrington Jacqueline Ellis
Paul Harrington Alan Tilvern
Michael Harrington Peter Arne

Director: Richard Doubleday

A Case of Dolls

w Frank Harbourne
When Crane and Orlando discover a box floating in the sea, its contents bring many surprises – not all of them welcomed by the two men, who find themselves prey to a group of very nasty rogues.
Smith John Barnett
Dr Jackson George Coulouris
Chatterji Alec Mango

Director: Christopher Hodson

Season Two
13 monochrome episodes

The Death of Marie Vetier

w Patrick Tilley
A beautiful and desperate women brings murder and treachery into Crane's life. The smuggler learns the hard way just how dangerous such a combination can be.
Marie Patricia Haines
Goddard Peter Vaughan
Darius Gertan Klauber

Director: Richard Doubleday

Epitaph for a Fat Woman

w Max Marquis
When his friend's son fails to arrive home from school, Crane and Orlando follow a trail that leads to death and heartbreak for his group of friends.
Selina Ingrid Hafner
Pasquale William Marlowe
Gant Emrys James

Director: Christopher Hodson

Dead Reckoning

w Bruno Christian and Reed de Rouen
Despite his reservations to do so, Crane allows himself to become involved in getting a man out of prison – unfortunately for all concerned, the man is a very nasty piece of work – and Crane nearly gets killed in the attempt.
Wolsey Richard Vernon
Lung Colin Gordon
Liz Jan Waters

Director: Christopher Hodson

Picture of My Brother

w Max Marquis
Faced with bringing The Venza gang – a ruthless bunch of killers – to justice, Colonel Mahmoud seeks Crane's help, and all hell breaks lose on the Morocco streets.
Abdul Louis Rayner
Venza Bill Nagy
Jasmina Jennifer White

Director: Peter Moffatt

Two Rings for Danger

w Raymond Bowers
The brother of a murdered man becomes suspicious when he's told that Crane was the last person to see his brother alive. So does Colonel Mahmoud – and that spells trouble for Crane
Charles Dudley Foster
Petra Annette Andre
Alphonse Job Stewart

Director: Richard Doubleday

Death is a Black Camel

w Gerald Wilson

Mahmoud and Crane share an uneasy alliance. The policeman must solve a baffling case, and Crane is asked to keep a strange rendezvous – a meeting from which he may not return.

Salbierre Philip Latham
Vanel Ric Hutton
Corto Lee Richardson

Director: Ronald Marriott

The Secret Assassin

w Ludovic Peters

Crane is invited to the palace of Mouley Ahmed as his honoured guest. But the reception he gets gives him cause to doubt the true nature of his 'friend's' invitation.

Ahmed Cyril Luckham
Zuida Isobel Black
Muller Donald Bisset

Director: Peter Moffat

A Mouthful of Ashes

w Gerald Wilson

When Crane gives Orlando a ticket for the theatre, he has no idea that he is sending his friend into danger – or that he himself will become involved before the day is through.

Stark Anthony Newlands
Freda Lang Maxine Audley
Pirelli Arthur White

Director: Michael Currer-Briggs

Recoil

w Max Marquis

When the Contessa d'Avezzano invites Crane and Orlando to her villa, she has more than a dinner date on her mind. It's an invitation to murder – with Crane as the main course.

Contessa Patricia Kneale
Dr Stampini Paul Eddington
Fausto Richard Hurndall

Director: Christopher Hodson

Gypsy's Warning

w Alan Plater

When Philipe plans to take revenge on a police informer, a turn of the cards from Gypsy leads Crane into violence and murder – and the shadow of death looms dark over his friends.

Philipe John Woodvine
Gypsy Howard Goorney
Jacko Harold Innocent

Director: Richard Doubleday

Knife in the Dark

w Phylis and Robert White

Orlando is suspected of murder. That night he left Crane's café after a quarrel, and the following morning he was found on the beach with blood on his hands.

Arif Derek Sydney
Abdoul Michael Mellinger
Mokahl Zoe Zephyr

Director: Ian Fordyce

Murder Is Waiting

w Eric Allan

A killer lies hidden in Casablanca. The police are on his trail – and so is Crane who, after receiving a strange invitation, finds himself faced with mortal danger.

Sweeper Keith Anderson
Raswani Basil Dignam
Marcel David Andrews

Director: Richard Doubleday

Man without a Past

w Carl Nystron

Crane finds himself up against a group of thieves who have decided that the only way to stop Crane clearing an innocent man's name is to have him shot on sight!

Hugo Krantz Patrick Troughton
Michaud Alan Wheatley
Sgt Miraz Anthony Baird

Director: Peter Croft

Season Three

13 monochrome episodes

Death Is a Closed Door

w Max Marquis

Though he desperately wishes to do so, Crane cannot help when a friend seeks his aid on a mission of great importance which could save the life of a threatened man.
Shafik Sandor Eles
Zena Valerie Sarruf
Raya Camilla Hasse

Director: Christopher Hodson

T.N.T.

w Anthony Scott Veitch

In the hands of experts, dynamite holds few dangers. But in the hands of men determined to use the explosive for their own greedy ambitions, it can – and does – become a dangerous threat to Crane's life.
Steve Hanna Edwin Richfield
Lisa Martes Delphi Lawrence
Harvey Troop Barry Linehan

Director: Marc Miller

The Third Bullet

w Gerald Wilson

A telephone call from an unknown woman puts Crane in the firing line – and the assassin's bullet has his name on it. Can Mahmoud find the killer before Crane ceases to be a 'problem'?
Shaab Leonard Trolley
Major Culcao Felix Felton
Dr Salas Laurence Hardy

Director: Christopher Hodson

A Danger to Others

w Guy Morgan and Doreen Montgomery

When Julie Lamont disappears, Crane and Orlando are asked to find her, but their investigations lead them to believe that the girl has been abducted – and most likely murdered. Neither are ready for the surprises in store.

Julie Lamont Sally Home
Dr Knunsden Eric Pohlmann
Francine Diana Lambert

Director: James Ormerod

Death Walks Beside Me

w Gerald Wilson

When his old friend Johnnie comes to Crane for help, the smuggler believes his request is impossible. Or is it? Crane must decide one way or the other – Johnnie's life depends on it.
Johnnie John Bonney
Jericho Christopher Carlos
Perrichon John Cazabon

Director: Ian Fordyce

The Man With the Big Feet

w Ludovic Peters

When a local mystic called The Master relates a prophecy of death to Orlando, Crane must decide if his powers are real – or simply a cover for something far more mysterious.
The Master Bruno Barnabe
Lewis Campbell Singer
Mrs Lewis Vanda Godsell

Director: Christopher Hodson

In Trust Find Treason

w Max Marquis

When Colonel Mahmoud's reputation comes under threat, Crane finds himself coming to Mahmoud's defence – news that breaks Orlando's face into laughter. He soon has cause to regret his merriment.
Aldo Romitu Ivor Dean
Allegria Yolande Turner
Gadulla Robert Cartland

Director: Richard Doubleday

The Painted Lady

w Ludovic Peters

Crane's meeting with Louisa may have been chance, but what happens shortly afterwards is cold-blooded and deliberate – and Crane has cause to rue the day he met the girl.

Louisa Moira Redmond
Barjou Richard Carpenter
Otto Harvey Hall

Director: Richard Doubleday

Moving Target

w Gerald Wilson

When Colonel Mahmoud's life comes under threat from an old enemy – a military man out to seek revenge – Crane once again steps into the firing line in an attempt to save the policeman's life.
Major Seaford Scott Forbes
Hennessey-Bodley John Carson
Stella Ursula Howells

Director: Richard Doubleday

A Cargo of Cornflour

w Dennis Butler

Offered a job transporting a cargo of flour, Crane becomes suspicious when his employers refuse to allow him to inspect the cargo prior to shipment, and his crew (Orlando) goes missing.
Vincent Moro Peter Bowles
Carmena Edina Ronay
Flavio Mark Kingston

Director: Ian Fordyce

A Violent Animal

w Arthur Swinson

A new threat to Crane's existence arrives in Morocco – a man brought from the mainland to execute our hero. It appears that Crane's smuggling activities have made him enemies – one of whom wants him dead.

Peter Garvey Peter Dyneley
Achmet Michael Mellinger
Pirelli Arthur White

Director: Marc Miller

The Death of Karaloff

w Ludovic Peters

Colonel Mahmoud has a problem. He's been ordered to keep Karaloff, a known criminal and a sworn enemy of Mahmoud's, alive, but he's loath to do so – so the policeman seeks Crane's help.
Karaloff Denys Graham
Brigadier Harris Tony Steedman
Ames Robert Gillespie

Director: Marc Miller

The Man in the Gold Waistcoat

w James Mitchell

If it hadn't been for the waistcoat, Crane wouldn't have become involved in the death of a man found in the desert. He did become involved – and now he's running for his life from a band of men intent on killing him.
Franz Bauer Steve Plytas
Dr Hilfe Alan Wheatley
Sheik Gamal William Devlin

Director: Christopher Hodson

CRANE
Created by Patrick Alexander and
Jordan Lawrence
Producer: Jordan Lawrence
Designer for series: Henry Federer
An Associated Rediffusion Network Production
Filmed on location in Morocco
39 monochrome 60-minute episodes
2 April – 25 June 1963
13 January – 15 June 1964
26 October 1964 – 25 January 1965

CRIBB

Based on the books by crime writer Peter Lovesey, this series of Victorian detective dramas depicted the cases solved by Detective Sergeant Cribb of the newly-formed Criminal

Investigation Department. A dour, solid, tenacious policeman, Cribb stalked the streets of London in the 1880s in pursuit of crime. His methods were neither glamorous nor flashy. His sense of humour was dry and his manner dogged. Yet somehow he always got his man – or woman. He out-thought the best brains of Scotland Yard and – together with his faithful companion, Constable Thackeray (and impeded by his superior, Inspector Jowett) – he brought the ne'er-do-well to justice almost single handed.

A splendid series in every department, the production values established the twilight world of the period in well-documented form and Alan Dobie, as Cribb, made for an attractive (though pretentious) hero.

REGULAR CAST

Sergeant Cribb **Alan Dobie**   *Constable Thackeray* **William Simons**
Inspector Jowett **David Waller**

Season One

1 90-minute pilot story and
7 60-minute episodes

Waxwork

w Peter and Jacqueline Lovesey
What appears to be a perfectly straightforward case – the confession by a young wife that she has murdered her photographer husband's assistant because he was blackmailing her – takes a dramatic turn when someone sends anonymously a photograph to the Home Secretary which casts doubt on her confession. Sergeant Cribb is called in – and it isn't long before he has a new suspect for the murder.
Miriam Cromer Carol Royle
Governor Bernard Archard
Insp. Waterlow Gerald Sim
Howard Cromer Laurence Payne

Director: June Wyndham-Davies

Swing, Swing Together

Adapted by Brian Thompson
Jerome K. Jerome's book, *Three Men in a Boat*, has just been published and everyone is talking about it. But fiction becomes grim reality when Harriet Shaw, a young lady at St Elfrids's College, goes for a moonlight swim and becomes a witness to

murder. Cribb is called in to investigate the murder – which appears to have been committed by three men and a dog in a boat!
Harriet Shaw Heather Moray
Percy Bustard Ronald Lacey
John Fernandez Mark Burns

Director: June Wyndham-Davies
Designer: Alan Price

Abracadaver

Adapted by Brian Thompson
When someone starts playing malevolent and highly dangerous jokes on music hall artists – and the jokes end in murder – Sergeant Cribb is called in. He soon begins to see a pattern behind an unscrupulous conspiracy.
Mrs Body Patsy Rowlands
Ellen Blake Julia Chambers
Buckmaster Derek Tansley

Director: Oliver Horsburgh
Designer: Alan Price

The Detective Wore Silk Drawers

Adapted by Brian Thompson
When a headless body fished out of the Thames bears the marks of a prize-fighter, Cribb sends police constable Jago to investigate the sinister disappearance of

several bare-fist fighters – and that could spell death for Jago, if his identity is exposed.
PC Jago Barry Andrews
Robert D'Estin David Hargreaves
Edmund Vibart Mark Eden

Director: Brian Mills
Designer: Chris Wilkinson

The Horizontal Witness

w Peter and Jacqueline Lovesey
Thackeray, Cribb's trusted partner, has a painful and embarrassing complaint, but Jowett can't spare him from duty – until an underworld king is murdered and Vokins, believed to be a witness to the crime, ends up in Charing Cross Hospital. Suddenly Thackeray is granted sick leave.
Vokins James Coyle
Sister Armstrong Elizabeth Bennett
Hepplewhite John Ringham

Director: June Wyndham-Davies
Designer: Unknown

Wobble to Death

w Peter and Jacqueline Lovesey
Charlie Darrell is determined to do the 'Wobble', a six-day marathon walking race. Nothing else matters – but by the second day, he is dead. The press calls it tragic. His wife calls it unfair. Cribb calls it murder, and sets out to prove it.
Cast unknown

Director: George Spenton-Foster
Designer: Tim Farmer

Something Old, Something New

Adapted by Brian Thompson
Daphne, Denise and their mother have a nice little line in matrimony. The girls take it in turn to find and marry an old man and then give him a helping hand into a grave – courtesy of Mamma's soup, laced with poison. It's not long before Cribb arrives on the scene.
Daphne Sally Osborne
Denise Alison Glennie
Mother Charlotte Mitchell

Director: Oliver Horsburgh
Designer: Unknown

A Case of Spirits

w Peter and Jacqueline Lovesey
Ghostly dismembered hands floating in mid-air. Spirits conjured from the grave. All good fun – until the seance ends with murder and Cribb and Constable Thackeray discover that Dr Probert has been dabbling in the occult.
Dr Probert Clive Swift
Miss Crush Judy Cornwell
Prof Quayle Michael Barrington

Director: Oliver Horsburgh
Designer: Alan Price

Season Two
6 60-minute episodes

Mad Hatter's Holiday

Adapted by Bill Macilwraithe
Brighton is horrified by the gruesome discovery of a severed hand in the crocodile pit at Brighton aquarium. Cribb and Thackeray investigate the crime – and find themselves flirting with death in their hunt for a dangerous cold-blooded killer.
Zena Prothero Fennella Fielding
Dr Prothero Conrad Phillips
Albert Moscrop Derek Fowlds

Director: June Wyndham-Davies
Designer: Alan Price

The Last Trumpet

w Peter and Jacqueline Lovesey
When Barnum and Bailey's American circus buy Jumbo, London Zoo's biggest and most celebrated elephant, there are those who oppose the sale – and won't stop at murder to achieve their aims. Cribb is called in to stop any further killings.
Mrs Pennycook Joyce Carey
Abraham Bartlett Geoffrey Keen
William Newman Garrick Hagon

Director: Brian Mills
Designer: Alan Price

The Hand That Rocks the Cradle

w Peter and Jacqueline Lovesey
A vacancy arises for a nanny at the VIP household of Princess Beatrice, youngest

daughter of Queen Victoria, and Nurse Grant is appointed. When it becomes clear that the woman isn't all she seems to be, Sergeant Cribb is called in to investigate her past.
Mrs Innocent Rosalie Crutchley
Princess Beatrice Irene Richard
Queen Victoria Jessica Spencer

Director: George Spenton-Foster
Designer: Tim Farmer

The Choir That Wouldn't Sing

w Peter and Jacqueline Lovesey
When Colonel Dawson is found dead at the bottom of a village quarry, the whole village knows what happened, but nobody is prepared to say. Sergeant Cribb must take steps to find out the truth – but should they be legal or human ones?
Mrs Gurney Elizabeth Spriggs
Joshua Alan Downer
Mr Jessop Barry McGinn

Director: Mary McMurray
Designer: Chris Wilkinson

Murder Old Boy

w Peter and Jacqueline Lovesey
A weekend which begins with jollity ends in murder, and Sergeant Cribb finds himself involved in a murder hunt in which his superior, Inspector Jowett, is a prime suspect. Before he can arrest a murderer,

Cribb must break down the sinister forces at work at a reunion of former pupils of a public school.
Russell Haygarth John Carson
Headmaster Terence Edmond
Matron Petra Davies

Director: George Spenton-Foster
Designer: Stephen Fineren

Invitation to a Dynamite Party

Adapted by Arden Winch
Is there a spy in Scotland Yard? Cribb won't believe it, but Inspector Jowett can name names. In order to uncover the treacherous informer, Cribb must infiltrate a gang of desperate Irish patriots who are conspiring to blow up a battleship.
Devlin Charles Keating
Rossana McGee Jeananne Crowley
Colonel Martin James Taylor

Director: Alan Grint
Designer: Chris Wilkinson

CRIBB
Producer: June Wyndham-Davies
Executive producer: Peter Eckersley
A Granada Television Network Production
1 colour 90-minute pilot and 13 60-minute episodes
13 April – 25 May 1980
29 March – 10 May 1981

CRIME SHEET

Following on directly from MURDER BAG (see entry under that title), Detective Superintendent Lockhart (now promoted to Chief Detective Superintendent) continued his fight against crime – not just murder, but all types of crime.

Beyond his promotion, little had changed, and he relied as much as ever on his wits and powers of deduction to get the job done.

The series proved to be equally as popular as its predecessor, and barely five months later, the detective reappeared in a series of new hour-long stories that depicted his appointment to Scotland Yard. (See entry under *No Hiding Place*)

REGULAR CAST
Chief Det. Supt. Lockhart Raymond Francis

Lockhart Rings the Bell
Lockhart Follows a Line
Lockhart Plays Safe
The Superintendent Hedges a
  Bet
The Superintendent Draws a
  Double Blank
Lockhart Chooses a Weapon
Lockhart Fits a Uniform

Lockhart Finds a Watch
Lockhart Goes Backstage
Lockhart Visits a Pawnshop
Lockhart Sees a Chemist
Lockhart Visits a Laundry
Lockhart Keeps an Appointment
Lockhart Meets a Romeo
Lockhart Closes a Door

(One further story was produced. Called
'The Superintendent Takes a Trip', Lockhart
wasn't featured, and the star character,
Chief Supt. Carr, was played by actor
Gerald Case)

CRIME SHEET
Producer: Barry Baker
Directors: Roger Jenkins, Penny Wooton,
Geoffrey Hughes, Ian Fordyce, Daphne
Shadwell
Writers: Peter Ling, Peter Yeldham, Barry
Baker, William Hitchcock, John Whitney
and Geoffrey Belman (Based on stories by
Glyn Davies)
An Associated Rediffusion Network Production
17 monochrome 30-minute episodes
8 April – 9 September 1959

DALGLIESH, ADAM

Four investigations handled by Chief Superintendent Adam
Dalgliesh (Commander Dalgliesh in the final story) a Scotland
Yard murder expert. Based on the novels by P. D. James, these
zipped along at a cracking pace, but proved a little strong for
some viewers' taste (each story contained two, three – sometimes
more – violent murders). They were nevertheless first-class
television, and are guaranteed to become classics of the genre.

REGULAR CAST
Adam Dalgliesh Roy Marsden

Death of an Expert Witness

Dramatised by Robin Chapman
(A 7-part story)
Police pathologist, Henry Kerrison, is called to the scene of a young girl's brutal murder, being investigated by Scotland Yard sleuth, Adam Dalgliesh. With the murder unsolved, both return to headquarters – but are called back when a second murder takes place. Prime suspects, laboratory assistant Bradley and the alluring Domenica Haworth, have strong alibis, but novelist Stella Mawson is caught out in her lies by Dalgliesh. Within hours, the detective finds himself investigating a third murder and trying to unravel the killings against the closely-knit community background which hides a murderer in its midst; a killer who will strike again unless Dalgliesh exposes him – or her!
Kerriston Ray Brooks
Haworth Barry Foster
Clifford Bradley Andrew Ray
Domenica Haworth Meg Davies

Director: Herbert Wise
Designer: Leo Austin

Shroud for a Nightingale

Dramatised by Robin Chapman
(A 5-part story)
Worried by the sinister political implications of a murder case under his investigation, Dalgliesh visits a hospital to see the gravely ill Martin Dettinger. The man's evidence proves helpful, but the detective's enquiries at the hospital are brought to a standstill when another horrific murder takes place. The nursing staff try to continue their lives and work normally, but the sleuth's murder inquiries dig deep into their private lives. Nerves finally reach breaking point when two nurses are brutally murdered and the detective's informant, Dettinger, ends up dead. With his inquiries inexplicably linked to the dead man, Dalgliesh must find enough evidence to trap a clever and determined killer.

Courtney-Briggs Joss Ackland
Mavis Gearing Liz Fraser
Mary Taylor Sheila Allen
Delia Dettinger Margaret Whiting

Director: John Corrie
Designer: Jon Pusey

Cover Her Face

Dramatised by Robin Chapman
(A 6-part story)
What begins as a social outing for Sally Jupp leads to her becoming the key witness in a murder hunt, when she discovers the body of a former colleague in the basement of the Select Book Club. Treading dangerous ground where one detective has already been killed, Dalgliesh centres his investigation on the Maxie household – until another girl is murdered, and the detective determines to dig deeper into Miss Jupp's secretive background. When she, too, is murdered, and gossip points an accusing finger at Derek Pullen, Dalgliesh has his own list of suspects and wastes little time in bringing the murderer to justice.
Eleanor Maxie Phyllis Calvert
Felix Hurst Julian Glover
Sir Reynold Price Bill Fraser
Sally Jupp Kim Thompson

Director: John Davies
Designer: Jon Pusey

The Black Tower

Dramatised by William Humble
(A 6-part story)
A violent death at Toynton Grange and a request for help from its pious warden, Wilfred Anstey, leads Adam Dalgliesh to the farm – but he arrives too late to prevent another death. This stuns the community and Maggie Hewson in particular, but the detective is nothing if not discreet and continues his investigations into the tragic events – until a fire in the Black Tower and

further tragedy returns to the troubled community. Another murder takes place, and Dalgliesh makes a grisly discovery – which places his own life in danger. The final inquest fails to satisfy the detective, who believes he is close to a solution – providing his ruthless adversary allows him to live long enough to expose the guilty party.

Wilfred Anstey **Martin Jarvis**
Maggie Hewson **Pauline Collins**
Julius Court **Art Malik**
Grace Willison **Rachel Kempson**

Director: **Ronald Wilson**
Designer: **Spencer Chapman**

DALGLIESH, ADAM
Producer: John Rosenberg (throughout)
Death of an Expert Witness
7 colour 60-minute episodes
8 April – 20 May 1983
Shroud for a Nightingale
4 colour 60-minute and 1 colour 90-minute episodes
9 March – 6 April 1984
Cover Her Face
6 colour 60-minute episodes
17 February – 24 March 1985
The Black Tower
6 colour 60-minute episodes
8 November – 13 December 1985
An Anglia Television Network Production

DANGER MAN (I)

The exploits of John Drake, a special security operative for the North Atlantic Treaty Organisation (NATO), who went wherever duty called in his unending crusade to rid the world of subversive elements. Handsome, athletic, fearless, Drake frequently took risks to achieve his aim, but they were calculated risks in the cause of world peace. A man who detested any form of physical violence (yet faced danger every day of his life), he was often forced to fight his unscrupulous enemies with whatever means were available to him.

International in both outlook and setting, no two stories found Drake in the same location. One week he'd be in Paris, the next, Brazil. One week later he'd be trudging through dense African undergrowth; Drake went wherever his own particular brand of justice could be used to best effect.

The stories themselves provided more than their fair share of thrills, but always remained logical and realistic and never went 'over-the-top' or insulted the viewers' intelligence.

Fans of the series will no doubt recall the opening sequence that introduced the 30-minute stories: a tall figure emerged from a federal building in Washington DC, crossed to a sleek white sports car, threw his mackintosh into the rear seat and drove away at speed. Throughout this sequence a voice-over narration informed us that: 'Every government has its Secret Service branch. America, the CIA; France, the Deuxième Bureau and England, MI5. NATO also has its own. A messy job. That's when they call on me – or someone like me. Oh yes, my name is Drake, John Drake.' The best of its genre, the series made an international name of its star, Patrick McGoohan.

REGULAR CAST
John Drake Patrick McGoohan

Season One
39 monochrome 30-minute episodes

View from the Villa

w Brian Clemens and Ralph Smart
An American banker in Rome in charge of gold worth $5 million is found dead, and the gold – which represented part of America's NATO contribution – is missing. Drake investigates, but is hampered by the attentions of a woman who deals in murder.
Gina Scarlotti Barbara Shelley
Stella Delray Delphi Lawrence
Mayne John Lee

Director: Terry Bishop

Time to Kill

w Brian Clemens and Ian Stuart Black
Despite being handcuffed to a beautiful woman, Drake succeeds in his mission to capture a vicious international killer. But first he has to prove himself innocent of a murder charge!
Lisa Orin Sarah Lawson
Colonel Keller Lionel Murton
Hans Voegler Derren Nesbitt

Director: Ralph Smart

Josetta

w Ralph Smart
Drake is assigned to protect a blind girl who heard her brother being shot and can recognise the killer's voice. When the girl's evidence proves insufficient to convict the killer, Drake is forced into tricking him into admitting his guilt.
Juan Kenneth Haig
Josetta Julia Arnall
Colonel Segar Campbell Singer

Director: Michael Truman

The Blue Veil

w Don Inglis and Ralph Smart
Drake is sent to the Arabian desert where, posing as a hard-drinking deadbeat, he gains access to a mine and finds the evidence he needs to help a stranded showgirl return to England.
Spooner Laurence Naismith
Clare Lisa Gastoni
The Moukta Ferdy Mayne

Director: Charles Frend

The Lovers

w Jo Eisinger and Doreen Montgomery
Drake receives a surprise telephone call from an old enemy, Miguel Torres. He requests Drake to work with him to guard 'The Lovers', a president and his wife visiting England.
President Ewan Solon
Maria Maxine Audley
Torres Martin Miller

Director: Peter Graham Scott

The Girl in Pink Pyjamas

w Ian Stuart Black and Ralph Smart   (From a story by Brian Clemens)
When a beautiful girl, wearing pink pyjamas, is found wandering in a dazed condition along a lonely road in a Balkan state, it provides Drake with a clue to an attempted assassination plot.
Girl Angela Browne
Dr Keller John Crawford
Major Minos Alan Tilvern

Director: Peter Graham Scott

Position of Trust

w Jo Eisinger
Drake is assigned to track down and destroy a Middle East drug syndicate who are

supplying opium on a worldwide scale. He becomes as much involved in the human tragedy as he does in the syndicate members
Captain Aldrich Donald Pleasance
Sandi Lewis Lois Maxwell
Fawzi Martin Benson

Director: Ralph Smart

The Lonely Chair

w John Roddick and Ralph Smart
Called in to tackle a politically sensitive case, Drake takes the place of a wealthy crippled industrialist to crack down on a gang who are holding his daughter ransom in exchange for secret design plans.
Noelle Laurence Hazel Court
Patrick Laurence Sam Wanamaker
Brenner Patrick Troughton

Director: Charles Frend

The Sanctuary

w John Roddick and Ralph Smart
Suspecting that a terrorist, about to be released from prison, has similar work awaiting him, the authorities assign Drake to impersonate him. Travelling to a remote part of Scotland, he discovers that a bird sanctuary hides a sinister secret.
Crawford Kieron Moore
Kathy Wendy Williams
Anders Charles Farrell

Director: Charles Frend

An Affair of State

w Oscar Brodny
Drake flies to a small Caribbean island where an American economics expert is reported to have committed suicide. British Intelligence have their doubts about the claim, and Drake must discover the true cause of the man's death.
Ortiz Patrick Wymark
Alvarado John Le Mesurier
Santiago Warren Mitchell

Director: Peter Graham Scott

The Key

w Jack Whittingham (From a story by Ralph Smart)
Called in by the American ambassador in Vienna to investigate how confidential information is being passed from the Embassy, Drake's enquiries bring him into contact with a fellow agent, posing as a newspaper man.
Harry Logan Robert Flemyng
Maria Logan Monique Ahrens
Alex Charles Gray

Director: Seth Holt

The Sisters

w Jo Eisinger (From a story by Brian Clemens)
A beautiful girl flees to England to seek political asylum. Drake is assigned to vet her request – but when a second girl arrives also seeking asylum, and claiming to be the sister of the first, he begins to suspect their identities.
Nadia Mai Zetterling
Gerda Barbara Murray
Hardy Richard Wattis

Director: Seth Holt

The Prisoner

w Ralph Smart and Robert Stewart
An American citizen in the Caribbean is accused of espionage and takes refuge in the American Embassy, which he cannot leave for fear of being arrested. Drake is assigned to help – and does so with the aid of a classical pianist.
Carpenter/Schumak William Sylvester
Sue Carpenter June Thorburn
Colonel Vasco William Lucas

Director: Terry Bishop

The Traitor

w John Roddick
Drake must find out what makes a man a traitor. When an English agent and his wife suddenly flee the country and head for Kashmir, Drake follows a known foreign courier to their destination. But danger shadows his every move.

Noel Goddard Ronald Howard
Louise Goddard Barbara Shelley
Banarji Warren Mitchell

Director: Terry Bishop

Deadline

w Jo Eisinger (From a story by Ian Stuart Black)
When an unsolved murder gives rise to a wave of terrorism in an African country, Drake plunges into the jungle to find an attractive native woman who can tell him the truth about the murder.
Khano William Marshall
Thompson Edric Connor
Mai Branara Chilcott

Director: Peter Graham Scott

Colonel Rodriguez

w Ralph Smart
An American reporter is arrested for allegedly spying in a Caribbean country, and Drake is sent out as another journalist – but he too is arrested by a crooked police chief who tries to frame him for murder.
Colonel Rodriguez Noel Willman
Martine Maxine Audley
Joan Bernard Honor Blackman

Director: Julian Aymes

The Island

w Ralph Smart and Brian Clemens
Stranded on a remote island after a plane crash with three other survivors – a beautiful heiress and two contract hit-men whom Drake had been taking for trial – the agent needs all his ingenuity to stay alive.
Wilson Allan Cuthbertson
Jones Peter Stephen
Bobby Ann Firbank

Director: R. Pennington Richards

Find and Return

w Jo Eisinger
Drake has to find a woman wanted for espionage – and possibly high treason. It means a trip to the Middle East and certain danger – other agents are interested in the woman and are closing in fast.
Vanessa Moira Lister
Nikolides Warren Mitchell
Hardy Richard Wattis

Director: Seth Holt

The Girl Who Liked GIs

w Marc Brandel and Ralph Smart
Was the death of an American soldier in Munich an accident or murder? Posing as a GI, Drake visits the soldier's girlfriend and father, but he cannot find definite proof – until he discovers a photograph the dead man had left to be developed.
Vicki Anna Gaylor
Lotsbeyer Anthony Bushell
Doyle Paul Maxwell

Director: Michael Truman

Name, Date and Place

w Ralph Smart and John Roddick
When three state officials are all murdered in an identical way, Drake is assigned to discover who is behind their deaths. He uncovers a very beautiful murderess and commissions her to murder someone – himself!
Nash Cyril Raymond
Hardy Richard Wattis
Kim Russell Joan Marsh

Director: Charles Frend

Vacation

w Ralph Smart
On a vacation to the Riviera, Drake recognises a notorious professional assassin. He changes places with the killer in order to discover his intended victim, but once he has done so, he finds the victim isn't so innocent as she makes out.
Veronica Jacqueline Ellis
Georges Barrie Ingham
Gautier Laurence Davidson

Director: Patrick McGoohan

The Conspirators

w Ralph Smart and John Roddick
A British diplomat is murdered to prevent
him giving evidence at an inquiry into
maladministration in Africa. Drake is sent
to protect the man's wife but she refuses to
concede that she's in danger – until someone
tries to kill her.
Lady Lindsay Patricia Driscoll
Saunders Terence Longdon
Craven Alfred Burke

Director: Michael Truman

The Honeymooners

w Ralph Smart and Lewis Davidson
A Chinese businessman is found dead in the
hotel bedroom of an English couple
honeymooning on an island in the Far East,
and the husband is arrested for murder.
Drake must take desperate action to obtain
the man's release from prison.
Ted Baker Ronald Allen
Joan Baker Sally Bazely
Cross Lee Montague

Director: Charles Frend

The Gallows Tree

w Ralph Smart and Marc Brandel
A car stolen in the Scottish highlands bears
the fingerprints of the organiser of a spy
ring who was reported dead ten years
previously. Drake traces him to a remote
island and finds a quite unexpected surprise.
Laing Paul Maxwell
Joan Wendy Craig
'Jock' Finlay Currie

Director: Michael Truman

The Relaxed Informer

w Ralph Smart and Robert Stewart
To Drake, a drastic situation (top security
leak) calls for drastic action. So he carries
out an audacious hold-up in Bavaria. The
recording wire he steals from a courier leads
him into dangerous waters.
Brenner Duncan Lamont
Ruth Moira Redmond
Colonel Doyle Paul Maxwell

Director: Anthony Bushell

The Brothers

w Ralph Smart
When a plane crashes off the coast of Sicily
and its occupants are shot and robbed by
bandits, who make off with a diplomatic
pouch, Drake is assigned to retrieve the
secret documents – at any cost.
Police Commissioner George Colouris
Lita Lisa Gastoni
Giuseppe Ronald Fraser

Director: Charles Frend

The Journey Ends Halfway

w Ian Stuart Black
Drake becomes involved in oriental intrigue
when, in the guise of a Czech engineer, he
travels to China to investigate the
disappearance of an eminent doctor who had
been trying to escape from the Communist
regime.
Dr Bakalter Paul Daneman
McFadden Willoughby Goddard
Miss Lee Anna May Wong

Director: Clive Donner

Bury the Dead

w Ralph Smart (From a story by Brian
Clemens)
A ticket for the opera in Palermo, received
by Drake in Washington, whirls the agent
into a dangerous adventure in Sicily. The
ticket contains a coded message that a
NATO agent has been killed: Drake is to
take over the dead man's mission.
Jo Harris Beverly Garland
Hugo Delano Dermot Walsh
Police Captain Paul Stassino

Director: Clive Donner

Sabotage

w Michael Pertwee and Ian Stuart Black
When a transport plane on its way from
Singapore to New Guinea suddenly breaks
radio contact with its base, and an explosion
sends it to its doom, Drake, posing as a
hard-drinking pilot, flies out to investigate.
Peta Maggie Fitzgibbon
Giselle Yvonne Romain
Benson Alex Scott

Director: Peter Graham Scott

The Contessa

w John Roddick and Ralph Smart

Cocaine found hidden in the jacket of an injured longshoreman in the New York dock sends Drake on a hectic chase to Genoa to await the return of the man's ship. Posing as a down-at-heel dockhand, he discovers a huge drug-smuggling operation.

Francesca Hazel Court
Julio John Wyse
Keller Lionel Murton

Director: Terry Bishop

The Leak

w Ralph Smart and Brian Clemens

Drake is sent to North Africa to investigate the frequency with which employees at an atomic energy plant are being taken ill – apparently suffering from radiation. He discovers the source of the leak, but needs proof that it is sabotage.

Dr LeClair Zena Marshall
Dr Bryant Bernard Archard
Sheik Ahmed Marne Maitland

Director: Anthony Bushell

The Trap

w Ralph Smart and John Roddick

When a clerk in the cipher office of the American Embassy walks out of her job and flies to Venice, Drake must discover if she is a willing or unwilling dupe in a game of international spying activities.

Beth Jeanne Moody
Gino Noel Trevarthen
Carla Maria Burke

Director: R. Pennington Richards

The Actor

w Marc Brandel

A security information leak takes Drake to a Hong Kong broadcasting station as a member of a team transmitting English lessons. He discovers that a code is being used to pass secrets to the Chinese – but the discovery almost costs him his life.

Colonel Greaves Rupert Davies
Jason Gary Cockrell
Chen Tung Burt Kwouk

Director: Michael Truman

Hired Assassin

w Ralph Smart and John Roddick

Hearing that an attempt is to be made to assassinate a foreign president when he visits a South American country, Drake infiltrates the terrorist group – and is immediately assigned the task of leading the assassination attempt.

Alexis Alan Wheatley
Luis Cyril Shaps
Pepe Frank Thornton

Director: Charles Frend

The Deputy Coyannis Story

w Jo Eisinger

Funds sent to a mid-European country for rehabilitation purposes do not appear to be reaching those in need, so Drake is assigned to find out who has misappropriated the funds and to put a stop to their activities.

Coyannis John Philips
Zameda Charles Gray
Lorraine Zameda Heather Chasen

Director: Peter Graham Scott

Find and Destroy

w Ralph Smart and John Roddick

When a prototype intelligence submarine is wrecked off the coast of South America, Drake is assigned to blow up the vessel before anyone can examine the sophisticated equipment on board – but foreign agents are already on their way.

Major Hassler Peter Arne
Melina Nadja Regin
Gordon Peter Sallis

Director: Charles Frend

Under The Lake

w Jack Whittingham

A train journey to Vienna affords Drake the opportunity to form a friendship with an attractive young woman whose father he

believes to be behind a worldwide forgery syndicate.
Mitzi Moira Redmond
Gunther Klaus Christopher Rhodes
Colonel Keller Lionel Murton

Director: Seth Holt

The Nurse

w Ralph Smart and Brian Clemens
A dramatic meeting with a Scots nurse in the heart of an Arabian desert plunges Drake into a mission to save the son and heir of an Arabian king who has been assassinated.
Mary MacPherson Eileen Moore
Innkeeper Eric Pohlmann
Prior Jack MacGowran

Director: Peter Graham Scott

Dead Man Walks

w Ralph Smart and Brian Clemens
When all the members of a research team experimenting in tropical plant diseases are believed to have died in suspicious circumstances, Drake is sent to Kashmir where crops are being devastated by a new strain of virus.
Hardy Richard Wattis
Natalie Smith Julia Arnall
Keith Smith Richard Pearson

Director: Charles Frend

DANGER MAN (II)

Three years after the 30-minute series ceased production, John Drake reappeared in a new series of adventures. However, changes had been made. Each episode was now of 60-minutes duration. Whereas the previous series had found Drake assigned as special investigator to an undesignated NATO department based in an American government building, he now found himself a fully-fledged member of Her Majesty's Secret Service and assigned as a Special Security Agent to a London-based ministry department designated MI9. He also had a new boss and was seen receiving his assignments directly from a desk-bound 'M'-type superior. (In the former series Drake was seen receiving orders from government ministers of all nationalities.) Unchanged were the keynotes of each story: Drake was still a loner, and continued to enter each new adventure with as much zeal and determination to succeed as he had shown previously. Action and suspense were still the order of the day, and no expense was spared to inject each story with a liberal sprinkling of nailbiting suspense. (Highlights of each story were the further development of Drake's 'software gadgets': tiepins that served as cameras; cherries containing miniature microphones; electric shavers which doubled as a tape-recorder/transmitter – all were housed in the agent's gimmick-ridden attaché case.)

Regular Cast

John Drake **Patrick McGoohan**   *Hobbs (his superior)*   **Peter Madden**

Season Two
32 monochrome 60-minute episodes

Yesterday's enemies

w Donald Johnson
When a former British agent appears to
have set up his own network of double
agents in the Lebanon, Drake is assigned to
bring the man to heel. He must first
penetrate his opponent's control
headquarters – and that proves a dangerous
task.
Archer Howard Marion Crawford
Jo Dutton Maureen Connell
Attala Anton Rodgers

Director: Charles Crichton

The Professionals

w Wilfred Greatorex and Louis Marks
A British businessman disappears, and to
discover his whereabouts Drake is appointed
to the Embassy staff in Prague. Learning
from the man's wife that he had money
problems and had left her for the exotic Ira
Frankel, Drake sets out to find the woman –
when he does so, he discovers more than he
bargained for.
Ira Frankel Nadja Regin
Mrs Pearson Helen Cherry
Milos Kaldor Alex Scott

Director: Michael Truman

Colony Three

w Donald Johnson
Drake takes the place of a defector and
discovers a special camp in Europe, which is
a reconstruction of an English village known
as Hamden. His assignment leads him into
dangerous waters.
Randall Glyn Owen
Richardson Peter Arne
Hobbs Peter Madden

Director: Don Chaffey

The Galloping Major

w David Stone
After an unsuccessful assassination attempt
on the life of the Prime Minister of a newly
independent African state, Drake is sent out
to investigate the situation and to help
shape the man's destiny.
Prime Minister William Marshall
Colonel Nyboto Errol John
Kasawari Earl Cameron

Director: Peter Maxwell

Fair Exchange

w Wilfred Greatorex and Marc Brandel
A British agent, who was captured and
tortured in East Germany, discharges herself
from hospital and returns to kill the man
who tortured her. Drake, posing as her
husband, has his hands full when she refuses
to forget the past.
Lisa Leila Goldoni
Frantz George Mikell
Young James Maxwell

Director: Charles Crichton

Fish on the Hook

w John Roddick and Michael Pertwee
The name 'Fish' hides the identity of the
controller of the British agents in the
Middle East. When his identity is in danger
of being exposed, Drake is sent to bring the
man to safety – but he must first discover
'Fish's' identity.
Gerdi Dawn Addams
Nadia Zena Marshall
Gamal Peter Bowles

Director: Robert Day

The Colonel's Daughter

w David Weir
Drake goes to India to investigate a leakage
of military secrets. The Chief of Police
proves to be an old friend, and the two men
are soon involved in investigating a series of
suspicious deaths.

Joanna Virginia Maskell
Colonel Blakeley Michael Trubshawe
Chopra Warren Mitchell

Director: Philip Leacock

Battle of the Cameras

w Philip Broadley

Secret documents which could be used in chemical warfare have been stolen and Drake traces them to a millionaire industrialist living in a heavily guarded villa. But all is not what it at first appears.
Martine Dawn Addams
Kent Niall MacGinnis
Hobbs Peter Madden

Director: Don Chaffey

No Marks for Servility

w Ralph Smart

Drake poses as a manservant to investigate a man suspected of being a big-time swindler. His 'master' is an arrogant and ill-mannered oaf and the open hostility between them makes life difficult for Drake.
Armstrong Mervyn Johns
Judy Francesca Annis
Hobbs Peter Madden

Director: Don Chaffey

A Man to be Trusted

w Raymond Bowers

Sent to Haiti to discover if two MI9 agents talked under torture – and subsequently death – Drake is suspicious that one of the local contacts he has been given is a traitor – but which one?
Lievens Harvey Ashby
Anne Patricia Donahue
Joanne Eunice Gayson

Director: Peter Maxwell

Don't Nail Him Yet

w Philip Broadley

Drake dons the disguise of a teacher in order to investigate claims that agent Rawson is handing over naval secrets. Wanting to trap the organisation behind Rawson, Drake plays a waiting game and follows him.

Rawson John Fraser
Diana Sheila Allen
Lucas Anthony Dawson

Director: Michael Truman

A Date with Doris

w Philip Broadley

When a British agent is framed for the murder of an actress, and the frame-up appears to be part of a revolution attempt, Drake travels to the Caribbean with orders to bring the man to safety.
Doris Jane Merrow
Euseff Eric Pohlmann
Richter Ronald Radd

Director: Quentin Lawrence

That's Two of Us Sorry

w Jan Read

When fingerprints are found on a briefcase from which valuable documents have been stolen, Drake finds himself in Scotland searching for a man believed dead for 20 years – and ducking the amorous advances of a beautiful girl.
Sheila Francesca Annis
Landlord Finlay Currie
Sutherland Nigel Greene

Director: Quentin Lawrence

Such Men Are Dangerous

w Ralph Smart

Drake masquerades as an ex-prisoner to penetrate an organisation that recruits and trains potential terrorists to eliminate political leaders. His first mission brings him into contact with deadly danger.
Major Latour Lee Montague
Shorty Pratt Jack MacGowran
Hobbs Peter Madden

Director: Don Chaffey

Whatever Happened to George Foster?

w David Stone

A wealthy British industrialist is involved in a plot to overthrow a Latin American government. Drake draws the matter to the attention of his superior – but is promptly told to forget about it!

Lord Ammanford Bernard Lee
Pauline Adrienne Corri
Certhia Jill Medford

Director: Don Chaffey

A Room in the Basement

w Ralph Smart

When the British Government finds its hands tied by diplomatic red tape, Drake gathers together a group of mercenaries to rescue a colleague being held prisoner in an Embassy building in Switzerland.

Bernard William Lucas
Embassy official Michael Gwynn
Susan Jane Merrow

Director: Don Chaffey

The Affair at Castelevara

w James Foster

When a defeated ex-leader returns to his country after a revolution, and is sentenced to death, Drake joins forces with an American agent on a mission to rescue him. But they must first defeat the threat of General Ventura.

Bisbal Eric Pohlmann
General Ventura Martin Benson
Sir Duncan Andre Morell

Director: Quentin Lawrence

The Ubiquitous Mr Lovegrove

w David Stone

A Treasury official accuses Drake of running up high gambling debts (a security risk for any agent); Drake denies the charge and visits the casino – where he is greeted as a long-standing client!

Mr Lovegrove Eric Barker
Mr Alexander Francis de Wolff
Elaine Adrienne Corri

Director: Don Chaffey

It's Up to the Lady

w Philip Broadley

When a British Government official defects and shortly afterwards his wife leaves the country, Drake follows her to Greece to persuade her husband to return. But where should a wife's loyalty lie when her husband is accused of being a traitor?

Paula Sylvia Syms
Charles Robert Urquhart
Hobbs Peter Madden

Director: Michael Truman

Have a Glass of Wine

w David Stone

A government employee photographs secret papers and then takes a 'holiday' in France with the documents in her luggage. Drake is assigned to follow her and discover her contacts – a trail which leads him to a French château.

Suzanne Ann Lynn
Lamaze Warren Mitchell
Police Chief George Benson

Director: Peter Maxwell

The Mirror's New

w Philip Broadley

Drake finds Paris far from gay when he is asked to investigate the disappearance of a British Embassy official. When Drake finds him, he claims to have amnesia and no memory of past events – but Drake thinks otherwise.

Bierce Donald Houston
Penny Wanda Ventham
Nikki Nicola Pagett

Director: Michael Truman

Parallel Lines Sometimes Meet

w Malcolm Hulke

When a couple employed at a top secret weapons research station are kidnapped while on holiday in Devon, Drake finds himself teamed with a beautiful Russian agent who has been assigned to the case.

Nicola Tarasova Moira Redmond
Dessiles Errol John
Darcy Earl Cameron

Director: Don Chaffey

You're Not in Any Trouble, Are You?

w Philip Broadley

In order to infiltrate a murder organisation and expose its leaders, Drake commissions a murder – his own! But matters are complicated when he befriends a young girl holidaying in Rome.

Sally Susan Hampshire
Peterson John Cazabon
Fredericks Bill Edwards

Director: Don Chaffey

The Black Book

w Philip Broadley

The brother of a high-ranking official at the British Embassy in Paris is being blackmailed and Drake is sent to discover why and by whom. His French contact is an unusual one – a husky-voiced girl on the telephone.

Simone Georgina Ward
Sir Noel Blanchard Griffith Jones
Serge Mike Pratt

Director: Michael Truman

A Very Dangerous Game

w Ralph Smart and David Stone

Posing as a defector in order to infiltrate a spy ring in Singapore, Drake is approached by the Chinese who want him to spy on British Intelligence! Faced with exposure, he offers to do so.

Lisa Lee Yvonne Furneaux
Chi Ling Peter Arne
Khim Burt Kwouk

Director: Don Chaffey

Sting in the Tail

w Philip Broadley

Drake takes a calculated risk in provoking the jealousy of Noureddine, a political assassin wanted by the Paris police, as a means of getting the man to leave the safety of Beirut.

Noureddine Derren Nesbitt
Alexandros Ronald Radd
James John Standing

Director: Peter Yates

English Lady Takes Lodgers

w David Stone

Drake heads for Lisbon to trace an agency suspected of exchanging stolen secrets – some of them British. He turns up a dead agent, and a landlady with a convenient sideline in forged passports.

Emma Gabriella Licudi
Pilkington RRobert Urquhart
Collinson Howard Marion Crawford

Director: Michael Truman

Loyalty Always Pays

w David Stone

The last message a British agent made before his sudden death confirms MI9's suspicions that the Chinese are about to gain a foothold in an African country in which Britain has financial interests. Drake is sent to Africa to discredit the Chinese and restore the status quo.

Beyla Johnny Sekka
Enugu Errol John
Prime Minister Earl Cameron

Director: Peter Yates

The Mercenaries

w Ralph Smart

When an MI9 agent is murdered while investigating the activities of a mercenary army in Africa, Drake is sent to complete his murdered colleague's assignment – and uncovers a plot to dispose of an African premier.

Prime Minister John Slater
Caroline Winter Patricia Donahue
Sgt. Bates Percy Herbert

Director: Don Chaffey

Judgement Day

w Donald Johnson (From a story by Michael Bird)

Sent to the Middle East to bring back a German scientist accused of having committed atrocities against prisoners of war, Drake finds himself acting as defending counsel in a bid to save the man's life.

Jessica Alexandra Stewart
Shimmon John Woodvine
Pilot Maurice Kaufmann

Director: Don Chaffey

The Outcast

w Donald Johnson
Assigned to investigate whether there is any
connection between the murder of a Wren
illegally found in possession of secret papers
and the disappearance of her boyfriend,
Drake finds himself pursuing a suspect to
Spain.
Leo Perrins Bernard Bresslaw
Nora Caslett Patricia Haines
Xavier Brian Worth

Director: Michael Truman

Are You Going to Be More Permanent?

w Philip Broadley
Which of three agents stationed in
Switzerland is a traitor? Drake must
discover the answer before any further MI9
agents are murdered. His plan involves
putting himself in the firing line – a move
which could cost him his life.
Kronenberger Maxwell Shaw
Laclos Howard Goorney
Lesley Arden Susan Hampshire

Director: Don Chaffey

Season Three
13 monochrome 60-minute episodes

To Our Best Friend

w Ralph Smart
Drake is reluctant to investigate MI9's
allegations that a fellow agent and close
personal friend is a traitor; nevertheless he
does so – and finds himself faced with a
dilemma between personal loyalties and
duty.
Bill Vincent Donald Houston
Leslie Vincent Ann Bell
Ivan T. P. McKenna

Director: Patrick McGoohan

The Man on the Beach

w Philip Broadley
Drake's mission to identify a double agent
in the MI9 network operating from a luxury
hotel in Jamaica leads to difficulties when he
finds himself being accused of being in the
pay of the enemy.
Angelica Barbara Steele
Davies Glyn Houston
Smith Peter Hughes

Director: Peter Yates

Say It With Flowers

w Ralph Smart and Jacques Gilles
When money is drawn from the account of a
man reported to have died at an exclusive
clinic in Switzerland, Drake investigates and
finds that the establishment is a cover for
selling secret information.
Wallace/Hagen Ian Hendry
Dr Brajanska John Phillips
Caroline Jemma Hyde

Director: Peter Yates

The Man Who Wouldn't Talk

w Donald Johnson and Ralph Smart
When an MI9 agent operating in Europe is
captured, Drake is assigned to ensure that
the man doesn't reveal the names of his
colleagues under torture. But other people
are interested in the man – and Drake, as
usual, finds trouble.
Meredith Norman Rodway
Lynda Jane Merrow
Interrogator Ralph Michael

Director: Michael Truman

Someone Is Liable to Get Hurt

w Philip Broadley and Ralph Smart
Drake is on a double mission: he's to
investigate reports that a Caribbean
country's pending election is threatened by
an illegal arms deal, and he must solve the
mystery of an agent's disappearance.
Volos Maurice Denham
Dr Sawari Zia Mohyeddin
Magda Geraldine Moffatt

Director: Michael Truman

Dangerous Secret

w Ralph Smart and Donald Johnson

A leading scientist has disappeared, taking with him the secret of a lethal mutant virus. Drake traces him to France where another scientist, a woman, has promised him work of a peaceful nature.

Louise Carron Elizabeth Shepherd
Colin Ashley Lyndon Brook
Fenton Derek Francis

Director: Stuart Burge

I Can Only Offer You Sherry

w Ralph Smart

When a young girl, Jean Smith, is suspected of leaking security secrets from her embassy in the Middle East, Drake, posing as a visiting journalist, is sent to find out what's behind her motives.

Jean Smith Wendy Craig
Ma'Suud Anthony Newlands
Nubar Bernard Archard

Director: George Pollock

The Hunting Party

w Philip Broadley

When a wealthy landowner is suspected of leaking confidential information to foreign newspapers, Drake becomes his butler to investigate the leak. He soon finds himself the human prey in a deadly hunt.

Basil Jordan Denholm Elliot
Claudia Jordan Moira Lister
Max Dell Edward Underdown

Director: Pat Jackson

Two Birds with One Bullet

w Jesse Lasky Jr and Pat Silver

Having discovered that one of the parties in a forthcoming election plans to murder their own candidate and lay the blame at Britain's door, Drake is sent to the Caribbean to prevent the killing.

Commissioner Winlow Geoffrey Keen
Pilar Lin Leila Goldoni
Dr Shargis Paul Curran

Director: Peter Yates

I'm Afraid You Have the Wrong Number

w Ralph Smart

Convinced that the betrayal of an organiser of one of MI9's networks in Switzerland could only have been accomplished by one of his own agents, Drake plays a deadly game of Russian roulette to discover the traitor.

Captain Schulman Paul Eddington
Leanka Jeanne Moody
Leontine Guy Deghy

Director: George Pollock

The Man with the Foot

w Raymond Bowers

When a freelance agent discovers his identity, Drake is ordered take a holiday. But even in an isolated Spanish hotel he cannot shake off his pursuers – until he devises a clever scheme to 'disappear'.

Monckton Robert Urquhart
Derringham Bernard Lee
Maruja Isobel Black

Director: Jeremy Summers

The Paper Chase

w Philip Broadley and Ralph Smart

When a briefcase containing confidential papers is stolen from a friend, Drake is asked to recover them. Following their trail leads the agent into acute danger in Rome.

Nandina Joan Greenwood
Eddie Gelb Kenneth J. Warren
Tamasio Aubrey Morris

Director: Patrick McGoohan

Not So Jolly Roger

w Tony Williamson

Drake is assigned to investigate the seaborne pirate radio station, Radio Jolly Roger, which is suspected of transmitting coded messages to Europe. When Andrews, an MI9 contact there, dies mysteriously, Drake takes his place in the guise of a disc jockey.

Marco Janson Edwin Richfield
Susan Wade Patsy Ann Noble
Corrigan Wilfred Lawson

Director: Don Chaffey

Season Four

2 colour 60-minute episodes

Koroshi

w Norman Hudis

An MI9 Japanese girl agent meets sudden death while transmitting a message from Tokyo, warning that a leading United Nations' mediator will be assassinated within hours of his arrival in New York. Drake is assigned to ensure the man's safety, and to discover how the girl's identity was blown.

Richards Kenneth Griffith
Ako Yoko Tani
Sanders Ronald Howard

Director: Michael Truman

Shinda Shima

w Norman Hudis

Assigned to take the place of an electronics expert arrested by Japanese customs men for being in possession of secret circuit designs, Drake follows a trail to Shinda Shima ('the murdered island') and finds himself up against a Japanese murder brotherhood.

Miho Yoko Tani
Pauline Maxine Audley
Controller George Coulouris

Director: Peter Yates

DANGER MAN
Series devised by: Ralph Smart

Season One
Producer: Ralph Smart
Associate producer: Aida Young
Music by: Edwin Astley
Distributed by ITC
Filmed at MGM Studios, Boreham Wood
39 monochrome 30-minute episodes
11 September 1960 – 13 January 1962
(USA: CBS 5 April – 14 September 1961 Syndicated)

Season Two
Producers: Aida Young, Sidney Cole
Executive producer: Ralph Smart
Music by: Edwin Astley
Script editor: Wilfred Greatorex
Distributed by ITC
Filmed at MGM Studios, Boreham Wood
32 monochrome 60-minute episodes
13 October 1964 – 26 November 1965

Season Three
Producer: Sidney Cole
Executive producer: Ralph Smart
Associate producer: Barry Delmaine
Music by: Edwin Astley
Script editor: Wilfred Greatorex
Distributed by ITC
Filmed at Shepperton Studios
13 monochrome 60-minute episodes
3 December 1965 – 7 April 1966

Season Four
Producer: Sidney Cole
Executive producer: Ralph Smart
Associate producer: Barry Delmaine
Music by: Edwin Astley
Script editor: George Markstein
Distributed by ITC
Filmed at Shepperton Studios
2 colour 60-minute episodes
5 and 12 June 1968

(USA: CBS 4 April – 11 September 1965
4 December 1965 – 10 September 1966
Syndicated under the title SECRET
AGENT)

(Author's note: KOROSHI and SHINDA SHIMA – shot as a project fourth series, were the only two stories made in colour. These were subsequently edited together (in reverse order, and with an added 'linking' sequence) and shown in the USA in 1968 as a full-length TV movie entitled *Koroshi*.)

DANGEROUS DAVIES
THE LAST DETECTIVE

Based on the Leslie Thomas book of the same name, this one-shot TV movie presented the story of Detective Constable Davies, a bumbling, out-of-touch copper who was a danger to everyone – except criminals. Frowned on by his superiors for his inept handling of previous investigations, he was dubbed 'the last detective' because whenever his division had a crime to solve Davies was the last man they were likely to call in – and only then as a last resort

The story concerned the events surrounding the detective's decision to reopen a 15-year-old unsolved murder.

As the title would suggest, this was played mainly for laughs. Though enjoyable, at 120 minutes duration, the mirth was thinly scattered.

REGULAR CAST

'Dangerous' Davies **Bernard Cribbins** *Chf Insp. Yardbird* **Joss Ackland**
Mod Lewis **Bill Maynard** *Sgt Ben* **Bernard Lee** *Fred Fennell* **Frank Windsor**
Ena Lind **Maureen Lipman** *Dave Boot* **John Leyton**

DANGEROUS DAVIES
THE LAST DETECTIVE
Producer: Greg Smith
Writer: Leslie Thomas
Director: Val Guest
An ATV Network Production
120 minutes colour
4 January 1981

DEAD RINGER AND DEATH
CALL

(Two Chief Inspector Jim Taggart adventures.)
See: *Taggart*

DEATH OF AN EXPERT WITNESS

(An Adam Dalgliesh Adventure)
See: *Dalgliesh, Adam*

DEMPSEY AND MAKEPEACE

A crash-bang-wallop, all action series that depicted the exploits of two undercover crimebusters, Lieutenant James Dempsey and Detective Sergeant Harriet Makepeace. The pilot episode set the format for the rest of the series: Dempsey, a tough, streetwise American cop from Manhattan's 9th Precinct ('the toughest precinct of all') found himself seconded to an elite British police undercover unit, SI (Special Intelligence) 10. He had shot dead his partner following a corruption scandal involving fellow police officers and the NYPD wanted him out of the way to allay reprisals. Teamed with a beautiful, but fiercely independent, policewoman, DS Harriet Makepeace, Dempsey — a man for whom actions invariably spoke louder than words (he carried a .357 Magnum to emphasise his claim) — found British police methods slow and irritating. A man used to getting his own way, he took an instant dislike to his plummy-voiced partner. To Makepeace, who constantly objected to the brash way the American went about his business and to the sometimes dubious methods he employed, the feeling was mutual. Ambitious and sharp-tongued, she didn't suffer fools gladly — particularly her new partner, whom she saw as an unnecessary delay in the progress of her career.

As time passed, their mutual antagonism gave way to an attraction that neither could ignore — an attraction that bordered on the side of romance though Makepeace, a sharp-witted woman with a heart of steel and a temper to match, would never have admitted to her emotions.

Trying to control the pair — and in particular, Dempsey, who flatly refused to 'hang up his gun' — was the head concho of SI10, Chief Superintendent Gordon Spikings, a tough Liverpudlian who had risen through the ranks to become a powerful figure of authority in the force. While resenting Dempsey's attitude, he nevertheless recognised a good copper, even if he was a 'Yank', and realised that he had a good team — although his 'boys' were far from happy with the partnership!

Rounding off the team was Detective Sergeant Chas Jarvis. Appearing on a semi-regular basis, his role was that of the unit's messenger boy (a sad piece of casting – Tony Osoba, a talented actor, deserved better).

Thereafter, the series was mayhem all the way. Fights, fisticuffs, daredevil stunts in bountiful number – you name it, the show had it. The plots were sometimes wafer-thin (a situation that improved as the series progressed) but this was more than offset by the overall format. A winner!

REGULAR CAST

Lieutenant James Dempsey Michael Brandon
Sergeant Harriet Makepeace Glynis Barber
Chf Supt Spikings Ray Smith   *Sergeant Chas Jarvis* Tony Osoba
Det Sgt Watson (3 stories in Season Two) Colin McFarlane

Season One

1 105-minute pilot story and 9 60-minute episodes

Armed and Extremely Dangerous

w Ranald Graham   *(Pilot Story)*
Transferred to London following a corruption scandal, Lieutenant James Dempsey, late of the NYPD, finds himself assigned to a crack police undercover unit, SI10 and 'on the beat' with glamorous surveillance expert, 'Harry' Makepeace. It isn't long before they find themselves involved with a plot to smuggle caviar – and Russian missile warheads!
Commander Duffield Terence Alexander
Lord Winfield Ralph Michael
Jo David Baxt

Director: Tony Wharmby
Designers: Colin Monk and Gordon Melhuish

The Squeeze

w Jesse Carr-Martindale
When a security van carrying half a million pounds is hijacked, Dempsey and Makepeace are detailed to investigate. The partnership almost meets an abrupt end when they find themselves trapped inside a car-wrecking plant.

Reynolds John Moreno
Charlie Colin Edwynn
Terry Jonathan Stratt

Director: Tony Wharmby
Designers: Colin Monk and Gordon Melhuish

Lucky Streak

w Dave Humphries
Involved in a search for a girl who wears a rare antique necklace, Dempsey and Makepeace find themselves facing a group of unscrupulous men who will kill to prevent anyone discovering their secret.
Prince Razul Raymond Brody
Crane Peter Cleall
Roz Genevieve Allenbury

Director: Tony Whamby
Designer: Mike Oxley

Given to Acts of Violence

w Jonathan Hales
London gangster Frank Egan plans to commit the perfect crime – but he has reckoned without the involvement of detectives Dempsey and Makepeace. The former falls out of a plane without a parachute, while 'Harry' has to land a plane by radio!

Frank Egan Brian Croucher
Ferguson Dave Cooper
McCallister Ian McCulloch

Director: William Brayne
Designer: Colin Monk

Hors de Combat

w Jonathan Hales
Dempsey and Makepeace find themselves involved with two rival underworld gangs, each hell-bent on taking over the other's territory, and Dempsey becomes involved with an American girl who is not all that she claims to be.
Frank Price Derek Ware
Bernie Silk Stephen Greif
Angie Hughes Catriona McColl

Director: Christian Marnham
Designer: Gordon Melhuish

Nowhere to Run

w Dave Humphries
When a terrorist group smuggles arms into the country in order to spring one of their number from prison, Dempsey and Makepeace face an action-packed gun battle on a motorway – and Spikings finds 'Chicago' on his doorstep.
Eddie Gary Shail
Masad Neville Rofalia
Piglet Nick Stringer

Director: Gerry Mill
Designer: Gordon Melhuish

Make Peace, Not War

w Jesse Carr-Martindale
On the trail of a consignment of T-shirts impregnated with heroin, 'Harry' Makepeace is forced to feign death, while Dempsey infiltrates a gang of thugs led by a mysterious veiled lady. But is she all she seems?
Lenny Chris Tajah
Ziggy Stephen Persaud
Davros Brian Coburn

Director: Tony Wharmby
Designer: Gordon Melhuish

Blind Eye

w Jesse Carr-Martindale
When Charlie Wilson, a convict, threatens to expose corruption in high places, Spikings discovers something rotten in MI10 – and immediately puts his life at risk. Dempsey and Makepeace face a hair-raising motorcycle chase to save their boss's life.
Charlie Wilson Desmond McNamara
Eileen Wilson Jacquie-Ann Carr
Sean Sean Scanlan

Director: Tony Wharmby
Designer: Colin Monk

Cry God for Harry

w Neil Rudyard
When a collection of priceless jade antiques is stolen from her father, Lord Winfield, Harriet Makepeace takes Dempsey along to investigate – a move which lands the two detectives into a spectacular battle against the baddies, with broadswords!
Lord Winfield Ralph Michael
Gerald Naismith Ralph Arliss
Ch'ien Cheng Tsu Keith Bonnard

Director: William Brayne
Designer: Colin Monk

Judgement

w Jesse Carr-Martindale
When Makepeace's best friend is murdered on a train, and her father, a respected judge, swears vengeance (but unfortunately grabs the wrong man), Dempsey and Makepeace discover that 'rough justice' is not always a simple solution to a crime.
Judge Hackett John Horsley
Atkins Graham Rowe
Sarah Hackett Sarah Sherborne

Director: William Brayne
Designer: Colin Monk

Season Two

10 60-minute episodes

Silver Dollar

w Ranald Graham
When a petrol station is blown up by masked raiders, and a major company is

blackmailed, Dempsey and Makepeace find
themselves involved with a gang of black
terrorists, who plan to poison bottles of
cough linctus!
Det Sgt Watson Colin McFarlane (Intro.)
Osuna George Harris
Wes Ben Thomas

Director: Tony Wharmby
Designer: Colin Monk

Wheelman

w Murray Smith
Hearing that a gang are planning a large
diamond robbery and need a driver,
Dempsey, posing as a 'wheelman', applies
for and gets the post. A daring game of
bluff and counter bluff ensues before he –
literally – smashes the gang's plans.
Jack Cade Tom Georgeson
Ass Com Webb Niall Toibin
Mickey the Shiv George Irving

Director: Tony Wharmby
Designer: Colin Monk

Love You to Death

w Roger Marshall
Dempsey is puzzled. During the last few
days someone has been sending him funeral
lilies. Then he is almost shot and begins to
receive threatening phone calls. Who is
behind the anonymous threats? Makepeace
must find out – before her partner receives a
bullet with his name on it!
Cathy Suzi Quatro
Mrs Barrett Elizabeth Sladen
Barrett Lex Molloy

Director: Tony Wharmby
Designer: Colin Monk

No Surrender

w Paul Wheeler
With Harriet badly injured in an attempted
bank robbery, and Det Sgt Watson severely
wounded, it is left to Dempsey to take over
the responsibility of bringing three vicious
youths to justice.

Det. Sgt Watson Colin McFarlane (Last)
Ramsey Jamie Foreman
Levey Tony London

Director: Victors Ritelis
Designer: Colin Monk

Tequila Sunrise

w Ranald Graham
During the course of an investigation into
extortion and blackmail, Makepeace
unwittingly gets a friendly informer badly
injured – Dempsey extols the virtue of
playing 'tough' and Harriet blows her top!
Stavros Edward Kelsey
Sid Lowe Milton Johns
Wee Jock Lou Hirsch

Director: Tony Wharmby
Designer: Colin Monk

Blood Money

w Dave Humphries
Undercover to trace some priceless Ancient
Egyptian antiquities, Dempsey and
Makepeace discover a large-scale gun-
running operation masterminded by a
Middle Eastern 'gentleman' – who issues
orders for them to be blown up!
Scott Derek Martin
Bailey Dudley Sutton
Colonel Raheed Stephan Kalipha

Director: Graham Theakston
Designer: Colin Monk

Set a Thief

w Dave Humphries
Discovering that a photographic model,
killed by a hit and run driver, had
connections at the highest level of
government circles, Dempsey and
Makepeace investigate further, and uncover
some disturbing facts.
Janine Jadie Rivas
Sullivan Edward Peel
Major Danby Malcolm Terris

Director: Tony Wharmby
Designer: Colin Monk

The Hit

w Murray Smith

When an undercover agent decides to stop and search a black drugs dealer accompanied by a streetwalker, it leads Dempsey and Makepeace into the twilight world of prostitution and drug dealing – and an all-out battle with a professional assassin.

Faith McColl Patti Boulaye
Tiffany Grace Amanda Pays
Picasso Anthony Morton

Director: Tony Wharmby
Designer: Colin Monk

In the Dark

w David Crane

A fanatical right-wing group plans to unseat Her Majesty's Government – unless they pay a ransom of 10 billion pounds. Dempsey finds himself distracted by a beautiful girl, and Makepeace is taken prisoner.

'Lucky' Livingstone Kenny Ireland
Adrian Lindsay Benjamin Whitrow
Sir Toby David Saville

Director: Graham Theakston
Designer: Colin Monk

The Bogeyman

w Ranald Graham

A tough opponent for Dempsey. A man who is his equal in every respect, save one – he's a cold-blooded, psychopathic killer! Obsessed with capturing him, Dempsey sets out alone – and Makepeace's patience is tested to the limit.

Lymon Nick Brimble
Kelly Michael Balfour
Terry Terry Downes

Director: Tony Wharmby
Designer: Colin Monk

Season Three

10 60-minute episodes

The Burning (Part 1)

w Ranald Graham

It had to happen one day. Dempsey's New York past catches up with him and he is forced to go undercover, with Makepeace as his control, when an old enemy threatens his life. Meanwhile, a mysterious woman enters his life – and personal conflict of a different kind leads Makepeace into a war with the Mafia.

The Burning (Part 2)

Dempsey's stunning female adversary, Mara, gets closer to her objective and it appears that the detective is cracking under the strain. Will he repeat his final hours with the NYPD? Or will Makepeace arrive in time to save his sanity? Whatever happens, things will never be quite the same.

Mara Jill St John
Det. Sgt Ward Jonathan Dockar-Drysdale
Conrad Michael J. Shannon
Joey David Baxt

Director: Baz Taylor
Designer: Mike Oxley

Jericho Scam

w Jeffrey Caine

When Dempsey falls foul of enemies in high places and is forced to go on the run, Makepeace must come up with the goods on the bad guys – before her partner achieves his objective of wiping out the blot on his career.

Simmons Michael Robbins
Det. Chf Insp. Lacey Lee Montague
Harris Jack Watson

Director: Robert Tronson
Designer: Mike Oxley

The Prizefighter

w Murray Smith

Undercover work is always dangerous, but when Dempsey and Makepeace infiltrate a murderous group of bare-knuckle fighters, and uncover a clever counterfeiting ring, they find their lives threatened by something far more deadly than the human fist.

Mrs Spikings June Barry
Ginger Danson Greg Powell
Horse Johnson Patrick Durkin

Director: Baz Taylor
Designer: Mike Oxley

Extreme Prejudice

w Jeffrey Caine

While under routine SI10 psychological assessment, Dempsey finds himself facing a life or death situation in which his split-second judgement could leave his life hanging by a thread – a situation which rapidly becomes a matter of dignity for the detective.

Dr Swann Kenneth Gilbert
'Big Ben' Davis Clive Mantle
Jimmy Mark Ryan

Director: John Hough
Designer: Mike Oxley

Bird of Prey

w David Wilks

Policework and death often walk hand in hand and Dempsey and his partner are no strangers to danger. This time, however, both find themselves placed in the firing-line – with very little hope of survival!

Det. Cons. Austin Andrew Dunn
Eddie Dean Robert Pereno
Christine Annabel Leventon

Director: Roger Tucker
Designer: Mike Oxley

Out of Darkness

w John Field

A girl is abducted from a launderette and the man responsible for the crime appears to leave countless clues to his identity, as obvious bait to lead Makepeace to him. Dempsey is concerned that she may be walking into a trap – his partner thinks otherwise.

Terry Julia Watson
Swabey Gary Cooper
Psychiatrist Tim Preece

Director: Christopher King
Designer: Mike Oxley

The Cortez Connection

w Guy Meredith

Busy with an old flame from New York, Dempsey appears unconcerned when a ruthless group of South American drug smugglers enters London's streets.

Makepeace, meanwhile, sets out alone – and storm clouds threaten to engulf their relationship.

Cortez Francisco Morales
Detective David Taylor
Cortez's man Vincenzo Nicoli

Director: Baz Taylor
Designer: Mike Oxley

Mantrap

w Murray Smith

With Dempsey and Makepeace hot on his trail, an evil criminal mastermind feeds them false clues to lead them into a carefully prepared trap. Unknowingly, the two detectives are heading to their own deaths!

Ryan Christopher Reich
Mick Walsh Jonathan McKenna
Danny Walsh Michael Watkins

Director: Roger Tucker
Designer: Mike Oxley

Guardian Angel

w Ranald Graham

Makepeace finally makes good her threat to end their partnership, by resigning from the force. Dempsey meanwhile finds himself teamed with another female cop, Joyce Hargreaves. It is her death that brings Makepeace to understand her partner's dilemma – but will she return to help him fight the latest threat to his life?

Joyce Hargreaves Kate O'Mara
Daish Richard Johnson
Corman Derek Newark

Director: Michael Brandon
Designer: Mike Oxley

DEMPSEY AND MAKEPEACE
Created and produced by: Tony Wharmby
Executive producer: Nick Elliot
Music by: Alan Parker
A Golden Eagle Films Production
for London Weekend Television
An LWT Network Presentation
1 colour 105-minute pilot story and 29 60-minute episodes
11 January – 15 March 1985
31 August – 2 November 1985
30 August – 1 November 1986

DEPARTMENT S

A tremendously popular series about the world's most unusual police department and its team of equally unusual investigators.

Department S, an offshoot of Interpol, was asked to solve the sort of cases which had baffled everyone else: those connected either with natural calamities or crimes that through their complexity or illogicality had left the best brains of Interpol scratching their heads in puzzlement.

The principal investigator for the department was Jason King. A successful author with a vivid imagination, he looked at each case as if it were the plot he'd devised for one of his books, then asked himself what his detective hero would do or think in the same circumstances. Something of a flamboyant character who liked to dress in dandified fashion, he never ceased to amaze (and sometimes amuse) his colleagues with wild theories – ideas which his down-to-earth, shrewd-thinking colleague Stewart Sullivan tended to shoot down at every available opportunity (while storing away those he thought as being practical). The third member of the team, Annabelle Hurst, approached each case from a scientific viewpoint. An expert with computer hardware, her eyes observed the smallest detail and she never thought twice about getting laboratory reports to back up her findings.

There was always an element of competition between the trio. Though they worked together towards a common end, each endeavoured to solve the problem before the other two. Their divergent approaches to each case may not have always brought an individual solution but, combined, they led to success.

Never far away from the action was Department Head, Sir Curtis Seretse, who was seen giving the team their assignments and occasionally joined them in the field. Devised by Monty Norman and Dennis Spooner, this highly inventive series was their shining hour.

REGULAR CAST

Jason King **Peter Wyngarde**   *Stewart Sullivan* **Joel Fabiani**
Annabelle Hurst **Rosemary Nicols**   *Sir Curtis Seretse* **Dennis Alaba Peters**

Six Days

w Gerald Kelsey

When an airliner goes missing for six days, then suddenly reappears – but the crew and passengers have no recollection of what has happened, or indeed that they were reported missing – the Department S team are asked to solve the mystery.

Captain Carter **Bernard Horsfall**
Hallet **Tony Steedman**
Borowitsch **Peter Bowles**

Director: **Cyril Frankel**

The Trojan Tanker

w Philip Broadley

What mystery lies behind a crashed tanker decked out like a luxury yacht, with only one occupant – a beautiful unconscious girl, who disappears before an ambulance arrives. Jason King arrives on the scene with an astonishing theory.

Veronica Bray Patricia Haines
Taylor Simon Oates
Cortoli Bill Nagy

Director: Ray Austin

A Cellar Full of Silence

w Terry Nation

The Department S team are called in to unravel the intriguing puzzle behind the discovery of four bodies, all in fancy dress, found in the cellar of a deserted house.

Martin Kyle Paul Whitsun-Jones
Walter Pally Robert Hawdon
Tronson Brandon Brady

Director: John Gilling

The Pied Piper of Hambledown

w Donald James

When it appears that all Hambledown's inhabitants have been kidnapped – save one, a young girl – the Department S investigators travel there to seek an answer to the baffling mystery which leads them into intrigue and danger.

Susan Lewis Gina Warwick
Colonel Loring Richard Vernon
Dr Brogan Jeremy Young

Director: Roy Ward Baker

One of Our Aircraft is Empty

w Tony Williamson

When a pilotless aircraft makes a perfect landing at London Airport, King, Sullivan and Hurst find the solution to the mystery in Ireland – but the outcome is far from what they expected.

Terrell Anton Rodgers
Howard Finch Basil Dignam
Julia Howarth Gillian Lewis

Director: Paul Dickson

The Man in the Elegant Room

w Terry Nation

When a dead girl and a gibbering demented young man are found in a beautiful room built inside a disused factory, the Department S team investigate a very unusual case of murder.

Trenton Stratford Johns
Trish Juliet Harmer
Doug John Hallam

Director: Cyril Frankel

Handicap Dead

w Philip Broadley

The Department S sleuths are assigned to discover the facts behind the deaths of several golfers – and find that the solution to the mystery lies a very long way from the lush, but deadly, playing green.

Eddie Curtis Neil McCallum
Dianne Lynne Dawn Addams
Sonny Dudley Sutton

Director: John Gilling

Black Out

w Philip Broadley

The connection between the kidnapping of a writer of food books and a new space product leads the team into a mystery fraught with danger and intrigue. Jason loses his cool, and Annabelle nearly loses her life.

Doctor Lang Neil Hallett
Brigitte Sue Lloyd
Wolf David Sumner

Director: Ray Austin

Who Plays the Dummy?

w Tony Williamson

Everyone knows that a dummy can't drive a car. So why should a crashed car have only a tailor's dummy at the wheel? The Department S team are assigned to find the answer – and place themselves in an explosive situation.

Pietra Kate O'Mara
Sarrat George Pastell
Gilford Alan McNaughton

Director: John Gilling

The Treasure of the Costa del Sol

w Philip Broadley
The Department S team take a well-earned break and immediately land themselves in hot water. They net some very strange fish indeed – a catch which plunges them into intrigue and mayhem.
Segres Peter Arne
Ramon David Healy
Trish Pippa Steel

Director: John Gilling

The Man Who Got a New Face

w Philip Broadley
The team of investigators find themselves faced with the strange mystery of a dead man found with a clown's mask on his face – a clue, perhaps, to a vicious vendetta between two millionaires' love for a beautiful film star?
Monique Adrienne Corri
Andre Eric Pohlmann
Nicole Alexandra Bastedo

Director: Cyril Frankel

Les Fleurs du Mal

w Philip Broadley
Three plastic flowers hold the secret of a grim robbery with murder. The Department S team must sniff out the clues to expose an extraordinary chain of events which leads them to a not-so-appealing crime.
Stacey Donal Donnelly
Weber Michael Gothard
Brandini Alex Scott

Director: Cyril Frankel

The Shift That Never Was

w Donald James
Why should an entire factory take the day off – and what connects a beauty parlour with an atomic generating station? The Department S investigators find themselves faced with an intriguing mystery.
Frank Bellman Eddie Byrne
George Parsons Toke Townley
Kate Mortimer Caroline Blakiston

Director: John Gilling

A Ticket to Nowhere

w Tony Williamson
The Department S sleuths investigate the strange disappearance of a Swedish scientist and the equally strange death of a financier. But how can they complete their investigations when they repeatedly forget everything they've discovered!
Drieker Michael Gwynn
Quince Neil McCarthy
Paula Juliet Harmer

Director: Cyril Frankel

The Man from X

w Tony Williamson
When a man wearing a spacesuit is found wandering through the streets of London and then dies before he can be questioned, the Department S team have only one clue to act upon – the man had recently been in a vacuum and has slight radiation burns.
Carter John Nettleton
Leila Wanda Ventham
Lowery Duncan Lamont

Director: Gill Taylor

Dead Men Die Twice

w Philip Broadley
A man dies. Three years later, his unfortunate double is murdered – twice, just to make sure. A strange case for the investigative talents of the team from Department S, who find that 'dead' men really do die twice.
Lomax/Reeves Kieron Moore
Tania Barbara Murray
Harlan David Bauer

Director: Ray Austin

The Perfect Operation

w Leslie Darbon

When a surgeon is interrupted during a brain operation – and another man takes over – the Department S team uncover an ingenious plot by a group of mysterious villains to infiltrate a spy network.
Walker Cyril Luckham
Allison Ronald Radd
Agatha Jean Marsh

Director: Cyril Frankel

The Duplicated Man

w Harry H. Junkin

It has taken double agent Anthony James ten years to build up a double identity, and the Department S team must uncover his new face within days – the Russians have shown their interest and they want to kill him.
Anthony James Robert Urquhart
May Ann Bell
Kirov Guy Deghy

Director: Paul Dickson

The Mysterious Man in the Flying Machine

w Philip Broadley

When the body of a murdered man is found inside a mock-up aircraft in a Paris warehouse, the Department S sleuths ask themselves why anyone should go to so much trouble to simulate a real flight? A message scrawled in lipstick provides the answer.
Gerrard Clinton Greyn
Lucky Hans Meyer
Francoise Virginia North

Director: Cyril Frankel

The Double Death of Charlie Crippen

w Leslie Darbon

The Department S team find themselves in Naples to investigate an unusual assassination attempt in which the 'victim'

was a dummy. A trail of clues leads them to uncover a sinister cold-hearted plot.
Slovik Peter Arne
Dupont Edward De Souza
Countess Yolande Turner

Director: John Gilling

Death on Reflection

w Philip Broadley

When an antique mirror sells for four times its value at an auction and the buyer is murdered shortly afterwards, Jason, Stewart and Annabelle have their work cut out sifting through the countless clues they uncover.
Yves Guy Rolfe
Comtesse Jennifer Hilary
Gresford Paul Whitsun-Jones

Director: Ray Austin

The Last Train to Redbridge

w Gerald Kelsey

Multiple murders on a tube train involve the Department S team in a case in which they uncover a devious espionage network behind the facade of a quiet country village in Sussex.
Draper Leslie Sands
Mrs Taylor Patricia English
Clark Derek Newark

Director: John Gilling

A Small War of Nerves

w Harry H. Junkin

Informed that a scientist has invented a poison gas which could kill a million people – and he intends to use it to hold England hostage – the Department S sleuths find themselves racing against time to prevent the man from doing so.
Dr Arkwright Frederick Jaeger
Mills Anthony Hopkins
Gina Isobel Black

Director: Leslie Norman

The Bones of Byrom Blain

w Tony Williamson

An intriguing mystery faces the investigative talents of the Department S

sleuths: on his arrival at a Ministry of Defence establishment, Byrom Blain disintegrated into a skeleton! The team must find out why.
Byrom Blain John Barron
Magda Jenny Hanley
Crawley Patrick Barr

Director: Paul Dickson

Spencer Bodily is 60 Years Old

w Harry H. Junkin
Despite looking no more than 20, an autopsy on Spencer Bodily's dead body proves he must have been at least 60 – an event that has startling repercussions for the Department S team, sent to investigate the crime.
Kendal Iain Cuthbertson
Mendham Garfield Morgan
Ingrid von Elzdorf Patricia Donahue

Director: Leslie Norman

The Ghost of Mary Burnham

w Harry H. Junkin
Is it the ghost of his wife that John Burnham keeps seeing and hearing, or just a clever plot to mentally unbalance the brilliant economist? That's the question facing the Department S team when they are asked to solve the mystery.
John Burnham Donald Houston
Mary Burnham Lois Maxwell
Dr Grant Anthony Nicholls

Director: Cyril Frankel

A Fish Out of Water

w Philip Broadley
When the body of an Interpol agent is found drowned in Beirut, Jason King is sent to take over his mission, to crack an international smuggling ring. The agent immediately finds his life threatened by a beautiful girl.
Sandra Maggie Wright
Rafic Lee Montague
Esplin Cyril Shaps

Director: Cyril Frankel

The Soup of the Day

w Leslie Darbon
Why should anyone wish to break into a bombed warehouse and steal dozens of cases of tinned soup? The Department S team investigate the break-in and discover that the soup contained some very strange ingredients indeed.
Fallon Michael Coles
Gregory Anthony Valentine
Standish Ronald Lacey

Director: Leslie Norman

DEPARTMENT S
Created by: Monty Berman and Dennis Spooner
Producer: Monty Berman
Music by: Edwin Astley
Executive story consultant: Dennis Spooner
An ITC Production
28 colour 60-minute episodes
9 March 1969 – 4 March 1970
(USA: Syndicated 1971)

DESTINATION DOWNING STREET

The adventures of Mike Anson, ITV's first all-British super spy. A former major in the Royal Marine Commandos, Anson was given the job of fighting the saboteur activities of The Big Enemy. (Just who was 'The Big Enemy' was tactfully never made clear.) Together with his four assistants: Jacques, an ex-resistance fighter; Sylva, a beautiful Czech undercover resistance worker; Colin, a university professor and explosives expert, and Phoebe, a WAAF officer assigned to 'manage' the team, Anson reported directly to the Prime Minister (hence the title), and was answerable only to him. (A nice touch was that the PM was never actually seen: Anson would be filmed standing or sitting at the other side of the PM's desk and the camera would be placed in the PM's chair.) The first story acted as a prologue to introduce the characters, and thereafter each story was told in weekly serialised episodes.

REGULAR CAST

Mike Anson John Stone   *Jacques* Donald Morley   *Sylva* Sylva Langova
Colin Graham Crowden   *Phoebe* Diana Lambert

The Machiavelli Touch

w St John Curzon   *(A 5-part story)*
When an atomic scientist disappears, a ship unaccountably sinks without trace and an African village disappears off the face of the map – and all three disasters appear to be the work of an organisation known only as ARKAB – the Prime Minister of England selects five special people to track down the organisation. Chosen because of their specialised talents, they are answerable to only one authority – the highest, the Prime Minister himself.
Machiavelli Richard Molinas
Dufresne David Garth
Romaine John Bailey

Director: Robert Tronson

The Green Patch

w St John Curzon   *(A 4-part story)*
When a helicopter crashes mysteriously, and someone lets secrets leak during a conversation in a Dar-es-Salaam bar, the code words 'The Green Patch' take on international significance, and Mike Anson is forced to set a trap by using his friend Tiny as bait.
Tiny McCrae Colin Douglas
Peter Sheldon Eric Lander
Loritzen Guy Deghy

Director: Robert Tronson

Mr Crazy

w St John Curzon   *(A 4-part story)*
ARKAB, the ruthless espionage organisation, have already had their previous attempts to rule the world dashed by Anson and his colleagues, but they try again. Their attack arrives at a very unexpected quarter, an American millionaire nicknamed Mr Crazy by the media. Meanwhile, the Prime Minister receives a ransom note.
Arkwright/Mr Crazy John McClaren
Charlesworth John Sharplin
Eisenstein Stratford Johns

Director: Jonathan Alwyn

Two Faces East

w St John Curzon   *(A 4-part story)*
Mike Anson and his friends are hot on the trail of Baron Immelmann, a man believed to be behind a nefarious 'face factory', which replaces agents with doubles that are indistinguishable from the original – and Anson is next on the man's list for an unwanted facelift!
Immelmann Josh Ackland
Club Foot Edward Burnham
Frau Kohne Wanda Rotha

Director: Jonathan Alwyn

The Empty Man

w St John Curzon   *(A 4-part story)*
With millions of pounds at stake, the manufacturers of a new top-secret all-British

experimental plane, 'The Emperor', are rightly concerned when it crashes off Beirut and breaks up. Mike Anson and his colleagues are called to Downing Street and given priority orders to recover the wreckage before enemy agents make off with the prototype engine.

Yaheez Raymond Adamson
Yilman Petra Davies
Djeunella Fenella Fielding

Director: Robert Tronson

Danger's End

w St John Curzon   *(A 4-part story)*
ARKAB make their final attempt to get rid of Anson and his friends. Using the beautiful Maria Voelckler as bait, they lead Mike and his colleagues into dangerous

territory. But the agent spies the opportunity to put an end to ARKAB's plans once and for all – even though his move places himself and his friends in mortal danger.

Machiavelli Richard Molinas
The Chief George Pastell
Maria Elizabeth Ross-Williams

Director: William Freshman

DESTINATION DOWNING STREET
Created and written by: St John Curzon
Producer: Eric Maschwitz
Music by: Peggy Cochrane
A TV Scripts Ltd Production
Presented by Associated-Rediffusion
25 monochrome 30-minute episodes
25 March – 9 September 1957

DIAL 999

An authentic police series which starred Robert Beatty as Inspector Mike Maguire of the Royal Canadian Mounted Police. Sent to the UK to study the methods used by British policemen in their fight against crime, Maguire found himself attached to the Metropolitan Police, given the acting rank of Detective Inspector, and teamed with Detective Inspector Winter and Detective Sergeant West

Made in cooperation with Scotland Yard, each episode showed the never-ending battle between the Yard and organised crime. With practically every scene being shot on location, the series was as authentic as anything that followed.

REGULAR CAST

Mike Maguire Robert Beatty   *Det. Insp. Winter* Duncan Lamont
Det. Sgt. West John Witty

The Killing Job	Mechanical Watchman
Thames Division	50,000 Hands
Robbery with Violence	Hunter Hunted
Illegal Entry	Extradition
Exception to the Rule	Honeymoon
Motor Bike Bandits	Rolling Racketeers
The Big Fish	Mined Area
Escape	Down to the Sea

22 Hours
Death Ride
Missing Persons
Special Edition
The Great Gold Robbery
Fashions in Crime
Old Soldiers Sometimes Die
Commando Crook
Night Mail
77 Bus
Gun Rule
Special Branch

Barge Burglars
Rat Trap
Living Loot
Payrole Job
Inside Job
Radioactive
Key Witness
Picture Puzzle
Deadly Blackmail
Ghost Squad
Heads or Tails

DIAL 999
Producer: Harry Alan Towers
Music by: Sidney Torch
(Harmonica solos by: Tommy Reilly)
Crime consultant: Duncan Webb
Police consultant: Ex-Supt Tom Fallon
A Towers of London Production
in association with ZIV TV Programmes
Filmed on location in London and at Elstree
Studios
39 monochrome 30-minute episodes
8 June 1958 – 13 June 1959
(USA: Syndicated 1959)

DIAMONDS

A well-made drama series revolving around the glittering world of the diamond industry, and those who dealt in them. The stories took us behind the scenes of a large diamond company in Hatton Garden, London, where money meant everything. The series depicted the calculated risks taken by the family of Coleman and Sons, diamond merchants in an exclusive club where dealers and merchants were all players in a multi-billion-pound power game.

A star-studded cast failed to make the diamonds sparkle.

CAST
Frank Coleman **John Stride**   *Margaret Coleman* **Hildegard Neil**
Dora Coleman **Doris Hare**   *Barry Coleman* **Ian McCulloch**
Joseph Coleman **Norman Woodland**   *Bernard de Haan* **Simon Ward**
Tom Fabricius **Mark Kingston**

DIAMONDS
Producer: John Cooper
Executive producer: David Reid
Writer/deviser: John Brason
An ATV Network Production
13 colour 60-minute episodes
9 September – 2 December 1981

DICK BARTON – SPECIAL AGENT

Sadly, he wasn't special at all. The original, the Dick Barton who kept 15 million listeners glued to their radio sets from October 1946 to March 1951, most certainly was special, very special. In his day, Barton was bigger than Bond. He attracted more fans than *The Man From Uncle* and Bond combined. Tuning in to his radio adventures became a national pastime and every 15-minute story was a pure joy. In short, he was unbeatable. But this new pretender to the throne was an impostor. Whereas the original had been bound by 13 rules of conduct which, take my word for it, kept the radio version well and truly on the straight and narrow, the television model looked (and acted) like a thug! (Heaven help us, he even dressed like a villain: brown trilby pulled low over his eyes; a military-style trenchcoat complete with wrap-around belt . . .)

A lacklustre attempt to inject new life into a national hero which, played for laughs, raised only guffaws. The producers should have known better – or paid more attention to the attributes which made the original the legend it became.

REGULAR CAST

Dick Barton Tony Vogel   *Snowey White* Anthony Heaton
Jock Anderson James Cosmo   *Sir Richard Marley* John Gantrel

Adventure One

w Clive Exton   *(An 8-part story)*
Just demobbed after an eventful six years in the army, Dick Barton and Snowey White are finding civilian life somewhat tame, when Barton receives a telephone call from an old friend, Sir Richard Marley, asking them to look into the disappearance of his daughter Virginia and son Rex, a singer.

Joined by Jock Anderson, an old army colleague, the three investigators soon find themselves up against master criminal, Melganik.
Virginia Marley Fiona Fullerton
Rex Marley Kevan Sheehan
Melganik John G. Heller

Director: Jon Scoffield
Designer: Lewis Logan

Adventure Two

w Julian Bond   *(An 8-part story)*
During a late-night celebration at the Blue
Parrot, Barton and his colleagues rescue a
young girl from being attacked. She
explains that her father, scientist George
Cameron, has been kidnapped by the
villainous Herr Muller – a man determined
to obtain the secret of a devastating weapon,
a poison discovered by Cameron. Before
they are through, the three investigators
will need more than luck to escape the
tortuous campaign of the depraved Muller.
Lucy Cameron Debbie Farrington
George Cameron Colin Rix
Muller Guy Deghy

Director: Jon Scoffield
Designer: Lewis Logan

Adventure Three

w Clive Exton   *(A 6-part story)*
Having thwarted Muller's plans to possess
George Cameron's deadly poison, Barton
and his colleagues settle down for a weekend
of rest. Their sojourn is interrupted by a
phone call from Dick's Aunt Agatha –
saying that her house has vanished! As they
are about to leave, a phone call from Sir
Richard Varley reveals that British research
scientist, Harold Jenkins, has perfected the
ultimate weapon. Barton and his comrades
will soon find themselves pitted once again
against their old enemy, the evil Melganik.

Melganik John G. Heller
Harold Jenkins Peter Godfrey
Aunt Agatha Stella Kemball

Director: James Hill
Designer: Lewis Logan

Adventure Four

w Julian Bond   *(A 4-part story)*
Having dispensed with Melganik's plans to
rule the world with Jenkins' weapon (which
has now been destroyed), Barton and his
two comrades take on the threat of the Drew
Brothers – leaders of the underworld. Dandy
Parkes, a middle-aged playboy, and
Amanda Aston, the young wife of a
respected Whitehall official, have had their
lives threatened. But what is the link
between the two? Finding the answer leads
Dick, Snowey and Jock to the very brink of
defeat.
Amanda Aston Marsha Fitzalan
Dandy Parkes Terence Seward
Ernie Drew Bernard Kay

Director: Jon Scoffield
Designer: Lewis Logan

DICK BARTON - SPECIAL AGENT
Producer: Jon Scoffield
Executive producer: Terence Baker (Advs 1
and 2)
Lewis Rudd (Advs 3 and 4)
Associate producer: David Pick
A Southern Television Network Production
26 colour 15-minute episodes
(Transmitted twice-weekly)
6 January – 8 April 1979

DICK AND THE DUCHESS

This situation comedy/adventure series starring Hazel Court
and Patrick O'Neal, proved highly successful when it was first
introduced to British viewers in the early sixties. Set around the
lives of newly-weds Dick and Jane Starrett, it depicted Dick's
adventures as an insurance claims investigator – cases which were
liable to come unstuck due to Jane's habit of sticking her nose
into his affairs. (The title took its name from Dick's habit of

calling his wife 'Duchess' – although she was in fact the daughter of an earl.) Also starring was Richard Wattis as Dick's boss.

Harmless fun for the family.

CAST

Richard Starrett **Patrick O'Neal** *Jane Starrett* **Hazel Court**
Peter Jamison **Richard Wattis**

The Brooch	The Swedish Story
The New Secretary	The Hospital
Jealousy	The Dress
Aunt Winifred	The Dog Collar
The Courtroom	Break In
The Bank Robbery	The Car Accident
The Missing Ring	The Painting
The Perfect Crime	Pop Goes the Weazel
Candlesticks	The Missing Earring
An American	The Armoured Car
The Nottingham Case	The Wild Party
The Kissing Bandit	Rodney's Romance
The Club	The Convention

DICK AND THE DUCHESS
Executive producer: Nicole Milinair
A Sheldon Reynolds Production
Filmed at Elstree Studios
26 monochrome 30-minute episodes
21 May 1959 – 8 July 1960
(USA: CBS September 1957 – May 1958)

DICK TURPIN

The swashbuckling exploits of the legendary eighteenth-century highwayman, from the prolific pen of master storyteller Richard Carpenter.

Having returned from military service in Flanders and found himself cheated out of his inheritance by an unscrupulous wealthy landowner, Turpin, convinced that being rich put one above the law, set out to obtain the first by breaking the latter. A devil-may-care soldier of fortune with nerves of steel, he was well-suited to the task and it wasn't long before his sense of chivalry and justice led him into the kind of situations he found hard to ignore – other people's troubles.

Joining him on his adventures was Nick Smith (renamed Swiftnick by Turpin in the first story), a young boy whose impetuous escapades had brought him to the attention of the authorities who had duly placed a price on his head. Turpin was convinced at first that the boy was too young to ride with him on the road, but as a favour to his mother Turpin allowed Swiftnick to join him and the two became close comrades.

Their main protagonist was the voraciously greedy Sir John Glutton. Having realised that Turpin, a folk hero to the masses, could become a threat to his position and a potential rallying point against his authority, Glutton, a man whose vast wealth and power had been gained by dubious means, became the highwayman's arch enemy. Helped by the sardonic, eighteenth-century fascist, Nathan Spiker – a man from a middle-class background who wished to rise to the aristocracy, but who was kept well and truly in his place by Glutton – the two men had one sole objective in life: to place Turpin's neck in the hangman's noose.

A smashing piece of television history. Carpenter's scripts were a joy and the casting of Richard O'Sullivan as Turpin was a triumph for all concerned.

REGULAR CAST

Dick Turpin **Richard O'Sullivan**   *Swiftnick* **Michael Deeks**
Sir John Glutton **Christopher Benjamin**   *Captain Spiker* **David Dakar**

Season One
13 colour 30-minute episodes

Swiftnick

w **Richard Carpenter**
When the evil Sir John Glutton and his steward, Captain Nathan Spiker, try to evict Mrs Smith and her son Nick from their inn, The Black Swan, the couple seek the help of Dick Turpin – a man who has an old score to settle with Sir John.
Swiftnick **Michael Deekes (Intro)**
Mrs Smith **Jo Rowbottom**
Dr Andrews **Alex McCrindle**

Director: **Charles Crichton**
Designer: **John Blezard**

The Capture

w **Richard Carpenter**
Undecided as to whether Swiftnick should join him on his travels, Turpin tries to get him a 'respectable' occupation, little

realising that Sir John Glutton has other plans in mind for both of them.
Jane Kelsey **Annabelle Lee**
Kate Doyle **Lesley Dunlop**
Tanner **Harold Goodwin**

Director: **Gerry Poulson**
Designer: **John Blezard**

The Champion

w **Richard Carpenter**
Mudbury village is being terrorised by the fanatical Nightingale and his bully, Hogg. Dick decides to help the villagers by enlisting a champion of his own, Tom Bracewell, a prizefighter whose alias is 'The Bristol Butcher'!
Bracewell **Don Henderson**
Nightingale **John Grillo**
Hogg **Robert Russell**

Director: **James Allen**
Designer: **John Blezard**

The Poacher

w Richard Carpenter

Under suspicion of poaching, Dick and Swiftnick must prove their innocence by netting the real culprit. They suspect a man named Vizard, but discover that the real culprit lies closer to home.
Willoughby Rupert Frazer
Vizard Michael O'Hagan
Big Nell Joan Rhodes

Director: James Allan
Designer: John Blezard

The Pursuit

w Richard Carpenter

The arrival of a mysterious highwayman to the district brings trouble and intrigue to Dick and his comrade. Not content with robbing the aristocracy – he has the nerve to rob Dick Turpin!
Belinda Stacy Dorning
Fenton Stewart Bevan
Grummit Joe Ritchie

Director: James Allen
Designer: John Blezard

The Blacksmith

w Richard Carpenter

When blacksmith Sam Morgan is thrown into jail by Turpin's arch enemy Nathan Spiker, the highwayman and Swiftnick take a hostage of their own – a very unwilling and irate prisoner, Sir John Glutton.
Sam Morgan Eric Mason
Isaac Rag Alfie Bass
Jones Stanley Price

Director: Charles Crichton
Designer: John Blezard

The Impostor

w Richard Carpenter

Worried that Turpin's increasing popularity with the villagers of Rookam could lead them into revolt, Sir John hires an impostor to pose as the highwayman. His first victim is Varley, Swiftnick's uncle.

Amos Varley William Moore
Isaac Rag Alfie Bass
Big Nell Joan Rhodes

Director: James Allen
Designer: John Blezard

The Upright Man

w Richard Carpenter

After discovering that Sal Hawk's husband has been ambushed and hanged by militiamen, Turpin goes to her aid. He finds she has been thrown out of her pub by Tyson Sarney – leader of the notorious brotherhood – and accused of betraying her husband.
Tyson Sarney Ray McAnally
Sal Hawk Bridget Price
Bassett Tony Haygarth

Director: Charles Crichton
Designer: John Blezard

The Whipping Boy

w Richard Carpenter

Furious at being robbed by Dick and Swiftnick, the Duke of Hertford sends for the most notorious thief-catcher in England, Colonel Tobias Moat, a man with an old score to settle with Turpin. His campaign of terror begins when he captures Swiftnick.
Colonel Moat John Hallam
Duke of Hertford Bernard Archard
Big Nell Joan Rhodes

Director: Dennis Abey
Designer: John Blezard

The Hero

w Richard Carpenter

When his sweetheart, Phylida, is captured by Sir John Glutton who arranges her marriage to Captain Spiker, Ffoulkes-Withers tries to prevent the marriage by pretending to be Dick Turpin.
Phylida Julie Dawn Cole
Ffoulkes-Withers James Woodley
Davy Keith James

Director: Charles Crichton
Designer: John Blezard

The Hostages

w Richard Carpenter

It is a sorry day when Dick and Swiftnick meet a stranger who turns out to be on the run from Captain Spiker. Worse still, the highwayman and his companion are suspected of harbouring him from justice.

Foxwell Forbes Collins
Isaac Rag Alfie Bass
Davy Keith James

Director: Charles Crichton
Designer: John Blezard

The Turncoat

w Richard Carpenter

Having received a letter implicating him in a Jacobite plot, Sir John Glutton seeks help from a most unexpected source – his arch enemy, Dick Turpin. But can Sir John's word of honour be trusted?

Major Gerhardt Stephen Greif
Foxwell Forbes Collins
Nabber Griffith Davies

Director: Gerry Poulson
Designer: John Blezard

The Jail-birds

w Richard Carpenter

Swiftnick's impetuousness has often got the better of him, and landed his comrade Dick in trouble. This time his foolishness ends in danger; both he and Turpin are captured and flung into jail.

Colonel Bingham William Lucas
Abel Jeames Bryan Pringle
Isaac Rag Alfie Bass

Director: Charles Crichton
Designer: John Blezard

Season Two

7 colour 30-minute episodes

The Fox (Part 1)

w Richard Carpenter

While trying to help a dying highwayman named Joe Cutler, Dick and Swiftnick are captured by the sinister Lord Manderfell, who offers Turpin the choice of being hanged or hunted like a fox. Dick chooses the latter.

The Fox (Part 2)

Pursued by Manderfell's men, Dick learns the secret of a rock formation called Devil's Chimney, and finds out the rightful owner of Joe Cutler's loot. Before he can return it, he must deal with his evil pursuer.

Manderfell Donald Pickering
Joe Cutler Godfrey Jackman
Warren Garfield Morgan

Director: Gerry Poulson
Designer: Martin Atkinson

Blood Money

w Richard Carpenter

Hotly pursued by Dragoons, Dick and his accomplice Swiftnick run into Sir John Glutton, who sets a price on his head for treason before retreating to Rookham Hall, where the wily old Isaac Rag has set himself up as lord of the manor.

Isaac Rag Alfie Bass
de Courcey Michael Culver
Dragoon Sergeant Sandy Sinclair

Director: Gerry Poulson
Designer: Martin Atkinson

Deadlier Than the Male

w John Kane

Turpin's warning, ignored by the beautiful Catherine Langford, not to marry Edward Faversham, places the highwayman's life in great danger. Swiftnick, meanwhile, has troubles of his own to contend with.

Catherine Lindsay Duncan
Faversham Simon Rouse
Wimple Julie Swift

Director: Dennis Abey
Designer: Martin Atkinson

The Elixir of Life

w John Kane

Waiting at Poll Maggot's inn, while a large amount of stolen jewellery is sold for them, Turpin and Swiftnick are roused from their sleep by the strange noises coming from the room of Dr Mandragola, a man who brews the 'elixir of life' – whisky!

Dr Mandragola John Junkin
Poll Maggot Annabelle Lee
Lieut. Venables Anthony Rudge

Director: Charles Crichton
Designer: Martin Atkinson

The Thief-taker

w Richard Carpenter
Posing as famous thief-taker Jeremiah Snare
and his assistant Jonathan Handy, Turpin
and Swiftnick fool their enemy Lord
Fordingham into letting them set out to
capture 'Dick Turpin' – all part of Dick's
plan to teach Captain Spiker a hard-earned
lesson.
Lord Fordingham James Villiers
Davy Keith James
Ollie Amanda Bell

Director: James Allen
Designer: Martin Atkinson

The Judge

w Charles Crichton
When Sir John Glutton threatens to enclose
the land which the villagers use for grazing
and John Radstock, a smallholder, is
arrested on false charges, Turpin decides the
time has come to deal with his enemy on his
home ground.
Radstock Ray Mort
Mary Jo Rowbottom
Judge Lambsfoot John Barrard

Director: Charles Crichton
Designer: Martin Atkinson

Season Three
5 colour 30-minute episodes

Dick Turpin's Greatest Adventure

w Richard Carpenter
Part 1:
American girl June Harding visits England
to seek justice from the Attorney General
for colonists suffering under the rule of the
corrupt and evil Governor Appleyard. She
travels to Bristol and meets Dick Turpin
and Swiftnick.

Part 2:
Having shared an adventure with the
highwaymen and found herself waylaid by
rogues, June escapes and decides that the
only way she can get to Bristol before the
Attorney General leaves the town is to steal
Black Bess, the highwayman's trusted steed
. . .

Part 3:
. . . Meanwhile, Dick and Swiftnick have
troubles of their own. They have
encountered ruffian Noll Bridger and are
fighting for their lives. Furthermore, Fytton
is hot on their trail, and the two comrades
find themselves sharing a prison cell . . .

Part 4:
. . . Having escaped from jail, Dick and
Swiftnick fall into the clutches of ex-priest
Ignasius Slake, a corrupt sect-leader, who
orders that Turpin be burnt at the 'stake' – a
giant flaming cartwheel . . .

Part 5:
. . . Freed by June Harding, Dick decides
to accompany her to confront Lord Melford
with her evidence of Governor Appleyard's
corruption, but they encounter danger along
the way.
Lord Melford Patrick MacNee
June Harding Mary Crosby
Noll Bridger Oliver Tobias
Ignasius Slake Donald Pleasance
Lady Melford Susan Hampshire
Sam Harding Ed Bishop
Fytton Patrick Ryecart
Governor Appleyard Wilfred Hyde-White

Director: Gerry Poulson
Designer: Michael Bailey

Season Four
6 colour 30-minute episodes

Sentence of Death (Part 1)

w Richard Carpenter
The sudden appearance of cut-throat
Barnaby Husk at Poll Maggot's inn brings
terror to the district – and danger to Dick
Turpin, who becomes involved when he is
asked to track down a young aristocrat.

Sentence of Death (Part 2)

Dick sets out to rescue the Duke of Hesse's son, and to settle accounts with the villainous Barnaby Husk – a man who has caused a great deal of unwanted trouble.
Barnaby Husk Bryan Marshall
Poll Maggot Annabelle Lee
Duke of Hess David de Keyser
Boy Arron Burchell

Director: James Allen
Designer: Martin Atkinson

The Godmother

w Richard Carpenter
Never one to deny his charm to the fairer sex, Turpin's latest romantic involvement leads to his attempted capture in a lady's bedroom and to a not so merry cross-country chase by Sir Richard Glutton.
Countess Joan Sims
Gooch John Bird
Sophonisba Dorothea Phillips

Director: James Allen
Designer: Martin Atkinson

The Secret Folk

w John Kane
Pursued by their enemies, Dick and Swiftnick take refuge in a remote forest – little realising that the tract of wooded foliage hides a danger far greater than anything their pursuers could offer.
Julsca Kay Adshead
Zsika Alan Lake
Karoly Bernard Kay

Director: Charles Crichton
Designer: Martin Atkinson

The King's Shilling

w Paul Wheeler
While helping some village lads escape from the clutches of two unscrupulous recruiting officers, Swiftnick finds himself a reluctant recruit to the colours. His only hope of rescue is his friend, Dick Turpin, but he's otherwise involved.
Willard Paul Angelis
Newell Ken Wynne
Sally Jane West

Director: Christopher King
Designer: Martin Atkinson

The Hanging

w Richard Carpenter
Dick finally decides to denounce the evil and corruption of Sir John Glutton and his aide, Captain Spiker. While trying to help the mysterious Mrs Brownlow, he finds himself captured – and sentenced to death by hanging.
Mrs Brownlow Jennie Linden
Lord Harrington Philip Locke
Ranby Leo Dolan

Director: Dennis Abey
Designer: Martin Atkinson

DICK TURPIN
Producers: Paul Knight, Sidney Cole
Music by: Dennis King
A Gatetarn, Seacastle Production in Association with London Weekend Television
Filmed entirely on location at Maidenhead
31 colour 30-minute episodes
6 January – 31 March 1979
16 February – 29 March 1980
16 May – 13 June 1981
30 January – 6 March 1982

ECHO FOUR-TWO

Fresh from fighting crime on London's streets with Detective Chief Superintendent Lockhart (see: *No Hiding Place*), Detective Sergeant Harry Baxter, now promoted to Detective Inspector, took over the command of London's E Division Q-car squad. Based in Bow Street in the heart of Hatton Garden, E Division covered a wide area from the River Thames to Euston Road. (The Q-cars bore no police symbol, which allowed them to patrol areas where police vehicles would have attracted unwelcome attention.) Together with his assistant, Detective Sergeant Joe York, DI Baxter was involved in fairly routine cases of robbery, minor arson, etc. – and struggled against awful scripts!

(Scheduled to run for 13 episodes, an actors' strike interrupted production and only 10 were made.)

REGULAR CAST

Det. Insp Baxter **Eric Lander**   *Det. Sgt York* **Geoffrey Russell**
Acting Supt Dean **Geoffrey Chater**

First Day Out

w Glyn Davies
DI Baxter takes charge of the Q-car Division – and soon finds himself making his first arrest.
Acting Supt Dean **Geoffrey Chater**
PC Bird **Jeremy Longhurst**
Thief **Paul Summers**

Director: **Geoffrey Hughes**

The Dummies

w Bill Strutton
DI Baxter must find out who planned the audacious robbery of a safe from a neon-lit shop window – in full view of passing pedestrians!
Joseph Marks **George Pastell**
Snelling **Barry Steele**
Joanna Chance **Jill Medford**

Director: **James Ormerod**

Bag and Baggage

w Leonard Fincham
DI Baxter and Sgt York find themselves up against a gang of clever – though petty – thieves, who have a nice line in thievery.
'Birdie' Martin **Neil McCarthy**
George Kelly **Dermot Kelly**
Doctor **Peter Glaze**

Director: **Geoffrey Hughes**

Innocent Informer

w John Roddick
Detectives Baxter and York become involved in two separate enquiries, both of which lead to a surprising result.
Carla Perigo **Olive Lucius**
Tulio Salvator **Bartlett Mullins**
Mickie Darrow **Tony Bronte**

Director: **James Ormerod**

Hot Money

w Leslie Watkins
DI Baxter discovers how money makes money, in an unusual way – a way that leads Owen Shelby into deep trouble.
Owen Shelby **Kevin Stoney**
Sid Fenstone **Philip Latham**
Angela Maxwell **Fiona Duncan**

Director: **Geoffrey Hughes**

Opportunity Taken

w Peter Yeldham
Stopping off for a quiet 'nightcap' at a nightclub leads DI Baxter and Sgt York into an intriguing case of 'who stole what, and why?'
Frank Delaney **Peter Elliott**
Sam Norman **Donald Morley**
Angela Russell **Yolande Turner**

Director: **Wilfred Eades**

Break Out

w Paddy Manning O'Brine

When DI Baxter miscalculates a villain's nerve, he and Sgt York are soon thankful for the intervention of the 'luck of the Irish'.

Pino Cervelli Harry Lockhart
Banjo Clegg Robert Desmond
Elsie Cervelli Joan Philips

Director: Geoffrey Hughes

Frozen Fire

w Michael Nelson

A case of arson leads DI Baxter to seek scientific help to find the culprit behind the flames – and a clever insurance fraud.

Mrs Dukes Betty Paul
Mr Dukes Dudley Foster
Barmaid Lucy Young

Director: John Frankau

There She Blows

w Frederick Gold

When careless talk about a payroll shipment leads to a robbery, DI Baxter and Sgt York find themselves working overtime to crack the case.

Hymie Martin Miller
Marie Perry Diane Hart
Frank Perry Anthony Sagar

Director: Geoffrey Hughes

The Kite Dropper

w Bill Strutton

A clever crook and an unusually cooperative 'stoolie' confuse the issue in a robbery case – but a lucky break solves DI Baxter's problem.

Cyril Skinner Leslie Dwyer
Katie Joan Hickson
Judge Brian Haynes

Director: Cyril Coke

ECHO FOUR-TWO
Producer: Richard Matthews
Music by: Laurie Johnson
An Associated Rediffusion Network Production
10 monochrome 30-minute episodes
24 August – 25 October 1961

FATHER BROWN

The adventures of G. K. Chesterton's clerical sleuth, Father Brown, whose individual approach to detection and his understanding of human nature provided the solution to many unusual mysteries. Set in the twenties, the stories depicted cases investigated by the gentle detective (motto 'Have Bible . . . Will Travel'), as he encountered many human and dramatic situations.

A short-lived though fondly-remembered series. Kenneth More was a perfect choice for the quiet and retiring detective and the entire proceeding reeked of class.

REGULAR CAST

Father Brown Kenneth More   *Flambeau* Dennis Burgess

The Hammer of God
The Oracle of the Dog
The Curse of the Golden Cross
The Quick One
The Man with Two Beards
The Head of Caesar

The Eye of Apollo   The Arrow of Heaven
The Dagger with Wings   The Secret Garden
The Actor and the Alibi

FATHER BROWN
Stories adapted by: Hugh Leonard, Peter
Wildeblood, Michael Voysey, John Portman
Producer: Ian Fordyce
Directors: Robert Tronson, Peter Jeffries
Music by: Jack Parnell
An ATV Network Production
11 colour 60-minute episodes
26 September – 5 December 1974

THE FELLOWS

A continuation of the successful THE MAN IN ROOM 17 series (see entry under that name), this picked up directly where the previous series left off.

Having handed in his resignation, Oldenshaw was once again teamed up with Dimmock, when both men were jointly appointed by the Home Office to the Peel Research Fellowship at All Saints College, Cambridge (a fellowship established in 1937 by Sir Robert Peel, during his term of office as Home Secretary). The two men were handed new crime sheets to study and given a new brief: 'To investigate the general proposition that in a period of rapid social change, the nature of crime – and therefore criminals – would change.'

No longer the celebrated 'magicians', with a host of helpers ready to obey their least request, they started from scratch. Nevertheless, their ingenuity (and plausibility) to outfox even the smartest of criminals soon brought them recognition as master sleuths among their fellow colleagues.

Helping the Fellows were, Mrs Hollinsczech, a research fellow who programmed their data for them, and their star servant, Thomas Anthem.

The programme itself was structured more as a serial than a series (the scripts themselves covered a finite time period between winter and spring), and character were continued from episode to episode. (All episodes were untitled, although stories one to four carried the sub-title 'Late of Room 17'.)

(Author's note: The series itself spawned a spin-off *Spindoe* (1968), which was centred around a gangster, Alec Spindoe (played by Ray McAnally), put 'away' by the Fellows midway through the series.)

REGULAR CAST

Oldenshaw **Richard Vernon**   *Dimmock* **Michael Aldridge**
Mrs Hollinsczech **Jill Booty**   *Thomas Anthem* **James Ottaway**
Alec Spindoe **Ray McAnally**

THE FELLOWS
Created by: Robin Chapman
Producers: Robin Chapman, Peter Plummer
Directors: Claud Whatham, Bob Hird,
Cormac Newell, Robin Chapman, Cyril
Coke
Writers: Robin Chapman, Michael Sullivan,
Alan Grant
A *Granada Television Network Production*
12 monochrome 60-minute episodes
19 May – 11 August 1967

FIREBALL XL5

Fireball XL5 – one of a fleet of rockets used by the twenty-first-century World Space Patrol to monitor and protect Sector 25 of the Solar System from alien invaders – was Gerry Anderson's second 'Supermarionation' outing.

Commanded by Colonel Steve Zodiac, 'a brave and fearless hero', and his crew – Venus, a Doctor of Space Medicine (and Zodiac's romantic interest!); Professor 'Matt' Matic, Fireball's science officer and navigator; co-pilot Robert the Robot (a transparent 'brain'); and Zoonie, Venus's pet Lazoon – Fireball zoomed around the galaxy confronting all kinds of strange alien creatures (armed with equally strange weapons) and making contact with new civilisations.

Assigned to their missions by Commander Zero and his aide, Lieutenant 90, the crew's main opponents were, believe it or not – Mr and Mrs Space Spy!

More popular today than when it was first transmitted (due to the legion of Fanderson devotees, a group which specialises in collecting anything and everything produced by Gerry Anderson), the series was – if you'll forgive the pun (intended in the nicest possible way) – wooden!

CHARACTER VOICES

Steve Zodiac Paul Maxwell *Prof. Matic* David Graham *Venus* Sylvia Anderson
Robert the Robot Gerry Anderson *Commander Zero* John Bluthal
Lieut 90/Zoonie David Graham

Planet 46

w Gerry and Sylvia Anderson
A missile capable of destroying the whole
world has been fired at Earth by Planet 46.
The crew of Fireball XL5 are assigned to
stop the missile reaching its target. They do
so – but find themselves captives of the
Subterraneans.
Director: Gerry Anderson

Hypnotic Sphere

w Alan Fennell
When several space tankers are put out of
action and their crews hypnotised, Steve
Zodiac and his crew escort another tanker
and find themselves hypnotised by a strange
light beam and an equally strange voice.
Director: Alan Pattillo

Planet of Platonia

w Alan Fennell
Landing on the Platinum Planet, to take its
king to Earth for trade talks, Steve and his
team have no way of knowing that Volvo,
the king's aide, has planted a bomb inside
Robert the Robot.
Director: David Elliott

Space Magnet

w Anthony Marriott
Sent to investigate the disappearance of
Fireball XL7, Steve and his crew discover
that the remains of FBXL7 are being used to
feed a giant power house, whose
electromagnet is being used to pull the
Moon out of its orbit.
Director: Bill Harris

The Doomed Planet

w Alan Fennell
When a flying saucer leads the crew of
Fireball XL5 to Membrono – a planet
doomed to be destroyed by another planet
which has come out of its orbit – Steve

Zodiac and Robert the Robot help an old
man to save the planet from destruction.
Director: Alan Pattillo

Plant Man from Space

w Anthony Marriott
A missile lands on Earth, but fails to
explode. Soon, a giant plant begins to
threaten Space City and Steve and his crew
become involved with a new enemy – Dr
Rootes, a man possessed with growing
plants.
Director: John Kelly

The Sun Temple

w Alan Fennell
Believing that missiles from Space City,
being used to destroy rogue meteorites, will
anger their God, the Rejuscans destroy the
Space City launching site. When Zodiac and
his crew investigate, Venus is captured –
and sentenced to death.
Director: Bill Harris

Space Immigrants

w Anthony Marriott
Flying to New Earth in Mayflower III, to
set up equipment to make the new planet
suitable for human life, Venus and engineer
Jock are threatened with extinction by
Lillispations. Becoming suspicious, Zodiac
jets off to investigate.
Director: Alan Pattillo

Space Monster

w Gerry Anderson
Trying to solve the disappearance of Fireball
XL2, Zodiac and his crew receive a distress
call from the planet Monotane. Landing on
the planet in Fireball Junior, they discover
the crew of FBXL2 – guarded by a giant
space creature.
Director: John Kelly

Flying Zodiac

w Anthony Marriott

When a circus visits Space City, the clowns Madame Mivia and Cosmo – in reality Mr and Mrs Space Spy – plan to use the big top to allow the Nomadians to take over Earth. Zodiac has other ideas.
Director: BIll Harris

XL5 to H₂O

w Alan Fennell

Sent to give aid to two survivors of a planet who are being attacked by a fish man, the crew of Fireball XL5 arrive to find the glass city of the planet destroyed and that the survivors have disappeared.
Director: John Kelly

A Spy in Space

w Alan Fennell

When Fireball XL9 is attacked and damaged, Zodiac and his crew are assigned to take over its patrol duties – an event which leads them into a trap laid by Mr and Mrs Space Spy, who plan to steal Fireball XL5.
Director: Alan Pattillo

Space Pirates

w Anthony Marriott

Hearing that Space Pirates from the planet Aridan are holding up freighters from planet Minera, Zodiac decides to take a spacecraft and trick the pirates into thinking it is helpless, but the pirates get to hear of his plans.
Director: Bill Harris

Convict in Space

w Alan Fennell

Captured by Steve Zodiac after stealing some top secret documents, the spy Deblis is sentenced to 20 years imprisonment on the prison planet Conva. Flying there, Fireball and its crew are captured by Mr and Mrs Space Spy.
Director: Bill Harris

Space Pen

w Dennis Spooner

After two crooks manage to steal some isotopes from the Space City vault, Zodiac and his crew chase them to the planet Conva, where Steve tricks the crooks into thinking he is a space pirate who has stolen Fireball XL5.
Director: John Kelly

The Last of the Zanadus

w Anthony Marriott

Kudos, the last inhabitant of the planet Zanadu, plans to kill all Lazoons and gives Zoonie a deadly virus. Steve and Venus face a race against time to take possession of an antidote from Zanadu's fountain of life
Director: Alan Pattillo

The Wings of Danger

w Alan Fennell

Two Subterraneans plan to kill Zodiac by using a robot bird, fitted with deadly radium capsules. Luring the Fireball XL5 crew to their planet, the bird begins to attack – and Zodiac receives a direct hit.
Director: David Elliott

The Triads

w Alan Fennell

The crew of Fireball XL5 are sent to investigate why nuclear explosions have taken place on the planet Triad. Crashlanding on the planet, Steve and his crew find themselves under attack by a giant tiger, but rescue is on the way in the shape of two giants, Graff and Snaff.
Director: Alan Pattillo

Prisoner of the Lost Planet

w Anthony Marriott

Landing on a strange planet in response to a distress call, Steve and his crew find a beautiful woman who tells them she has been exiled there, but wants to go to Earth. When Steve tells her that isn't possible, she threatens to activate a nearby volcano and destroy the entire planet.
Director: Bill Harris

Flight to Danger

w Alan Fennell

Trying to gain his astronaut wings, Lieutenant 90 attempts a solo orbit of the Moon, but something goes wrong and his capsule explodes. Steve and his crew attempt to find him, but fail to do so.
Director: David Elliott

Sabotage

w Anthony Marriott

A bomb, planted by two Arcon warriors aboard XL5, explodes and puts the rocket out of control and the two warriors use their Gamma ray to transport Steve and his crew to their spaceship, where they are taken prisoner.
Director: John Kelly

Space Vacation

w Dennis Spooner

Zodiac, Venus and the Professor land on the planet Olympus for a holiday. At a party given in their honour, Venus is taken hostage in an attempt to get Steve to take on a secret mission.
Director: Alan Pattillo

Robert to the Rescue

w Dennis Spooner

Sent to investigate a new planet, which suddenly appears then disappears, Fireball XL5 is brought down by unseen forces. Leaving the craft, Zodiac and his crew find themselves in total blackness – and Robert the Robot disappears.
Director: Bill Harris

Mystery of TA2

w Dennis Spooner

Having discovered the wreckage of TA2, a spaceship which disappeared 50 years ago, Steve and his crew find a map which proves that Colonel Denton, the pilot of TA2, intended to reach the planet Arctan. Zodiac sets out to find him.
Director: John Kelly

The Forbidden Planet

w Anthony Marriott

Having discovered the planet Nutopia by using an ultrascope which can look into deep space, Zodiac and his crew are unaware that the Nutopians plan to use their transmission device to kidnap Venus – as their eternal companion.
Director: David Elliott

Dangerous Cargo

w Dennis Spooner

After surveying a derelict planet, Steve and his crew return to Space City and are told to return to the planet with Vesium Nine – the most powerful explosive known to man – and destroy it.
Director: John Kelly

The Granatoid Tanks

w Alan Fennell

About to leave the glass-surfaced Planet 73, two scientists see Granatoid tanks (hostile robots) coming towards them. In panic, they send a message to Space City for help, and Fireball XL5 is assigned to rescue them.
Director: Alan Pattillo

1875

w Anthony Marriott

As a joke, Steve, Venus and Commander Zero enter Professor Matic's time machine – and find themselves back in 1875, in a western town. Steve is elected Sheriff and Venus become Frenchi Lil, a bandit, with Commander Zero as her accomplice.
Director: Bill Harris

The Robot Freighter Mystery

w Alan Fennell

Suspecting that the Biggs Brothers are behind a spate of recent robot freighter sabotage, Steve is assigned to check that the brothers really are responsible for collecting 'space salvage' by dubious means.
Director: David Elliott

Drama at Space City

w Anthony Marriott

Looking after Zoonie, while Steve and Venus take a well-earned holiday, Commander Zero goes into the cabin of Fireball XL5 with the Lazoon, who gives

the order 'Full Power' – which Robert the Robot takes literally, and launches the spacecraft!
Director: Alan Pattillo

Whistle for Danger

w Dennis Spooner
Sent to the planet Floran, to launch a bomb in the atmosphere to destroy the plant disease Planetoid 3, the crew of Fireball XL5 are taken prisoner by two Florans, drugged and imprisoned in a tall tower.
Director: John Kelly

The Day the Earth Froze

w Alan Fennell
A note found in the hand of an unconscious patrol crewman leads Zodiac and his crew to a distant planet. The crew are captured by two icemen, who inform them that they plan to destroy the Earth by reflecting the Sun's rays.
Director: David Elliot

Faster Than Light

w Dennis Spooner
The supply line to Space City is placed in jeopardy when Fireball XL5's stabilisers break down. In this condition, Fireball – which travels faster than light – could prove highly dangerous for its crew.
Director: Bill Harris

Invasion Earth

w Dennis Spooner
When two Fireball patrol ships, sent to investigate a strange cloud in space, explode, and strange alien spaceships emerge from the cloud and land at Space City, Zodiac and his crew face mortal danger.
Director: Alan Pattillo

The Ghost of Space

w Alan Fennell
When Earth geologist Frazer, discovers electronic rock on the planet Electron, he asks Zodiac to take it back to Space City. The astronaut refuses – and strange things begin to happen to Steve and his crew.
Director: John Kelly

A Day in the Life of a Space General

w Alan Fennell
When Lieutenant 90 becomes General 90, things begin to go wrong. Steve Zodiac falls into a swamp while on holiday and General 90 orders a red alert to intercept an alien invasion. What can lie behind the strange events?
Director: David Elliot

Trial by Robot

w Alan Fennell
The only clue to the disappearance of robots from several planets points to the fact that wherever Professor Himber – the world's greatest authority on robots – gave lectures, robots disappeared. Zodiac must discover why.
Director: Bill Harris

Space City Special

w Dennis Spooner
Returning to Space City on one of the new supersonic airlines, Venus, in the company of General Rossiter, has no idea that the vehicle's pilot, Major Todd, has been brainwashed by the Subterraneans – and intends to crash the airliner.
Director: Alan Pattillo

The Fire Fighters

w Alan Fennell
When balls of fire begin to fall on Earth from a cloud in space, the crew of Fireball XL5 are assigned to avert the threat – a mission that ends with Zodiac risking all to save Earth from total destruction.
Director: John Kelly

FIREBALL XL5
Created by: Gerry and Sylvia Anderson
Producer: Gerry Anderson
Associate producer: Reg Hill
Music by: Barry Gray
Visual effects by: Derek Meddings
Script supervisors: Gerry and Sylvia Anderson
An AP Films Production in association with ATV and distributed by ITC
39 monochrome 30-minute episodes
25 March – 16 December 1963
(USA: NBC 5 October 1963 – 25 September 1965
Syndicated)

FOUR FEATHER FALLS

Set in a fictitious western town (the Four Feather Falls of the title), this series was Gerry Anderson's second outing into television puppetry (the first being *Torchy, the Battery Boy,* one year earlier), and depicted the cowboy exploits (antics?) of Sheriff Tex Tucker – a man who had a simple formula for dealing with lawbreakers ('Git outa town – and don't come back'). Helped by his unofficial deputies Dusty his dog and Rocky his horse (both of whom talked) and his magical guns, Tex ('One of the nicest cowpokes you could ever meet') was the scourge of cattle-rustlers and badmen in general – though his methods were so successful that he never had to kill anyone (not even his worst enemies, Pedro the Bandit and Big 'Bad' Ben)! Tex was no ordinary cowboy, you see, he had 'somethin' special' – four magical feathers given to him as a reward for saving the life of friendly Injun Chief Kalamakooya's son: provided he wore the feathers in his stetson, Tex was nigh on invincible. (One feather gave the power of speech to Dusty, another did the same for Rocky, and the remaining two feathers made Tex's guns swivel at remarkable speed and fire automatically whenever his life was in peril.)

The town was also populated by such notable 'goodies' as store owner Ma Jones, 'Doc' Haggety, and Tex's friends, Grandpa Twink and his grandson 'Little' Jake. Oh yes, in the true tradition of cowboy heroes, Tex would occasionally burst into song (particularly his favourite 'Two Gun Tex') whenever he felt the need.

(Author's note: Two episodes were often transmitted back to back to fill out a 30-minute time slot.)

CHARACTER VOICES
Tex Tucker **Nicholas Parsons** (Singing voice: Michael Holliday)
Rocky/Dusty/Pedro **Kenneth Connor**
Grandpa Twink/Fernando **David Graham** *Ma Jones/Little Jake* **Denise Bryer**

Pilot story (This episode had no o/s title)

w Barry Gray
Riding home, Tex Tucker meets a young Indian boy shivering from the cold night air, and gives him shelter for the night. During his dreams the boy calls out the name 'Kalamakooya' and a great Indian chieftain (his father) appears. As a reward for finding and caring for his son, Chief Kalamakooya gives Tex four magical feathers – and the cowboy's adventures begin.
Director: **Gerry Anderson**

(Author's note: At the time of going to press, I have been unable to discover the writers and directors of the following episodes)

Trouble at Yellow Gulch

When Mexican bandits Pedro and Fernando hold Four Feather Falls to ransom, newly-elected Sheriff Tex Tucker dons his magical six guns to save the day.

The Phantom Horseman

It appears that all the townsfolk know the legend of the phantom horseman – save one, Sheriff Tex Tucker – who rides off alone to camp in the desert.

Pedro Has a Plan

Pedro and Fernando devise a clever scheme to rid themselves of Sheriff Tex Tucker – the trouble is, they forgot to tell Tex how the story ends!

Sheriff for a Day

When Tex is called away on business, he hands over his magic guns to Little Jake so that he can protect the townsfolk – as it turns out, a foolish move.

Indian Attack

It seems that Pedro and Fernando will never learn. They try to steal Tex's magical feathers – with disastrous results.

A Close Shave

Continuing their campaign against Sheriff Tex Tucker, Pedro and Fernando think up another brilliant scheme to defeat their enemy. It goes wrong, of course.

Pedro's Pardon

Swearing to behave himself, Pedro becomes a respectable citizen. Tex, meanwhile, wonders how long this latest ruse to defeat him will last.

The Toughest Guy in the West

Grandpa Twink's boastful tales of his youthful exploits against the Indians have frequently amused his kinfolk, but now he has the chance to prove his worth – the 'Injuns are attackin'.

Gunrunners

Tex has no time for villains, so when he hears that someone is selling guns to the Indians, he sets off with Dusty to find the varmint.

Jailbreak

A $500 reward is offered for desperado Zack Morrill, and Pedro and Fernando intend to claim it. As usual, they are outwitted by Tex.

Trapped

When Jake and his litte Indian friend, Makooya, find themselves trapped while exploring treasure caves, Dusty proves his worth by finding them.

Dusty Becomes Deputy

There's trouble afoot in Four Feather Falls. With Tex away on business, Pedro and Fernando see their chance to rob the bank – but they've reckoned without Deputy Sheriff Dusty.

A Lawman Rides Alone

Against his better judgement, Sheriff Tex Tucker rides out alone to bring in two dangerous outlaws wanted for robbing the Wells Fargo stage.

Buffalo Rocky

Tex uses a bit of horse-sense (Rocky's) to track down a clever thief who has been robbing townsfolk of their mail.

Gunplay

Magical guns are useful, but when he's challenged to a shootout by a team of cattle-rustlers, Tex proves he has no need to rely on magic.

Escort

Hearing that a shipment of gold is being brought to the town, Pedro and Fernando make yet another unsuccessful bid to outwit Sheriff Tex Tucker.

A Little Bit of Luck

Taking advantage of Tex's absence, robbers decide to raid the town bank. It all seems too easy – but what if Tex returns before they make their getaway?

Best Laid Plans

This time Pedro and Fernando have devised a foolproof scheme for dealing with the Sheriff – so how come Tex is ready and waiting when they arrive in town?

The Ma Jones Story

When two strangers arrive in town with plans to put Ma Jones out of business, Tex needs all his guile to defeat them.

Election Day

It seems a forgone conclusion that Tex will be reelected as Sheriff, but Pedro has other plans – ones that don't include Tex Tucker.

Gunfight on Main Street

When Cass Morgan, an old friend of Tex Tucker's, arrives in town seeking two gunmen who shot down his brother, Tex must choose between loyalty and duty – if he is to keep the peace.

Ghost of a Chance

Mr Jackson wants to sell his valuable gold mine, but there's just one problem – the mine is haunted by ghosts. Can Tex help him lay the curse?

Once a Lawman

It appears that Tex's days as Sheriff are numbered. Someone has robbed the bank three times in as many weeks. Can the cowboy find the robber?

Landgrabbers

When greedy neighbours try to force Tex's friend to sell them his land, Tex becomes involved in a dangerous situation that could get him killed.

A Cure for Everything

The arrival in town of a medicine man spells trouble for 'Doc' Haggety. The newcomer professes to have a cure for anything – including a snoopy Sheriff!

Bandits Abroad

With $200 reward offered to anyone bringing notorious bandit, Pancho Gomez, to justice, it isn't long before Pedro and Fernando devise another crackpot scheme to get the reward.

Safe as Houses

When a silver-tongued talker comes to town and casts doubt on the bank's security system, Tex has his hands full helping the bank manager to convince people their money really is safe where it is.

Gold is Where You Find It

Confident of success, Pedro and Fernando lay plans to swindle the townsfolk out of their savings – but Tex beats them at their own game.

Gold Diggers

Why should Pedro and Fernando be anxious to spend a night in jail? Tex has his own ideas as to why – but he certainly doesn't mind locking them up.

First Train Through

When an avalanche threatens the new Canyon Railroad through Four Feather Falls, Tex must decide whether the rockfall was manmade or an act of God.

A Bad Name

When his friend Ben is framed on a charge of cattle rustling, Sheriff Tex Tucker puts his six guns to good use to prove his innocence.

Kidnapped

Serious times for Four Feather Falls. Little Makooya is critically ill – and Pedro and Fernando take 'Doc' Haggety as their hostage.

Teething Troubles

When Rocky gets a toothache, Tex must come up with a clever scheme to make him visit the dentist. You can lead a horse to water, but dentists are an entirely different matter.

Fancy Shootin'

With a circus coming to town, everyone is making plans for the big day. Tex, however, aware that gunman Lightnin' Lew has escaped from jail, suspects that he'll attempt to disrupt the festivities.

Ride 'em Cowboy

Offered a pair of new boots by the townsfolk if he rides for them in the rodeo, Tex accepts the challenge – but Pedro the bandit has other plans for the boots.

Ambush

When the railroad payroll is stolen by 'bad injuns', Tex uses Rocky's speaking abilities – not to mention his horse-sense – to save the day.

Horse Thieves

When Pedro and Fernando's horse rustling plans go wrong and place Tex's horse, Rocky, in peril, he decides to teach the bandits a hard-earned lesson.

Happy Birthday

It's round-up time in Four Feather Falls. The townsfolk throw a party in Tex's honour for all that he has done as their Sheriff.

FOUR FEATHER FALLS
Producer: Gerry Anderson
Special effects: Reg Hill
Songs: Michael Holliday
An AP Films Production for Granada TV
39 monochrome 15-minute episodes
25 February – 17 November 1960

THE FOUR JUST MEN

Based on the world famous novel by Edgar Wallace, this popular late '50s series told how Ben Manfred MP (cum amateur detective) summoned together three ex-World War II comrades at the deathbed request of their former unit commander Colonel

Bacon, who asked that they band together again to form a secret union to provide justice in a world where injustice was rife. Calling themselves The Four Just Men, Manfred and his colleagues – Poccari, one of the world's wealthiest hoteliers; American journalist Tim Collier; and brilliant freelance lawyer, Jeff Ryder – set out to administer their own brand of law wherever injustice spread its ugly tentacles. No problem proved too large or too small to merit their attention – provided the cause was worthy. Wherever they travelled, whatever they did, they were never far from danger.

Overseen by Manfred, each of the team shared their adventures with their personal secretary/assistant: Collier placed his trust (and sometimes his life) in the hands of the beautiful Nicole; Ryder's confidant was Vicky; and Italian beauty, Guilia, was never far from Poccari's side.

Each story was screened on a rotational basis – allowing each member of the team to star in their own story – though all four did sometimes work together, with Collier and Ryder's adventures being the more spectacular.

REGULAR CAST

Ben Manfred Jack Hawkins   *Tim Collier* Dan Dailey   *Jeff Ryder* Richard Conte
Ricco Poccari Vittorio De Sica   *Nicole* Honor Blackman   *Vicky* June Thorburn
Guilia Lisa Gastoni

(Author's note: the initials given after each episode denote the actor starring in that story.)

The Battle of the Bridge All
The Prime Minister D.D.
Village of Shame J.H.
The Judge R.C.
The Crying Jester V.D.S.
The Beatniques D.D.
The Deserter J.H.
Dead Man's Switch R.C.
The Night of the Precious
   Stones V.D.S.
The Deadly Capsule D.D.
Their Man in London J.H.
Maya V.D.S.
National Treasure J.H.
Panic Button R.C.
The Man with the Golden
   Touch V.D.S.

The Man in the Road D.D.
Money to Burn J.H.
Crack up R.C.
The Miracle of St Philipe D.D.
The Slaver V.D.S.
The Princess D.D.
The Protector R.C.
The Man in the Royal Suite
   V.D.S.
The Grandmother D.D.
The Man Who Wasn't There
   J.H.
The Bystanders R.C.
Rogue's Harvest V.D.S.
The Godfather D.D.
Riot R.C.
The Heritage J.H.

Marie D.D.
The Survivor J.H.
The Discovery R.C.
The Rietti Group V.D.S.
Treviso Dam V.D.S.

The Last Days of Nick
    Pompey R.C.
The Moment of Truth D.D.
Justice for Gino R.C.
The Boy without a Country J.H.

THE FOUR JUST MEN
Producers: Sidney Cole, Jud Kinberg
Executive producer: Hannah Weinstein
Directors: Basil Dearden, Don Chaffey,
Anthony Bushell, Will Fairchild,
Harry Watt
Writers: Louis Marks, Leon Griffiths
Marc Brandel, Jan Read, Lindsay Galloway
A Sapphire Films Production for ATV
Distributed by ITC
39 monochrome 30-minute episodes
17 September 1959 – 22 June 1960
(USA: Syndicated 1957)

THE FOURTH FLOOR

A slick, fast-moving cops and villains drama by Ian Kennedy Martin that starred two supercop detectives in *The Professionals'* Bodie and Doyle tradition, and depicted (sometimes violently) how Collis and Miller of Scotland Yard's serious robberies squad (based on the fourth floor of that illustrious institution – hence the title), found themselves on the trail of a crooked accountant who planned to pull off the biggest crime of the century. The story took in all the major police thriller ingredients: a 'Mr Big' behind the operation, contract Mafia killers, blackmail and extortion, a large shipment of heroin, etc., and zipped along at cracking pace.

Transmitted in three 60-minute parts over three nights, this was sparkling stuff. (Sadly, though this was intended as a pilot for a projected series, changes to the management at the production company put paid to any idea of a follow-up.)

CAST

Detective John Miller Christopher Fulford   *Detective Jim Collis* Richard Graham
Payne Kenneth Haig   *Det. Chf Supt Haladene* Brian Cox
Hanley Derrick O'Connor   *Monroe* Geoffrey Whitehead

THE FOURTH FLOOR
Created by: Ian Kennedy Martin
Producer: Ian Toynton
Executive producers: Johnny Goodman,
Lloyd Shirley
Script executive: Linda Agran
*A Euston Films Production for Thames
Television*
Networked
1 colour story of 180-minutes duration
14, 15, 16 April 1986

FRAUD SQUAD

This series brought us to the 'inside story' of Scotland Yard's Fraudulent Crimes Squad and centred around investigations handled by Detective Inspector Gamble and his aide Detective Sergeant Vicky Hicks, whose job it was to solve cases of fraud at all levels of society.

A reasonably innovative idea that became bogged down by the domestic problems of Detective Gamble.

REGULAR CAST

Det. Insp. Gamble Patrick O'Connell   *Det. Sgt Hicks* Joanna Van Gyseghem

Season One

13 colour 60-minute episodes

Turbot on Ice

w Robert Holmes
Turbot, an old lag known to the police, is picked up carrying a holdall containing £4,000. Gamble and Hicks trace the bag to its owner, Jessie Stewart, a wages clerk at a family firm, but she denies any knowledge of the money!
Frank Turbot Andrew Sachs
Jessie Stewart Margaret Vines
Derek Hollister Derek Fowlds

Director: Michael Currer-Briggs
Designer: Don Fisher

Brother Simple

w Joshua Adam
Hearing that Mrs Butcher, the wife of a wealthy businessman, has given £20,000 to a fellowship, Gamble assigns Vicky to join the sect and investigate the integrity of its leader, Brother Simple.
Brother Simple Michael Coles
Mrs Butcher Elvi Hale
Det Cons Fox Geoffrey Kenion

Director: Michael Currer-Briggs
Designer: Don Fisher

Last Exit to Liechtenstein

w Jack Trevor Story
Rex Lucien, on bail with a fraud charge hanging over his neck, gatecrashes the Policeman's Ball to 'settle accounts' with Gamble, the man who arrested him. But is there another reason for his untimely intrusion?
Rex Lucien Michael Gambon
Diana Lucien Angela Brown
Harry Drew Richard Carpenter

Director: Paul Annett
Designer: Anthony Waller

Run for Your Money

w Basil Dawson

A simple confidence trick hardly seems
worthy of Gamble's attention – until the
wily detective realises that he may have
underestimated Kay Pilgrim, the boss of a
con team preying on houseowners.
Kay Pilgrim Caroline Blakiston
Jacky Joyce Michael Gothard
Det. Cons. Fox Geoffrey Kenion

Director: Raymond Menmuir
Designer: Anthony Waller

All Claims Paid For

w Jack Trevor Story

A fraud with a difference is brought to
Gamble's attention: someone is getting rich
by selling undelivered domestic appliances
to an old folks' home. The detective digs
deeper to find out who is behind the con
game.
Marchmont Martin Shaw
Kathy Finbow Collette O'Neil
Supt Proud Ralph Nossek

Director: Paul Annett
Designer: Trevor Patterson

Over a Barrel

w Basil Dawson

The blackmailing of an illegal immigrant
appears to be outside the duties of the Fraud
Squad, but Gamble and Hicks nevertheless
become involved, which revives a bitter
conflict within Gamble's own family.
Helen Gamble Elizabeth Weaver
Lucy Gamble Katherine O'Connell
Nala Cheudray Christopher Benjamin

Director: Paul Annett
Designer: Trevor Patterson

Where's George

w Jack Trevor Story

Everyone is asking the same question.
Where *is* George? His wife wants to know,
so does his business partner, his father-in-
law, and Inspector Gamble – who suspects
that George can help him account for a
missing £50,000!

George Carroway John Aberini
Joy Carroway Jan Waters
Angus Dalziel Donald Douglas

Director: Raymond Menmuir
Designer: Anthony Waller

The Front Man

w George Lancaster

Tommy Morrissey has a nice line in
swindles. He's a conman with a heart of
stone. He moves into town, sets up his
prey, than leaves – with his pockets
crammed full of other people's cash. He's on
Gamble's patch – and the detective wants
him!
Tommy Morrissey John Nettleton
Meredith John Kidd
Capt. Oakes Graham Crowden

Director: Paul Annett
Designer: Don Fisher

The Biggest Borrower of All

w Robert Banks Stewart

When a building society executive who has
tried to kill himself mutters the word 'fraud'
from his hospital bed, Gamble takes an
interest – and discovers that the building
society manager has booked a one-way ticket
to Zurich.
Joseph Horden Paul Eddington
Mrs Keever Noel Dyson
Brophy Richard Hampton

Director: Robert D. Cordona
Designer: Trevor Patterson

Pros and Cons

w Geoffrey and Rosemary Bellman

One con merchant on his patch is one too
many for Inspector Gamble. So when he
hears that Harry, a comparative minnow in
a major school of fraudulent activities, is
swimming back to town, he takes note of
the man's activities.
Harry Roddy McMillan
Grant Terence Seward
Emberton Arthur Cox

Director: Raymond Menmuir
Designer: Anthony Waller

Cold as Charity

w Basil Dawson

Mindful that 'duty comes before everything', Gamble enters into his latest case – a fraud in which Gamble's friend, Stefan Pastek, appears to be implicated – with misgivings that he may have to choose between loyalty and duty.

Stefan Pastek Philip Stone
Lord Griffin Laurence Hardy
Supt Proud Ralph Nossek

Director: Michael Currer-Briggs
Designer: Don Fisher

Two Kinds of Crash

w Anthony Marriott

Arthur New's troubles really begin when he crashes his new car. Claiming off his insurance proves tricky, especially when it appears that someone has made off with his – and other people's – premium payments. Gamble investigates.

Arthur New Geoffrey Palmer
Olly West Colin Welland
Madge New Jane Watson

Director: Michael Currer-Briggs
Designer: Don Fisher

Anybody Here Seen Kelly?

w Jack Trevor Story

A valuable painting believed to have been destroyed in a fire turns up in Ireland, and Gamble travels to Dublin to interview Kelly, an elderly art dealer. But Kelly has disappeared – why?

Captain Maclennan William Dexter
Kelly Liam Redmond
Jacklin Gerald James

Director: Michael Currer-Briggs
Designer: Don Fisher

Season Two

13 colour 60-minute episodes

The Martin Kessel File

w Basil Dawson

Hot on the trail of a forger who has caused him many a problem over the years, Inspector Gamble applies for a warrant to search the man's premises – only to be told that the Kessel case is closed.

Martin Kessel Rupert Davies
Supt Proud Ralph Nossek
Gilbey Noel Johnson

Director: Paul Annett
Designer: Anthony Waller

The White Abyss

w Stuart Douglas

Hearing that Henry Cornwallis – believed to have died in a climbing accident and for whom a memorial fund was set up – has been seen in Switzerland, Inspector Gamble leaves to investigate.

Percy Sayers Alan Browning
Angela Cornwallis Wendy Gifford
Henry Cornwallis Peter Jeffrey

Director: John Sichel
Designer: Gerry Roberts

Robbing Peter . . . to Pay Paul

w Alan Falconer

When Taylor, a retired railway clerk, informs Gamble that a young woman called Phyllis has conned him out of his savings, Vicky is assigned to the case . . . and finds herself with a bit of a problem.

Phyllis Stewart Dilys Laye
Peter Taylor Arthur Brough
Mrs Brodny Dandy Nichols

Director: Paul Annett
Designer: Anthony Waller

Double Deal

w Lewis Greifer

Hearing that conman Charlie Dickens is 'going straight' and has found a 'respectable' job, the cynical and experienced Gamble is sceptical of Charlie's claims. Vicky, however, is prepared to give him the benefit of the doubt – an unwise move.

Charlie Dickens Dinsdale Landen
Sir Roy Prentice Richard Vernon
'Soapy' Richards Peter Woodthorpe

Director: Paul Annett
Designer: Anthony Waller

The Harland Affair

w Martin Worth

Building tycoon Jim Harland's firm can only survive if he forms a partnership with a Dutch firm – a building company Gamble suspects of fraudulent activities. An inspection of Harland's books is called for, which, when checked reveals some surprising discrepancies.

Jim Harland Andrew Keir
Dr Ashley Jeremy Longhurst
Alec Thornton Anthony Woodruff

Director: Ron Francis
Designer: Don Fisher

Inquest

w Richard Harris

A shock awaits Detective Gamble when he is called into his superiors' office. Laughton, a tax investigator asks the detective a lot of disturbing questions – questions relating to the left-wing activities of Gamble's wife, Helen.

Laughton Brewster Mason
Helen Gamble Elizabeth Weaver
Lucy Gamble Katherine O'Connell

Director: Paul Annett
Designer: Michael Eve

People Can Go So Far . . .

w Ivor Jay

Gamble is asked to investigate the activities of a retired spinster, a woman responsible for administering a charity fund for the sick and needy – to which only one payment has been granted in three years.

Grace Miles Patience Collier
Major Brampton Clive Morton
June Anstruther Joyce Carey

Director: Paul Annett
Designer: Michael Bailey

Remission – Negative

w Richard Harris

After receiving a complaint from a man whose wife died after being admitted to a clinic specialising in nervous diseases, Gamble investigates the establishment and discovers a ruthless doctor exploiting the sick for his own gain.

Dr Matthews Anton Rodgers
Virginia Matthews Veronica Hurst
Stamford Roger Hammond

Director: John Sichel
Designer: Anthony Waller

Whizz Kid

w Paul Wheeler

Roger Simms' youthful zest and flair for management has been a shot in the arm for Burton Investments, but he doesn't get along with the older and more experienced Arthur Mills, the man he replaced. Is that the reason behind Mills' accusations of discrepancies in the firm's books?

Roger Simms Edward Petherbridge
Arthur Mills Tenniel Evans
Liz Simms Hilary Pritchard

Director: David Foster
Designer: Don Fisher

The Great Blanket Factory Swindle

w Stuart Douglas

The Cozy Lamb Blanket Factory is losing money fast – partly due to its chairman, 80-year-old Lady Flanders, but mostly due to petty pilfering. But does £40,000 come under that heading? Gamble thinks not – and investigates the firm.

Lady Flanders Fay Compton
Mr Bender John Moore
Herbert Pitt Donald Eccles

Director: John Sichel
Designer: Stanley Mills

The Hot Money Man

w Roy Russell

The Fraud Squad team investigate a currency leak by keeping tabs on wealthy Harry Killett, whom they suspect of making his fortune by smuggling money out of the country. So when he deposits a large suitcase with an Investment Company, Gamble swoops – but the criminals are one jump ahead of him.

Harry Killett Kevin Brennan
Aubrey Downsmith Julian Curry
Liz Downsmith Deborah Stanford

Director: John Sichel
Designer: Stanley Mills

Golden Island

w Lewis Greifer

Winifred Holland, a wealthy spinister, lives with her mother and works for Captain Garland, a writer and explorer wishing to mount an expedition to search for Spanish treasure. Winifred is prepared to finance the treasure hunt – until Gamble points out that the real Captin Garland died five years earlier.

Winifred Holland **Phyllida Law**
Bill Garland **George Baker**
Yvonne Schenk **Lisa Daniely**

Director: **Paul Annett**
Designer: **Michael Bailey**

The Price of a Copper

w Robert Holmes

Fraud, extortion, vice . . . the Dysart Brothers are in for a percentage of everything. Outwardly respectable, their legitimate business is a front for criminal activities. Gamble is intent on tearing down their empire – by whatever means it takes.

Tony Dysart **Donald Burton**
Mickey Dysart **David Calder**
Lady Sarah **Doris Rogers**

Director: **Paul Annett**
Designer: **Michael Bailey**

FRAUD SQUAD
Created by: Ivor Jay
Producer: Nicolas Palmer
Associate producer: Robert D. Cordona
An ATV Network Production
26 colour 60-minute episodes
20 May – 12 August 1969
19 September – 12 December 1970

FUNERAL RITES

(A Chief Inspector Jim Taggart adventure)
See: *Taggart*

THE FUZZ

This seven-part comedy series took a light-hearted look at the day-to-day happenings of a small city police force based 'north of Watford'.

Played strictly for laughs, it had three things going for it: scripts by Willis Hall (creator of *BUDGIE*), character actor Michael Robbins (always reliable), and actress Lynda Bellingham (always enticing). The former played Detective Sergeant Marble, who was forever in danger of losing his own (marbles, that is) because he was required to pick up the pieces and carry the can for the disastrous results obtained by the two constables under his command, PCs Cordwainer and Dickinson – two of the most inept coppers ever to don police uniform. Assigned to drive the station's sole 'Panda' car (for Panda read Z – for Zany!), the two coppers were let loose on an unsuspecting public and created havoc on their patch, spending much of their on-duty hours daydreaming that one day they would be assigned to investigate 'the big one' – a major crime. (In reality they found themselves chasing after handbag snatchers, pantie thieves or checking into a break-in at the local fish and chip shop!) Meanwhile, Miss Bellingham, the station's only WPC, would almost certainly find herself staving off the advances of the station's Chief Superintendent Allardyce – and who could blame him.

REGULAR CAST

Det. Sgt Marble Michael Robbins   *PC Cordwainer* Nigel Lambert
PC Dickinson Mike Savage   *WPC ('Purrfect') Purvis* Lynda Bellingham
Supt Allardyce Colin Jeavons

THE FUZZ
Created by: Willis Hall
Producer: Stuart Allen
Director: Stuart Allen

A Thames Television Network Production
7 colour 30-minute episodes
8 September – 20 October 1977

THE GAY CAVALIER

'Three hundred years ago, England was locked in Civil War. From this struggle emerged many colourful figures. Cavaliers, highwaymen, adventurers – men of reckless courage who loved and laughed at danger. Captain Claude Duval is a little of all of them – and he fights injustice wherever he finds it.'

A par-for-the-course swashbuckler that raised more smiles than the scripts intended.

REGULAR CAST

Captain Duval (The Gay Cavalier) Christian Marquand
Dinny O'Toole Larry Burns   *Major Mould* Ivan Craig

Springtime for Julia

w Charlotte Hastings
Vast sums of money are needed to finance the new state and its armies to fight those opposing King Charles. Loyal subject, Claude Duval, sees an opportunity to earn himself some gold – at Cromwell's expense.
Julia Greta Gynt
Peckstaff Roddy Hughes
Major Jawkins Bruno Barnabe

Director: Terence Fisher

Dragon's Heart

w Brock Williams
If Captain Claude Duval and his comrade Dinny O'Toole can seize the 'Dragon's Heart' – a priceless ruby, and part of the Crown Jewels – from a traitorous Dutch merchant, England will be a safer place for subjects loyal to the King.
Cathie Joyce Linden
Bulstrode Willoughby Goddard
Sergeant Russell Waters

Director: Lance Comfort

The Lady's Dilemma

w Jack Andrews

With Cromwell and his Roundheads selling off state property, King Charles looks powerless to intervene. But he has reckoned without the aid of Claude Duval, who has more than one way of dealing with the enemy.

Lady Jane Jean Anderson
Colonel Jeffries Christopher Lee
Lord Drayton Roger Maxwell

Director: Lance Comfort

The Masked Lady

w Charlotte Hastings and Gordon Wellesly

Having made away with secret Roundhead documents, Duval is astonished when he himself is robbed of the papers by a mysterious masked girl on a black horse. Following her, he discovers two masked ladies. But who is who?

Elizabeth Barribell Colette Wilde
Margaret Pamela Thomas
Grindly Henry Oscar

Director: Lance Comfort

Angel Unawares

w Charlotte Hastings

When the Court of St Mary's is plundered by Cromwell's troops, Captain Duval is asked to retrieve 'The Angel' – a priceless carved statuette which belongs to the church and was carried away during the raid.

Mother Therese Nora Gorsen
Clo Simone Silva
Deacon Charles Farrell

Director: Lance Comfort

Flight of the Nightingale

w Brock Williams

Believing that if one sets a thief to catch a thief one will reap rich rewards, Major Mould, Cromwell's chief intelligence officer, lays a trap for Duval. But the Cavalier turns the tables – and Mould is soon regretting his move.

Major Mould Ivan Craig
Purdy Sydney Bromley
Rosie O'Dowd Charlotte Mitchell
Director: Lance Comfort

The Sealed Knot

w Jack Andrews

Duval's life depends upon him exposing which member of 'The Sealed Knot' – a secret Royalist organisation in which the Roundheads are interested – is a spy in Cromwell's pay.

Lady Travers Christine Hayward
Sir Richard John Le Mesurier
Sir Robert Conrad Philips

Director: Terence Fisher

The Lost is Found

w Anthony Verney

A dying man, Sir Edward Claydon, asks Captain Duval to find his son, who joined the Roundheads when they took over power. Duval's attempts to find the boy are hampered by the boy's sister, Mary. Why?

Mary Claydon Hazel Court
Sir Edward Anthony Dexter
Ralph Claydon Nigel Stock

Director: Lance Comfort

Girl of Quality

w Brock Williams

Assigned by the King to rescue Lady Hamilton, a school teacher in Rye – the scene of recent revolts and street fighting – Claude and Dinny find themselves engaged in more than a simple rescue attempt.

Lady Hamilton Judy Bloom
Purdy Sydney Bromley
De Freitas Frank Pettingel

Director: Terence Fisher

The Little Cavalier

w Anthony Verney

It's nothing new when children's fathers go missing under Cromwell's rule – his men round up all the able-bodied menfolk, and set them to work building his fortresses. But this time Duval is on hand to save a young child from becoming an orphan.

Nicolas Michael Brook
Clo Simone Silva
The Deacon Charles Farrell

Director: Lance Comfort

Return of the Nightingale

w Brock Williams
Captain Duval and Dinny O'Toole must
rescue Beatrice from an unwanted marriage
to Roundhead, Captain Moorfield, before he
finds out that her dowry has been given to
the Royalist cause.
Captain Moorfield Robin Bailey
Beatrice Sara Gregory
Malpass Hector Young

Director: Lance Comfort

Forsaking All Others

w Charlotte Hastings and Gordon Wellesly
Young Philip Desmond is suspected of
treachery by his Royalist friends. Duval
believes him innocent of the charge – but he
must first convince himself of the truth and
the motives behind Philip's actions.
Philip Desmond Paul Hansard
Mary Christine Labiez
Lord Suffolk G. H. Mulcaster

Director: Lance Comfort

A Throne at Stake

w Jack Andrews
Duval and Dinny face the greatest test of
their lives. They must locate the
whereabouts of a Loyalist who can save the
throne of England from falling into
Cromwell's hands. But the man, hunted by
Roundheads, has gone to ground, and they
have no idea of where to begin their search.
Cathie Joyce Linden
Purdy Sydney Bromley
Peter Sacks Richard Bobb

Director: Lance Comfort

THE GAY CAVALIER
Producer: George King
*A George King Production for Associated
Rediffusion TV*
13 monochrome 30-minute episodes
12 July – 20 September 1957

THE GENTLE TOUCH

A detective drama series that documented the exploits of
Detective Inspector Maggie Forbes – British television's first
female detective – and her colleagues at Seven Dials police
station adjacent to London's Soho district.

Having joined the Metropolitan Police as a rookie cadet
straight from school and worked her way up to the rank of DI,
Maggie Forbes was a plain clothes cop with a gentle approach to
her police work – but nevertheless found life tough. Recently
widowed, she was forced to combine her duties as a detective
with the task of rearing her teenage son – and thereby lay the
problem with the first dozen or so episodes of the series; they lost
sight of their objective and became bogged down with Maggie's
domestic problems.

With stories that seldom strayed far from the established cops
and robbers format (week in, week out investigations into rape,
murder, violent crime, and so on), it is difficult to sum up the
series' appeal to the public, who warmed to Maggie's adventures
in droves and made the programme a resounding success.

Sharing the spotlight with DI Forbes were Detective Chief Inspector Russell — Maggie's boss — Detective Sergeant Jake Barratt, Detective Inspector Bob Croft, Detective Sergeant Jimmy Fenton, and (from series four) Detective Sergeant Peter Philips, who made up the CID division at Seven Dials.

REGULAR CAST

DI Maggie Forbes Jill Gascoine   *Det. Chf. Insp. Russell* William Marlowe
DS Jake Barratt Paul Moriarty   *DI Bob Croft* Brian Gwaspari
DS Jimmy Fenton Derek Thompson   *DS Peter Philips* Kevin O'Shea
Steve Forbes (Maggie's son) Nigel Rathbone

Season One

7 60-minute episodes

Killers

w Brian Finch   *(A 2-part story))*
Maggie Forbes, just promoted to Detective Inspector in the Metropolitan Police, reaches a crossroads in her life. Within hours of her promotion her police constable husband is shot dead by two brothers. Maggie is ordered to stay at home while her colleagues investigate the killing.
PC Ray Forbes Leslie Schofield
Dale Bladen Jason Savage
Harry Bladen Brian Croucher

Director: Tony Wharmby
Designer: Gordon Melhuish

Recoil

w Brian Finch   *(Part 2 of debut story)*
Tired of sitting at home, Maggie disobeys orders and sets out to find her husband's killers. Having received a tip-off from a contact in the criminal world that the gun used in the crime was supplied by illicit arms dealer Jackie Frost, she hands her information to Chief Inspector Russell — and tells him she is resigning from the force.
Jed Bladen Stephen Yardley
Harry Bladen Brian Croucher
Frost Michael Tudor Barnes

Director: Christopher Hodson
Designer: John Clements

Help

w Roger Marshall
Having withdrawn her resignation, Maggie tries to sort out the problems facing her friend Susan Scott and her daughter. What she doesn't know is that trouble is on her own doorstep — her son Steven has taken to drinking.
Susan Scott Beth Harris
Linda Kate Dorning
Station officer Peter Spraggon

Director: David Askey
Designer: Gordon Melhuish

Shock

w Roger Marshall
When a woman is found dead in a 'love nest', Det. Insp. Maggie Forbes is handed the case. She builds up a strong picture of how the crime was carried out, but further investigations lead to several shocks for the people involved.
Peter Rylands Christopher Bramwell
Brian Rylands Robert Austin
Linda Trudi Styler

Director: Tony Wharmby
Designer: John Clements

Blade

w Roger Marshall
A young man found murdered in the London Underground one morning has been stabbed with a knife. The nature of the crime points to a homosexual encounter — which eventually leads Maggie to a blazing row with her colleague, DI Croft.
Thorne Kenneth Gilbert
Mrs Thorne Patricia Garwood
Larry John Wheatley

Director: Christopher Hodson
Designer: John Clements

Rogue

w Pat Hooker

Interviewing an unsuccessful businessman who is suspected of deliberately setting fire to his premises for the insurance, Maggie takes offence when the man offers her a bribe. But even stranger offers are waiting around the corner – ones that Maggie can't ignore.
No cast credits available

Director: David Askey
Designer: Gordon Melhuish

Melody

w Terence Feely

Maggie investigates the death of Melody, a call-girl found murdered in her flat. When none of the other call-girls can offer any insight into Melody's background, Maggie suspects that their pimp, Miller, has put the 'frighteners' on them.
No cast credits available.

Director: Paul Annett
Designer: Unknown

Season Two
10 60-minute episodes

Something Blue

w Tony Hoare

Resigned to a life without her husband – but still having problems with Steven, her teenage son – Maggie finds solace in an unusual case of robbery, one that will test her investigative powers to the full.
Chris Adams Linda Robson
Jenny Burns Diana Malin
Sue Williams Judy Lloyd

Director: John Reardon
Designer: Frank Nerini

Decoy

w Terence Feely

When a girl is attacked and raped, DI Maggie Forbes goes undercover and poses as a barmaid to try and trap the rapist – but acting as a decoy places her life in great danger.

Dr Bill Ryder Richard Owens
Tommy Hunter Peter Davidson
Turot David Sterne

Director: John Reardon
Designer: Frank Nerini

Break-in

w Terence Feely

A burglary at the office of a solicitor who prosecutes for the police leads to a crisis situation between Maggie and one of her superiors, when the detective uncovers some incriminating evidence.
Noel Simpson David Gant
Jack Ledley Colin McCormack
Mrs Ledley Linda Redwick

Director: Tony Wharmby
Designer: Gordon Melhuish

Menaces

w Roger Marshall

Ivor Stocker, JP and successful businessman, is being blackmailed. Maggie, assigned to investigate the blackmail threats, uncovers a can of worms in the offices of a 'respectable' law company.
Ivor Stocker Joss Ackland
June Stafford Judy Loe
Phil Rae Robert Morgan

Director: Paul Annett
Designer: Andrew Gardner

Hammer

w Tony Parker

When a series of robberies with violence – all bearing a similar pattern, and all carried out by women – break out on Maggie's patch, the detective must decide whether the crimes were committed by a team, or one woman in several disguises.
Frances West Rossalind Ayres
Nellie Jackson Derek Martin
Maureen Leslie Ash

Director: Tony Wharmby
Designer: John Clements

Chance

w Pat Hooker

Having spent several frustrating hours at the law courts, Maggie is anxious to get back to the paper work piling up on her desk. But even paperwork has its drawbacks — particularly when a clue to a major crime lies hidden among its sheets.

Simon Fox John Gregg
Bert Prendergast Rio Fanning
Mr Johnson Graham Rowe

Director: David Askey
Designer: John Clements

Loyalties

w Tony Parker

When Mrs Beresford, wife of a wealthy and respected businessman, is threatened with a knife by a menacing masked figure, who then runs away, leaving her unharmed, DI Maggie Forbes find herself assigned to the case.

Mary Beresford Honor Shepherd
Victor Beresford John Barron
Alan Lawson Ray Lonnen (Intro.)

Director: James Gatward
Designer: Andrew Gardner

Maggie's Luck

w David Crane

Maggie is looking forward to a hard-earned weekend break and a date with Alan Lawson. Her son Steve wants mum 'out of the way'. But it looks as though both plans could be thwarted — until help arrives from an unexpected source.

Alan Lawson Ray Lonnen
Elaine Jennifer Hilary
McNally Don Fellows

Director: Nic Phillips
Designer: Gordon Melhuish

Shame

w Roger Marshall

When a badly beaten young boy refuses to name his attackers, DI Maggie Forbes and DS Fenton's enquiries lead them to suspect that they are dealing with something far more alarming than child cruelty.

Peter Lee Whitlock
Dr Winner Angus MacKay
Dennis Tilley Michael Melia

Director: Peter Moffatt
Designer: David Catley

The Ring

w Neil Rudyard

Maggie's delight at being courted by the rich, unattached and amorous Dave Connally soon changes to suspicion when he gives her a Victorian ring — part of a jewel haul being investigated by her colleagues at Seven Dials.

Dave Connally George Sewell
Solly Goldmeir Bernard Spear
Frank Cowley Tim Pearce

Director: Paul Annett
Designer: Michael Minas

Season Three

13 60-minute episodes

Gifts

w Terence Feely

When Maggie and Steve begin to receive gifts in the post, both are puzzled and ask themselves who their mysterious benefactor can be? An admirer? Someone with a crush on Maggie . . . or someone playing a very dangerous game?

Mr Selby Jim Wiggins
Mr Allenby Roger Ostime
Mr Pusey Ray Gatenby

Director: Christopher Hodson
Designer: Mike Oxley

Doubt

w Anthony Biggam

A young PC is badly injured by villains, and Maggie Forbes begins to wonder whether a woman can really handle police work when the police themselves are no longer respected or welcomed by the general public.

Sam Taylor David Dakar
Ian Harding Christopher Villiers
Jacko Edward Peel

Director: Paul Annett
Designer: Frank Nerini

The Hit

w Terence Feely

A marksman with a highpowered rifle is loose on Maggie's patch and she is assigned to take over the case. Against her better judgement she allows herself to be led into the marksman's rifle sights.
Johnny Delvaux Nick Tate
Gerald Harvey George Baker
Mrs Chandler Trudi Goodwin

Director: Nic Phillips
Designer: David Catley

Scapegoat

w Roger Marshall

Investigating a break-in at a community centre, DI Maggie Forbes and DS Jake Barratt uncover clues which lead them to suspect that the crime was carried out by people harbouring racial prejudice – but no one will confirm their suspicions.
Martin Hersh Harry Towb
Sylvia Hersh Gillian Raine
Rick Sloan Gary Holton

Director: John Reardon
Designer: Colin Monk

Knife

w Ray Jenkins

Maggie must find a potentially violent teenager who has escaped from a top-security remand centre. Her assignment is a difficult one. The girl hates men, her parents – and has sworn to kill Maggie on sight!
Debbie Sylvestra Le Touzel
Ralph Burwell Neil McCarthy
Jimmy Paris Nick Stringer

Director: Christopher Baker
Designer: Frank Nerini

Protection

w Roger Marshall

Should a policewoman seek the help of friends when investigating a crime? That's the question Maggie must ask when she places the life of an old acquaintance on the line in her search for protection racketeers.

Harry Warren Tony Selby
Maria Lina Maryan
Dave Connally George Sewell

Director: Carol Wiseman
Designer: Andrew Gardner

Paint it Black

w Kenneth Ware

Is a young girl suspect really behind the killing of a café proprietor? Before she can answer that question, Maggie must first of all find her suspect – and a possible witness to the crime.
Jane Dean Tammi Jacobs
Andy Golding Tony Scannell
Cynthia Collins Gayle Runciman

Director: Nic Phillips
Designer: David Catley

Affray

w James Doran

Tempers run high at Seven Dials. A WPC is in Intensive Care after some youths started a riot at a student meeting. DI Maggie Forbes and DS Jake Barratt have to deal with a generation who show intense dislike of the police – and their methods.
WPC Evans Jean Hastings
Douglas James Simmons
Hodges Roy Alexander

Director: Christopher Baker
Designer: Richard Dunn

Black Fox, White Vixen

w Jeremy Burnham

When a famous actress in a long-running TV series begins to receive death threats, Maggie Forbes and her team are assigned to protect her – but trouble springs from a most unexpected quarter.
Marcia Bancroft Elizabeth Counsell
Keith Bristow Martyn Jacobs
Brian Spencer Ronald Hines

Director: Nic Phillips
Designer: David Catley

One of Those Days

w Neil Rudyard

A drunken bank robber is causing havoc at Seven Dials, but only Maggie seems to be taking him seriously. Everyone else is busy coping with their own problems – until the situation turns nasty.
Dooley David Kelly
Doyle Tony Doyle
Edna Slater Liz Smith

Director: Nic Phillips
Designer: David Catley

Vigil

w Tony Parker

DS Barratt and DS Fenton are delighted when they learn that a beautiful policewoman has been seconded to Seven Dials. So is DI Croft – and he outranks them. Maggie meanwhile smiles knowingly.
WPC Whittaker Lynne Ross
Amanda Scott Susan Tracy
Annette Dilys Laye

Director: Peter Cregeen
Designer: Frank Nerini

Damage

w P. J. Hammond

Maggie Forbes, assigned to investigate the plight of Mr Pascoe, whose small son Peter is in trouble, has tragedy of her own to deal with. But what comes first, one's duty or one's family loyalties?
Mr Pascoe Robert Longden
Peter Peter Thistleton
Mrs Appleton Helen Cherry

Director: Carol Wiseman
Designer: Andrew Gardner

Solution

w P. Hammond

When confronted with personal tragedy, DI Maggie Forbes and Det. Chf Insp. Russell are forced to examine their feelings about mercy killings. Maggie in particular has to examine her own judgement of the case.

George Taylor James Ottaway
Dr Tyson John Pennington
Jean Fiona Walker

Director: Carol Wiseman
Designer: Andrew Garden

Season Four

13 60-minute episodes

Right of Entry

w Neil Rudyard

A day in the life of a policewoman. DI Maggie Forbes has more than enough on her plate – a dead burglar, a severe case of paranoia – without the finicky nit-picking of a new sergeant to the team.
DS Peter Philips Kevin O'Shea (Intro.)
Leo Frank Thornton
Auntie Win Avis Bunnage

Director: John Reardon
Designer: Andrew Gardner

Be Lucky Uncle

w Geoff McQueen

When Maggie's most reliable informant disappears, and dangerous allegations are made about DI Bob Croft, Maggie and her team have their hands full dealing with their own problems, let alone crimebusting.
Turk Art Malik
Fisher Oliver Smith
Eskimo Ben Thomas

Director: Gerry Mill
Designer: Rodney Cammish

Cause and Effect

w Guy James

When an articulate, well-educated coloured boy confesses to a crime he did not commit, and her son Steve seeks advice which only a father can give, Maggie's problems go from bad to worse.
Mark Brian Bovell
Mr Coombes Frank Mills
Paula Livesey Mary Peach

Director: Nic Phillips
Designer: Richard Dunn

Auctions

w Chris Barlas

When two outwardly gentle old ladies cause havoc at a sale of major paintings, Maggie enters into the world of art collecting, with the aid of Scotland Yard art expert, Sgt Sid Bryant.

Sgt Sid Bryant Michael Cronin
Lucius Peter Cellier
Finnerman Bernard Kay

Director: Gerald Blake
Designer: Rae George

Dany

w Ray Jenkins

If she is to save the life of an important witness, Maggie must gain the confidence of a beautiful French student – the only one who knows the whereabouts of a man who is running from a gang of pornography merchants.

Dany Joanne Whalley
Helmut Ritter Frederick Jaeger
DI Mary Woods Gwynneth Powell

Director: Gerald Blake
Designer: David Catley

Victims

w P. J. Hammond

Two events threaten the peaceful surroundings of Seven Dials. DS Jake Barratt becomes smitten with a beautiful mugging victim, and Maggie encounters a case of a wife sharer – with a very persistent suitor.

Adela Baker Sheila Gish
Mike Turnbull Bernard Holley
WPC Evans Jean Hastings

Director: Christopher Hodson
Designer: John Emery

The Meat Rack

w Roger Marshall

A dangerous mission for DI Maggie Forbes. A maniac is slashing prostitutes who work out of a London pub and she is assigned to go 'on the game' with a very convincing pimp – a CID detective.

Det. Chf. Insp. Grout John Brown
Christine Mitzi Rogers
Sally Leslie Dane

Director: Gerald Blake
Designer: Rodney Cammish

Joker

w Ray Jenkins

When a frustrated detective with an oddball sense of humour makes things happen to cop an arrest or two, and things get out of hand when an elderly man is wrongfully arrested for jewel robbery, Maggie shows him the joker in her hand.

DC Power Enn Reitel
Jimmy Ogden Arthur English
Malcolm Webster Alan Lake

Director: Nic Phillips
Designer: Bryan Bagge

Tough Mrs Rudge

w Tony Couch

Why is Mrs Rudge so terrified of Ginger? When the old lady is arrested for shoplifting, DI Maggie Forbes and her team become involved in a hunt for a vicious gang who prey on pensioners.

Mrs Rudge Kathleen St John
Mike Turnbull Barry Johns
Police Doctor David Hanson

Director: Nic Phillips
Designer: Andrew Gardner

Private Views

w Tony Parker

When a grass reports that a gang of thieves is about to enter the Seven Dials' manor, every officer is put on standby and all weekend leave is cancelled until the matter is cleared up.

Finch Mark Botham
Foxy Roberts Gary Dean
The Colonel Hugh Cross

Director: John Davies
Designer: Rae George

Pressures

w Kenneth Ware

Most policemen become hardened to the long line of gory crimes they investigate as part of their day to day duties. But how long does it take for one of them to crack. Maggie is about to find out.

Supt Parker Richard Borthwick
Ray Gillespie Stewart Bevan
Det. Chf Insp. Smedley Chris Johnson

Director: Nic Phillips
Designer: Andrew Gardner

Weekend

w P. J. Hammond

Though Mr and Mrs Issard live in the same house, they live completely different lives. When DS Peter Philips calls at the house in response to a complaint, and Mrs Philips accuses her husband of trying to poison her, Maggie takes an interest.

Mrs Philips Anne McCarthy
Mr Philips Arthur Rowe
Police Constable Jerry Waring

Director: John Davies
Designer: Andrew Gardner

Who's Afraid of Josie Tate

w Neil Rudyard

It's a sad day for DI Maggie Forbes when she encounters Mrs Tate – a wife who is determined to help her jailed husband get justice. Her explosive challenge takes the detective unawares – and Maggie leaves Seven Dials on a stretcher.

Jocelyn Tate Paola Dionisotti
Dr Gladstone Colin Rix
Wally Tate Ralph Bates

Director: Gerry Mill
Designer: David Catley

Season Five

13 60-minute episodes

Finders, Keepers

w Neil Rudyard   *(A 2-part story)*

Having moved house, Maggie returns to Seven Dials for the first time since the explosion wrecked her office, and almost cost her her life. She arrives at a time when her colleagues are investigating a gang of small-time crooks.

DI Mike Turnbull Bernard Holley
Alice Fairbrother Lynda Bellingham
Dudley Fairbrother Eamon Boland

Director: Gerry Mill
Designer: Bryan Bagge

Losers, Weepers

w Neil Rudyard

Having stumbled across millions of pounds in forged notes, a gang are determined not to hand the money back. Maggie and her team must help them change their minds.

Eskimo Ben Thomas
Oscar Derrick O'Connor
Simeon Platt Peter Machin

Director: Gerry Mill
Designer: Bryan Bagge

Do It Yourself

w Guy James

When Maggie becomes involved in the antics of a group of vigilantes administering rough justice on an housing estate, she finds life further complicated by the arrival of a new DI to the team.

DI Jack Slater Michael Graham Cox
Joey Felix Ray Burdis
Mrs Felix Margery Mason

Director: Bill Turner
Designer: Richard Dunn

The Conference

w Guy James

When the Seven Dials team attend a crime seminar about a series of thefts from London hotels, and new boy DI Slater 'sets up' DS Philips, things go with a bang – but not as Slater intended.

Tanner Steve Alder
Det. Chf Insp. Macfarlain Sean Scanlan
Det. Insp. Mary Woods Gwynneth Powell

Director: Gerry Mill
Designer: Richard Dunn

The Good, the Bad and the Rest

w Anthony Couch
When Maggie's son Steve uncovers a swindle at his college, Mother comes to the rescue, although her mind is elsewhere – worrying that a vicious thug may slip through a legal loophole.
Bursar Frank Gatliff
Jimmy Jonathan Caplan
George Taylor James Ottaway

Director: Gerald Blake
Designer: Gordon Melhuish

Mad Dog

w Terence Feely
When animal rights campaigners free some dogs from a laboratory, but fail to realise that one of the animals is dangerously ill, a children's birthday party becomes a terrible nightmare for Maggie Forbes.
Lennie Muldoon Robin Hayter
Emma Saunders Louise Jameson
Dr Davies Andrew Burt

Director: Peter Cregeen
Designer: Gordon Melhuish

Wise Child

w Guy James
When a well-dressed con man begins harassing a rich middle-aged widow, Maggie doubts he's up to much good. But DI Jack Slater thinks otherwise – until Maggie Forbes plants doubt in his mind.
Roland Rupert Frazer
Lady Morrell Diana Fairfax
WPC Joan Frazer Natalie Forbes

Director: Gerald Blake
Designer: Bryan Bagge

Appearances Can Be Deceptive

w Neil Rudyard
A brutal wife-beating husband is killed by the desperate woman. Maggie investigates and draws the conclusion that she has an open and shut case of self-defence – until circumstances change for the worse.

Elaine Campbell Adrienne Posta
Karen Lysette Anthony
Duncan James Wood

Director: Gerald Blake
Designer: Rodney Cammish

Fox and Hounds

w Tony Hoare
An old man is mugged and dies from his injuries, but the young suspect refuses to help the police. Faced with getting to the bottom of the crime, Maggie finds her own investigations hampered by a local man – with a bizarre protest.
Leroy Winston Jones Victor Romero-Evans
Marcus Williams Oscar James
Sgt Harry Cooper Peter Spraggon

Director: John Reardon
Designer: Gordon Melhuish

Secrets

w P. J. Hammond
Her name is Cecily. She's sophisticated, well-liked – and dangerous, as DI Maggie Forbes will soon find out when she makes enquiries at Cecily's elegant flat, a place which conceals a grim secret.
Cecily Amanda Boxer
Thorne Malcolm Tierney
James Patrick Newell

Director: Jonathan Wright-Miller
Designer: Rodney Cammish

Cure

w P. J. Hammoond
Does Mr Armour really have the gift of healing he claims? DI Maggie Forbes and DS Jake Barratt, searching for the truth, decide to test his powers – with frightening results.
Mr Armour John Grillo
Mrs Armour Ann Morrish
Mrs McAvoy Patricia Lawrence

Director: Gerry Mill
Designer: John Clements

A Woman's Word

w Simon Masters

Locked in a feud regarding how far she should go to keep her word to an informer, Maggie welcomes the news that Det. Chf Insp. Russell has some interesting revelations about Maggie's colleague, DI Slater.

Betty Farrell **Angela Douglas**
Malcolm Sinclair **Nigel Humphries**
Goodwin **Steve Humpoletz**

Director: **Gerald Blake**
Designer: **John Emery**

Exit Laughing

w Neil Rudyard

When a minor civil servant is found dead in rather exotic surroundings, Maggie and her team believe they have an open and shut case of a lover's quarrel that ended in death. Nothing could be further from the truth.

Selina De Sade **Wanda Ventham**
WPC Virginia Hankie **Debbi Blythe**
Sgt Dave Bryant **Michael Cronin**

Director: **Gerry Mill**
Designer: **John Emery**

THE GENTLE TOUCH
Season One
Producers: Kim Mills, Jack Williams
Executive producer: Tony Wharmby
7 colour 60-minute episodes
11 April – 23 May 1980

Season Two
Producers: Jack Williams, Kim Mills, Michael Verney-Elliott
Executive producer: Tony Wharmby
10 colour 60-minute episodes
5 September – 7 November 1980

Season Three
Producer: Michael Verney-Elliott
Executive producer: Tony Wharmby
13 colour 60-minute episodes
6 November 1981 – 5 February 1982

Season Four
Producer: Michael Verney-Elliott
Executive producer: Tony Wharmby
13 colour 60-minute episodes
22 October 1982 – 28 January 1983

Season Five
Producer: Michael Verney-Elliott
Executive producer: Nick Elliott
13 colour 60-minute episodes
1 September – 24 November 1984

An LWT Network Production
(All Series)

GHOST SQUAD
GS5

This suspense-filled detective/spy drama series was inspired by the real-life exploits of the men and women of Scotland Yard's legendary undercover unit (dubbed by ex-Detective John Gosling as the 'Ghost Squad' in his book of that name). Distinguished by two formats (Ghost Squad and GS5), it documented the adventures of a team of crimebusting agents whose brief was to infiltrate their way into the inner sanctums of major underworld gangs and international espionage agencies, and snuff out their activities by whatever means were available to them – including assassination. Known only to their immediate superiors, there was nothing to identify them with the governing body they represented. Often working alone, their missions were a closely guarded secret between themselves and their controllers (a GS agent could work side by side with other members of the unit without knowing his or her identity). If operating abroad, they could expect no help from their superiors, the police, or anyone else. They were alone and shared a common bond – hazardous missions, in which the mortality rate was high.

The principal GS operator in the first series was American, Nick Craig. Paid to disappear into the underworld for weeks – even months – at a time in order to trap his adversary, his expertise in the field of deception and knowledge of theatrical make-up techniques led him through numerous identity changes, and brought him the kind of cases he loved best – the dangerous ones, on which his life (or death as it later turned out) hung by a shoestring. Seen giving Craig his assignments was GS chief, Sir Andrew Wilson, and/or his secretary, Helen Winters.

Three new characters were introduced midway through the second series: agent Tony Miller, a two-fisted, merciless defender of justice; Geoffrey Stock, the department's new chief administrator (Sir Andrew and his secretary Helen had been posted to a new unit); and Jean Carter, primarily Stock's secretary, but later a fully-fledged agent.

It was this series that saw Nick Craig killed off (by an explosive device), but a new series of adventures was just around the corner and the programme continued for 13 further stories under the title GS5 with the introduction of another new character, Peter Clarke, a soft-spoken agent who abhorred violence (until he was aroused) and preferred to get his quarry through slow, methodical investigation – which, to Miller's mind, made him a 'soft' replacement for his dead friend Craig. Nevertheless, the partnership worked and the final outing by the GS team was among the best of the entire series – helped no doubt by the script-editing attributes of Brian Clemens, who was only months away from his successful association with *The Avengers*.

Another notable point: the series gave rise to one of the more memorable television theme tunes, a haunting piece (whistled throughout) by composer Philip Green.

Author's note: To avoid confusion in the transmission order, I have resisted the urge to include in the first season running order three stories, denoted *, which were filmed for the first season, but tagged onto the beginning of the videotaped second season. Production of these was held back by an actors' strike.

REGULAR CAST

Nick Craig **Michael Quinn**   Sir Andrew Wilson **Sir Donald Wolfit**
Helen Winters **Angela Browne**   Tony Miller **Neil Hallett**
Geoffrey Stock **Anthony Marlowe**   Jean Carter **Claire Nielson**
Peter Clarke **Ray Barrett**   Billy Clay (a GS5 agent) **Ray Austin**

Season One

13 monochrome 60-minute episodes

Ticket for Blackmail

w Lindsay Galloway

Newly-appointed Ghost Squad operative Nick Craig is assigned to expose an illicit diamond smuggling gang. To do so he travels to the South of France as a passenger on a holiday coach tour.
Karolides **Paul Stassino**
Ivor Tobias **Ronald Leigh-Hunt**
Graham Tobias **Alex Scott**

Director: **Norman Harrison**

Bullet with My Name on It

w Lindsay Galloway

Investigating a murder-for-sale bureau in Rome, Nick Craig, impersonating an American criminal lawyer, plays his role too well – and finds his life threatened by professional assassins.
Clive Charles **Peter Williams**
Kane **Alfred Burke**
Gina **Catherine Feller**

Director: **Don Sharp**

Hong Kong Story

w Lindsay Galloway

When an assassin's bullet misses its target, a VIP, and kills an airline steward standing next to him, Sir Andrew Wilson, responsible for the dignitary's safety, assigns Nick Craig to investigate the incident.
Wang **George Pastell**
Dr Siligi **Leonard Sachs**
Wacker **Bill Kerr**

Director: **Don Sharp**

High Wire

w Lewis Davidson

Craig dons the disguise of a wall of death motorcycle rider to infiltrate a gang

responsible for a series of audacious robberies. His ability to ride the machines leads to him being offered the role of look-out on the gang's next job.
Fred **William Hartnell**
Simon **Tom Adams**
Moker **John Cairney**

Director: **Norman Harrison**

The Broken Doll

w Patrick Campbell

Three things link the deaths of four British girls murdered in Marseilles: all worked at the same nightclub, all were blonde, and all were beautiful. Nick Craig finds a fourth clue – and sets out to solve the murders.
Julie **Julia Arnall**
Federoff **Simon Lack**
Tante Marie **Jean Anderson**

Director: **Don Sharp**

The Eyes of the Bat

w Robert Stewart

Craig's latest assignment could cost him his life: impersonating a safe blower, he must infiltrate a gang planning a major bank robbery and blackmailing fashion models for their secrets.
Ambrose Jerome **William Lucas**
Simone **Jean Clarke**
Peter **Edward Judd**

Director: **Don Sharp**

Still Waters

w Max Marquis

Masquerading as a crooked Dutch diamond merchant, Craig attempts to infiltrate a worldwide smuggling racket and expose the head man. His disguise is penetrated – and he barely escapes with his life.

Arny Long John Carson
Captain Starr Stratford Johns
Hanson Victor Beaumont

Director: Robert Lynn

Assassin

w Dick Sharples and Gerald Kelsey
Called in to help save the life of a young
American framed for the killing of Kubitz,
a mid-European Prime Minister, Nick Craig
finds himself facing a task as difficult as any
he has previously encountered.
Ricci Christopher Witty
Anna Jill Ireland
Koster Joseph Furst

Director: Robert Lynn

Death from a Distance

w Lindsay Galloway
Recruited into the GS team on a special
mission to ensure the safety of a visiting
president, Det. Insp. Brett's methods raise a
few eyebrows – none higher than Craig's,
who asks if the newcomer is all that he
seems.
Brett William Sylvester
Jackie Hazel Court
Router Anton Diffring

Director: Robert Lynn

Million Dollar Ransom

w Dick Sharples and Gerald Kelsey
Craig is sent to Sweden to thwart the plans
of a ruthless gang of kidnappers who intend
to use the Monte Carlo motor rally as a
cover to smuggle a kidnapped scientist out
of the country.
Bob Royston Bruce Beeby
Phil Slade Peter Dyneley
Pat Miller Jennifer Joyce

Director: Don Sharp

Season Two
26 monochrome 60-minute episodes

The Green Shoes

w Robert Holmes*
Hearing that an attempt will be made to
kidnap a research scientist, Nick Craig visits

a Nuclear Research Centre with orders to
protect the man. Strange things begin to
happen – and the GS operative faces a
deadly enemy.
Dr Gordon Ewan Solon
Marie Gordon Joyce Blair
Scientist John Welsh

Director: Don Sharp

Catspaw

w Bill Craig*
When a man's body is discovered in a crate
unloaded from a boat at a Baltimore dock,
Craig flies to South America with orders to
infiltrate a 'hit' squad, a team of assassins
prepared to kill anyone for money.
Torres Paul Stassino
Ribas Michael Goodliffe
Anita Moira Redmond

Director: Robert Lynn

The Princess

w Dick Sharples and Gerald Kelsey*
Craig finds himself in an unexpected but
pleasurable location – a girl's finishing
school in Switzerland. His mission: to
chaperone a princess whose life has been
threatened after her betrothal to the crown
prince.
Laura Honor Blackman
Princess Nadia Barbara Evans
Alfiat Warren Mitchell

Director: Robert Lynn

The Big Time

w Leon Griffiths
Pop stars and the fashion world act like a
magnet for young innocents dreaming of
stardom, but Nick Craig's involvement in
the glitter and tinsel world draws him into
very dangerous waters.
Peter Welcome Derek Waring
Slattery George Murcell
Rooney Paul Farrell

Director: Peter Sady

Death of a Sportsman

w Basil Dawson
Newly-commissioned GS agent, Tony
Miller, probes an illicit diamond-buying

organisation based in Cairo. Acting on a hunch when he recognises a man presumed dead, he almost bites off more than he can chew.

Spencer Deeds John Longden
Beni Peter Diamond
Major Mahmoud Warren Mitchell
(Miller and Stock introduced in this story)

Director: James Firman

Interrupted Requiem

w Bill Craig

When a scientist swears to blow up a new British missile programme unless his kidnapped daughter is released unharmed, Nick Craig is given the job of finding the kidnappers and rescuing the girl from danger.

Anton Brissac Leonard Sachs
Jan Kupra Richard Dare
Helen Kupra Ellen McIntosh

Director: John Nelson-Burton

East of Mandalay

w Bill Craig

Investigating the sale of illegal arms to a revolutionary group, Tony Miller, posing as a mercenary soldier, discovers a plot to overthrow a foreign country – an event which could signal the end of peace in the country.

Sir Charles Ian Fleming
Surato Barry Shawzin
Sara Jacqui Chan

Director: Dennis Vance

Escape Route

w Peter Yeldham

Nick Craig and Jean Carter pursue a wealthy embezzler to Sydney, Australia, where he is believed to have set up an escape route for wanted criminals. Their mission: to locate and destroy the organisation.

Elliot Chapman Terence Alexander
Johnson John Junkin
Insp. Monroe John Scott
(GS agent Jean Carter Introduced)

Director: Anthony Kearney

The Last Jump

w Richard Harris

When a paratrooper's chute fails to open during a training exercise and secret telemetry equipment is stolen from a top secret base and then turns up in Germany, agent Tony Miller is assigned to investigate.

Captain Horstead Jack Watling
Lt Col. Trent Thomas Heathcote
Lt Blanchford John Bailey

Director: Dennis Vance

Polsky

w Tudor Gates

A series of cleverly executed robberies has GS agent Tony Miller donning a false identity to infiltrate an army training establishment believed to be next on the thieves' hit list.

Joe Dunning Ray Austin
Jack Berg Tom Bowman
Constable Alec Ross

Director: Dennis Vance

The Heir Apparent

w Julian Bond

Heir apparent to a wealthy oil-rich state, Prince Karim enrols at an English school. Craig is assigned to protect him from danger – and that leads him into dark and deadly danger.

Karim Julien Sherrier
Ben Ali Roger Delgado
Commander Frank Middlemass

Director: Dennis Vance

The Magic Bullet

w Maurice Wiltshire

Assigned to protect the life – and secrets – of an eminent metallurgist attending a science conference at a country retreat, Nick Craig springs an elaborate trap on a group of foreign spies.

Prof. Baker David Markham
Dr Ibanez Mary Morris
Sir David Maurice Hedley

Director: James Ferman

The Menacing Mazurka

w John Lucarotti
What at first seems an enviable task –
looking after a troupe of girl dancers – soon
turns into a highly dangerous situation for
GS operative Tony Miller, when he has to
foil a cruel game of diplomatic blackmail.
Ilse Virany Jacqueline Ellis
Laslo Radiv George Pravda
Andret Ray Austin

Director: Hugh Rennie

The Retirement of the Gentle Dove

w Philip Levene
In disguise, GS controller Geoffrey Stock
enters an old people's home on the trail of a
notorious foreign counter-spy known only as
the Gentle Dove and believed to be seeking
political asylum in Britain.
Siegfried Mia Karan
Lieber Barbara Berkley
Sir Kenneth Clare Maxwell Foster

Director: Dennis Vance

Mr Five Percent

w Louis Marks
When large consignments of arms threaten
to destroy the uneasy truce in a foreign
state, GS forcibly enlist the services of a
known dope-pedlar in order to introduce
agent Tony Miller to the 'right people'.
Durkavic Guy Deghy
Tony Esposito Edwin Richfield
Liz Esposito Naomi Chance

Director: Phil Brown

Gertrude

w Bill McIllwraithe
GS agents Miller and Carter are sent to
Scotland to protect a female double-agent
who holds the secret of a plan to overthrow
a pro-British government. Jean finds herself
used to bait to lure the enemy into the
open.
Gertrude Mary Mackenzie
Henry Cameron Archie Duncan
Police Insp. Douglas Wilmer

Director: Anthony Kearey

Sabotage

w Reed de Rouen
On his way to assist Mallory, a local GS
operator based in the Philippines, Miller is
picked up as a saboteur. Under threat of his
life, he is ordered to blow up a British secret
service headquarters.
Mallory Maurice Durant
Ali Ray Austin
Rand-Fuller Maurice Colbourne

Director: Hugh Rennie

The Thirteenth Girl

w Joshua Adam
When a Swiss au pair girl is murdered,
overseas GS operator Sally Lomax is assigned
to investigate. She uncovers the existence of
a white slave organisation – little realising
that she could become their next victim.
Sally Lomax Patricia Mort
de Souza Maurice Kaufmann
Franz Hartmann John Carson

Director: Peter Sasdy

Sentences of Death

w Geoffrey Bellman and John Whitney
Investigating the activities of a dope-
smuggling ring in Singapore, agent Nick
Craig finds his identity blown – and is
forced to tell state secrets under the
influence of drugs.
Paul Ronald Leigh-Hunt
Phillipa Ann Lynn
Insp. Morse Norman Chappell

Director: Peter Sasdy

The Grand Duchess

w Julian Bond
Tony Miller acts as a private investigator to
recover priceless gems stolen from the wife
of a British diplomat – unaware that his
movements are being monitored by a
ruthless blackmailer.
Downes Garfield Morgan
Voygee William Gaunt
Lazenger John Barron

Director: Chris Morahan

The Desperate Diplomat

w Joshua Adam

Working undercover as butler to a foreign diplomat, GS agent Tony Miller discovers that the man is being blackmailed by an unscrupulous foreigner, who threatens to make known the man's gambling debts.

Clive Errington Derrick de Marney
Margaret Errington Barbara Shelley
Neville Shand Ferdy Mayne

Director: Anthony Kearey

Hot Money

w Louis Marks

Giuseppe del Piazzo, a dealer in secondhand books, pays a forged banknote into his bank, the serial number of which corresponds with that of a genuine note stolen in a major bank robbery. Craig is assigned to discover the link between the two.

del Piazzo Andreas Malandrinos
Granger Lloyd Lamble
Max Michael Coles

Director: John Nelson Burton

Quarantine at Kavar

w Anthony Dawson

Sent to the Middle East to trace a lost expedition, Nick Craig meets a beautiful girl who claims she has proof that a group of terrorists intend to blow up a seat of government. The agent attempts to deliver her film of the terrorists' activities to the authorities – but the terrorists are closing in around them.

Dr Hussain Maurice Kaufmann
Suzi Keller Elvi Hale
Major Sayid Roger Delgado

Director: Geoffrey Nethercott

The Golden Silence

w John Lucarotti

Mike Ferrers has a nice line in travel arrangements. His travel bureau will book you into a high-class hotel – and his employees will ensure the holiday is permanent! Posing as a would-be tourist, agent Nick Craig books for a holiday with death.

Mike Ferrers Gordon Jackson
Max Leach David Lodge
Miss Armstrong June Straw

Director: John Nelson-Burton

Lost in Transit

w Philip Levene

Investigating the upsurge of a new Nazi party, GS operator Tony Miller finds himself up against a modern-day Fuhrer who is planning to overthrow the British Government and take over the country.

Van Tempel Anthony Jacobs
Lise Delphi Lawrence
Eppler John Woodvine

Director: John Nelson-Burton

The Man with the Delicate Hands

w Philip Levene

When, against all the evidence, Helen Lambert insists that the man dragged from a wrecked car is not her brother Paul, GS agent Tony Miller is assigned to investigate her claim.

Helen Lambert Anne Blake
Peter Brenner Derek Francis
Paul Lambert Brian Nissen

Director: Peter Sasdy

The Missing People

w Peter Yeldham

Tony Miller must find the link between the murder of several nightclub hostesses and a mysterious advertisement placed in a Polish newspaper. He finds more than he bargained for – and danger lurking in the shadows.

Slim Salmon Willoughby Goddard
Cresswell Nigel Green
Josie Pamela Ann Davy

Director: Peter Sasdy

P. G. 7

w Joshua Adam

Sally Lomax assists a young girl who is helping the Ghost Squad to track down the man behind a series of murders in Switzerland. The women find themselves

taken prisoner and used as guinea pigs in the man's experiments.
Lofts Simon Oates
Clarke John Carson
Insp. Duclos Richard Leech

Director: Peter Sasdy

A First Class Way to Die

w John Lucarotti
Assigned to protect an eminent scientist on board a luxury cruiser, agent Nick Craig doesn't find the sea air beneficial to his health. Someone is out to kill him – and does so – in this explosive finale to the season.
Larry Arnell Peter Dyneley
Nesterenko Laurence Hardy
Stewardess Mitzi Rogers

Director: Peter Sasdy

Season Three
GS5

13 monochrome 60-minute episodes

An Eye for an Eye

w Kenneth Hayles
Mourning the death of his fellow agent and friend Nick Craig, Miller, and new GS5 operator Peter Clarke, are sent to check out the explosion at sea. Their investigations bring surprising – and to Miller – highly satisfactory results.
Laura Adams Dilys Laye
Dixon Brian Oulton
McKay William Marlowe

Director: Eric Price

A Cast of Thousands

w Larry Forrester
Working undercover, GS5 agent Sally Lomax discovers that an elusive typewriter holds the key to her investigations into 'accidents' on a film set. Suspecting sabotage, she uncovers a murder cartel.
Sally Lomax Patricia Mort
Josef Farago George Pravda
Lambert Edwin Richfield

Director: Peter Sasdy

Death of a Cop

w Roger Marshall
Masquerading as a news reporter, Tony Miller investigates the death of a policeman suspected of being 'on the take' from gamblers. His search for the cop killer leads him into the world of high finance.
Betty Asher Betty McDowell
Kaufmann Robert Brown
De Souza Roger Delgado

Director: Dennis Vance

Party for Murder

w Nicholas Palmer
Assigned to investigate a series of sabotage incidents involving a new machine being designed for South America, Clarke 'defects' to the Fascist party responsible for the crime – with dangerous results.
Elisabeth Creasey Lois Maxwell
Billy Clay Ray Austin
Withers Brian Haines

Director: Dennis Vance

Dead Men Don't Drive

w Tudor Gates
GS5 operative Tony Miller finds himself facing a tough problem: how could a man be seen driving a car through a village and yet, when the vehicle crashed, the man is found to have been dead for several hours?
Yvonne Marsden Zena Marshall
Hayman Geoffrey Chater
Doctor Colin Douglas

Director: Peter Sasdy

Pay Up or Else

w Dave Cummin
When a protection racket gang declare war on innocent people, GS5 agent Tony Miller is assigned to infiltrate the gang and force the opposing sides into a showdown. He achieves this – with startling results.
Demaris Felix Felton
Harry Mason Harry Towb
Helen Mason Toni Palmer

Director: Eric Price

Dr Ayre

w Brian Clemens

Stock's disbelief that a 'master criminal' is behind a series of brilliantly executed robberies is severely shaken when operative Peter Clarke brings him conclusive proof that successful criminal Dr Ayre is masterminding further audacious crimes.

Paul Morris Garfield Morgan
Jill Norman Jennifer Wilson
Sydney Grafton Gerry Duggan

Director: Eric Price

Scorpion Rock

w Guy Morgan

The island of Baleric hides a sinister secret which GS5 operator Tony Miller must solve if he is to have any chance of locating the whereabouts of a fellow undercover agent believed kidnapped by dictator Zafre.

Emilio Zafre Paul Whitsun-Jones
Nicola Webb Catherine Woodville
Stripey Hawkins Michael Robbins

Director: Bill Stewart

The Goldfish Bowl

w Tudor Gates

Sent to check out the strange goings on at a secret missile base, GS5 operatives Clarke and Miller find their cover blown and the enemy awaiting their arrival – a dangerous situation when you're seeking a sadistic killer.

Smart Talfryn Thomas
Jean Carter Claire Nielson
Crawford Gerald Sim

Director: Bill Stewart

Seven Sisters of Wong

w Brian Clemens

Masquerading as a dope-pedlar, agent Tony Miller meets a beautiful Chinese girl and finds hmself involved with a secret patriot army, who intend to use his services – whether he likes it or not!

Freddie Morgan Donald Morley
Mary Sin Lau Maureen Beck
Deprae Leonard Sachs

Director: Bill Stewart

Rich Ruby Wine

w Joshua Adam

Stock assigns his entire department to locate Franz Rudolph Gruber, a former Nazi chief in Hungary. Gruber is known to have in his possession the Howarth jewel collection – which Stock suspects will be used to finance a new Nazi regime.

Ernest Hartmann Geoffrey Bayldon
Mayer Harold Goldblatt
Anna Adina Mandlova

Director: Eric Price

Hideout

w Malcolm Hulke

Undercover operative Sally Lomax is assigned to delve into the past of a man whom Stock believes to be a murderer. The man, Dawson, is now managing a holiday camp – at which several 'accidents' have taken place. Sally books in – but her holiday is far from peaceful.

Sally Lomax Patricia Mort
Leslie Dawson Emrys Jones
Billy Clay Ray Austin

Director: Peter Sasdy

It Won't Be a Stylish Marriage

w Brad Ashton

After a whirlwind courtship on the French Riviera, GS5 agent Peter Clarke, posing as a shy businessman, 'marries' Yoette, an attractive French girl – in order to discover the secret behind another French girl's mysterious death.

Yoette Nyree Dawn Porter
Duval David Garth
Count Marais Carl Duering

Director: Bill Stewart

GHOST SQUAD
Season One
Producer: Connery Chappell
Associate producer: Dennis Holt
Music by: Philip Green
13 monochrome 60-minute filmed episodes
9 September – 11 November 1961

Season Two
Producer: Anthony Kearey
Music by: Philip Green
26 monochrome 60-minute videotaped
episodes

GS5
Producer: Dennis Vance
Music by: Philip Green
Script editor: Brian Clemens
13 monochrome 60-minute videotaped
episodes

A Rank Organisation TV Film
in association with Associated Television Ltd
(Season 1)
An ATV Network Production
(Seasons 2 and 3)
9 September – 11 November 1961
29 December 1962 – 4 May 1963
22 February – 27 June 1964

(USA: Syndicated 1960
10 Filmed episodes)

GIDEON'S WAY

Based on the character created by John Creasey, this superior mid-'60s 'documentary'-style police series (the last joint production between Robert S. Baker and Monty Berman), centred around the criminal investigations of Commander George Gideon of Scotland Yard, a solid hard-working policeman with a nose for sniffing out crime. With his second-in-command, Chief Inspector David Keen, the two men formed a formidable crimebusting team. Both had come up through the ranks, and both men worked towards the same objective: solving (and wherever possible) preventing serious crime.

Remembered for its extensive use of location photography (almost every story was filmed in and around London), the series was notable in all departments.

REGULAR CAST

Commander Gideon **John Gregson**   *Chf Insp. Keen* **Alexander Davion**
Kate Gideon **Daphne Anderson**   *Matthew Gideon* **Richard James**
Malcolm Gideon **Giles Watling**

State Visit

w Jim O'Connolly
Commander Gideon and Inspector Keen are assigned to protect the life of a visiting German statesman who has received threats to his life from Max Fischer, a former victim of Nazi persecution.

Max Fischer **Alfie Bass**
Sarah Fischer **Catharine Lacey**
Kate Gideon **Daphne Anderson**

Director: **John Moxey**

The 'V' Men

w Alan Falconer

When Sir Arthur Vane's neo-fascist activities begin to prove a thorn in Scotland Yard's side, and Vane complains that his life has been threatened, Commander Gideon and Inspector Keen are instructed to protect Vane from danger.

Sir Arthur Vane Ronald Culver
Cathy Miller Angela Douglas
Chf Supt Allan Cuthbertson

Director: Cyril Frankel

The Firebug

w David Chantler

An outbreak of fires in old buildings leads Gideon and Keen to a man motivated by circumstances not of his own making. But if he is really an arsonist, shouldn't Gideon arrest him? Why then does he fail to do so?

Bishop George Cole
Det. Sgt Grady Aubrey Richards
Mrs Termison Avril Elgar

Director: Roy Baker

The Big Fix

w Jack Whittingham

Gideon and Keen enter the world of horse-racing – a world in which money can save a man's life or lead him to lose it, suddenly – particularly if the man owes a fortune in gambling debts.

Joe Short Michael Ripper
Colonel Middleton Maurice Hedley
Janet Middleton Penelope Horner

Director: James Hill

The Housekeeper

w David Chantler

Gideon faces a race against time to unmask a shrewd, calculating opponent – a killer who dares him to attempt to halt his next crime. Gideon's dilemma: which of two potential victims is the next on the madman's hit list?

Ralph Marriott Harry Fowler
Mark Marriott Kay Walsh
Delia Marriott Marje Lawrence

Director: Leslie Norman

The Lady Killer

w David Chantler

A killer stalks the streets murdering pretty young girls. Inspector Keen, aroused by the intuition of his girlfriend, leads the search for the mysterious modern-day Bluebeard – and lands himself in great danger.

Robert Carne Ray Barrett
Rina Justine Lord
Marion Grove Rosemary Leach

Director: Leslie Norman

To Catch a Tiger

w Iain MacCormick

Words whispered by a dying nurse lead Commander Gideon and Inspector Keen to re-open an old case. By doing so, they unwittingly unleash a new chain of tragic events on an old Scotland Yard colleague.

Sir Percy Richmond Raymond Huntley
June Kennet Delphi Lawrence
Supt Fred Lee Norman Bird

Director: Leslie Norman

Big Fish, Little Fish

w Alan Falconer

When a young pickpocket plies his trade on the London streets, it begins a chain of events that leads Commander Gideon to the existence of a well-organised group of thieves intent on pulling off a major crime.

'Happy' Roden Jack McGowran
Gabriel Lyon Sydney Tafler
Bessie Cowran Avis Bunnage

Director: Cyril Frankel

The White Rat

w Harry H. Junkin

When a robbery case turns to a murder enquiry, Commander Gideon and Inspector Keen are assigned to the case. Hearing that his old friend Syd Taylor is heading the enquiry, Gideon expects fast results – but events prove him wrong.

Sgt Syd Taylor David Davies
Rose Lenman Virginia Maskell
Mickey Keston Ray McAnnaly

Director: Roy Baker

How to Retire without Really Working

w Norman Hudis

Outwardly the epitome of middleclass respectability, Robert Gresham actually lives on the proceeds of petty crime. The crime he's planning now is far from petty and will cause Commander Gideon much aggravation.

Robert Gresham Eric Barker
Margaret Gresham Joyce Grant
Mr Pater William Mervyn

Director: George Pollock

Subway to Revenge

w Norman Hudis

A vicious murder on the London Underground brings Commander Gideon an investigation he'd rather be without – and his enquiries lead him to question his department's methods of investigation.

James Lane Donald Churchill
John Stewart Bryan Pringle
Ella Winters Anne Lawson

Director: Roy Baker

The Great Plane Robbery

w Alan Falconer

It's one of the most audacious crimes of the century – the theft of gold bullion from an aircraft in flight! Commander Gideon has few days left to discover who is behind the robbery – and how it was achieved.

Barley George Baker
Dobson Edwin Richfield
Harold Jeremy Burnham

Director: Leslie Norman

Gang War

w David Chantler

No copper likes to have a gang war break out on his patch, but that's what could happen if Gideon cannot stave off the plans of an ambitious, scheming woman who plans to pull off a major crime.

Lollo Romano Jane Merrow
Frank Romano Ray Brooks
Jerry Blake Ronald Lacey

Director: Quentin Lawrence

The Tin Gold

w Harry H. Junkin

Alerted to the fact that two dangerous prisoners have broken out of jail, Commander Gideon spreads a wide net over London to catch them – but they give him the slip and take refuge in the home of a young mother.

'Benny' Benson Derren Nesbitt
Freddy Tinsdale John Hurt
Ruby Benson Jennifer Wilson

Director: John Gilling

The Alibi Men

w Iain MacCormick

Convinced that he knows the identity of a murderer, Gideon must find sufficient proof to arrest him – a task made doubly difficult when a professional alibi-seller gives the man a new identity.

Bruce Carroway Jack Hedley
Mary Calloway Sheila Allen
Cathy Bellman Nicola Pagett

Director: Cyril Frankel

Fall High, Fall Hard

w Malcolm Hulke

A two-year-old unsolved murder mystery attracts the attention of Gideon and Keen. Reopening the case, they find that history appears to be repeating itself – with murderous effect.

Erickson Donald Houston
Joan Erickson Sarah Lawson
Randle Victor Maddern

Director: Leslie Norman

The Wall

w David Chantler

Everyday domestic affairs are not usually brought to Gideon's attention, but when a husband disappears without trace the policeman takes an interest in the circumstances surrounding the case.

Will Rikker John Barrie
Liz Rikker Megs Jenkins
Michael Penn Richard Carpenter

Director: Leslie Norman

The Prowler

w Harry H. Junkin

When a mentally disturbed young man brings terror to the streets of London by clipping young girls' hair, Commander Gideon and Inspector Keen begin an extensive search to trap him – before the pranks turn into murder.

Det. Sgt Brown Richard Burrell
Det. Supt Lemaitre Reginald Jessup
Sophie Murdoch Rosemary Dunham

Director: Robert Tronson

The Thin Red Line

w Iain MacCormick

The theft of silver trophies commemorating past glories of an army regiment involve Gideon and Keen in a search for a man's past memories – memories which may (or may not) hold a clue to the crime.

General MacGregor Finlay Currie
Major Ross Allan Cuthbertson
Sgt McKinnon Gordon Jackson

Director: Cyril Frankel

A Perfect Crime

w Alan Falconer

What appears to be the perfect crime – a major robbery of jewels which were never recovered – points Commander Gideon to a man who has led a very successful double life – until the detective deflates the man's ego.

Spender 'Todd' Patrick Allen
Ann Beaumont Ann Lynn
Police Commissioner Basil Dignam

Director: Leslie Norman

The Millionaire's Daughter

w Norman Hudis

The arrival in London of an American millionaire with his wife and daughter involves Gideon in a very unusual kidnapping – one which isn't all it appears to be, and one that disastrously misfires.

Elliot Henderson David Bauer
Felissa Henderson Lois Maxwell
Philip Guest Donald Sutherland

Director: Cyril Frankel

Morna

w Alan Falconer

Commander Gideon faces a severe test of his investigative abilities when asked to discover the identity of a killer who has murdered a beautiful young girl without apparent motive.

Morna Angela Douglas
Chay Johnny Sekka
Leonard Bright John Junkin

Director: Cyril Frankel

Boy with a Gun

w Iain MacCormick

Threatened by three bullies, Chris, the son of an eminent police surgeon working in Gideon's department, pulls a gun and shoots one of the boys. The outcome brings unexpected friends for Chris, and a tough case for Gideon.

Chris Kirk Howard Knight
Doctor Kirk Anthony Bate
Tim Murphy George Sewell

Director: Jeremy Summers

The Reluctant Witness

w Norman Hudis

Gideon discovers that a man found dead is Tony Bray, a police informer whom he wrongly convicted and who consequently spent four years in jail. Gideon determines to find his killer – at any price.

Red Carter Mike Pratt
Syd Carter David Gregory
PC Moss Trevor Bannister

Director: Jeremy Summers

The Rhyme and the Reason

w Jack Whittingham

When the sister of a boy suspected of murder comes to him for help, Commander Gideon politely refuses. But later that day a tragic event causes him to rethink his position – with dreadful results for all concerned.

Mary Rose Jo Rowbottom
Bill Rose Alan Rothwell
Det. Supt Smedo Duncan Lamont

Director: John Gilling

The Night-lifers

w Iain MacCormick

Young people who live for 'kicks' and have an irresponsible outlook on life present Commander Gideon with a problem. Which one of them is responsible for a selfish crime? Or can it be all three?

Peta Stone Anton Rogers
Sue Young Annette Andre
Tim Coles Derek Fowlds

Director: John Moxey

GIDEON'S WAY

Based on characters and a theme by John Creasey
Producers: R. S. Baker and Monty Norman
Music by: Edwin Astley
Script supervisor: Harry H. Junkin
An ATV Presentation
Distributed by ITC
Filmed on location in London and at Elstree Studios
26 monochrome 60-minute episodes
18 March 1965 – 10 May 1966

GLENCANNON

A rusty old boat. A crusty old sea captain. Hardly a combination for a successful television programme, but this series (based on the Glencannon stories by Guy Gilpatrick) scored with the viewers and became a substantial money-earner. The stories, played mainly for laughs, depicted the adventures of Glencannon, an old sea dog who was constantly getting into trouble – but always came out on top.

REGULAR CAST

Glencannon Thomas Mitchell   *Bosun Hughes* Patrick Allen

The Ancient Mariner
Artful Mr Glencannon
Balloon Story (aka Glasgow Phantom)
Captain Snooty
Champagne Charlie
Chinaman's Chance
Crocodile Tears
Double Trouble Deal and Trouble
The Donkey Man's Widow
Early Falls the Den
Gabriel's Trumpet
The Glencannon Collection
Hair of the Dog
Home Stretch
Jungle Story
Love Story
The Loving Cup

Mean Man of Genca
Milk Blossom
Monte Carlo Massacre
Glencannon and the Ailing Turtle
Mud Bottom Mulligan
Mutiny on the Thornecliffe Castle
Nearly a Bridegroom
Nosegay for Montgomery
Pearl of Panama
The Rolling Stone
Sign of the Brass Knuckle
Scot from Scotland Yard
Smugglers of San Diego
Souse of the Border
Stardust and Corn
Three Lovesick Swains from Gibraltar

Man with a Mermaid
The Masked Monster
The Toothless Hag of Cadiz

Toad Man of Tamarog
Yogi of West 9th Street
Wailing Lady of Limehouse

GLENCANNON
Executive producer: Donald Hyde
Associate producer: Howard Cornell
Director: John Knight
Writers: Basil Dawson, John Touron,
Ian Dallas
A Gross-Krasne Films Production
39 monochrome 30–minute episodes
4 May – 27 December 1959

THE GLORY BOYS

A tense thriller of international political intrigue, which dramatised the events surrounding the combined attempts of two IRA and Arab terrorists, McCoy and Famy (the 'Glory Boys' of the title), to assassinate Sokarev, an Israeli nuclear scientist who, disillusioned with his work, wished to seek political asylum in Britain. The task of safe-guarding the man's life was handed to Jones, head of British security, who reluctantly handed the assignment to Jimmy – a down-on-his-luck, whisky-swilling security agent.

The story depicted Jimmy's attempts to keep Sokarev alive, by staying one jump ahead of the terrorists – as they threaded their way to their target through the body-strewn streets of London.

Overlong – but impressive.

CAST

Sokarev Rod Steiger   *Jimmy* Anthony Perkins   *Jones* Alfred Burke   *Helen* Joanna Lumley   *Mrs Sokarev* Sheila Allen   *Fairclough* Robert Lang   *Famy* Gary Brown   *McCoy* Aaron Harris   *Director General* Anthony Steel   *Minister* Ian Cutherbertson   *Sir Humphrey* Alan MacNaughton

THE GLORY BOYS
Producer: Michael Glynn
Executive producer: David Cunliffe,
Alan Landsbury
Written by: Gerald Seymour
Designer: David Crozier
A Yorkshire Television Production
Transmitted in 3 60-minute parts
colour
1–2–3 October 1984

THE GOLD ROBBERS

Written by John Hawkesworth and Glyn Jones, this action-packed, cops and robbers oater centred around the participants in a multi-million pound bullion robbery, and the tough CID officer who doggedly tracked them down.

Tough and uncompromising in its approach, this was strong stuff, and a winner all the way.

REGULAR CAST

Det. Chf Supt Cradock Peter Vaughan   *Det. Sgt Tommy Toms* Artro Morris
Inspector Tompkins Michael Wynne

The Great Bullion Robbery

w J. Hawkesworth and Glyn Jones
A bullion aircraft, carrying five-and-a-half million pounds of gold bars approaches an airfield in the South of England. Before the day is out, Det. Chf Supt Cradock will find himself assigned to track down the team behind 'the crime of the century'.
Richard Bolt Richard Leech
Ashe Michael Barrington
Grierson Donald Morley

Director: Don Leaver
Designer: Frank Nerini

Grounded

w David Whittaker
From his temporary headquarters on Westmarsh Airfield, Detective Cradock begins his unenviable task of discovering how the robbery was executed.
Derek Hartford Joss Ackland
Lingwood Peter Madden
Fay Hartford Alethea Charlton

Director: Peter Sasdy
Designer: John Emery

Crack Shot

w C. Scott Forbes
Pressurised by his superiors – not to mention the Home Office – Cradock must make his move and deliver the marksman who shot out the tyres of the police car escorting the bullion.

Freddy Lamb Roy Dotrice
Rosemary Lamb Ann Lynn
Eric Michael Forrest

Director: Don Leaver
Designer: Frank Nerini

The Big Spender

w Allan Prior
'Hello. Tango One To Base. Hello Dave.' Cradock, is certain that the voice who mimicked a police operator's relay call belongs to Barry Porter, a second-rate conman. But how can he prove it?
Barry Porter George Cole
Milly Porter Eve Pearce
Valerie Towers Kathleen Blake

Director: Don Leaver
Designer: Frank Nerini

Dog Eat Dog

w Leslie Sands
Did someone pay £30,000 to spring a convict to help pull off the job? It seems a high price to pay – but death is an even higher price, and the criminal fraternity aren't always to be relied on.
Josef Tyzack Alfred Lynch
Mary Tyzack Collette O'Neill
Terry Craddock Nicolas Ball

Director: Cyril Coke
Designer: John Emery

Rough Trade

w Pixie Weir

Cradock finds a weak line in the bullion robbers' armour. Peter Conroy, the man who drove the escape van, has run to Austria to escape arrest. But he's left his wife behind – and Cradock can use her.

Stephanie Conroy Jennifer Hillary
Peter Conroy Geoffrey Whitehead
Edward Lancing Donald Hewlett

Director: Lionel Harris
Designer: Frank Nerini

An Oddly Honest Man

w David Weir

A ray of hope – or just another tough nut to crack? Tom Goodwin, the pilot who flew the robbery plane, appears to want to 'opt out' and is prepared to spill the beans. But can Cradock really trust the man's evidence?

Tom Goodwin Ian Hendry
Dee Lattery Wanda Ventham
Edward Makin Christopher Benjamin

Director: Bill Bain
Designer: John Emery .

The Arrangement

w Eric Coltart

A chance to get on the robbers' trail – or yet another clever counter-bluff? Cradock must decide if the outcome of a meeting is worth the risk of wading even deeper into the depths of the underworld.

Eddie Makin Johnny Wade
Tilt Donald Webster
Forman Jeremy Child

Director: Alan Clarke
Designer: Colin Piggot

Account Rendered

w Jeremy Paul

A major turning point at last. Harry Oscroft, a brilliant accountant and paymaster to the gold robbers, is desperate when violence enters his safe suburban retreat and threatens his family. Perhaps with a little squeeze . . .

Harold Oscroft Bernard Hepton
Mrs Oscroft Daphne Slater
Anderson Frederick Bartman

Director: Bill Bain
Designer: Andrew Drummond

The Cover Plan

w Berkley Mather and John Hawkesworth

Why should an informer put the finger on the Hon. Timothy Fry, DSO, who was found smuggling a girl out of the country. Of more interest to Craddock is how – if at all – is the Honourable Timothy mixed up in the bullion snatch?

Hon. Timothy Fry Patrick Allen
Terry Lardner John Bindon
Anderson Frederick Bartman

Director: Cyril Coke
Designer: Roger Hall

The Midas Touch

w Donald Jackson

'Mr Big arrested in Paris' reads the newspaper headline. Cradock has got his man – the brain behind the gold robbery. But he knows all too well that there's someone bigger still at large and sets out to find him.

Victor Anderson Frederick Bartman
Opel Noel Willman
Richard Bolt Richard Leech

Director: Lionel Harris
Designer: Andrew Drummond

The Man with Two Faces

w George Lansbury

The net tightens. The hunter closes in on his prey, but Nechros swallows the bait and not the hook, and Cradock comes under further pressure by powerful men behind his superiors.

Nechros Johnny Shannon
Ass. Com. Farr Peter Copley
Jenny Bolt Louise Pajo

Director: Cyril Coke
Designer: John Clements

The Kill

w John Hawkesworth and Martin Hall
In spite of warnings to the contrary,
Cradock closes in for the kill. He knows his
man and is determined to get him at any
cost. But his final fling leads him into
deadly territory.
Stockbroker Peter Bowles
Nobby Clarke Ronald Clarke
Dillo George Innes

Director: Bill Bain
Designer: Frank Nerini

THE GOLD ROBBERS
Producer: John Hawkesworth
Music by: Max Harris
Story editor: Martin Hall
An LWT Network Production
13 colour 60-minute episodes
6 June – 29 August 1969

HADLEIGH

Always interesting, this pot-boiler about the adventures (and troubles) of James Hadleigh, the squire of Melford Park – and Yorkshire's most eligible bachelor – became an instant hit with female viewers everywhere.

As played by Gerald Harper, Hadleigh was a man for whom only the exclusive best was good enough. Hadleigh had everything: wealth, status and, later in the series, a beautiful wife; but he also had the problems that came from success. His main objective in life was finding the finance to hold onto the family estate, Melford Park, and his stable of thoroughbred horses. To this end, Hadleigh occasionally 'sold' his services to the highest bidder (more often than not, the British Treasury) and undertook well-paid duties for them – or anyone else who was prepared to pay the going rate for his services.

Author's note: The Hadleigh character actually began life in an earlier series, *GAZETTE,* which centred on a Yorkshire weekly newspaper owned by Hadleigh's father. Hadleigh himself only appeared on a semi-regular basis (more often than not when the paper was faced with libel suits, take-over bids and so on) but the producers of that series believed the character was strong enough to carry his own show – and *HADLEIGH* was born.

REGULAR CAST

James Hadleigh Gerald Harper   *Jennifer (his wife)* Hilary Dwyer
Charlie (his father-in-law) Gerald James   *Sutton (his manservant)* Peter Dennis
Aunt Helen Ambrosine Phillpots

HADLEIGH
Producers: Terence Williams, Jacky Stoller
Executive producers: Peter Willes,
David Cunliffe
Directors: Tony Wharmby, Peter Cregeen,
Derek Bennett, Raymond Menuir, Peter
Moffatt, Mike Newell, Michael Ferguson,
James Goddard, Chris Hodson
Story editor: Alfred Shaughnessy
Writers: Michael J. Bird, Ian Kennedy
Martin, Jeremy Paul, David Ambrose,
Raymond Bowers, Ian Curteis
A Yorkshire Television Production
Four seasons
52 colour 60-minute episodes
29 October 1969 – 29 March 1976

THE HANGED MAN

A top-notch thriller which told how Lew Burnett, a successful businessman who had built a small empire in the international construction industry, made enemies along the way – men who decided to rid themselves of the competition by having Burnett killed. After three such attempts on his life, Burnett decided to stay 'dead' in order to stay alive and seek out those who loved him, hated him and envied his success enough to want to see him dead. He was a man living on borrowed time, a man given a second chance to come to terms with his success and delve deep into his past to discover which of nine men (and women) wished to see him destroyed.

Written and created by Edmund Ward, this was strong stuff and as a consequence was given a late-night Saturday evening prime-time transmission slot.

REGULAR CAST
Lew Burnett Colin Blakely   *John Quentin* Gary Watson
Alan Crowe Michael Williams

Wheel of Fortune

w Edmund Ward
After three attempts on his life, Lew Burnett decides to remain 'dead' as his only means of staying alive. But one man, ex-mercenary soldier, Alan Crowe, doesn't believe that Lew is dead.

Alan Crowe Michael Williams
Elizabeth Haydon Angela Browne
Sammy Grey Brian Croucher

Director: Marc Miller
Designer: Alan Pickford

Tower of Destruction

w Edmund Ward

Having discovered Burnett's reasons for 'staying low', Alan Crowe joins his friend on a trip to a power station under construction. But sad memories wait for the construction boss – and danger interferes with his reverie.

George Pilgrim William Lucas
Joe Denver Julian Glover
Druscilla Lowndes Jenny Hanley

Director: Marc Miller
Designer: Alan Pickford

Knave of Coins

w Edmund Ward

An embezzler in Switzerland badly needs Burnett's money to buy a revolution. What's more, he could hold the secret behind the attempts on Lew's life. Crowe endeavours to hook the man with the help of his mercenary friends.

Peter Kroger William Russell
Hans Ericksen Michael Coles
Gilbert Webb Frederick Treves

Director: Tony Wharmby
Designer: Alan Pickford

Chariot of Earth

w Edmund Ward

Burnett's search for the man who wants to kill him leads him to Scotland where his former partner, Charlie Galbraith, has bought a Highland estate. Lew wonders where he found the money to do so?

Charlie Galbraith Alan MacNaughton
Louisa Galbraith Barbara Shelley
Douglas McKinnon Jack Watson

Director: Tony Wharmby
Designer: Alan Pickford

The Bridge Maker

w Edmund Ward

When he was in Scotland earlier, the locals called Lew Burnett 'The Bridge Maker'. Now he's back to ask: 'Who's trying to kill me?' He soon finds himself accused of corruption – and under sentence of death.

Leonid Frengel James Maxwell
Josef Milojek Ray Smith
Eddie Malone Gareth Hunt

Director: Tony Wharmby
Designer: Mary Rea

Grail and Platter

w Edmund Ward

When a Detroit gang of organised criminals learn that Burnett is still alive, and can provide something they want, they send a contract killer to deal with him – a man who has an old score to settle with Burnett.

Hans Dieter Frederick Jaeger
Joe Shapiro Al Mancini
Jane Cowley Naomi Chance

Director: Tony Wharmby
Designer: Mary Rea

Laws of Fortune

w Edmund Ward

Still on the run and under cover of darkness, Lew Burnett and Alan Crowe break into Lew's business offices to put the firm's books under scrutiny – and see if they hold any clue as to who their opponents are.

Capt. Jane Ashley Jan Francis
Sam McGuire James Grout
James Prendergast Laurence Payne

Director: Marc Miller
Designer: Alan Pickford

Ring of Return

w Edmund Ward

The last link in the chain begins to fall into place, but Lew and Alan are in no position to complete the chain. They are wanted for murder – and all this as Lew's daughter Laura returns from Switzerland.

Laura Burnett Jane Seymour
Margaret Burnett Ann Morrish
Turtle John F. Landry

Director: Marc Miller
Designer: Alan Pickford

THE HANGED MAN
Producers: Marc Miller and Edmund Ward
Executive producer: Peter Willes
A Yorkshire Television Production
8 colour 60-minute episodes
15 February – 5 April 1975

HARRY'S GAME

Transmitted in three parts, this critically-acclaimed political thriller depicted how, when faced with a secret manhunt in Ireland, the British Government elected to call on the services of specialist Captain Harry Brown, who was given the task of locating an IRA killer in the bomb-strewn streets of Belfast. Having infiltrated the IRA ranks, Harry was forced to play a deadly game of cat and mouse with his quarry in which the loser had to pay with his life.

Sizzling stuff. Loads of action and a cracking story by Gerald Seymour.

CAST

Harry Brown **Ray Lonnen**   *Home Secretary* **Geoffrey Russell**
Bannen **Nicolas Day**   *Colonel Frost* **Geoffrey Chater**
Seamus Duffryn **Charles Lawson**   *Mrs Duffryn* **Rita Howard**

HARRY'S GAME
Producer: Keith Richardson
Executive producer: David Cunliffe
Director: Lawrence Gordon Clark
Designer: Mike Long
Music by: Mike Moran
(Award-winning) end music by: Clannad
A Yorkshire Television Network Production
180 minutes
Colour
25–26–27 October 1983

HAZELL

'The name's 'azell. James 'azell. 33 years old, divorced, I got a dodgy ankle and the only ambition I got is never to grow up.'

The hilarious (sometimes violent) escapades of James Hazell, an ex-cop turned private eye. Dogged with failure after being invalided out of the police force (he hit the alcohol trail, watched his marriage disintegrate, and sank 'as low as a snake's belly'), Hazell picked up the crumbling pieces of his life and set up anew as a private detective. A brash, noisy, cockney Jack the Lad, who was bright without being brainy, kindhearted without being a softy, Hazell fancied his chances with the best of them (but sometimes got scared in the process).

His main enemy was cop 'Choc' Minty, a no-nonsense CID

copper, who was seldom seen doing anything but putting Hazell in his place by threatening to withdraw his investigator's licence.

Ideally cast as Hazell, actor Nicholas Ball injected a new meaning to descriptive one-liners: 'He's as bent as a boomerang' or, referring to wine, 'It tastes like a wet sheepdog.' A cracking performance. Sizzling scripts. Wonderful!

REGULAR CAST

James Hazell **Nicholas Ball**   *'Choc' Minty* **Roddy McMillan**
Dot Wilmington **Barbara Young**   *Cousin Tel* **Desmond McNamara**

Season One

10 colour 60-minute episode

Hazell Plays Solomon

w Gordon Williams and Terry Venables
Asked to investigate young Trish Abrey, who lives with her parents in London's East End, Hazell's enquiries lead him to suspect that the girl is not really their daughter – so why should her 'parents' want her checked out?
Trish Abrey Lisa Moss
Cliff Abrey George Innes
Georgina Gunning Jane Asher

Director: Jim Goddard
Designers: Davis Ferris/Bill Palmer

Hazell Pays a Debt

w Gordon Williams
Seeking vengeance on Hazell, whom he believes framed him, released prisoner O'Rourke gets set to 'fix' his enemy. Hazell meanwhile, trying to earn some money by debt-collecting, is unaware of the storm clouds brewing overhead.
O'Rourke Derrick O'Connor
Mrs Hazell Betty Hardy
Dornford Richard Murdoch

Director: Alastair Reid
Designers: Davis Ferris/Bill Palmer

Hazell and the Walking Blur

w Richard Harris
Hazell investigates the strange facts behind a drunken Scotsman woken up with £1,000 in his pocket – but no knowledge of how it got there, or who it belongs to.

Alex Galbraith Bill Henderson
Tommy Griffiths Michael Elphick
Gordon Gregory James Faulkner

Director: Brian Farnham
Designers: Gordon Toms/Bill Palmer

Hazell Settles the Accounts

w Gordon Williams and Tony Hoare
Engaged by a Soho nightclub to investigate a fall in takings, Hazell finds himself on the trail of a crooked accountant – and becomes involved in the affairs of a seedy Soho gang running a protection racket.
Dobson Freddie Jones
Gloria Pamela Stephenson
Graves John Rhys Davies

Director: Jim Goddard
Designers: Bill Palmer/David Ferris

Hazell Meets the First Eleven

w Tony Hoare and Gordon Williams
Hired to check into the background of a whizz-kid financier to determine if he's a suitable husband for a 'First Eleven' family, Hazell gets an insight into how the 'other arf' spend their leisure hours.
Gordon Gregory James Faulkner
Jonathan Clayton David Robb
Pamela Courtney Celia Gregory

Director: Moria Armstrong
Designers: David Ferris/Bill Palmer

Hazell and the Rubber-heel Brigade

w Richard Harris
Hazell reacquaints himself with his old police colleagues – but it's a far from happy

event. The detective finds himself on the carpet – accused of taking a bribe eighteen months before he left the force.
Det. Supt Bull John Phillips
Det. Sgt Fenner Colin Burns
Mrs Hazell Betty Hardy

Director: Peter Duguid
Designers: David Ferris/Bill Palmer

Hazell Goes to the Dogs

w Tony Hoare
Ida Wiggins employs Hazell to investigate her bookmaker husband, whom she believes is having an affair. A fairly straightforward assignment? Not when you're James Hazell!
Wally Wiggins Dave King
Ida Wiggins Marji Lawrence
Melina Marina Sirtis

Director: Jim Goddard
Designers: Bill Palmer/David Ferris

Hazell and the Weekend Man

w Richard Harris
Though outwardly an upright citizen, Mrs Bradley becomes suspicious enough of her weekend-only lodger to get Hazell to check into his background. He does so – with some surprising results.
Mrs Bradley Pat Heywood
Mr Arnold Sam Dale
Mr Bradley Roger Sloman

Director: Don Leaver
Designers: David Ferris/Bill Palmer

Hazell Works for Nothing

w Peter Ransley
Why should the cops be after him? Hazell has no idea, but he's nevertheless on the run from the law and needs to resolve the situation as fast as possible. Perhaps 'Choc' Minty can help?
Glad Betty Hardy
Maureen Maggie Riley
Pearl Gretchen Franklin

Director: Moira Armstrong
Designers: Bill Palmer/David Ferris

Hazell and the Maltese Vulture

w Trevor Preston
Checking out the character of a business executive for an American consortium seems a routine enquiry for Hazell, but he's soon involved in murder – and finds himself facing unfriendly questioning by a group of villains.
T. P. Eades Ben Aris
Sheena Dana Gillespie
Big Arti Pat Roach

Director: Colin Bucksey
Designers: Bill Palmer/Colin Ferris

Season Two

12 colour 60-minute episodes

Hazell and the Baker Street Sleuth

w Gordon Williams and Terry Venables
Hazell meets Neville Fitch, a private investigator currently trying to get evidence for Anne McGeegan against her husband Michael in a divorce case. Neville asks Hazell to join him – and the Cockney sleuth ends up having a punch-up.
Fitch Clive Swift
Anne McGeegan Lorna Heilbron
Michael McGeegan Ken Hutchinson

Director: Brian Farnham
Designers: Philip Blowers/Peter Elliott

Hazell and the Deptford Virgin

w Leon Griffiths
Hired by Fiona Sutton to retrieve a missing family heirloom – a statuette of the Virgin St Wanda of Cracow – Hazell discovers a local dustman has it and is offering it for sale – but he soon finds that others are interested in the statuette.
Fiona Mel Martin
Heller Peter Miles
Brownhill Charles Gray

Director: Alan Grint
Designers: Philip Blowers/Peter Elliott

Hazell Bangs the Drum

w Jim Hawkins
Believing that her cousin Raiji is being blackmailed, Dr Angela Patel employs

Hazell to investigate. Hazell and cousin Tel decide to keep an eye on the restaurant where Raiji works as a cook – and discover that more than curry is on the menu.
Dr Patel Anna Nicholas
Raiji Dino Shafeek
Sheila Lois Daine

Director: Brian Farnham
Designers: Philip Blowers/Peter Elliott

Hazell Gets the Boot

w Willis Hall
Big Dave Castle calls himself a legitimate businessman, but he's really a villain. His Bentley has been stolen and he employs Hazell to find it – quickly. Hazell does so, but ends up involved in a big gang feud.
Big Dave Billy Murray
Patsy Flanagan Cindy O'Callaghan
Cynthia Liz Crowther

Director: Carol Wilkes
Designers: Philip Blowers/Peter Elliott

Hazell Gets the Bird

w Andrew Nickolds and Stan Hey
When Caroline Bancroft arrives at Hazell's office to collect a case of Camberwell Beauty butterflies, her visit leads Hazell into meeting the King of the Jungle – and learning that Camberwell Beauty is not always a harmless species.
Caroline Bancroft Carolyn Seymour
Scouse Benny Michael Angelis
Anderson Christopher Asante

Director: Baz Taylor
Designer: Bill Palmer

Hazel and the Big Sleep

w Trevor Preston
Homeless, and sleeping on the office floor, Hazell is given a case trying to find a thief at a London hotel. But he falls asleep on the job and wakens to find himself involved with the Mafia!
Sheel Geraldine Gardner
Giant Peter Mayhew
Lugosi Ken Parry

Director: Baz Taylor
Designers: Philip Blowers/Peter Elliott

Hazell and the Suffolk Ghost

w Jim Hawkins
On a trip to the seaside Hazell smells out a rat in a brewery and uncovers a cruel attempt to cheat a man out of his bequest. Dead chickens in a lavatory, blood smeared on his car – events which place the sleuth's life in danger.
Peter Harlow Michael Gaunt
Bell Desmond Llewelyn
Stephanie Harlow Meg Davies

Director: Mike Vardy
Designers: Philip Blowers/Peter Elliott

Hazell and Hyde

w P. J. Hammond
Hired by Mr Clive to find his runaway daughter, Hazell finds she has joined a group of down-and-out squatters – and discovers dope and violence among the drop-outs.
Mr Clive John Rapley
Annie Katherine Stark
Claudine Maev Alexander

Director: Baz Taylor
Designer: Robin Parker

Hazell and the Happy Couple

w Richard Harris
Helen Bryers has left her husband. He wants her back and hires Hazell to find her. The sleuth eventually crosses his client – to his cost. He discovers that even pathetic men are capable of revenge.
Helen Bryers Anna Massey
Bryers Ronald Lacey
Pamela Nell Campbell

Director: Marek Kanievska
Designer: David Ferris

Hazell Gets the Part

w Dave Humphries
Film starlet Jean Curzon hires Hazell to find her emerald necklace, stolen at the studios where she is making an X-certificate film. In order not to arouse suspicion, he acts as her chauffeur – but another actress decides he's ready for stardom!

Jean Curzon Toby Robins
Vanessa Lynda Bellingham
Mort Berman Richard Parmentier

Director: Mike Vardy
Designer: Anthony Cartledge

Hazell and the Greasy Gunners

w Brian Glover
Hazell learns to keep his ear to the ground
in more ways than one when he meets up
with an officer, who is far from being a
gentleman, and Harry the Ear – so called
because he has a nasty habit of biting
people's ears off!
Captain Baldwin Alex Scott
Harry the Ear Brian Glover
Samantha Cyd Hayman

Director: Gerry Mill
Designer: Bill Palmer

Hazell and the Public Enemy

w Murray Smith
Bank robber Ned Barrow has escaped from
Parkhurst Prison, and 'Choc' Minty is on his
trail. Hazell, hired by a newspaper to get a
murder confession from a gangster, nearly
ends up being murdered himself.
Ned Barrow Larry Lamb
Jack Horner John Bindon
Rita Green Lynne Miller

Director: Marek Kanievska
Designers: Philip Blowers/Peter Elliott

HAZELL
Producer: June Roberts (Season 1)
Tim Aspinall (Season 2)
Associate producer: Juliet Grimm
Story editor: Richard Harris
A Thames Television Production
22 colour 60-minute episodes
16 January – 20 March 1978
19 April 1979 – 30 January 1980

THE HIDDEN TRUTH

A short-lived series which set out to show the inner workings of
a modern department of forensic science, and depicted how its
pathologists handled investigations (accidents, drug addiction,
disease, arson and so on), and assisted not just the police, but
sometimes the defence.

Chief pathologist in the series was Professor Robert Lazard, a
man whose working day could often take in a post mortem,
giving evidence in a coroner's court, offering expert advice to the
police on a poisoning enquiry and investigating the cause of an
epidemic. (A pathologist's lot was a busy one.) Working with
him were his first assistant Dr Henry Fox, Dr Ruth Coliton and
Ceylon-born Dr Hamavid de Silva. All were guided by Professor
Lazard's dictum: 'Stay clear of involvement'. (It was an unwritten
law that nothing in relation to the work in hand should be
discussed while they were working – and even more important,
after they had completed their investigation.)

REGULAR CAST

Professor Lazard **Alexander Knox**   *Dr Henry Fox* **James Maxwell**
Dr Ruth Coliton **Elizabeth Weaver**   *Dr Hamavid de Silva* **Zia Mohyeddin**

Cause of Death

w Martin Woodhouse
A charred body is found in the remains of a
burnt-out warehouse, and Lazard and his
team are given the macabre task of proving
whether the man was murdered or simply
the victim of unfortunate circumstance.
[No cast credits available]

Director: Lionel Harris

The Final Analysis

w Peter Lambda
The birth of a baby brings three people into
conflict over a paternity suit. Professor
Hazard and Dr Coliton must tread carefully
if they are to avoid allowing their personal
feelings to colour their judgement.
Stan Garnet George Moon
Dr Roberts Simon Lack
Henry Barker David Lodge

Director: Peter Sasdy

Missing, Believed Killed

w John Hawkesworth
When a crashed wartime bomber is
discovered, Professor Lazard is asked to
provide the answer behind a 20-year-old
mystery. His conclusions could bring a
major insurance fraud to light – and help
the pilot's wife to find justice.
Lloyd Geoffrey Keen
Tua Ling Jacqui Chan
Vice Marshall Colin Gordon

Director: Lionel Harris

One Of the Hampshire Pargeters

w Ludovic Kennedy
How was Barry Pargeter killed? That's the
question facing Professor Lazard when called
to give evidence at the Old Bailey. But he
must sift through some gruesome evidence
before he can provide the answer.
Chf Insp. Greaves Anthony Sagar
Quayle William Sylvester
Judge Anthony Marlowe

Director: John Frankau

THE HIDDEN TRUTH
Devised by: John Whitney and
Geoffrey Bellman
Producer: Stella Richman
A Rediffusion Network Production
4 monochrome 60-minute episodes
24 September – 13 October 1964

HINE

More of an anti-hero than hero, this series told the story of Joe
Hine, a freelance arms dealer (his passport read: Profession –
'salesman'!) living in 'a world made for Civil Servants and
company executives' (men like Walpole Gibb and Astor Harris –
Hine's two main rivals). Hine decides to make his fortune before
retiring from the hypocritical world of double think, forever.
Having set himself a target of a £100 million-plus package for
radar equipment, jet fighters and missiles, he found himself
facing stiff opposition from rival arms dealers – men who would
stop at nothing to 'break Hine', by whatever means it took.

A controversial subject for its day, the series was nevertheless compulsive viewing, with Barrie Ingham stealing the acting plaudits from such notables as Colin Gordon, Michael Goodliffe and Maxwell Shaw.

REGULAR CAST

Joe Hine **Barrie Ingham**   *Walpole Gibb* **Colin Gordon**
Astor Harris **Paul Eddington**   *Sir Christopher Pendle* **Michael Goodliffe**
Susannah Grey **Sarah Craze**   *Jeremy Windsor* **John Steiner**
Raschid **Maxwell Shaw**

HINE
Created by: Wilfred Greatorex
Producer: Wilfred Greatorex
Associate producer: Robert D. Cordona
Directors: Robert Tronson, Cyril Coke
Writers: Wilfred Greatorex, Ray Jenkins,
Peter Draper, Robert Holles, Arden Winch
An ATV Network Production
13 colour 60–minute episodes
7 April – 30 June 1971

THE HUMAN JUNGLE

The series depicted how Dr Roger Corder M.D., D.P.M., a London psychiatrist, attempted to help people through emotional problems and the turmoil of mental breakdown. He was assisted by his secretary Nancy and the young Dr Jimmy Davis (a man who lacked Dr Corder's experience and knowledge, but was nevertheless capable at his job). Though Corder was good at sorting out other people's problems, he couldn't always cope with his own. His relationship with his daughter Jennifer wasn't always a happy one. There was friction between them and Corder couldn't always get on the same wavelength as his headstrong offspring.

An extremely popular series, the public demanded its return after the series ended, but only 26 stories were made.

REGULAR CAST

Dr Roger Corder **Herbert Lom**   *Dr Jimmy Davis* **Michael Johnson**   *Jennifer Corder*
Sally Smith   *Nancy Hamilton* **Mary Yeomans**   *Jane Harris (Assistant to Dr Corder)*
Mary Steele

Season One
The Vacant Chair
The Flip-side Man

Season Two
Struggle for the Mind
Success Machine

Run with the Devil
Thin Ice
The Lost Hours
A Friend of the
  Sergeant Major
Fourteen Ghosts
Fine Feathers
The Two-edged Sword
A Woman with Scars
Time Check
Over and Out
The Wall

The 24-hour Man
Solo Performance
Ring of Hate
Conscience on a Reck
The Quick and the Dead
The Man Who Fell Apart
Dual Control
Skeleton in the Cupboard
Wild Goose Chase
Enemy Outside
Heartbeats in a Tin Box

THE HUMAN JUNGLE
Created by: Julian Wintle
Producers: Julian Wintle and Leslie Parkyn
Theme music composed by: Bernard
Ebbinghouse (Played by John Barry)
Directors: James Hill, Sidney Hayers, Don
Sharp, Vernon Sewell, Robert Day, Charles
Crichton, Roy Baker, Alan Cook
Writers: John Kruse, Robert Stewart, Bill
MacIlwraith, Lewis Davidson, Ann Francis,
Marc Brandel
*An Independent Artists Production for ABC
Television*
First season filmed at Beaconsfield Studios,
Second season at Elstree.
26 monochrome 60-minute episodes
30 March – 29 June 1963
20 February – 17 May 1965
(USA: Syndicated 1964)

HUNTER'S WALK

Created by Lord Ted Willis, this 'coppers on the beat' crime series (reputedly turned down by the BBC, who saw it as a latter-day Z cars), was about small town crime and the policemen who solved it.

Given the premise that the dividing line between a respectable citizen and a law-breaker was razor-thin, the stories – set in the fictional town of Broadstone – depicted how the local villains were kept in check by the town's police force, who were: Detective Sergeant 'Smithy' Smith, a dedicated CID detective; Sergeant Ken Ridgeway, the station officer; Smithy's young protégé, Detective 'Mickey' Finn; and anxious-to-please Constables Fred Pooley and Harry Coombes – Broadstone's resident boys in blue.

REGULAR CAST
DS Smith **Ewan Hooper**   *Sgt Ken Ridgeway* **Davyd Harries**
DC 'Mickey' Finn **David Simeon**   *PC Fred Pooley* **Duncan Preston**
PC Harry Coombes **Charles Rea**   *Betty Smith* **Ruth Madoc**

Season One
13 colour 60-minute episodes

Disturbance

w Richard Harris
Led by DS Smith, the Broadstone police
force suddenly find themselves in a manhunt
for a disturbed and potentially dangerous
man. All leave is cancelled and the boys are
off and running.
PC Glenn Mike Lewin
Dennis Kenwright Doug Fisher
Janet Kenwright Helen Fraser

Director: Robert Tronson
Designer: Gerry Roberts

Local Knowledge

w Richard Harris
A case of assault. A sick man at large. DS
Smith, awakened from his slumbers by PC
Pooley, is having none of it – but the
experience will affect both him and the
people of Broadwater.
Christine Lewis Frances White
Philip Lewis Ian Thompson
McLean Michael Ripper

Director: Ron Francis
Designer: Trevor Paterson

Outcast

w Nicolas Palmer
When Smokey Haines returns to Broadstone
after serving a two-year prison sentence for
killing his baby, DS Smith must look for
mitigation circumstances in the case – and
the sympathy of the town's citizens.
Smokey Haines Jim Norton
Alice Haines Mary Healey
Arthur Harry Walker

Director: Robert Tronson
Designer: Ken Wheatley

Behaviour

w P. J. Hammond
What is DS Smith to make of Raymond
Flack, a new arrival in Broadstone – and
why should local villain Jimmy Walker wish
to leave the town?
Raymond Flack Terence Rigby
Jimmy Walker Andrew McCulloch
Mrs Flack Bella Emberg

Director: Robert Tronson
Designer: Ken Wheatley

Vanishing Trick

w Nicolas Palmer
Certain that there is a connection between a
housebreaker who has eluded the police for
months and the recent death of Ben
Lawrence, DI Smith has trouble proving it.
His only clue is Lawrence's 16-year-old
daughter.
Sally Lawrence Zuleika Robson
Irish Lawrence Jane Hylton
Mrs Purdey Ann Tirard

Director: John Cooper
Designer: Trevor Paterson

Reasonable Suspicion

w Richard Harris
The Criminal Law Act 1967, Section Two,
sub-sections four and five states 'A constable
may arrest, without warrant, any person
whom he – with reasonable cause – suspects
either to be guilty of an offence or about to
commit an offence – but how should one
apply the act, that's Smithy's problem?
Neil Yeldham Brendan Price
Ruth Mary Tamm
Geoff Peter Settelen

Director: Robert Tronson
Designer: Gerry Roberts

Discretion

w P. J. Hammond

When Sergeant Ridgeway begins to receive anonymous complaints of petty offences – people parking without lights, a householder who has no dog licence – DS Smith has little sympathy for his colleague, until a routine enquiry pays unexpected results.

Saxon David Collings
Lorry Driver Alun Armstrong
Mr Davenport James Hayter

Director: Robert Tronson
Designer: Gerry Roberts

Care and Protection

w Richard Harris

Two separate cases, both concerning children, confront DS Smith and his colleagues with a harsh look at reality and the detective must find the link which connects both events.

WPC Carey Joy Ring
Bridget Bailey Elain Donnelly
Mrs Morris Pauline Devaney

Director: Ron Francis
Designer: Colin Andrews

Incident

w Ted Willis

When George Lomax, a down-on-his-heels dealer in double glazing, leaves a pub drunk and disgruntled, it sets off a chain of events which require the assistance – and understanding – of the Broadstone police.

George Lomax Glyn Owen
Linda Lomax Patricia Denys
Matt Raymond Mason

Director: Ron Francis
Designer: Trevor Paterson

The Old Folks at Home

w James Doran

It's the old story all over again. Someone moves into Broadstone, sets up a con, takes easy pickings from the old and helpless – then moves on. But this time the smoothie has charmed someone to death and Smithy is anxious to nab him.

Anne Jill Browne
Philips Ken Jones
Turner Michael Turner

Director: Desmond McCarthy
Designer: John Newton Clarke

All Too Tidy

w Roger Ormerod

When Les comes out of prison and his father tries to establish a new rapport with him – but the bored and spoiled Les gets up to his old tricks – DS Smith takes an interest in the boy's welfare.

Les Carter John Labanowski
Tom Carter Robert Keegan
Jess Carter Mary Chester

Director: Ron Francis
Designer: Vic Symonds

Lost Dog

w Bill Barron

A number of seemingly unrelated events after a robbery suddenly fall into place and give DS Smith and his team something to work on – but in which direction will it lead them?

Jack Foster Norman Rossington
Lil Foster Wendy Gifford
Beatrice Hill Mary Morris

Director: Robert Tronson
Designer: Colin Andrews

Skeletons

w Leslie Duxbury

When an elderly woman is found dead in her shop and the clues all add up to murder, the Broadstone policemen are fishing in the dark – but routine door-to-door enquiries bring some unexpected results.

Det. Chf Supt Dunstan Leslie Schofield
Brian Kirby Roderick Smith
Joyce Kirby Sarah Grazebrook

Director: Gareth Davies
Designer: Colin Andrews

Season Two
13 colour 60-minute episodes

Help

w Richard Harris
DC Finn is feeling well pleased. He's looking after his mate, Leslie, who's getting married the following morning. They are out on the town, making the most of Leslie's 'freedom' – but in the process Les causes a breach of the peace.
Leslie Cope Larry Dann
Mrs Mason Jennifer Hill
Ron Leo Dolan

Director: Malcolm Taylor
Designer: John Newton Clarke

Perspectives

w P. J. Hammond
When an old-age pensioner is badly beaten for a few pence, and a wealthy landowner is robbed of some valuable antiques, DS Smith reflects that though neither would understand the other's loss – justice for both is equal.
Maunder Hugh Latimer
Old Woman Jean Marlowe
PC East Stephen Yardley

Director: Robert Tronson
Designer: Michael Eve

Villain

w Bob Baker and Dave Martin
When Bobby Dawes, a big-time crook with a reputation to uphold, is released from prison and returns to Broadstone, DS Smith gets set to prevent the crime he's convinced will take place. The question is what stroke will Dawes pull?
Bobby Dawes David Dakar
John Dix John Rolfe
Elaine Dix Karin McCarthy

Director: John Cooper
Designer: Roger Allen

Blind Eye

w Brian Finch
Assigned to investigate the evidence of his old friend Bert Jackson, a security officer

who says he neither saw nor heard the thieves who tried to rob his employers, PC Pooley draws some uncomfortable conclusions about himself.
Bert Jackson Colin Douglas
Alice Jackson Shelia Raynor
Bernie Pilling Roy Holder

Director: Hugh Munro
Designer: Roger Allan

Lost Sheep

w Bob Baker and Dave Martin
Sheep-rustling can be a very lucrative business, but though DS Smith has a shrewd idea of who is responsible he finds country people have their own brand of law and justice.
Billy Silk Bryan Marshall
Harrop Thorne Mike Pratt
Jake Thorne Norman Jones

Director: Tony Wharmby
Designer: Roger Allan

Charlie

w James Doran
A bit of a villain he may be, but Charlie is everybody's friend. You're never short of a laugh or a joke whenever Charlie's around, but this time it appears he's gone too far – and his family need police assistance.
Charlie Mead Bill Maynard
Annie Mead Margaret John
Pam Mead Pam Scotcher

Director: Malcolm Taylor
Designer: Ray White

Digger

w Peter Hill
DS Smith will rue the day he was confined to bed when some odd developments took place in Broadstone. He shouldn't really have to worry, his 'boys' can handle anything that comes along – can't they?
Digger Davies Ronald Radd
Chf Insp. Terry David Nel
Frank Daley William Maxwell

Director: Robert Tronson
Designer: John Newton Clark

Ella

w Brian Finch

A policeman's private life should be clean as silk. So say DS Smith and Sergeant Ridgeway. So when one of their 'boys' starts tongues wagging by calling on an attractive widow, they take an interest.

Ella Minton Jane Collins
Chuck Minton Ron Welling
Ronnie Grimshaw Milton Johns

Director: Tony Wharmby
Designer: Roger Allan

Witness

w Leslie Duxbury

The friendly association between solicitor Jimmy Briggs and DS Smith is severely strained when Briggs' stepdaughter is accused of organising a series of shoplifting offences. Smith has concrete evidence – but the Briggs family close ranks to give the girl an alibi.

Jimmy Briggs Derek Farr
Mrs Briggs Heather Canning
Claire Briggs Judy Buxton

Director: Malcolm Taylor
Designer: Ray White

Steady Job

w Bill Barron

A small boy sleepwalking; a series of offences against children; a working men's club using cheap labour – all apparently unrelated events which are drawn together in an unexpected way by DS Smith.

Doris Pope Mitzi Rogers
Michael Pope Geoffrey Chapman
Rupert Symes Patrick Connor

Director: Victor Menzies
Designer: Colin Andrews

Visitors

w Tony Hoare

When DS Smith receives a Scotland Yard tip-off that two London villains are on their way to Broadstone – intention unknown – he sets in motion a chain of events that the citizens of the town will find it hard to forget.

Bernie Fleet Christopher Coll
Charlie Bachus Ray Lonnen
Roy Lock Richard Vanstone

Director: Hugh Munro
Designer: Roger Allan

Free While Wednesday

w Bill Barron

When Ken Ridgeway's father dies, he comes under heavy pressure to leave the force, enter the family business, and marry his girlfriend Brenda. Meantime DS Smith has his hands full with problems of his own.

Brenda Diana Rayworth
Joe Ridgeway Julian Somers
Richard Burke Sean Arnold

Director: Hugh Munro
Designer: Roger Allan

Kids

w Richard Harris

DS Smith and his boys have to deal with all kinds of villainy – but the latest outbreak of 'crime' has them well and truly puzzled. It appears that a new gang of villains have entered their patch – seven young kids!

Elen Smith Carole Shadbolt
David Smith Dale Owen
Stephanie Coe Patricia Smith

Director: Robert Tronson
Designer: Richard Lake

Season Three

13 colour 60-minute episodes

Intent

w Bob Baker and Dave Martin

When a violent row breaks out at a wedding reception between the groom and the bride's ex-boyfriend, and the groom is badly injured, DS Smith must ask himself the age old question: did he fall, or was he pushed?

Roger Jenkins John Rhys Davies
Brenda Diana Hayworth
Houseman Simon MacCorkindale

Director: John Nelson-Burton
Designer: Michael Bramhall

Reprisals

w Bob Baker and Dave Martin

Colin Parfitt is an ambitious copper – too ambitious perhaps. He's arrested 38 criminals within three months, and it now appears that someone is seeking revenge. DS Smith investigates a fire at Parfitt's home and asks: Is it an accident?

Colin Parfitt Mark Griffith
Mrs Parfitt Emily Richard
Roley Higwood Desmond Hill

Director: Richard Bramall
Designer: Stanley Mills

Sudden Death

w Jack Ronder

A head-on collision between two cars. One driver dead, the other intoxicated and driving without a licence. PC Pooley believes he has an open and shut case – Ken Ridgeway thinks otherwise.

Mr Danby Stuart Fell
Mrs Danby Barbara Ewing
Johnny Adam Bridge

Director: Richard Bramall
Designer: Michael Bramhall

Outsiders

w Bob Baker and Dave Martin

Hearing that a volatile and aggressive West Indian youth, picked up for speeding, is wanted for questioning in Birmingham, DS Smith, too, turns aggressive. But does he overstep the mark because of racial prejudice?

Lance Dodds Ram John Holder
PC Glenn Mike Lewin
DS Gladstone Clifton Jones

Director: Peter Jeffries
Designer: Roger Allan

Echoes

w P. J. Hammond

It's a tough case to crack, but DS Smith is determined to get to the bottom of the villainy – even though he may turn up a connection which proves that a copper and a villain have more than a little in common.

Raymond Mint Edward Judd
Eileen Patricia Mort
Supt Hanbury David Waller

Director: Richard Bramall
Designer: Michael Bramhall

Say Nothing

w Brian Finch

When the annual Broadstone fête finds police and local hooligans on show before the whole town and Special Constable Alec Richards is put to a severe test, DS Smith and his boys lend a hand.

Alec Richards Ray Smith
Jimmy Snout Michael Deeks
Bert Brown Derek Benfield

Director: Richard Bramall
Designer: Michael Bramhall

Not Me

w Richard Harris

PC Pooley, on night patrol, finds a man covered in blood. DS Smith and Sergeant Ken Ridgeway must find out who is responsible for the man's injuries, and why it happened.

Dr Clark Glynn Edwards
Collins George Innes
Mrs Collins Mary Healey

Director: John Nelson-Burton
Designer: David Chandler

Interference

w Richard Harris

When Len Summers, who runs a local youth club in his spare time, is accused by a club member's father of sharing a relationship with his son which is closer than it should be, DS Smith foresees personal tragedy.

Len Summers Godfrey James
Mr Ferris Norman Jones
Mrs Summers Marji Lawrence

Director: John Nelson-Burton
Designer: Roger Allan

Job

w Brian Finch

No one other than his wife seems concerned when PC Pooley fails to arrive home one evening. But when his empty car is found at the scene of a break-in, it becomes a job for the Broadstone police – who view it as a serious matter.

Joe Tanner *Jonathan Adams*
Vic *Johnny Wade*
PC Glenn *Mike Lewin*

Director: **Richard Bramall**
Designer: **Michael Bramhall**

Missing

w Richard Harris
When a local girl 'disappears', everyone, including her mother, assumes she has 'Gone off again' – but PC Harry Coombes, acting on instinct, sets out to prove that such is not the case this time around.

Mrs Fielding **Wendy Gifford**
Jack Dale **Barry Stanton**
Don Beatty **Graham Ashley**

Director: **Richard Bramall**
Designer: **Roger Allan**

Spinsters

w Roger Marshall
Neighbours can be a problem. With no love lost between Mrs Sheldon and the Grahams next door, what kind of petty irritation escalates into a crime which DS Smith and PC Pooley must investigate?

Barry Graham **Graham Weston**
Mrs Sheldon **Anna Barry**
Alice Graham **Amanda Murray**

Director: **Ron Francis**
Designer: **Don Fisher**

Take Away

w Richard Harris
Take two drunken, penniless Scotsmen returning from a cup final abroad, two

Chinamen, one of them running around a restaurant with a meat cleaver, add a pregnant wife, and you have more problems for DS Smith to sort out.

Lee Peng **Burt Kwouk**
Alec Guthrie **Freddie Earlle**
Hugh Fairbairn **Michael McKevitt**

Director: **Richard Bramall**
Designer: **Roger Allan**

Kicking and Screaming

w Bob Baker and Dave Martin
Why should a man systematically destroy his own home? Sergeant Ken Ridgeway is landed with the job of finding the answer. He soon finds that he's dealing with a very violent customer indeed.

Cp Kirby **Ken Hutchinson**
Eileen Kirby **Dorothy White**
Ray Huntley **Arnold Peters**

Director: **John Cooper**
Designer: **Michael Bramhall**

HUNTER'S WALK
Created by Ted Willis
Season One
Producer: John Cooper
Music by: Derek Scott
Script editor: Nicholas Palmer
13 colour 60-minute episodes
4 June – 3 September 1973

Seasons Two and Three
Producer: John Cooper
Music by: Derek Scott
Script editor: Richard Harris
2×13 colour 60-minute episodes
22 April – 22 July 1974
1 June – 24 August 1976
An ATV Network Production

THE INFORMER

As a departure from private eyes and super-cool policeman, the mid-sixties saw the emergence of this series, one that introduced a new kind of television hero – the professional informer: a man who traded information for high rewards, and hoped he'd live long enough to enjoy the fruits of his success.

Such a man was Alex Lambert, a disbarred barrister turned police informant. Posing as a business consultant, Lambert used the contacts he had made on both sides of the law to carry out his new and dangerous profession. Like others of his ilk, he was a man alone, a man with no close friends. Not even his wife knew of his activities. Information was an informer's stock in trade and he could share his problems with no one – his life depended on secrecy and the fact that nobody except his police contact knew (or suspected) his real profession.

People turned informer for many reasons. Lambert took risks – tremendous risks – strictly for the huge financial rewards his information brought him from insurance companies, knowing that any second he could be found out and removed by his enemies.

REGULAR CAST

Alex Lambert **Ian Hendry**   *Helen Lambert* **Heather Sears**
Piper (Lambert's business partner in series 1) **Neil Hallett**
Cass (Lambert's business partner in series 2) **Tony Selby**

THE INFORMER
Created by John Whitney and Geoffrey
Bellman
Producers: Stella Richman and Peter
Collinson (Series 1)
John Whitney (Series 2)
Executive producer: Stella Richman
(Series 2)
Script editor: John Whitney (Series 1)
Alfred Shaughnessy (Series 2)
A Rediffusion Television Presentation

Season One
8 colour 60-minute episodes
3 August – 21 September 1966

Season Two
13 colour 60-minute episodes
25 September – 18 December 1967

(USA: Syndicated 1965 – 8 episodes)

THE INSIDE MAN

A series of mystery dramas that depicted the investigations of Dr James Austen – a criminologist/psychiatrist who specialised in seeking out the 'dark places of the mind where unsolved problems could often lead to acts of sudden violence'.

Austen sometimes worked for 'The Department', a secret British Government department. Sometimes he was hired by large business combines. On other occasions he found himself sorting out the problems of private individuals. Whatever the nature of his employment, he was never far from excitement or danger, and always living close to other people's fears.

Helped by his colleagues, Sarah Worth, James Dawnay and Michael Barnett – all specialists in their chosen field, Austen guaranteed success.

An interesting though sometimes confusing series, the production got bogged down with its own format. As usual, Frederick Jaeger took the acting honours.

REGULAR CAST
Dr James Austen **Frederick Jaeger**   *Sarah Worth* **Petra Davies**
James Dawnay **Basil Henson**   *Michael Barnett* **Robin Ellis**

Delayed Action	An East-West Affair
Relapse	The Spy Vanishes
Crosscheck	A Day of Angels
Death of a Friendship	The Case of the Abandoned
Discord	Wife
Recall	Revenge for a Visitor
Lady in the Bath	

THE INSIDE MAN
Producer: David Cunliffe
Executive producer: Derek Granger
Music by: Don Harper
Directors: Bob Hird, Anthony Kearey,
Shaun O'Riordan, David Cunliffe, Richard
Martin
Writers: David Ellis, Martin Hall, Paul
Erikson, Paul Wheeler, Robert Holmes,
George Landry
A London Weekend Television Production
12 colour 60-minute episodes
17 January – 4 April 1969

INSPECTOR MORSE

Three classic whodunnits taken from the *Inspector Morse* books by Colin Dexter, which gave actor John Thaw (so good in *The Sweeney*) the opportunity to get back to a part worthy of his talents.

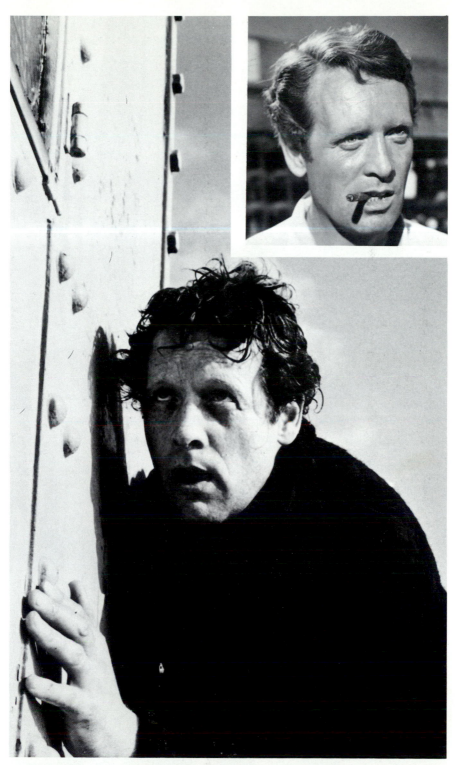

Danger Man John Drake (Patrick McGoohan).

Dempsey and Makepeace Dempsey, Chf Supt Spikings and Makepeace.

Dial 999 Mike Maguire.

Dick Turpin (Richard O'Sullivan).

The Fellows Dimmock, Mrs Hollinsczech, Thomas Anthem and Oldenshaw.

(Above) **Ghost Squad** Left to right, Tony Miller,
Nick Craig and Geoffrey Stock.

(Right) **GS5** Agent Peter Clark (Ray Barrett).

Hazell Cockney Jack the Lad, cum-private eye, James Hazell (Nicholas Ball).

The Invisible Man Brady and his sister Diane (Lisa Daniely).

Ivanhoe (Roger Moore).

Jason King (Peter Wynegard).

Jemima Shaw Investigates (Patricia Hodge).

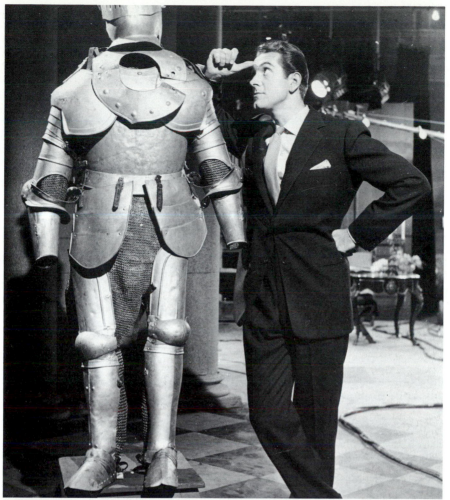

Knight Errant John Turner as Adam Knight.

The Man in Room 17

Mark Saber Donald Gray (seated) as Saber.

Marlowe – Private Eye Philip Marlowe and Annie Riordan.

Minder Left to right, Terry McCann, Arthur Daley and Dave.

As Inspector Morse (his first name was never given), he was a laid-back, classical-music-loving, Oxford-based sleuth with a quirky cerebral approach to solving crime. Brilliant at his job but occasionally erratic (his theories sometimes backfired in his face), Morse enjoyed nothing better than poetry, music and booze – especially real ale. Somewhat prejudiced to people of slightly lesser intellect, his don't-muck-me-about manner camouflaged a gentle nature – though he could (and did) harangue his partner, Detective Sergeant Lewis, for his plodding approach to crime.

Wonderful. Clever and cryptic (sometimes too cryptic for their own good), the stories are destined to become classics of the genre.

REGULAR CAST

Inspector Morse **John Thaw**   *Det. Sgt Lewis* **Kevin Whately**

The Dead of Jericho

w Adapted by Anthony Minghella
When an attractive woman is found dead at her home in Oxford's Jericho district, the evidence points to suicide, but Inspector Morse has his own personal reasons for believing that the victim was murdered. Hours before, he had invited the woman to supper and she had agreed to meet him – so why should she have committed suicide in the intervening period?
Anne Staveley **Gemma Jones**
Chf Insp. Bell **Norman Jones**
George Jackson **Patrick Troughton**
Alan Richards **Richard Durden**

Director: **Alistair Reid**
Designer: **David McHenry**

The Silent World of Nicholas Quinn

w Adapted by Julian Mitchell
Overhearing a conversation he wasn't meant to hear, Nicholas Quinn finds out something he should not know – something that costs him his life. Inspector Morse and DS Lewis have an abundance of suspects among Quinn's colleagues from Oxford University's examinations board. But the thing that bothers Morse the most is: How did Quinn overhear a conversation when he was stone deaf?

Dean **Frederick Treves**
Philip Ogleby **Michael Gough**
Mrs Bartlet **Elspet Gray**
Donald Martin **Roger Lloyd Pack**

Director: **Brian Parker**
Designer: **David McHenry**

Service of All the Dead

w Adapted by Julian Mitchell
A quiet country church is an unlikely setting for murder, and the vicar and his voluntary helpers are equally unlikely suspects. But murder has taken place on the hallowed ground of the parish church of St Oswald – and will almost certainly take place again unless Inspector Morse and his colleague DS Lewis can solve the macabre mystery.
Harry Josephs **Maurice O'Connell**
Chief Supt Bell **Norman Jones**
Doctor Starkie **Michael Hordern**
Mrs Rawlinson **Judy Campbell**

Director: **Peter Hammond**
Designer: **David McHenry**

INSPECTOR MORSE
Producer: Kenny McBain
Executive producer: Ted Childs
A Zenith Production for Central TV
3 colour 120-minute episodes
6–13–20 January 1987

INTERNATIONAL DETECTIVE

Based on the secret files of the William J. Burns International Detective Agency, whose head office was in New York (actually a studio set at Elstree Studios), this first-rate series introduced Agency man Ken Franklin – a man who rarely carried a gun, preferring to solve crimes by cool and methodical brain work. Head operator for the agency, each story began with Franklin being given his latest assignment by W. J. Burns, then jetting off to wherever his adventures took him. (Apart from the top of his head or his hand, 'Burns' himself was never actually seen.) While this was taking place, an off-screen announcer told us that: 'Though these stories are based on real cases from the secret files of the W. J. B. Detective Agency, the names of clients and locations have been changed to protect their privacy.'

Produced in documentary style, the series was among the best of its genre.

REGULAR CAST

Ken Franklin **Arthur Fleming**

The Conway Case
The Carrington Case
The Dimitrios Case
The Cumberland Case
The Winthrop Case
The Whitley Case
The Prescott Case
The Dudley Case
The Rose Bowl Case
The Broker Case
The Steibel Case
The Bremner Case
The Dennison Case
The Barnaby Case
The Robbins Case
The Oakland Case
The Carter Case
The Marino Case
The Daniels Case
The Kempton Case

The Stevenson Case
The Raffael Case
The Bristol Case
The Buxton Case
The Joplin Case
The Santerno Case
The Bismark Case
The Marlowe Case
The Rashid Case
The Orlando Case
The Sheridan Case
The Somerset Case
The Anthony Case
The Dolores Case
The Stanton Case
The Dunster Case
The Martos Case
The Washington Case
The Madonna Case

INTERNATIONAL DETECTIVE
Producer: Gordon L. T. Scott
Associate producer: Jeremy Summers
Music by: Edwin Astley and Harry Booth
(Theme music composed by: Le Roy Holmes)
Story editor: Guy Morgan

A Delfry Production for ABC Television
Filmed on location and at Elstree Studios
39 monochrome 30-minute episodes
26 December 1959 – 4 June 1961
(USA: Syndicated 1959)

INTERPOL CALLING

'Set in a dignified building in Paris, lies the headquarters of the International Criminal Police Organisation (Interpol for short). Some of the most extraordinary stories in the annals of crime have happened here. Interpol Calling tells just some of those stories.'

That announcement introduced every episode in this superior crime series which told how the world famous organisation brought criminals to justice on a worldwide scale.

REGULAR CAST

Inspector Paul Duval **Charles Korvin**   *Inspector Mornay* **Edwin Richfield**

The Angola Brights
The Thirteen Innocents
The Money Game
The Sleeping Giant
The Two-headed Monster
The Long Weekend
You Can't Die Twice
Diamond SOS
Private View
Dead on Arrival
Air Switch
The Chinese Mask
Slave Ship
The Man's a Clown
Last Man Lucky
No Flowers for Onno
Mr George
The Thousand Mile Alibi
Act of Piracy
Game for Three Hands

The Collector
The Heiress
Payment in Advance
Fingers of Guilt
The Girl with Grey Hair
Trial at Craby's Creek
Ascent to Murder
Slow Boat to Amsterdam
White Blackmail
A Foreign Body
In the Swim
The Three Keys
Eight Days Inclusive
Dressed to Kill
Cargo of Death
Desert Hi-jack
Pipeline
The Absent Assassin
Checkmate

INTERPOL CALLING
Producers: Anthony Perry, Connery Chapel
Executive producer: F. Sherwin Green
Produced by Rank/Wrather
An ATV Presentation
39 monochrome 30-minute episodes
14 September 1959 – 20 June 1960
(USA: Syndicated 1961)

INTRIGUE

'In the cut-throat business world, competing firms resemble competing governments fighting for supremacy – and they also use ruthless weapons. There is a need for strong men who can temper the excesses of industry with the skill of diplomats. Such a man is Gavin Grant, a management consultant whose speciality is *Intrigue*'. So ran the narration (episodes 1–3 only) which introduced this industrial spy pot-boiler.

The stories themselves related how Grant, a freelance troubleshooter with a high tech business degree(!), specialised in preventing the theft of ideas by industrial espionage agents or in retrieving those stolen. Partnered by his beautiful sidekick, Val Spencer, they sold their skills to whomever paid best.

REGULAR CAST
Gavin Grant Edward Judd   *Val Spencer* Caroline Mortimer

INTRIGUE
Based on an idea by Tony Williamson
Producer: Robert Banks Stewart
Directors: John Moxey, Robert Tronson,
Kim Mills,
Jonathan Alwyn, Bill Bain, Patrick
Dromgoole
Writers: David Weir, Anthony Skene,
Raymond Bowers, Robert Banks Stewart,
Brian Clemens, Robert Holmes
An ABC Weekend Network Production
12 colour 60-minute episodes
1 October – 17 December 1966

THE INVISIBLE MAN

'A man who can investigate crimes without being seen. A man who can go where no ordinary man could hope to enter. A man searching for the answer to his invisibility . . . *The Invisible Man*.'

The story of how scientist Peter Brady tested his theory of optical density, discovered how to render any matter invisible – then become invisible himself when further experiments misfired (an optical conductor fused and showered him with chemicals mixed with oxygen).

Thereafter the series followed his adventures as he tried, together with his girlfriend Tania, to discover a formula that would restore him to visible form – while staving off the forces of evil who attempted to discover the secret of his invisibility. (During the first story, Brady was hunted down and imprisoned by British ministry scientists who saw him as a national menace – before being convinced otherwise and releasing him to continue his research. In consideration of this, Brady elected to use his strange power for 'the benefit of mankind' and undertook many hazardous missions for the British Government.)

On screen, Brady appeared swathed in bandages, overcoat or laboratory overall, and sunglasses! Oddly enough, the actor who played the role was never credited – though his voice belonged to actor Tim Turner.

Author's note: I can confirm the existence of an episode from this series which contains a different origin scenario of how Peter Brady came to be The Invisible Man to that given in the story 'Secret Experiment'!

The story, usually transmitted with its o/s title blanked out, closely follows the storyline of 'Bank Raid', but contains several differences in the o/s action – the most notable being that the first eight minutes or so retells how, by accident, Brady became the-man-who-wasn't-there, in a *totally different* scenario to that contained in the first story!

In this episode, the actor playing the bandage-swathed scientist is *not* the thespian who played the role in all other stories! He is of smaller stature and the voice used to convey Brady's dialogue sounds suspiciously like that of Canadian actor Robert Beatty!(?) Young Deborah Watling sports a short, straight-cut hairstyle (in all other stories it was curly) and Brady's sister Diane, is referred to as 'Dee'!

Viewing the story compels uncalled-for amusement. The actor playing The Invisible Man bumps into furniture and doors, his 'headless' shoulder-padding is clearly visible, and the 'special effects' are far removed from the technical expertise of the other stories.

Conclusion: *two* pilot stories were filmed, of which this was the first. One look at the results and the producers decided to think again and call for a remake.

REGULAR CAST

Peter Brady ?   *Diane (his sister)* Lisa Daniely
Sally (his young niece) Deborah Watling   *Tania* Zena Marshall
Colonel Ward Ernest Clark

Secret Experiment

w Michael Connor and Michael Cramoy
A secret experiment has dramatic results for scientist Peter Brady – he vanishes into thin air! Or does he? He's just a man who isn't there – an invisible man! Accepting his fate, he decides to use his newly-found power to aid others.

Daine Brady Lisa Daniely (Intro.)
Sally Deborah Watling (Intro.)
Dr Hanning Lloyd Lambie (Intro.)

Director: Pennington Richards

Crisis in the Desert

w Ralph Smart
Colonel Warren, of British Military
Intelligence, seeks Brady's aid. His mission:
to rescue a British agent from the secret
police of a foreign country. *Sans* clothes, the
Invisible Man flies into danger.
Colonel Warren Douglas Wilmer
Hassan Eric Pohlmann
Omar Martin Benson
Director: Pennington Richards

The Locked Room

w Lindsay Galloway and Ralph Smart
Tania, a scientist from behind the Iron
Curtain working in London, is ordered to
return home for criticising her government.
Brady, believing she can help him to regain
his visibility, gives her some unseen
assistance.
Tania Zena Marshall (Intro.)
Dushkin Rupert Davies
Philip Noel Coleman

Director: Pennington Richards

Behind the Mask

w Stanley Mann and Leslie Arliss
Tricked into visiting the home of the
disfigured Raphael Constantine, Peter Brady
receives a strange request. He is asked to use
his invisibility to recover a secret document
which incriminates his host in a crime he
didn't commit.
Constantine Dennis Price
Max Edwin Richfield
Marcia Barbara Chilcott

Director: Pennington Richards

Play to Kill

w Robert Westerby and Leslie Arliss
Was actress Barbara Crane really responsible
for a cliff-top accident which cost a hobo his
life? She believes she was – the Invisible
Man thinks otherwise and sets out to prove
her innocence.
Barbara Crane Helen Cherry
Colonel Colonel Gordon
Tom Hugh Latimer

Director: Peter Maxwell

The Mink Coat

w Leonore Coffee and Ian Stuart Black
Unknown to Penny Page, the mink coat she
is carrying to France contains vital stolen
documents hidden in its lining. Fortunately
for her, her fellow passengers include Diana
and Peter Brady – the Invisible Man.
Penny Page Hazel Court
Walker Derek Godfrey
Bunny Harold Behrens

Director: Pennington Richards

Picnic with Death

w Leonard Fincham and Leslie Arliss
Through the friendship of his niece Sally,
Brady becomes involved with a woman
whose husband and sister-in-law are
plotting to murder her. However, Brady's
invisibility allows him to stay one jump
ahead of their plans.
Derek Norton Derek Bond
Carol Norton Faith Brook
Lindy Norton Margaret McCourt

Director: Pennington Richards

Blind Justice

w Ralph Smart
The Invisible Man becomes a blind woman's
eyes to help her find the gang of cut-throats
responsible for her husband's death. The
woman's blindness allows her to 'see' Brady,
which makes his task that much easier.
Katherine Holt Honor Blackman
Arthur Holt Philip Friend
Det. Insp. Heath Robert Raglan

Director: Pennington Richards

Strange Partners

w Michael Cramoy
Being invisible is a defence against detection
from any human being. But when Brady
accepts a mission from Colonel Ward, he
discovers that invisibility is no protection
against man's canine friends.
Lucien Currie Griffith Jones
Vickers Patrick Troughton
Colonel Ward Ernest Clark

Director: Pennington Richards

The Gun-runners

w Ian Stuart Black

When the pocket-sized Mediterranean state of Bay Akim looks like becoming a trouble spot and a haven for gun-runners, the British Government asks Brady to help it rid the state of Sardi, a ruthless dictator.
Sardi Paul Stassino
Ali James Booth
Zena Fleming Louise Allbritton

Director: Peter Maxwell

Odds Against Death

w Ian Stuart Black and Stanley Mann

To save the daughter of brilliant scientist, Professor Owen, from danger, Brady uses his invisibility to manipulate the casino tables in Italy in Owen's favour.
Unknowingly, the scientist is gambling his daughter's life away.
Prof. Owens Walter Fitzgerald
Suzy Owens Julia Lockwood
Croupier Peter Elliott

Director: Pennington Richards

Jailbreak

w Ian Stuart Black

Convinced that Joe Green, a man sentenced for robbery, was falsely accused, Peter Brady strips off his clothes and helps Green to locate a blonde who can prove his alibi and bring the real criminal to justice.
Joe Green Dermot Walsh
Robson Maurice Kaufmann
Prison Governor Ralph Michael

Director: Pennington Richards

Bank Raid

w Doreen Montgomery and Ralph Smart

When his niece, Sally, is kidnapped and held hostage by a gang of criminals, Brady has to rob a bank to save her life – but the Invisible Man has a trump card up his unseen sleeve.
Crowther Willoughby Goddard
Williams Brian Bradford
Headmistress Patricia Marcel

Director: Ralph Smart

Death Cell

w Michael Cramoy

A beautiful woman escapes from a mental home and appeals to Brady to help her prove her fiancé innocent of the murder of a policeman. Brady pays an unseen visit to the man – and receives a surprise.
Ellen Summers Lana Morris
Dr Trevor Ian Wallace
George Wilson William Lucas

Director: Peter Maxwell

Point of Destruction

w Ian Stuart Black

When three test pilots lose their lives in identical plane crashes, then a fourth narrowly escapes death, Peter Brady investigates the failure of a top secret fuel diffuser which is suspected of causing the accidents.
Scotty Duncan Lamont
Stefan Derren Nesbitt
Controller Barry Letts

Director: Quentin Lawrence

The Vanishing Evidence

w Ian Stuart Black

Peter Thal, an international spy, murders Professor Harper and steals vital secrets on which he had been working. Colonel Ward seeks out the Invisible Man's help to follow Thal to Holland.
Peter Thal Charles Gray
Colonel Ward Ernest Clark
Jenny Wryden Sarah Lawson

Director: Peter Maxwell

The Prize

w Ian Stuart Black

Arriving in Scandinavia to collect a prize for his contribution to science, Brady becomes involved in the strange affair of Tania Roskoff, a brilliant Soviet writer who has been arrested while crossing the border.
Tania Roskoff Mai Zetterling
Ganzi Anton Diffring
Professor Koenig Tony Church

Director: Quentin Lawrence

Flight into Darkness

w Ian Stuart Black and W.H. Altman
Believing that his discovery in the field of
anti-gravity will endanger mankind, Dr
Stephens destroys all his papers and
disappears. *Sans* clothes, the Invisible Man
is asked to bring him to England.
Dr Stephens Geoffrey Keen
Wilson Esmond Knight
Dr Wade John Harvey

Director: Peter Maxwell

The Decoy

w Brenda Blackmore
When one of two identical twins, Terry and
Toni West, a musical act touring Britain,
disappears, the Invisible Man volunteers to
help. Terry disappeared at a Soho hotel — at
which Brady arrives as an unseen guest.
Terry and Toni Trent Betta St John
Captain Rubens Robert Gallico
Andreas Wolf Morris

Director: Quentin Lawrence

The White Rabbit

w Ian Stuart Black
When a young woman doctor in France sees
a white rabbit materialise out of thin air,
and her evidence points to a Fascist plot to
use the discovery of making things invisible
to launch a revolt, Peter Brady is soon on
the scene.
Carla Marla Landi
Roberts Paul Daneman
Colonel Ward Ernest Clark

Director: Quentin Lawrence

Man in Disguise

w Brenda Blackmore and Leslie Arliss
Tricked into handing over his passport to a
beautiful girl in Paris, enabling the girl's
accomplice to impersonate him and smuggle
dope into England, Brady finds himself
involved in an international drugs racket.
Matt Lee Montague
Madeleine Leigh Madison
Det. Insp. Robert Raglan

Director: Quentin Lawrence and Peter
Maxwell

Man in Power

w Ian Stuart Black
A Middle East king is murdered by his
power-crazy army chief. The Invisible Man
finds himself involved in helping the king's
sister and brother regain their father's
throne.
General Shafari Andre Morrell
King Raschid Vivian Matalon
Princess Jonetta Madeleine Scott

Director: Peter Maxwell

The Rocket

w Michael Pertwee
When gambling losses lead one of Brady's
ex-colleagues into selling off secret
information to a foreign power, the
scientist's invisibility proves a very valuable
asset in retrieving the documents.
Dr Brown Glyn Owen
Tony Fayer Russell Waters
Ernest Robert Brown

Director: Quentin Lawrence

Shadow Bomb

w Tony O'Grady (aka Brian Clemens) and
Ian Stuart Black
When his friend risks being blown up by a
new type of bomb detonator, Brady steps
into danger as his replacement. Should even
a shadow fall across the new device, the
bomb will explode — instantly.
Captain Finch Conrad Phillips
Betty Jennifer Jayne
Captain Lloyd Walter Gotell

Director: Peter Maxwell

The Big Plot

w Tony O'Grady
When a plane crash reveals that someone
was smuggling into England a canister of
Uranium 235, used in the manufacture of
atomic weapons, The Invisible Man needs
all his guile to smash a plot to start World
War III.
Rubesch William Squire
Angela Barbara Shelley
Colonel Ward Ernest Clark

Director: Peter Maxwell

Shadow on the Screen

w Ralph Smart and Philip Levene
In the belief that he's helping the wife of a refugee to get her scientist husband from behind the Iron Curtain, Brady finds himself the victim of a clever trap. The woman is a communist spy who intends to learn the Invisible Man's secret.
Rostov Edward Judd
Gretchen Rostov Greta Gynt
Colonel Ward Ernest Clark

Director: Pennington Richards

THE INVISIBLE MAN
Producer: Ralph Smart
Music by: Sydney John Kay
Associate Director: David Tomblin
Production Supervisor: Aida Young
An Official Films Production
for Incorporated Television Programmes Ltd
Made at National Studios, Elstree
An ATV Presentation
26 monochrome 30-minute episodes
18 June 1959 – 22 October 1961
(USA: Syndicated 1958)

IT's DARK OUTSIDE

'A weird, edgy, neurotic, high-powered and sometimes frightening picture of the modern world, with characters as tortured and possessed as so many people are today', is how producer Derek Bennett described this series, which continued the adventures of the vinegary tongued Chief Inspector Rose and the sensitive copper with a conscience, Detective Sergeant Swift, last seen six months earlier in *The Odd Man* series (see entry under that name). But that's where the connection ended. In *The Odd Man*, Rose and Swift were two of five running characters. In this series, they shared the spotlight with newcomers Anthony Brand, a barrister who became involved in the twilight world of crime through his friendship with Rose, and his journalist wife, Alice. (For the second eight stories, DS Swift, Brand and Alice were replaced by DS Hunter, Rose's new colleague; Claire, Hunter's girlfriend; and Fred Blaine, a drunken journalist friend of Claire's.)

Though each episode in the series had its own separate story, the final three episodes of the second eight were transmitted in serialised format and told how CI Rose and DS Hunter found themselves up against Sebastian (a young Oliver Reed) who led his gang of drop-outs into all sorts of illegal activities and trouble with the policemen.

The series spawned a number one best seller, *Where Are You Now?* for singer Jackie Trent.

At the time unmissable, the series was television drama at its very best.. (See also: *Mr Rose*)

REGULAR CAST

DI Rose **William Mervyn**   *DS Swift* **Keith Barron**   *Brand* **John Carson**
Alice **June Tobin**   *DS Hunter* **Anthony Ainley**   *Claire* **Veronica Strong**
Blaine **John Stratton**   *Sebastian* **Oliver Reed**

Season One

8 monochrome 60-minute episodes
The Grim World of the Brothers Tulk
One Man's Right
Speak Ill of the Living
More Ways of Killing a Cat
Wake the Dead
A Room with No View
A Case for Indentification
You Play the Red and the Black Comes Up

Producer: Derek Bennett
Directors: Derek Bennett (Ep. 1)
Gerald Dynevor (Ep. 2–8)

Season Two

8 monochrome 60-minute episodes
The Guilty World of Horsea Pitt
Specimens Walk on Their Hind Legs Too
Arrangement in Black and White
A Dream of Maggie – A Greed of Money
A Slight Case of Matrimony
The Party
The Prevalence of Liars
The Gatling's Jammed and the Colonel's
    Dead

Produced and Directed by: Derek Bennett
A Granada TV Network Production
2 seasons × 8 monochrome 60-minute
episodes
3 January – 21 February 1964
26 February – 23 April 1965

IVANHOE

'Ivanhoe, Ivanhoe, to adventure, bold adventure watch him go.
   There's no power on earth can stop what he's begun; with
            Bart and Gurth, he'll fight 'till he has won.
Ivanhoe, Ivanhoe. He's a friend who will defend the people's foe.
   He'll strike with speed like lightning bold brave and game,
            In justice he is fighting, to win the fairest dame.
Shout a cheer, adventure is here; riding with Ivanhoe – Ivanhoe.'
   The title theme song accurately summed up this series.
Ivanhoe, defender of justice, a knight who fought to win the
heart of a fair lady and defended the people against King John's
tyranny. An unmasked avenger who battled against the forces of
injustice wherever he found it, then rode away Lone-Ranger-
style on his white steed to seek further adventures in a land
oppressed by the evil King John, who sought to usurp King
Richard of England's throne. (He obviously hadn't learned his
lesson during his encounters with Robin Hood 12 months
earlier!)
   A well-mounted production which gave the then relatively
unknown Roger Moore his first taste of stardom. Bearing little or
no resemblance to Sir Walter Scott's hero, the series was greeted

with universal approval and vied with *Robin of Sherwood* in the popularity stakes.

(Author's note: Transmitted in this country in monochrome, hearsay has it that the series was in fact produced in colour. I have been unable to verify the rumour.)

REGULAR CAST

Ivanhoe **Roger Moore** *Gurth* **Robert Brown** *Bart* **John Pike**
Prince John **Andrew Keir**

Freeing the Serfs

w Joel Carpenter
Returning to England from the Crusades, Ivanhoe discovers that his homeland is under the oppression of King John. His first act is to free two ill-fated serfs, Gurth and his son Bart – who insist on becoming his squires in return for their freedom.
Gurth Robert Brown (Intro.)
Bart John Pike (Intro.)
Sir Rufus Alex Scott

Director: Lance Comfort and David MacDonald

Slave Traders

w Saul Levitt
When several young children are kidnapped and sold into slavery, Ivanhoe and his friends decide to set matters right by engineering their release –and teaching their kidnapper, Sir William of Bedford, a lesson.
Sir William Martin Wyldeck
Prince John Andrew Keir
Sir Guilbert Patrick Holt

Director: Lance Comfort

Wedding Cake

w Thomas Law
Sir Maurice, a treacherous nobleman, plans to win possession of a lady's estates by marrying off his idle nephew to her. Ivanhoe and Gurth dent his plans by springing a surprise or two of their own.
Sir Maurice John Bailey
Sir William Martin Wyldeck
Prince John Andrew Keir

Director: Pennington Richards

Black Boar

w Richard Fielder
In order to save Gurth's life, Ivanhoe allows himself to be accused of poaching and is thrown into prison – a risky business: if found guilty of the charge, he will be sentenced to death by hanging.
Sir William Martin Wyldeck
Martha Betty McDowell
Ned Edwin Richfield

Director: Lance Comfort

Whipping Boy

w Larry Forrester
Ivanhoe and his friends discover that young Philip of Wexford is being held in the castle of Sir Waldermar as a whipping boy – boys who are punished for their master's misdeeds – and with Sir Baldwin's help they plan to teach the knight how to temper justice with mercy.
Sir Waldermar Terence Longden
Sir Baldwin Leslie Perrins
Harold Alan Coleshill

Director: Lance Comfort

The Witness

w Geoffrey Orme (From a story by Jane Hilton)
Ivanhoe and Gurth must stop King John from discovering – and silencing – the one man in England who has proof that King Richard is still alive. Openly greedy for his brother's throne, King John has announced his coronation.

Prince John Andrew Keir
Sir William Martin Wyldeck
Sir Guilbert Patrick Holt

Director: Lance Comfort

The German Knight

w Saul Levitt

Ivanhoe engages in mortal combat to ensure a serf's right to gain freedom after remaining at liberty for over one year. But the man, Ralph, a friend of Ivanhoe's, jeopardises his freedom by visiting his mother – why?

Sir Otto Christopher Lee
Ralph Richard Martin
Sir Waldermar Terece Longdon

Director: Pennington Richards

Face to Face

w Shirl Hendryx

While Ivanhoe is away in the North, gathering money for the resistance, a strolling player, strongly resembling Ivanhoe, robs a church. Gurth has 24 hours to find the stranger – or Ivanhoe will be hunted down by King John's troops.
Sir Humphrey Derek Aylward
Black Gordon Danny Green
Burst Paul Hansard

Director: Bernard Knowles

Rinaldo

w Saul Levitt

Ivanhoe and Gurth search the villages for a mysterious Moor – the only man in England who can save the life of Sir Robert of Thornton, a man falsely accused by treason. The Moor carries on ornate dagger which holds a clue to the real traitor's identity.
Sir Robert Alex Archdale
Rinaldo Bruno Barnabe
Prince John Andrew Keir

Director: Bernard Knowles

The Escape

w Saul Levitt

Advancing his plan to seize the throne, Prince John has friends of King Richard –

Ivanhoe among them – thrown into his dungeon. Escape seems impossible – but help arrives from a most unlikely source.
Blackheath Ivan Craig
Rufus Alex Scott
Warren Kenneth Cope

Director: Bernard Knowles

The Swindler

w Bill Strutton

Gurth is tricked into exchanging his money for fake gold ingots and vows to hunt down the peddler and seek retribution – but when he and Ivanhoe catch up with the man, they are in for a surprise.
Peter the Peddler Jon Pertwee
Eric the Blacksmith Brian Wesker
Rand the Goldsmith Ballard Berkely

Director: Pennington Richards

The Princess

w Felix Van Lieu

Hearing that Prince John is holding Princess Deirdre prisoner in Blackheath's castle, Ivanhoe and Gurth join forces with Brian Boy O'Neil, to arrange her escape – but the girl leads Ivanhoe a merry chase before her freedom is assured.
Princess Deirdre Delphi Lawrence
Brian Boy O'Neil Rufus Cruikshank
Blackheath Ivan Craig

Director: Arthur Crabtree

The Fledgling

w Larry Forrester

Determined to help young Roland achieve his ambition to become a knight, Ivanhoe allows the youth to replace him in a tournament – but the evil ally of Prince John, Baron Courcey, has arranged for the boy to be killed.
Roland Anthony Wager
Baron Courcey John Bailey
Firman Ernie Butcher

Director: Arthur Crabtree

The Devil's Dungeon

w Aubrey Feist

While trying to retrieve gold stolen by Baron Courcey's men-at-arms, Ivanhoe and

Gurth are thrown into the dreaded Devil's Dungeon, a place from which no one has ever escaped – Ivanhoe and Gurth intend to be the first to do so.

Baron Courcey John Bailey
Sir Robert John Carson
Roger of Relford Howard Lang

Director: Pennington Richards

The Night Raiders

w Anthony Verney

When three black-hooded riders terrorise a Kentish farmer and his daughter, Ivanhoe sets out to give them aid before the girl Marcia, an old friend, is harmed. As he arrives at the farm, the hooded horsemen attack – and Gurth is wounded.

Marcia Joan Rice
Gwain Jerry Verno
Sir Robert Ray Young

Director: Pennington Richards

The Prisoner in the Tower

w M. L. Davenport

Hearing that Prince John has threatened to throw loyal servants of King Richard into prison, Ivanhoe and Gurth approach their friend Sir Damon, who suspects that his father-in-law, Lord Malvern, is supplying Prince John with loyalists' names.

Sir Damon Michael David
Lord Malvern Leonard Sachs
Lady Eleanor Jennifer Jayne

Director: Bernard Knowles

The Masons

w Felix Van Lieu

When an informer brings news that Prince John is planning to build fortresses along the English coast to prevent King Richard's return, Ivanhoe and Gurth ride North to thwart his evil plans – but Blackheath hears of their plans and arranges a trap.

Lord Blackheath Ivan Craig
Cronyn Michael Ripper
Sir William Emerton Court

Director: Arthur Crabtree

Freelance

w George Baxt and Bill Strutton

Out riding, Ivanhoe and Gurth come across Simon, who is being attacked by Sir Oliver's men. They send the villains packing and Simon tells them a sorry tale of villainy afoot in his village. Ivanhoe decides to investigate the man's claims.

Simon Roy Purcell
Sir Oliver Peter Reynolds
Sir Edgar Robert Cawdron

Director: Pennington Richards

The Circus

w Felix Van Lieu

Travelling the land singing King Richard's praises is a worthwhile occupation – until Prince John gets to hear of it. Ivanhoe and Gurth become involved when a group of minstrels are arrested for treason.

Dick O'Devon John Warner
Sir Mark Robert Cawdron
High Constable Brian Sumner

Director: Pennington Richards

The Ransom

w Sheldon Stark and Larry Forrester

Told that their friend Sir Guilbert has been thrown into jail for refusing to pay Prince John's taxes, Ivanhoe and Gurth fight their way to Sir Edmund's castle to rescue him – but treachery awaits their arrival.

Sir Guilbert Patrick Holt
Sir Edmund Maurice Kaufmann
Sir Walter Charles Stapley

Director: Bernard Knowles

Ragen's Forge

w Sheldon Stark and Larry Forrester

To save the beautiful Donella from a loveless marriage, Ivanhoe dons the disguise of a madcap jester. But Sir William gets to hear of his plans and arranges a far-from-friendly welcoming committee for the knight.

Donella Ann Sears
Sir William Martin Wyldeck
Bruno Cecil Brook

Director: Lance Comfort

Murder at the Inn

w Felix Van Lieu
Hearing that his friend Sir William is being taken to London to face execution, Ivanhoe leads a group of friendly villagers in a rescue bid – but a treacherous innkeeper's intervention leads the party into deadly danger.
Sir William Maurice Kaufmann
Innkeeper Neal Arden
Bess Leigh Madison

Director: Bernard Knowles

Lyman the Pieman

w Geoffrey Orme (From a story by Joseph Cochran)
Ivanhoe and Gurth meet Lyman, a pieman plying his trade before a hanging. Told that Sir Robert is to be hanged for stealing a donkey and cart, the two men set off to right an injustice – but trouble waits along the way.
Lyman Michael Ripper
Sir William Martin Wyldeck
Prince John Andrew Keir

Director: Bernard Knowles

Brothers in Arms

w Larry Forrester
Five monks have disappeared while gathering church taxes and the Lord Abbot seeks Ivanhoe's help. His search for the killers leads to a very strange resting place – a country inn run by far from friendly innkeepers.
Brother Gareth Rupert Davies
Brother Wynford Guy Deghy
Lord Abbot Oliver Johnson

Director: Bernard Knowles

The Weavers

w Geoffrey Orme
Aided by Gurth, Ivanhoe manages to save the weavers of Quincey from an attack by a band of mysterious black-garbed brigands working for Sir William. Content that all is well, Ivanhoe leaves Quincey town, but Sir William refuses to concede defeat.

Sir William Martin Wyldeck
Willaloom Leslie Duggan
Abel Reginald Beckworth

Director: Bernard Knowles

The Gentle Jester

w Larry Forrester
Hearing that one of King Richard's loyalist supporters, Sir Maverick, has lost his beloved jester, Ivanhoe and Gurth attempt to rectify the matter by choosing a replacement. A rival knight sees this as a chance to capture some glory by killing Ivanhoe.
Sir Maverick Paul Whitsun-Jones
Judith Patricia Breddin
Brother Aubrey John Stewart

Director: Arthur Crabtree

The Raven

w Bill Strutton
The appearance of a jet black raven on Sir Murdock's estate foretells danger and his guards desert him, leaving the knight to fight the 'unknown' alone. Ivanhoe and Gurth scoff at the omen of doom – until a mysterious event overtakes their arrival at the castle.
Sir Murdock Ralph Truman
Will the Simple Michael Bate
Sergeant Derek Sydney

Director: Arthur Crabtree

The Widow of Woodcote

w Geoffrey Orme
Suffering from wounds sustained in a tournament, Ivanhoe is taken to the home of Widow Marigold – a healer. While there, he overhears some news of interest to King Richard – but in his present state he is unable to pass on the information.
Widow Woodcote Peggy Marshall
Garn Neal Arden
Robber Paul Eddington

Director: Bernard Knowles

The Kidnapping

w Bill Strutton and Lawrence Hazard
When Prince Arthur is taken prisoner by Prince John's men, Eleanor, the Queen

Mother, seeks Ivanhoe's help. He is to rescue the boy and take him to the safety of her friends in the North – but Ivanhoe must first find out where the Prince is being held.
Queen Eleanor Phyllis Neilson-Terry
Prince John Andrew Keir
Prince Arthur Michael Anderson

Director: Bernard Knowles

Treasures from Cathay

w Larry Forrester and Bill Strutton
Baron Treville's men flee from Westworth Castle after seeing a flaming star shoot across the sky. Ivanhoe must ponder the question: is it an ill omen; or a slice of trickery? With Gurth's help, he provides a simple – but sinister – solution.
Baron Treville Arthur Gomez
Lady Maude Naomi Chance
Cedric the Simple Bill Shine

Director: Bernard Knowles

By Hook or by Crook

w Bill Strutton
Given the task of finding a lost charter signed by King Richard which, if found, would ensure the freedom of a village – to the dismay of an unscrupulous knight – Ivanhoe and Gurth come within inches of death.
Baron Courcey John Bailey
Village Elder John Cazabon
Shepherd Peter Madden

Director: Bernard Knowles

Double-edged Sword

w Tania Lawrence and Bill Strutton
Believing that King Arthur's sword, Excalibur, will help him seize King Richard's throne, Prince John steals the original and orders a replica to be made. Ivanhoe discovers his plan – but must fight for his life in a one-sided battle for justice.
Baron Mauney Peter Dyneley
Prince John Andrew Keir
Sir Randall John Fabian

Director: Arthur Crabtree

Search for Gold

w Saul Levitt
Ivanhoe and Gurth are asked to discover the hiding place of a copy of a treasure map and substantiate a fake which has been given to Sir Arnold. Finding they are on a wild goose chase, the knights decide to teach all involved a lesson.
Sir Arnold Derick De Marney
Sir Romer Noel Johnson
Bordo Tom Bowman

Director: Lance Comfort

The Masked Bandits

w Geoffrey Orme
When serfs are robbed by masked bandits, who take the money they have been saving to buy their freedom, Sir Ivanhoe and Gurth set out to discover under whose orders the bandits are operating.
Earl of Pembroke Wensley Pithey
Jack Ludlow John Schlesinger
Sir Roger Derek Waring

Director: Bernard Knowles

Arms and the Women

w Aubrey Feist
Attacked by Prince John's men, Ivanhoe and Gurth seek refuge in Robert Castle. Discovering all the men are absent, Ivanhoe persuades Lady Ursula and her handmaidens to help them repel their enemy.
Lady Ursula Gwynn Whitty
Sir Robert Emerton Court
Sir Geoffrey Alex Scott

Director: Pennington Richards

The Cattle Killers

w Larry Forrester
When Sir Rufe is accused of killing his neighbour's cattle to send up the price of his own stock, his wife, Lady Violette, seeks Ivanhoe's help to plead her husband's innocence. Ivanhoe has a dilemma – he suspects Sir Rufe is guilty of the charge!
Sir Rufe Alex Scott
Lady Violette Moira Landi
Sir Erwynn Andrew Faulds

Director: Pennington Richards

Three Days to Worcester

w Larry Forrester

When his friend Sir Maurice is unwittingly duped into buying worthless land by a beautiful woman, Ivanhoe suspects Sir Geoffrey of being involved in the deception. His dilemma is made more difficult when Simon, Sir Geoffrey's ward, offers to help Ivanhoe expose the knight!

Simon **Meadows White**
Edith **Adrienne Corri**
Sir Maurice **Geoffrey Toone**

Director: **Pennington Richards**

The Monk

w Alan Reeve Jones

Arriving at Shene, a village under the tyrannical rule of Sir Roger, Ivanhoe and Gurth devise a clever scheme to rid the villagers of the knight for good. Dressed as monks, they set out to teach Sir Roger a lesson in piety.

Sir Roger **Leonard Sachs**
Father Benedict **Ronald Leigh-Hunt**
Sir Roderick **John Carson**

Director: **Arthur Crabtree**

Counterfeit

w Samuel B. Wells

Ivanhoe and Gurth set out to retrieve a fabulous treasure stolen by Prince John's troops. Before their adventure is done, they rescue a young girl from a loveless marriage, and battle with lance and sword to uphold a knight's honour.

Edwina **Susan Beaumont**
Sir Clive **John Bailey**
Prince John **Andrew Keir**

Director: **Bernard Knowles**

IVANHOE
Producer: Bernard Coote
Executive producer: Peter Rogers
Music by: Albert Elms
A Sydney Box Television Presentation
Filmed at Beaconsfield Studios
39 monochrome 30-minute episodes
5 January 1958 – 7 May 1959
(USA: Syndicated 1957)

JANGO

It is seldom that an actor is given the opportunity to star in a programme that he himself devised, but that's exactly what Robert Urquhart achieved with this amiable detective series.

Having created the character to appear in a one-off comedy whodunnit called *Murder Stamp*, Urquhart was delighted when the viewers took to the character and demanded to see him again. Two months later the character was reborn for a series of eight further adventures.

A cross between Jacques Tati's Monsieur Hulot and G. K. Chesterton's Father Brown, Jango – a professor of criminology – was an unpretentious, intelligent, tough (but never violent), smooth-talking, 'thoroughly nice guy' – but bad news for villains. A scruffy man, with glasses, a dirty raincoat, tweed hat and twisted walking stick, he operates a one-man (unofficial) detective business.

Looking at him, you'd have been forgiven for thinking he was as twisted as his walking stick – and people did just that, until he started asking awkward questions and plodded away until he had got to the bottom of some seedy affair. Divorced (but still inordinately fond of his wife Dee, a fashion boutique owner (on whose settee he spent his nights), Jango favoured keeping in with both sides of the law and led a somewhat complicated life.

REGULAR CAST

Jango Smith Robert Urquhart   *Dee Smith* Moira Redmond

A Little of What She Fancied

w Albert Henry Webb
Called in to assist Scotland Yard ('unofficially, of course'), Jango's unorthodox methods of investigation provide an ingenious solution to how a woman was poisoned.
Supt Ballock Derek Francis
Insp. Gold Manning Wilson
Helen Drye Anita Webb

Director: Cyril Coke

Mind the Doors, Please

w Peter Ling and Shelia Ward
Wherever there's crime, you'll find Jango. This time, he's behind the locked doors of a bank vault. But that won't worry the unorthodox sleuth too much – will it?
Graham James Cairncross
Harris Harold Goodwin
Parkinson Richard Vernon

Director: Cyril Coke

The Bumbling Burglar

w Mike Watts
Confused as to why a burglar should break into a house and then leave – empty handed – Jango decides to retrace the robber's steps to see if he can solve a crime that never took place.
Hymie Bernie Winters
Thompson Richard Cooke
Humpernickel Richard Warner

Director: Cyril Coke

The Itching Fingers of Lady Ffoulkes

w Peter Ling and Sheila Ward
When Lady Ffoulkes arrives home with her shopping and discovers lots of things she didn't buy – or pay for – she decides it is time to call on her friend Jango Smith.
Lady Ffoulkes Athene Seyler
Store Manager Dudley Foster
Mr Cartwright Patrick Newell

Director: Cyril Coke

Great Day for Jango

w Don Matthews
What appears to be a very implausible alibi – first the lorry was there, then it wasn't – leads Jango to solve a very unusual case of blackmail with menaces.
Alf Sam Kydd
Mr Murphy Patrick McAlinney
Mrs Murphy Elizabeth Begley

Director: Cyril Coke

Seven Swords of Haversham

w Albert Henry Webb
Lord Haversham's famous sword – the one with the jewelled hilt – has disappeared. Asked to solve the mystery, Jango comes up with a very odd solution – and an even odder way of tracing the treasure.
Lord Haversham William Kendal
Harkness Noel Howlett
Mrs Harkness Diana King

Director: Cyril Coke

Treacle on Three Fingers

w Mike Watts
When a burglar takes a short cut through a cemetery, Jango must follow suit and get to work among the headstones – and that's when things become sticky.

Oscar Grant **Peter Sallis**
Cemetery Attendant **Brian Wilde**
Insp. Clarke **Robert Raglan**

Director: **Cyril Coke**

Champagne for Dee

w Don Matthews
When Jango decides to make some easy
money on the side – and makes it pay –
there must be something he's not telling
Dee. There is, but that's Jango's little secret
– and he's not telling.

Hermond **Alan Gifford**
Gaston **Jean Driant**
Gendarme **Michael Barber**

Director: **Cyril Coke**

JANGO
Created by Robert Urquhart
Produced and directed by: Cyril Coke
An Associated Rediffusion Network Production
8 monochrome 30-minute episodes
25 January – 22 March 1961

JASON KING

The return of the urbane, extravagantly with-it, dandy secret
agent from *Department S* (see entry under that name), this time in
a series of run-of-the-mill adventure stories which did little to
further the mystique of the character – or recapture the thrills
and excitement of the previous series.

This time around King no longer worked for that elite
organisation, had no baffling crimes to solve and filled his over-
indulgent life by investigating straightforward (sometimes
comical) escapades involving blackmail, murder and girls . . .
lots and lots of beautiful girls. He did, however, become
involved in the occasional 'espionage' adventure when coerced
into working for British Intelligence by Sir Brian, a British civil
servant, who threatened to shop him to the Inland Revenue for
unpaid taxes unless King undertook various missions for him.
The remaining stories found King up to his neck in problems –
usually of his own making. That said, the series *was* fun, and
among the better offerings around at that time.

REGULAR CAST
Jason King **Peter Wyngarde**   Nicola Harvester (his publisher) **Ann Sharp**
Sir Brian **Dennis Price**   Ryland (Sir Brian's assistant) **Ronald Lacey**

Wanna Buy a Television Series

w Dennis Spooner
Deciding that it's time for Mark Caine to
reach a wider audience, Jason tries to sell his
character to a TV producer by telling him
the story of his greatest adventure.

Harry Carmel **David Bauer**
Umberto Bellini **Derek Francis**
Michelle André **Anna Palk**

Director: **Jeremy Summers**

A Page Before Dying

w Tony Williamson
Everyone is reading the new Mark Caine novel: the British, the Americans, and the West Germans. It's from the latter that Jason receives an invitation to sell the film rights – and the next thing he knows, he is in a safe, in East Berlin!
Sir Brian Dennis Price
Ryland Ronald Lacey
Lanik Carl Duering

Director: Jeremy Summers

Buried in the Cold, Cold Ground

w Philip Broadley
Jason really should have known better than to give a lift to a pretty young girl. This one turns out to be a newly-released prisoner – and she leads him a not-so-merry chase through the South of France.
Felicity Michele Dotrice
Dacre Frederick Jaeger
Sandes Gary Raymond

Director: Jeremy Summers

A Deadly Line in Digits

w Tony Williamson
It's a case of 'anything you can do, a computer can do better' when Jason gets involved with several large-scale robberies, which must have had inside information. Jason's problem: the info was known only to Scotland Yard's computer!
Sir Brian Dennis Price
Kenworthy Donald Houston
Julia Marsh Joanna Jones

Director: Jeremy Summers

Variations on a Theme

w Philip Broadley
Jason has little time to enjoy the splendours of Vienna, when rival gangs try to use him as bait to snare double agent Alan Keeble – whom Jason believed dead, until he received a message asking him to visit Vienna.
Keeble Ralph Bates
John Julian Glover
Kolkov Eric Pohlmann

Director: Cyril Frankel

As Easy as A B C

w Tony Williamson
The fact that every Mark Caine novel is the subject of thorough research by Jason hasn't escaped Charles and Edward, two petty crooks. They pull off a job by copying the plot of Jason's latest book – and leave the author to carry the can.
Charles Nigel Green
Edward Michael Bates
Mireille Ayesha Brough

Director: Jeremy Summers

To Russia – with Panache

w Tony Williamson
An honour indeed. Believing that Jason is the only man alive capable of solving a mystery which is baffling them, the Russians engage his services – by abducting him and transporting him to Moscow in a wooden crate!
Alexandra Lanova Pamela Salem
Colonel Kolkov John Malcolm
Porokov Jeffrey Wickham

Director: Paul Dickson

A Red, Red Rose Forever

w Donald James
When a fellow passenger on a flight to Switzerland collapses en route, with a bunch of roses in his hand, Jason helps him into an ambulance and is left holding the roses. Before he knows it, the flowers are swopped for a rifle with the comment that instructions will follow . . .
Ryland Ronald Lacey
Simone Barbara Murray
Dr Claudel Alan McNaughton

Director: Cyril Frankel

All That Glisters (Part 1)

w Philip Broadley
Jason becomes involved in a complicated game of bluff and counter-bluff when he is asked to introduce adventurer John Mallen to Phillipe de Brion – a man who wishes to buy a golden antique for a cool half a million dollars . . .

All That Glisters (Part 2)

Jason finds himself a pawn in a deadly game when the search for the stolen antique switches from Paris to Rome and the author finds that chasing gold can lead to certain death.
Frank Lucas Lee Patterson
John Mallen Clinton Greyn
Phillipe de Brion Anton Rodgers

Director: Cyril Frankel

Flamingoes Only Fly on Tuesdays

w Tony Williamson
Opposition parties may be essential in a democracy, but as Jason finds out during a trip to the Caribbean, in a state of revolution they only get in the way – particularly if you're mistaken for a gun-runner.
Pelli Hugh McDermott
Lyra Hildegard Neil
Drakin David Healey

Director: Jeremy Summers

Toki

w Philip Broadley
Seeking inspiration to finish his latest novel and meet his publisher's deadline, Jason visits a Paris café and meets Toki, a girl for whom a king would abdicate. But Toki already has a leader – Le Grand, a ruthless gangster – and that's when Jason's troubles begin.
Le Grand Kieron Moore
Toki Felicity Kendall
Oliver David Buck

Director: Jeremy Summers

The Constance Missal

w Harry H. Junkin
Jason has girl trouble again. This time two beautiful females hypnotise him and steal the only copy of a film manuscript he's written. But the girls have more than film scripts on their mind – as their unwilling accomplice Jason soon discovers.

Claudia Geraldine Moffat
Elaine Janet Key
Lord Barnes Clive Revill

Director: Jeremy Summers

Uneasy Lies the Head

w Donald James
Jason is concerned and confused when a friend shows him newspaper cuttings with pictures of him in Istanbul – but he is in Paris! Who is impersonating him, and why? Jason determines to find out – and steps straight into danger.
Trim Lance Percival
Shelly Blackman Juliet Harmer
Ryland Ronald Lacey

Director: Cyril Frankel

Nadine

w Philip Broadley
Always seeking inspiration for his Mark Caine novels, Jason meets Nadine, a girl who seems to provide all the inspiration he needs. But the girl is playing her own deadly game – with Jason as the joker in the pack.
Nadine Ingrid Pitt
Ringo Alfred Marks
Achille Patrick Mower

Director: Cyril Frankel

A Kiss for a Beautiful Killer

w Gerald Kelsey
Does Jason really hold the key to the secret that both sides of a South American revolution are seeking so desperately? He thinks not. They think otherwise – and are prepared to go to any lengths to extract his information
Delphi Kate O'Mara
Cordobier Clifford Evans
Rodriguez Alex Scott

Director: Cyril Frankel

If It's Got to Go – It's Got to Go

w Tony Williamson
Why has Jason been tricked into visiting a German health farm? Whatever the reason,

his stay at the establishment proves far from healthy – someone keeps trying to help him lose weight, with a diet of bullets.

Dr Litz John Le Mesurier
Myra Jennifer Hilary
Dr Wilstein Felix Aylmer

Director: Cyril Frankel

A Thin Band of Air

w Harry H. Junkin

Accompanied by a beautiful young photographer, Lee Bailey, who is working on the publicity for the author's new book, Jason visits Paris – where a dead man's Russian accent and a ten-year old kidnapping endanger both their lives.

Lee Bailey Francisca Tu
Rene Chenard T. P. McKenna
Jean Cazette Cyril Shaps

Director: Cyril Frankel

It's Too Bad about Auntie

w Harry H. Junkin

A little old lady who accuses a young girl of murder. An extraordinary surplus of vacuum cleaners. Two links in an unusual puzzle which Jason finally clears up – but only after some daring undercover work.

Mary Trevor Sarah Lawson
Det. Sgt Roddick Dinsdale Landen
Geoffrey Winters Jack Watling

Director: Jeremy Summers

The Stones of Venice

w Donald James

Arriving in Venice for a holiday, Jason is surprised to find he's been awarded a special prize for his latest Mark Caine novel *The Stones of Venice* – a book he hasn't written! Further surprises arrive in the shape of two thugs carrying guns.

Ingrid/Teresa Anna Gael
Capitano Garrozo Roger Delgado
Colonel Gardner William Squire

Director: Jeremy Summers

A Royal Flush

w Philip Broadley

Nothing appeals to Jason's vanity more than a beautiful girl seeking his help. But he soon finds trouble when he arrives at a suite she booked for him at a Capri hotel – and the girl fails to keep the rendezvous.

Karen Elaine Taylor
Princess Vania Penelope Horner
Boris Terence Lodge

Director: Roy Ward Baker

Every Picture Tells a Story

w Robert Banks Stewart

Having your character presented to a wider audience is all very well – providing you agree to the promotion. But an unauthorised strip cartoon based on his Mark Caine character has sinister implications for Jason when it is translated into Chinese.

Tsung Clifford Evans
Finnigan Neil McCallum
Lucy Cameron Kara Wilson

Director: Cyril Frankel

Chapter One: the Company I Keep

w Donald James

Has Jason become clairvoyant? When all the ingredients of his latest Mark Caine novel actually start to happen, the author believes he has. But sinister forces are behind the puzzling affair.

Contessa Toby Robins
Alfred Thistle Ronald Radd
Giorgio Paul Whitsun-Jones

Director: Cyril Frankel

Zenia

w Philip Broadley

When the young daughter of a foreign president is kidnapped by revolutionaries, Jason is asked to find her. Finding her is one thing, obtaining her freedom another. But Jason has a plan in mind – one based on a Mark Caine adventure.

Leila Patricia English
President Michael Goodliffe
Zenia Zienia Meron

Director: Roy Ward Baker

An Author in Search of Two Characters

w Dennis Spooner

A stranger runs towards Jason, a shot rings out and the man dies. A Frankenstein-like monster beats the author unconscious. Dreams? Hardly, these are just two of the events in Jason's new film script – and they are taking place around him!

Chf Insp. Hughes Ivor Dean
Ackroyd Dudley Foster
Claire Liz Frazer

Director: Cyril Frankel

That Isn't Me, It's Somebody Else

w Dennis Spooner

A bogus Jason King sets a problem for the adventure-loving author. The double has set out to kill a gangland boss. But Jason seems unconcerned – until, to escape from marriage, he takes refuge in the Italian villa of the big-time gangster.

Bonisalvi George Murcell
Bennett Patrick Troughton
Broggi Simon Oates

Director: Roy Ward Baker

JASON KING
Created by: Dennis Spooner and Monty Berman
Producer: Monty Berman
Executive story consultant: Dennis Spooner
Music by: Laurie Johnson
Creative consultant: Cyril Frankel
A Scroton Production for ITC
Filmed on location and at EMI/MGM Studios
26 colour 60-minute episodes
15 September 1971 – 5 May 1972

JEMIMA SHAW INVESTIGATES

A series centred around the adventures of Jemima Shaw, a TV reporter turned private investigator.

The stories remained faithful to the novels by Antonia Fraser and depicted how Jemima, a woman with a love of the high life, became entangled in a series of murders, blackmails and high drama in the high society set.

Par-for-the-course material given added interest by the stunningly beautiful Patricia Hodge.

REGULAR CAST
Jemima Shaw Patricia Hodge

A Splash of Red – Part 1
A Splash of Red – Part 2
The Crime of the Dancing Duchess
A Chamber of Horrors
Dr Ziegler's Casebook
A Greek Bearing Gifts
A Model Murder
Death à la Carte
A Promising Death
High Style
The Damask Collection
A Little Bit of Wildlife

JEMIMA SHAW INVESTIGATES
Created by: Antonia Fraser
Producer: Tim Aspinall
Directors: Robert Tronson, Alan Grint,
Neville Green, Brian Farnham, Christopher
Hodson
Writers: Dave Humphries, Tim Aspinall,
Philip Mackie, Simon Brett, Gilly Fraser
A Thames Television Network Production
12 colour 60-minute episodes
8 June – 24 August 1983

JOE 90

The tenth of Gerry Anderson's unique television puppet creations – but this time with less emphasis on machinery and space-type action, and a nine-year-old star character.

The first episode (untitled on screen, but widely known as *Most Special Agent*) told how Professor Ian McClaine gave his adopted son, Joe, amazing powers provided by a pair of special glasses which fused the boy's brain impulse to his own. Called the BIG RAT (Brain Impulse Galvanascope, Record and Transfer), Joe could then assume the skills and personality of whoever's brain pattern was entered into the machine. As a result he became a brilliant scientist who worked for and with Commander Shane Weston of the World Intelligence Network (WIN) and his deputy Sam Loover, and undertook dangerous missions on their behalf.

With the reduction of special effects and gadgetry (the only major item of hardware was Professor McClaine's Jet Car), and the first ever location work used for an Anderson puppet series (Episode 13, *The Unorthodox Shepherd*), the series should have been every bit as successful as Anderson's earlier work, but failed to capture the viewers' attention.

CHARACTER VOICES

Joe 90 **Len Jones**   *Prof. McClaine* **Rupert Davies**
Shane Weston **David Healey**   *Sam Loover* **Keith Alexander**

Most Special Agent

w **Gerry and Sylvia Anderson**
Persuaded that by using his new invention BIG RAT on his nine-year-old adopted son, Joe, he could become an invaluable agent for WIN, Commander Weston tells Joe a story of what might happen if he did become an agent: he could steal a new Russian prototype plane. Joe does just that, and becomes WIN's youngest 'Most Special Agent'.

Director: **Desmond Saunders**

Most Special Astronaut

w Tony Barwick
With the aid of a top astronaut's brain pattern, Joe saves an Earth space station from destruction.

Director: Peter Anderson

Project 90

w Tony Barwick
The only way Joe can save his kidnapped father is to acquire the brain patterns of a balloonist.

Director: Peter Anderson

Hi-jacked

w Tony Barwick
Joe must devise a plan to stop the world's most dangerous gun-runner and smuggler from achieving his aims.

Director: Alan Perry

Colonel McClaine

w Tony Barwick
Using the brain patterns of an explosives expert and a top Army driver, Joe transports a dangerous cargo across Africa.

Director: Leo Eaton

The Fortress

w Shane Rimmer
Joe is assigned to rescue a fellow WIN agent from a San Marino jail, before the man can tell his WIN secrets.

Director: Leo Eaton

King for a Day

w Shane Rimmer
To prevent a Middle Eastern heir to the throne being kidnapped, Joe impersonates him – and gets kidnapped himself.

Director: Leo Eaton

International Concerto

w Tony Barwick
A world famous pianist needs a replacement for a broadcast recital. With the aid of BIG CAT, Joe plays a lively tune.

Director: Alan Perry

Splashdown

w Shane Rimmer
When two electronics experts are killed, Joe assumes the persona of a crack test pilot to investigate their deaths.

Director: Leo Eaton

Big Fish

w Tony Barwick
Joe must find a way to gain access and retrieve a secret submarine stranded at the bottom of the sea – in enemy waters.

Director: Alan Perry

Relative Danger

w Shane Rimmer
Using the brain patterns of a leading underground explorer, Joe must save three men trapped deep in a cavern.

Director: Peter Anderson

Operation McClaine

w Gerry Anderson and David Lane
When a famous writer needs brain surgery, and the leading specialist is injured in a plane crash, Joe performs the operation – but gives someone else the credit.

Director: Ken Turner

The Unorthodox Shepherd

w Tony Barwick
Joe, his father and Sam Loover investigate a supposedly haunted church that is being used as a cover for dubious activities.

Director: Ken Turner

Business Holiday

w Tony Barwick

Joe is given the brain patterns of a colonel to complete a top secret Army mission of major importance.

Director: Alan Perry

Arctic Adventure

w Tony Barwick

A nuclear bomb is lost somewhere in the Arctic wasteland. Joe is sent to recover it and secure its time mechanism.

Director: Alan Perry

Double Agent

w Tony Barwick

By accident, Joe gains the brain pattern of a double agent. WIN have to find him before he can cause mischief.

Director: Ken Turner

Three's a Crowd

w Tony Barwick

Joe has to step in when his father's new girlfriend appears to have more on her mind than a romantic interlude.

Director: Peter Anderson

The Professional

w Donald James

Joe's liable to end up in trouble – unless he can avoid it. Someone is playing a deadly game of cat and mouse – a very dangerous game.

Director: Leo Eaton

The Race

w Tony Barwick

Joe is given the brain pattern of a Monte Carlo rally driver after WIN receives a challenge they dare not refuse.

Director: Alan Perry

Talkdown

w Tony Barwick

Joe becomes a test pilot to discover why a hypersonic fighter plane crashed in mysterious circumstances.

Director: Alan Perry

Breakout

w Shane Rimmer

Two escaped convicts capture a cannon and destroy the track carrying a prime minister's train. Using the brain pattern of a bobsleigh champion, Joe saves the day.

Director: Leo Eaton

Child of the Sun God

w John Lucarotti

Having stumbled across a lost Indian tribe, Joe has to prove that he is their lost sun god – or lose his life.

Director: Peter Anderson

See You Down There

w Gerry and Sylvia Anderson

Being a WIN agent can have its drawbacks, as Joe and his father find out when given a somewhat unusual mission.

Director: Leo Eaton

Lone Handed 90

w Des Saunders

Joe dreams of becoming a western sheriff, and finds himself involved in shoot-outs and a life on the open range.

Director: Ken Turner

Attack of the Tiger

w Gerry and Sylvia Anderson

Joe finds himself one step away from danger – and two steps behind his enemy – when asked to undertake a mission for WIN.

Director: Peter Anderson

Viva Cordova

w Tony Barwick

When a Mexican president's life is threatened, Joe enters the scene – and finds himself in the firing line.

Director: Peter Anderson

Mission X-14

w Gerry and Sylvia Anderson/Pat Dunlop

The formula for a new antibody has to be learned. Joe adopts the brain pattern of a top scientist to gain its secrets for WIN.

Director: Ken Turner

Test Flight

w Donald James

Joe stops a sabotage threat with the aid of a computer specialist and an explosives expert's brain patterns.

Director: Peter Anderson

Trial at Sea

w Donald James

Joe finds himself held hostage aboard a transatlantic super liner – and only he can prevent a major disaster.

Director: Leo Eaton

The Birthday

w Tony Barwick/Gerry and Sylvia Anderson

As a special birthday treat for Joe, Professor McClaine and his friends recall some of his son's greatest adventures.

Director: Leo Eaton

JOE 90
Producer: David Lane
Executive producer: Roy Hill
Music by: Barry Gray
Script editor: Tony Barwick
AN ITC/Century 21 Production
Presented by ATV
30 colour 30-minute episodes
29 September 1968 – 20 April 1969

JOHN SILVER'S RETURN TO TREASURE ISLAND

Specially written for television by John Goldsmith, this eight-part sequel to Robert Louis Stevenson's *Treasure Island* (set ten years after the events in the original story) depicted how Jim Hawkins and Long John Silver were reunited and shared one final adventure.

Containing all the elements which made the original story a classic, it told how Jim Hawkins, having graduated from Oxford University, returned to The Admiral Benbow for a brief stay before taking up an appointment as agent to Squire Trelawney's plantation – and resumed his friendship with the one-legged rascal, 'Captain' John Silver, who had broken into Jim's home to retrieve a treasure map he'd secreted there before going on the run from the law.

Thereafter the story unfolded in sprightly form and told how Silver –mellowed slightly, but still a scoundrel – set about cajoling Hawkins to help him return to Treasure Island. ('For old times' sake, Jim – for old times.') Along the way they encountered intrigue and danger, faced pirates and bounty-hunters after Silver's blood and so on – until the wooden-legged rogue achieved his aim and the story ended in a not-too-surprising manner.

Swashbuckling stuff, Brian Blessed walked away with both the treasure and the acting plaudits.

REGULAR CAST

Long John Silver Brian Blessed   *Jim Hawkins* Christopher Guard
Ben Gunn Ken Colley   *Squire Trelawney* Bruce Purchase   *Dr Livesey* Peter Copley
Captain Smollet Richard Beale   *Van Der Brecken* Reiner Schone
Isabella Deborah Poplett   *Rev Morgan* Artro Morris

The Map

w John Goldsmith   *(120-minute introductory story)*
Having graduated from Oxford University, Jim Hawkins returns home to spend some time with his mother, before setting out to take up his appointment as Squire Trelawney's plantation agent. His plans are changed by the intervention of his old 'friend', Long John Silver.
Mrs Hawkins Charlotte Mitchell
Sir Soloman Pridham Willoughby Goddard
Captain Parker John Hallam

Director: Piers Haggard
Designer: Doug James/Phil Williams

Island of the Damned

w John Goldsmith
Adrift at sea in a small boat, Jim and his companions beach at Santa Anna, where Van Der Brecken says he has friends who will help them – but shocks await the crew and Jim Hawkins in particular.
Mrs Huysmans Jeanne Watts
Don Pedro Mark Lewis
Major Moreda Reggie Carter

Director: Piers Haggard
Designer: Colin Pocock

Jamaica

w John Goldsmith
Having arrived at Jamaica, Silver manages to persuade Jim Hawkins to set him ashore at a secluded cove before putting to Kingston. Bidding their companion

goodbye, Jim and Ben Gunn sail to Squire Trelawney's plantation – and trouble.
Abed Peter Lloyd
Hallows Donald Pickering
Devereaux Christopher Goodwin

Director: Piers Haggard
Designer: Colin Pocock/Doug James

Manhunt

w John Goldsmith
Overhearing a conversation between Jim Hawkins and Silver, Sharpe informs Hallows of their next move. When Jim arrives to confront Caleb Lewis, he walks into a well-sprung trap – and is arrested for murder.
Caleb Lewis Robert Putt
Hallows Donald Pickering
Devereaux Christopher Goodwin

Director: Piers Haggard
Designer: Colin Pocock/Doug James

The Crow's Nest

w John Goldsmith
Van Der Brecken is persuaded to drop Long John Silver at Machado Island – a pirate stronghold, from which Silver hopes to mount an expedition to Treasure Island. But the wily old sea dog has failed to take into account the pirate's greed.
Keelhaul Nick Brimble
Boakes Morgan Shepherd
Gaynes Dicken Ashworth

Director: Piers Haggard
Designer: Colin Pocock/Doug James

Fugitives

w John Goldsmith

Though their arrival in Mexico is greeted with an outbreak of gold fever, Jim, Conchita and their friends manage to reach their destination – from which Jim proposes to leave for England to clear his name. But circumstances bring the wrath of Garcia down on them.

Conchita Aixa Moreno
Garcia John Bennett
Lopez Aldo San Brell

Director: Piers Haggard
Designer: Colin Pocock/Doug James

In Chains

w John Goldsmith

Imprisoned, all appears lost for Jim and his companions. But help is at hand – from an unexpected quarter. They escape and make their way inland – to a far greater danger than they left behind.

Don Felipe Arthur Bostrum
Dr Leach Malcolm Terris
Boakes Morgan Shepherd

Director: Piers Haggard
Designer: Colin Pocock/Doug James

Treasure

w John Goldsmith

After being tried by a kangaroo court and sentenced to death, Jim Hawkins's life hangs in the balance. But the pirates have reckoned without the wily old Long John Silver who, with the aid of Dr Leach, releases his friend – and pockets the booty.

Garcia John Bennett
Dr Leach Malcolm Terris
Colonel Fenton Roy Boyd

Director: Piers Haggard
Designer: Colin Pocock/Doug James

JOHN SILVER'S RETURN TO TREASURE ISLAND
Series devised by: Robert S. Baker
Producer: Alan Clayton
Executive producer: Patrick Dromgoole
Music by: Terry Oldfield and Tom McGuinness
Produced by HTV in association with Primetime Television
2 episodes of 120-minute duration
6 of 60-minutes duration
8 episodes
5 July – 23 August 1986

JUDGE DEE

Described by the critics as 'a curiosity shop of murder mysteries' this medieval-flavoured oddity in the television 'detective' stakes depicted the investigations of Judge Dee, an actual character who lived in China from A.D. 630 to 700 and served as a Minister for State in the Tang Empire.

If the thought of a Chinese detective conjures up comparisons with Charlie Chan, forget it. Dee was an unassailable, crime-busting magistrate who shrewdly sifted the evidence and sought a rational explanation for the 'unexplainable'.

The series failed to attract viewers, and only six stories were produced – five of which were actually transmitted.

REGULAR CAST

Judge Dee Michael Goodliffe   *Tao Gan* Garfield Morgan
Hoong Norman Scace   *Ma Joong* Arne Gordon   *Rose Tree* Pamela Roland
Sun Dew Penny Casdagli   *Innocence* Susan Lefton

Traitors in High Places

w John Wiles

When Judge Dee and his entourage arrive in Canton, supposedly to conduct a trade enquiry, he discovers corruption in the local government. With the help of a blind girl he exposes the corrupt element and moves on.
Lan Lee Jill Kerman
Censor Lew Tan David Blake Kelly
Governor Weng Basil Dignam

Director: Howard Baker
Designer: Peter Phillips

The Haunted Pavilion

w John Wiles

Attending a party to celebrate the remarriage of Ko, a wealthy businessman whose first wife died, Judge Dee presents Ko with a bizarre letter which he claims is from his dead wife. Ko reads it, and throws himself from a balcony to his death – a mystery which tests Dee's investigative talents to the limit.
Ko Chin Yuan David Langton
Leng Chien Harold Innocent
Madame Ko Rosemary Leach

Director: Howard Baker
Designer: Peter Phillips

A Festival of Death

w John Wiles

Although there are sinister superstitions surrounding the Festival of the River Goddess, the last thing Judge Dee expects to find there is murder. But he does so when Tong, a wrestler, dies in mysterious circumstances during a contest.
Tong Michael Goldie
Sia Alan Chuntz
Kou Yuan Donald Hewlett

Director: Richard Doubleday
Designer: Colin Rees

The Day of the Scavengers

w John Wiles

When the Imperial City is gripped by plague, the Scavengers – corpse-clearers who rule by terror – the indiscretions of an eminent general's wife, and a prophesy of murder all add up to another exciting challenge for Judge Dee.
Yuan Michael Robbins
Madame Yee Ursula Howells
Hoo Pen John Woodnutt

Director: Howard Baker
Designer: Peter Phillips

A Place of Great Evil

w John Wiles

Forced to shelter at an ancient monastery until a storm breaks, Judge Dee discovers that it is not the serene and holy place it appears. Three people have already died in mysterious circumstance, as did the Abbot, one year earlier. Under cover of darkness, Dee himself is attacked – and he vows not to leave until the mystery is solved.
(Note: This episode replaced the following story.
No cast or further production credits available.)

The Curse of the Lacquer Screen

w John Wiles

The panels of an elaborately inlaid screen tell a story – and Teng Kan bought it because the story related closely to his own life. But the screen has taken on prophetic power: overnight its strip-cartoon frames have changed from marital bliss to scenes of murder. When the change is followed by the death of his beloved Silver Lotus, Teng seeks the help of his old friend Judge Dee to find a solution to the mystery that threatens him with madness.

Teng Kan **John Moffatt**
Silver Lotus **Jan Gamble**
Kun Shan **Kenneth Colley**

Director: **Richard Doubleday**
Designer: **Peter Phillips**
(Note: This episode was not transmitted.)

JUDGE DEE
Stories adapted from the novels by
Rober Van Gulik
Producer: Howard Baker
Music by: Derek Hilton
A Granada Television Network Production
5 colour 60-minute episodes
8 April – 13 May 1969

JUSTICE

Compulsive viewing for courtroom addicts at the time, this series showed the law from the viewpoint of junior barrister, Harriet Peterson, a lawyer earning her living moving from lawcourt to lawcourt, doing a job she believed in – pursuing the law in the cause of justice.

The first 13 stories were set in the North of England, but as the series grew in status – it proved enormously popular – the producers felt the need to move Harriet and her practice to London. Persuaded to sell her cottage and move to the 'smoke' by her head of chambers, Sir John Gallagher, she soon found herself working on a succession of exciting cases.

Notable for its attention to detail (all scripts were vetted by a real life barrister) the programme showed the law as it really was. Pompous at times. Hilarious at others – but always rigid and infallible (although Harriet was seen to lose the odd case or two).

With scripts from writers James Mitchell (*Callan*) and Edward Ward (*The Main Chance*), among others, the show's popularity was assured. It ran for three seasons – of which the final 13 stories (co-starring Anthony Valentine – taking a break from his Toby Meres *Callan* role) were the best.

REGULAR CAST
Harriet Peterson **Margaret Lockwood**
Sir John Gallagher **Philip Stone** (Seasons 1 and 2)
Dr Ian Moody **John Stone** (Seasons 2 and 3)
William (Clerk of Chambers) **John Bryans** (Seasons 2 and 3)
James Eliot **Anthony Valentine** (Season 3)

JUSTICE
Producer: James Ormerod (Seasons 1 and 2)
Jacky Stoller (Season 3)
Executive producer: Peter Willes
Directors: Tony Wharmby, John Frankau, Alan Bromly, Christopher Hodson, Brian Farmham

A Yorkshire Television Network Production
39 colour 60-minute episodes
8 October 1971 – 14 January 1972
9 February – 4 May 1973
17 May – 16 August 1974

KILLER

(A Chief Inspector Jim Taggart adventure.)

See: *Taggart*

KING AND CASTLE

Mooted as a successor to *Minder*, this drama series about an ex-policeman, Ronald King, and his young partner, David Castle, who set up the Manor Debt Collection Agency, failed to live up to expectations. Panned by the critics, it ran for only six episodes.

REGULAR CAST

Ronald King **Derek Martin**   *David Castle* **Nigel Planer**
Mr Hodinett **Andrew Cruikshank**   *Deirdre Aitken* **Laura Davenport**

Exodus

w Ian Kennedy Martin

Ex-detective Ronald King sets up the Manor Debt Collection Agency and cons young David Castle into becoming his partner. Castle is not too sure about his new post – he's busy moving into a new flat.
Ernest Midgeley **Kenneth Cope**
Katrina Midgeley **Linda Marlowe**
Det. Chf Supt Hinkley **Tony Doyle**

Director: **Peter Cregeen**
Designer: **Philip Blowers**

Villains

w Ian Kennedy Martin

Why have King and Castle been asked to investigate Charlie Casson's death in a motor-accident? It *was* an accident – wasn't it? Then why are the police so interested – and who is behind the attempts to scare them off?
George Casson **Peter Rutherford**
Det. Chf Insp. Caley **Norman Bowler**
Det. Insp. Brownjohn **Richard Hampton**

Director: **Henry Herbert**
Designer: **Philip Blowers**

Partners

w Ian Kennedy Martin

Hired by wealthy Devas to find Fitch-Courtney, a man whose wine business has gone bust and who owes many thousands to Devas, Ronald King sees this as a way to 'make a killing' and increase their wealth – that's when he discovers that neither man is quite what he seems.
Devas **David Suchet**
Fitch-Courtney **Jeremy Nicholas**
Marshall **Malcolm Rogers**

Director: **Alan Bell**
Designer: **Philip Blowers**

Friends

w Ian Kennedy Martin

When some young boys steal a stereo and fit the crime on Roger Gray, a friend of ex-matinee idol Dale Danbury, King and Castle, investigating Danbury for a client, become involved with the matinee star's search for justice.

Dale Danbury Terence Morgan
Roger Gary Jerome Willis
Mrs Chalmers Liz Smith

Director: Peter Cregeen
Designer: Philip Blowers

Romance

w Ian Kennedy Martin
The Hon. Lisa Berkeley owes over £10,000
in unpaid debts. King and Castle are given
the job of investigating her background.
But the woman is far from being a lady – as
David Castle discovers when he is given a
free hand by his partner.
Lisa Berkeley Isla Blair
Roger Hilton Gary Watson
Harold Medley Paul Rogers

Director: Henry Herbert
Designer: Philip Blowers

Rivals

w Ian Kennedy Martin
When the Hercules Debt Recovery service,
a rival debt-collecting agency, moves into
Ronnie King's area and sets up in direct
opposition, things take on a decidedly
unwelcome atmosphere. One firm must go –
but which?
Herbert Parish Peter Cellier
Milbray Peter Bruce
Det. Chf Insp. Caley Norman Bowler

Director: Alan Bell
Designer: Philip Blowers

KING AND CASTLE
Created by: Ian Kennedy Martin
Producer: Chris Burt
Executive producer: Lloyd Shirley
Music by: Sound Lab
(Title theme sung by: Nigel Planer)
A Thames Television Network Production
6 colour 60-minute episodes
3 September – 8 October 1986

KINVIG

Hated by some, loved by others (including yours truly), this
piece of science-fiction-cum-sit-com hokum – written by Nigel
Kneale of *Quatermass* fame – totally bemused the critics, most of
whom didn't understand it (others didn't really care). It was,
nevertheless, a splendid departure from the norm.

In a nutshell, the series told how Des Kinvig, a nondescript
little man who ran a run-down electrical repair shop in Bingleton
(few of the items he repaired ever left the shop in working order)
found an escape from his humdrum life by 'searching the skies'
for UFOs. Together with his equally nondescript mate – and
fellow sky watcher – Jim Piper, he pursued his outdoor activity
to escape from his nagging wife, Netta, and their 'baby' – a huge
dog named Cuddley.

Life changed for Kinvig when he met a woman from outer
space – and what a woman she was. As portrayed by sexy
Prunella Gee (decked out in some of the skimpiest female attire
ever to grace the female form . . . so *that's* why I enjoyed it so
much!), 'Miss Griffin' – as the extra-terrestrial called herself –
was every hot-blooded male's fantasy dream come true.

With trips to Mercury in Miss Griffin's silver spaceship – not to mention Kinvig's habit of physically transporting himself to the planet by the use of Doctor Murgatroyd's Patent Tonic (!) – and humanoids, set against a sit-com background, it's little wonder that the critics (and public) found the entire proceedings not to their taste.

A wonderfully funny, exhilarating slice of science-fiction hokum.

REGULAR CAST

Des Kinvig **Tony Haygarth**   Netta Kinvig **Patsy Rowlands**
Jim Piper **Colin Jeavons**   Miss Griffin **Prunella Gee**
Mr Horseley **Patrick Newell**   Buddo **Simon Williams**
Bat **Alan Boredham**   Loon **Stephen Bent**

Contact

w Nigel Kneale

Des Kinvig and his friend Jim Piper share a mutual obsession – watching the skies for UFOs. One day a new customer enters his shop, a stunning but oddly-dressed woman. That night, while walking his dog, Des discovers a spaceship – and his life will never be the same again.

Director: **Brian Simmons**
Designer: **Mike Oxley**

Creature of Xux

w Nigel Kneale

By using Doctor Murgatroyd's Patent Tonic and a special coin given to him by Miss Griffin, Kinvig transports himself to Mercury, where Miss Griffin and Bobby recruit him in their war against the Xux – insect-like creatures, planning to invade earth.

Director: **Les Chatfield**
Designer: **Mike Oxley**

Double, Double

w Nigel Kneale

Hearing from his wife that she has seen his 'double' walking a 'dog thing' through the town, Des and Jim, convinced it is a Xux humanoid, set out to track it down – with surprising results.

Director: **Les Chatfield**
Designer: **Mike Oxley**

The Big Benders

w Nigel Kneale

When Miss Griffin warns Des and Jim that the Xux plan to give all Earthlings the power to bend cutlery – a degrading prospect that will allow them to invade Earth unopposed – Kinvig and Piper hatch a plot to expose their villainy.

Director: **Les Chatfield**
Designer: **Mike Oxley**

Where Are You, Miss Griffin?

w Nigel Kneale

Miss Griffin takes a job at the BBC as secretary to Horseley, whom she suspects of being a Xux humanoid. Des and Jim meanwhile have troubles of their own. Having been arrested, they escape and storm the BBC to rescue Miss Griffin from Horseley's clutches.

Director: **Les Chatfield**
Designer: **Mike Oxley**

The Humanoid Factory

w Nigel Kneale

Kinvig dreams that hundreds of civil servants, led by Horseley, are emerging from a blazing BBC building. Fearing that the invasion has begun, together with Jim he breaks into a disused warehouse – and discovers hundreds of humanoids. They smash the lot.

Director: **Les Chatfield**
Designer: **Mike Oxley**

The Mystery of Netta

w Nigel Kneale

Concerned that his wife Netta is jealous of Miss Griffin (his wife has started to take an interest in 'space people', and developed a friendship with Jessop, a Town Hall official), Des turns down Miss Griffin's offer to go with her to Mercury. To complicate matters further, Jessop sells encyclopaedias – one of which contains a picture of two astronauts. Des and Miss Griffin! Confused? So was Des, who thought the entire adventure had been a dream – but was it?

Director: Les Chatfield
Designer: Mike Oxley

KINVIG
Created by Nigel Kneale
Producer: Les Chatfield
Music by: Nigel Hess
A London Weekend Television Production
7 colour 30-minute episodes
4 September – 16 October 1981

KNIFE EDGE

(A Chief Inspector Jim Taggart adventure.)
See: *Taggart*

KNIGHT ERRANT

'Knight Errant '59. Quests undertaken, dragons defeated, damsels rescued. Anything, anywhere, for anyone, so long as it helps. Fees according to means.' Within days of inserting that advertisement in the personal column of the national newspaper, Adam Knight, the hero of this late-fifties adventure series, become involved in the first of his many adventures. Having tried a variety of jobs and decided that his interest lay in other people's problems, Adam set up the Knight Errant agency, donned a business suit ('a twentieth-century Sir Lancelot – a Knight Errant') and set out to help anybody, in any situation.

Helping him to fulfil his crusade were Liz Parish, former *Daily Clarion* newspaper columnist, and Peter Parker, a young author who expressed a liking for Adam's aims and signed on as his leg man (a part tailor-made for a young actor named Richard Carpenter – later to achieve wider fame as creator/writer of *Catweazle, Dick Turpin, Robin of Sherwood* and so on).

Midway through the first season, the series adopted a name change to *Knight Errant '60* (for obvious reasons – it was now 1960) and a fourth member joined the group – Tony Hollister, a cigar-smoking liquor tycoon, who signed on as Adam's business adviser.

Season two saw a further name change – the business had now become *Knight Errant Limited* – and the introduction of a new head of the firm, publisher Stephen Drummond (Adam Knight had left to manage his uncle's farm in Canada). Having taken over the business because he thought the project too worthwhile to stagnate after Adam's departure, Drummond, a man more interested in people than books, picked up the reins and steered the firm to new heights. Liz Parish was still around, but this time she, too, had an assistant – Frances Graham, Drummond's private secretary. Two other new faces were added to the roster midway through this season: Greg Wilson, Parker's replacement (Peter had left to write an opus called *What is Wrong with Britain Today*) and Colonel Cope-Addams, a retired Army officer, who brought his wide knowledge of military procedure and enjoyment of adventure to the series ('Knight errantry is a tremendous lark').

Extremely popular in its day, the series ran to 78 episodes and had some notable guest stars: David McCallum appeared twice, as did Honor Blackman, and a young actor named Oliver Reed took a step up the ladder to fame.

REGULAR CAST

Adam Knight John Turner   *Liz Parish* Kay Callard
Peter Parker Richard Carpenter   *Tony Hollister* William Fox
Stephen Drummond Hugh David   *Frances Graham* Wendy Williams
Greg Wilson Stephen Cartwright   *Colonel Cope-Addams* Alan Webb

---

KNIGHT ERRANT

Season One
Producer: Warren Jenkins
Directors: Cliff Owen, James Ormerod, Derek Bennett, Michael Scott, Herbert Wise, Eric Fawcett
Writers: Philip Levene, John Whitney, Geoffrey Bellman, Robert Holmes, Robert Banks Stewart
30 monochrome 60-minute episodes
13 October 1959 – 21 June 1960

Season Two
Producer: Kitty Black
Directors: Derek Bennett, Roger Jenkins, Eric Price, Douglas Hurn, Bill Hitchcock, Chris McMaster
Writers: Robert Banks Stewart, Roger Marshall, John Kruse, William Hood, H. V. Kershaw, Lewis Davidson
39 monochrome 60-minute episodes
15 September 1960 – 22 June 1961

LADIES IN CHARGE

A novel idea. Set in the twenties, this told how three young women, Babs Palmer, Diana Granville and Vicky Barton, defied their parents and twenties convention (women shouldn't go out to work, but stay at home and rear a family), and set up their own agency to help solve people's post-war problems.

From varying backgrounds, all three shared the same common interest – a dedication to help the needy.

Quaint, but fascinating material (the period was depicted in authentic detail), I for one wouldn't mind seeing more.

REGULAR CAST

Babs Palmer Julia Hills   *Diana Granville* Carol Royle
Vicky Barton Julia Swift

Zoe's Fever

w Fay Weldon
The 'Ladies in Charge' trio are asked to solve the mystery behind the disappearance of a young mother. Is she dead or has she simply run away? Eager to please, the redoubtable trio begin their first investigation.
Ernest Julian Glover
Zoe Natasha Matalon
Mrs Harris Heather Tobias

Director: Richard Bramall
Designer: David Ferris/Graham Guest

Dangerous Prelude

w Paula Milne
The girls take an interest in the affairs of Edward Cane, a successful novelist visiting London with his sister to employ a housekeeper. There are certain stipulations, however: she must be young, unmarried and of a high moral standard. Vicky discovers why.
Edward Cane David Rintoul
Clara Cane Suzanne Bertish
Arthur James Michael Gough

Director: John Wood
Designer: David Ferris/Graham Guest

Double Act

w Julia Jones
Babs, Diana and Vicky expected to receive some odd requests but none so strange as the one from music hall ventriloquist Cosmo Keble and his dummy. It appears that Cosmo has a very unusual predicament.

Cosmo Keble Gavin Richards
Lord Brompton Richard Vernon
Edith Imelda Staunton

Director: John Woods
Designer: David Ferris

A Public Mischief

w Anne Valery
Diana and her friends look for evidence to explain the strange goings on surrounding Madame Morgan – a medium who reputedly hears voices from the grave. Is she for real – or just a fraud?
Madame Morgan Eileen Kennally
Mrs Spriggs Maggie Wilkinson
Maggie Cecily Hobbs

Director: Jane Howell
Designer: David Ferris/Graham Guest

The Shadow

w Julia Jones
When Florence Potter, obsessed with the idea that a mysterious 'shadow' is following her, seeks the girls' help, Diana sets out to uncover the prowler's identity.
Florence Potter Lavinia Bertram
George Potter Andrew Wilde
Philip Courtauld Nigel le Vaillant

Director: Richard Bramall
Designer: David Ferris/Graham Guest

All That Glitters

w Anne Valery
The reward for finding a set of Imperial family jewels – and one aristocratic nephew, who is held responsible for their loss – is one sparkling diamond. Can the girls resist

the challenge and intrigue of a Czarist family squabble?
Countess Kutuzov **Irene Worth**
Count Litvinoff **Nigel Davenport**
Henri **Jonathan Kydd**

Director: **Neville Green**
Designer: **Graham Guest/David Ferris**

LADIES IN CHARGE
Based on an idea by: Kate Herbert-Hunting
Producer: Peter Duguid
Executive producer: Lloyd Shirley
A Thames Television Network Production
6 colour 60-minute episodes
6 May – 17 June 1986

LUKE'S KINGDOM

A full-blooded, no-punches-pulled tale of the hardships and heartbreak, injustice and vengeance which faced the Firbeck family, newly-arrived settlers to the wild and brutal Australia in the 1830s.

Jason Firbeck, a retired naval Lieutenant, recently widowed, and his family, sons Samuel and Luke, and daughter Jassy, arrived in Sydney to claim land bequeathed to them by a wealthy friend in Whitehall.

After an exhausting journey from Sydney to the blazing hot hinterland the family found their 'promised' land had been claimed by someone else. Led by Luke they plunged deeper into the outback to face the challenge of the untamed wilderness – and found themselves opposed on every side by ruthless land barons, escaped convicts, marauding aborigines and red-coated soldiers.

Beyond the limits of the colony's law, with no justice to protect them, the family faced turmoil and hardship in their quest to settle a new homestead. They were 'squatters', illegal tenants of crown land in the wilderness of Australia, threatened on all sides, by the ruthless original settlers, and the land itself. One mistake and their lives were forfeit.

REGULAR CAST

Luke Firbeck **Oliver Tobias**   *Jason Firbeck* **James Condon**
Jassy Firbeck **Elizabeth Crosby**   *Samuel Firbeck* **Gerrard Maguire**

LUKE'S KINGDOM
Producer: Tony Essex
Title music by: Francis Essex
Directors: Peter Hammond, Peter Weir, Hugh David
Writers: Keith Raine, Robert Wales, Donald Bull

A Trident International/TCN9 Co-Production
A Yorkshire TV Presentation
13 colour 60-minute episodes
31 March – 8 July 1976

THE MAIN CHANCE

A fast-moving, sometimes abrasive series about the career and cases of David Main, an ambitious and successful solicitor.

Young, calculating, brash and tough, Main worked on his own terms, or not at all. Nearing the top of his profession, he was always looking for 'the main chance' – the opportunity to better himself and secure his share of the profitable law business. With a sumptuous, super-efficient office suite, staffed by the most advanced methods of communication available (he had a mania for efficiency and kept his own case records on microfilm), he was a man possessed by a relentless, uncontrollable ambition to succeed.

Using his wits, energy, and dedication to justice, he ploughed his way through his legal struggles bulldozer fashion, with only his knowledge of the law standing between his professional survival and extinction.

The series was not only about solicitors and legal struggles, it told of people. Main would help anyone: the rich, the poor, the strong, the weak – all were treated with equal process by the ambitious but caring solicitor.

Super solicitor, super programme.

REGULAR CAST

David Main **John Stride**   *Julia Main* **Kate O'Mara** (First season)
Sarah Courtenay (Later Lady Radchester – Main's secretary) **Anna Palk**
Henry Castleton **John Wentworth**   *Margaret Castleton* **Margaret Ashcroft**
Walter Clegg **Glynn Edwards**   *Laura Grafton* **Ingrid Hafner**
Andrew Redford **Gary Bond**

THE MAIN CHANCE
Created by: Edmund Ward
Producer: Peter Willes, John Frankau
Executive producer: David Cunliffe
Directors: John Frankau, Derek Bennett,
Marc Miller, Chris Hodson, Cyril Coke,
Michael Ferguson, Tony Wharmby
Writers: Edmund Ward, Ray Jenkins,
John Bett
A Yorkshire Television Production
46 colour 60–minute episodes
18 June 1969 – 18 July 1975

THE MAN FROM INTERPOL

A low-budget oater from the Danziger Brothers' stable which depicted how crack Interpol agent, Commander Anthony Smith, was seconded on active duty to Scotland Yard and rounded up the baddies against a backcloth of cardboard sets.

Dull – notable only for the imput of writer Brian Clemens, who penned around two-thirds of the stories.

REGULAR CAST

Anthony Smith **Richard Wyler**   *Det. Insp. Mercer* John Longden

Nest of Vipers
The Feathered Friend
Soul Peddlers
Odds on Murder
The Key Witness
Escape Route
Love by Extortion
No Other Way
The Trap
The Dollmaker
No Entry
The Man Who Sold Hope
The Murder Racket
Death via Parcel Post
Out of Thin Air
The Case of Mike Crello
Killer with a Long Arm
Murder in the Smart Set
The Front Man
The Last Words

The Maharajah of Den
Murder Below Decks
Diplomatic Courier
State Secret
International Incident
Inside Job
A Woman in Paris
Man Alone
Mistaken Identity
Missing Child
My Brother's Keeper
The Big Thirst
Death in Oils
Multi Murder
Latest Fashion in Crime
The Art of Murder
The Child of Eve
The Big Racket
The Golden Shirri

THE MAN FROM INTERPOL
Produced by: The Danziger Brothers
Music by: Tony Crombie
39 monochrome 30-minute episodes
1960
(Various dates across the regions)
(USA: NBC January – October 1960)

THE MAN IN ROOM 17

They could solve a crime without ever leaving their headquarters – a room a stone's throw away from the House of Parliament. They were called in only when crimes had beaten the best brains of police and espionage agents. Crooks and spies were brought to justice by them. Even the Prime Minister was sometimes kept in the dark about their activities. They were *The Man in Room 17* – Oldenshaw and Dimmock, two academic criminologists who solved crime by logic, without ever leaving their room (their only contact with the 'outside' world being Sir Geoffrey Norton, a civil servant).

The 'man' of the title referred to Oldenshaw, the senior member of the team. An ex-barrister and 'backroom boy' for Churchill during the war (not to mention his five years as a special war correspondent), he was asked to set up 'Room 17', a special Government department whose brief it was to research into crime and the criminal mind. He agreed to do so for a maximun of one year but stayed with the unit for 22 months.

It was at Oldenshaw's direct request that Dimmock joined the department. Younger than his colleague, Dimmock had discovered his fascination for crime and the criminal mind while studying at Ohio University's Institute for Criminology. Someone there mentioned his name to Oldenshaw and on his return to the UK he found a letter from his future colleague waiting for him. Since the two men shared a keen interest in the oriental game of *Wai ch'i* (known to Westerners as 'Go'), they played together rather than conducting the interview. Dimmock got the job.

The type of cases they dealt with varied from espionage to cloak-and-dagger mysteries, but all came under the rarified talents of the 'super sleuths'.

One notable point of interest: the 'Room 17' sequences in each story were written, designed and directed separately to the main production, to give the stories more scope.

During the second season, Dimmock was replaced by a new character, Imlac Defraits, played by Denholm Elliott. (Michael Aldridge who played Dimmock was indisposed – although the two men did renew their partnership in *The Fellows* one year later. See entry under that name.)

REGULAR CAST
Oldenshaw **Richard Vernon**   *Dimmock* **Michael Aldridge**
Defraits **Denholm Elliott**   *Sir Geoffrey* **Willoughby Goddard**

Season One
13 monochrome episodes

Tell the Truth

w Reed de Rouen

Under pressure from the Government, Scotland Yard have pooled their best brains to investigate a case of industrial sabotage. When no progress is made, Det. Chf Supt Cannon suggests to the Police Commissioner that they call in Room 17.

Supt. Cannon **Jonathan Adams**
Peter Nash **Dinsdale Landen**
Max Opals **Vladek Sheybal**

Director: **Richard Everitt**

Note: The 'Room 17' sequence in this and consecutive stories was produced separately to the main action by:

Director: **David Boisseau**
Designer: **Dennis Parkin**
Writer: **Robin Chapman**

Hello, Lazarus

w Gerald Wilson
Room 17 are invited to investigate the disappearance of Mark Cranshaw, a young tycoon. His home and offices are wired for sound, and the team discover an unsavoury romance – and a two million pound credit fraud.
Henderson **Brian Wilde**
Cranshaw **David Burke**
Lynn Cranshaw **Bettina John**

Director: **David Cunliffe**

The Years of Glory

w Patrick Thursfield
When a retired general's home is burgled and his secretary murdered, the general is forced to admit that the diary he kept from the war has been stolen. Should this fall into the wrong hands its contents could embarrass the Government. Room 17 investigate.
General Colquhoun **Laurence Hardy**
Violetta Petrovic **Jean Anderson**
Glynnis Hughes **Meg Wyn Owen**

Director: **Peter Plummer**

Confidential Report

w John Lucarotti
Someone has stolen a highly confidential report written by Fredi Moon for British Intelligence on a foreign government. If published, its contents could have a devastating effect. Room 17 are asked to recover it.

Fredi Moon **Zena Walker**
General Gavieau **Leonard Sachs**
Morden-Cross **Laurence Payne**

Director: **Philip Casson**

The Millions of Mazafariyah

w Ludovic Peters
Room 17 makes contact with the Middle East when an attempt is made on the life of a Foreign Office official who was involved in a brawl. Though he swears he was stabbed only once, he now has two wounds!
Dullendorf **Barbara Jefford**
Charles Morrow **Hugh Burden**
Osman **Gerrald Healy**

Director: **Peter Plummer**

The Seat of Power

w N. J. Crisp
When a foreign agent enters Britain and his Embassy states his task is a menial one, Room 17, discovering that the agent isn't quite what he seems, investigate and disclose the man's sinister intentions.
Andrei Konev **Michael Gough**
Lord Bowers **David Horne**
Dr Pearson **Colin Jeavons**

Director: **David Cunliffe**

Safe Conduct

w John Burke
When an ex-president of a Latin American state, exiled in Britain, receives a letter from the son he presumed dead, Room 17 are asked to bring the boy out of his country to the safety of Britain.
Johnson **Robert Dorning**
Manuel **Eric Thompson**
Maria **Barbara Evans**

Director: **Philip Casson**

A Minor Operation

w Martin Woodhouse
A newspaper report describing how a man walked out of a hospital casualty ward, taking surgical instruments with him,

makes fascinating reading for Room 17.
They soon find themselves involved in the
man's espionage activities.
Peter Mandell Michael Johnson
Dr Boddington Brian Wilde
Magra Ference Carol Cleveland

Director: Peter Plummer

Find the Lady

w John Lucarotti
Room 17 face a question of priorities. They
are requested to decide the real identity of a
mysterious young girl and act on their
findings to decide whether to save her life or
stop a revolution by handing her back to her
enemies.
Lieutenant Achara Mike Pratt
Ambassador Diego John Moffatt
Ambassador's wife Eira Heath

Director: Peter Plummer

The Bequest

w Bill Strutton
When a businessman asks for a government
loan to develop a revolutionary new fibre,
Room 17 find themselves involved with
personal intrigue, murder – and the
unsavoury face of professional rivalry.
Marcus Oliver George Benson
Katherine Hewitt Melissa Stribling
Moira Leigh Jill Dixon

Director: David Cunliffe

Up against a Brick Wall

w Ian Stuart Black
When a man's body is discovered lying
partly in one country and partly in another,
Room 17 are given the task of deciding who
should investigate his death and take overall
responsibility for the case.
Karen Dilys Laye
Martha Ross Barbara Mullonoy
Sefton Arthur Jenkins

Director: Philip Casson

Out for a Duck

w Reed de Rouen
An English millionaire, liable to the Inland
Revenue for a large sum of unpaid income
tax, flees to a Caribbean island. Room 17

are handed the task of bringing him home
to face the music.
Milo Vine Desmond Walter-Ellis
Major Myers Scott Forbes
Juliet Servone Jan Walters

Director: Peter Plummer

Black Anniversary

w John Kruse
Room 17 are given the job of finding the
connection between the strange death of a
British Army general and a Colonial
governor – men who died exactly one year
apart, presumably of an ancient curse!
Huston Dennis Quilley
Kumano Johnny Sekka
Pat Hardacre Delina Kidd

Director: David Cunliffe

Season Two
13 monochrome episodes

How to Rob a Bank – and Get Away with It

w John Kruse
When a continental film director employs
unusual methods to create the right
atmosphere for his productions, and fiction
and reality begin to merge, Room 17 are
hard pressed to decide which is which.
Yasha Soroya Vladek Sheybal
Jack Simpson Mike Pratt
Horton Brian Wilde

Director: Claude Whatham

Vendetta

w Keith Cavander
When a man lost at sea appears to be the
only survivor of a damaged ship, Room 17
are asked to decide whether the crew's death
has political implications, or was just a
personal tragedy for those concerned.
Petty Officer Bradshaw Michael Robbins
Lieut Quatrane David Burke
Fabbri Neil Stacy

Director: Gerard Dynevor

The Black Witch

w John Hawksworth

Room 17 are asked to solve the mystery of a man found dead near an old abbey. Found in his pocket were objects used for devil worship. Oldenshaw and Defraits must find out why – and how – the man died so mysteriously.

Tracey Peverill Amber Kummer
'The Devil' Abbet Hopner
Boote Charles Abbot

Director: Peter Plummer

First Steal Six Eggs

w Ian Stuart Black

When a Hungarian interior designer is commissioned to convert the home of a well-known London hostess, Room 17 employ an agent to ensure that the man's activity does not extend to more sinister motives.

Paul Panacek Peter Wyngarde
Tracey Peverill Amber Kummer
Yvonne Cass Judy Parfitt

Director: Richard Everitt

The Catacombs

w Keith Cavander

Hoping to discover a treasure in the Middle East, a British millionaire enlists the help of a man with a very dubious background. Room 17 are handed the task of vetting the man's credentials.

Haynes Lyndon Brook
Crawford Edward Chapman
Petropolous Warren Mitchell

Director: Peter Dews

Where There's Will

w John Lucarotti

Tracey Peverill, a part-time agent of Room 17, asks Oldenshaw to sort out the cross currents of hatred and intrigue surrounding an eccentric millionaire's will – a bequest disputed by his scheming family.

Tracey Peverill Amber Kummer
Nigel Hendry Paul Williamson
Ester Hendry Geraldine Newman

Director: Peter Plummer

The Fissile Missile Makers

w John Kruse

When a number of foreign spies become interested in photographs of a new missile, and will kill to learn more about it, Room 17 are more intrigued than usual – the British Government know nothing of the missile's existence!

Shelton George Sewell
Sheila Bladen Ann Castle
Hatton Michael Glover

Director: Bob Hird

Goddess of Love

w Reed de Rouen

Three students decide to steal the statue 'The Goddess of Love' and return it to its rightful home in Greece. Hearing of the plan, the Room 17 sleuths take the unusual step of helping them to do so.

Bruce Derek Fowlds
Hatton Michael Glover
Mr Crabtree George Moon

Director: Peter Dews

Under Influence

w Michael Gilbert

When a judge begins to make some very odd decisions during the course of a trial, Room 17 become involved. The judge has been assigned to conduct the trial of a famous pop singer accused of murder, and the media interest could lead to trouble.

Mr Justice Easterbrook Alan MacNaughton
Ricky Mayne Tim Barrett
Corinna Easterbrook Jennifer Jayne

Director: Gerard Dynevor

Lady Luck's No Gentleman

w David Weir

An infallible system for winning at roulette – the dream of millions. Ruthless men will stop at nothing to obtain the system. Room 17 must decide how the system works – and who is behind it.

Alf Gover Ray Barrett
Hatton Michael Glover
Hodgen Paul Dawkins

Director: Peter Plummer

The Standard

w Patrick Thursfield

How far should a group of Army officers go to obtain a highly prized award? Room 17 must find a solution to the dilemma – and investigate the threats to the life of a visiting foreign prince.

Major Winton Charles Tingwell
Moulay El Gharbi David Cole
Lieut Stanton Roy Marsden

Director: Bob Hird

Saints Are Safer Dead

w Anthony Linter

When a valuable painting is sold at a London auction for an inflated price, Room 17 send Tracey Peverill to Venice to locate the source of the buyer. She uncovers a strange world of greed, vengeance and jealousy.

Tracey Peverill Amber Kummer
Fidessa Elphinstone Lisa Daniely
Pentodopolis David Sumner

Director: Peter Plummer

Never Fall Down

w Robin Chapman

A public figure has been indiscreet and his ability as a government adviser is under question. Assigned to clear the man's name, Room 17 are unable to do so – until the obvious solution to the problem provides an answer.

Hatton Michael Glover
Robert Grimes Geoffrey Keen
Leonard Finch John Strutton

Director: Peter Dews

THE MAN IN ROOM 17
Created by: Robin Chapman
Producer: Richard Everitt
A Granada Television Network Production
26 monochrome 60-minute episodes
11 June – 3 September 1965
8 April – 1 July 1966

MAN IN A SUITCASE

A rough and tumble adventure series in the *Danger Man* mould, this portrayed the adventures of ex-CIA man, turned freelance investigator, McGill.

Kicked out of American Intelligence through no fault of his own (he was framed by his superiors in the cause of international intrigue), his career in ruins, his reputation lost, McGill was forced to start life anew. He became the 'Man in a Suitcase' – a bounty hunter working for anyone who would hire him. ('$500 a day – plus expenses'.)

The tools of his trade were few. A leather suitcase containing a change of clothes and a gun. Sometimes he found himself acting as a private eye in order to save a wrecked marriage. One week later he'd be hired to protect the life of a threatened man. But because of his past, McGill could claim no protection from the authorities – even when cheated by clients, which he was, on several occasions.

He made mistakes and was always aware that hidden in the shadows were those who knew of his former CIA background and who wouldn't think twice about using their knowledge to obtain his help or discredit him.

They didn't come any tougher than McGill – but how he managed to work his way through a no-holds-barred fight, say, across a garage forecourt, down subway steps and onto a station platform, without ever once removing his cigarette from his mouth, is beyond the author!

Originally produced under the title *McGill*, the series adopted the first episode title (*Man in a Suitcase*) prior to transmission.

REGULAR CAST
McGill Richard Bradford

Brainwash

w Frances Megahy and Bernie Cooper
Kicked out of American Intelligence, McGill begins his life anew as a freelance trouble-shooter. But always at the back of his mind is the suffering he faced as a result of someone else's treachery – a man he'll meet again, one day.
John Colin Blakely
Colonel Davies Howard Marion Crawford
Judy Suzan Farmer

Director: Charles Crichton

The Sitting Pigeon

w Edmund Ward
Hired to guard a crook who has ideas of grandeur and is willing to sell out his brothers, McGill finds himself facing a ruthless enemy – one who is prepared to kill to achieve his ambitions.
Rudyard Robin Bailey
Rufus Blake George Sewell
Valerie Lois Daine

Director: Gerry O'Hara

Day of Execution

w Philip Broadley
Will a threat to kill him be carried out? That's the dilemma facing McGill as he whiles away the time wondering if every tick of the clock will bring him closer to his unknown assassin.

Jarvis Robert Urquhart
Moria Rosemary Nicols
Willard Donald Sutherland

Director: Charles Crichton

Variation on a Million Bucks (Part 1)

w Stanley R. Greenberg
A million dollars has been hidden away in a Lisbon bank. Believing that he is the only man with the key to the safe deposit, McGill travels to Lisbon. But he is not the only man after the money – as he finds to his cost . . .

Variation on a Million Bucks (Part 2)

w Stanley R. Greenberg
Blackmailed and under escort, McGill reaches the safe deposit box containing the answer to his prayers. But his troubles are far from over: someone else has plans for the loot – and McGill.
Michaels Ron Randell
Taiko Yoko Tani
Max Stein Anton Rogers

Director: Pat Jackson (Part 1)
Robert Tronson (Part 2)

Man from the Dead

w Stanley R. Greenberg
News of vital interest to McGill appears in a newspaper – the sighting by Rachel Thyssen of her supposedly dead father – and McGill determines to find Harry Thyssen by shadowing the girl when she visits him.

Harry Thyssen John Barrie
Rachel Thyssen Angela Brown
Coughlin Lionel Murton

Director: Pat Jackson

Sweet Sue

w Philip Broadley

An apparently straightforward case concerning a walthy man's wayward daughter takes a decidedly nasty turn when McGill digs too deep into the man's business affairs.
Sue Judy Geeson
Mandel George A. Cooper
Charles David Cole

Director: Robert Tronson

Essay in Evil

w Kevin B. Laffan

When three respectable businessmen take it upon themselves to remove the opposition, McGill finds himself involved in a business arrangement with a very nasty sting in its tail.
George Masters Donald Houston
Felix De Burg Peter Vaughan
Peters John Cairney

Director: Freddie Francis

The Girl Who Never Was

w Donald Jonson

Hired to trace a missing painting, McGill enters the shady world of art dealers. He discovers that the ownership of a masterpiece brings out the best in some, the worst in others – and McGill is dealing with one of the latter.
Kershaw Bernard Lee
Todd Basil Dignam
Mavis Priscilla Morgan

Director: Robert Tronson

All That Glitters

w Stanley R. Greenberg

Called in to investigate the disappearance of a little boy, McGill finds that in place of the usual distraught parents, two apparently unconnected people are faced with a joint emotional crisis.

Dolores Hornsby Barbara Shelley
Tommy Duncan Lamont
Michael Hornsby Michael Goodliffe

Director: Herbert Wise

Dead Man's Shoes

w Edmund Ward

Danger looms its ugly head in a peaceful village. McGill, asked to undertake a straightforward case, suddenly finds himself the target for a group of vicious gangsters waiting to kill him. But why?
Lucas Guardino Derren Nesbitt
John Gilsen John Carson
Peters James Villiers

Director: Peter Duffell

Find the Lady

w Philip Broadley

'Find the Signora', a dying man's last words provide McGill with a puzzle. Who is the Signora? The answer leads him to a hotel room in Rome – and a man who has vowed to kill him on sight.
Commandante Patrick Cargill
Guilio Maxwell Shaw
Francesca Jeanne Roland

Director: Robert Tronson

The Bridge

w Robert Muller

Engaged to discover the truth behind a young man's attempted suicide, McGill uncovers more trouble than he bargained for in the shape of Annabelle Fenchurch.
Lord Gormond Bill Owen
Annabelle Fenchurch Jane Merrow
Sir Walter Fenchurch Anthony Nicholls

Director: Pat Jackson

The Man Who Stood Still

w Raymond Bowers

Tricked into arranging a meeting between two old war comrades, McGill has a problem on his hands. One betrayed the other and seeks revenge – but which is which?

Gomez Rupert Davies
Palma Cyril Shaps
Teniente Alex Scott

Director: Peter Duffell

Burden Of Proof

w Edmund Ward

Henry Faversham, the English adviser to a
Central American republic, is accused of
stealing the country's gold reserves. McGill
is assigned to watch his movements –
unobserved.
Faversham John Gregson
Carla Faversham Nicola Pagett
Ambassador Roger Delgado

Director: Peter Duffell

The Whisper

w Morris Farhi

A difficult and, if he gets it wrong,
unrewarding case for McGill. He must
decide if Father Loyola, a Jesuit priest in
Africa, is genuine – or a crook using his
religion as a means to benefit himself.
Marcus Spencer Patrick Allen
Father Loyola Colin Blakely
Penelope Spencer Sheila Brennan

Director: Charles Crichton

Why They Killed Nolan

w Donald Jonson

Framed for the murder of a seedy private
investigator who came to him for advice,
McGill has one chance to save himself and
stay alive. He must find out why the man
was killed – and by whom.
Nolan Sam Kydd
Mrs Arnoldson Ursula Howells
Mr Arnoldson Griffith Jones

Director: Charles Crichton

The Boston Square

w Wilfred Greatorex

When a noted oceanographer disappears
with secret information – the results of his
research into commercial sea farming – his
employers ask McGill to find out why. He
ends up by fishing in murky and dangerous
waters.

Rudnik Peter Arne
Dalby Vincent Ball
Sir Eric Basil Dignam

Director: Don Chaffey

Somebody Loses, Somebody . . . Wins?

w Jan Read

McGill takes on a strange assignment in
East Berlin – and finds himself back in the
world of espionage, with the dormant
embers of an almost-forgotten romance
about to burst into flame again.
Ruth Jacqueline Pearce
Kommandant Philip Madoc
Colonel Carl Duering

Director: John Glen

Blind Spot

w Victor Canning

McGill is hired to protect a blind girl, the
innocent victim of circumstance whose
presence at the scene of a murder she could
not see has brought threats to her life from a
killer who has no knowledge of her
handicap.
Henry Thibaud Marius Goring
Marcelle Felicity Kendall
Maurice Derek Newark

Director: Jeremy Summers

No Friend of Mine

w John Stanton

McGill finds himself a job in Africa as a
mercenary and becomes involved in intrigue
between white settlers and natives whose
concept is 'Let the blood come, because after
the blood comes freedom.'
Cameron Clive Morton
Masuto Errol John
Turner Allan Cuthbertson

Director: Charles Crichton

Jigsaw Man

w Stanley R. Greenberg and Reed de
Rouen

McGill has the difficult task of piecing
together two parts of a human jigsaw – two

brothers, one of whom keeps running away from the huge family fortune. Why should this be? McGill seeks the answer.

Silvio Paul Bertoya
Tony Michael Sarne
Ugo Maurice Kaufmann

Director: Charles Frend

Web with Four Spiders

w Edmund Ward

Dr James Norbert, a brilliant American lawyer, receives photographs of himself in the arms of a girl. He assigns McGill to track down the person who took them – and discover why. Blackmail seems unlikely, Norbert has received no demands.

Dr Norbert Ray McAnally
Martha Jacqueline Ellis
Simon Croft Simon Oates

Director: Robert Tronson

Which Way Did He Go, McGill?

w Frances Megahy and Bernie Cooper

When a released prisoner searches for his share of the loot stolen in a major crime, McGill finds himself the unwilling pawn in a deadly treasure hunt – a game with danger on all sides.

Earle Donald Sutherland
Joy Jennifer Jayne
Soames Hugh McDermott

Director: Freddie Francis

The Property of a Gentleman

w Wilfred Greatorex

When a veteran actor gets carried away with the role he is playing and reveals the truth about a bizarre plot, McGill finds cause to have his gun ready to repel any emergency that springs to the fore.

Gerald Farson Terence Alexander
Jane Farson Justine Lord
Dr Vance Derek Francis

Director: Peter Duffell

The Revolutionaries

w Jan Read

Seeking to help a political exile's campaign to restore his North African country to rightful rule, McGill takes on the role of peace-maker – but finds himself up against ruthless men who wish to see him dead.

Dr Maza Hugh Burden
Haidar Ferdy Mayne
Chantal Sonia Fox

Director: Peter Duffell

Who's Mad Now?

w Roger Parkes

Called in to help an old friend, McGill begins to wonder who is telling the truth. She says she is being followed, her husband says she's neurotic – who is right?

Jason Robert Hutton
Joan Audine Leith
Dr Forsythe Philip Madoc

Director: Freddie Francis

Three Blinks of the Eyes

w Vincent Tilsley

McGill has trouble on his hands – but that's nothing new. This time, however, he's been accused of murder, and faces the guillotine, unless he can find the wealthy woman who hired him to bring her playboy husband to heel.

Eleanor Faith Brook
Bernard Drew Henley
Magistrate Charles Lloyd-Pack

Director: Charles Crichton

Castle in the Clouds

w Jan Read

A senior civil servant's entanglement with a beautiful – but dangerous – adventuress leads McGill into a delicate case with murder as the outcome. McGill finds himself chased by foreign agents seeking to right an injustice.

Sir Dennis Gerald Flood
Magda Gay Hamilton
Ezard Edward Fox

Director: Peter Duffell

Night Flight to Andorra

w Jan Read and Reed de Rouen

McGill takes on a desperate mission to engineer the release of an innocent victim

held in a fortified mansion in the Pyrenees. But things begin to go wrong almost from the start. Why? Is there a traitor in his team?
Radek **Peter Woodthorpe**
Rafael **Zia Mohyeddin**
Eddy **Ewan Hooper**

Director: **Freddie Francis**

MAN IN A SUITCASE
Devised by Richard Harris and
Dennis Spooner
Producer: Sidney Cole
Music by: Albert Elms
(Title music by: Ron Grainer)
Executive story consultant: Stanley R. Greenberg
Script editor: Jan Read
An ITC Production
30 colour 60-minute episodes
27 September 1967 – 17 April 1968
(USA: ABC. 3 May – 20 September 1968
28 episodes. Syndicated)

MAN OF THE WORLD

The assignments of freelance photographer-cum-journalist Mike Strait, 'a man with the world in his lens, and his finger on the trigger'.

Strait's assignments for some of the world's leading fashion magazines took him all over the globe – and he was seldom far away from trouble. Cameras were the tools of his trade, but intrigue appeared to be his business. No matter where he went trouble followed him like a magnet, and he was drawn into all kinds of exciting adventures along the way. Tough and intrepid, action was the keynote of his adventures.

A so-so adventure series that had lots of snap, but very little crackle or pop!

REGULAR CAST
Mike Strait **Craig Stevens**   *Maggie* **Tracey Reed**   *Hank* **Graham Stark**

Season One
13 monochrome 60-minute episodes

Death of a Conference

w **Tudor Gates and R. E. Thompson**
When a man falls dead from an assassin's bullet and with him dies the hopes for peace in a South American country, Mike Strait is sent to cover a peace conference that has no chairman.
General Montreaux **John Philips**
Thiboeuf **Patrick Troughton**
Alexi **Warren Mitchell**

Director: **David Green**

Masquerade in Spain

w **Lindsay Hardy**
Assigned to take exclusive pictures of one of the world's richest women, Strait finds himself taking an involuntary part in a fantastic kidnapping plot – with himself and the girl as hostages.
Denzo **Clifford Evans**
Gomez **George Coulouris**
Sebastian **George Pastell**

Director: **David Greene**

Blaze of Glory

w John Roddick

When Strait meets an ace racing driver whose eyesight is failing, he sees the opportunity to help a young man achieve his aim of driving in a top racing rally — but another man is interested in the driver for different reasons.
Kim Patricia Donahue
Tony Gardner Peter Dyneley
Ricci Norman Florence

Director: Harry Booth

The Runaways

w Michael Pertwee

Falling in love at first sight can have disastrous results, as Mike Strait discovers when he meets a young couple who have become romantically involved — the problem being the man is a compulsive faller-in-love.
Joanne Erica Rogers
Martin Leon Peers
Mrs Van Kempson Renee Houston

Director: Charles Crichton

The Frontier

w Lindsay Galloway

On a photographic assignment close to the Indian-Chinese border, Strait becomes entangled in a beautiful doctor's sacrifice to bring peace to a village threatened by a group of evil would-be dictators.
Hossari Gary Raymond
Chang Peter Arne
Dr Bahandi Leela Naidu

Director: Anthony Bushel

The Sentimental Agent

w Jack Davies

Thrown into prison for taking unauthorised photographs in an area of South America, Mike asks Maggie to enlist the help of Borella — an import merchant, and rogue — to secure his release . The man does so — at a price.
Borella Carlos Thompson
Lee Shirley Eaton
Minister Peter Jones

Director: Charles Frend

The Highland Story

w Lindsay Galloway

Assigned to report on the Scottish highland clan system, Strait finds the residents of a Scottish village less than friendly when he enquires about 'sacred' highland traditions.
McDonald Finlay Currie
The MacGillie John Laurie
Charles West Ray Barrett

Director: Charles Frend

The Nature of Justice

w Tudor Gates

Professor O'Connor claims to have discovered an engraved stone tablet which provides a link to an early civilisation. Assigned to cover the story for a science magazine, Mike finds that all is not as it first appears.
O'Connor Robert Flemyng
Sheikh Ben Said Bernard Archard
Gault Ewan Solon

Director: Harry Booth

The Mindreader

w Ian Stuart Black

Does Carla really have unearthly powers which enable her to read other people's minds? Her reputation — and life — depend on Mike Strait getting to the truth of the matter.
Carla Juliet Mills
Downing Patrick Wymark
Linda Moira Redmond

Director: David Greene

Portrait of a Girl

w Lindsay Galloway

Having already saved Joanne's life during an earlier assignment, Strait is not too surprised when his latest rendezvous with her leads them into intrigue surrounding an ingenious scheme to exact money from tourists by selling them fake Gainsborough paintings.
Joanne Erica Rogers
Langford Colin Gordon
Galsworth Michael Goodliffe

Director: Charles Frend

Specialist for the Kill

w Lindsay Hardy

A casual assignment in Berlin to photograph the latest fashions for his magazine turns into a nightmare for Mike Strait when he uncovers a plot to assassinate a visiting industrialist.

Colonel Cutler Paul Maxwell
Polikoff Derren Nesbitt
President Majek George Pravda

Director: Jeremy Summers

A Family Affair

w Tudor Gates

In Paris to photograph fashion models, Strait finds himself literally blown into a tense situation when the fashion salon is wrecked by a violent explosion. He is then asked to join the search for a missing man – with startling results.

Helene Lisa page
Insp. Sanglett Richard Warner
Corbet Eugene Decker

Director: Jeremy Summers

Shadow of the Wall

w Ian Stuart Black

Hearing that a friend in West Berlin has been arrested for espionage, Mike visits the city and soon finds himself the target of a group of men plotting to overthrow a government minister.

Colonel Cutler Paul Maxwell
Linda Suzanne Neve
Wilhelm Joseph Furst

Director: Harry Booth

Season Two

7 monochrome 60-minute episodes

The Bandit

w John Pudney and Ian Stuart Black

On assignment in Mexico, Mike becomes involved in the affairs of a tempestuous film star who seems unconcerned when she receives threats to her life. When she is kidnapped by a Sicilian bandit, Mike is asked to rescue her.

Maria Natasha Parry
Nicko Sam Wanamaker
Chivario Robert Rietty

Director: Charles Crichton

The Enemy

w Julian Bond

Mike is assigned to discover the hiding place of a fashionable Italian doctor who, having rejected 'civilisation', has gone to work in the African jungle. The man was secretly working on a new virus, and Mike must confirm if it exists.

Dr Moretti Anthony Quayle
Souen Tsai Chin
Major Teong John Meillon

Director: John Moxey

Double Exposure

w Jack Davies

On holiday behind the Iron Curtain, Strait receives an unexpected plea for help from an old lady who asks him to solve the mystery of her missing son – a military leader.

Mrs Rosewall Cicely Courtneidge
Grabowsky Nigel Davenport
Washington official John Tate

Director: Jeremy Summers

Jungle Mission

w Lindsay Galloway

While gathering material for a report on a rebel leader in the Amazon, Strait encounters an order of nuns who wish to establish a mission in the jungle – but someone is out to stop them. Mike takes an interest in their affairs.

Mother Superior Noelle Middleton
Padron Alexander Davion
Acquilma Isobel Black

Director: Harry Booth

In the Picture

w Brian Clemens

Although he doesn't realise it, a picture taken by Mike reveals the secret of a plot to assassinate a European president. But the group behind the murder plot are aware of

the photograph's existence – and order the photographer's death.
Troyan Albert Lieven
Maria Nadja Regin
Debar Peter Madden

Director: John Moxey

The Bullfighter

w Marc Brandel
In Spain on a 'simple' assignment, Strait finds an air of mystery surrounding his 'model' – a bullfighter. It appears that someone is prepared to go to any lengths to stop the man becoming a success – including murder.
Luiz Joseph Cuby
Carmen Marla Landi
Ramos Ferdy Mayne

Director: Harry Booth

The Prince

w Arthur Berlin
In order to avert a rebellion, Mike helps to establish the true identity of a young boy who had been kidnapped years earlier and who claims he is the rightful heir to the throne. But is the boy really a prince?
Tulan Michael Sirr
Count Korshin Geoffrey Keen
Burton Larry Cross

Director: Charles Crichton

MAN OF THE WORLD
Producer: Harry Fine
Music by: Henry Mancini
Script Editor: Ian Stuart Black
An ATV Presentation
filmed on location and at Shepperton Studios
20 monochrome 60-minute episodes
29 September – 22 December 1962
11 May – 23 June 1963
(USA: Syndicated 1962)

MARK SABER

The adventures of Mark Saber, a gun-slinging, one-armed detective, who got into lots of trouble but always emerged triumphant.

Loved by some, hated by others, the series nevertheless became one of the longest-running cop shows on television – and one of the first all-British programmes to be sold to the United States.

An enigma, its success was difficult to understand. For the main part the stories were totally inept, the production values cheap (as was most of the material produced by the company) and the acting seldom raised itself above the level of schoolroom amateur dramatics. That said, Saber and his long line of assistants stayed around for over five years of new adventures (over 130 of them), then started all over again for four years of repeats – many of which were aired in a primetime transmission slot, such was its popularity.

Under the guise of *Mark Saber*, the show ran to a total of 52 episodes, with Saber being assisted by Stephanie, his breezy blonde secretary; Barny O'Keefe, his leg man; and Scotland Yard detectives, Inspectors Brady and Chester.

Scarcely had *Mark Saber* ended when the detective reappeared under the guise of *Saber of London*. The location was the same (although the detective ventured farther afield by investigating cases in Europe), but the cast were different. This time around, Saber was assisted by Peter Paulson, who was soon replaced by Bob Page, before the line-up stopped with Eddie Wells, a reformed thief who assisted Saber in the field. Stephanie had departed to be replaced by Ann Summers – Saber's girlfriend (seen in only six episodes). Scotland Yard was still represented, this time in the form of Inspector Parker (same actor, different name).

The only notable writer on the series was a young, up-and-coming scribe named Brian Clemens.

REGULAR CAST
Mark Saber Donald Gray   *Stephanie Ames* Diana Decker
Barny O'Keefe Michael Balfour   *Peter Paulson* Neil McCallum
Bob Page Robert Arden
Eddie Wells Jerry Thorne   *Ann Summers* Jennifer Jayne
Insp. Brady Patrick Holt   *Insp. Chester/Parker* Colin Tapley

MARK SABER
52 monochrome 30-minute episodes
18 September 1957 – 22 June 1959

SABER OF LONDON
83 monochrome 30-minute episodes
Produced by Edward and Harry Lee
Danziger
Filmed at Associated British Studios, Elstree
12 August 1959 – 30 August 1961
(USA: Saber of London
NBC. October 1957 – September 1959
Syndicated title: **Uncovered**)

MARLOWE – PRIVATE EYE

Raymond Chandler's world-famous sleuth brought vividly to life in a glossy television series that picked up huge ratings on both sides of the Atlantic, won dozens of awards (including the best series on cable TV in the US, and the coveted 'Edgar' best script award for Jo Eisinger), and proved that the British could match the Americans at their own game.

With the magnificent Powers Boothe as Chandler's gumshoe, class oozing out of every frame (Maurice Binder designed and produced the title sequence), careful attention to detail (the series was filmed partly on location in Santa Monica, California, partly in London) each of the five stories was a pure visual delight.

Reports have it that plans to produce a new series have reached an advanced stage – personally I can't wait.

REGULAR CAST

Philip Marlowe **Powers Boothe**   *Lt. Magee* **William Kearns**
Annie Riordan **Kathryn Leigh Scott**

The Pencil

w Jo Eisinger
What significance is held by a pencil received by Marlowe in the mail? What does it mean? Marlowe knows only too well – the Syndicate has marked someone for death. Can he find the victim before the killers strike?
Don Luigi Bruce Boa
The Ringer Ron Travis
Sal Vaccaro David Healey

Director: Peter Hunt

Nevada Gas

w David Wickes
When a big-time lawyer is gassed in his car, Marlowe's investigations lead him to suspect that a vicious mobster and the lawyer's wife share a sordid secret. But there is more to the case than he first suspects.
George Dial John Terry
Candless Bill Bailey
Mrs Candless Jill Medford

Director: David Wickes

Finger Man

w Jo Eisinger
Investigating corruption at City Hall and the sudden death of a high official place Marlowe's life on the line. But who is trying to kill him – and why? On the run, Marlowe seeks help – but his 'friends' are conspicuous by their absence.
DA Ed Bishop
Sally Glenn Gayle Hunnicutt
Sneyd David Baxt

Director: Sidney Hayers

The King in Yellow

w Jesse Lasky Jr and Pat Silver
Death comes suddenly to a famous jazz musician in a girl's bedroom. Hunting the killer, Marlowe finds himself the prey in a deadly game of cat and mouse – a game that can only end in death.
King Leopardi Michael Billington
Gaff Talley John Alderson
Kitty Delorme Nancy Wood

Director: Bryan Forbes

Smart-Aleck Kill

w Jesse Lasky Jr and Pat Silver
The death of a Hollywood movie star leads Marlowe through the seedy twilight world of narcotics and prostitution, where killers can hide behind the glitter and gloss of the film-making industry.
Det. Murphy Shane Rimmer
J. P. Magnus Paul Maxwell
Dr Sutro Michael J. Shannon

Director: Peter Hunt

MARLOWE – PRIVATE EYE
Based on stories by: Raymond Chandler
Producer: David Wickes
Music by: John Cameron
Title sequence by: Maurice Binder
Art directors: William Alexander, Robert Cartwright
A David Wickes Television Production in association with London Weekend Television
5 colour 60-minute episodes
27 April – 25 May 1984

MARTIN KANE, PRIVATE INVESTIGATOR

After nine years of success as a 'live' television show in America (*Martin Kane, Private Eye*), William Gargan, the actor who had played Kane during the first three years of its run, crossed the Atlantic to star in this all-British version.

He shouldn't have bothered. The result was an uneasy marriage between a wise-cracking New York cop, who believed in cooperating with the police, and a desk-bound, tea-drinking Scotland Yard detective, both of whom seemed to do little beyond discussing a case over a cup of tea, or answering endless telephone calls.

REGULAR CAST

Martin Kane William Gargan   *Supt Page* Brian Reece

Smash and Grab
Munich Story
Airport Story
The Heiress
Bank Robbery
GI Returns
Taxi Story
Alpine Story
Escape Story
Inside Dope
Family Story
Barge Story
Bus Ticket
Swindle
Racing Car
Burglary
Passport Ring
Art Forgery
Amsterdam Story
Murder without Motive

Amnesia
Counterfeit Story
Night Ferry
Violin Story
Kidnap Story
Breakdown
Brother Story
Absconder
Music Hall
Hyde Park Story
Dinosaur Story
Film Studio
Lady Killer
Race Track
Break-in
Museum Story
Paris Story
Lisbon Story
Copenhagen Story

MARTIN KANE, PRIVATE
INVESTIGATOR
Producer: Harry Alan Towers
Directors: Pennington Richards,
Cliff Owen, Lance Comfort
Writers: Ken Taylor, Peter Holliday
*A Towers of London Production
for ABC TV*
Filmed at Elstree Studios
39 monochrome 30-minute episodes
14 September 1957 – 1 June 1958

THE MIND OF MR J. D. REEDER

Set in the 1920s, this agreeable series centred around the investigations handled by J. D. Reeder, a criminal-hunter for the Department of Public Prosecutions.

A mild, self-effacing little man, Reeder was a gentle genius with a criminal mind – but meticulous and tough in his investigative approach to crime. Bespectacled, his greatest attribute was his seedy and mild-mannered appearance which led the criminal fraternity to underrate the brilliance of his tortuous criminal mind.

Assisted by Mrs Houchin, Miss Belman and head of the department, Sir Jason Toovey, Reeder's talent for seeking out the truth (and ability to change his appearance at the drop of a hat) made him a legend among his peers.

REGULAR CAST

J. D. Reeder **Hugh Burden**   *Sir Jason Toovey* **Willoughby Goddard**
Mrs Houchin **Mona Bruce** (Season One)
Miss Belman **Gillian Lewis** (Season Two)

Season One
8 colour 60-minute episodes

The Treasure Hunt

w Donald Churchill
'Unfortunately I see evil in everything. It's a horrible handicap to possess a criminal mind.' The words of J. D. Reeder. The foretelling of future events, as the mild-mannered criminal-hunter sets out to trap a murderer.
Lew Kohl **John Bennett**
Albert **Michael Balfour**
Sir James **Mark Dignam**

Director: Kim Mills
Designer: Tony Borer

The Stealer of Marble

w Vincent Tilsley
Called to investigate the disappearance of Billingham, Managing Director of Telfers Trust, who has absconded with £150,000, Mr Reeder finds himself involved in a complex case of murder and extortion.

Sidney Telfer **David Gooderson**
Margaret Belman **Virginia Stride**
Det. Sgt Perryman **Dallas Cavell**

Director: Kim Mills
Designer: Terry Gough

The Green Mamba

w Vincent Tilsley
When the emeralds of Suleiman the Magnificent are stolen and the sentry guarding them dies from a snake bite, Mr Reeder has good reason to be grateful for the intuition of a woman.
Mo Liski **Joe Melia**
El Rahbul **Harold Kasket**
Chief Insp. Payne **Richard Butler**

Director: Kim Mills
Designer: Eddie Wolfram

Sheer Melodrama

w Vincent Tilsley
An attempted robbery in India links Reeder in London to the mysterious case of a man

sentenced to six months'imprisonment in India for attempting to steal the jewels of a policeman's wife. The man has sworn revenge.
Lal Punjabi Michael Bates
Tommy Fenalow Ken Campbell
Insp. Greyash Denis Goacher

Director: Guy Verney
Designer: Mike Hall

The Strange Case

w Vincent Tilsley
Reeder becomes involved in a duel of wits with Lassard, a man who has accused the disowned son of Lord Sellington of stealing £5,000 destined for a charity. But trying to reconcile father and son results in tragedy.
Lord Sellington John Robinson
Lassard John Malcolm
Sir Harry Carlin Edward Fox

Director: Dennis Vance
Designer: Mike Hall

The Poetical Policeman

w Hugh Burden
When young PC Burnett discovers a bank robbery in progress and arrests Green, the bank manager, on what he believes to be overwhelming incriminating evidence, it is left to Mr Reeder to clear the man's name.
PC Burnett Paul Shelley
Green John Barrard
Police Sergeant Windsor Davies

Director: Mike Vardy
Designer: Eddie Wolfram

The Troupe

w Michael Potter
When international confidence trickster Art Lomer arrives in Britain to complete another shady operation – a plan to dupe wealthy businessman Bertie Staffen – he reckons without the involvement of Mr J. D. Reeder who has more than one trick up his sleeve.
Art Lomer Patrick Bedford
Bertie Staffen Peter Cellier
Becket William Moore

Director: Robert Tronson
Designer: Jim Nicolson

The Investors

w Gerald Kelsey
Twelve people – all of private income – have disappeared from London over a period of twelve months. Assigned to investigate the latest disappearance, Mr Reeder finds himself racing against time to stop further people vanishing.
Ernest David Garth
Joseph Bracher John Le Mesurier
Wilson Harold Goodwin

Director: Kim Mills
Designer: Sylva Nadolny

Season Two
8 colour 60-minute episodes

The Duke

w Bill Craig
Mr Reeder makes the acquaintance of 'Duke' Dorsey, a Chicago gangster come to England to claim his inheritance of a country estate. No sooner has he arrived, when someone tries to kill him. Reeder must discover who – and why?
The Duke Ray McAnally
Major Blundell Anthony Woodruff
Moscrop Bruno Barnabe

Director: Mike Vardy
Designer: Mike Hall

Man with a Strange Tattoo

w Gerald Kelsey
Called in to investigate a robbery attempt during which someone was accidentally shot and killed by Lady Rothbard, Mr Reeder's examination of the body leads him to suspect someone is guilty of lying.
Lady Rothbard June Baxter
Lord Rothbard George Innes
Sir Clive Geoffrey Lumsden

Director: Peter Duguid
Designer: Peter Le Page

The Shadow Man

w Trevor Preston
When a bank manager draws a huge sum in cash from his bank, converts it into foreign currency, and then vanishes without trace,

Mr Reeder is assigned to find him and discover the reason for his strange actions.
Hallaty Michael Collins
Lena Ingrid Hafner
Mr Piper Arthur James

Director: Mike Vardy
Designer: Bernard Spencer

Death of an Angel

w Gerald Kelsey
A man has been arrested for the murder of Clara White, a silent movie actress, but Sir James Toovey, believing him innocent, sends Mr Reeder to visit the man in his cell. The meeting provides the detective with food for thought.
Dudley Vernon Michael Gywnn
Rev Oswald Harris Peter Williams
Shiner Bright Victor Maddern

Director: Peter Duguid
Designer: Neville Green

The Willing Victim

w Gerald Kelsey
Why should anyone wish to kill Mr Reeder? After a bomb arrives in his office, a car almost runs him down, and a piece of masonry narrowly misses him while walking home, the mild-mannered detective determines to find out.
Lew Kassio Harry Towb
Miss Clutterbuck Madeline Smith
Insp. Todd George A. Cooper

Director: Jonathan Alwyn
Designer: Stan Woodward

The Fatal Engagement

w Louis Marks
When several Peers of the Realm appear to be implicated in the murder of Hetty Malone, a popular music hall star, Sir Jason Toovey gives Mr Reeder 48 hours to prove the men innocent of their involvement with the woman.

Chief Insp. Pyne Windsor Davies
Lord Nettleford Basil Dignam
Sir Christopher Norman Claridge

Director: Mike Vardy
Designer: Mike Hall

Find the Lady

w Emanuel Litvisoff
As she is about to be announced at the palace, a young debutante is spirited away. Mr Reeder is appointed to find her – and uncovers a dastardly traffic in white slavery.
Earl of Colebrook John Barron
Count Vigaretti Tony Anholt
Lady Cynthia Alison Hughes

Director: Reginald Collin
Designer: Stan Woodward

The Treasure House

w Emanuel Litvisoff
When someone attempts to kill a reformed safe-breaker, Mr Reeder must discover what lies behind the threats to the man's life. What he discovers leads him to suspect that a villain's word can't always be trusted.
Olbude Richard Vernon
Lidgett Milton Johns
Larry O'Ryan Lawrence Douglas

Director: Voytek
Designer: Roger Burridge

THE MIND OF MR J. D. REEDER
Based on stories by Edgar Wallace
Producer: Kim Mills (Season One), Robert Love (Season Two)
Executive producer: Lloyd Shirley
Story editor: Monica Menell (Season One), Maggie Allen (Season Two)
A Thames Television Network Production
16 colour 60-minute episodes
23 April – 11 June 1969
19 April – 7 June 1971

MINDER

The incomparable adventures of Cockney entrepreneur Arthur Daley, an incorrigible wheeler-dealer in shady merchandise who was always getting into scrapes which his luckless 'minder' Terry McCann usually had to sort out.

Arthur was the sharp member of the team, an artful dodger who made his living through loopholes in the law. Not quite an outright villain (but very close to it), he believed in helping himself – usually at other people's expense. Flash but canny, he was a keen supporter of local charities (especially if there was the prospect of making an 'easy earner'). Respected in some circles, abhorred in others, his word was his bond (nearly) and he'd let Terry fight to the death to prove it!

Terry, a young streetwise tearaway with dozens of dead-end jobs behind him (plus two short stays at Her Majesty's pleasure for robbery and GBH), was unemployed but not on the dole. (When he first heard about National Insurance stamps he decided not to 'join'.) Rough and tough, but with a heart of gold, (when he gave *his* word, he usually kept it), he was Arthur's knight in shining armour, *sans* sword – the hero on a white horse (in Terry's case a white Ford Capri), Arthur's chucker-out – Arthur's 'boy'.

When not out 'pulling a stroke', the two men could be found plotting their next cynical scam at the Winchester Club, run by their friend and ally, Dave – usually downing drinks at Dave's expense.

Never too far away from the action – or Arthur's dubious activities – were policemen Detective Sergeant Chisholm, Sergeant Rycott and Detective Constable Jones; three hapless coppers whose sole ambition in life was to feel the collars of Daley and McCann – two of the most lovable rogues ever to grace the television screen.

REGULAR CAST

Arthur Daley **George Cole**   *Terry McCann* **Dennis Waterman**
Dave **Glynn Edwards**   *Des* **George Layton**   *Det. Sgt Chisholm* **Patrick Malahide**
Sgt Rycott **Peter Childs**   *DC Jones* **Michael Povey**

Season One

11 colour 60-minute episodes

Gunfight at the OK Launderette

w Leon Griffiths

The day begins with an Italian wedding – and ends up with a siege. Terry is held hostage and has to use all his ingenuity to wriggle out of the mess, while Arthur sees an easy earner in publicising the event.

Alfie **Dave King**
Stretch **Trevor Thomas**
Det. Sgt Chisholm **Patrick Malahide**

Director: **Peter Sasdy**

Bury My Half at Waltham Green

w Paul Wheeler

When Arthur tells Terry 'It's the easiest bread you'll ever earn', you can bet there will be unforeseen complications — especially when Terry finds that he's been hired to mind an ex-jailbird intent on recovering his share of the spoils.

George Nicky Henson
Rose Ann Lynn
Jack Tony Selby

Director: Christopher King

The Smaller They Are

w Leon Griffiths

Changing a $100 note for Big Stan leads Arthur into trouble, and Terry into problems with international crooks and several other interested parties — including Sergeant Rycott.

Big Stan David Jackson
Maurine Bonnett Hans Meyer
Sergeant Rycott Peter Childs

Director: Roy Ward Baker

A Tethered Goat

w Murray Smith

Terry is hired to mind an Arab banker, who appears concerned that his minder doesn't carry a gun. But when the chips are down Terry shows his prowess at fisticuffs — much to Arthur's annoyance.

Bassam Sayin Lee Montague
Dai Kenneth Griffith
Frankie Jenny Lee-Wright

Director: James Gateward

The Bounty Hunter

w Bernie Cooper

Jo, a young widow tricked into parting with her savings, approaches Arthur for help. He sends Terry to recover the money, but, as usual, things don't go too smoothly for the cheerful minder.

Jo June Ritchie
Des George Layton
Harold Christopher Biggins

Director: Peter Sasdy

Aces High — and Sometimes Very Low

w Leon Griffiths

Maurice, Arthur's professional gambling friend, is so good at his occupation that he's been banned from casinos — and mugged for minding him while he tries to settle an old score.

Maurice Anthony Valentine
Ari Anthony Scott
Zardinidis Dimitri Andreas

Director: Roy Ward Baker

The Bengal Tiger

w Leon Griffiths

When Terry is hired to wrap up the troubles of Arthur's newsagent, Mr Mukerjee, who has had bricks thrown through his shop window and is having problems with his daughter Indira, Terry finds himself up against trouble from two quarters.

Mukerjee Saeed Jaffrey
Indira Shireen Anwar
Gibbons Clive Hornby

Director: Peter Sasdy

Come in T-64, Your Time Is Ticking Away

w Tony Hoare

Never one to pass up an easy earner, Arthur takes a business interest in a minicab firm. When the company is threatened, he sends Terry to find out what's going on — and that's just the start of Terry's problems.

Kevin Alfred Burke
Katie Daphne Anderson
Des George Layton

Director: Frances Megahy

Monday Night Fever

w Leon Griffiths

Arthur falling in love? When he takes an interest in Sharon, a would-be singer, and promises to make her a star, that appears to be the case. Terry, however, has doubts — which soon lead to concern about Arthur's welfare.

Sharon Sheila White
Big John Brian Croucher
Det. Sgt Chisholm Patrick Malahide

Director: Mike Vardy

The Desert Song

w Andrew Payne

When Terry rescues Charlie, a young Greek Cypriot, from a street brawl, it leads him and his boss Arthur to an encounter with vicious men determined to take over a rival restaurant's trade.
Charlie Peter Bland
Christina Diane Keen
Omar Godfrey James

Director: Roy Ward Baker

You Gotta Have Friends

w Leon Griffiths

When Arthur does his friend Whaley a favour, things end up nasty. Terry becomes involved in an intriguing affair, and Arthur thinks he's scored 'the big un' – but when Daley's around, things seldom work out right.
Billy Gilpin David Buck
Whaley Roy Kinnear
Det. Sgt Bennett Alan Surtees

Director: Ian Toynton

Season Two
13 colour 60-minute episodes

National Pelmet

w Willis Hall

An invitation to the seaside from Arthur finds Terry doing the last thing he expected on a holiday – minding a horse. Arthur meanwhile weighs up the odds in favour or against doubling his stake money.
Jocelyn Liza Goddard
Everitt Jeremy Young
O'Brady Jim Norton

Director: Martin Campbell

Whose Wife Is it Anyway?

w Tony Hoare

When Arthur visits Alex, an old friend who has been beaten up, Terry finds himself

moving in to mind the man's antique shop while he is laid up in hospital. Things soon begin to go awry and Terry finds himself far from happy with his latest job.
Alex David Dakar
Grandma Molly Veness
Chas David Auker

Director: Roy Ward Baker

You Lose Some, You Win Some

w Jeremy Burnham

When a casino boss threatens the life of Maurice, Arthur's gambling friend, Terry and Arthur find themselves watching the gamblers to see fair play. But Maurice has more than one card up his sleeve.
Maurice Anthony Valentine
Alnutt Clifford Parrish
Sadie Lynda Baron

Director: James Gateward

Don't Tell Them Willie Boy Was Here

w Paul Wheeler

Ex-boxer Terry has to mind Willie, a champion boxer who is making a comeback after two years out of the ring. A simple task? Not when Arthur sees money to be earned by placing a side bet on both fighters!
Willie Paul Barber
Pug Dinny Powell
Barney Mather Alfred Marks

Director: Dennis Abey

Not a Bad Lad, Dad

w Tony Hoare

It's a job neither Terry nor Arthur had anticipated. Terry arrives home to find a nine-year-old boy sitting on his doorstep. Why or how the lad came to be there leads him a merry chase before the day is through.
Peter Warren O'Neill
Beryl Sharon Duce
Bob Martin Pax

Director: Ian Tonyton

The Beer Hunter

w Willis Hall

When Arthur goes out on the town with Yorkie, an old mate from his army days, and manages to lose him, Terry is given the job of getting Yorkie to the bus station in time to return home – providing he can find him!

Yorkie Brian Glover
Coliver Rupert Blythe
Renee Georgina Hale

Director: Tom Clegg

A Nice Little Wine

w Stanley Price

When Arthur purchases dozens of crates of wine – 'A nice little earner, Tel' – and things turn sour on him, Terry finds the enterprise highly amusing – until things take a decidedly unfunny sidestep.

Clive Peter Jeffrey
Bettina Rachel Davies
Det. Sgt Chisholm Patrick Malahide

Director: Chris Menaul

All Mod Cons

w Andrew Payne

When Terry is hired to remove some squatters from Harry's apartment, Arthur fancies his chances of breaking into the property development business. His dreams are swiftly shattered when things don't go as he planned.

Harry Harry Towb
Kate Toyah Wilcox
McQueen Michael Robbins

Director: Ian Sharp

Diamonds Are a Girl's Worst Enemy

w Paul Wheeler

Dreaming of riches and reputation are seldom far from Arthur's mind, but when he hires out Terry to help mind an old adversary's Mercedes, Arthur's dreams come tumbling down around him.

Tajvir Zia Mohyeddin
Sid Sam Kydd
Des George Layton

Director: Chris King

The Old School Tie

w Jeremy Burnham

An old school friend of Terry's escapes from prison. He claims he's innocent and Terry wants to help him – but they must travel a rocky road before the matter is resolved.

Palmer Peter Copley
Tommy Nick Stringer
Sergeant Rycott Peter Childs

Director: James Gateward

All About Scoring, Innit?

w Wills Hall

Danny Varrow is a footballer. He's also a gambler, a drinker and an womaniser. Like it or not, Terry becomes his reluctant minder – and that's when the game really gets tough.

Danny Varrow Karl Howman
Arklow Forbes Collins
Raikes Anthony Douse

Director: Martin Campbell

Caught in the Act, Fact

w Tony Hoare

Arthur is up to something – something particularly fishy. Terry doesn't know what, and he's not too concerned. He's got problems of his own helping his mate Des who is in danger of being run in by the police – twice!

Des George Layton
Det. Sgt Chisholm Patrick Malahide
Det. Cons. Jones Ken Sharrock

Director: Terry Green

A Lot of Bull and a Pat on the Back

w Tony Hoare

Arthur is into the repossession business with a difference. He's signed on to collect a prize bull. But Terry doesn't fancy his chances as a matador, and Arthur finds himself up to his neck in trouble – amongst other things!

Penny Ginnie Nevinson
Smith Leon Sinden
Brown Derek Benfield

Director: Terry Green

Season Three

13 colour 60-minute episodes

Dead Men Do Tell Tales

w Tony Hoare

When Terry and Arthur are lumbered with a dead weight – a coffin – Terry's loyalties are divided between his friendship with Monty, and Nancy, a girl whose lifestyle he finds attractive. Using gentle persuasion he tries to reform her.

Monty Harry Fowler
Nancy Suzi Quatro
Det. Sgt Chisholm Patrick Malahide

Director: Robert Young

You Need Hands

w Andrew Payne

Just when Arthur needs some impressive muscle, Terry gets himself badly beaten up. 'He's what you might call "horse des combat' says Arthur – who could use Terry's services as never before.

Gerald Matthews Julian Holloway
Vernon Mike Reid
Des George Layton

Director: Ian Sharp

Rembrandt Doesn't Live Here Anymore

w Dave Humphries

Hired to mind a nightclub, Terry settles in with great reluctance. Arthur meanwhile spies the opportunity to venture into the world of fine art – a world filled with professional tricksters. And there's none trickier than Arthur Daley.

Rory Quinn Ewan Hooper
Frank George Sewell
Max John Tordoff

Director: Tom Clegg

Looking for Mickey

w Tony Hoare

When 'Mad Mickey' goes on the run, Arthur sees the chance of scooping the pool. Terry is hired to mind Mickey, while Arthur cooks up a shady deal which brings him nothing but trouble – in the shape of Chisholm, his 'favourite' policeman.

Mickey John Labanowski
Det. Sgt Chisholm Patrick Malahide
DC Jones Michael Povey

Director: Tom Clegg

Dreamhouse

w Andrew Payne

When a superstar is away in Las Vegas, Terry is hired to look after his sumptuous manor house. Arthur meanwhile plans to break into show business on a grand scale – but he has reckoned without Beryl, the superstar's wife.

Beryl Wanda Ventham
Silver Roger Sloman
Derek Richard Griffiths

Director: Tom Clegg

Another Bride, Another Groom

w Willis Hall

The troubles mount up for Arthur. On his niece's wedding day the last thing he wants to do is shift a load of porno magazines. But that's what he and Terry must do – even if it entails using the bride's wedding transport!

Darrel Mark Botham
Bernie John Hartley
Trina Jane Lester

Director: Mike Vardy

Birdman of Wormwood Scrubs

w Leon Griffiths

When Ernie Dodds is released after a 14-year prison sentence and swears never to go back inside, Terry and Arthur have their hands full – Ernie has a few old scores to settle.

Ernie Max Wall
Grundy Joe Ritchie
Bank Manager Frederick Treves

Director: Ian Toynton

The Son Also Rises

w Paul Wheeler

Shifty property developer Ted Standen's son is threatened – but he doesn't seem to care. So Terry reluctantly renews his contact with

school in order to teach Standen senior a costly lesson.
Ted Standen Gareth Hunt
John Standen Stephen Garlick
Julie Bobbie Brown

Director: Francis Megahy

Why Pay Tax?

w Leon Griffiths
When Barry the Bookie gets cleaned out, Terry loses his heart to Dolly, Barry's clerk. Arthur meanwhile sees yet another way of turning a no-win situation into a money-making venture.
Dolly Kika Markham
Ray Nigel Davenport
Mr Wong Cecil Cheng

Director: Roy Ward Baker

Broken Arrow

w George Day
Terry introduces a drinking partner to Arthur, who decides that a darts tournament is an untapped avenue to make a few bob on the side – that is providing the players see things your way.
Daffyd Sean Mathias
Wally Michael Graham Cox
Sherry Maggie Steed

Director: Roy Ward Baker

Poetic Justice – Innit?

w Tony Hoare
While Arthur is away doing a stint of jury service, Terry is left in charge of the lock-up. Arthur meanwhile gets his teeth into a nice little earner – a hung jury who, because of Arthur's 'wisdom', find it difficult to bring in *any* sound verdict.
Judge James Cossins
Det. Sgt Chisholm Patrick Malahide
DC Jones Michael Povey

Director: Terry Green

Back in Good Old England

w Andrew Payne
Terry's pleasure at seeing Jack 'Oily' Wragg again is short lived when he realises that

there are others who want to meet him – to settle old scores. Arthur meanwhile shows his true colours.
Jack Peter Postlethwaite
Des George Layton
Sergeant Rycott Peter Childs

Director: Francis Megahy

In

w Leon Griffiths
When Arthur's secondhand car business comes under the scrutiny of the police – and in particular Klingmann, a German detective – Terry has to hunt down two tough Scots to clear Arthur's name.
Insp. Klingmann Frederick Jaeger
Sergeant Rycott Peter Childs
Frank Brian Cox

Director: Ian Toynton

Season Four
11 colour 60-minute episodes

Rocky Eight and a Half

w Leon Griffiths
When Arthur has a bright idea, it usually spells trouble for Terry. This time Arthur decides the time is ripe to lure Terry back to the boxing ring – but Terry's reluctance to do so costs Arthur dearly.
Harry Lynch George Innes
Sergeant Rycott Peter Childs
Darrow Frank Gatliff

Director: Ian Toynton

Senior Citizen Caine

w Andrew Payne
Arthur's ambition to own a Rolls Royce takes second place when Terry is asked to protect Cecil – an elderly, recently-widowed garage owner – from his greedy family.
Cecil Caine Lionel Jeffries
Johnny Caine Keith Barrow
Derek Caine John Carlin

Director: Robert Young

High Drains Pilferer

w Dave Humphries
Who would want to rob Mickey the Fish? That's the question Terry must answer,

when he has the misfortune to be hired to mind Mickey, an ex-villain whose girlfriend's jewels have been stolen.
Mickey David Calder
Det. Sgt Chisholm Patrick Malahide
DC Jones Michael Povey

Director: Robert Young

Sorry Pal, Wrong Number

w Leon Griffiths
Having decided that a race-tipping scheme demands his fullest attention, Arthur leads Terry up the garden path and gets him to 'mind' three public telephone boxes – but certain unfriendly people take an interest.
J. J. Mooney T. P. McKenna
Det. Sgt Chisholm Patrick Malahide
Sprott Shaun Curry

Director: Terry Green

The Car Lot Baggers

w Trevor Preston
When a secondhand car dealer friend of Arthur's has the frighteners put on him, Arthur suspects a group of local gypsies of being responsible. Terry thinks otherwise – and sets out to prove so.
Arnie Ray Winstone
Det. Sgt Chisholm Patrick Malahide
Fribbins Colin Jeavons

Director: Francis Megahy

If Money Be the Food of Love, Play On

w Tony Hoare
Both Arthur and Terry are captivated by Dee, a young Australian girl searching for her fiancé. Both men learn a lesson they won't easily forget.
Dee Rogers Penny Downie
Greg Collins Larry Lamb
Sergeant Rycott Peter Childs

Director: Terry Green

A Star is Gorn

w Tony Hoare
When Arthur accidentally takes possession of a valuable master-tape, he has visions of

making an earner in a big way. But the tape's owners and other interested parties are determined to dent his ambitions.
Cyril Ash Mel Smith
Zack Zolar Mike Holoway
Sergeant Rycott Peter Childs

Director: Ian Toynton

Willesden Suite

w Andrew Payne
Arthur sees greater respectability at hand when he is asked to speak to a local Rotary Club at a hotel when Terry is acting as temporary house detective. It bodes ill for all concerned.
Pongo Harris William Simmons
Charles Riding Bernard Kay
Chf Insp. Baxter John Rowe

Director: Francis Megahy

Windows

w Geoff Case
Arthur's plans for the Daley Health Club flounder when Terry intercedes in a tug-of-love dilemma between a young thug and his mistress.
Johnny Petselli Tony Anholt
Joe Mancini Patrick Troughton
Louise Catherine Rabett

Director: Robert Young

Get Daley!

w Andrew Payne
Arthur's stay in hospital is far from tranquil when a friend of Terry's is framed for a job Arthur witnessed – but apparently Arthur can't remember clearly enough to be of help to either Terry or the police.
Keith Wendell Ian Bartholomew
Det. Sgt Chisholm Patrick Malahide
DC Jones Michael Povey

Director: Ian Toynton

A Well Fashioned Fit-Up

w Barry Purchese
Arthur's entry into the fashion world lacks not only the glamour he expected, but also the profits he gambled on. Terry receives a

dressing down from his irate colleague – and things go from bad to worse.
Billy Christopher Fulford
Nigel Trevor Steedman
Ronnie Shyvers Stanley Meadows

Director: Jim Hill

Season Five
9 colour 60-minute episodes

Goodbye Sailor
w Andrew Payne
Anything 'on the cheap' takes Arthur's interest. This time he's up to his neck in illicit tobacco – but the smoke rings swiftly turn to smouldering embers and Arthur is left to sift through the ashes of defeat.
Larry Patel Rashid Karapiet
Det. Sgt Chisholm Patrick Malahide
DC Jones Michael Povey

Director: Francis Megahy

What Makes Shamy Run?
w Leon Griffiths
The appearance of fake £20 notes at the Winchester Club rekindles Det. Sergeant Chisholm's interest in the activities of Arthur Daley – with surprising results for all concerned.
Shamy Art Malik
Det. Sgt. Chisholm Patrick Malahide
DC Jones Michael Povey

Director: Terry Green

A Number of Old Wives' Tales
w Tony Hoare
Arthur and Terry attend wedding celebrations being held for a friend, and you can bet Arthur won't allow a money-making opportunity to slip by unnoticed. He doesn't – and that's when the trouble starts.
Clive Cosgrove Patrick Mower
Det. Sgt Chisholm Patrick Malahide
DC Jones Michael Povey

Director: Francis Megahy

The Second Time Around
w Geoffrey Case
When Terry is hired to mind a woman writer of romances and finds she has a

penchant for the bottle, a simple task takes on the proportions of a full-scale minding contract – much to Arthur's disapproval.
Ruby Hubbard Beryl Reid
Ronnie Todd John Landry
Barney Todd Bill Maynard

Director: Francis Megahy

Second Hand Pose
w Tony Hoare
When Arthur deliberately leaves Terry out in the cold, he takes up with a new partner – and a rather unusual alternative line of employment.
Roly-Poly Peter Johnny Shannon
Abigail Collins Stacy Dorning
Sergeant Rycott Peter Childs

Director: Roy Ward Baker

The Long Ride Back to Scratchwood
w Leon Griffiths
Arthur's 'easy-earner' this time are some black-market football tickets. With Terry's help he succeeds in scoring an own goal – one that costs him both money and reputation.
Justin James Mark Farmer
Joe Eldon Peter Needham
Mario Nicolas Chagrin

Director: Terry Green

Hypnotising Rita
w Alan James
In an effort to square his debts, Arthur takes over a cleaning business – an enterprise which, far from squaring away his problems, gets Terry all steamed up – and leads to his competitors making a clean sweep of things.
Mr Sharma Renu Setna
Jimmy Ray Burdis
Sudbury Donald Sumpter

Director: Terry Green

The Balance of Power
w David Yallop
When Arthur's car lot comes under threat, it leads him into the world of local politics,

with Terry as his campaign manager-cum-minder — but votes are not the only thing Arthur has on his mind.
MacIntyre Alex McAvoy
Det. Sgt Chisholm Patrick Malahide
DC Jones Michael Povey

Director: Ian Toynton

Around the Corner

w Tony Hoare
Arthur finds himself cornered once again with Terry as his only means of defence against some not-so-tasty villains intent on doing Arthur some harm.
Det. Sgt Chisholm Patrick Malahide
Sergeant Rycott Peter Childs
DC Jones Michael Povey

Director: Roy Ward Baker

Season Six
6 colour 60-minute episodes

Give Us This Day Arthur Daley's Bread

w Andrew Payne
When Arthur ventures into the landscape gardening business with some old lags who would rather be wielding a jemmy than a spade, it falls on Terry's shoulders to set matters straight.
Marion Ellis Dale
Det. Sgt Chisholm Patrick Malahide
DC Jones Michael Povey

Director: Francis Megahy

Life in the Fast Food Lane

w Alastair Beaton
When Terry decides to take too great an interest in the upper-class Sarah Bates and Arthur enters the car telephone business, lines are certain to become crossed — when they do Arthur gets wet, and Terry loses out on romance.
Sarah Jan Francis
Det. Sgt Chisholm Patrick Malahide
DC Jones Michael Povey

Director: Terry Green

Return of the Invincible Man

w Leon Griffiths
Arthur offers to help his friend, garment manufacturer Solly, but his offer seriously misfires — and leaves Arthur feeling far from cheerful with his latest money-making enterprise.
Solly John Bluthal
Painter Pat Roach
Det. Sgt Chisholm Patrick Malahide

Director: Roy Ward Baker

Arthur Is Dead, Long Live Arthur

w Tony Hoare
Tired of the pressures of entrepreneurialism — and constant demands from the Inland Revenue — Arthur decides life is no longer worth living — especially when there's an 'earner' to be made from being 'dead'.
Freddie the Fly Robert Austin
Mr Muir Jonathan Elsom
Det. Sgt Chisholm Patrick Malahide

Director: Terry Green

From Fulham with Love

w Tony Hoare
What price success? For Arthur no price is too high — providing there's a nice little earner at the end of the day. But Arthur's schemes frequently cost Terry more than himself — and this time's no exception.
Sergie Michael Gothard
Natasha Rula Lenska
Det. Sgt Chisholm Patrick Malahide

Director: Francis Megahy

Waiting for Goddard

w Leon Griffiths
When Arthur tries to hijack an eccentric senior citizen who may inherit a fortune, Terry sides with the angels, loses patience with his colleague and storms out of his life for good (?).
Albert Goddard Ronald Fraser
Det. Sgt Chisholm Patrick Malahide
Scooter Kenneth Cope

Director: Roy Ward Baker

Minder on the Orient Express

w Andrew Payne

When Terry accepts a pair of tickets from a beautiful young heiress for a trip on the Orient Express, he believes his luck has changed. Until he discovers that his girlfriend has been left behind – and that Arthur Daley is his new travelling companion, together with an assortment of rogues who would do justice to an Agatha Christie whodunnit.

Det. Sgt Chisholm Patrick Malahide
DC Jones Michael Povey
James Crane Adam Faith
Meredith Gascoyne Maurice Denham
Sergeant Rycott Peter Childs
Helen Spender Honor Blackman
Judge Robert Beatty
Harry Ridler Ronald Lacey

Director: Francis Megahy

MINDER
Series devised by Leon Griffiths
Producers: Lloyd Shirley, George Taylor
(Seasons 1–3) George Taylor (Seasons 4–6 – Orient Express)
Executive producers: Verity Lambert (Seasons 1–4); Lloyd Shirley (Seasons 4–6 – Orient Express)
Associate producer: Ian Toynton
Executive in charge of production: Johnny Goodman
Script editor: Linda Agran
Title song sung by: Dennis Waterman
Incidental music by: Mike Moran
A Thames Television Network Production
63 colour 60-minute episodes
1 colour 120-minute special
11 September – 11 December 1980
13 January – 7 April 1982
11 January – 21 March 1984
5 September – 26 December 1984
4 September – 9 October 1985
25 December 1985

MR PALFREY OF WESTMINSTER

A peep into the shadowy world of spies and spy-catchers, as seen through the activities of Mr Palfrey, a master of the art of counter-espionage.

A man of mystery (we never learned his first name), Palfrey was 'something to do with the Ministry of Defence' – in reality Britain's Special Intelligence Service – and worked from a sparsely-furnished office adjacent to Westminster, under the direct command of his business-like female boss the Coordinator (also unnamed) – a woman who ruled her roost with a rod of iron.

Not a man of action, Palfrey was basically an inquisitor and an observer – but if 'heavy' work was required, the spy-catcher could always call upon the services of Blair, the department's 'hit' man – a nasty piece of work.

First class – and greatly missed.

REGULAR CAST

Mr Palfrey Alec McCowen   *Coordinator* Caroline Blakiston   *Blair* Clive Wood

Season One

4 colour 60-minute episodes

Once Your Card Is Marked

w George Markstein

Mr Palfrey moves to his new office, meets
his new boss, and finds himself at the centre
of an intriguing mystery which leads to a
web of murder and deceit.
Springer David Buck
Dr Crawley Alan MacNaughton
Susan Valerie Holliman

Director: Christopher Hodson
Designer: David Ferris

The Honeypot and the Bees

w Michael Chapman

Mr Palfrey turns his professional gaze on the
private life of a senior RAF Officer and
NATO Commander (the 'Honeypot') and
watches with interest as the enemy ('the
bees') home in on his well-prepared trap.
Air Vice-Marshall Richard Johnson
Melissa Leonie Mellinger
Admiral Frobisher Frederick Treves

Director: Peter Cregeen
Designer: Robert Ide

The Defector

w Philip Broadley

When a famous Russian novelist contacts
the department with defection on his mind,
Mr Palfrey's highly-tuned antennae pick up
different signals to those intended. Playing
a hunch, the investigator puts one over on
the enemy.
Volkov Julian Glover
Duggie Ronald Hines
Kilpeck Anthony Brown

Director: Christopher Hodson
Designer: David Marshall

A Present for Leipzig

w Anthony Skene

Seeking the owner of a stolen icon, Mr
Palfrey finds that the present from Leipzig is
not exactly what at first it seems – but he
must discover the true owner of the item
before the jigsaw puzzle falls into place.
Armitage Martin Jarvis
Dieter Louis Sheldon
Velliadis Forbes Robinson

Director: Peter Cregeen
Designer: David Ferris

Season Two

6 colour 60-minute episodes

Freedom from Longing

w Philip Broadley

Mr Palfrey matches wits against Martina, a
beautiful foreign spy – an investigation
which leads to personal betrayal of the most
brutal kind.
Martina Estelle Kohler
Grant Brian Deacon
Bunny Kingston Donald Douglas

Director: Christopher Hodson
Designer: David Ferris

Return to Sender

w Philip Broadley

When Baliev, an ex-spy homesick for the
scenes of a less-troubled youth, contacts the
department, Mr Palfrey finds himself faced
with the harsh reality of his occupation – a
job in which there are few easy decisions.
Baliev Clive Francis
Frankie Fiona Walker
Becky Vivienne Ritchie

Director: Gerald Blake
Designer: Bill Palmer

Music of a Dead Prophet

w Michael Chapman

Special Intelligence investigator Mr Palfrey
finds himself using a murder victim as a
sprat to catch a mackerel – a fish wanted by
both sides of the diplomatic fence.

Forbes David Saville
McNair David Quilter
Dearborn Paul Herzberg

Director: John Davies
Designer: Robert Ide

Official Secret

w George Markstein
When old suspicions are re-awakened by
new betrayals, Mr Palfrey sets a trap that
produces unexpected results for everyone
concerned in a plot to flush out traitors.
Benedict Maurice Denham
Zoltan George Roubicek
Garforth Gary Waldhorn

Director: Christopher Hodson
Designer: David Ferris

Spy Game

w Barry Appleton
When old battles, refought centuries later
in a London flat, end in the death of a
modern spy, Mr Palfrey needs all his guile
to uncover a trail of deceit that threatens to
intrude into his private domain.

Madison David Baxt
Roche Dallas Adams
Turnbull Dennis Edwards

Director: Gerald Blake
Designer: Bill Palmer

The Baited Trap

w Philip Broadley
It had to happen one day. Mr Palfrey
confronts one of his own exclusive kind and
is forced to back his own judgement against
his Iron Lady – the Coordinator.
Baliev Clive Francis
Col Piscarov Roger Heathcott
Standing Jim Norton

Director: John Davies
Designer: Robert Ide

MR PALFREY OF WESTMINSTER
Producer: Michael Chapman
Executive producer: Lloyd Shirley
A Thames Television Network Production
10 colour 60-minute episodes
18 April – 8 May 1984
7 May – 11 June 1985

MR ROSE

The return of Chief Inspector Rose, last seen in *It's Dark Outside*
(see entry under that name), now plain *Mr Rose*.

In this series, Rose had retired to write his memoirs and to
indulge in his hobby of growing roses. Having inherited a large
private income from the death of two of his maiden aunts, he
could now afford to live the life of a gentleman of leisure – except
that he didn't know how, and chose not to do so. Being released
from the straight-jacket of duty had left him bored and irritable
– but this didn't last for long. The word went out that he was
going to reveal all, which disturbed one or two of his former
acquaintances and things started happening which engaged his
natural curiosity, demanded his professional skill and satisfied
his taste for action.

The series started at this point, with Rose installed in his
country cottage with his manservant, Halifax (whom we later
learned had been an ex-detective himself and one-time protégé of
Rose) and his pretty, but rather humourless secretary, Drusilla.

(During the second series he was joined by a new secretary, Jessica, and a new male assistant, Trent, turned up in season three.) As he tried to get down to writing his memoirs – he had fortunately kept copious private notes on each of his cases, which were piled up in a spare room – the old police dog in him set him once again on the trail of wrongdoers. As a private person, he had no rights of interrogation or arrest, but he now had complete freedom of action: he was no longer bound by police methods or police rules. He had the freedom of choice to go on with an investigation or drop it. He could make known his findings, or keep them to himself. He could hand a man over to the law or let him go free – and he found himself busier than ever and caught up in even more hair-raising adventures than before.

REGULAR CAST

Mr Rose **William Mervyn**   *John Halifax* **Donald Webster**
Drusilla Lamb **Gillian Lewis**   *Jessica Dalton* **Jennifer Clulow**
Robert Trent **Eric Woolfe**

Season One

13 colour 60-minute episodes

The Bright Bomber

w Philip Mackie
Retired from the police force, Mr Rose encounters the first of many old enemies, Bomber Bolt, who threatens to blow Rose's cottage and ambitions to smithereens if the ex-policeman mentions his name in his memoirs.
Bomber Bolt George Sewell
Edwin R. Eager John Strutton
Mrs Prior Melissa Stribling

Director: David Cunliffe

The Naked Emperor

w Philip Mackie
Rose is asked to name his price by a large newspaper tycoon – not for the serial rights to his memoirs, but to find out why someone is trying to kill him, and who?
Lord Chedworth Ronald Radd
Tomlinson Ivor Dean
Elinor Gray Adrienne Corri

Director: Michael Cox

The Noble Roman

w Philip Mackie
Anonymous telephone calls from a caller who rings off when the call is answered. Hints that someone is trying to contact Rose. The ex-policeman is confused – until he discovers the truth about an unsolved murder case.
Prentice Colin Jeavons
Ransome Allan Cuthbertson
Ursula Ransome Colette O'Neill

Director: David Cunliffe

The Black Beast

w Philip Mackie
When a friend of Mr Rose is falsely accused of murder, the ex-policeman finds himself in a head-on clash with his old enemy, Chief Inspector Entwhistle. The outcome of their meeting could save a man's life.
Chf Insp. Entwhistle Campbell Singer
Martin Strand Kevin Stoney
Heather Nerys Hughes

Director: Michael Cox

The Jolly Swagman

w Robert Holmes
Offered free passage on a luxury cruise, Rose willingly accepts. Once aboard he meets two

old friends and a dangerous adversary from his past – a man who swore to kill him should they ever meet again!
Pichot Paul Whitsun-Jones
Hugo Varney Derek Farr
Purser John Le Mesurier

Director: David Cunliffe

The Unquiet Ghost

w Robert Holmes
Why should anyone feel threatened by a scandal that is about to break in the Brazzini case. To Rose's knowledge he was never involved in such a case! Someone thinks otherwise – and is after his blood.
Oscar Malleson Lloyd Lamble
Mr Jago Donald Hewlett
Philip Portbridge Roger Hammond

Director: Michael Cox

The Tin God

w Martin Worth
When his old adversary David Maxton turns up on Rose's doorstep, the ex-policeman wonders whether Maxton has come to confess – or to take his revenge for past battles?
David Maxton Thorley Walters
Shirley Judy Geeson
Eve Gwendolyn Watts

Director: David Cunliffe

The Bad Halfpenny

w Philip Mackie
When Drusilla keeps a secret rendezvous alone, Mr Rose sets out to find her – and finds himself face to face with an old enemy he would rather not have met again.
Colonel Travers William Kendall
Peacock Arthur Pentelow
Aubrey Derek Tansley

Director: David Cunliffe

The Honest Villain

w Martin Worth
Mr Rose sets aside his memoirs again to pursue the evidence given to him by a villain who calls at his cottage with news about an escaped murderer.

O'Leary Bernard Gallagher
Sgt Harris Donald Douglas
Sgt Matherson Roy Maxwell

Director: Michael Cox

The Deadly Doll

w Martin Worth
When he gives refuge to a beautiful girl seeking advice, Rose finds himself implicated in murder and intrigue – with himself as the main suspect!
Wendy Lee Dilys Watling
Ted Alan Bird
Fred Chater Derren Nesbitt

Director: David Cunliffe

The Avenging Angel

w Philip Mackie (**from a story by Anthony Linter**)
Drusilla disappears. Worried about her safety, Rose sets out on a trail that leads him into a well-devised trap from which he barely escapes alive.
Ruvanski Barrie Ingham
Ambrose Poster John Cater
Virginia Joyce Heron

Director: Michael Cox

The One Woman

w Philip Mackie
When his friend Nigel Chinney and his employees Drusilla and John get into bad trouble through helping a beautiful girl, Rose asks himself what attracted his friends to her in the first place?
Nigel Chinney Graham Armitage
Susan Nicola Pagett
Angela Suzan Farmer

Director: David Cunliffe

The Good Loser

w Philip Mackie
Rose discovers the truth about his manservant John Halifax and learns a few home truths along the way. But when the evidence comes to a dead end, who is the ex-policeman to turn to?

Sir Hadforth O'Grady **Jack Gwillam**
Insp. Pritchett **David Morrell**
Clulow **Michael Barrington**

Director: **Michael Cox**

Season Two
6 colour 60-minute episodes

The Frozen Swede

w Robert Holmes
When Rose returns from his holiday and
moves into his ultra-modern, push-button
flat designed by a Swedish architect, his first
case is a surprising one. He must find out
who shot the designer – and placed him in
Rose's deep freeze.
Jessica Dalton **Jennifer Clulow (Intro.)**
Det. Cons. Jackson **John Challis**
Letitia Jolly **Barbara Shelley**

Director: **Ian Fordyce**

The Fifth Estate

w David Whitaker
Rose embarks on his most challenging case.
What secret lies behind 'The Fifth Estate'?
And who is trying to destroy it? A merry
chase ensues before he learns its secret.
John Hesaltine **Robert Urquhart**
Annis Hurley **Anne de Vigier**
Lord Deerson **John Bailey**

Director: **Barry Davis**

The Golden Frame

w William Emms
Considering his past, it's hardly surprising
that more than one person is out to frame
Mr Rose. But before he can discover who is
trying to frame him, the private investigator
must discover why.
Insp. Davidson **Tenniel Evans**
Det. Insp. Rogers **William Corderoy**
Janey Hedley **Pamela Ann Davy**

Director: **Ian Fordyce**

The Unlucky Dip

w Michael J. Bird
When a pickpocket chooses Mr Rose as his
next victim, the sleuth must ask himself: is

there a method to the man's madness? If so,
why chance his arm picking on an
ex-policeman?
David Unwin **John Barcroft**
Harry Croaker **Kevin Lindsay**
Vincent Pelling **John Welsh**

Director: **Barry Davis**

The Dead Commercial

w Peter Wildeblood
Of course Mr Rose would be delighted to
take part in a commercial. But what exactly
do they want him to do? Drop dead? If so,
he's having none of it – until intrigue takes
his fancy.
Mrs Johnson **Lisa Daniely**
Celia Watson **Madeline Mills**
Johnson **Paul Williamson**

Director: **Ian Fordyce**

The Heralds of Death

w Michael J. Bird
Does the death of one person herald the
death of others? That's the intriguing
question facing Mr Rose as he tries to solve
the latest in a long line of unsolved crimes.
Ron Field **Frederick Bartman**
Mark Tabler **Patrick Holt**
Insp. Crawley **Robert Cartland**

Director: **Barry Davis**

Season Three
6 colour 60-minute episodes

The Less-Than-Iron Duke

w Roy Clarke
Mr Rose is back on the crime-fighting trail
again: this time with a new assistant, Bob
Trent. No sooner has he settled into his new
activities then he finds himself up against a
vicious protection gang.
Harry Duke **Peter Madden**
Two Tone **Harry Towb**
Eddie **Eric Lander**

Director: **Barry Davis**

The Bogey Man

w Bryan Thompson
When Mr Rose witnesses a traffic accident
on his way to the library and discovers that

he knew the dead driver, he finds himself investigating an identical accident that happened two years earlier – and face to face with 'The Bogey Man'.
Det. Sgt Willis **Glynn Edwards**
Bruce **Hugh McDermott**
Harcourt **William Moore**

Director: **Barry Davis**

The Missing Chapter

w David Whitaker
Why should Rose book a one-way ticket to Tangier? Is he evading blackmail? Or does something far more sinister lie behind his actions. Those who know him well are confused – as are the police.
Vera Tate-Farlie **Geraldine Newman**
Harry Quist **John Dearth**
Colin Durrows **Derek Williams**

Director: **June Howson**

The Jolly Good Fellow

w Michael J. Bird
Invited to lecture on criminology to the pupils of St Stevens College, Mr Rose finds his journey there interrupted by students – who kidnap him and hold him for charity ransom.

Prof. Cosgrove **Manning Wilson**
Sir Gilbert Treece **Walter Fitzgerald**
Philip Mostyn **Mark Allington**

Director: **June Howson**

Free and Easy

w Jack Russell
Why should Mr Rose play dead? Is he foxing? If so who is the lookalike stranger who has appeared on Rose's patch, calling himself Mr Rose?
Rose/Marcus Despard **William Mervyn**
Thomas Landry **Derek Newark**
Guardsman Francis **Nicolas Ball**

Director: **Barry Davis**

(Author's note: I have been unable to trace a sixth episode, although it has been confirmed that one exists.)

MR ROSE
Series devised by: Philip Mackie
Producer: Philip Mackie (Season 1),
Margaret Morris (Seasons 2 and 3)
A Granada Television Network Production
25 colour 60 minute episodes
17 February – 12 May 1967
31 May – 5 July 968
7 November – 5 December 1968

MISS ADVENTURE

A short-lived but thoroughly enjoyable 'girl around town looking for romance but finding only adventure' series centred around Stacey Smith, a confidential investigator for the Stanton Detective Agency – a penny-pinching enquiry firm run by Henry Stanton, who sent Stacey into all kinds of mischievous escapades.

REGULAR CAST
Stacey Smith **Hattie Jacques**   *Henry Stanton* **Jameson Clark**

Strangers in Paradise

w Peter and Marjorie Yeldham
(A 6-part story)
Stacey Smith, a bubbly enquiry agent working for Henry Stanton, sets off on her first adventure aboard a number 22 London bus – but somehow finds herself stranded in Greece. She then loses her briefcase and stumbles across a blackmail attempt – before solving a jewel robbery and a complicated murder case.

Andreas Maurice Kaufmann
Max Parish Bill Kerr
Sophia Yvonne Ronain

Director: Jonathan Alwyn

The Velvet Touch

w Peter and Marjorie Yeldham
(A 4-part story)
Seeking a handsome chaperon, Stacey winds up stumbling across a confidence trickster who is romancing wealthy women for their money, and uncovers a double murder plot – ending up in the lap of Scotland Yard.
Rodney Stephens Tony Britton
Roberts Alan Browning
Philip Costain John Stone

Director: Jonathan Alwyn

Journey to Copenhagen

w Peter Yeldham   *(A 3-part story)*
Stacey's new assignment – to follow a young man suspected of dubious activities – leads her on a merry chase on land and at sea, off the Danish coast. Along the way she encounters more than her fair share of trouble.
Alexie Adakov Paul Whitsun-Jones
Hastings Eric Flynn
Captain Logan David Davies

Director: Jonathan Alwyn

MISS ADVENTURE
Producer: Ernest Maxim
An ABC Weekend Network Production
13 45-minute monochrome episodes
5 July – 13 October 1964

MURDER BAG

Originally intended as a mid-Autumn filler, this became a runaway success and snowballed into a series of 55 30-minute investigations.

Beginning with *Murder Bag – Case One, September 16* (the first 30 stories carried no on-screen title beyond the case number and transmission date), the series detailed the authentic methods of murder detection that took place each time a police superintendent and his sergeant were assigned to a murder enquiry with their Murder Bag. (It was rare for the investigating officer to have the same sergeant helping him on successive cases, so the superintendent was the only regular member of the cast.)

The Murder Bag itself – actually a black leather briefcase – contained over 42 items of equipment that the officers would need to probe out clues leading eventually to a killer's arrest. Carelessly discarded cigarette butts, strands of human hair found on the body, a few specks of dried blood and so on, all would be transferred to airtight glass containers from the bag, before being labelled and sent to the forensic laboratory for tests.

Produced live in the studio (the only piece of film used was a brief title sequence that showed a Scotland Yard detective checking the contents of the bag), the series introduced Superintendent Lockhart – a character whose television career was destined to span a decade and over *300* adventures! (see entries under *Crime Sheet* and *No Hiding Place*.)

REGULAR CAST
Superintendent Lockhart Raymond Francis

Season One
30 untitled monochrome 30-minute episodes

Season Two
25 monochrome 30-minute episodes

Lockhart Casts a Net
Lockhart Bags a Brooch
Lockhart Lays a Ghost
Lockhart Turns a Key
Lockhart Reads a Letter
Lockhart Sets a Trap
Lockhart Counts the Shots
Lockhart Finds a Needle
Lockhart Finds a Hat
Lockhart Listens to the Birds
Lockhart Foretells the Future
Lockhart Finds a Gun
Lockhart Follows a Dog

Lockhart Finds a Flaw
Lockhart Fits the Shoe
Lockhart Breaks Even
Lockhart Visits a Hospital
Lockhart Seeks a Driver
Lockhart Ditches a Car
Lockhart Sees the PM
Lockhart Misses a Clue
Lockhart Watches a Film
Lockhart Opens a Door
Lockhart Makes a Tally
Lockhart Misses the Plane

MURDER BAG
Created by: Glyn Davies
Producer: Barry Baker
Written by: Barry Baker and Peter Ling
(From stories by Barry Baker)
Directors: Jonathan Alwyn, Cyril Coke,
Roger Jenkins, Jean Hamilton,
David Boisseau
An Associated Rediffusion Network Production
16 September 1957 – 31 March 1958
30 June 1958 – 1 April 1959

MURDER IN SEASON

(A Chief Inspector Jim Taggart adventure)
See: *Taggart*

THE NEW ADVENTURES OF CHARLIE CHAN

The adventures of Earl Derr Biggers's astute and inscrutable Chinese detective from Honolulu who, together with his 'Number One Son' Barry, investigated a series of 39 thinly-plotted cases during the late 1950s.

Hidden beneath masses of make-up, actor J. Carrol Naish (as Charlie Chan) had little to do beyond spouting the sayings of Confucius – which apparently proved helpful to him when deliberating over some newly-found clue.

REGULAR CAST

Charlie Chan J. Carrol Naish   *Barry* James Hong   *Inspector Duff* Rupert Davies
Inspector Marlowe Hugh Williams

THE NEW ADVENTURES OF CHARLIE
CHAN
Producers: Sidney Marshall and
Rudolph Flothow
Executive producer: Leon Fromkess
Directors: Don Chaffey, Alvin Rakoff, Leslie
Arliss, Charles Bennett, Charles Haas
Writers: John Butler, Richard Grey,
Terence Maples
An ITC Production
39 monochrome 30-minute episodes
Various transmission dates across the region
from 1957 to 1961
(USA: Syndicated 1957)

THE NEW AVENGERS

The return of John Steed and *The Avengers*. Well, not quite. This series introduced the legion of Avenger's fans (termed Avengerphiles by fellow Australian Avengers buff, Geoff Barlow) to two new members of Steed's department: Purdey and Mike Gambit.

The former (described by producers Albert Fennell and Brian Clemens as 'a girl for the eighties') was a more than worthy successor for the role as Steed's Girl Friday. Soft and feminine (but with a kick like a tornado), she packed as much power into her graceful frame as Emma Peel and Tara King combined – and had a brain to match. A chauvinist pig's dream, Purdey could shoot the pips out of an apple at 20 paces and had a fighting style far-removed from the kung-fu, karate talents of her predecessors (a shoulder-high kicking technique which gave lots of glimpses of her shapely thighs).

Mike Gambit, an ex-mercenary soldier, was the quiet member of the team – until aroused, when he would strike with dazzling displays of the martial art technique of kung-fu. Steed's number one boy, an expert with firearms, longbow and all manner of weapons, Gambit was a valuable addition to Steed's team.

Steed himself had hardly changed. A little older, true, but with age had come presence of mind. He still believed in honour and duty. Steed retained his charm, but had mellowed slightly and now preferred to spend much of his time at 'Steed's Stud', his large country mansion where he bred horses and entertained an endless succession of beautiful women. As tough and as immaculate as ever (the bowler and brolly were still in evidence), John Steed was back in a series which compared favourably with any of his earlier adventures.

REGULAR CAST

John Steed **Patrick Macnee**   *Purdey* **Joanna Lumley**   *Mike Gambit* **Gareth Hunt**

Season One
13 colour 60-minute episodes

The Eagles Nest

w **Brian Clemens**
Steed, Purdey and Gambit get tangled up with a new Nazi regime. Posing as monks, the German baddies take over the Isle of St Dorca, where they intend to bring the comatose body of Hitler to life – until the New Avengers get a whiff of their plans.
Von Claus **Peter Cushing**
Father Trasker **Derek Farr**
Karl **Frank Gatliff**

Director: **Desmond Davis**

House of Cards

w **Brian Clemens**
The House of Cards – a deadly game to kill off members of Steed's department. His name is on the King of Hearts, Gambit's name is on the Knave, and Purdey is destined to become the assassinated Queen – unless they can stop Perov's diabolical plan in time to save a Russian defector.

Perov **Peter Jeffrey**
Vasil **Gordon Sterne**
Roland **Frank Thornton**

Director: **Ray Austin**

The Last of the Cybernauts . . . ?

w **Brian Clemens**
Steed renews his acquaintance with the unstoppable Cybernauts. Purdey and Gambit haven't met them before. When they do all hell breaks loose, and Gambit must face hand-to-hand combat with the machines to save Purdey from becoming a dead agent.
Kane **Robert Lang**
Malov **Oscar Quitak**
Goff **Robert Gillespie**

Director: **Sidney Hayers**

The Midas Touch

w **Brian Clemens**
To touch his hand spells instant death. He's Midas, a carrier of every disease known to man. Steed and Gambit are hot on his trail,

but Purdey, working alone, has been captured – and promised to Midas on completion of his latest mission!
Vann Ed Deveraux
Midas Giles Millinaire
Freddy John Carson

Director: Robert Fuest

Cat amongst the Pigeons

w Dennis Spooner
A man who has control over birds. A man who intends to use his feathered army to rule the world. The New Avengers take on the greatest challenge of their career. Purdey finds a bird in the hand leads to others in the bush – and Gambit and Steed are caught cat-napping.
Zacardi Vladek Sheybal
Waterflow Peter Copley
Rydercroft Basil Dignam

Director: John Hough

Target!

w Dennis Spooner
Targets that shoot back deadly curare-tipped darts. A joke by Gambit that misfires. Secret antidotes hidden beneath Steed's bowler. Purdey, trying to outdo Steed's 'hit' record, lies at death's door – and Steed is injected by small fry.
Draker Keith Barron
Illenko Robert Beatty
KloeKoe Deep Roy

Director: Ray Austin

To Catch a Rat

w Terence Feely
Hot on the trail of 'The White Rat', Gambit plays a lethal game of follow-the-leader, Purdey unzips a man's trousers and Steed meets a 'retired' agent who re-enters his life on a very uneven keel.
Gunner Ian Hendry
Cromwell Edward Judd
Quaintance Robert Fleming

Director: James Hill

The Tale of the Big Why

w Brian Clemens
What secret lies hidden in the pages of *The Tale of the Big Why*, a western hero paperback? Purdey dons her motorcycle outfit to find out, while Gambit takes a plane ride without paying. The outcome is a barrel of laughs for all concerned.
Harmer Derek Waring
Turner Roy Marsden
Roach Gary Waldhorn

Director: Robert Fuest

Faces

w Brian Clemens and Dennis Spooner
Three New Avengers are quite enough for anyone, so why should two lookalikes cause Steed and Gambit any problem? Gunning for a helping of double trouble leads Gambit to the bottle and Purdey into danger before Steed saves face by exposing himself!
Prator David De Keyser
Mullins Edward Petherbridge
Craig Richard Leech

Director: James Hill

Sleeper

w Brian Clemens
The New Avengers discover that playing around with S.95, a new anti-terrorist weapon, can prove tiresome for themselves and the enemy. Purdey goes to sleep on the job and her colleagues employ the help of the Post Office to give their enemy nightmares.
Brady Keith Buckley
Tina Sara Kestelman
Chuck Mark Jones

Director: Graeme Clifford

Three-handed Game

w Dennis Spooner and Brian Clemens
'Minding' the Three-handed Game provides The New Avengers with thrills they hadn't counted on. Steed's memory is good, but Juventor's is better. And what price Gambit as a nude model – or Purdey as a music hall dancing act?

Ransom David Wood
Juventor Stephan Greif
Ivan Tony Vogel

Director: Ray Austin

Dirtier by the Dozen

w Brian Clemens
Colonel 'Mad Jack' Miller's Special 19th
Commando unit is up to dirty tricks and
Steed and his colleagues are out to nab
them. Gambit is given an army commission
and Purdey tiptoes through a minefield –
before receiving an 'in-flight' glass of bubbly
from Steed.
Colonel Miller John Castle
Sergeant Bowden Shaun Curry
Travis Colin Skeaping

Director: Sidney Hayers

Gnaws

w Dennis Spooner
There's something nasty down in the sewers
– something that likes human flesh. Purdey
goes underground to flush out the enemy,
while Gambit and Steed concoct a witch's
brew before they too join the rat race.
Thornton Julian Holloway
Carter Peter Celier
Walters Morgan Shepherd

Director: Ray Austin

Season Two
13 colour 60-minute episodes

Dead Men Are Dangerous

w Brian Clemens
When Steed twice escapes death from a
sniper's bullet and someone sends him a
wreath bearing the inscription JOHN
STEED – R.I.P., Gambit goes belltower
climbing and Steed finally rings the bell –
to save Purdey's life.
Mark Clive Revill
Perry Richard Murdoch
Penny Gabrielle Drake

Director: Sidney Hayers

Angels of Death

w Terence Feely and Brian Clemens
When Pelbright, a friend of Steed's, keels
over and dies for no apparent reason, Steed
decides it's time to visit a health farm – not
to get fit, but to weave his way through a
complicated maze of clues – which finds
him nearer to Purdey than ever before.
Manderson Terence Alexander
Tammy Caroline Munro
Reresby Michael Latimer

Director: Ernest Day

Medium Rare

w Dennis Spooner
When Victoria Stanton, a medium,
'foresees' Steed's death, Gambit and Purdey
are thrown headlong into a race to save their
colleague's life. Steed meanwhile foresees
future events – and forecasts lengthy prison
sentences for the men who tried to frame
him.
Victoria Stanton Sue Holderness
Wallace Jon Finch
Richards Jeremy Wilkin

Director: Ray Austin

The Lion and the Unicorn

w John Goldsmith*
The Unicorn, an international spy with a
triple D-rating, kidnaps a Royal personage
as hostage for a British minister. Steed lifts
the lid off the Unicorn's scheme, while
Gambit sees the sights of Paris, leaving
Purdey to display her football prowess.
Unicorn Jean Claudio
Leparge Maurice Marsac
Henri Raymond Bussieres

Director: Ray Austin

Obsession

w Brian Clemens
Larry Doomer, Purdey's ex-boyfriend, now
Squadron Leader Doomer, intends to play a
modern-day Guy Fawkes by firing a rocket
at the Houses of Parliament. Purdey blows
her top and Steed is left to put a stopper on
Doomer's unprofessional plans.

Larry Doomer **Martin Shaw**
Kilner **Lewis Collins**
Morgan **Anthony Heaton**

Director: **Ernest Day**

Trap

w **Brian Clemens**
Heeding a department 'Red Alert' code, Steed and his colleagues board a plane which crash lands in the territory of Soo Choy, a Chinese overlord. Using Purdey's bra, Gambit plays Robin Hood, while Steed and Purdey book in for a Chinese 'takeaway'.
Soo Choy **Terry Wood**
Arcarty **Ferdy Mayne**
Dom Carlos **Robert Rietty**

Director: **Ray Austin**

Hostage

w **Brian Clemens**
Steed stealing departmental secrets? It appears so – but why? Gambit is ordered to find out, and receives a lesson from the master, while Purdey plays a waiting game – until Gambit regains his reputation on a Ghost Train ride!
McKay **William Franklyn**
Spelman **Simon Oates**
Walters **Michael Culver**

Director: **Sidney Hayers**

K is for Kill (Part 1 'The Tiger Awakes')

w **Brian Clemens** *
1965, and a young Russian soldier bursts into an old Nissen hut, mows down a Salvation Army Band, then dies – his face has changed to that of an old man! Steed rings his ex-colleague Mrs Peel and tells her it is a mystery they will never solve until . . . 1977, and another young Russian officer dies – then ages within seconds of death.

K is for Kill (Part 2 'Tiger by the Tail')

Hot on the trail of the babyfaced 'K' agents – each of whom is over 60 years old – Steed receives a health warning when a sniper's bullet shatters his cigarette case, Gambit and Purdey search for a son whose father is younger than his heir, and Steed rings a note of discord to avert an assassination.
Turkov **Maxence Mailfort**
Stanislav **Charles Millot**
Toy Paul **Emile Deiber**

Director: **Yvon Marie Coulais**

Complex

w **Dennis Spooner** **
What connection does an ultra-modern security building in Toronto have with enemy agent Scapina? That's the question facing the New Avengers. Finding the answer sees Gambit arrested and Purdey held prisoner by a computer! Enter undercover man John Steed – in a deluge.
Baker **Cec Linder**
Talbot **Harvey Atkin**
Karavitch **Vlasta Vrana**

Director: **Richard Gilbert**

The Gladiators

w **Brian Clemens** **
Karl Sminsky and his aides are supermen. They can punch their way through solid steel and catch bullets in their hands! Tough they may be, but when Sminsky and his army meet an unbeatable force – Steed's steel-lined bowler – their aspirations and pride are dented.
Karl Sminsky **Louis Zorich**
Peters **Neil Vipond**
O'Hara **Bill Starr**

Director: **George Fournier**

Emily

w **Dennis Spooner** **
Hot on the trail of the Fox, a double agent, the New Avengers find themselves hard-pressed to keep abreast of their prey, until Purdey decides to take a mid-adventure car wash shampoo, and Steed becomes hunted by the police – for driving a car wearing a bowler!
Collins **Les Carlson**
Miss Daly **Jane Mallet**
Phillips **Richard Davidson**

Director: **Don Thompson**

Forward Base

w Dennis Spooner **

Somewhere in the heart of Canada lies a Mark VI circuit control unit which proves that the Russians have moved ahead in missile guidance. The New Avengers must find it. So Steed goes fishing on dry land and catches a submarine complete with its pirate captain – Long John Purdey!

Hosking Jack Creley
Ranoff Marilyn Lightstone
Milroy Maurice Good

Director: Don Thompson

THE NEW AVENGERS
Producers: Albert Fenell and Brian Clemens
Music by: Laurie Johnson
An Avengers (Film and TV) Enterprises Ltd Production and IDTV TV Productions, Paris
26 colour 60-minute episodes
(Episodes * filmed in France, ** filmed in Canada)
22 October 1976 – 28 January 1977
9 September – 25 November 1977
(Note: The episode entitled *Emily* was cancelled on its original transmission date and replaced by *The Gladiators*. This episode resurfaced in 1978.)
(USA: Premiered 15 September 1978. CBS Two episodes (titles unknown) were edited together as a TV movie of 75 minutes duration.)

NEW SCOTLAND YARD

A tough, gritty, no-punches-pulled series that accurately portrayed the crime-fighting exploits of the men from New Scotland Yard's CID division.

A departure from the 'cardboard-cut-out' television detectives, the programme introduced the viewer to a new breed of policemen – men with emotions and everyday down-to-earth problems, the kind of coppers who seldom found time to strip off the burden of duty and go home to relax.

Such men were Detective Superintendent Kingdom and Detective Inspector Ward, of the Central Office of the CID; men with quiet authority who dealt with crimes of importance: murder, robbery with violence, extortion, blackmail and so on. Kingdom was the efficient and reasonable member of the team, Ward the hard man with a ruthless approach to his work. Their relationship was often abrasive and tolerant, but the two men shared a mutual respect for each other.

The Kingdom/Ward partnership lasted through three seasons before two new men were added to the production roster for the final series, Detective Chief Superintendent Clay and Detective Sergeant Dexter (played by Clive Francis, the son of another well-known TV cop, Raymond Francis of *No Hiding Place* fame.) Enjoying a father-and-son-type relationship, Clay and Dexter brought the programme to a conclusion.

(One notable point of interest to trivia buffs: scriptwriter Richard Harris named two of his characters after two real-life television producers, Detective Sergeants Clemens and Fennell.)

REGULAR CAST

Det. Chf Supt John Kingdom **John Woodvine**   *Det. Insp. Alan Ward* **John Carlisle**
Det. Cf Supt Clay **Michael Turner**   *Det. Sgt Dexter* **Clive Francis**

Season One

12 colour 60-minute episodes

Point of Impact

w Don Houghton
Superintendent Kingdom and Inspector
Ward investigate a case that puts their
relationship under severe strain.
Sgt Grainger Brian Rawlinson
PC Tyrell Bryan Marshall
Major Lofthouse Basil Henson

Director: Tony Wharmby
Designer: Roger Hall

The Comeback

w Tony Hoare
The murder of a bank manager for no
apparent motive leads Kingdom and Ward
to discover a second unsolved murder.
Dobson Geoffrey Morris
Collins Kenneth Cranham
Mrs Rawlings Sheila Wilcox

Director: Tony Wharmby
Designer: John Clements

Memory of a Gauntlet

w Don Houghton
Detectives Kingdom and Ward come up
against a new and deadly enemy – a group
of Nazi sympathisers.
Lutstein Cyril Shaps
Harman Vernon Dobtcheff
Bruchler Guy Deghy

Director: Christopher Hodson
Designer: John Clements

The Palais Romeo

w Stuart Douglas
Despite evidence to the contrary, Kingdom
is convinced that a young man is the one
he's looking for in connection with a
murder.

Det. Sgt Bates Colin Rix
Det. Sgt Wilson Godfrey Jackman
Det. Con. Davies Peter Porteous

Director: Bill Bain
Designer: Roger Hall

Hard Contract

w Philip Martin
Two apparently unrelated murders – with
both victims killed by the same gun. A
poser for detectives Kingdom and Ward.
Det. Sgt Hadley Windsor Davies
Peter Gould Michael Ripper
George Rennell Patrick O'Connell

Director: Paul Annett
Designer: John Clements

Shock Tactics

w Patrick Alexander
Archer claims his wife's death was the result
of a practical joke. Can Kingdom prove it
was murder?
Archer John Normington
Arthur Cleveden QC Ray Smith
Pauline Archer Joyce Cummings

Director: John Reardon
Designer: John Clements

The Wrong 'Un

w Tony Hoare
When an inmate at a prison dies of knife
wounds, it looks like a simple case of
murder – until events force Kingdom to dig
deeper.
Read Billy Murray
White Christopher Sandford
Det. Sgt Dawson Robert Tunstall

Director: Paul Annett
Designer: Roger Hall

Fire in a Honey Pot

w Robert Banks Stewart
A series of fires in betting shops leads
Kingdom and Ward to a web of vicious
racketeers demanding protection money.
Leach Ken Halliwell
Det. Sgt Gilson Peter Blythe
Dunbar John J. Cairney

Director: Bryan Izzard
Designer: Bryan Bagge

The Banker

w Don Houghton
When a Mayfair couturier is found shot at
the wheel of his car, his financial affairs
come under the scrutiny of Kingdom and
Ward.
Marty Lewis Milton Johns
Det. Sgt Gilson Peter Blythe
St Clare Hugh Latimer

Director: James Ormerod
Designer: Roger Hall

Ask No Questions

w Lewis Greifer
A girl found dead on a rubbish dump leads
Det. Chf-Supt Kingdom into the seedy
world of society drop-outs.
Jack Freeman Tenniel Evans
Paul Freeman David Horovitch
Det. Sgt Bates Colin Rix

Director: James Ormerod
Designer: David Catley

Reunion

w Nicholas Palmer
On the same night that Steve Thomas
escapes from prison, a solicitor is found dead
in his office. Kingdom and Ward
investigate.
Thomas Robin Ellis
Tricia Sharon Duce
Diana Thomas Virginia Stride

Director: David Cunliffe
Designer: Bryan Bagge

And When You're Wrong?

w Alan Falconer
Though Ward expects to catch the brain
behind a major art robbery through the
latter's connection with shady insurance
agent, Prentice, things go terribly wrong.
Prentice Robert Fyfe
Joan Prentice Sheila Fearn
Kost Keith Marsh

Director: Bryan Izzard
Designer: John Clements

Season Two

13 colour 60-minute episodes

Nothing to Live for

w Tony Hoare
Demoted to uniformed sergeant on charges
of misconduct, Ward considers his career
prospects – but a vicious murder enquiry
will soon give him something more to
occupy his mind.
Dr Mason Mark Jones
Belmont Phillip Madoc
Det. Con. Sidley John Peel

Director: Bryan Izzard
Designer: John Emery

A Case of Prejudice

w Stuart Douglas
Kingdom and Ward investigate a race
killing among a predominantly black
community – but the police are treating it
as a case of robbery with violence.
King Daniels Mark Heath
Andrew Perks Ian Gelder
Det. Sgt Bates Colin Rix

Director: Oliver Horsbrugh
Designer: Roger Hall

A Gathering of Dust

w Don Houghton
When a demolition team uncover a cellar on
a building site and the remains of a skeleton
are found, Kingdom and Ward must
discover if murder has been committed.

Bill Derek Martin
Matterson Tony Steedman
Det. Insp. Willis Alan Downer

Director: Bryan Izzard
Designer: David Catley

Evidence of Character

w Peter Wildeblood

When a girl is found murdered and a local man becomes the victim of village gossip, Kingdom finds their vitriolic tongues lead to further complications.
Ronnie Johnson Gary Raymond
Vera Noone Joan Scott
Det. Sgt Buss Michael Beint

Director: Bryan Izzard
Designer: John Emery

Prove It

w Richard Harris

Police attempts to nail Bowers, a London villain, have proved unsuccessful, but when small-time crook, Slee is killed, Kingdom loses no time in bringing a charge against Bowers.
Bowers Ray Lonnen
Det. Sgt Clemens Anthony Sagar
Det. Sgt Fennell Richard Borthwick

Director: Peter Moffatt
Designer: Frank Nerini

Shadow of a Deadbeat

w Don Houghton

Arthur and Daniel, two down-and-outs, cause a major headache for Detective Kingdom and Sergeant Ward when one of them drops dead in a condemned house.
Arthur John Rees
Daniel Richard Mathews
Ashley John Graham

Director: Bryan Izzard
Designer: David Catley

Papa Charlie

w Stuart Douglas

When someone breaks into Kingdom's house and tries to strangle Angela, his wife, the detective is forced to make an unenviable decision.

Angela Sally Home
Charles Change Tony Melody
PC Noble Ken Haward

Director: John Reardon
Designer: John Emery

Error of Judgement

w Victor Pemberton

Was the hanging of Thomas Stevens 12 years earlier a miscarriage of justice? Kingdom and Ward investigate.
Mrs Stevens Carmel McSharry
Tony Stevens Billy Hamon
Kenneth Fraser Bryan Stanion

Director: Oliver Horsbrugh
Designer: Martin Johnson

Two into One Will Go

w Alun Falconer

When one of Sgt Ward's suspects in a stolen car racket is shot in a telephone kiosk, Kingdom steps in and takes up the enquiry.
Det. Insp. Willis Alan Downer
John Randall George Baker
Det. Sgt Bliss Ruth Madoc

Director: Howard Ross
Designer: David Catley

The Money Game

w Basil Dawson

When Audrey Miller is mugged and her shopping bag is found to contain £20,000 in forged bank notes, Kingdom and Ward embark on a search for a forger.
Audrey Miller Pauline Delaney
Fred Larch Michael Balfour
WDC Carol James Carolyn Jones

Director: Bill Turner
Designer: David Catley

We Do What We Can

w Tony Hoare

When Macey came out of prison, Sergeant Ward helped him to get a job. Macey's wife, suspecting that her husband is mixed up in something fishy, gives Ward a call.

Donald Macey Robert Morris
Jenny Macey Susan Glanville
DC Thomas Dennis Blanch

Director: John Reardon
Designer: Bryan Bagge

Hoax

w Stuart Douglas
When Ward and his mother fall victim to hoaxers, it is thought that someone is having a go because they don't like policemen. Kingdom thinks otherwise.
Mrs Ward Betty Bascombe
Det. Insp. Clough John Ringham
Det. Sgt Bates Colin Rix

Director: John Reardon
Designer: Bryan Bagge

My Boy Robby?

w Tony Hoare
The discovery of a young girl's body by a woman out walking her dog, leads Detective Superintendent Kingdom and Sergeant Ward to a vicious murderer.
Det. Con. Thomas Dennis Blanch
Harry Watson Don Henderson
Robby Baylis Dennis Waterman

Director: Paul Annett
Designer: David Catley

Season Three

13 colour 60-minute episodes

Where's Harry?

w Tony Hoare
Assigned to investigate a prison escape, Detective Kingdom and Sergeant Ward have good reason to thank their experience in the field.
Harry Logan Derek Newark
Kenny Hall Geoffrey Hinsliff
Det. Insp. Mayer Anthony Langdon

Director: John Reardon
Designer: Andrew Drummond

Diamonds Are Never Forever

w Tony Hoare
When two masked men burst into the home of rich jeweller Eliot Ryan and his wife

Carlotta, Kingdom and Ward suspect an 'inside' job.
Eliot Ryan Gerald Sim
Carlotta Ryan Denise Buckley
George Reed Michael Culver

Director: Oliver Horsbrugh
Designer: Roger Hall

Bullet in a Haystack

w Don Houghton
William Radkin lies dead beside his bedroom window. He was murdered by a bullet fired from outside his house and Kingdom must discover the sniper's hiding place.
Radkin Peter Miles
PC Gunter Ken Halliwell
Sammy Cutler Sam Kydd

Director: Bill Turner
Designer: David Catley

Weight of Evidence

w Andrew Brown
When Kingdom and Ward bring two bank robbers to trial, but are unhappy with the verdict, things take a decidedly unpleasant turn.
Eddie Wharton Bob Hoskins
Al Farmer Michael Elphick
Det. Con Thomas Dennis Blanch

Director: Jim Goddard
Designer: Bryan Bagge

Crossfire

w Nicholas Palmer
When Manuel Barrios disappears in London, it looks like a straightforward case of kidnapping. But things are not always as they seem.
Manuel Barrios Nicholas Hoye
Sebastian Barrios Tony Robbins
Miguel Salvador Richard Dennis

Director: Paul Annett
Designer: Michael Yates

Property, Dogs and Women

w Stuart Douglas
It's Christmas – and a busy time for Kingdom and Ward who are called in to

investigate reports that a local police
division are treating juvenile gangs badly.
PC Trent Tony Selby
Mr Percy **Vic** Wise
Det. Insp Ridge Denys Hawthorne

Director: Paul Annett
Designer: Bryan Bagge

Exchange Is No Robbery

w Peter Hill
Investigations into a major bank robbery
lead Kingdom into a head-to-head
confrontation with a rival Regional Crime
Squad detective.
Chf Supt Piggot Peter Jeffrey
Alfie Brian Hill
Commander Connor Charles Morgan

Director: Bill Turner
Designer: David Catley

Daisy Chain

w Andrew Hall
Double-dealing and double death rears its
ugly head when Kingdom and Ward are
faced with clearing up an unsolved murder.
Det. Sgt Ross David Henry
Det. Sgt Coates Michael O'Hagen
Paget Maurice Good

Director: John Reardon
Designer: John Clements

Don't Go Out Alone

w Peter Wildeblood
What appears to be a straightforward
murder investigation takes an awkward turn
when Kingdom discovers the crime has an
unexpected link with the Foreign Office.
Leonid Vectis Sandor Eles
Enid Flint Pauline Taylor
Det. Sgt Murphy Roy Boyd

Director: Bill Turner
Designer: Andrew Gardner

The Stone

w James Andrew Hall
What should a civil servant do when he
finds his colleague dead – and his
confidential papers strewn across his desk?
Call in New Scotland Yard.

Jameson John Grieve
Secker Richard Cornish
PC Benson Adrian Shergold

Director: Bill Turner
Designer: Bryan Bagge

Monopoly

w Stuart Douglas
Why was Sidney Preece shot to death while
playing monopoly? Kingdom must find out
the facts before a second death takes place.
Sidney Preece Peter Birrel
Pamela Preece Susan Tracy
Det. Sgt Bates Colin Rix

Director: Cyril Coke
Designer: David Catley

Rogues Gallery

w John Lucarotti
When a Constable painting is stolen from a
collection and subsequently turns up on an
easel in the Hartmann Gallery, Kingdom
and Ward investigate.
Duschene Julian Glover
Sgt English Brian Osborne
Jean Rossen Janet Key

Director: Bill Bain
Designer: Roger Hall

Pier

w P. J. Hammond
Kingdom and his wife Angela take a holiday
to try to sort out their crumbling marriage
– but even an 'off-duty' policeman is a
policeman.
Angela Kingdom Sally Horne
Det. Sgt Edge Colin McCormack
Adams Ray Lonnen

Director: Cyril Coke
Designer: Rodney Cammish

Season Four

7 colour 60-minute episodes

Comeback

w P. J. Hammond
When Roper, a Borstal boy, is found
stabbed near his home, Detective Supt Clay

and Detective Sgt Dexter find several people have motives for the crime – including the boy's parents.

Mr Roper Richard Davies
Mrs Roper Julia McCarthy
Det. Insp. Moss Roger Hume

Director: Philip Casson
Designer: John Wood

The Trojan Horse

w Basil Dawson

A case of hijacking takes the interest of Detectives Clay and Dexter when a lorry driver is killed while attempting to stop his load being stolen.

Driver Peter Brayham
Joe Morris Arthur White
Det. Sgt Bradley Gil Sutherland

Director: Colin Cant
Designer: Rodney Cammish

Death by Misadventure

w Peter Wildeblood

When Det. Sgt Dexter investigates a burglary at a retired General's home and the burglar is found dead shortly afterwards, he must decide if there is a connection between the two incidents.

Joss Adrian Michael Elphick
General Travers Esmond Knight
Jessie Travers Miranda Bell

Director: Derek Goodwin
Designer: Barbara Bates

For All Their Faults

w Tony Hoare

Businessman Herbert Morris is arrested in connection with the murder of a young girl. Clay believes him innocent, Dexter thinks otherwise.

Herbert Morris William Lucas
Det. Insp Hall Ray Lonnen
Norma Morris Mary Kenton

Director: Oliver Horsbrugh
Designer: David Catley

A Man of His Word

w Peter Hill

When Warner is released from prison and finds his wife Polly has deserted him, he

vows to seek her out – and kill her. Clay and Dexter determine to stop him.

Warner Don Henderson
Polly Warner Heather Canning
Joe Shotter Robert Gary

Director: Oliver Horsbrugh
Designer: David Catley

All That Glitters

w Tony Hoare and Keith Bacchus

When gold is stolen from a ship's makeshift strongroom and a steward mysteriously disappears, Clay and Dexter investigate a case of murder near the Thames estuary.

Jack McNeil Stephen Yardley
Charlie Palmer Billy Murray
Bernard Hobbs Bill Dean

Director: Bill Turner
Designer: John Emery

A Year to Kill

w Stuart Douglas

The suspicious death of schoolmaster Graham Pitman draws the attention of Clay and Dexter – particularly when two teenagers confess to being responsible for the man's death.

Tommy Downs George Collis
Amber Thomas Jenny Duggan
Mr Duggan Tony Caunter

Director: Oliver Horsbrugh
Designer: Andrew Gardner

NEW SCOTLAND YARD
Producer: Jack Williams (throughout)
Executive producer: Rex Firkin (Seasons 1 and 2)
Story editor: Basil Dawson (throughout)
A London Weekend Television Network Production
45 colour 60-minute episodes
22 April – 15 July 1972
13 October 1972 – 12 January 1973
23 June – 15 September 1973
13 April – 25 May 1974

No Hiding Place

Further highlights from the career of Chief Detective Superintendent Lockhart, ITV's best-known policeman.

Having celebrated two years on air in *Murder Bag* and *Crime Sheet* (see entries under those names), Lockhart plunged into a new series of adventures, this time ensuring that villains had no place to hide from the long arm of the law.

As genial as ever, though with a slightly tougher edge to his character, the snuff-taking detective now found himself assigned to Scotland Yard, in a fast-paced series of exciting adventures whose slickness and regard to authenticity attracted even higher ratings than before — and would take him through over 8 further years with 230 investigations along the way, making the character a strong contender for British television's longest-running detective.

Along the way he had numerous assistants — the best remembered being Detective Sergeant Harry Baxter, a brilliant young detective who remained at Lockhart's side from episode 1 through 141 stories. (Midway through the series Baxter was transferred to E Division's famous Q car squad, and promoted from Sergeant to Inspector — a rank he retained when he returned to the Yard in 1963. See entry under *Echo Four Two*.)

When Baxter retired from the force we met Detective Sergeants Russell and Perryman, who stayed around for 70-odd episodes, and Lockhart's final assistant, Detective Sergeant Gregg, who appeared during the final season.

The series proved so successful that when it was cancelled in July 1965, protests from the public (and police) poured in and Lockhart was reinstated for a further two years.

With scripts supplied by the likes of Terence Feely, Leon Griffiths, Roger Marshall, Dennis Spooner and Terry Nation during its first two years, and a cross-over story in which Lockhart teamed up with spy chief Garetta from the *Top Secret* series to investigate an arson/murder case in London, it is little wonder that the series is regarded with fondness by viewers old enough to remember one of British television's best-loved detective heroes.

REGULAR CAST

Chf Det. Supt Lockhart **Raymond Francis**　*Det. Sgt Baxter* **Eric Lander**
Det. Sgt Russell **Johnny Briggs**　*Det. Sgt Perryman* **Michael McStay**
Det. Sgt Gregg **Sean Caffrey**

NO HIDING PLACE
Producers: Ray Dicks ('59/'62),
Richard Matthews ('62), Johnny Goodman
('62/'64), Peter Wiles ('65), Geoffrey
Nugus('65/'66),
Michael Currer-Briggs ('67)
Directors include: Cyril Coke, Ian Fordyce,
Jonathan Alwyn, Richard Gilbert, Bill
Hitchcock, Richard Doubleday, James
Ormerod, Chris Hodson
An Associated Rediffusion Network Production
236 monochrome 60-minute episodes
16 September 1959 – 22 June 1967

THE ODD MAN

The series that reached semi-cult status when it exploded onto an unwary public in the summer of 1962 – though contrary to popular belief it didn't introduce Chief Inspector Rose, the urbane, imperturbable policeman from Scotland Yard's CID division – at least not immediately. The detective of the piece in season one was Chief Inspector Gordon, a dour-faced, efficient and implacable policeman. (Rose actually made his debut in the second season.)

The series itself – a dark, weird and wonderful crime series with Hitchcockian overtones – was told in serial format (although each episode was complete in itself and had its own separate story) and related how five recurring characters interacted when faced with crimes of murder, vengeance and international intrigue. The main characters were: Steve Gardiner, a theatrical agent and part-time private investigator, who somehow always found himself mixed up in murder and mayhem; his wife Judy (who was 'murdered' in the first season – but miraculously returned for season three); a mysterious silent killer known only as South (first season only); CIs Gordon and Rose; and their police colleague Detective Sergeant Swift.

With the introduction of Chief Inspector Rose – at that time a rather unfriendly, sometimes harsh (to the point of inhumanity) detective – the series gained momentum and became avid viewing for devotees of detective drama. (See entries under *It's Dark Outside* and *Mr Rose*.)

REGULAR CAST

Steve Gardiner **Edwin Richfield**   *Chf Insp. Rose* **William Mervyn**
DS Swift **Keith Barron**   *Judy Gardiner* **Sarah Lawson**
Chf Insp. Gordon **Moultrie Kelsall**   *South* **Christopher Quinee**

Season One

8 monochrome 60-minute episodes
Note: No cast list available for first season.

The Raggle-Taggle Gypsy

w Edward Boyd

When an ex-Hungarian turns up mysteriously after having been missing for a whole year, is taken ill and then dies from an overdose of drugs, Steve Gardiner sets out to retrace the man's footsteps – and discovers a sinister clinc run by an ex-SS doctor.
Director: Derek Bennett

South American Way

w Edward Boyd

When Gardiner organises a British tour for a South American dance company and discovers a plot to discredit their patron, he intervenes on behalf of the British Government. But South, a hired killer, stalks his every move.
Director: Derek Bennett

The Circular Escape

w Edward Boyd

When Professor Preece is sent to prison for passing secrets to a foreign agent but escapes to settle accounts with the real traitor (his son), a chance meeting with Judy alerts Steve Gardiner to Preece's plans.
Director: Derek Bennett

A Hundred Feet of Film

w Edward Boyd

Before Gardiner can arrive at a sleazy hotel to keep a rendezvous with a man claiming to have important news, South kills the informer. Steve discovers the man's body and a reel of film – which sets him on the trail of a powerful, evil villain.
Director: Derek Bennett

Francis the Third

w Edward Boyd

A young boy 'adopts' Judy and declares that he will stay with her and Steve, and then produces a £100 note to pay his rent. This odd event leads Steve to uncover an assassination plot against a French politician, whom South has been hired to kill.
Director: Derek Bennett

A View to a Death

w Edward Boyd

When Judy has a nightmare during which she is murdered by a mute killer and then meets South, the man from her dreams, in the corridor of a train, Steve finds more than he bargained for on his return home - Judy is dead!
Director: Derek Bennett

The Great Big Question Mark

w Edward Boyd

Steve is approached by a young girl who asks him to sign a petition on behalf of the man who killed his wife and who is applying for a reprieve. They argue and the incident places both their lives in danger when Steve is mistaken for an American journalist.
Director: Derek Bennett

The House of D'Arblay

w Edward Boyd

The body of an actor, covered with flowers and found in a car, leads Steve to bait a trap for the killer – South, the mysterious assassin who murdered Judy. Steve unmasks the killer and South is brought to justice and hanged.
Director: Derek Bennett.

Season Two

8 monochrome 60-minute episodes

The Pretty Silver Game

w Edward Boyd

Enter Inspector Rose: 'Once you know me better, Sergeant, you will realise the most terrifying thing about me. I never get angry.' But what happens when Rose comes face to face with Gardiner's 'dead' wife Judy?
Ruth Jenkins Anna Cropper
Miss Twilight Jean Anderson
Linda Jordan Marina Martin

Director: Richard Everitt

The Last Bright Hours of Georgia Snow

w Edward Boyd

Rose and Swift find themselves tangled up in the mystery of Georgia Snow, a young girl who requested Steve Gardiner's assistance, but is now beyond help. She lies dead in her flat – her face a mask of terror.

Georgia Snow Lynne Furlong
Michael Dent Philip Anthony
Erica Somers Valerie Hanson

Director: Richard Everitt

The Double Image of Mother Eve

w Edward Boyd

Why should a nun request police protection? CI Rose and DS Swift will gladly assist the woman – providing they know what they are letting themselves in for – but Mother Eve has taken a vow of silence.

Mother Eve Noel Dyson
Acolyte Dennis Edwards
George Newman Anthony Bate

Director: Richard Everitt

Yesterday is for Psychiatrists

w Edward Boyd

Murder. Extortion. Policemen Rose and Swift have dealt with both. But when Steve Gardiner gets himself into hot water, Rose must do some quick thinking before he and Swift find themselves engulfed in mayhem of a different variety.

Mohammed Ali Steve Plytas
Simpson Gerrard Hely
Tina Sylvia Bidmead

Director: Richard Everitt

The Town That Dies at Eight

w Edward Boyd

A town where nobody sets foot outside after dark draws the attention of CI Rose. Why should everyone be so afraid? What dark mystery lurks in the shadows? Why is everyone running scared?

Sayers Jack May
Johnny Sayers Tim Seely
Delia Gwendoline Watts

Director: Eric Price

This Stuff's Thicker Than Water

w Edward Boyd

Jake Justice is a very determined man. When he wants CI Rose to reopen an unsolved case, the CID man has no option but to do so. At least that's what Justice believes – but then Rose is equally determined to allow the law to run its own course.

Jake Justice James Bolam
Brother Paul Alfred Burke
Weaver Ivor Dean

Director: Eric Price

The Betrayal of Ambrose Fleech

w Edward Boyd

'The people of this country have begun to lose faith in their country's security system. Do you agree, Inspector?' Rose does. But he won't allow a cover-up to stand in the way of his investigations.

Captain Burgan Michael Barrington
Maxine Higson Ingrid Hafner
Joshua Higson Donald Hewlett

Director: Richard Everitt

Prince on a White Horse

w Edward Boyd

'Last time, I offered you money. I offered you mercy. But you were too big for either. Next time it will be different. Tomorrow brings no mercy.' Inspector Rose has spoken. Villains beware.

Minerva Dane Kay Callard
Caroline Sutton Amanda Reiss
Victor West Peter Butterworth

Director: John Moxey

Season Three

8 monochrome 60-minute episodes

The Saga of Johnny Mac

w Harry Driver and Jack Rosenthal

Someone is out to send Johnny Mac to heaven – at least that's what Rose is expected to believe. But when someone leaves an explosive device in an empty office, the policeman plays a perilous game to find the motive.

Johnny Mac Toke Townley
Chemist Rex Boyd
Sergeant Bryan Mosely

Director: Richard Everitt

The Sheep 'Neath the Snow

w George Reed
CI Rose and DS Swift find themselves up
against a man determined to see the
Inspector drummed out of the force. 'Your
head will roll for this, Rose. And all I can
say is that I never saw a better shape for
rolling!'
Junkie Jeremy Kemp
Vera Annette Robinson
Drunk Henry McGee

Director: John Moxey

Portrait of Caroline

w John Finch
A confusing case for CI Rose. Day one: a
girl almost gets strangled and her husband
vanishes. Day two: he returns and gets
strangled, and then the wife vanishes!
What's amiss? Rose has 24 hours to solve
the mystery.
Harry Kapp Colin Jeavons
Lisa Kapp Judy Parfitt
Caroline Amanda Reiss

Director: Gerald Dynevor

Two Hundred and Forty-nine Pounds Twelve

w Edward Boyd
Tommy Fryer is a very methodical man. On
May 3, he had one shilling. May 6, one
shilling and sixpence. May 11 – five
shillings! Entries in a cash book which lead
CI Rose and DS Swift into a most unusual
affair.
Tommy Fryer Kenneth Nash
Cody Jeremy Bullock
Policeman Jack Austin

Director: Richard Everitt

A Pattern of Little Silver Devils

w Edward Boyd
Why do people become policemen?
Someone has to do the job. But this is one
time Rose wishes he had chosen another

profession. Digging into the private lives of
strangers isn't the most social activity.
Hugo Loveday Paul Whitsun-Jones
Aunt Jane Joan Haythorne
Mitch Scott Donald Sutherland

Director: Richard Everitt

The Long Wound

w Harry Driver and Jack Rosenthal
When a murderer appears to have left his
calling card, and wishes to be found, CI
Rose finds himself investigating an unusual
murder to which his theatrical friend Steve
Gardiner may hold the answer.
Osaku Donald Chann
Kosugi Robert Lee
Travis Patrick O'Connell

Director: Gerald Dynevor

A Kind of Wild Justice

w Edward Boyd
Murder comes in all shapes and all sizes.
The victim can be a person's mother, niece
or brother. Rose gets the impression that all
is not as it first appears when he is asked to
investigate a murder in family circles.
Mrs Gray Annette Kerr
Paul Ross Harry Landis
Sarah Ross Leonie Forbes

Director: Gerald Dynevor

A Last Tilt at the Windmill

w H.V. Kershaw and Peter Eckersley
'Look, you've had £10,000 worth of
publicity already. A murder arrest right in
your back pocket. Cut your losses. They
may be heavy.' – CI Rose. But will
Gardiner take his advice?
Bruce Dominic Donald Hewlett
Myra Keen Patricia Healey
Mrs Gianconelli Clare Kelly

Director: Stuart Latham

THE ODD MAN
Created by: Edward Boyd
Producer: Stuart Latham
A Granada TV Network Production
24 monochrome 60-minute episodes
11 May – 29 June 1962
5 April – 24 May 1963
26 July – 13 September 1963

OPERATION JULIE

This three-part dramatisation, based on a true story, charted how Inspector Richard Lee of the Thames Valley Drugs Squad mounted Britain's biggest drug hunt to smash a major international drugs syndicate.

In dramatic form it depicted how after a first-hand encounter with a teenage girl hooked on the devastating effects of the drug LSD, and discovering that the men responsible had set up a distribution network on his own patch, Lee mounted Operation Julie – a 13-month-long enquiry to track down the manufacturers, the distributors and the pushers behind the international drugs syndicate.

Armed only with a handful of rundown vehicles and two dozen police officers, he sidestepped opposition from other police forces and brought the gang to justice.

Tough and brutal in its portrayal of police undercover work and the stark reality of the effects of LSD, the programmes made for compulsive – though at times, harrowing – viewing.

CAST

DI Lee **Colin Blakely**   *DC Garrett* **Peter Baldwin**   *DS Creasey* **John Ainley**
DS Bates **Melanie Hughes**   *DC Wooley* **Clare Bonass**
DC Johnstone **Selena Carey-Jones**   *Truscott* **Michael Carter**
Chief Templeton **Alan Downer**   *Longfellow* **James Cosmo**
Det. Insp. Gough **Jon Laurimore**   *Ass. Chief Soames* **Robert McBain**

OPERATION JULIE
Dramatised by: Gerry O'Hara, Keith
Richardson and Bob Mahoney
(From a book by Colin Pratt and Dick Lee)
Producers: Malcolm Hayworth and
Peter Holmans
Executive producer: Keith Richardson
Director: Bob Mahoney
Designer: Ashley Wilkinson
A Tyne Tees Television Network Production
Produced in association with Chatsworth
Television
3 colour 60-minute episodes
4–5–6 November 1985

ORLANDO

The further adventures of Orlando O'Connor, the lovable rogue from *Crane* (see entry under that name), this time in a series of adventures made for children.

The first story set the series' format. Having returned to England and bought a rundown boat-building business, which swiftly fell into debt, Orlando packed his bags and headed for London's dockland to renew his friendship with Tony, an ex-Navy comrade – and hopefully to find work. But Tony was dead.

In the process of trying to discover how his friend died, Orlando struck up a friendship with Steve and Jenny Morgan, two teenagers who had inherited a private detective agency from their uncle.

Thereafter the stories depicted how Orlando and his friends always seemed to find themselves mixed up in adventures in and around London's busy dockland.

Popular material for the younger generation, the series spanned three years of less-than-intriguing adventures. (It transpired that Orlando was gifted with an ancient Arabic talisman (the *Gizzmo*) which sent out radio beams in emergencies and protected his life when in peril!!)

The first 13 episodes were self-contained stories, while the remaining 12 adventures (told in serialised format) spanned a further 63 episodes.

REGULAR CAST
Orlando **Sam Kydd**   *Steve* **David Munro**   *Jenny* **Judy Robinson**

ORLANDO
Producer: Ronald Marriott
Directors: Ronald Marriott, Hugh Munro,
Adrian Cooper
An Associated Rediffusion Production
76 colour 30-minute episodes
13 April 1965 – 10 June 1968

O.S.S.

A series of spy adventures with a difference – each story related actual events which took place in the tense atmosphere of World War II. This well-made collection of espionage adventures told the story of the Office of Strategic Services (a forerunner of the

CIA and wartime equivalent of Britain's MI5) and in particular, the exploits of ace spy-smasher, Major Frank Hawthorne.

Set up to fight sabotage, enemy spy groups and wartime intrigue, the OSS team were empowered to travel the world in the service of their country – though this series dealt mainly with the unit's activities in England and Europe.

With first-class, thrill-a-minute scripts, there was plenty to entertain the viewer – many of whom found themselves unable to resist the grab-you-by-the-throat opening title teaser: a Morse signal code superimposed over the OSS title, from which emerged a large document envelope with the words TOP SECRET emblazoned across its cover (plus that week's story title – usually prefixed by the word OPERATION). While this was taking place, an announcer's voice was heard to exclaim: 'Stories straight from the annals of one of America's most effective wartime intelligence services . . . the OSS!'

REGULAR CAST

Major Frank Hawthorne **Ron Randell**   *His OSS Controller* **Lionel Murton**

OSS
Producer: Jules Buck
An ITC/Buckeye Enterprises Production
26 monochrome 30-minute episodes
22 September 1957 – 9 March 1958
(USA: September 1957 – March 1958
ABC Syndicated)

PATHFINDERS

The further adventures of the Wedgwood family, introduced four months earlier in *Target Luna* (see entry under that name).

Hardly *Star Wars*, these made-on-a-shoestring children's space adventures were nevertheless good, clean, Boy's Own-type adventure fare which kept younger viewers glued to their seats. (All three serials were transmitted as part of the early afternoon 'Family Hour' programme.)

For easy reference, the adventures have been listed in chronological transmission order.

REGULAR CAST

Professor Wedgwood **Peter Williams** Conway Henderson **Gerald Flood**
Geoffrey Wedgwood **Stewart Guidotti** Valerie Wedgwood **Gillian Ferguson**
Jimmy Wedgwood **Richard Dean** Professor Meadows **Pamela Barney**

Story One

Pathfinders in Space

w Malcolm Hulke and Eric Paice
(A 7-part serial)

Having successfully put a man into space, Professor Wedgwood himself blasted off to pilot man's first mission to set foot on the Moon. Having landed on its surface, the Professor found himself stranded when his back-up supply rocket refused to function properly due to the breakdown of its automatic pilot.

His mission looked doomed until his children and science journalist Conway Henderson set out to save the day by taking a second supply rocket into space – before they, too, found their rescue mission jeopardised by a strange alien spacecraft which blocked their flight path. Having negotiated their way past the space intruder, they landed on the lunar surface and saved the Professor's life. Along the way they made a startling discovery that an ancient civilisation had landed on the moon years before them, and they shared an exciting flight home when their spaceship was threatened once again (this time by a shower of rogue meteorites) before they successfully returned to Terra Firma!

Convoy to the Moon
Spaceship from Nowhere·
Luna Bridgehead
The Man in the Moon
The World of Lost Toys
Disaster on the Moon
Rescue in Space

Director: **Guy Verney**
Designer: **Tom Spaulding** (Eps 1, 3–7)
          David Gillespie (Eps 1–2)

Story Two

Pathfinder to Mars

w Malcolm Hulke and Eric Paice
(A 6-part serial)

Following directly on the tail of the previous story, this picked up shortly after Professor Wedgwood and his team's triumphant return to Earth. Almost immediately, the scientist made plans to mount a second expedition to Mars.

Due to an injury he'd received on the previous mission (a broken arm), Wedgwood himself was unable to lead the mission so he entrusted the job of piloting his new inter-stellar rocket MR4 to his friend Henderson. Together with the Professor's son Geoffrey and Henderson's niece Margaret, Professor Meadows (the world's leading female authority on space) and her pet hamster Hamlet, the crew awaited the arrival of the last crew member, Professor Hawkins, an Australian space expert.

Unknown to them, the real Hawkins had been replaced by Harcourt Brown – a fanatical scientist who believed that there was life on Mars and who was looking to prove his theory at the MR4 crew's peril.

Having taken control of the spaceship and reprogrammed its on-board computer to take them to Mars, Brown's theories faded to nothing when they actually landed on the red planet. All they found were airless deserts and dust, which forced the crew to make a hazardous journey to find water – a trek which found them attacked by huge lichen plants which grew at incredible speed (courtesy of time-lapse camera work) and facing certain extinction on the planet's barren surface. (They managed to escape of course, thus leaving the way open for a third adventure.)

The Impostor
Sabotage in Space
The Hostage
Lichens
Zero Hour on the Red Planet
Falling into the Sun

Professor Wedgwood **Peter Williams**
(Ep 1 only)
Harcourt Brown **George Coulouris**
Director: **Guy Verney**
Designer: **David Gillespie**

Story Three

Pathfinders to Venus

w Malcolm Hulke and Eric Paice
(An 8-part serial)

While returning from their hazardous mission to Mars, the crew of MR4 picked up a distress signal from the vicinity of the planet Venus. This turned out to be an SOS from a rival space explorer Captain Wilson, an American astronaut.

Together with Brown, the ship's uninvited guest, Henderson led a rescue mission to Venus – but all they found were the ransacked remains of the American's spaceship, and evidence of an alien lifeform.

Leaving the rest of the crew to ponder this puzzle, Brown found the missing astronaut and listened with interest as Wilson told of his encounter with a strange race of primitive men who worshipped flying reptiles. Having forced the astronaut to lead him to the tribe's camp site, Brown and Wilson found themselves held prisoner – leaving the way open for Henderson to rescue them from the reptiles (pterodactyls) and escape under cover of an erupting volcano, before Henderson and his crew discovered that fate had dealt them a cruel hand – the MR4 had been engulfed in flames by the volcanic ash.

Did they escape? Of course they did (this was a children's programme, remember) – but no further episodes were forthcoming.

SOS from Venus
Into the Poison Cloud
The Living Planet
The Creature
The Venus People
The City
The Valley of Monsters
Planet on Fire

Captain Wilson **Graydon Gould**
Director: **Guy Verney** (Eps 1–5, 7)
          Reginald Collin (Eps 6, 8)
Designer: **David Gillespie** (Eps 1–8)
          Douglas James (Eps 6–8)

PATHFINDERS
Created by Malcolm Hulke and Eric Paice
Producer: Sydney Newman
Programme adviser: Mary Field
An ABC Weekend Network Production
21 monochrome 30-minute episodes
11 September – 23 October 1960
11 December 1960 – 15 January 1961
5 March – 23 April 1961

THE PERSUADERS

Take Daniel Wilde, an irrepressible, fun-loving American who had dragged his way out of the New York slums, and made (and lost) his first million before his thirtieth birthday. A man with a remarkable talent for making money – but who used that gift solely to squander away his riches pursuing the life of an international thrill-seeking playboy. Team him with Lord Brett Sinclair, a 'flower of the British aristocracy', a man born to a family motto of honour, justice and fair play – but who had side-stepped his pedigree in favour of womanising, fast cars and an easy lifestyle; and add Judge Fulton, a retired lawkeeper who had spent his life defending the innocent and punishing the guilty, while watching the justice he served to allow others not worthy of its mercy to slip through the net to continue their life of crime. Put them together and you had *The Persuaders*, two daredevil playboys seeking adventure who were blackmailed into becoming the lawman's 'instruments of justice' – defenders of the law as dispensed by Judge Fulton in his campaign to rid the world of villainy.

Projected to run for five seasons of 26 episodes, the series was cancelled when it failed to attract an audience in the US (it was beaten to the punch by *Mission Impossible* – then at the height of its success) and only 24 episodes were produced.

A glossy, lively comedy/suspense adventure series which earned its stars a fortune – for playing themselves!

REGULAR CAST

Danny Wilde Tony Curtis   *Lord Brett Sinclair* Roger Moore
Judge Fulton Laurence Naismith

Overture

w Brian Clemens

Danny and Brett set out on their first assignment – to find a brunette whose heart-shaped birthmark could prove her real identity. An exciting prospect, but one that leads them into danger and intrigue
Maria Imogen Hassall
Coley Alex Scott
Dupont Michael Godfrey

Director: Basil Dearden

The Gold Napoleon

w Val Guest

Is there gold beneath the bronze of Napoleon gold replicas? That's what Danny and Brett must find out – providing someone allows them to do so – after setting up Danny as a real live (but almost dead) target.
Pullicino Alfred Marks
Michelle Susan George
Devigne Harold Goldblatt

Director: Roy Ward Baker

Take Seven

w Terry Nation

The mysterious reappearance of a 'long lost brother' seeking his share of a rich estate finds the Persuaders in the firing line when they try to help a young girl with family problems on her mind.

Jenny Lindley Sinead Cusack
Mark Lindley Christian Roberts
Maggie Sue Lloyd

Director: Sidney Hayers

Greensleeves

w Terence Feely

When a derelict old mansion suddenly reopens its doors without the knowledge of its owner, Brett Sinclair, Danny finds new employment – as butler to Brett Sinclair, who impersonates himself to uncover the mystery.
Melanie Rosemary Nicols
Sir John Andrew Keir
Congoto Cy Grant

Director: David Greene

Powerswitch

w John Kruse

A dead girl found floating in a Côte d'Azur bay. Her beautiful flatmate with something to hide. Two pieces of a puzzle that plunge Danny and Brett into dangerous waters – inhabited by human sharks.
Pekoe Annette Andre
Insp. Blanchard Paul Whitsun-Jones
Crane Terence Alexander

Director: Basil Dearden

The Time and the Place

w Michael Pertwee

Beautiful girls and the Persuaders go hand in hand. But when the playboys offer to help a young girl stranded on a country road, the 'damsel in distress' proves quite incapable of keeping her honour.

Lord Croxley Ian Hendry
Marie Anna Palk
Ryder Patrick O'Connell

Director: Roger Moore

Someone Like Me

w Terry Nation

One Brett Sinclair is almost too much for Danny to handle, but two prove unbearable – particularly when Danny finds himself on the receiving end of the fake Brett's activities. Danny's dilemma: who is the real one and who is the impostor?

Dr Fowler Reginald Marsh
Nurse Crane Anne de Vigier
Milford Bernard Lee

*Director:*Roy Ward Baker

Anyone Can Play

w Tony Williamson

Danny discovers a gold mine. Gambling in a Brighton casino and finding he isn't allowed to lose, he plays for high stakes – and finds that he has difficulty in disposing of his winnings. Until death plays its hand.

Lyn Cyd Hayman
Ryker Ed Deveraux
Sir Maxwell Richard Vernon

Director: Leslie Norman

The Old, the New and the Deadly

w Brian Clemens

Birds have always been Danny's weakness – the female variety of course. But when he becomes involved with a fanatical ex-Nazi, a girl who is trying to clear her father's name, and a statuette of a bird, he's guaranteed to make the feathers fly.

Suzy Anna Gael
Groski Derren Nesbitt
Verner Kenneth J. Warren

Director: Leslie Norman

Angie . . . Angie

w Milton S. Gelman

A weekend of fun and champagne at the Cannes Film Festival turns into a deadly life-taking scenario, when Danny meets up with Angie, a boyhood friend from the Bronx – a man with murder on his mind.

Angie Larry Storch
Marissa Kirsten Lindholm
Ben Lionel Murton

Director: Val Guest

Chain of Events

w Terry Nation

Life under canvas for Brett means deep freezers and feather beds, while Danny makes do with roughing it. So while Brett digests his ready-made breakfast, Danny casts a fishing line to catch his – and hooks a load of trouble for both men.

Schubert Peter Vaughan
Emily Suzanna Leigh
Britten George Baker

Director: Peter Hunt

That's Me Over There

w Brian Clemens

Thaddeus Krane has grown fat on famine and wealthy on war. Someone is out to expose him for the crook he is – which results in the informer being killed, Brett being kidnapped and Danny posing as a not-so-likely English lord!

Thaddeus Krane Geoffrey Keen
Anne Summers Susan Farmer
Colonel Wright Allan Cuthbertson

Director: Leslie Norman

The Long Goodbye

w Michael Pertwee

The discovery by Danny and Brett of a skeleton in a crashed plane in the Scottish Highlands leads the two thrill-seekers into an adventure from which they emerge smelling ever-so-slightly from murder.

Sir Hugo Chalmers Leo Genn
Carla Nicola Pagett
Theopolos Noel Willman

Director: Roger Moore

The Man in the Middle

w Donald James

When Brett is captured while trying to trap a British traitor and Danny has to rescue him before his cover is blown, who better to help him than another noble Sinclair – Archibald Sinclair Beauchamp. A mistake – as Danny discovers to his cost.

Archie Terry Thomas
Kay Suzy Kendall
Krilov Stephen Greif

Director: Leslie Norman

Element of Risk

w Tony Barwick

When someone mistakes Danny for the undisputed mastermind of crime, a planner of pure genius, Danny is prepared to play along – even though his life depends on the outcome. Brett meanwhile has troubles of his own.

Lomax Shane Rimmer
Carl William Marlowe
Joan Karen Kessey

Director: Gerald Mayer

A Home of One's Own

w Terry Nation

When Danny buys a 'little piece of England' – a cottage in the country – and the locals turn nasty, his dreams of becoming an English squire end up in ashes. Brett meanwhile meets a lady birdwatcher – who carries a gun!

Lucy Hannah Gordon
Hatherway John Ronane
Abel Gaunt Leon Greene

Director: James Hill

Five Miles to Midnight

w Terry Nation

Opening a travel business can have its drawbacks, as Danny and Brett discover when their first customer turns out to be Frank Rocco, a New York hoodlum on the run from a gang of Italian mobsters.

Frank Rocco Robert Hutton
Sidonie Joan Collins
Torino Robert Rietty

Director: Val Guest

Nuisance Value

w David Wolfe and Tony Barwick

When someone forcibly takes away Danny's latest girlfriend, heiress to a fantastic fortune, the Bronx-born playboy and his partner Lord Brett Sinclair decide to nip their adversary's passion-flower in the bud – with somewhat unexpected results.

Lisa Vivienne Ventura
Mary Sarah Lawson
Michel Ralph Bates

Director: Leslie Norman

The Morning After

w Walter Black

When Brett awakens after a heavy night's drinking party and finds he has a wife – a very glamorous one, too – it takes more than Danny's friendship to untangle the surrounding web of intrigue.

Kristen Catherine Schell
Jon Tony Bonner
Christianson Bernard Horsfall

Director: Leslie Norman

Read and Destroy

w Peter Yeldham

When Felix Meadows, a man wanted after an audacious East-West double cross, turns to Brett for sanctuary, Sinclair sends him to his stately home in Berkshire – but someone watches their every move and things don't turn out as planned.

Meadows Joss Ackland
Cavendish Nigel Green
Heidi Kate O'Mara

Director: Roy Ward Baker

A Death in the Family

w Terry Nation

The Sinclair clan is shrinking. Some distant relative is playing out his own game of 'Kind Hearts and Coronets' by killing off everyone who stands between him and the Sinclair title. Will Brett be the next to die? Whose face lies behind the killer's smile?

The General/The Admiral/
Lady Agatha Roger Moore
Kate Diane Cilento
Roland Denholm Elliot

*Director:*Sidney Hayers

The Ozerov Inheritance

w Harry H. Junkin
The Grand Duchess Ozerov requires Brett
and Danny's help. Someone has laid claim
to ownership of the family jewels and they
must prove the Duchess's right. Doing so
leads them to uncover a death in the past –
and one in the present.
Duchess Gladys Cooper
Sergie Gary Raymond
Yelker Jospeh Furst

Director: Roy Ward Baker

To the Death, Baby

w Donald James
Hired to break up the friendship between
Shelley Masterson, a beautiful heiress and
her dubious boyfriend, Danny and Brett
find that a bit of soft soap can make anyone
slip – right into the dirty money laundry
business.

Shelley Jennie Linden
Foster Terence Morgan
Hatton Thorley Walters

Director: Basil Dearden

Someone Waiting

w Terry Nation
The victim, Lord Brett Sinclair – the
suspect, Danny Wilde?! When Danny gets
whiff that someone is out to sabotage his
friend's dreams of becoming a world-beating
motor-racing driver, his efforts to avoid
disaster leave Brett at the starting gate.
Carrie Penelope Horner
Brothers John Cairney
Louise Lois Maxwell

Director: Peter Medak

THE PERSUADERS
Created by: Robert S. Baker
Producer: Robert S. Baker
Associate producers: Terry Nation and
Johnny Goodman
Music by: Ken Thorne
(Persuaders theme by: John Barry)
Story consultant: Terry Nation
Co-story consultant: Milton S. Gelman
A Tribune Production
Made on location and at Pinewood Studios
24 colour 60-minute episodes
17 September 1971 – 25 February 1972
(USA: ABC 18 September 1971 – 14 June
1972
Syndicated 24 Episodes)

POLICE SURGEON

Centred around the medical casebook of Dr Geoffrey Brent, a
young police surgeon assigned to the Bayswater area police
division, this short-lived doctor-encounters-crime and can't
resist becoming involved in his cases oater, is best remembered
for giving Ian Hendry his first crack at television stardom. This
outing failed to set the pulses beating, and barely five weeks later
Hendry would unpack his stethoscope in the cause of justice as
Dr David Keel in *The Avengers*.

REGULAR CAST

Dr Geoffrey Brent Ian Hendry   *Insp. Landon* John Warwick
Amanda Gibbs Ingrid Hafner

Easy Money

w Julian Bond

Called on to give evidence in connection
with a young man arrested for robbery, Dr
Geoffrey Brent gives his opinion – but one
that is far-removed from that expected by
the arresting officer.
Sgt Manning Alistair Williamson
Young thief Michael Crawford
Insp. Landon John Warwick

Director: John Knight

Under the Influence

w Julian Bond

A man arrested for drunken driving leads Dr
Brent into conflict with a fellow practitioner
who believes the man guilty as charged.
Brent thinks otherwise – but must prove his
theory to the satisfaction of the police.
Insp. Landon John Warwick
Herbert Drew Bernard Archard
Barrister Heron Carvic

Director: Don Leaver

Lag on the Run

w Julian Bond

Police surgeon Geoffrey Brent plays the role
of private detective when a girl confesses to
a crime she obviously didn't commit – a
confession that brings unforeseen
consequences for both himself and the girl.
Jean Young Olive McFarland
George Drake Harry H. Corbett
Amanda Gibbs Ingrid Hafner (Intro.)

Director: Don Leaver

Smash but No Grab

w Julian Bond

When Sally Hughes, an attractive woman
injured in a road accident, presses her claim
for damages, Dr Brent finds himself in a
situation which neither he nor the police can
overcome.

Sally Hughes Joyce Heron
PC Gregson Neil Wilson
Peter Hughes Geoffrey Palmer

Director: Don Leaver

Wilful Neglect

w Julian Bond

When two children are discovered,
apparently abandoned, Police Surgeon
Geoffrey Brent uncovers the unsolvable
problems which lie behind the outwardly
happy faces of loving parents.
Harry Davis Nigel Stock
Jean Davis Hazel Hughes
Mrs Carver Patience Collier

Director: Don Leaver

You Won't Feel a Thing

w Julian Bond

Desperately seeking a way to save a patient's
life, Dr Brent must first overcome a small
girl's fear of doctors – and of hypodermic
needles in particular. Without an injection,
the girl faces certain death.
Helen Graham Mavis Ransom
PC Robinson Ivor Salter
Insp. Landon John Warwick

Director: Robert Hartford-Davis

A Home of Her Own

w Bill MacIllwraithe

Accident-prone Mrs Lamond presents a
danger to herself and her neighbours, but
her independence adds to Dr Brent's
dilemma when he has to decide whether to
place the old lady in a nursing home – as
requested by her far from loving in-laws.
Mrs Lamond Jane Eccles
George Lamond Donald Morley
Insp. Landon John Warwick

Director: Don Leaver

Sunday Morning Story

w Julian Bond

Called in to give evidence on the cause of death of a young female refugee, Dr Brent finds himself facing a tough case. It appears that neither he nor the police have sufficient evidence to lay the blame on the person responsible.

Miss Pears Jean Anderson
PC Jordan Donald Churchill
Second Police Surgeon Michael Harrison

Director: Don Leaver

Three's a Crowd

w Julian Bond

What appears to be an unsurmountable problem – a charge of assault by a domineering woman and her daughter-in-law – ends up as a test of strength between Dr Brent and a defending barrister.

Mrs Carroll Elizabeth Begley
Kathy Baker Maureen O'Reily
Baker Percy Herbert

Director: Don Leaver

Man Overboard

w Bill MacIllwraithe

A body found beneath a balcony draws Police Surgeon Geoffrey Brent into a tough case involving two women – and a possible charge of murder. His evidence can prove one or the other guilty of murder.

Miss Perkins Anne Castle
Mrs Perkins Helen Lindsay
Insp. Landon John Warwick

Director: Guy Verney

Operation Mangle

w W. F. Woodlands

When George Bates rallies his neighbours against an unscrupulous landlord, Dr Brent finds himself as pig in the middle – trying to breach the barricade erected by the tenants to reach an injured man.

George Bates Dudley Foster
Alice Bates Edna Petrie
Insp. Landon John Warwick

Director: James Ormerod

The Bigger They Are

w Richard Harris

Called in to attend to a nightwatchman's wounds caused by robbers, Dr Brent and Inspector Landon discover another wounded man clinging for his life to a ledge near the warehouse roof. Their dilemma: what's he doing there and is he one of the robbers?

Nightwatchman Blaise Wyndham
West James Cilliford
Insp. Landon John Warwick

Director: Don Leaver

POLICE SURGEON
Producer: Julian Bond (Eps 1–3 and 8)
Leonard White (remainder)
Story editor: Julian Bond
Designer for series: Alpho O' Reily
An ABC Television Network Production
12 monochrome 30-minute episodes
10 September – 3 December 1960

PRETORIUS

Heralding the arrival of a new television detective, Inspector Andries Pretorius, of the Belgian police, this two-hour pilot, starring actor Clive Wood – so convincing as Blair, Mr Palfrey's 'heavy' in *Mr Palfry of Westminster* – introduced viewers to the hard-nosed, no-nonsense detective as he attempted to carry out a job he would much rather not have had, tracking down a consignment of South American cocaine meant for the streets of

Bruges, and finding out who was behind the related death of a colleague.

Thwarted at every turn by a criminal who cleverly let others do the dirty work and thereby kept his own hands – and reputation – clean, Pretorius found that there was more than one way to trap a rat.

Slow, but thoroughly entertaining, one hopes that a series will follow.

CAST

Pretorius Clive Wood   *Klosters* John Labanowski   *Huizinga* Tony Melody
Foster Bruce McGuire   *De Jong* Michael Turner   *Vaneck* Stephen Grief
Tanji Elsa O'Toole   *'Foxy' Rynaert* Cyril Appleton   *Le Brun* Timothy Morand

PRETORIUS
Created & written by: Michael Chapman
Producer: Michael Chapman
Executive Producers: Lloyd Shirley and
Brian Walcroft
Director: Alex Clarke
A thames Television Network Production
Colour – 115 minutes
1 September 1987

THE PRISONER

The series that elevated television adventure series to the pinnacle of success and aroused so much interest that even today, 20 years after its first transmission, it remains one of the oddest and most thought-provoking television experiences of all time. A series so stunningly different that it became a major cult and spawned a worldwide appreciation society (Six of One) which is viewed as the frontrunner among the many television-related fan clubs which have sprung up to commemorate what many believe to be television's silver years – the decade between 1960 and 1970.

Following closely on the heels of Patrick McGoohan's successful *Danger Man* series (see entry under that name), viewers who expected a continuation of the exploits of the super-cool agent John Drake were in for a rude awakening. With few exceptions, viewers all over the world were totally bemused by what they saw: the surrealistic adventures of a man with no name – only a number. An ex-spy known only as Number Six. A man marooned in a mysterious village from which he would never escape – but spent each waking hour attempting to do so.

Imprisoned in his cottage/cell, watched on every side by closed circuit television cameras, he determined to outwit his chief adversary Number Two, and discover the identity of Number One — a man set on brainwashing the secrets from the mind of his tormented captive. ('Where am I? In the village. What do you want? Information. You won't get it!')

Without debating the longevity of the programme, or trying to qualify its lasting appeal, it's enough to say that this was Patrick McGoohan's personal *tour de force*. He thought up the idea, wrote and directed some of the episodes, was executive producer for the entire series — and starred in the title role.

Like it or hate it, the programme was (and remains) a slice of television history. There has been nothing like it before or since, and it remains a challenging, inventive tribute to its creator.

REGULAR CAST

Number Six Patrick McGoohan   *The Butler* Angelo Muscat
Number Two Leo McKern   Colin Gordon   Peter Wyngarde   Mary Morris
Guy Doleman   *Number Forty-eight* Alexis Kanner

Arrival

w George Markstein and David Tomblin
A menacing roll of thunder. A tiny sports car zooming through the streets of London. Doors that are flung back to the sound of thunderclaps as an unnamed man slams down his resignation on his superior's desk. A return drive home to pack for a holiday. An ominous black hearse parked outside his window. A cloud of billowing gas and the man falls unconscious . . . to awaken in a strange and mysterious village.
The man has become . . . *The Prisoner*, a man with no name, just a number.
The reason for his abduction — his resignation. 'They' wish to know why he resigned. *He* won't tell. He attempts to escape. But there is no escape. He has become Number Six — a man who can trust no one but himself.
Number Two Guy Doleman
Cobb Paul Eddington
The Woman Virginia Maskell
The New Number Two George Baker

Director: Don Chaffey

The Chimes of Big Ben

w Vincent Tilsley
Nadia, a new arrival in the village, is moved into the cottage next to Number Six. She too has recently resigned her job. She too tries to escape — alone, before accepting her neighbour's help. Using her contacts they escape to London — or do they?
Number Two Leo McKern
The General Finlay Currie
Nadia Nadia Grey
Fotheringay Richard Wattis

Director: Don Chaffey

A, B and C

w Anthony Skene
In a bid to discover why the Prisoner resigned, Number Two decides to risk subjecting him to a new experimental process in which his dreams can be penetrated. Under its influence, Number Six *must* relay the truth — or is he playing a game of cat and mouse with his captors?

Number Two Colin Gordon
Engadine Katherine Kath
Number Fourteen Sheila Allen
'A' Peter Bowles

Director: Pat Jackson

Free for All

w Patrick McGoohan
The Prisoner stands for election as the new Number Two, but finds that his rights are just as limited as before. Is the election genuine or just another trick? And why should the current Number Two appear to greet his election speech with enthusiastic applause?
Number Two Eric Portman
Number Fifty-eight Rachel Herbert
Labour Exchange Manager George Benson

Director: Patrick McGoohan

The Schizoid Man

w Terence Feely
Number Two puts into operation his latest ploy to break the Prisoner – his exact double and a girl who claims a telepathic link with Number Six. While he sleeps, a form of brainwashing reverses his brain pattern – but not his instinct for survival or his determination to escape!
Number Two Anton Rodgers
Alison Jane Merrow
Supervisor Earl Cameron

Director: Pat Jackson

The General

w Lewis Greifer
'Speedlearn' and a sublimator device. The latest process to keep the village occupants subservient. Both are distrusted by Number Six who, with the help of Number Twelve, a young man, manages to thwart Number Two's latest project – though not without loss of life.
Number Two Colin Gordon
Number Twelve John Castle
The Professor Peter Howell

Director: Peter Graham Scott

Many Happy Returns

w Anthony Skene
When the Village appears abandoned – so far as he can tell, the Prisoner is alone – Number Six sees the chance to escape. Building a raft he does so, but finds himself a prisoner once more – this time in the hands of his friends and colleagues in London.
The Colonel Donald Sinden
Thorpe Patrick Cargill
Mrs Butterworth Georgina Cookson

Director: Joseph Serf

Dance of the Dead

w Anthony Skene
Having discovered a body washed up on the shore and removed the dead man's wallet and a radio which works but emits only cryptic messages, Number Six puts his own identification on the body and refloats it in the barren hope that it will be found and a search initiated. Returning to the Village he discovers the drowned man – and is placed on trial.
Number Two Mary Morris
The Doctor Duncan Macrae
The Observer Norma West

Director: Don Chaffey

Checkmate

w Gerald Kelsey
The Prisoner plays a dangerous game when invited to take part in an unusual game of chess: the board is a lawn, the chess pieces people. Unknown to the Prisoner, the Queen has been brainwashed by Number Two, who intends to use her attraction to Number Six to destroy him.
Number Two Peter Wyngarde
The Rook Ronald Radd
The Queen Rosalie Crutchley
Man with the Stick George Coulouris

Director: Don Chaffey

Hammer into Anvil

w Roger Woddis
Swearing to avenge the death of a girl whose appeals for help when being persecuted by

Number Two go unheard, Number Six attempts to trick Number Two into believing that he is a decoy sent from the outside world to spy on him.
Number Two Patrick Cargill
Number Fourteen Basil Hoskins
Psychiatrist Norman Scace

Director: Pat Jackson

It's Your Funeral

w Michael Cramoy
Number Two promotes his latest weapon in the fight to gain information from Number Six – misinformation. In order to stop the Prisoner foiling an assassination attempt, Number Six is fed incorrect information which leads him to cry 'wolf' just once too often.
Number Two Derren Nesbitt
Watchmaker's daughter Annette Andre
Number One Hundred Mark Eden

Director: Robert Asher

A Change of Mind

w Roger Parkes
The Prisoner falls foul of further attempts to gain his secrets – he becomes the latest victim of an instant social conversion process designed to change the villager's attitudes. The attractive Number Eighty-six is the bait – but will the Prisoner bite?
Number Two John Sharpe
Number Eighty-six Angela Browne
The Doctor George Pravda

Director: Joseph Serf

Do Not Forsake Me

w Vincent Tilsley
The Prisoner's nightmare continues. Awaking in his own London flat – but with the body of a stranger and his memory tampered with – he finds that no one recognises him: not his fiancée, her father, nor even Sir Charles, one of his former employers. Has Number Two finally won the game?
Number Two Clifford Evans
Janet Zena Walker
The Colonel Nigel Stock

Director: Pat Jackson

Living in Harmony

w David Tomblin   (**From a story by Ian L. Rakoff**)
When the Prisoner suddenly finds himself in a Western town where he has been appointed sheriff, he faces mental conflict when he refuses to wear guns – even though a gunfight is unavoidable.
The Kid Alexis Tanner
The Judge David Bauer
Kathy Valerie French

Director: David Tomblin

The Girl Who Was Death

w Terence Feely
She calls herself Death. A worthy opponent for Number Six – the Survivor. When the two meet something must give. But who will remain when the two pit themselves in a head-to-head battle? A bedtime story with a difference, or the Prisoner's flight of fantasy?
Sonia Justine Lord
Schnipps Kenneth Griffith
Potter Christopher Benjamin

Director: David Tomblin

Once upon a Time

w Patrick McGoohan
When the Prisoner and Number Two face a deadly conflict of wills, one man must break. For the loser it spells the end, but Number Six is well aware of the risks he's undertaking. Prepared for the ordeal he faces relentless interrogation to discover why he resigned – but will his secrets be known when the challenge is over?
Number Two Leo McKern
Supervisor Peter Swanick
Umbrella Man John Cazabon

Director: Patrick McGoohan

Fall Out

w Patrick McGoohan
The final trial begins. Its outcome will decide the Prisoner's fate. Will he remain entombed in the village or finally win the right to be treated as a free man? Will he escape to begin life anew? Will Number

One finally be unmasked? The question is resolved when, together with Number Forty-eight and the Butler they engineer their freedom and return to London . . .

. . . A menacing roll of thunder. A tiny sports car zooming through the streets of London. We see the driver's face. His expression is grim . . .

The end – or the beginning?

Number Two **Leo McKern**
Number Forty-eight **Alexis Kanner**
The President **Kenneth Griffith**

Director: **Patrick McGoohan**

THE PRISONER
Producer: David Tomblin
Executive producer: Patrick McGoohan
Music by: Albert Elms
(Prisoner theme by: Ron Grainer)
Script editor: George Markstein
An ITC Production by Everyman Films
Made on location at Hotel Portmeirion, Penrhyndeudraeth, North Wales
and at MGM Studios, Borehamwood
17 colour 60-minute episodes
29 September 1967 – 2 February 1968
(USA: CBS 1 June – 21 September 1968)
The story entitled 'Living in Harmony' was never transmitted during the series' network schedule, but reappeared in syndication.

THE PROFESSIONALS

The activities of the men who worked for a special undercover crimebusting unit, Criminal Intelligence 5 (CI5) – a select group of men (and women) who were professionals by trade and professionals by nature. Men who had a very special brief: to elevate criminal intelligence to the sophisticated levels that already existed in military intelligence, and thereby attempt to defuse criminal situations before they had the chance to escalate, or strike at the heart of such activities if and when they got out of hand.

Men like George Cowley (affectionately referred to as 'The Cow'), controller of CI5. Having accepted the challenge of forming the unit to combat an increasing wave of terrorism, Cowley, a tough, straight-talking, no-nonsense ex-MI5 administrator, set about selecting the right men for the job – tough, hard men to deal with tough, hard situations. Men who could shake down the enemy and crush their criminal activities before they even started to grow. Men who could get in first and ensure that the streets of England were safe and 'smelling, even if ever so faintly, of roses and lavender' – a motley crew whom Cowley welded together into an exceptional crimefighting squad who fought violence with violence and organised crime with dedication and panache.

His two most dedicated assistants were Bodie and Doyle – dubbed by their controller as 'The Bisto Kids'.

If there was anyone in CI5 tougher than Bodie, they hadn't proved it. A tough ex-SAS and Parachute Regiment veteran, Bodie feared nothing. A powerful, pugnacious man who exuded the confidence of a man who knew he could handle himself in any situation, Bodie was the unit's star turn.

Sharing a spirited, often abrasive relationship with Bodie (but one that was always tempered by a mutual respect), was Ray Doyle. An ex-CID detective from London's infamous East End beat, Doyle's deceptively quiet exterior camouflaged a deadly temper. When he was aroused, there was no place to hide – until the job was safely under wraps.

Abounding with spectacular action, the series performed consistently well in the ratings (maintaining a top five place with each outing) and became an enormous success (although the majority of its critics described the programme as over violent).

REGULAR CAST

George Cowley Gordon Jackson *Bodie* Lewis Collins
Doyle Martin Shaw *Murphy* Steve Alder (eight appearances Seasons Four/Five)

Season One
13 colour 60-minute episodes

Old Dog with New Tricks

w Brian Clemens
The adventures begin. George Cowley gathers together his newly-formed intelligence squad, but soon finds himself donning the role of the Home Secretary, whose life has been threatened by a ruthless escaped prisoner.
Charley Turkel Jonny Shannon
Henry Turkel Anthony Morton
Drapper Stephen Chase

Director: Sidney Hayers

Private Madness, Public Danger

w Anthony Read
When an executive and his secretary working for World Chemical Products die in mysterious circumstances, CI5 are asked to clear up the mystery. Bodie and Doyle's investigations lead them into dangerous waters – to stop a deranged killer.
Nesbitt Keith Barron
Susan Fenton Di Trevis
Gerald Harvey Angus Mackay

Director: Douglas Camfield

The Female Factor

w Brian Clemens
When Cowley discovers the Prime Minister's private telephone number doodled on a notepad in the flat of a girl dragged from the Thames, he instigates an investigation that turns into a shooting-match between his men and the Russians – and exposes the indiscretions of a government minister.
Sir Charles Milvern Anthony Steel
Baker Walter Gotell
Sara Felicity Dean

Director: David Wickes

Killer with a Long Arm

w Brian Clemens
Bodie and Doyle seek a man armed with a deadly new rifle capable of killing at a distance of two miles. Together with Cowley, they scan the faces of the VIPs attending the Wimbledon tennis finals – any one of whom could be the sniper's target.
Georgi Michael Latimer
Hilda Diane Keen
Costa Milos Kirek

Director: David Wickes

Heroes

w James McAteer

Watched with horror by motorists, a gang of terrorists blow open the door of a security van and kill Patterson, a man under Cowley's protection – events which plunge the CI5 team into a race against time to save the lives of innocent people.
Latymer Anthony Bailey
Tommy John Castle
Raider Damien Thomas

Director: William Brayne

Where the Jungle Ends

w Brian Clemens

The robbery of a London bank by a highly-trained group of professional killers led by Krivas, sends Bodie and Doyle on a wild cross-country goose chase – while Cowley, unable to keep up with them, becomes the target of the enemy.
Krivas David Suchet
Sinclair Geoffrey Palmer
Franky Paul Humpoletz

Director: Raymond Menmuir

Close Quarters

w Brian Clemens

When four German terrorists come to Britain to kill a prominent businessman, Cowley's team are assigned to find them – all save Bodie who, injured during a recent case, is ordered to stay at home. As things turn out it is he who becomes the terrorists' next target.
Inge Madlena Nedeva
Julia Gabrielle Drake
Myer Clive Arrindell

Director: William Brayne

Everest Was Also Conquered

w Brian Clemens

A death-bed confession leads Cowley to reopen a ten-year-old corruption and murder scandal. When one of his agents is killed by a ruthless villain, the CI5 chief digs deeper – and uncovers corruption in high places.

Lord Derrington Michael Denison
Neil Turvey Richard Greene
Goodman Charles Keating

Director: Francis Megahy

When the Heat Cools Off

w Brian Clemens

When Doyle receives a visit from Jill Haydon, who begs him to reopen a case the CI5 man investigated when a policeman – her father has served seven years of a thirty-year prison sentence on Doyle's evidence – and he agrees to do so, events take a very nasty turn which culminate in the girl joining her father in jail.
Bill Haydon Peter Hughes
Jill Haydon Lalla Ward
Harry Scott Bernard Kay

Director: Ray Austin

Stake-out

w Dennis Spooner

A stake-out at a bowling alley plunges Bodie and Doyle into a deadly game of cat and mouse with a gang who intend to put pressure on the British Government by exploding a nuclear device in a government building.
Frank David Collings
Bob Barry Jackson
Blonde Pamela Stephenson

Director: Benjamin Wickers

Long Shot

w Anthony Read

Assigned to protect former US Secretary of State Harbinger when he attends a top secret anti-terrorist conference, Bodie and Doyle soon find themselves under attack from all sides, which forces Cowley to agree to the terrorists' demands – or does it?
Ramos Roger Lloyd-Pack
Sammy Martin Robert Gillespie
Harbinger Ed Bishop

Director: Ernest Day

Look after Annie

w Brian Clemens

Cowley has a special interest in Annie Irving – he had once wanted to marry her. Now

Annie has returned. But far from rekindling old passions, her arrival plunges the CI5 chief into deadly danger.

Annie Diane Fairfax
Stanley Langdon Clifton Jones
Ben Hymer Keiith Buckley

Director: Charles Crichton

Klansman

w Brian Clemens   (**From a story by Simon Masters**)

When a black community comes under threat from men wearing Klansman robes, Doyle and Bodie are sent to investigate. While talking to a group of black youths, Bodie is knifed and left for dead – and Doyle finds himself beaten up and flung into a cellar.

Milier Jules Walter
Zadie Trevor Thomas
Dinny Anthony Booth

Director: Pat Jackson
(Note: This episode, deemed too violent by the production company, has never been transmitted on British television – though it has been aired in Australia and other international markets.)

Season Two
10 colour 60-minute episodes

Hunter, Hunted

w Anthony Read

When Cowley asks Bodie and Doyle to field test a new gun – the American 180, which has enormous destructive power, long range and a new type of laser aiming device – and the weapon is stolen from Doyle's home, the CI5 agents must recover the rifle before someone turns its sights on Ray Doyle.

Preston Bryan Marshall
Kathie Mason Cheryl Kennedy
Richards Tony Caunter

Director: Anthony Simmons

The Rack

w Brian Clemens

When Bodie and Doyle bring in for questioning John and Paul Coogan, two men suspected of criminal activities, and the latter attacks Doyle who retaliates by punching him in the stomach – but nevertheless finds himself accused of brutality when Coogan dies – it places the very existence of Cowley's department in jeopardy.

John Coogan Michael Billington
Geraldine Mather Lisa Harrow
David Merlin Robert James

Director: Peter Medak

First Night

w Gerry O'Hara

When a gang of kidnappers drag an important Israeli Minister, Biebermann, away from his police escort, CI5 are handed the task of finding him. But the gang give Cowley's Bisto Kids a long run for their money before the speed of their attack and firepower win the day.

Biebermann Julian Holloway
Frank Tony Vogel
John Arnold Diamond

Director: David Wickes

Man without a Past

w Jeremy Burnham and Michael Armstrong

When Bodie's late-night dinner rendezvous with his girlfriend comes to an explosive climax, leaving Bodie unhurt but two people dead and the girl injured, Cowley orders him to stay out of the investigation – but a second attempt on his life forces Bodie to ignore his superior's orders.

Brian Forrest John Carson
Peter Crabbe John Castle
Madge Forrest Rachel Herbert

Director: Martin Campbell

In the Public Interest

w Brian Clemens

Given information which indicates that the police force in a certain city are corrupt, Cowley sends Bodie and Doyle to visit the city. Their arrival is greeted by Chief Constable Green and his deputy Inspector Chives – two corrupt policemen who issue death warrants for the agents.

Green Paul Hardwick
Chives John Judd
Pellin Stephen Rea

Director: Pennant Roberts

Rogue

w Dennis Spooner
Working closely with Hunter, Head of the
Special Branch, to bring Cuthbertson, a
major criminal, to justice, Cowley assigns
tough CI5 agent Martin to accompany
Bodie and Doyle when they are sent to
bring a witness to headquarters – but
Martin is not all he seems.
Barry Martin Glyn Owen
Cuthbertson Tony Steedman
Hunter Neil Hallett

Director: Ray Austin

Not a Very Civil, Civil Servant

w Edmund Ward
Alarmed that his reputation could be
tarnished by a corruption trial, a
government minister seeks Cowley's help.
The CI5 boss uncovers large-scale corruption
and bribery in the building industry – and
contrary to the minister's denials, his role in
the sordid affair.
Sir James Maurice Denham
Colonel Summerville Bill Fraser
Logan Blake Robert Swann

Director: Anthony Simmons

A Stirring of Dust

w Don Houghton
Alarmed and astonished when he learns that
the notorious spy Thomas Darby wishes to
return to England after he escaped
prosecution for treason by fleeing to Russia,
Cowley plays a waiting game in order to
discover the secret of the 'Fourth Man' – a
spy banker whose identity has never been
revealed.
Darby Robert Urquhart
Brigadier Stadden Andre Morell
Sorenson Alan MacNaughton

Director: Martin Campbell

Blind Run

w Ranald Graham
Assigned to escort a visiting foreign
politician to two addresses for talks and then
return him to their original rendezvous,
Bodie and Doyle come under fire from
several carloads of terrorists. Ignoring
orders, Bodie returns to base – and finds
Cowley and several guests watching Doyle's
progress on a TV monitor!
Leia Jasmina Hilton
Minister Kevin Brennan
Hanish Kevork Malikyan

Director: Tom Clegg

Fall Girl

w Ranald Graham
When Marika, a beautiful East German film
starlet, pays a brief visit to London, it sets
in motion a series of events that finds Bodie
accused of murder, Ray Doyle assigned to
kidnap the girl, and Bodie finally seeking
refuge on top of a gasometer to defend
himself against the enemy – and his own
colleagues.
Marika Pamela Salem
Schuman Frederick Jaeger
Krieber Sandor Eles

Director: William Brayne

Season Three

8 colour 60-minute episodes

(Note: episodes denoted with an asterisk
were filmed for season two, but transmitted
during season three)

The Purging of CI5

w Stephen Lister
Someone is out to eliminate CI5: Cowley
narrowly escapes with his life when a bomb
explodes in his office, but two field agents
aren't so lucky. When the unknown killer
plants bomb number three in Bodie's home,
the situation turns very nasty indeed.
Lisa Wakeman Martha Nairn
Catrall Terry York
Billy Chris Fairbank

Director: Dennis Abey

Backtrack *

w Don Houghton
Suspecting that Pulman, a solicitor, is
mixed up with a group of Arab terrorists
whose activities are being investigated by
his department, Cowley orders Bodie and
Doyle to burgle the homes of two VIPs.
What they discover puts their lives in the
firing line.
Kammahmi Anthony Scott
Pulman Brian Gwaspari
Sgt Garbett Michael Elphick

Director: Christopher King

Stopover

w John Goldsmith
When Meredith, an old friend of Cowley's,
reappears after two years and swears he has
information that a senior British
Intelligence agent, codenamed Iron Sphinx,
is working for the enemy, the CI5 chief
becomes involved in a treacherous affair
which almost costs him his life.
Meredith James Laurenson
Kodai Michael Gothard
Radouk Morris Perry

Director: William Brayne

Dead Reckoning

w Philip Loraine
Asked to handle the debriefing of Batak, a
British spy exchanged by the Russians for
one of their own, Cowley and his men find
themselves involved in treachery and
double-dealing – with the enemy waiting on
the sidelines to close in for the kill.
Batak 1 Derek Godfrey
Batak 2 Alan Tilvern
Anna Batak Carol Royle

Director: Denis Lewiston

The Madness of Mickey Hamilton *

w Christopher Wicking
When St Jacques, a foreign ambassador, is
shot while visiting London, Cowley and his
team find themselves facing a killer without
a cause, in a holocaust of hospital
shoot-outs.

Mickey Hamilton Ian McDiarmid
Kay Costa Majorie Yates
Frank Barry Stanton

Director: William Brayne

A Hiding to Nothing

w Ted Childs
When CI5 are called in to tighten up the
security arrangements during vital Foreign
Office peace talks, Bodie and Doyle find
themselves under rocket attack by a group
of terrorists determined to smash the peace
conference.
Frances Cottingham Sylvia Kay
Shelley Lise Hilbolt
Alousha Adam Hussein

Director: Gerry O'Hara

Runner

w Michael Feeney Callan
When a secret code words heralds all-out
war between the authorities and a Mafia
network, CI5 explode into action. Doyle
escapes death by inches, and Bodie is
compelled to use strong tactics to rout the
enemy.
Sylvie Barbara Kellerman
Duffy Michael Kitchen
Albie Ed Devereaux

Director: Martin Campbell

Servant of Two Masters *

w Douglas Watkinson
When Mr Plum, a ministry official,
approaches Bodie and Doyle with 'classified'
information that their boss, Cowley, is a
traitor, the two agents find themselves
stalking 'The Cow' when he sets up a deal
with the enemy.
Plum John Savident
Alfred Cole Glynn Edwards
Jutta Christina Ward

Director: Ferdinand Fairfax

Season Four

15 colour 60-minute episodes

The Acorn Syndrome

w John Kruse
Bodie and Doyle pursue a group of East
German agents who are blackmailing a

government engineer whose daughter's life is being held hostage against the plans of a new jet-engine tank.

Guthrie Michael Craig
Copeland Ronald Hines
Sandy Cona Kirsch

Director: Martin Campbell

Wild Justice

w Ranald Graham

Is Bodie cracking up? If not, why should he disobey orders and arrange a mysterious – and deadly – motorcycle race with the leader of a gang of Hell's Angels? Doyle is assigned to keep an eye on his partner – with high-speed results.

King Billy Ziggy Byfield
Dr Ross Sarah Douglas
Cheryl Frances Low

Director: Dennis Abey

Fugitive

w Gerry O'Hara   (**From a story by Anthony Read**)

On the trail of a young female terrorist, the CI5 agents find themselves up against an enemy determined to settle old scores – and Bodie becomes a walking time bomb in an attempt to smash a gang of international gun-runners!

Karen Vickie Turner
Werner Michael Byrne
Christina Brigitte Kahn

Director: Dennis Lewiston

Involvement

w Brian Clemens

When Doyle's friend Benny dies after being savagely beaten in an attempt to silence him, Doyle and Bodie find themselves racing against time to smash a major drug-smuggling ring – led by Holly, the father of Doyle's girlfriend.

Ann Patricia Hodge
Charles Holly William Russell
Buzz Valentine Pringle

Director: Chris Burt

Need to Know

w Brian Clemens   (**From a story by Chris Menaul**)

When Cowley gets word that Gorky, a senior KGB official, plans to snatch Drake, a senior MI5 man suspected of being a double agent, from custody, Bodie and Doyle are assigned to take the prisoner to safety – but come under immediate attack.

Manton Patrick O'Connell
Drake Norman Jones
Gorky Niall Buggy

Director: William Brayne

Take Away

w Roger Marshall

Asked to investigate a drug-smuggling operation that could have international repercussions, Cowley assigns Bodie and Doyle to the case. The latter goes undercover as a street-market trader, while Bodie moves in with a gang of drug addicts.

Proll John Rumny
Chi Sang Arnold Lee
Ciu Sang Fiesta Mei Ling

Director: Douglas Camfield

Blackout

w Brian Clemens

The CI5 team find themselves driving around London to find a gang of villains who plan to assassinate a lobby of international diplomats with a powerful anti-tank gun. Once located, Bodie does his mountain-climbing act to smash the gang's activities.

Gerda Linda Hayden
Stuart Ben Cross
Murphy Steve Alder

Director: William Brayne

Blood Sports

w Gerry O'Hara

Following a political assassination, CI5 uncover an international terrorist organisation operating from South America. Bodie and Doyle go undercover to save the life of a foreign diplomat, and Cowley plans a game of golf.

Lacoste Yves Beneyton
Anita Cabreros Michell Newell
Radio operator Pierce Brosnan

Director: Phil Meheaux

Slush Fund

w Roger Marshall
Bodie and Doyle investigate a Euro-
consortium building a death-trap fighter
plane. They have already killed 50 pilots –
and mean to rub out anyone standing in
their way . . . including the two CI5
agents.
Van Neikerk Stuart Wilson
Hope Matthew Long
Sir Kenneth David Swift

Director: William Brayne

The Gun

w Christopher Wicking
When two young boys find a gun in a
garden, a trail of murders leads Bodie and
Doyle to an illegal heroin consignment
being smuggled into Britain. Cowley plays
a hunch and Bodie saves a schoolteacher
from death.
Inger Celia Gregory
Gary Robert Gwilym
Franco Peter Kelly

Director: Dennis Lewiston

Hijack

w Roger Marshall
An East European offical uses a swoop on
the London Bullion Market to escape behind
the Iron Curtain – but he hasn't reckoned
with CI5's involvement. Doyle prevents a
murder attempt and Cowley derives great
satisfaction from denting the man's plans.
Merhart Dennis Lil
Walter Dave King
Amanda Jill Baker

Director: Martin Campbell

Mixed Doubles

w Brian Clemens
Assigned to protect a Middle Eastern leader,
in England to sign a peace treaty, Bodie and

Doyle have no way of knowing that Rio, the
world's greatest assassin, has inside
information – and has been sent to kill
them.
Rio Michael Coles
Macklin Ian McCulloch
Joe Nicholas Grace

Director: Roger Tucker

A Weekend in the Country

w Gerry O'Hara
When Bodie and Doyle spend an idyllic
weekend in the country with their
girlfriends, it isn't long before they find
themselves back in business – defending a
farmhouse under siege from a gang of
escaped prisoners.
Vince Ray Burdis
Georgie Brian Croucher
Judy Louisa Rix

Director: James Allen

Kickback

w Stephen Lister
Bodie's loyalty to CI5 is placed on the line
when a ghost from his SAS past reenters his
life. Lured into joining a gang of ruthless
terrorists in the role of a hired assassin, he
finds his allegiances tested to the full.
Keller Norman Eshley
Benedek Peter Whitman
Murphy Steve Alder

Director: Ian Sharp

It's Only a Beautiful Picture

w Edmund Ward
What link can there be between industrial
espionage and the theft of several art
treasures? CI5 agents Bodie and Doyle
uncover the crimes of Colonel Sangster, a
criminal mastermind who leads them a
merry dance before the case is over.
Colonel Sangster Moray Watson
Tibbs Jonathan Newth
Galbraith Dennis Burgess

Director: Dennis Lewiston

Season Five

11 colour 60-minute episodes

(Note: Episodes denoted with an asterisk were filmed for season four, but transmitted during season five.)

Foxhole on the Roof *

w Brian Clemens

Roddy Barker and his henchman Stacey combine to make life difficult for Cowley's team. Armed with an arsenal of weapons, they build a rooftop fortress and place a nearby hospital under siege.

Barker Stanley Meadows
Stacey Karl Howman
Murphy Steve Alder

Director: William Brayne

Operation Susie *

w Ranald Graham

Two teenage overseas students are found to be drug traffickers. But why does somebody in high places want them dealt with quietly? Cowley and his team discover the answer – and Bodie and Doyle find themselves hunted men.

Diana Alice Krige
Northcott Harold Innocent
Rudiger Ewan Stewart

Director: Ian Sharp

You'll Be All Right *

w Gerry O'Hara

Notorious villain Jack Stone seeks the services of Bodie and Doyle when his family become the pawns in a long-standing underworld vendetta. Someone is putting the frighteners on his wife and kids – but why?

Jack Stone Derrick O'Connor
Chrissie Stone Geraldine Sherman
Murphy Steve Alder

Director: John Crome

Lawson's Last Stand

w Ranald Graham

Lieutenant Colonel Peter Lawson vanishes from an army hospital. He is in possession of valuable NATO secrets and may have been abducted by the Russians. Bodie and Doyle are sent to find him – with explosive results.

Peter Lawson Michael Culver
Tug Willis John Hallam
Brigadier Tennant Donald Pickering

Director: Ian Sharp

Discovered in a Graveyard *

w Christopher Wicking

The victim of a terrorist bullet, Doyle lies close to death, a deep-seated despair depriving him of the will to live. Together with other CI5 agents, Bodie tracks down the girl responsible – but arrives too late to save her life.

Mayli Megumi Shimanuki
Hogan Philip Latham
Murphy Steve Alder

Director: Anthony Simmons

Spy Probe

w Tony Barwick

Bodie and Doyle infiltrate an organisation which is hiring killers. Their victims – nobodies. Why? Cowley orders them to find the link, but is there someone in the background hindering their progress?

Dawson Paul Daneman
Minister Graham Crowden
Miss Walsh Joyce Grant

Director: Dennis Abey

Cry Wolf

w Paul Wheeler

Is Susan Grant crying wolf? The police are convinced she is – Cowley is not so sure. What part does Henry Laughlin play in the scenario? Bodie and Doyle are sent to find out.

Susan Grant Sheila Ruskin
Mrs Grant Rona Anderson
Laughlin Alan MacNaughton

Director: Phil Meheux

The Untouchables *

w Brian Clemens

When Bodie loses heavily at poker and a foreign diplomat buys his marker, things

look desperate for Cowley's department. As Bodie sinks lower and lower into a bottomless pit of treachery, Cowley plays his trump card.
Romero **Keith Washington**
Anna **Marilyn Galsworthy**
Sir John **Robert Flemyng**

Director: **William Brayne**

The Ojuka Situation *

w **Dave Humphries**
President Ojuka, the deposed head of the African state of Battan, is in London seeking Britain's help to regain his position. Agents Bodie and Doyle are assigned to guard him – but treachery follows their every step.
Ojuka **Clarke Peters**
Avery **Geoffrey Palmer**
Murphy **Steve Alder**

Director: **Christopher King**

A Man Called Quinn

w **Tony Barwick**
Unaware that he is being controlled by the enemy, ex-CI5 agent Quinn sets out to kill his ex-superiors. Cowley, Bodie and Doyle find themselves playing a deadly game of cat and mouse – with Cowley as Quinn's number one target.
Quinn **Del Henney**
Krasnov **Steven Berkoff**
Granger **Bernard Archard**

Director: **Chris Burt**

No Stone

w **Roger Marshall**
What is the connection between Jimmy Gilpin, a terrorist group, and the deaths of a Judge, a Clerk of Court and a QC? Cowley and his team must put the jigsaw together to prevent further explosive deaths.
Ulrike **Sarah Neville**
Gilpin **John Wheatley**
Hockley **Philip York**

Director: **Chris Burt**

THE PROFESSIONALS
Created by: Brian Clemens
Producers: Sidney Hayers (Season 1)
Raymond Menmuir (remainder)
Executive producers: Albert Fennell and Brian Clemens
Music by: Laurie Johnson
Script editors: Kenneth Ware, Dennis Spooner,
Gerry O'Hara, Tony Barwick
An Avengers Mark 1 Production
for London Weekend Television
57 colour 60-minute episodes
30 December 1977 – 17 March 1978
7 October – 9 December 1978
27 October – 15 December 1979
7 September – 27 December 1980
7 November 1982 – 6 February 1983

THE PROTECTORS

No, not *that* one, this mid-sixties crime-prevention series preceded its namesake by eight years. Short-lived (due to a wages dispute among the production team), it depicted the attempts of three do-gooders to fight crooks and prevent crime taking place.

Leading the team from their lavishly-furnished central London office was Ian Souter, a bearded Scot whose easy, relaxed manner concealed a quick, ruthless intelligence when it came to safeguarding his clients' interests. After seven years' experience of investigating claims for a company of loss adjusters, Souter set up his own security agency in partnership with his ex-policeman friend Robert Shoesmith.

A man dedicated to making the agency a high-powered link between the twilight borderland that separated the underworld from the policeman's beat, Shoesmith admired a clever criminal and had sympathy for his opponent – unless the criminal was ruthless or cruel, in which event the ex-policeman would come down on him like a ton of bricks.

The third, indispensable member of the team, a woman with an experienced eye for spotting art fakes and forgeries, was Heather Keys, Souter and Shoesmith's private secretary-cum-confidante.

Dubbing themselves SIS (Specialists in Security), they advertised their services in the newspaper personal columns under the heading: 'Need protection. Wish to stay one jump ahead of the competition? Call Welbeck 3269 and ask for *The Protectors*.'

REGULAR CAST

Ian Souter Andrew Faulds   *Robert Shoesmith* Michael Atkinson
Heather Keys Ann Morish

Set Up

w Martin Woodhouse
'The criminals and us – we're all in the same business. The difference being, our clients pay us to keep one jump ahead of the criminal mind' – Ian Souter. The SIS team open their doors for the first time.
Souter Andrew Faulds
Shoesmith Michael Atkinson
Heather Ann Morish

Director: Raymond Menmuir

Happy Is the Loser

w Stan Woodward
Accepting what appears to be a routine assignment, the SIS team suddenly find themselves involved with violence when they are framed by a gang of ruthless racketeers.
Det. Sgt Jarrett John Ringham
Happy Dwyer Brian Wilde
Hon. Arthur Kerr Gerald Harper

Director: Jonathan Alwyn

The Bottle Shop

w Martin Woodhouse
Invited to discover why a research laboratory is losing money, even though they have a monopoly in the medical research trade, the Protectors discover that someone is making overtures to the competition and is prepared to sing – for a price.
Dr Fothergill Peter Bowles
Dr Bradbury Faith Brook
Fairchild Donald Hewlett

Director: Bill Bain

No Forwarding Address

w Fiona McConnell
Following up a lead, Souter and Shoesmith find themselves in a deserted warehouse which should contain the answer to a riddle they are determined to solve. They find nothing of interest – beyond a dead body.
Barnaby Norman Bird
Jason Michael Wynne
Pop Masters Reg Lye

Director: Raymond Menmuir

The Loop Men

w Larry Forrester

An injured railwayman, a loop-line rendezvous at midnight: clues which the Protectors must crack to discover the headquarters of a gang of hijackers – and deliver a young man from a life of crime.
The Corporal Jeremy Kemp
Tusky Franks Harvey Ross
Stodgey Payne Derren Nesbitt

Director: Peter Hammond

The Stamp Collection

w Ian Kennedy Martin

Guarding a world-famous stamp collection which is locked in a bombproof vault hardly seems a dangerous assignment. But the Protectors will need all their guile when they come up against a brilliant criminal.
Banding Edwin Richfield
Farrell Glyn Edwards
Miss Nicholson Beryl Baxter

Director: Laurence Bourne

It Could Happen Here

w Malcolm Hulke

The SIS team find themselves up against a gang who intend to infiltrate a union to play a sordid game of industrial espionage which could destroy a union official and his family.
Brian Winters Mike Pratt
Jean Winters Jayne Muir
Cynthia Colette Wilde

Director: Bill Bain

Freedom!

w Bill Strutton

A young girl's bid for political asylum and a team of vigilant security men spell trouble for Souter and Shoesmith when they are assigned to investigate the validity of the girl's claims.
Tamara Mary Miller
Slankin Roger Delgado
Yarasov Anthony Newlands

Director: Jonathan Alwyn

The Pirate

w John Lucarotti

Conman Smokey Grey is anxious to unload £30,000 worth of stolen jewels. But the Protectors have other more important things to occupy their minds – Heather has been kidnapped!
Smokey Grey John Carson
Hugh Denver Leslie French
Trussler Lee Fox

Director: Peter Hammond

The Deadly Chameleon

w Tony O'Grady (aka Brian Clemens)

How – and why – is a timid bank clerk connected to a baffling case of fraud? If they are to save an innocent man's life, the Protectors must find the answer – their dilemma: their chief suspect has disappeared!
Anson Basil Dignam
Tilsworth Peter Barkworth
Gerry Bates John Barcroft

Director: Laurence Bourne

Who Kidnapped Lazoryck?

w Larry Forrester

When the past catches up with a highly-placed spy, Souter and Shoesmith find themselves facing a race against time to find the connecting link between the man and a recently-released political prisoner.
Lord Keele Peter Williams
The Major Hamilton Dyce
Joyce Kester Patricia English

Director: Mark Lawton

Channel Crossing

w Malcolm Hulke

When personal disaster strikes terror into the heart of a prominent government minister, the Protectors, assigned to guard the man during a luxury cruise, find themselves in very dangerous waters.
James Benson Alan Wheatley
Janine Benson Mary Kenton
Jack Morgan Barry Lineham

Director: Kim Mills

Mr Palfrey of Westminster and The Coordinator.   **Mr Rose** (William Mervyn).

The New Avengers John Steed, Purdey and Mike Gambit.

No Hiding Place Chf Det. Supt Lockhart and Det. Sgt Baxter.

The Odd Man Steve Gardiner and Chf Insp. Rose.

The Persuaders (Above) Lord Brett Sinclair (Below) Danny Wilde.

Police Surgeon   (Above and below) The Prisoner.

The Professionals Left to right: Doyle, George Cowley, Bodie.

Public Eye Alfred Burke as Frank Marker.

The Rat Catchers Peregrine Smith, Brig. Davidson, Richard Hurst.

Redcap John Thaw as Sergeant John Mann.

The Adventures of Sherlock Holmes
Sherlock Holmes (Jeremy Brett) and Dr Watson (David Burke).

The Return of Sherlock Holmes Sherlock Holmes and Dr Watson (Edward Hardwicke) set out to right another wrong.

Riviera Police Left to right: Lt Col. Sorel (Frank Lieberman), Supt Hunter (Geoffrey Frederick), Insp. Legrand (Brian Spink), Supt Johnson (Noel Trevarthan).

Robin of Sherwood Michael Praed (back row, third from right) as Robin of Loxley.

Robin of Sherwood (Season Three) Robin of Huntingdon (Jason Connery) now heads the outlaws.

Cargo for Corinth

w John Lucarotti

Returning from their last assignment, the Protectors are asked to guard a valuable statue in transit from Corinth to Venice: a mission that once again finds them all at sea and surrounded by sharks – the human variety.

Jack Morgan Barry Lineham
Nicos Maurice Kaufmann
Captain Brian Sadler

Director: Jonathan Alwyn

The Reluctant Thief

w Bill Strutton

When Heather falls victim of a wages snatch, Souter and the thief find themselves in very strange company. Shoesmith meanwhile discovers a surprising motive for the robbery.

Hughie Derek Fowlds
Insp. Tarrant Tony Steedman
Wally David Batley

Director: Laurence Bourne

THE PROTECTORS
Producer: Michael Chapman
An ABC Weekend Network Production
14 monochrome 60-minute episodes
28 March – 27 June 1964

THE PROTECTORS

A glossy but less-than-interesting cops aand robbers series which chronicled the activities of Harry Rule, Paul Buchet and Caroline, the glamorous Contessa di Contini – collectively known as *The Protectors*, three experts at protecting those in peril, who came together to battle evil from their international crimefighting agency.

No risk was too great. No assignment too challenging. The team handled dangerous and highly sensitive investigations across the world.

Head of the agency was Harry Rule, an ice-cool professional investigator who set out to grab his share of the action from his ultra-modern detective office in London. (He could just as easily be found cavorting around his luxury Tudor-style country home which he shared with his au pair Suki, and his Irish wolfhound 'Gus'.) Wealthy to the point of being crass, Lady Caroline Oglivie (aka the Contessa), lived in a lavishly furnished villa in Rome. Like her partners she, too, operated a detective agency – although her speciality was seeking out art and antiques fakes. Buchet, a baby-faced French-born intellectual, operated from his Paris apartment – at least he did so whenever he wasn't otherwise occupied by the attentions of a seemingly endless stream of beautiful girlfriends! The youngest member of the trio, his bland exterior concealed a tough and sophisticated alertness whenever he was called in to partner his colleagues.

With the accent placed firmly on action, what should have been a star-studded, thrill-a-minute experience wasn't! Without wishing to offend its fans, the show was awful!

REGULAR CAST

Harry Rule Robert Vaughan   *Contessa di Contini* Nyree Dawn Porter
Paul Buchet Tony Anholt   *Suki* Yasuko Nagazami   *Chino* Anthony Chinn

Season One

26 colour 30-minute episodes

2,000ft to Die

w Terence Feely
Freddie Reiwald, a daredevil film stuntman, has good reason to be frightened – someone is out to kill him. Enter Harry Rule.
Reiwald Harvey Hall
Carozzo Paul Stassino
Ransome Nicholas Scott

*Director:*Johnny Hough

Brother Hood

w John Goldsmith
At the request of industrial tycoon Bela Karoleon, the Protectors engineer an audacious prison escape for his brother.
Bela Karoleon Patrick Troughton
Sandor Karoleon Vladek Sheybal
Maria Jill Bacon

Director: Don Chaffey

See No Evil

w Donald Johnson
The Protectors become involved with a blackmailed senator, a ruthless gang of cut-throats and a sinister blind man in Rome.
Max James Bolam
Blind Man Alan Webb
Senator Leonard Sachs

Director: Jeremy Summers

Disappearing Trick

w Brian Clemens
The Contessa di Contini finds herself in deep trouble when she tries to help her friend Brad Huron win a wager.

Brad Huron Derren Nesbitt
Carl Huron David Bauer
Walters Don Henderson

Director: Jeremy Summers

Ceremony for the Dead

w Donald James
A game of bluff and counter-bluff with a gang of kidnappers places the Contessa di Contini's life in danger.
President Medina Stanley Lebor
Madame Rue Toby Robins
Julie Jenny Lee Wright

Director: Jeremy Summers

It Was All Over in Leipzig

w Donald James
When the Contessa meets up with two men from her past, the Protectors find themselves investigating a plot to overthrow a government.
Jim Palmer Ron Randell
Lintar Paul Weston
Chino Anthony Chinn

Director: Don Chaffey

The Quick Brown Fox

w Donald James
A wrongly-dated typewritten note helps the Protectors expose the mastermind behind a new Nazi organisation.
Keller Morris Perry
Osuna Mark Malicz
Helga Anna Matisse

Director: Don Chaffey

King Con

w Tony Barwick
When Alan Sutherland swindles Irena Gleskova out of a 12th-century icon, the

Protectors decide the time is ripe to con a conman.

Sutherland Anton Rodgers
Irena Izabella Telezynska
Cribbs Ronald Lacey

Director: Jeremy Summers

Thinkback

w Brian Clemens

When Harry Rule wakes up in a hospital bed, his first thought is for his passenger, the Contessa – but the doctor swears that there was no one else in the crashed car!

Insp. Wilson Ian Hendry
Doctor Donald Burton
Nurse Penny Sugg

Director: Cyril Frankel

A Kind of Wild Justice

w Donald James

Savage justice against Harry Rule. A girl first of all shoots him – then poisons him for jailing her father.

Kate Anna Palk
Reagan Patrick O'Connell
Soaper Barry Stanton

Director: Jeremy Summers

Balance of Terror

w John Goldsmith

When a Russian scientist goes missing in London armed with a phial of toxin which could wipe out the entire city, the Russians call in Harry Rule.

Karassinkov Nigel Green
Schelpin Laurence Naismith
Grodny Angus Lennie

Director: Don Chaffey

Triple Cross

w Lew Davidson

Framed for the theft of some rare jewels, Harry Rule and the Contessa find themselves involved with murder and bombs as they try to get them back.

Charlie John Neville
Kofax Peter Bowles
Detective Del Henney

Director: John Hough

The Numbers Game

w Ralph Smart

A letter in code opens up new avenues and alleyways when Harry Rule and the Contessa set out to crack a dope smuggling gang.

Frank Henry McGee
Sir Walter Frederick Treves
Luigi George Innes

Director: Don Chaffey

For the Rest of Your Natural . . .

w Tony Barwick

The Contessa finds herself on trial for her life – with a grotesque jury of cut-outs, and a psychopathic killer as prosecutor!

Colin Grant Norman Rodway
Visitor Damien Thomas
Chino Anthony Chinn

Director: Johnny Hough

The Bodyguards

w Dennis Spooner

Why would a dead man need protection? And why did someone fire several bullets into his coffin to ensure he remained so? The Protectors find the answer.

Robard Freddie Jones
Mason Manning Redwood
Insp. Newman Ken Watson

Director: Don Chaffey

A Matter of Life and Death

w Donald James

When Harry Rule is cunningly lured to Africa, his colleagues find themselves involved in a strange smuggling racket.

Mallory Patrick Allen
Goran Barrie Houghton
Baruna Maxwell Shaw

*Director:*Don Chaffey

The Big Hit

w Donald James

When a pretty girl slips a drug into Paul Buchet's drink and attempts are made on Harry's life, the Protectors go underground to unmask the enemy.

Howard Derek Smith
Assassin Bob Anderson
Suzanne Morag Hood

Director: Roy Ward Baker

One and One Makes One

w Jesse and Pat Lasky
The Protectors find themselves faced with
finding a foreign agent who has killed and
replaced a top Canadian spy.
Shkoder Michael Gough
Maria Georgia Brown
Bennett Neil McCallum

Director: Don Chaffey

Talkdown

w Pat and Jesse Lasky
Someone with a vendetta against Harry Rule
lures the detective into a deadly trap – a
speeding plane which Harry has no idea how
to control.
Foster Derren Nesbitt
Insp. Hill John Nettleton
Air Controller John Joyce

Director: Jeremy Summers

Vocal

w Brian Clemens
Paul Buchet and the Contessa find
themselves in desperate situations when they
are held prisoner by a mysterious man called
Azon.
Azon David Buck
Gregg Ian Hogg
Vickers Shane Rimmer

Director: Cyril Frankel

With a Little Help from My Friends

w Sylvia Anderson
Assigned to protect a president during his
stay in London, Harry Rule finds, to his
cost, that his involvement brings a threat to
his family.
Kahan Jeremy Brett
Laura Hannah Gordon
President Martin Benson

Director: Jeremy Summers

Chase

w Brian Clemens
When the Contessa gives Harry a new
shotgun for his birthday, the detective soon
has need to put it to good use.
Gardner Patrick Magee
Kurt Keith Buckley
Perston Donald Eccles

Director: Harry Booth

Your Witness

w Donald James
Chrissie is the key witness in a murder
investigation. The Protectors are hired to
protect her – but she protests, and then
disappears.
Chrissie Stephanie Beacham
Dixon George Baker
Monique Judith Arthy

Director: Jeremy Summers

It Could Be Practically Anywhere on the Island

w Tony Barwick
When Linda McCall's poodle Muffin is
stolen, Harry Rule finds himself racing
around the island searching for – er, dog
droppings!
Linda McCall Linda Staab
Felix Costa Sherwood Price
Jonathan P. Hacket Dervis Ward

Director: Robert Vaughan

The First Circle

w Tony Barwick
Called in to protect Colonel John Hunter, a
Vietnam war veteran whose life is filled with
nightmares of war horrors, Harry Rule finds
himself in the firing line.
Colonel Hunter Ed Bishop
Slade John Collin
Mrs Hunter Sally Bazely

Director: Don Chaffey

A Case for the Right

w Jesse and Pat Lasky
When they gatecrash a prince's party, the
Protectors find themselves involved in a
sinister affair amid some Roman tombs.

Carplano Milo O'Shea
Fabrizzio Jacques Sernas
Chino Anthony Chinn

Director: Michael Lindsay-Hogg

Season Two
26 colour 30-minute episodes

Quin

w Trevor Preston
The Protectors become involved in a grim
search for Quin, one of the most dangerous
men in the world.
Quin Peter Vaughan
Allen Brian Glover
Garcia Anthony Langdon

Director: Don Leaver

Bagman

w Terry Nation
The Protectors play a game of hunt the
criminal when a ransom demand in
Copenhagen leads them to an abandoned
fort.
Christian Stephen Chase
Chino Anthony Chinn

Director: Johnny Hough

Fighting Fund

w John Kruse
Well supported by the river police, Harry
Rule leads the hunt for a gang of terrorists
who have stolen valuable treasures to
auction for arms.
The Marquesa Lisa Daniely
Dr Blanco Mischa de la Motte
Bishop Hugh Morton

Director: Jeremy Summers

The Last Frontier

w Tony Barwick
The Protectors are assigned to smuggle a
beautiful Russian scientist into England –
but their plan is exposed and the enemy is
out to stop them.
Irena Gayevska Hildegard Neil
Eastbrook William Lucas
Khukov Yuri Borienko

Director: Charles Crichton

Baubles, Bangles and Beads

w Terry Nation
A doublecross in Denmark leads the
Protectors face to face with danger – with
the Contessa's life depending on the
outcome.
Bergen Frederick Jaeger
Kate Bergen Yvonne Antrobus
Executive John Barron

Director: Jeremy Summers

Petard

w Tony Barwick
Espionage rears its ugly head when Harry
Rule gets involved in the cutthroat world of
international business.
Wyatt Iain Cuthbertson
Weston Cyril Luckham
Leo Ralph Bates

Director: Cyril Frankel

Goodbye George

w Brian Clemens
Intent on discovering what has happened to
George, the Contessa di Contini finds
herself surrounded by macabre and strange
events.
Caspar Paul Jones
Maria Geraldine Moffatt
Parton Lionel Murton

Director: Michael Lindsay-Hogg

Wam (Part One)

w Tony Barwick
Why should Monica Davies write to her
father, who has cut her out of his will, that
she will soon be rich without his help? . . .

Wam (Part 2)

. . . The Protectors are hired to find the
answer – and find themselves involved in a
drama on a mountain top in Salzburg,
where holiday-makers are being held to
ransom.
Monica Davies Jill Townsend
William Arthur McKay Prentis Hancock
Insp. Luhrs Michael Sheard

Director: Jeremy Summers

Implicado

w Tony Barwick

Harry Rule and Paul Buchet are assigned to investigate the case of an English boy arrested in Spain on drug-smuggling charges.

Raphael Santana Patrick Mower
Stephen Douglas Peter Firth

Director: Jeremy Summers

Dragon Chase

w John Kruse

The Protectors find that protecting a Russian they have smuggled into Britain offers the greatest challenge of their career.

Nikkolai William Dexter
Lockier Donald Houston
Peter Lockier Bruce Robinson

Director: Charles Crichton

Decoy

w Brian Clemens

When a 'dead' man steps out of Harry Rule's past, it spells danger for the detective – and intrigue for the Contessa di Contini.

Jerry Butler Ronald Radd
Nick Archer Mark Damon
Joe Terry Canner

Director: Michael Lindsay-Hogg

Border Line

w Anthony Terpiloff

The Protectors are asked to help an Hungarian-born actress to smuggle her father's body across the border.

Ilona Tabori Georgia Brown
Kilas Oscar Homolka
Reporter Jon Lauriemore

Director: Charles Crichton

Zeke's Blues

w Shane Rimmer

When Harry Rule meets up with an old adversary he finds little comfort in a drama played out to music.

Zeke Shane Rimmer
Patrick Ray Lonnen
Kasankas Paul Curran

Director: Jeremy Summers

Lena

w Trevor Preston

When a young female journalist faces danger while seeking to expose a politician in Venice, the Protectors lend a hand.

Lena Judy Parfitt
Pursuer Mario Depita
Russi Roger Lloyd Pack

Director: Don Leaver

The Bridge

w Tony Barwick

A kidnapped girl leads Harry Rule into an explosive situation when he is charged with handing over her ransom.

Anna Diane Quick
De Santos Michael Goodliffe
Mitchell James Maxwell

Director: Jeremy Summers

Sugar and Spice

w David Butler

Threats to an industrialist's schoolgirl daughter lead to Harry Rule and the Contessa mounting counter-abduction plans.

Charles Standish Norman Ettlinger
Vicky Standish Debbie Russ
Manning Derek Anders

Director: Charles Crichton

Burning Bush

w Trevor Preston

Harry Rule finds himself involved with the strange world of the supernatural when a Canadian heiress disappears in London.

Anne Ferris Sinead Cusack
Mark Jenner Ken Hutchinson

Director: Don Leaver

The Tiger and the Goat

w Trevor Preston

Paul Buchet finds himself racing against time to save the Contessa's life – she is

being used as bait to lure an assassin into the open.
Commander Whiting Douglas Wilmer
Barsella Derek Godfrey
Reece Derek Newark

Director: Jeremy Summers

Route 27

w Terry Nation
Working alone, Harry Rule finds himself following the trail of a drug-smuggling gang, operating from a brewery.
Sandom Michael Coles
Insp. Bergen Jeremy Wilkin
Revell Carl Bohun

Director: Don Leaver

Trial

w Robert Banks Stewart
When someone attempts to interfere with the course of justice by threatening a judge, the Protectors enter the scene.
Judge Cronin Richard Hurndall
Arthur Gordon Joss Ackland
Anne Gordon Gwen Cheryl

Director: Charles Crichton

Shadbolt

w Tony Barwick
Shadbolt is a cruel, professional assassin. He doesn't mind who he kills – providing it pays well. Shadbolt's next victim is Harry Rule!
Shadbolt Tom Bell
Girl Passenger Georgina Hale
Police Inspector Stanley Stewart

Director: Johnny Hough

A Pocketful of Posies

w Terry Nation
Is cabaret singer Carrie Blaine losing her mind, or is she really being haunted? The Protectors become ghost-busters to save her sanity.

Carrie Blaine Eartha Kitt
Mario Toza Kieron Moore
Sara Trent Kate O'Mara

Director: Cyril Frankel

Wheels

w Tony Barwick
Attempting to stop a daring Swiss bank robbery, Harry Rule finds himself running circles around the thieves.
Manning Dinsdale Landen
Sneider George Pravda
Anton Robert Coleby

Director: David Tomblin

The Insider

w Trevor Preston
The Protectors take positive action to lay their hands on a stolen film – but receive a negative response from its owner.
Smith Stuart Wilson
Chambers Donald Hewlett

Director: Don Leaver

Blockbuster

w Shane Rimmer
The Protectors are assigned to probe a series of plutonium robberies and discover how a convoy of it disappeared.
Birch Stanley Meadows
Bailey Christopher Neame
Slater Maurice O'Connell

Director: Jeremy Summers

THE PROTECTORS
Producer: Gerry Anderson and Reg Hill
Music by: John Cameron
(End theme sung by: Tony Christie)
Script editor: Tony Barwick
A Group Three Production for ITC
Filmed on location and at EMI/MGM Studios, Elstree
52 colour 30-minute episodes
29 September 1972 – 30 March 1973
21 September 1973 – 15 March 1974
(USA: Syndicated 1972)

PUBLIC EYE

The less-than-glamorous adventures of Frank Marker, a seedy, down-to-earth private enquiry agent whose lacklustre, prepared-to-work-for-next-to-nothing lifestyle came as an attractive antidote to the scores of clean-cut, wealthy American detectives on the TV screen during the mid-sixties.

The kind of private eye who couldn't afford to employ a private secretary and operated from wherever the rent was cheapest (usually a dimly-lit, rundown third-storey backroom, well away from the harsh flare of the city neon lights), Marker was a new kind of hero – a disenchanted, foot-weary private eye who usually found himself working for people who had more money than he would ever earn in two lifetimes, but nevertheless plodded along taking wry satisfaction from his role as a willing – but battered – 20th-century Robin Hood (for Lincoln green substitute a shabby grey raincoat). Describing himself as an expert at walking the fine red line between the law and the unlawful, he played out his daydreams at someone else's expense by investigating other people's problems, most of which were more exciting than his own.

Unlike his contemporaries, who undertook their crimefighting activities in exotic locations, Marker's world was the streets of London, Birmingham and, latterly, the sand-strewn streets of Brighton. Places occupied by all manner of sleazy law-breakers, people who would see you dead rather than pay their bill or, as Marker found out to his cost, the clever criminal fraternity who wouldn't think twice about leaving him to carry the can. (During his stay in Birmingham, Marker foolishly acted as middleman between insurers and villains, got caught in possession of stolen jewellery and went to prison.)

Authentic in its portrayal of the twilight world frequented by his profession, the series was riveting stuff.

(Author's note: The first three seasons were notable for their use of off-beat story titles; in each case these were made up from words spoken by – or to – Marker in that particular story.)

REGULAR CAST

Frank Marker **Alfred Burke**
From Season Five
Mrs Mortimer **Pauline Delaney**   *Det. Insp. Firbank* **Ray Smith**
Ron Gash **Peter Childs**

Season One
15 monochrome 60-minute episodes

All for a Couple of Ponies

w Roger Marshall

Accused of robbery, Marker has a hard time proving his innocence to the police. Stone, the one man who çan verify his alibi, has disappeared.

Dick Stone Griffith Davies
Valerie Stone Pauline Munro
Joey Stone Jack Smethurst

Director: Don Leaver

Nobody Kills Santa Claus

w Roger Marshall

When Paul Garston employs Marker to find out who's blackmailing him, it isn't long before Marker himself is in sore need of a bodyguard.

Paul Garston Keith Baxter
Eva Garston Caroline Blakiston
Eric Hart Peter Barkworth

Director: Don Leaver

They Go off in the End, Like Fruit

w Martin Worth

Requested to repossess a client's car for ten per cent of the finder's fee, Marker issues a cheque – and almost winds up broke.

Brown Garfield Morgan
Maxwell Philip Latham
Madely Henry McGee

Director: Robert Tronson

Dig You Later

w Roger Marshall

When a client asks him to find his office telephonist, a young blonde to whom he was getting married, Marker finds more than he bargained for.

Paul Brooks Alan Browning
Anne Julia Foster
Inspector Barry Glyn Edwards

Director: Kim Mills

I Went to Borrow a Pencil, and Look What I Found

w Terence Frisby

Engaged to keep his eye on the wife of a man who suspects her of playing around, Marker becomes suspicious when the man requests no evidence – just her boyfriend's name.

Colin Reynolds Peter Sallis
Sheila Reynolds Nyree Dawn Porter
Raymond Franks Gerald Harper

Director: Jonathan Alwyn

But the Jones Never Get Letters

w William Emms

When his daughter starts to receive anonymous letters, Mr Hordern employs Marker to keep an eye on his daughter's flat – a place that Marker finds empty.

Mr Hordern Derek Francis
Marion Hordern Judy Parfitt
Paul Obukwe Clifton Jones

Director: Laurence Bourne

A Harsh World for Zealots

w Michael Cahill

Assigned to check into reports that a shop assistant is helping himself to more than his share of the takings, Marker uncovers some very odd behaviour.

Chambers Willoughby Goddard
Gates Peter Butterworth
Freddy Peter Bowles

Director: Laurence Bourne

'And a Very Fine Fiddle Has He'

w Robert Holmes

Hired to check into reports that a solicitor's client is being blackmailed, Marker finds himself earning his fee the hard way – nose down on the pavement!

Donald Halston Geoffrey Palmer
Robert Spanser John Carson
Judith Spanser Patricia Haines

Director: Laurence Bourne

My Life — That's a Marriage

w Michael Hastings

Marker's enquiries into why George left the girl he loves, Alice, in the lurch bring some very surprising results — not all of which Alice wants to hear.

Alice Benjamin Avis Bunnage
Alfred Benjamin Harry Ross
Janet Benjamin Pauline Delaney

Director: Kim Mills

You Think It'll Be Marvellous — But It's Always a Rabbit

w Robert Holmes

James Sale, the occupant of Ward C in the County Hospital, employs Marker to discover the driver of the car that ran him down. But where does Marker begin?

James Sale Maurice Good
Sue Jefferson Dilys Laye
DS Wimpole Gary Watson

Director: Mark Lawson

Protection Is a Man's Best Friend

w Mike Watts

Marker's attempts to track down the head man behind a betting shop extortion racket lead him into trouble with the law — and the unlawful.

Nancy Heuston Margaret Whiting
Ben Heuston Reginald Marsh
Shoemaker Griffith Jones

Director: Laurence Bourne

The Morning Wasn't So Hot

w Roger Marshall

Looking for a missing girl in the densely populated London streets isn't Marker's idea of fun — but when you need a bob or two . . .

Drummond Richard Butler
Dammon Philip Madoc
Sue Forbes Susan Burnet

Director: Kim Mills

You Should Hear Me Eat Soup

w Terence Frisby

When an old adversary sets foot on his doorstep, Marker decides to book a seat on the first available plane to anywhere — but his adversary has other ideas.

Happy Holliday David Lander
Tony Naylor Ray Brooks
Sonia Jennie Linden

Director: Patrick Dromgoole

You Have to Draw the Line Somewhere

w Martin Worth

Why is a solicitor so upset that his marriage has broken down? Employed to find the answer, Marker learns more than he's supposed to know.

Harry Lawford Peter Jeffrey
Jean Lawford Zena Marshall
John Fordyce James Cairncross

Director: Toby Robertson

Have It on the House

w Roger Marshall

Hired to track down a military man who has duped a woman out of £700, Marker's instinct tells him he's being taken for a fool — but conning an expert can prove dangerous.

Mrs Warboys Mona Bruce
Major Dorning Barry Letts
Mrs Ames Sally Bazely

Director: Guy Verney

Season Two
13 monochrome 60-minute episodes

All the Black Dresses She Wants

w Martin Worth

A meeting with a Birmingham solicitor and a pile of unpaid bills sees Marker leaving London for the smoke-filled skies of Birmingham — and even more trouble.

Beck Basil Dignam
Steve Burrell John Carson
Liz Lodge Delena Kidd

Director: Kim Mills

Don't Forget You're Mine

w Roger Marshall

Marker moves into his new Handsworth district office, and waits for the phone to ring. When it does — he wishes it hadn't.

Mrs Jessup Pauline Delaney
Donald Roy Dotrice
Karen Scott Virginia Stride

Director: Kim Mills

I Could Set It to Music

w Julian Bond
Who is blackmailing a highly-placed
director of industry by threatening to release
photographs of his indiscretions? Marker
thinks he knows – but can he prove it?
Hugh Clayton Hugh Burden
Jean Clayton Isobel Dean
Hetheridge William Moore

Director: Basil Coleman

It's a Terrible Way to Be

w Hugh Leonard
A meeting with an Irishman and a pile of
unpaid bills spell trouble for Marker. Paddy
wants his debts settled – but who'll pay
Marker's fee?
Gannon Harold Goldblatt
Mrs Gannon Marie Kean
Con David Kelly

Director: Guy Verney

You Can Keep the Medal

w Julian Bond
Hired to find out how a girl drowned in a
canal, Marker soon finds that the country air
doesn't suit everyone – particularly
snoopers.
Ella Bowen Miranda Connell
Phil Lyons William Lucas
David Bowen Barry Letts

Director: Guy Verney

You're Not Cinderella, Are You?

w Roger Marshall
Employed at the Hotel Railton as house
detective during World Cup week, Marker
has his work cut out keeping his eye on the
strange behaviour of the hotel's guests.
Kurt Heller William Franklyn
Marty Rose John Junkin
Hostess Georgina Hale

Director: Quentin Lawrence

Works with Chess – Not with Life

w Roger Marshall
Hired by a firm of solicitors to prove that
their client is the victim of food poisoning,
Marker finds himself dining alone.
Faulkner Laurence Hardy
Alan Sherrett Derek Waring
Nancy Sherrett Susan Dowdall

Director: Basil Coleman

It Had to Be a Mouse

w Robert Holmes
Marker's problems are twofold. A local
paper won't run his agency ad, and someone
asks him to run to ground claims against a
local tenant – on the cheap, of course.
Leonard Minster Ronald Adam
Mary Hollobread Wendy Gifford
Ansell Dudley Foster

Director: Kim Mills

Tell Me About the Crab

w Jack Trevor Story
Mr Madison wants Marker to find out who
is pestering his wife – and why? It's hardly
the stuff that dreams are made of, but
Marker's rent is due.
Madison Robin Bailey
Jill Jacqueline Pearce
Catherine Gwen Cheryl

Director: Jonathan Alwyn

No, No, Nothing Like That

w Andrew Hall
Nothing in his diary. No outstanding cases.
Sitting in an empty office waiting for the
phone to ring. Marker's career has reached a
new low.
Harris Munro Glyn Houston
Anna Munro Rona Anderson
Dr Pringle Geoffrey Palmer

Director: Quentin Lawrence

There Are More Things in Heaven and Earth

w Julian Bond
Hired to undertake some difficult
negotiations for Miss Barnes, Marker can't

help but wonder what he's let himself into.
Things turn nasty from the start.
Miss Barnes Helen Lindsay
Stella Rouse Stephanie Bidmead
Tony Hart Patrick Mower

Director: Tony Robertson

Twenty Pounds of Heart and Muscle

w Robert Holmes
Marker finds himself hired as a bodyguard
with a difference. The difference being that
the body is resting peacefully in a velvet-
lined coffin!
Pauline Garrity Mary Webster
Enoch Garrity George A. Cooper
Charlie Knox Garfield Morgan

Director: Piers Haggard

What's the Matter? Can't You Take a Sick Joke?

w Hugh Leonard
Who has robbed Mrs Wyncherley's husband
of his final resting place? Marker finds
himself undertaking enquiries in a graveyard
to learn the truth.
Mrs Wyncherley Sheila Keith
Fowler Peter Vaughan
Brampton Clive Morton

Director: Guy Verney

Season Three
13 colour 60-minute episodes

If This is Lucky, I'd Rather be Jonah

w David Whittaker
A wife with expensive tastes. A husband
anxious to please. As Marker finds out, a
combination for trouble.
Valarie Kitson Sheila Fearn
Eric Kitson Edward Fox
DS Willows Alister Williamson

Director: Patrick Dromgoole

But What Good Will the Truth Do?

w Martin Worth
Marker is hired to dig into the facts
surrounding a fourteen-year-old sailing
accident. Supposing he finds the facts –
what then?

Liz Chambers Georgina Hale
Sarah Chambers Maureen Pryor
Harry Chambers Harold Goodwin

Director: Quentin Lawrence

Memories of Meg

w Robert Banks Stewart
Memories. Everyone has them. Some will
share them with others. But some wish to
hide them away like some forgotten dream.
Marker's memories turn to nightmares.
Nat Harold Lang
Mrs Briggs Sonia Dresdel
Arthur Leslie Dwyer

Director: Dennis Vance

Have Mud, Will Throw

w Roger Marshall
What seems like a straightforward case for
Marker turns, because of an accident, into a
complex human situation.
Jackson Barry Stanton
Rowan Arthur Brough
Mrs Burditt Katharine Parr

Director: Peter Duguid

But They Always Come Back for Tea

w Roger Marshall
Marker discovers that a little corruption
goes a long way – and sometimes the
innocent have to pay for it.
Harry Warren Evan Hooper
Paula Warren Rhoda Lewis
Robin Warren Christian Comber

Director: Kim Mills

Mercury in an Off-white Mac

w Roger Marshall
New lodgings and some interesting police
work. Marker looks set to improve his lot –
until some strange people destroy his
dreams.
George Caroline Blakiston
DI Wilson Philip Brack
DS Davidson Bernard Lee

Director: Kim Mills

Strictly Private and Confidential

w Robert Wynatt

Why did Brenda leave home? Was it because of what her parents said to her? Or are there more sinister reasons? Marker finds out.

Ron Baker Martin Shaw
Brenda Smedley Karol Keyes
Arthur Smedley George A. Cooper

Director: Patrick Dromgoole

Honesty is the Best Policy – but Who Can Afford the Premiums!

w Bill Braig

Never one to turn down a 'juicy' case, Marker finds himself playing for high stakes when he is hired to follow a wayward wife.

Marchmont Donald Hewlett
Vera Burnside Jan Holden
Lewis Burnside Garfield Morgan

Director: Robert Tronson

The Bromsgrove Venus

w Anthony Skene

A nude and nasty young man add up to trouble when Marker is hired to follow a ten-year-old trail – to murder.

Pauline Marjie Lawrence
Ainsworth Leon Sinden
Marge Ainsworth Sylvia Kaye

Director: James Goddard

It Must Be The Architecture – Couldn't Be the Climate

w Robert Holmes

The death of a young girl. Malicious gossip. A man's career in trouble. Three elements that provide Marker with food for thought.

Jessica Hinckman Hilary Mason
Dr Howlett Gary Hope
Murchinson Alan Lake

Director: James Goddard

It's Learning About the Lies That Hurts

w Robert Holmes

It's the morning after the night before, and some night it must have been – someone

died as a result, and Marker is faced with finding out why.

Lawrence Friend Michael Barrington
Blythe Dallas Caveli
Docherty Geoffrey Quigley

Director: Kim Mills

There's No Future in Monkey Business

w Brian Hayles

When the director of a firm finds someone fixing the books, Marker finds himself on the factory floor – and up to his neck in monkey business.

Jago Ray Brooks
Harry Latham Wilfred Pickles
Barney Christopher Benjamin

Director: Alan Gibson

Cross That Palm When We Come to It

w Roger Marshall

It's an interesting propostion that Marker should have left alone. Someone must foot the bill – and end up eating porridge.

Wheldon Tony Steedman
Pratt Arthur Cox
Arresting officer John Bailey

Director: Peter Duguid

Season Four

7 colour 60-minute episodes

Welcome to Brighton

w Roger Marshall

Released from jail and facing a life of bread and butter jobs, Marker finds himself alone in a strange new environment.

Jackerman George Sewell
Freda Jackerman Anne Ridler
Grace Heather Canning

Director: Kim Mills
Designer: Mike Hall

Divide and Conquer

w Roger Marshall

Once a private eye, always a private eye. Working at a building firm, Marker spots two youths pulling a con – and he's soon back into trouble.

Harry Terence Rigby
Frank Richard O'Callaghan
Enright Peter Cellier

Director: Kim Mills
Designer: Stan Woodward

Paid in Full

w Roger Marshall
Still struggling to find his feet while
working at the building firm, Marker just
can't seem to keep his nose out of trouble.
Jenny Tania Truck
Hull John Grieve
Wilson Maurice Good

Director: Guy Verney
Designer: Stan Woodward

My Life's My Own

w Roger Marshall
Marker meets a girl who, for the next two
days, has him running around in circles.
But then things change dramatically.
Shirley Marlowe Stephanie Beacham
Dr Nourse Gary Watson
Mrs Nourse Katherine Blake

Director: Kim Mills
Designer: Fred Pusey

Case for the Defence

w Roger Marshall
Things are looking up. Marker is invited to
join an enquiry agency. But why should
they wish to employ a man with a record?
Osborne William Lucas
DC Broom Leslie Dawson
Dorothy Milner Pauliine Challoner

Director: Guy Verney
Designer: Neville Green

The Comedian's Graveyard

w Roger Marshall
Struggling against the way his new
employers handle cases, Marker is assigned
to find a stagestruck teenager who has run
away from home.

Billy Raybold Joe Melia
Judy Tessa Wyatt
Arthur Mack Leslie Dwyer

Director: Jonathan Alwyn
Designer: Colin Andrews

A Fixed Address

w Roger Marshall
Why is it that when you decide to make
some changes in your life, something – or
someone – always gets in your way?
Rosemary Deborah Grant
Peter Barrie Rutter
Mortimer Philip Brack

Director: Kim Mills
Designer: Peter Le Page

Season Five

13 colour 60-minute episodes
(Episodes denoted with asterisk
transmitted in b/w)

A Mug Named Frank *

w Michael Chapman
Settled into his new enquiry office with
things looking sweet, a case of shoplifting
leads Marker to becoming involved in a
family feud.
Mrs Stuart Nora Nicholson
Gerry Stuart Barry Foster
Robert Stuart Andre Morrell

Director: Quentin Lawrence
Designer: Stan Woodward

Well – There Was This Girl, You See*

w Philip Broadley
When he takes on an enquiry for a young
girl, it isn't long before Marker wishes he'd
never laid eyes on her.
Mary Freeman Susan Broderick
James Walker Paul Harper
DI Firbank Ray Smith (Intro.)

Director: James Goddard
Designer: Fred Pusey

Slip Home in the Dark *

w Ray Jenkins
Marker is hired to find out who is making
threatening phone calls to a woman living

alone. His furtive observations bring unexpected results.

Barbara Pitt Estelle Kohler
Ken Pitt James Laurenson
Polly Susan Engel

Director: Peter Duguid
Designer: Roger Allen

I Always Wanted a Swimming Pool

w Philip Broadley
Framed! Marker, hired to watch the antics of a wayward husband, finds himself hooked up in a very unusual affair of the heart.
Charles Luce Cyril Luckham
Alan Grove James Bolam
Gustaffson John Savident

Director: Dennis Vance
Designer: Fred Pusey

The Beater and the Game

w Michael Chapman
A routine enquiry involving a small debts claim involves Marker in shaking off the overtures of a group of wealthy ladies.
Gorman Terence Rigby
Maureen Alethea Charlton
DI Firbank Ray Smith

Director: Peter Duguid
Designer: Stan Woodward

Come into the Garden, Rose *

w Douglas Livingstone
The ladies of Cheviot House have sharp tongues, as Marker finds out to his cost when his client Rose Mason sets them wagging.
Rose Mason Madge Ryan
Harry Brierly George Sewell
Cora Saunders Dulcie Bowman

Director: Bill Bain
Designer: Peter le Page

And When You've Paid the Bill, You're None the Wiser

w Trevor Preston
His latest assignment leads Marker into the centre of a family squabble over who gets what, from whom.

Geoffrey Kulman George Pravda
Mrs Kulman Kathleen Michael
Martin Kulman David Suchet

Director: Piers Haggard
Designer: David Marshall

Who Wants to be Told Bad News?

w John Kershaw

Marker finds himself at the centre of hypocrisy and villainy when he is hired to look after a client's welfare.
Miss Bain Mollie Maureen
Alfred Bain Glyn Edwards
Suresh Dhamar Madhav Sharme

Director: Douglas Camfield
Designer: Mike Hall

The Man Who Didn't Eat Sweets

w Richard Harris
When Mrs Meadows finds the photograph of a beautiful young girl in her husband's wallet, Marker is contacted – and receives a surprise from what he uncovers.
Julia Meadows Marjie Lawrence
Eddie Meadows Peter Sallis
Adele Jean Harvey

Director: James Gateward
Designer: Norman Garwood

Ward of Court

w James Doran
A case full of surprises – the kind Marker enjoys. This time it appears as though his interests and those of DI Firbank are the same – but are they?
Smythson Barry Warren
Ann Wilson Julie Samuel
DI Firbank Ray Smith

Director: William S. Stewart
Designer: Mike Hall

Transatlantic Cousins

w James Doren
Marker must sort out a fascinating case involving a streetwise old reprobate and a young American visiting Britain.

L'Ettrell Warren Stanhope
Nell Brenda Cavendish
Barbra L'Ettrell Patricia Cutts

Director: Dennis Vance
Designer: Roger Allan

Shades of White

w Robert Muller
When Marker takes on an investigation he'd
rather be without, he finds himself
manipulated by several people – including
DI Firbank.
Alan Biddersloe John Collin
Anne Biddersloe Lesley Ann Down
DI Firbank Ray Smith

Director: Piers Haggard
Designer: David Marshall

John VII, Verse 24

w Peter Hall
Faced with a head-on collision with DI
Firbank, Marker is more determined than
ever to get to the bottom of his latest
investigation.
Alec Payton George A. Cooper
Mr Holland Jeremy Bullock
DI Firbank Ray Smith

Director: David Wickes
Designer: Neville Green

Season Six

13 colour 60-minute episodes

The Bankrupt

w James Doren
Hired to enquire into the activities of
bankrupt shirt manufacturer Hayden-Peters,
Marker uncovers a web of deceit and
treachery.
Hayden-Peters Ray Barrett
Sandra Hayden-Peters Susan McCready
Tom Lewis Gareth Thomas

Director: James Gateward
Designer: Allan Cameron

Girl in Blue

w Roger Marshall
Her name is Janice Summers, and she has
disappeared. Marker is hired to discover her
whereabouts and bring her back home.

Mr Summers Richard Leech
Janice Summers Rosalyn Elvin
DI Firbank Ray Smith

Director: Dennis Vance
Designer: Norman Garwood

Many a Slip

w John Kershaw
A routine credit inquiry leads Marker to
uncover some strange discoveries concerning
an eminent doctor's wife.
Dr Pembroke Michael Culver
Felicity Pembroke Ann Curtboys
DI Firbank Ray Smith

Director: David Wickes
Designer: Norman Garwood

Mrs Podmore's Cat

w Philip Broadley
It's hardly the stuff of detective novels when
Marker is hired to babysit Mrs Podmore's
pet cat, Bertie. But things have a way of
turning awkward.
Mrs Podmore Jean Kent
Major Byers Dudley Foster
DI Firbank Ray Smith

Director: Bill Bain
Designer: Allan Cameron

The Man Who Said Sorry

w Richard Harris
When an oddly-dressed man visits his office
and explains that Marker is the only man
capable of helping him, the enquiry agent
begins to see problems ahead.
Barrett Paul Rogers
Holmesdean Patrick Phillips
DI Firbank Ray Smith

Director: Jonathan Alwyn
Designer: David Marshall

Horse and Carriage

w Richard Harris
When a husband hires Marker to investigate
his wife – but he, too, 'carries on' with
another woman – Marker finds the season of
goodwill a little hard to bear.

Harry Tony Melody
Lil Pat Heywood
PC Tony Selby

Director: Bill Bain
Designer: Graham Guest

A Family Affair

w John Kershaw
Marker's job: to prove a woman guilty or
innocent of putting pressure on her deceased
employer to leave her his entire wealth.
John Knight Norman Henry
Henry Knight Ralph Michael
Harriet Thorne Peggy Ann Wood

Director: Douglas Camfield
Designer: Allan Cameron

The Golden Boy

w Philip Broadley
Reveldale has everything going for him. So
what reason could he have for throwing
everything up and disappearing? His father
asks Marker to find out.
Sir John Reveldale David Gwillim
Vyv Reveldale Richard Hurndall
Clifton Philip Ray

Director: Douglas Camfield
Designer: Bryan Graves

The Windsor Royal

w Philip Broadley
Clement Lawrence is justifiably proud of
The Windsor Royal – a new breed of rose –
so when his rose bushes disappear he hires
Marker to investigate.
Lawrence Raymond Francis
Pamela Lawrence Nina Thomas
Thornton Julian Somers

Director: Douglas Camfield
Designer: Peter Le Page

It's a Woman's Privilege

w Michael Chapman
Surprised but happy to receive a visit from
his former landlady, Mrs Mortimer,
Marker's pleasure soon evaporates when she
tells him her problem.

Mrs Mortimer Pauline Delaney
Gordon Richard Thorpe
Nick Mortimer Brian Deacon

Director: Jim Goddard
Designer: Norman Garwood

Home and Away

w Brian Finch
Suspecting that there's another woman in
her husband's life, Madge Reading seeks
Marker's help. His enquiries bring
surprising results when her husband cries
'Foul'.
Madge Reading Barbara Young
Donald Reading Bryan Pringle
Gladys Mottram Barbara Keogh

Director: Robert Knight
Designer: Allan Cameron

Egg and Cress Sandwiches

w Michael Chapman
An unconventional vicar. A breath of
scandal and a pillar of the community. All
three combine to bring Marker trouble of
one kind or another.
Maj. Gen. Felcourt Robert Flemyng
Peter Palfrey Angus MacKay
DI Firbank Ray Smith

Director: Graham Evans
Designer: Graham Guest

The Trouble with Jenny

w Roger Marshall
While spending the night at a dingy hotel,
the strange activities of a young female
guest come to Marker's attention.
Jenny Petra Markham
Mrs Barnes Marjie Lawrence
DS Colin Donald Burton

Director: David Wickes
Designer: Tony Borer

Season Seven
13 colour 60-minute episodes

Nobody Wants to Know

w James Doran
Marker has one week in which to find a
witness. When he does so, he'll never forget
the girl – or what his involvement cost her.

Janice Harper **Judy Buxton**
Jackson **Trader Faulkner**
DI Firbank **Ray Smith**

Director: **Douglas Camfield**
Designer: **Bill Palmer**

How About a Cup of Tea

w **John Kershaw**
Bruised and battered during his last case,
Marker receives a surprise visitor to his
hospital bed – DI Firbank – who has a
proposition to put to him.
DI Firbank **Ray Smith (Last)**
Helen Mortimer **Pauline Delaney (Last)**
Ronnie Gash **Peter Childs (Intro.)**

Director: **Bill Bain**
Designer: **Mike Hall**

How About it, Frank?

w **James Doran**
A new beginning for Marker. Ron Gash
wants him as his new partner. But are
Gash's methods of detection compatible
with Marker's?
Chf. Insp. Tyson **Ray McAnally**
Ruby **Maggie Smith**
Ron Gash **Peter Childs**

Director: **Bill Bain**
Designer: **David Ferris**

They All Sound Simple at First

w **John Kershaw**
Called in by a cabinet-maker to recover
£700 he's owed for an antique clock, Marker
finds that even the easiest of cases isn't all
that simple.
Dominic Anders **Philip Madoc**
Nina **Diane Keen**
Croxley **Peter Bowles**

Director: **David Wickes**
Designer: **Harry Clark**

The Fall Guy

w **Brian Finch**
A girl named Tuesday brings more than
beauty into Marker's life when he gets
mixed up with the less-than-hospitable Lord
of the Manor.

Tuesday Simpson **Susan Penhaligon**
Julian Bradley **Ronald Lewis**
Alison **Iris Russell**

Director: **Douglas Camfield**
Designer: **Peter Le Page**

What's to Become of Us?

w **Richard Harris**
Finding himself facing a very strange client,
Marker decides it is time to head for fresh
fields – providing his client allows him to
leave.
Hooper **John Woodnutt**
Mrs Grahame **Rosemarie Dunham**
Ron Gash **Peter Childs**

Director: **Douglas Camfield**
Designer: **Peter Le Page**

Hard Times

w **James Doran**
A new 'home', a new 'office', and his first
client. A day to remember – a day of
trouble. Marker's new starting point leaves a
lot to be desired.
Watson **Joseph Grieg**
Pearce **Tenniel Evans**
Knaggs **Ray Lonnen**

Director: **Simon Langton**
Designer: **Richard Harrison**

No Orchids for Marker

w **Philip Broadley**
A chance to make £1,000 for 'keeping an
eye on things'. An offer too good to refuse
finds Marker all at sea – without a
lifejacket.
Eileen Sanders **Joan Scott**
Freddie **Lewis Flander**
DS Evans **Anthony Langdon**

Director: **Graham Evans**
Designer: **Frank Gilman**

The Fatted Calf

w **Brian Finch**
Marker's search for a young university
student brings him face to face with
violence – and a group of revolutionaries.

Giles Robinson **Peter Settelen**
Janet Frisby **Jan Harvey**
Vince Gregson **Alun Armstrong**

Director: **Jonathan Alwyn**
Designer: **Alex Clarke**

Lifer

w **Bob Baker and Dave Martin**
An anonymous tip-off sets Marker on the
trail of a man seeking vengeance for a crime
committed ten years earlier.
Arthur Biddle **Norman Bird**
Brian Stafford **Tony Calvin**
Kay Price **Ingrid Hafner**

Director: **David Wickes**
Designer: **Eric Shedden**

Take No for an Answer

w **Roger Marshall**
Hired to find a missing wife, Marker's
enquiries lead him to unearth something
nasty in suburbia – and something odd in a
garden shed.
Carter **Stephen Yardley**
Paula **Delena Kidd**
Graham **Michael Turner**

Director: **Kim Mills**
Designer: **Bill Palmer**

Fit of Conscience

w **David Ambrose**
Is there more than the eye can see behind
Marker's latest assignment – an enquiry into
a bribe of a public servant? Marker uncovers
deeper issues – and finds himself without
friends.
Overton **Peter Welch**
Brightwell **Kevin Brennan**
Evelyn Friendly **Margaret Whiting**

Director: **Mike Vardy**
Designer: **Graham Guest**

Unlucky for Some

w **Philip Broadley**
Case number 87. Marker bows out with a
strange and intriguing case involving two
villains who appear to have it made – until
Marker arrives on the scene.
Jeremy Fellows **Julian Holloway**
Keith **John Quayle**
Ethel **Joyce Heron**

Director: **Jonathan Alwyn**
Designer: **Norman Garwood**

PUBLIC EYE
Based on an idea by Roger Marshall and
Anthony Marriott
Producers:
Don Leaver and John Bryce (Season 1)
Richard Bates (Season 2)
Michael Chapman (Seasons 3–7)
Kim Mills (Seasons 4–5)
Robert Love (Season 6)
Executive producers:
Lloyd Shirley (Season 4)
Robert Love (Season 6)
Theme music: Robert Earley
Story editors:
Richard Bates (Seasons 1–3)
Michael Chapman (Seasons 5 and 6)
An ABC Weekend Network Production
(Seasons 1–3)
A Thames TV Network Production
(Seasons 4–7)
87 monochrome and colour 60-minute
episodes
23 January – 1 May 1965
2 July – 24 September 1966
20 January – 13 April 1968
30 July – 10 September 1969
7 July – 29 September 1971
8 November 1972 – 14 February 1973
6 January – 7 April 1975

THE PURSUERS

Take a jaded Hollywood film star. Bring him to England and
partner him with a large black German Shepherd dog (not
forgetting a dumb-headed personal assistant) and you had *The*

Pursuers, the lacklustre adventures of Detective Inspector Bollinger of Scotland Yard, a cop who patrolled the streets of London with his sidekicks, delving into 'the strange and complicated vagaries of human behaviour'.

As 'complicated' as lighting matches, the series' only redeeming feature were the dozen or so scripts by Phillip Levene.

REGULAR CAST

DI Bollinger **Louis Hayward**   *DS Steve Wall* **Gaylord Cavallaro**

The Sailor
The Husband
Bessie
The Face
The Mine
Master Key
The Hunt
The Holiday
The Gun
The Jungle
Masquerade
The Silent Witness
The Frame
The Othello Murder
The Return
The Lost Key
The Poacher
The Scientist
Tomorrow's Ghost
Supreme Court

Breakout
The Countess
The Suspect
The Colonel
The Escape
Inside Job
Confession
The Web
The Track
Model Crime
Persuasion
The George Webber Story
The Convention
The Amateur
The Accident
Runaway
The Contract
Double Alibi
The Painting

THE PURSUERS
Executive producer: Donald Hyde
Directors: Robert Lynn, Wilfred Eades,
Peter Bez
Writers: Phillip Levene, John Warwick,
Leonard Fincham, Basil Dawson
A Crestview Production
for ABC TV
39 monochrome 30-minute episodes
1 April 1961 – 21 April 1962

QUATERMASS

The return of Professor Bernard Quatermass, the man whose three earlier adventures struck terror into viewers' hearts and frightened the living daylights out of millions. After a 20-year retirement, Quatermass returned for a new four-part story which, though nowhere near as scary as its predecessors, was nevertheless meaty enough to provide the viewer with a memorable final adventure.

No monsters this time around, just a story set in the near future concerning people being 'taken over' by some unseen alien life-form. Set against the backdrop of a world gone mad (law and order had broken down and the streets of Britain were amok with marauding gangs of 'Planet People' – youngsters who believed they had been chosen to lead the human race to a new world), the story concerned the Professor's attempts to convince the authorities that in reality the alien civilisation was harvesting the young people for *food*.

REGULAR CAST

Quatermass **John Mills**   *Kapp* **Simon MacCorkindale**
Clare Kapp **Barbara Kellerman**   *Kickalong* **Ralph Arliss**
Caraway **Paul Rosebury**   *Bee* **Jane Bertish**   *Hetti* **Rebecca Saire**
Sal **Toyah Wilcox**

Ringstone Round

w Nigel Kneale

After several years' retirement in Scotland, Professor Quatermass returns to London to appear on a TV show which is celebrating the latest co-venture in space – the linking of two USA/USSR orbiting vehicles to form a joint space station. Astonished by the savagery he has encountered in the streets, he condemns the super-powers during the broadcast. As he does so, the space station is destroyed by an unseen force! Outside, the 'Planet People' start to converge on the stone circle of Ringstone Round.

Director: Piers Haggard

Lovely Lightning

w Nigel Kneale

Having seen hundreds of 'Planet People' obliterated by the beams of light from space, Quatermass joins forces with Kapp to rescue a young girl who escaped from the holocaust, though she is now deaf and blind. Meanwhile, more youngsters converge at Ringstone Round and, as it is later discovered, similar places across the world.

Director: Piers Haggard

What Lies Beneath

w Nigel Kneale

Rescued by a group of old people from a gang fight, Quatermass takes shelter with them, while Kapp returns to his home to find that his family have been killed by the beam of light from space. As thousands of 'Planet People' converge at the gates of Wembley Stadium, the Professor realises the awful truth – the aliens are in fact, harvesting the human race.

Director: Piers Haggard

An Endangered Species

w Nigel Kneale

Annie is killed but Quatermass survives the latest blast from space. Joined by a group of aged experts, the Professor lays plans to thwart any further harvesting of the 'lemmings' – a threat that can only be overcome by someone giving their life to destroy the aliens . . .

Director: Piers Haggard

QUATERMASS
Created by: Nigel Kneale
Producer: Ted Childs
Executive producer: Verity Lambert
Associate producer: Norton Knatchbull
Executive in charge of production: Johnny
Goodman
Music by: Marc Wilkinson and Nic Rowley
Director: Piers Haggard
*A Euston Films/Thames Television Network
Production*
4 colour 60-minute episodes
24 October – 14 November 1979

THE RACING GAME

Based on the best-selling books by former champion jockey turned thriller writer, Dick Francis, this short though thoroughly watchable series packed more thrills and excitement into its 6-week run than other programmes did in a 13-week schedule.

The star of the series was ex-jockey turned detective Sid Halley. Crippled by an accident on the turf, Halley was forced to look for alternative employment and found it as a roving private investigator who hired out his services to the wealthy racehorse-breeding stables. With the odds stacked firmly against him, he probed the million-pound racing industry for intrigue and brought those bent on turning their meagre wagers into a fortune – by fair means or foul.

(Author's note: Each episode title was preceded by the words: *The Dick Francis Thriller* . . . These have been omitted for brevity.)

REGULAR CAST

Sid Halley **Mike Gwilym**   *Chico Barnes* **Mick Ford**

The Dick Francis Thriller – Odds Against

w Terence Feely
Ex-jockey turned private eye Sid Halley investigates his first case – and finds that the odds are against him when he trys to uncover who is behind a major betting coup.

Charles Roland **James Maxwell**
Howard Graves **Gerald Flood**
Dora Graves **Rachel Davies**

Director: **Lawrence Gordon Clarke**
Designer: **Vic Symonds/Mike Long**

— Trackdown

w Terence Feely

Employed to find out who's behind a betting swindle, Halley finds himself faced with a list of unlikely outsiders and uncovers a devious blackmail plot – which culminates in murder.

Jack Beater Leslie Sands
Tom Mansell Jeremy Clyde
Trish Latham Carol Royle

Director: Lawrence Gordon Clarke
Designer: Vic Symonds/Mike Long

— Gambling Lady

w Evan Jones

Investigating a routine insurance claim for a valuable racehorse leads Sid and Chico to unearth a major international swindle – one that could leave the bookmakers smarting from huge losses.

Sylvia Guiccoli Caroline Blakiston
Count Guiccoli Anthony Steel
Charles Roland James Maxwell

Director: Peter Duffell
Designer: Vic Symonds/Mike Long

— Horses for Courses

w Leon Griffiths

Trying to run down a clever confidence trick behind a get-rich-quick racket, Sid and Chico find themselves facing bribes, a doublecross and – when all else fails – murder.

Kate Ellis Jan Francis
George Benson Maurice O'Connell
Terry Flynn John Bindon

Director: John Mackenzie
Designer: Vic Symonds

— Horsenap

w Trevor Preston

When a valuable racehorse disappears, its owner seeks the help of race-going private eye Sid Halley – who finds himself trying to piece together the clues against a backdrop of organised crime.

Lankester Iain Cuthbertson
Carol Tomes Susan Penhaligon
Steve Larry Lamb

Director: Colin Bucksey
Designer: Vic Symonds/Mike Long

— Needle

w Terence Feely

A dead racehorse points the way for Halley to take on a gang of ruthless crooks who are leaving a trail of dead horseflesh across the country. As Halley discovers, a hypodermic needle spells trouble on the turf.

Sally Meg Davis
John Fenby Davyd Harries
Insp. Kilbride Andrew Downie

Director: Peter Duffell
Designer: Vic Symonds/Mike Long

THE RACING GAME
Producer: Jacky Stoller
Executive producer: David Cunliffe
Music by: Mike Moran
A Yorkshire Television Network Production
6 colour 60-minute episodes
21 November 1979 – 9 January 1980

RAFFLES

First introduced in *Raffles – The Amateur Cracksman* in 1975, viewers had to wait another 14 months for further exploits of E. W. Hornung's gentleman jewel thief, L. J. Raffles and his trusted confidant, Bunny.

Little had changed since the first story (an adventure which depicted how Raffles helped himself to a £10,000 necklace, from under the very noses of the police.) Raffles was still performing daring – sometimes foolhardy – robberies to prove that his main adversary, Scotland Yard policeman Inspector Mackenzie, was a 'bungling oaf, with little talent and no imagination'. (Mackenzie suspected Raffles of being a thief, but never found enough evidence to incriminate him.) The thief still had his inborn talent for mischief that had led him into his amateur, but highly-skilled pastime. He continued to distrust the word of politicians (but remain a true patriot); he *knew* that the police were 'bad losers, and not always the good sports they might be'; and he was always willing to try the 'impossible' – that daring theft of any priceless object that took his fancy, and left the police baffled by his impudence – and its owners aggrieved by its loss.

Only one man in England knew Raffles's secret: that he wasn't simply an all-round good egg, who played third bat for the English cricket team, while exploiting his sophisticated man-about-town manner for personal gain – Bunny Manders.

Raffles's fag at college, Bunny had never lost his schoolboy admiration for his colleague. His only desire was to be of use to his schoolboy hero – by defending Raffles from the searching enquiries of the police. Constantly reminding Raffles of his gentleman's code, Bunny was his mentor's conscience – a subordinate certainly, but nevertheless his trusted friend.

REGULAR CAST
Raffles **Anthony Valentine** *Bunny* **Christopher Strauli**
Insp. Mackenzie **James Maxwell** (1975) *Victor Carin* (1977)

Raffles – The Amateur Cracksman

Adapted by **Philip Mackie** *(Pilot Story)*
An invitation to play cricket at the home of the Earl of Milchester gives Raffles and his friend Bunny the opportunity to help themselves to the Dowager of Melrose's £10,000 diamond necklace.
Earl of Milchester **Michael Barrington**
Dowager of Melrose **Margot Lister**
Inspector Mackenzie **James Maxwell**

Director: **Christopher Hodson**
Designer: **Roger Andrews**

The First Step

w Philip Mackie
It's over a year since Raffles and Bunny pulled off their last major coup, and Bunny seeks out his friend again to embark on a new set of adventures. But Raffles appears to be otherwise engaged – to the beautiful Lady Maud.
Lord LochMaben **Thorley Walters**
Lady Maud **Susan Skipper**
Sgt Groom **Godfrey James**

Director: **Christopher Hodson**
Designer: **Roger Andrews**

A Costume Piece

w Philip Mackie
Reuben Rosenthall is a self-made millionaire – which makes him an obvious attraction for Raffles. But can the amateur cracksman succeed in fleecing Rosenthall and saving his friend Bunny from certain death at gunpoint?

Rosenthall Alfred Marks
Billy Purivs Brian Glover
Dolly Jill Gascoine

Director: Christopher Hodson
Designer: Roger Andrews

The Spoils of Sacrilege

w Philip Mackie

Raffles himself is always on the lookout for the unexpected. Bunny, however, isn't – and that's what leads him into trouble . . . and Raffles into a seemingly innocent encounter to save his partner from harm.
Osborne William Mervyn
Mrs Osborne Barbara Hicks
George Osborne William Humbert

Director: Christopher Hodson
Designer: Roger Andrews

The Gold Cup

w Philip Mackie

Someone is seeking to convince the police that Raffles is responsible for a series of audacious thefts. He isn't. So he sets out to give the stranger and the police something to think about.
Lord Thornaby Tony Britton
Kingsmill Peter Sallis
Insp. Woodward Charles Rea

Director: David Cunliffe
Designer: Roger Andrews

A Chest of Silver ·

w Philip Mackie

Though Bunny is well aware of his friend's activities, he'd be more than grateful if Raffles kept him informed of which law he intends to break – and when. Dealing with Inspector Mackenzie is difficult at the best of times – but alarming when he has no idea what Raffles is up to.
Bank official Geoffrey Hutchins
Insp. Mackenzie Victor Carin
Sergeant Mike Murray

Director: Alan Gibson
Designer: Chris George

The Last Laugh

w Philip Mackie

Raffles never could resist a challenge or an appeal to his gallantry. This time, however, a combination of the two lead him into deadly danger and he finds himself facing the dreaded villain, Pinelli.
Pinelli Cyril Shaps
Count Corbucci Robert Lang
Insp. Mackenzie Victor Carin

Director: Jim Goddard
Designer: Roger Andrews

A Trap to Catch a Cracksman

w Philip Mackie

When Raffles's pride in his amateur status as a sportsman is outraged, he finds himself fighting a solo battle. Bunny, sober, could be of help; but Bunny drunk can – and does – confuse the issue.
Swigger Morrison Lloyd Lamble
Florrie Carol Drinkwater
Sgt Thompson John Stratton

Director: John Davies
Designer: Chris George

To Catch a Thief

w Philip Mackie

Somewhere in Mayfair there appears to be another Raffles. One thief on his patch is more than enough for Inspector Mackenzie, who doesn't take the intruder's appearance lightly. Neither does Raffles – who determines to trap his impersonator.
Lord Belville Robert Hardy
Insp. Mackenzie Victor Carin
PC John Flint

Director: Christopher Hodson
Designer: Chris George

A Bad Night

w Philip Mackie

While his friend Raffles is busy taking on the Australian test cricketers at Manchester, Bunny sets out to go burgling alone. His attempts to impress his friend lead him into deadly peril.

Netje Jan Francis
Mrs Van Der Berg Brenda Cowling
Sgt Holly Norman Bird

Director: Christopher Hodson
Designer: Chris George

Mr Justice Raffles

w Philip Mackie
Raffles often takes the law into his own hands, but when an unscrupulous money-lender grabs his attention and a beautiful suffragette steals his heart, he decides its time to deliver some poetic justice of his own.
Brigstock John Savident
Lady Belsize Lynette Davies
Teddy Garland Charles Dance

Director: Christopher Hodson
Designer: Roger Andrews

Home Affairs

w Philip Mackie
An irresistible challenge: to take on the Home Secretary, Scotland Yard *and* Inspector Mackenzie. Could Raffles refuse? No way, but he decides to give them a chance by planning nothing in advance – just brilliant improvisation. A mistake!
Sir Arthur Graham Crowden
Dodson Eric Chitty
Insp. Mackenzie Victor Carin

Director: James Goddard
Designer: Chris George

The Gift of the Emperor

w Philip Mackie
'Politicians are not to be trusted – any more than criminals, Bunny.' When MP Carstairs tries to con our hero, Raffles takes an interest in international politics. Needless to say, he gets the upper hand.
Carstairs John Carson
Von Heumann John Hallam
Insp. Mackenzie Victor Carin

Director: Jim Goddard

An Old Flame

w Philip Mackie
Has Raffles finally met his match? Lady Paulton is rich, beautiful, eager and determined. She's also aware of Raffles's midnight hour activities. Will she give him away? Is there no escape this time?
Lady Paulton Caroline Blakiston
Lord Paulton Gerald Flood
Insp. Mackenzie Victor Carin

Director: James Goddard
Designer: Roger Andrews

RAFFLES
Based on stories by: E. W. Hornung
Adapted by: Philip Mackie
Producers: Peter Willes (1975)
Jacky Stoller (1977)
Executive producer: David Cunliffe (1977)
Music by: Anthony Isaac
A Yorkshire Television Network Production
1 colour 60-minute pilot story
13 colour 60-minute episodes
10 September 1975
25 February – 20 May 1977

RANDALL AND HOPKIRK (DECEASED)

'There's something different about this pair of private eyes . . . one of them is dead!' So ran the billing for this oddball entry into the sixties cops and robbers stakes, which starred a different kind of investigative duo: private eye Jeff Randall and his partner Marty Hopkirk – a ghost!

Partners in a private enquiry agency, Jeff and Marty appeared to have everything going for them – until the day when Marty was run down and killed by a car. Thus began one of the most unusual partnerships in television detective fiction. Barely minutes after his death, Marty returned as a ghost to help his partner track down his killer (his death had been arranged to keep him silent regarding a divorce enquiry) – and by so doing, had outstayed his welcome in heaven (or wherever detectives lay down their guns), by invoking an ancient curse which stated that: 'Before the sun shall rise, each ghost unto his grave must go. Cursed be the ghost who dares to stay and face the awful light of day.' Ergo, Marty was fated to remain on earth as a ghost – but one seen only by his partner Jeff, to whom he quickly became a welcome (sometimes unwelcome) spiritual adviser.

With lots of high-speed action, some better-than-most plots (plus some stinkers), the show was guaranteed success – in all save the most profitable market of all, the USA. Syndicated there under the title *My Partner the Ghost* (with a redone title sequence), it failed to find an audience and disappeared almost as fast as Marty's spectre.

REGULAR CAST

Jeff Randall Mike Pratt   *Marty Hopkirk* Kenneth Cope   *Jean Hopkirk* Annette Andre

My Late Lamented Friend and Partner

w Ralph Smart
The enquiry team of Randall and Hopkirk loses a partner, but not its spirit. Jeff goes hunting for shadows, while Marty plays peek-a-boo with people who'd rather he remained unseen and unheard.
Sorrenson Frank Windsor
Beatnik Ronald Lacey
Mrs Sorrenson Anne Sharp

Director: Cyril Frankel

A Disturbing Case

w Mike Pratt and Ian Wilson
Talking to 'himself' lands Jeff in hospital and further trouble when a hypnotist who is using patients to rob their homes takes on Marty who, though unseen, gives the doctor a sight to remember.
Dr Conrad David Bauer
Dr Lambert Gerald Flood
Insp. Nolan Michael Griffiths

Director: Ray Austin

That's How Murder Snowballs

w Ray Austin
Jeff discovers that an ability to read minds doesn't always pay the rent. It can in fact get you into an awful lot of trouble – and it does. But when Marty's around, anything can happen.
Barry Jones Patrick Holt
Gloria Marsh Grazina Frame
Insp. Nolan Michael Griffiths

Director: Paul Dickson

Never Trust a Ghost

w Tony Williamson
Why should Marty continue to report that people have been murdered when no bodies are found to confirm his accusations? Jeff knows that *something* is going on – but what? Has Marty started seeing things?
James Howarth Peter Vaughan
Karen Howarth Caroline Blakiston
Insp. Clayton Donald Morley

Director: Leslie Norman

Who Ever Heard of a Ghost Dying?

w Tony Williamson

Marty in danger of being exorcised! Jeff has his work cut out protecting his ghostly partner from the overzealous attentions of Hellingworth and Purley – two ghostbusters, who want Marty out of the way to further their own plans.

Hellingworth John Fraser
Purley Charles Lloyd Pack
Insp. Large Ivor Dean

Director: Ray Austin

The House on Haunted Hill

w Tony Williamson

Who ever heard of a ghost being scared of – ghosts? Jeff Randall did. Far from helping Jeff to get to the bottom of the secret of a haunted house, Marty's white suit develops goosebumps.

Jennifer Judith Arthy
Frederick P. Waller Peter Jones
Walter Previss Jeremy Nurnham

Director: Ray Austin

When Did You Start to Stop Seeing Things?

w Tony Williamson

Is Jeff really free of his spiritual helper? When Marty fails to make contact with his partner, it appears so. Bad timing. If ever Jeff needed a partner to help him crack a case, this is it!

Sir Oliver Clifford Evans
Jarvis Keith Barron
Insp. Large Ivor Dean

Director: Jeremy Summers

Just for the Record

w Donald James

Jeff and Jean are hired to look after two beauty contestants. Jeff's task is an agreeable one – looking after Miss Russia. Language proves no problem – but the involvement of a ghost certainly does!

Pargiter Ranald Radd
Anne Olivia Hammett
Lord Dorking Nosher Powell

Director: Jeremy Summers

Murder Ain't What It Used to Be!

w Tony Williamson

A vendetta between a notorious Chicago gangster and a ghost proves to be a somewhat difficult case for Jeff Randall. It appears that the gangster's rival is reaching out from the grave to settle old accounts – and Marty is the unwilling third party!

Bugsy Spanio David Healy
Paul Kristner Alan Gifford
Mrs Maddox Joyce Carey

Director: Jeremy Summers

But What a Sweet Little Room

w Ralph Smart

When his client dies in an 'accidental' car crash, Jeff seeks Marty's help to expose a phoney medium who makes her living by duping her clients into believing that she can contact the deceased.

Arthur De Crecey Michael Goodliffe
Madame Hinska Doris Hare
Elliot Norman Bird

Director: Roy Ward Baker

Who Killed Cock Robin

w Tony Williamson

Hired to guard a tropical bird aviary, Jeff finds himself investigating a complicated plot to strip his friends of their feathers. But birds can be killed – not murdered . . . can't they?

Sandra Joyce Jane Merrow
Laverick Cyril Luckham
Beeches David Lodge

Director: Roy Ward Baker

The Ghost Who Saved the Bank at Monte Carlo

w Tony Williamson

She has perfected a gambling system that will win her a fortune. So why doesn't her number come up? Because Marty's spectral hand is operating the roulette wheel, that's why – and the ghost has even more games up his sleeve.

Aunt Clara Mary Merrall
Larsey Brian Blessed
Suzanne Veronica Carlson

Director: Jeremy Summers

For the Girl Who Has Everything

w Donald James

When death strikes in a haunted castle, Jeff finds himself investigating a weird mystery, and Marty discovers that a ghost-hunting psychic can see him – and seeing is believing, isn't it?

Kim Wentworth Lois Maxwell
Mrs Pleasance Marjorie Rhodes
McAllister Freddie Jones

Director: Cyril Frankel

You Can Always Find a Fall Guy

w Donald James

You don't expect a nun, of all people, to doublecross you – unless she turns out to be something quite different. Jeff is held prisoner, and Marty tries to break the habit of a lifetime.

Miss Holliday Juliet Harmer
Yateman Patrick Barr
Edwards Garfield Morgan

Director: Ray Austin

The Smile Behind the Veil

w Gerald Kelsey

Whose face hides behind the veil of a funeral mourner – and why is she smiling? Jeff finds himself looking for the answer – and Marty performs miracles to wipe the smile off the face of a murderer.

Cynthia Hilary Tindall
Seaton Alex Scott
Donald Seaton Gary Watson

Director: Jeremy Summers

A Sentimental Journey

w Donald James

When a consignment of 'goods' worth £10,000 turns out to be an attractive blonde, Jeff concedes that the assignment is to his liking – until trying to escort her from Glasgow to London takes on murderous implications.

Dandy Tracey Crisp
Seymour William Squire
Tony Drew Henley

Director: Leslie Norman

When the Spirit Moves You

w Tony Williamson

There are some things a ghost detective can do better than his mortal counterparts. One is to act as an unseen bodyguard. But what happens when the client can not only see you – but wants to hear your side of the story?

Niklos Corri Kieron Moore
Calvin P. Bream Anton Rodgers
Insp. Large Ivor Dean

Director: Ray Austin

The Trouble with Women

w Tony Williamson

When Jeff is hired to find out if a woman's husband is having an affair, he finds that having a ghost for a partner has its uses – especially if you're gambling for your life with the cards stacked against you.

Alan Corder Paul Maxwell
Susan Lang Denise Buckley
Paul Lang Edward Brayshaw

Director: Cyril Frankel

It's Supposed to Be Thicker Than Water

w Donald James

Playing postman to deliver an envelope to an escaped convict strikes Jeff as a simple affair – until he discovers that the envelope contains an invitation to murder and he finds his own life on the line.

Crackan Felix Aylmer
Fay Crackan Liz Fraser
Rev. Henry Crackan Neil McCallum

Director: Leslie Norman

The Man from Nowhere

w Donald James

Why should a stranger enter Jean's flat and claim to be her husband? Everyone knows that Marty died – don't they? One man who wishes to get to the bottom of the strange event is the ghostly Hopkirk himself – but Jeff doesn't appear to be interested!

'Marty' Ray Brooks
Hyde Michael Gwynn
Mannering Patrick Newell

Director: Robert Tronson

Could You Recognise the Man Again?

w Donald James

When Jeff and Jean observe gangster George Roden leaving their car – and find a dead body in the back seat – it leads to Jean being held hostage to stop her giving evidence, and Marty enlisting unusual help to find her.

George Roden Stanley Meadows
Mrs Roden Madge Ryan
Insp. Large Ivor Dean

Director: Jeremy Summers

Vendetta for a Dead Man

w Donald James

Jansen, a vengeance-seeking escaped prisoner, decides that since Hopkirk, the man who put him away, is dead, his widow Jean must suffer – but he's reckoned without the ghostly guardian's devotion to his wife.

Jansen George Sewell
Cavallo-Smith Barrie Ingham
Mrs Cavallo-Smith Ann Castle

Director: Cyril Frankel

Money to Burn

w Donald James

Hot money proves a big temptation for Jeff Randall – but puts him in a hot spot. He finds himself accused of stealing money intended for incineration, and when there's smoke there's fire – this time in the shape of a sultry torch singer.

Elizabeth Saxon Sue Lloyd
O'Malley Ray Desmond
Insp. Large Ivor Dean

Director: Ray Austin

The Ghost Talks

w Gerald Kelsey

With Jeff confined to a hospital bed, Marty seizes the opportunity to increase his ill-temper by telling his partner about a spy drama he handled before they became partners.

Major Brennan Alan MacNaughton
Jackson John Collin
Captain Raschid Marne Maitland

Director: Cyril Frankel

All Work and No Pay

w Donald James

Why are the Foster brothers trying to convince Jean Hopkirk that her late husband is trying to contact her? The subject of some strange psychic phenomena, Jean is distraught enough to believe them – until Marty lends a hand.

Henry Foster Alfred Burke
George Foster Dudley Foster
Laura Adrienne Corri

Director: Jeremy Summers

Somebody Just Walked Over My Grave

w Donald James

People popping in and out of Marty's grave! Men dressed in tricorn hats! What's it all about? Marty finds himself accusing his partner of seeing things and Jeff gets plastered – twice!

Mandrake George Murcell
Dighton Bernard Kay
Martha Patricia Haines

Director: Cyril Frankel

RANDALL AND HOPKIRK
(DECEASED)
Created by: Dennis Spooner
Producer: Monty Berman
Executive story consultant: Dennis Spooner
Creative consultant: Cyril Frankel
Music by: Edwin Astley
An ITC Production
Made on location and at Elstree Studios
26 colour 60-minute episodes
26 September 1969 – 31 July 1971
(Note: ATV Midlands dropped the show after 20-odd episodes had been transmitted)
(USA: Syndicated 1973 under the title MY PARTNER THE GHOST)

THE RAT CATCHERS

Smith, Davidson and Hurst. Three names that struck terror in the hearts of their enemies. A trio of dedicated British Secret Service men who staffed a most secret unit of British Intelligence – a department so secret that its existence was known only to the highest government authority, a unit that had no name (not even an acronym).

Their brief: to obey orders without question and defend England's shores against its enemies with unfailing efficiency. Three men licensed to kill. Three men who worked alone and trusted no one.

Masquerading as a millionaire playboy was the unit's number one operative, Peregrine Pascale Smith, a fearless professional with 12 years experience under his belt. Equally as efficient was the Brigadier (we never learned his first name) – the brains of the department, a man with a brain like a computer, feeding in facts, getting answers and never letting sentiment or emotion stand in the way of results.

As the series opened, Richard Hurst was the newcomer of the unit. An ex-Scotland Yard Superintendent, with years of police discipline to support him, he was trained to obey orders, but his first faltering steps in the shadowy world of Smith and Davidson found him out of step with their objectives, until a series of tests proved him to be exactly what his colleagues were looking for – a man every bit as dangerous as themselves!

With the exception of the first story, the episodes were transmitted in serialised format (though only one or two had a 'cliffhanger' ending). Closer to the Le Carré school of thought than the glamorised antics of James Bond, the series was a tough and uncompromising look at the British spy network.

(Author's note: The Hurst role was originally written for Raymond Francis, the actor who had established the role of Detective Chief Superintendent Lockhart in *No Hiding Place*, and intended to show how a man trained to stay within the rules would react when thrown into the anything-goes world of espionage. Francis changed his mind at the last minute, and the role was given to Owen.)

REGULAR CAST

Peregrine Smith **Gerald Flood**   *Brigadier Davidson* **Philip Stone**
Richard Hurst **Glyn Owen**

Season One

13 colour 60-minute episodes

Ticket to Madrid

w Raymond Bowers

With surprise and disgust, ex-policeman Richard Hurst begins to learn what his new job entails – a job that will lead him into the darkest corners of espionage, where danger and intrigue walk hand-in-hand.
Commissioner Norman Scace
Dr Peters Jeffrey Gardiner
Miss Larks Jan Waters

Director: James Ormerod

The Captain Morales Story

w Raymond Bowers

While carrying out a 'simple' task in Madrid, Hurst comes face to face with the cold horror of the new world to which he has been admitted – a world which respects nothing save violence, and leaves a man little time for honour.
Captain Morales Edward de Souza
Alpha James Kerry
Teniente Peter Dennis

Director: James Ormerod

The Unwitting Courier

w Raymond Bowers

A beautiful and friendly foreign agent places Hurst in the firing-line and leaves the Brigadier little room for manoeuvre when faced with the task of remitting a secret document to his Madrid contact.
Jane Dawson Jeanne Moody
Harry Beschman David Bauer
Chinese girl Tsai Chin

Director: James Ormerod

Madrid Delivery

w Raymond Bowers

With the vital information passed to other hands, Hurst believes his Madrid connection is over and looks forward to returning home. But he soon finds that his task is unfinished – and this time he will need the Brigadier's help.

Miniver Tom Gill
Betty Patricia English
Vergora Alex Scott

Director: James Ormerod

The Missing Agent

w Paul Lee

Stockholm, the Venice of the North. But it isn't the city sights that Smith and Hurst are concerned with as they search for missing agent Dorothy Hansen – there are others in Stockholm equally determined that she should not be found.
Dorothy Hansen Pamela Sholto
Miss Hansen Anne Dyson
Kjellin Wanda Ventham

Director: Bill Hitchcock

The Baited Hook

w Paul Lee

With danger dogging their every step, Smith and Hurst continue their search for the missing girl. Their meeting with a student anxious to learn English springs a surprise – the girl has a gun, and intends to use it.
Nils Sandor Eles
Fru Lovberry Stella Courtnay
Swedish girl Jayne Sofiano

Director: Bill Hitchcock

The Umbrella

w Jeremy Paul

It is called the Umbrella Project. Once it is in operation, all of Britain will be protected from aerial attack. But someone has threatened to sabotage the project by breaching security – Smith and Hurst must discover who.
Supt. Blythe Robert Raglan
Charles Lysaght Ronald Howard
Arnold Bennett Tenniel Evans

Director: Don Gale

Thieves' Market

w Jeremy Paul

Somewhere there lurks a traitor. He could be one of many as Hurst finds out when he

travels to Lisbon. Meantime, Smith tries to find the connection between a Nazi general's memoirs and a golf bag flown to Lisbon.
Miss Fairbrother **Wendy Gifford**
Lemnitz **Edward Underdown**
Watkins **Max Kirby**

Director: **Don Gale**

Return of Evil

w Jeremy Paul
Following the trail of a possible traitor, Smith and Hurst find themselves facing a threat from the past: the return of the one man whose shadow still looms large over Europe – and who could rise from the ashes unless they stop his progress.
Ann Meadows **Monica Grey**
Miss Mellbuish **Carmilla Brockman**
Herr Gideon **Frederick Schrecker**

Director: **Don Gale**

The Edge of Disaster

w Paul Lee
It hangs in the air around us. It is invisible and yet pointed with deadly accuracy. As a nation we are threatened unless it is isolated and destroyed. Smith and Hurst are handed the task of staving off disaster.
Barlow **Reginald Marsh**
Rowena Blythe **Sylvia Kay**
Wilson **Basil Moss**

Director: **Bill Hitchcock**

Operation Lost Souls

w Victor Canning
A trail of traitors for sale leads Smith and Hurst to Geneva to discover who is behind the brain drain. To their astonishment they discover that the organisation's headquarters are stationed in Ireland.
Arlette Maylam **Patricia Haines**
Conrad Bymans **Bernard Kay**
John Savage **Tom Watson**

Director: **Bill Hitchcock**

Operation Irish Triangle

w Victor Canning
The operation brewing in Ireland seems to have all the trademarks of being both vital and dangerous. Smith and Hurst investigate – and find out more than they bargained for when the beautiful Arlette Maylam shows her true colours.
Irving Caldwell **John Macklin**
Wally Turnsell **Alan Gifford**
Henri Dupont **Eugene Deckers**

Director: **Bill Hitchcock**

Operation Big Fish

w Victor Canning
Everything is set for the kill. But what exactly is the operation? And when will it take place? With the Brigadier's help, can Smith and Hurst smash what promises to be one of history's most spectacular crimes?
Valerie Warner **Rachel Gurney**
Armstrong **Edward Palmer**
Shamus O'Neil **P. G. Stephens**

Director: **Bill Hitchcock**

Season Two
12 colour 60-minute episodes

Showdown Vienna

w Jeremy Paul
Find and destroy! The Brigadier's orders would be simple emough but for a dangerous problem called Leopold Donner. Smith and Hurst's one-off mission seems doomed to failure – before they've even had a chance to begin.
Leopold Donner **Frank Gatliff**
Angelique Donner **Lucy Fleming**
Josef Donner **Vernon Dobtcheff**

Director: **Bill Hitchcock**

Mission to Madeira

w Victor Canning
Working undercover, Hurst infiltrates the Midas Consortium. A dangerous job, but there are fringe benefits in the shape of the lovely Lea. Hurst's problems are compounded by having to decide if he can trust the girl.
Lea **Hannah Gordon**
Angelo Cornoldi **Richard Warner**
Captain Maldonado **John Abineri**

Director: **Don Gale**

Death in Madeira

w Victor Canning

Is Hurst lovesick? It appears that way when he threatens to resign – for personal reasons. But the Brigadier is having none of it and his plan to prevent Hurst from leaving results in a particularly unpleasant interlude.

Ellerton Frederick Treves
Lea Hannah Gordon
Francine Susan Engel

Director: Don Gale

Midnight over Madeira

w Victor Canning

The death of one particular man would send the world's stock markets crashing and make a gigantic fortune for the Midas Consortium. The Brigadier sees a way to prevent this taking place – no matter how strongly Hurst protests.

Midas Kevin Storey
Lt. Col Hyman Jerry Stovin
Captain Maldonado John Aberini

Director: Don Gale

Wednesday in Dubrovnik

w Raymond Bowers

Faces from the past threaten to bring disorder and confusion to the ranks of the British Secret Service and rock the Brigadier's little lot to its very foundations. Smith and Hurst are handed the job of protecting their pensions.

Alpha James Kerry
Peter Jeffrey Gardiner
Miss Larks Jacqueline Ellis

Director: James Ormerod

Murder in Mostar

w Raymond Bowers

A very unpleasant murder and the Brigadier's miscalculations place Smith and Hurst in a state of revolt. Can the Brigadier really be serious when he orders them to eliminate a public figure?

Arthur Dent Reginald Marsh
Charles Dinley Derren Nesbitt
Albert Michael Peake

Director: James Ormerod

Dead-End – Dubrovnik

w Raymond Bowers

A series of events have culminated with the Brigadier forming a strange alliance to get rid of a common enemy. The outcome is violence of the worst kind – and death stalks the streets of Dubrovnik.

Alpha James Kerry
Arthur Dent Reginald Marsh
Charles Dinley Derren Nesbitt

Director: James Ormerod

Big Grab – Amsterdam

w Raymond Bowers

An American agent carrying vital secrets in his head disappears in Amsterdam. Washington presses for action, but the Brigadier seems unconcerned. Why – and what part does the mysterious Vol play in the affair?

Sir James Tinsell Raymond Huntley
Vol Cyril Shaps
Alpha James Kerry

Director: James Ormerod

Retribution Amsterdam

w Jeremy Paul

A hostage spy – and an enemy agent with a brain as acute as the Brigadier's. The only way out is for Smith and Hurst to follow their chief's orders to the letter – orders that could produce horrifying results.

Vol Cyril Shaps
Abbot Hugh McDermott
Shebenen Toke Townley

Director: James Ormerod

The Heel of Achilles

w Stanley Miller

Helped by Gerde, a turncoat spy, Smith and Hurst find violence in Athens. The sun-drenched beaches of Corfu will run red with blood unless they can find the man behind an international espionage ring.

Lord Corbridge Anthony Marlowe
Gerde Dora Reisser
Maria Hilary Tindall

Director: Don Gale

The Seven Pillars of Hercules

w Stanley Miller

High up in the mountains of Greece a man is hiding. The Brigadier has ordered his capture – but so has Madame Achmet – and her weapons are likely to be far more deadly than those available to Smith and Hurst.
Madame Achmet Catherine Lacey
Ziranov Wolfe Morris
Yin Paul Tann

Director: Don Gale

The Mask of Agamemnon

w Stanley Miller

Can Smith and Hurst rescue the man being held aboard Madame Achmet's yacht?

Should they even attempt the snatch? If they rescue the man, the Brigadier has ordered him dead! Death and destruction disturb the peaceful Corfu harbour.
Madame Achmet Catherine Lacey
Ziranov Wolfe Morris
Alpha James Kerry

Director: Don Gale

THE RAT CATCHERS
Producer: Cyril Coke
A Rediffusion TV Network Production
25 colour 60-minute episodes
2 February – 27 April 1966
15 December 1966 – 9 March 1967
(USA: Syndicated 1966 13 episodes)

REDCAP

Ten years before actor John Thaw donned his kipper ties to make life tough for villains as Detective Inspector Jack Regan in *The Sweeney*, he could be found equally well at home wearing the white-belted uniform of the Royal Military Police (Special Investigation Branch), as Sergeant John Mann, an uncompromising policeman who set out to track down serious crime involving British troops.

A bad-tempered policeman with a chip on his shoulder, Mann could be aggressive with underlings, but quiet and understanding with the families of soldiers who had suffered a loss. Wherever serious crime threatened to escalate into a dangerous situation, Mann could be found sifting through the evidence and using his military training to get to the bottom of things.

The series looked at crime as it affected soldiers, their wives and their families.

REGULAR CAST
Sergeant John Mann John Thaw

Season One
13 monochrome 60-minute episodes

It's What Comes After

w William Emms

SIB officer John Mann is appointed to investigate a vicious crime which no one,

including the victim, wishes him to solve. But Mann's insistence on getting the job done surprises everyone – including his CO.
Captain Lynne Keith Barron
Mess Sergeant Derek Newark
CO Tenniel Evans

Director: Raymond Menmuir

A Town Called Love

w Anthony Steven and Jack Bell
Following the trail of a deserter, SIB officer
Sergeant Mann finds a highly unusual
'black-market' activity – a 'love town'
frequented by officers and lower ranks alike.
What's more, it appears that a high ranking
military man is behind the enterprise.
Sgt Coulter Glynn Edwards
Col Matthews Peter Copley
Pvt Pentlebury Michael Robbins

Director: Raymond Menmuir

Epitaph for a Sweat

w Richard Harris
In Aden on active service to investigate the
background to a vicious murder, Sgt Mann
uncovers more than he bargained for. His
suspects are many, but he must first of all
find the motive for the crime.
Sgt Rolfe Leonard Rossiter
Sgt Bailey Mike Pratt
Sapper Russell Ian McShane

Director: Peter Graham Scott

Misfire

w Roger Marshall
Sgt Mann's suspicions are aroused when a
soldier confesses to a crime he obviously
didn't commit. Mann's determination to
prove the man's innocence unearths an
unusual love interest.
Pvt. Staples Gary Bond
Insp. Paish John Collin
Iris Pearson Diana Coupland

Director: Raymond Menmuir

Corporal McCann's Private War

w Troy Kennedy Martin
Detailed to investigate a charge that a
soldier serving in Cyprus is guilty of black-
market activities – and suspected murder –
Sgt Mann finds that he needs his wits about
him to track down a determined criminal.
Corporal McCann Ian McNaughton
Police Insp. Warren Mitchell
Sergeant Major Windsor Davies

Director: Peter Graham Scott

The Orderly Officer

w Julian Bond
Investigating a difficult case, Sgt Mann
finds his movements restrained by 'internal
arrangements'. Much to the anger of a
superior officer, he skilfully sidesteps his
orders – and makes a surprising discovery.
Colonel Ronald Leigh-Hunt
Sgt Greatrex Barry Keegan
Sgt Merritt Colin Rix

Director: Bill Bain

Nightwatch

w Troy Kennedy Martin
When a regiment returns from Borneo and
complains that their unit is being haunted
by a ghost, Sgt Mann turns ghostbuster to
allay their fears – but investigating ghost
stories can prove ill-advised.
Brown Hywel Bennett
CO Joseph O'Connor
Major Stokely Allan Cuthbertson

Director: Bill Bain

The Boys of 'B' Company

w Robert Holles
What criminal activity lies behind the
facade of a Boy Soldier training unit? Sgt
John Mann unearths some strange goings-on
– and produces a surprising solution to the
mystery.
Boy CSM Duffy Richard O'Sullivan
Tug Wilson Barry Evans
CSM Hobbis Bryan Mosely

Director: Raymond Menmuir

A Regiment of the Line

w Leon Griffiths
Hunting a killer is always a dangerous
game, but when Mann is assigned to track
down a killer among a battalion of men
trained to kill – and the killer turns his
training against the SIB officer – Mann
needs all his wits . . .
Insp. Heller Walter Gotell
Pvt. Scanlon Colin Blakely
Major Carl Duering

Director: Raymond Menmuir

The Man They Did

w Michael Ashe

Was a soldier's death from natural causes, or is Sgt Mann investigating a murder? The SIB officer finds himself facing a difficult case. No one is prepared to help him – and everyone appears to have an alibi!
Pvt. Jedd Bryan Marshall
Corporal Scott Richard Coleman
Lt. Golden Michael Gaunt

Director: Guy Verney

A Question of Initiative

w Jeremy Paul

Mann learns the hard way that, although a case has reached a successful conclusion, it doesn't necessarily follow that it's over – particularly when the culprit is free to continue his crimes.
Captain Ritchie Ewan Solon
Major Silk Gary Watson
Insp. Barwick John Aberini

Director: Jonathan Alwyn

A Place of Refuge

w Troy Kennedy Martin

Mann discovers the truth behind what appears to be a suicide attempt. But things are seldom as they appear – or as people wish them to appear. Digging into the dead man's background unearths some startling evidence.
Captain Pelly Philip Bond
Staff Sgt John Collin
Wendy Stuteland Barbara Jefford

Director: Laurence Bourne

The Patrol

w Troy Kennedy Martin

Assigned to look into accusations that a British Army patrol unit ransacked a jungle village, SIB officer Sgt Mann ends up by unmasking a dangerous killer – and war comes to the Borneo jungle.
Sgt Job Ewan Hooper
Pvt. Burroughs David Burke
John Bell Robin Bailey

Director: Guy Verney

Season Two

13 monochrome 60-minute episodes

Crime Passionel

w Troy Kennedy Martin

When a Sergeant is mysteriously shot dead in a Borneo jungle, Sgt Mann investigates the man's death – and finds that all is not as it first seems in a jungle survival camp.
Major Vance Barry Letts
Corporal Ball Richard Owens
Corporal Fish Michael Wynne

Director: Guy Verney

The Pride of the Regiment

w Arden Winch

It's a tricky situation: why, particularly in the light of a royal visit, does a Victoria Cross holder go beserk and place himself and his regiment in trouble. The answer surprises everyone – including Sgt Mann.
Captain Bane Neil Hallett
Barratt George Sewell
Huntley Philip Locke

Director: Quentin Lawrence

The Killer

w Troy Kennedy Martin

After several deaths among the men of a special Commando Unit in Malaysia, Sgt Mann flies out to investigate. His arrival at the training camp is greeted by another death – and he is soon at war with the killer.
Sgt. O'Keefe Garfield Morgan
Corporal Murdoch Ian Cullen
Ass. Provost Peter Williams

Director: Guy Verney

Buckingham Palace

w Troy Kennedy Martin

Investigating a murder in a blizzard on a Cyprus mountain top, Sgt Mann discovers that the stately homes of England are being offered for sale to the locals. Pick of the crop is 'a prime residence' – Buckingham Palace!
Pvt. King Patrick Bedford
Sgt. Buckett William Lucas
Butros Peter Bowles

Director: Guy Verney

Rough Justice

w Julian Bond

Assigned to investigate strange events at an exclusive Cavalry Regiment based in Germany, Sgt Mann uncovers prejudice, deceit and violence between the officers and the serving ranks.

John Richardson Edward Fox
Sgt Rees Philip Madoc
Colonel Wright Terence Longdon

Director: Quentin Lawrence

The Moneylenders

w Eric Coltart

Investigating a series of mysterious beatings-up at a regimental reunion dinner, Sgt Mann is amazed to discover that when each of the victims is questioned their response is that they all tripped over!

CSM Moore Windsor Davies
Lance Corporal Farrington Alan Lake
Sgt Collins Patrick O'Connell

Director: Raymond Menmuir

Strictly by the Book

w Richard Harris

Military Policemen are disliked. It's a fact that Mann and his colleagues live with. But why should several people be so eager to show their dislike in such a violent fashion? Mann investigates – and reaches a surprising conclusion.

Sgt Laurie Peter Andrews
Lt. Wilmer Allan Cuthbertson
Sgt Andrews Peter Raymond

Director: Quentin Lawrence

Peterson's Private Army

w Marshall Pugh

It's a case with a difference. Instead of solving the crime, Sgt Mann must get to the bottom of strange events at a Scottish regiment undergoing jungle training, and prevent a massacre from taking place.

Lt Peterson Michael McKevitt
Sgt Burns John Junkin
Pvt. Macgregor David Jackson

Director: Quentin Lawrence

Stag Party

w Julian Bond

Investigating a trail of bomb outrages in Cyprus, Sgt Mann discovers a very unusual stag party – one at which a murder is being planned. But can he prevent the crime from taking place?

Ivy Williams Anne Lynn
Sgt Mason Barrie Ingham
Nicco Panos Steve Plytas

Director: Raymond Menmuir

An Ambush Among Friends

w Roger Marshall

Why should the Chinese be so helpful when Sgt Mann is investigating an ambush in Singapore? What have they to hide? Suspicious, the SIB officer digs deeper – and uncovers a startling bunch of facts.

Corporal Pond David Burke
Captain Walton Russell Hunter
Sgt Amiss Awan Hooper

Director: Quentin Lawrence

The Alibi

w Thomas Clarke

Assigned to get to the bottom of a strange mystery, Sgt Mann visits the Navy to decide if Corporal Harkness is telling the truth – or lying in an attempt to cover up the biggest blunder in naval history.

Corporal Harkness Keith Barron
Insp. Harding David King
Lt Cdr Jaden Anthony Bate

Director: Laurence Bourne

The Proper Charlie

w Robert Storey

What at first appears to be a case of simple assault leads Sgt Mann to investigate a far from simple love-affair between a serving soldier and a married civilian. But why would the soldier wish to bring his regiment into disrepute?

Pvt. Ringwold John Pickles
Sgt Cole Richard Leech
Joyce Cole Carole Mowlam

Director: Guy Verney

Information Received

w Richard Harris

It's the kind of investigation Mann likes least – investigating another colleague. But his inquiries into what happened between a military policeman and a prisoner in his care lead to an unexpected outcome.

Captain Benning Michael Goodliffe
Corporal Donlon Anthony Sagar
CSM Greer Tony Cauntner

Director: Raymond Menmuir

REDCAP
Devised by: Jack Bell
Producer: John Bryce
Story editor: Ian Kennedy Martin
An ABC Weekend Network Production
26 monochrome 60-minute episodes
17 October 1964 – 16 January 1965
2 April – 25 June 1966

REGAN

The film which was the forerunner of *The Sweeney* (see entry under that name) and introduced Detective Inspector Jack Regan and Detective Sergeant George Carter to television.

When a policeman was mysteriously murdered, Regan and Carter broke all the rules to track down his killer. But they found that there were men in the Flying Squad who were equally determined to break them.

REGULAR CAST

Det. Insp. Regan John Thaw   *Det. Sgt. Carter* Dennis Waterman
Det. Chf Insp. Haskins Garfield Morgan
Arthur Dale Lee Montague   *Tusser* David Dakar   *Annie* Maureen Lipman
Det. Supt Maynon Morris Perry   *Det. Insp. Laker* Stephen Yardley

Writer: Ian Kennedy Martin
Producer: Ted Childs
Executive producers: Lloyd Shirley and George Taylor
Associate producer: Mary Morgan
Director: Tom Clegg
A Euston Films Production
for Thames Television
Colour – 90-minutes
4 June 1974
(Transmitted under the Armchair Cinema banner)

REILLY – ACE OF SPIES

Vaunted as one of the most lavish and dramatic television series ever produced, this programme certainly lived up to expectations – although the facts surrounding Reilly's real life contribution to the British Secret Service were glamorised somewhat to add a dash of artistic licence to the proceedings. (In reality, Reilly was far from being the 'patriot' depicted in the series.)

The entire enterprise was nevertheless energetic and enjoyable in its depiction of the extraordinary career of the man who was possibly Britain's first 'secret agent', a man who endeavoured to change the course of history by plotting to overthrow the Bolsheviks and replace them with a new government – headed by himself. (His plans to do so floundered when Lenin was shot by an anarchist and Reilly and his colleague, Lockhart, were sentenced to death by a Revolutionary Tribunal in Moscow.)

A high-budget, thrill-packed slice of television drama.

REGULAR CAST

Sidney Reilly Sam Neill   *Fothergill* Peter Egan   *Bruce Lockhart* Ian Charleston
Cummings Norman Rodway   *Dzerzhinsky* Tom Bell   *Stalin* David Burke
Lenin Kenneth Cranham   *Zaharov* Leo McKern   *Margaret* Jeananne Crowley
Baldwin Donald Morley   *Count Massino* John Castle

REILLY – ACE OF SPIES
Producer: Chris Burt
Executive producer: Verity Lambert
Ex. in charge of production:
Johnny Goodman
Writer: Ian Kennedy Martin
Music by: Harry Rabinowitz
Script executive: Linda Agran
Directors: Martin Campbell (Eps 2–4, 9,
10, 11, 13)
James Goddard (Eps 1, 5–8, 12)
A Euston Films Production
for Thames Television
Networked
·12 colour episodes
(Ep. 1 90 minutes, remainder 60 minutes)
5 September – 16 November 1983

THE RETURN OF SHERLOCK HOLMES
(The Adventures of Sherlock Holmes)

Acclaimed by the critics and Holmes aficionados alike, this series, torn from the pages of the *Strand Magazine*, depicted the adventures of Conan Doyle's legendary Baker Street detective in such painstaking detail that it exorcised forever the spectre of Hollywood's archetypal Holmes as played by Basil Rathbone.

In his place was actor Jeremy Brett, who had us – and possibly himself? – totally convinced that the great detective had returned from the grave and had taken up residence in Castlefield (the location which served as the series' London backdrop). Brett *was* Holmes. Everything we'd ever read about the detective was brought vividly to life. As played by David Burke (and later Edward Hardwicke), his trusted confidant Watson *was* Watson. 221b Baker Street *was* the residence immortalised in the novels. Due entirely to producer Michael Cox's prudent judgement in steering the production back to its literary roots (the original stories as serialised in the *Strand Magazine* and, in particular, the illustrations of Sidney Paget – recreated with loving care throughout the series), the programme was by far and away the closest yet to the spirit of Conan Doyle.

REGULAR CAST
Sherlock Holmes **Jeremy Brett**   *Mrs Hudson* **Rosalie Williams**
Dr Watson **David Burke** *(Adventures of)*   **Edward Hardwicke** *(Return of)*

The Adventures of Sherlock Holmes
Season One
7 colour 60-minute episodes

A Scandal in Bohemia

(Dramatised by **Alexander Baron***)*
Sherlock Holmes and Dr Watson are requested by a masked nobleman to save one of the royal houses of Europe from ruin. The game is afoot and Holmes meets a shadow from his past – the beautiful Irene Adler.
Irene Adler **Gayle Hunnicutt**
King of Bohemia **Wolf Kahler**
Godfrey Norton **Michael Carter**

Director: **Paul Annett**
Designer: **Michael Grimes/ Margaret Coombes/Tim Wilding**

The Dancing Men

w **Anthony Skene**
A row of absurd little figures drawn in chalk on a garden seat puzzled Mr Cubitt and terrified his young wife, Elsie. A childish prank? Enter Sherlock Holmes to get to the bottom of the strange mystery.
Hilton Cubitt **Tenniel Evans**
Elsie Cubitt **Betsy Brantley**
Abe Slaney **Eugene Lipinski**

Director: **John Bruce**
Designer: **Michael Grimes**

The Naval Treaty

w **Jeremy Paul**
The French and the Russians will pay a fortune to learn the contents of a secret

treaty between Great Britain and Italy – but the document has disappeared. Apart from the Minister himself, only one man in the foreign office had access to it – and that man, a friend of Dr Watson's, turns to Holmes for help.

Percy Phelps David Gwillim
Dr Ferrier John Taylor
Annie Harrison Alison Skilbeck

Director: Alan Grint
Designer: Margaret Coombes

The Solitary Cyclist

w Alan Plater

Who is the mysterious man on a bicycle who follows music teacher Violet Smith each time she cycles to and from Chiltern Grange to give music lessons to the daughter of widower Robert Carruthers? At Watson's request, Holmes looks into the matter.

Violet Smith Barbara Wilshere
Carruthers John Castle
Woodley Michael Siberry

Director: Paul Annett
Designer: Michael Grimes

The Crooked Man

w Alfred Shaughnessy

Holmes and Watson investigate the violent death of Colonel Barclay at Aldershot and the scandal that is threatening the good name of the Royal Mallows Regiment. They meet the crooked man and his curious companion and bring to light a tragic love story.

Henry Wood Norman Jones
Nancy Barclay Lisa Daniely
Young Henry Wood Michael Lumsden

Director: Alan Grint
Designer: Margaret Coombes

The Speckled Band

w Jeremy Paul

When Holmes ignores the threats of Doctor Grimesby Roylott not to meddle in his affairs, the detective and his friend Dr Watson find themselves involved in a chilling case and they finally confront the 'speckled band' itself – a deadly snake.

Dr Roylott Jeremy Kemp
Helen Stoner Rosalyn Landor
Julia Stoner Denise Armon

Director: John Bruce
Designer: Michael Grimes

The Blue Carbuncle

w Paul Finney

The stone is not yet 20 years old, but it has a sinister history. Two men who once possessed it have committed suicide. When the gem is stolen from its latest owner, the Countess of Morcar, Holmes enters the scene.

Henry Baker Frank Middlemass
James Ryder Ken Campbell
Peterson Frank Mills

Director: David Carson
Designer: Tim Wilding

Season Two

6 colour 60-minute episodes

The Copper Beeches

(Dramatised by Bill Craig)

Violet Hunter arrives at Baker Street to seek advice. She has been offered a new job at double her usual salary to act as governess to Jephro Rucastle's young son – on condition that she cuts off her luxuriant chestnut hair before taking up the post! Intrigued, Holmes travels with her to Rucastle's home.

Violet Hunter Natasha Richardson
Jephro Rucastle Joss Ackland
Mrs Rucastle Lottie Ward

Director: Paul Annett
Designer: Michael Grimes

The Greek Interpreter

w Derek Marlowe

The game's afoot with a difference. This time Holmes is invited by his redoubtable brother, Mycroft, to solve the intriguing case of a Greek interpreter he was to cross-examine – a man with sticking plaster all over his face.

Mycroft Holmes Charles Gray
Mr Melas Alkis Kritikos
Wilson Kemp George Cosigan

Director: Alan Grint
Designer: Margaret Coombes

The Norwood Builder

w Richard Harris

When a young solicitor named John McFarlane is arrested by Inspector Lestrade of Scotland Yard, for murder minutes after he has entered 221b Baker Street, Holmes sets out to prove the man's innocence.
Lestrade Colin Jeavons (Intro.)
John McFarlane Matthew Solon
James Oldacre Jonathan Adams

Director: Ken Grieve
Designer: Tim Wilding

The Resident Patient

w Derek Marlowe

In return for three-quarters of all his fees, Dr Trevelyan was set up in practice in London's West End by Mr Blessington. It worked out well – until the patient became frightened for his life. An obvious case for the Baker Street detective.
Blessington Patrick Newell
Dr. Trevelyan Nicholas Clay
Biddle Tim Barlow

Director: David Carson
Designer: Michael Grimes

The Red-headed League

w John Hawkesworth

Two months after reading the advertisement: 'To the Red-headed League. There is a vacancy open which entitles a member of the League to a salary of £4 a week for purely nominal services. All red-headed men sound in body and mind are eligible', Jabez Wilson desperately needs the services of Sherlock Holmes
Jabez Wilson Roger Hammond
Mr Merryweather John Woodnutt
Moriarty Eric Porter

Director: John Bruce
Designer: Margaret Coombes

The Final Problem

w John Hawkesworth

If the criminal escapes the net, his revenge will be terrible. The criminal is Professor Moriarty, and Holmes believes there is no price too high to rid the world of his monstrous crimes. At Reichenbach Falls, the two men face each other for the final showdown.
Moriarty Eric Porter
Director of the Louvre Olivier Pierre
Minister of the Interior Claude Le Sache

Director: Alan Grint
Designer: Tim Wilding

The Return of Sherlock Holmes Season One

7 colour 60-minute episodes

The Empty House

(Dramatised by John Hawkesworth)

Three years after Dr Watson believed his friend Sherlock Holmes had died during his encounter with the evil Professor Moriarty at the Reichenbach Falls, Watson himself is faced with an intriguing unsolved murder mystery – and receives help from a strange source. Holmes has returned from the dead!
Doctor Watson Edward Hardwicke (Intro.)
Colonel Sebastian Moran Patrick Allen
Inspector Lestrade Colin Jeavons

Director: Howard Baker
Designer: Margaret Coombes

The Abbey Grange

w Trevor Bowen

When the wicked Sir Eustace Brackenstall is found murdered, Sherlock Holmes and Inspector Hopkins soon arrive on the scene. It appears like an open-and-shut case – until Holmes finds a dog's burnt collar.
Inspector Hopkins Paul Williamson
Sir Eustace Brackenstall Conrad Phillips
Lady Brackenstall Anne Louise Lambert

Director: Peter Hammond
Designer: Tim Wilding

The Musgrave Ritual

w Jeremy Paul

When the aristocratic Reginald Musgrave seeks out the great detective's help to get to the bottom of the death of the Musgrave butler, Holmes discovers the dead man's secret – and the hiding place of the long-lost crown of Charles I.

Reginald Musgrave Michael Culver
Richard Brunton James Hazeldine
Rachel Howells Johanna Kirby

Director: David Carson
Designer: Michael Grimes

The Second Stain

w John Hawkesworth
Holmes heeds a call from the Prime
Minister asking for his assistance in
obtaining a letter stolen from Westminster.
Its contents could start a war and Holmes
must recover the letter to avert a great crisis
– and prevent a murder.
Lady Trelawney Hope Patricia Hodge
Prime Minister Harry Andrews
Inspector Lestrade Colin Jeavons

Director: John Bruce
Designer: Tim Wilding

The Man with the Twisted Lip

w Alan Plater
Holmes is asked to delve through the clues
to search for Neville St Clair, who has
disappeared from his home. His wife is
distraught by the attentions of a mysterious
beggarman, Hugh Boone, whom Holmes
unmasks – with unwanted results.
St Clair/Hugh Boone Clive Francis
Mrs St Clair Eleanor David
Isa Whitney Terence Longdon

Director: Patrick Lau
Designer: Tim Wilding

The Priory School

w T. R. Bowen
With Holmes sworn to secrecy, he begins to
gather the clues that will lead him to the
people behind the kidnapping of the Duke
of Holdernesse's son – a case which proves
one of the most baffling of his career.
Dr Huxstable Christopher Benjamin
Mr Aveling Michael Bertenshaw
Duke of Holdernesse Alan Howard

Director: John Madden
Designer: Margaret Coombes

The Six Napoleons

w John Kane
Why should a burglar steal six identical
busts of Napoleon – then smash them to
bits? When the body of an unknown man is
found not far from the remains of one of the
busts, Holmes unravels the mystery – and
earns the acclaim of Scotland Yard.
Harker Eric Sykes
Hudson Gerald Campion
Venucci Steve Plytas

Director: David Carson
Designer: Tim Wilding

SHERLOCK HOLMES
Developed for television by:
John Hawkesworth
The Adventures of
Producer: Michael Cox
Associate producer: Stuart Doughty
Music by: Patrick Gowers
13 colour 60-minute episodes
24 April – 5 June 1984
25 August – 29 September 1985

The Return of
Producer: June Wyndham Davies
Executive producer: Michael Cox
Music by: Patrick Gowers
7 colour 60-minute episodes
9 July – 20 August 1986

THE RETURN OF THE SAINT

The further adventures of Simon Templar, alias the Saint. A
daredevil 20th-century swashbuckler who lived for excitement
and danger. A pirate or a philanthropist as the occasion
demanded. A freelance troubleshooter whose debonair outlook

on life brought him into contact with the life he loved best – those triumphant moments when, having rescued the damsel in distress, or solved the affairs of the British Secret Service, he could stand back to proclaim that victory was his alone.

The adventures as before – well, not quite. The original recipe concocted by his creator Leslie Charteris had been juiced up in an attempt to garner worldwide sales and this series was no better (though certainly no worse) than its contemporaries.

'The Saint is back', proclaimed the media, 'The King of swashbucklers returns to television in a new series of adventures that will delight his fans.'

But it wasn't the 'King', just a lookalike pretender to his throne. The real Simon Templar had abdicated some 16 years earlier, leaving behind a legacy that the newcomer found difficult to replace. The King was dead – long live the King. The newcomer was an impostor – and his 'subjects' hardly raised a cheer! (see *The Saint*)

REGULAR CAST
Simon Templar Ian Ogilvy

The Judas Game

w Leslie Charteris
Simon takes on a dangerous mission amid the Italian Alps. His task: to rescue a girl he once loved from a group of ruthless terrorists. But treachery dogs his every step and he soon finds himself in trouble.
Selma Morell Judy Geeson
Wilcox Maurice Roeves
Vlora Olga Karlatos

Director: Jeremy Summers

The Nightmare Man

w John Kruse
Simon must find out why an assassination has been arranged – and by whom? He winds up to his neck in danger, which could result in his own death – as Big Ben tolls a death knell for The Saint.
Gunther Joss Ackland
Livia Moreno Moira Redmond
Colonel Perez John Bennett

Director: Leslie Norman

Duel in Venice

w John Kruse
A quiet interlude in Venice with Sally, the daughter of an old friend, erupts into more mayhem for Simon. The girl is kidnapped by a killer who uses her as bait to lure Simon into a trap – with violent results.
Sally Cathryn Harrison
Jed Blackett Maurice Colbourne
Caludia Carole Andre

Director: Jeremy Summers

One Black September

w John Goldsmith
The Saint finds himself teamed up with the beautiful Leila Sabin, an Israeli agent, when he is asked to track down a terrorist hiding somewhere in London. But where – and why is Simon being followed?
Leila Sabin Prunella Gee
Hakim Garrick Hagon
Yasmina June Bolton

Director: Leslie Norman

The Village that Sold its Soul

w John Goldsmith

Simon's arrival at the isolated village of Santa Maria spells upheaval for the gang behind a series of violent outbreaks in the area. He is made far from welcome, but repays his hosts – explosively.

Boldini Giancarlo Prete
Moreno Cyrus Elyas
Prince Castracano Maurice Denham

Director: Leslie Norman

Assault Force

w Moris Farhi

Overhearing a young Eurasian girl pleading for her life, Simon intervenes – and soon finds himself involved in a dangerous web of political intrigue in the East. No stranger to trouble, he needs his wits this time around.

Jeanette Kate O'Mara
Hula Bert Kwouk
O'Hara Bryan Marshall

Director: Peter Sasdy

Yesterday's Hero

w John Kruse   (From a story by Roger Parkes)

When a 'dead' man returns to pursue his trail of vengeance and seeks Simon's help, the Saint finds himself involved in a deadly escapade of treachery and blackmail – with an unknown victim waiting marked for death.

Roy Gates Ian Hendry
Sandy Annette Andre
Cleaver Gerald Flood

Director: Roy Ward Baker

The Poppy Chain

w John Kruse

Simon finds himself infiltrating a drugs syndicate to teach its board members that it doesn't pay to rake in millions at the expense of lives – or try to get one jump ahead of the Saint!

Sandy Jenny Hanley
General Platt Laurence Naismith
Scorbesi Gregoire Aslan

Director: Charles Crichton

The Arrangement

w Anthony Terpiloff

Never one to resist overtures from a beautiful woman, Simon's meeting with two lovely girls develops into a nightmare situation. The women are arranging to murder their husbands – and require Simon's assistance!

Lady Stevens Carolyn Seymour
Sheila Northcott Sarah Douglas
Guy Northcott Michael Medwin

Director: Peter Medak

The Armageddon Alternative

w Terence Feely

When a man threatens to blow up London if a beautiful girl is not guillotined in public, Simon finds himself chasing shadows in an attempt to run his quarry to earth – before he can carry out his threat.

Fred George Cole
Lynn Jackson Anouska Hempel
Commander Denning Donald Houston

Director: Leslie Norman

The Imprudent Professor

w Terence Feely

When two pretty girls attempt to use Simon in their scheme to lure a learned professor into defecting to a foreign power, the Saint teaches them that those who play with fire should expect to get burned.

Samantha Catherine Schell
Max Boothroyd Anthony Steel
Emma Susan Penhaligon

Director: Kevin Connor

Signal Stop

w John Kruse

The Saint takes a train ride into murder and intrigue when he meets a young girl who leads him into a very nasty affair. Simon soon finds himself under the scrutiny of two policemen who make him bemoan the retirement of Claude Eustace Teal.

Janie Lennox Claran Madden
Insp. Grant Frederick Jaeger
Sgt Taylor Ian Cullen

Director: Ray Austin

The Roman Touch

w John Goldsmith   (From a story by William Fairchild)
The beautiful city of Rome holds danger for pop star Michelle. And when Simon tries to help her, it looks like the end for the Saint – with Michelle left to sing his requiem.
Michelle Kim Goody
Bruno Walters Laurence Luckinbill
Diamond Linda Thorson

Director: Jeremy Summers

Tower Bridge is Faling Down

w Leon Griffiths
When asked to help expose an embezzler and killer, The Saint believes that he has found the perfect ploy. He intends to sell off Tower Bridge to draw the villain into the open!
Ray Dennis John Woodvine
Sammy Alfie Bass
Jenny Fiona Curzon

Director: Roy Ward Baker

The Debt Collectors

w George Markstein
When Simon rescues a young girl from a runaway horse, he soon discovers that she is not all she seems to be. Or is she? And what part in the mystery does Christine, her sister, play? It's double trouble, whatever the outcome.
Gerri Hanson Mary Tamm
Christine Diane Keen
Geoffrey Connaught Anton Rodgers

Director: Leslie Norman

Collision Course (Part 1 'The Brave Goose')

w John Kruse
After her husband is killed in a power-boat race, Simon befriends the beautiful Annabel and decides to help her overcome the threats to her life. But who is behind the threats?

Collision Course (Part 2 'The Sixth Man')

Surrounded by danger and intrigue, Simon and Annabel set out to unravel the mystery of buried gold. Who holds the secret to a bullion robbery? And who is behind the attempts on their lives?
Annabel Gayle Hunnicutt
Duchamps Stratford Johns
Lebec Derren Nesbitt

Director: Cyril Frankel

Hot Run

w Tony Williamson
An avalanche of danger threatens to engulf Simon when he books into an Alpine resort for a holiday. Murder strikes shortly afterwards, and the Saint finds himself on a ski ride that could result in a man's death – his own!
Diana Rula Lenska
Korvis John Nolan
Marland Barry Andrews

Director: Peter Sasdy

The Murder Cartel

w John Goldsmith
An assassination attempt on a powerful – but despised – oil sheik propels Simon into doing a little undercover work for the CIA to expose a murder cartel who are killing for profit.
Laura Britt Ekland
Vidal Helmut Berger
Kemal Marne Maitland

Director: Tom Clegg

The Obona Affair

w Michael Pertwee
When the son of a visiting African president is kidnapped in London, who better to turn to than Simon Templar for help. But as the African soon discovers, the Saint has his own way of dealing with treachery.
President Obona Thomas Baptiste
Colonel Dyson Jack Hedley
Wright Derek Newark

Director: Peter Sasdy

Vicious Circle

w John Goldsmith   (From a story by Michael Armstrong and John Kruse)
When former racing-driver Robert Lucci – husband of a leading Italian fashion designer

– dies in a car crash, Simon finds himself seeking a killer and trying to find a girl on the run.

Anna Tessa Wyatt
Dr Brogli Mel Ferrer
Renata Elsa Martinelli

Director: Sam Wanamaker

Dragonseed

w John Kruse
When a rich man's son meets his death in a helicopter accident and Simon finds evidence to prove the boy was murdered, it spells trouble for the assassins as the Saint metes out his own kind of justice.

Carla Annamaria Macchi
Domenico Sam Wanamaker
Doctor Michael Graham

Director: Leslie Norman

Appointment in Florence

w Philip Broadley
When his close friend Christian is kidnapped and murdered by Italian terrorists, Simon vows to avenge his death. But his attempts to track down the killers are distracted by a beautiful girl.

Manfred Stuart Wilson
Ingo James Aubrey
Lea Carla Romanelli

Director: Peter Sasdy

The Diplomat's Daughter

w Michael Pertwee
A chance encounter with a beautiful girl leads Simon into the deadly world of drug smuggling and an encounter with a gang who are prepared to remove anyone who gets too close to their secret.

Maria Lyn Dalby
Pierre Murray Head
Shriver Karl Held

Director: Charles Crichton

RETURN OF THE SAINT
Producer: Anthony Spinner
Executive producer: Robert S. Baker
Music by: Johnny Scott
(Saint theme by: Brian Dane)
An ITC Production
24 colour 60-minute episodes
10 September 1978 – 12 March 1979
(USA: CBS 21 December 1979 –
14 March 1980, 13 episodes
10 May – 15 August 1980,
12 episodes)

RICHARD THE LIONHEART

In Olden days when knights were bold, there was none bolder than King Richard the Lionheart, the gallant English sovereign who led his armies to rout the Saracens in Palestine and successfully defeated the Mohammedan rulers of the Holy Land. Perhaps so. But if this series was anything to go by, the Lionheart was also one of the dumbest (and most boring) rulers in history! After four long years away from England, Richard received news that there was intrigue afoot in his beloved homeland (his younger brother Prince John was seeking to usurp the English throne). Laying down his arms, the Lionheart returned home to quell his brother's ambitions – then promptly returned to his Crusade in Palestine, thereby leaving his brother to plot anew.

Yet another super-cheapo series from the Danziger Brothers that failed to please either younger or older audiences.

REGULAR CAST

King Richard Dermot Walsh   *Lady Berengaria* Sheila Whittington
Blondel Iain Gregory   *Sir Gilbert* Robin Hunter   *Sir Geoffrey* Alan Hatwood
Prince John/King Philip of France Trader Faulkner
Leopold of France Francis de Wolfe   *Hugo* Glyn Owen   *Marta* Anne Lawson

Long Live the King

w Mark Grantham

King Henry of England lies gravely ill. His eldest son Richard, away training his armies, knows nothing of the plot being hatched by his brother John, who with the evil Sir Philip intends to usurp the throne for himself.
Sir Philip Peter Reynolds
Prince John Trader Faulkner
King Henry Dominic Roche

Director: Ernest Morris

The Lion and the Eagle

w Paul Tabori and Stanley Miller

Hearing that Prince John is mounting a rebellion in the North, Richard sets out to thwart his plans – but encounters more trouble than he bargained for along the way.
De Glanville John Gabriel
Edward the Saxon Glyn Owen
De Bohm Raymond Rollett

Director: Ernest Morris

The Robbers of Ashdown Forest

w Paul Tabori and Stanley Miller

Having returned to London to prepare for his coronation, Richard discovers that his brother Prince John has fled the country – taking with him Queen Eleanor, as hostage.
Queen Eleanor Prudence Hyman
Baron Rheinfrid Tom Bowman
Ulric Steve Plytas

Director: Ernest Morris

The Wolf of Banbury

w Paul Tabori and Stanley Miller

In defiance of Richard's orders, Baron Giles gives protection to fugitives from justice. To add insult to injury, he abducts the Lady Rosalie, recently betrothed to Sir Geoffrey.

Baron Giles Francis de Wolfe
Lady Rosalie June Alexander
La Motte Humphrey Lestocq

Director: Ernest Morris

School for a King

w Paul Tabori and Stanley Miller

Anxious to learn the plight of his subjects at first hand, Richard sallies forth in disguise – and soon finds himself arrested for not paying his taxes.
Stephen de Tours Peter Illing
Lady Blanche Dawn Beret
Steward Richard Hearne

Director: Ernest Morris

Crown in Danger

w Paul Tabori and Stanley Miller

Having sent several of his friends in pursuit of three escaped prisoners, Richard is concerned when he hears that they have taken refuge in the castle of a knight who feeds his foes to his wild animals.
Sir Miles Tony Doonan
Robert Howard Green
Bertram Kevin Brennan

Director: Ernest Morris

The Pirate King

w Paul Tabori and Stanley Miller

Believing himself to be Richard's equal, Forked Beard, a self-styled 'King', seeks a treaty between himself and the English king. Having rejected his proposal, Richard is taken prisoner.
Forked Beard Martin Benson
Pirate Captain Michael Peake
Harbour master Norman Wynne

Director: Ernest Morris

The Alchemist of Rouen

w Paul Tabori and Stanley Miller
Lady Rosalie's appeal to Richard to help her
father, whom she believes has fallen under
the spell of Villanus, an alchemist, almost
costs Richard his life.
Rosalie June Alexander
Villanus Trader Faulkner
Villa Soraya Rafat

Director: Ernest Morris

The King's Champion

w Paul Tabori and Stanley Miller
Led by a bogus pretender to the English
throne, a Black Knight issues a challenge
that Richard, with too few knights at court,
must accept – or forfeit his throne.
King William John Scott
The Pretender Trader Faulkner
Black Knight John Bey

Director: Ernest Morris

King Arthur's Sword

w Paul Tabori and Stanley Miller
Richard leads his men to capture the thieves
who have stolen King Arthur's sword
Excalibur, from Arthur's tomb at
Glastonbury Abbey. But danger dogs his
path.
Merlin Ferdy Mayne
Black Knight David Davenport
Lady Guinivere Daphne Anderson

Director: Ernest Morris

The Challenge

w Paul Tabori and Stanley Miller
Zara and her brother Umbaldo issue a
challenge to Richard. He must choose a
champion to defeat Umbaldo. Should
Umbaldo win, Richard will pay service to
Zara – should he be defeated, Zara will
become Richard's bride.
Zara Zena Marshall
Umbaldo Trader Faulkner
Sir Roland Ian Curry

Director: Ernest Morris

The Bride

w Paul Tabori and Stanley Miller
Urged by his counsellors to take a bride,
Richard sets out in disguise to visit the
court of Prince Frederick, to take a cautious
look at his daughter.
Prince Frederick Ian Fleming
Lady Berengaria Sheila Whittington
Lady Alice Susan Shaw

Director: Ernest Morris

The Great Enterprise

w Paul Tabori and Stanley Miller
Queen Berengaria, honeymooning with her
new husband, is unaware that someone is
plotting treachery at Richard's court –
returning home, she faces a charge of
treason.
Abbas Richard Shaw
Mahmoud Olaf Pooley
Knight Michael McStay

Director: Ernest Morris

The Norman King

w David Nicholl
Unaware that King Tancred of Sicily and
King Philip of France are plotting his
death, Richard accepts their invitation to a
banquet given in his honour.
Tancred Elwyn Brook-Jones
King Philip Trader Faulkner
Laki Roger Delgado

Director: Ernest Morris

When Champions Meet

w David Nicholl
Pursuing his plot to have Richard killed,
King Philip joins forces with Richard's
brother, Prince John. Together they
challenge Richard to face Saladin, in a
'friendly' tournament.
King Philip Trader Faulkner
Saladin Marne Maitland
Guy Conrad Philips

Director: Ernest Morris

Warrior from Scotland

w Stanley Miller
Determined to join Richard's Crusade,
Kenneth, a young Scottish warrior, arrives

at Richard's castle. While attempting to impress Richard, he loses the King's banner – and is sentenced to death.
Kenneth Anton Rodgers
Leopold Francis de Wolfe
Nectobanus Roy Kinnear

Director: Ernest Morris

The Conjurer

w Mark Grantham

Ali, a Saracen youth with a flair for conjuring – but a fear of killing – is ordered to infiltrate Richard's camp and slay the monarch.
Ali Riggs O'Hara
Gamal George Pastell
Nur Eric Dodson

Director: Ernest Morris

The Lord of Kenak

w David Nicholl

Arnold, master of Kernak Castle, is a Crusader in name only. So when he hears that the King is travelling to query his absence from court, he plans to have Richard killed.
Arnold Willoughby Goddard
Conrad Michael Peake
Sir Humphrey Francis Matthews

Director: Ernest Morris

The Saracen Physician

w Stanley Miller

Gravely ill with fever, Richard is taken to the camp of his allies where, unknown to his friends, the attendant physician is in the pay of Saladin – Richard's enemy.
Simeon Peter Elliott
Sir Kenneth Anton Rodgers
Theodore Christopher Carlos

Director: Ernest Morris

A Marriage of Convenience

w Stanley Miller

On the pretence of opposing Lady Edith's marriage to Sir Kenneth, Richard sends his confidant to Saladin to propose that the Moslem leader consolidate the peace between them by marrying the girl.

Guy Conrad Philips
Lady Edith Jennifer Daniel
Saladin Marne Maitland

Director: Ernest Morris

Queen in Danger

w David Nicholl

When Queen Berengaria sets out on a pilgrimage, Conrad of Montferrat arranges to have her abducted – hoping that by effecting her 'rescue' he will gain Richard's confidence.
Conrad Michael Peake
Kermal John Bennett
Salivor Laurence Hardy

Director: Ernest Morris

Prince Otto

w Stanley Miller

Prince Otto's castle is the only barrier in the Crusader's path. He insists on being paid before he'll allow anyone to pass – including the British sovereign.
Otto Walter Gotell
Marianne Jill Ireland
De Fleury Trader Faulkner

Director: Ernest Morris

The Vision Fades

w Stanley Miller

With their objective in sight, Richard and his men are determined to capture Jerusalem in one final assault – but the king proceeds slowly. Why?
Leopold Francis de Wolfe
Farah Anna Gerber
Arab Robert Robinson

Director: Ernest Morris

The Strange Monks of Latroun

w Stanley Miller

Masquerading as a wounded felon, Richard sets out alone to unmask a group of 'monks' who have robbed a poor pilgrim and left him to die in the forest.
Abbot Edgar Wreford
Red Hugh Alistair Williamson
Pilgrim Olaf Pooley

Director: Ernest Morris

The Fugitive

w Stanley Miller

The sole survivor of a shipwreck, Richard
scrambles ashore to safety. Unfortunately
he's landed on the land of Duke Leopold –
his sworn enemy!

Leopold Francis de Wolfe
Count Rolfe Elwyn Brook-Jones
Hugo Glyn Owen

Director: Ernest Morris

Knight Errant at Large

w David Nicholl

Following his knight's vows, Richard helps
a young woman in distress – and quickly
finds himself a prisoner of the tyrannical
Lord Rudolph.

Rudolph David Davies
Marta Anne Lawson
Hugo Glyn Owen

Director: Ernest Morris

Guardian of the Temple

w David Nicholl

With his new friends, Hugo and Marta,
Richard stops at a market-town to purchase
fresh mounts – and finds himself arrested as
an enemy spy.

Farmer Robin Hunter
First soldier Alan Haywood
Second soldier Iain Gregory

Director: Ernest Morris

Capture

w David Nicholl

Within sight of escape from Austria, Marta
collapses from fatigue. Though he risks
capture, Richard refuses to continue until
she has recovered.

Michael Peter Reynolds
Duke Leopold Trader Faulkner
Count Rolfe Elwyn Brook-Jones

Director: Ernest Morris

A King's Ransom

w David Nicholl

Hearing that Leopold demands a price of
150,000 marks for Richard's release, Queen

Berengaria commands Sir Gilbert and Sir
Geoffrey to raise the money.

Prince John Trader Faulkner
Queen Eleanor June Haythorne
Queen Berengaria Sheila Whittington

Director: Ernest Morris

The Devil Unloosed

w David Nicholl

Told by a fortune-teller that Richard is
dead, Prince John makes plans to proclaim
himself King. He has reckoned without
Robin Hood and his Merry Men – Richard's
loyal subjects.

Robin Hood Ronald Howard
Little John Robert Percival
Prince John Trader Faulkner

Director: Ernest Morris

The Little People of Lynton

w Paul Tabori and Stanley Miller

Hearing that someone is using the royal seal
to collect illegal taxes, Richard, disguised as
a tax-inspector, journeys to the country to
set matters right.

Baron John Scott
Tom Jack Smethurst
Michael Roy Kinnear

Director: Ernest Morris

The Raiders

w Mark Grantham

Out hunting, Richard and Gilbert find the
body of a murdered man – a discovery
which leads them to the castle of a
murderous knight, responsible for several
killings.

Brian McFergus Philip Latham
Lemuel Neil Hallett
Father Benedict Robert Raglan

Director: Ernest Morris

An Eye for an Eye

w Paul Tabori and Stanley Miller

Richard finds himself abducted by a knight
with a grievance against the English
Throne. Put on trial for treason, Richard is
sentenced to be hanged.

Rudolph David Davies
Mary Jennifer Jayne
James Sean Kelly

Director: Ernest Morris

The Caveman

w Mark Grantham
While spending some time at a friend's
castle, Richard is asked to intervene in a
dispute between his host and his workers.
Baron Brentlock Guy Deghy
Hermit Nigel Greene
Diane June Thorburn

Director: Ernest Morris

A Year and a Day

w Paul Tabori and Stanley Miller
Alan, a serf, is promised his freedom if he
joins the Crusaders instead of Baron
Fitzgeorge – who plans to kill Alan on his
return.
Alan Derek Sherwin
Fitzgeorge Richard Caldicot
Rose Eira Heath

Director: Ernest Morris

The Crown Jewels

w Mark Grantham
Unknown to Queen Berengaria, her cousin
Miguel, who has arrived in London to train
as a knight, is actually involved in a plot to
kill her husband and steal the crown jewels.
Miguel Maurice Kaufmann
Martha Lisa Daniely
Queen Berengaria Sheila Whittington

Director: Ernest Morris

The Man Who Sold Pardons

w David Nicholls
Masquerading as Sir Richard of Kent,
Richard sets out to find the man responsible

for selling forged 'pardons' to ex-colleagues
of Prince John.
Nicholas Nigel Greene
Friar Thomas Gerald Greene
Innkeeper Leon Cortez

Director: Ernest Morris

The Heir of England

w David Nicholl
Travelling to invite the Duchess of Brittany
and her son Prince Arthur to Richard's
coronation, Sir Gilbert is ambushed. His
attacker takes his place and continues the
journey disguised as Richard's emissary.
Duchess Margaret Scott
Prince Arthuur Christopher Witty
Marvel Trader Faulkner

Director: Ernest Morris

The Peoples' King

w David Nicholl
Lord Roger, Richard's enemy, plans to slay
the newly-crowned King, by attending
Richard's coronation in disguise.
Attempting to do so he is unmasked by Sir
Gilbert and the two men engage in a fierce
battle for the King's life.
Lord Roger Anthony Jacobs
Sir Gilbert Robin Hunter
Megan Jane Hylton

Director: Ernest Morris

RICHARD THE LIONHEART
Produced by the Danziger Brothers
Associate producer: Brian Taylor
39 monochrome 30-minute episodes
11 June 1962 – 13 December 1963
(USA: Syndicated 1963)

THE RIVALS OF SHERLOCK HOLMES

Based on an anthology by Sir Hugh Greene, these 26 crime and mystery stories depicted the investigations of Sherlock Holmes's contemporaries in the criminal world of Victorian and Edwardian London – other sleuths (of one kind or another) who were almost as famous in their day.
(Note: The name immediately after the story title relates to the writer who dramatised the episode. The name in brackets refers to the lead character's creator.)

SEASON ONE
13 colour 60-minute episodes

A Message from the Deep Sea

w Philip Mackie   *(R. Austin Freeman)*
A dastardly crime. A girl is found with her throat cut in an East End lodging house. Dr Thorndyke discovers a vital clue, previously overlooked by the police.
Dr Thorndyke John Neville
Dr Hart Paul Darrow
Sam Turner Ray Lonnen

Director: James Goddard
Designer: Fred Pusey

The Missing Witness Sensation

w Philip Mackie   *(Ernest Bramah)*
When a young post-office clerk is gunned down at her counter, blind detective Max Carrados discovers vital evidence to her killer.
Max Carrados Robert Stevens
Insp. Beedel George A. Cooper
Stringer Christopher Cazenove

Director: Jonathan Alwyn
Designer: Peter Le Page

The Affair of the Avalanche Bicycle and Tyre Co. Ltd.

w Paul Erickson   *(Arthur Morrison)*
Horace Dorrington, private enquiry agent, investigates a case of sabotage on a bicycle track – but danger is waiting around every bend.

Dorrington Peter Vaughan
Farrish Kenneth Colley
Stedman John Carlisle

Director: James Goddard
Designer: Fred Pusey

The Duchess of Wiltshire's Diamonds

w Anthony Steven   *(unknown)*
It appears that every jewel thief in Europe and America is intent on stealing the Duchess of Wiltshire's diamonds – but Simon Carne devises an ingenious way to protect them.
Simon Carne Roy Dotrice
Duchess Barbara Murray
Chf Supt Vyvyan Dudley Foster

Director: Kim Mills
Designer: Neville Green

The Horse of the Invisible

w Philip Mackie   *(W. Hope Hodgson)*
An invisible horse that haunts a family on the eve of a wedding. Is it really a ghost? Enter ghost-hunter Carnacki to throw some light on the mystery.
Carnacki Donald Pleasance
Captain Higgins Tony Steedman
Mary Higgins Michele Dotrice

Director: Alan Cooke
Designer: Stan Woodward

The Case of the Mirror of Portugal

w Julian Bond   *(Arthur Morrison)*
Ace sleuth Horace Dorrington is prone to
forget his obligations to his client – but not
too forgetful to clear up the mystery
surrounding the theft of a valuable
diamond.
Dorrington Peter Vaughan
Solomons Arnold Diamond
Nephew Jeremy Irons

Director: Mike Vardy
Designer: Patrick Downing

Madame Sara

w Philip Mackie
(L. T. Meade and Robert Eustace)
Asked by an old school-friend to investigate
a murder case, detective Dixon Druce meets
up with Madame Sara whose business is . . .
murder?
Dixon Druce John Fraser
Insp. Vandeleur George Murcell
Madame Sara Marianne Benet

Director: Piers Haggard
Designer: Neville Green

The Case of the Dixon Torpedo

w Stuart Hood   *(Arthur Morrison)*
A secret weapon. Forged roubles. An
eccentric inventor and a trained assassin –
more than enough to occupy the mind of ace
detective/spy-trapper Jonathan Pride.
Jonathan Pride Ronald Hines
Hunter Cyril Shaps
Roberts James Bolam

Director: James Goddard
Designer: Fred Pusey

The Woman in the Big Hat

w Alan Cooke   *(Baroness Orczy)*
When a respectable man is murdered, the
only clue the police have is a mysterious
woman in a big hat – a challenge for Lady
Molly of Scotland Yard, who is asked to find
her.
Lady Molly Elvi Hale
Kate Harris Una Stubbs
Insp. Saunders Peter Bowles

Director: Alan Cooke
Designer: Stan Woodward

The Affair of the Tortoise

w Bill Craig   *(Arthur Morrison)*
The police are baffled: the body of a
murdered man has disappeared. Enter
Arthur Hewitt to solve the mystery – and
find himself involved with voodoo.
Arthur Hewitt Peter Barkworth
Miss Chapman Cyd Hayman
Insp. Nettings Dan Meaden

Director: Bill Bain
Designer: Norman Garwood

The Assyrian Rejuvenator

w Julian Bond   *(Clifford Ashdown)*
Hearing about the results being guaranteed
by the makers of the Assyrian Rejuvenator,
private investigator and conman Romney
Pringle exposes a clever swindle – and
makes a profit.
Romney Pringle Donald Sinden
Col. Sandstream Michael Bates
Sgt Hawkins Victor Platt

Director: Jonathan Alwyn
Designer: David Marshall

The Ripening Rubies

w Anthony Skene   *(Max Pemberton)*
Outraged by a spate of audacious jewel
robberies, Lady Faber seeks the help of
detective Bernard Sutton – who agrees to act
as watchdog at the woman's society ball.
Bernard Sutton Robert Lang
Lady Faber Lally Bowers
Mrs Kavanagh Moira Redmond

Director: Alan Cooke
Designer: Peter Le Page

The Case of Laker, Absconded

w Philip Mackie   *(Arthur Morrison)*
When a bank clerk disappears with the sum
of £15,000, detectives Arthur Hewitt and
Jonathan Pride put their heads together to
solve the mystery.
Arthur Hewitt Peter Barkworth
Jonathan Pride Ronald Hines
Charles Laker Roger Cartland

Director: Jonathan Alwyn
Designer: Mike Ball

Season Two

13 colour 60-minute episodes

The Mysterious Death on the Underground Railway

w Alan Cooke   *(Baroness Orczy)*
When a beautiful young girl is discovered dead on the seat of an underground train, detective Polly Burton offers to assist the police with their enquiries.
Polly Burton Judy Geeson
Laura Stanley Cyd Hayman
Insp. Thornton Dennis Blanch

Director: Graham Evans
Designer: Patrick Downing

Five Hundred Carats

w Alexander Baron   *(George Griffith)*
When the theft of a diamond weighing 500 carats leads to lust and murder, Inspector Lipinzki is asked to solve the crimes.
Lipinzki Barry Keegan
Mr Arundel Patrick Barr
Lomas Richard Morant

Director: Jonathan Alwyn
Designer: Patrick Downing

Cell 13

w Julian Bond   *(Jacques Futrelle)*
Professor Van Dusen sits alone in the condemned cell of the country's toughest security prison. His crime – he swore he could 'think his way out'. But can he?
Van Dusen Douglas Wilmer
Governor Michael Gough
Fielding Donald Pickering

Director: Reginald Collin
Designer: Mike Hall

The Secret of the Manifique

w Gerald Kelsey   *(E. Phillips Oppenheim)*
With the aid of two ex-convicts, Detective Laxworthy conceives a plan of great importance – he plots to steal the plans for the first ever French torpedo.
Laxworthy Bernard Hepton
Wing Christopher Neame
Admiral Christador John Nettleton

Director: Derek Bennett
Designer: Peter Le Page

The Absent-minded Coterie

w Alexander Baron   *(unknown)*
France's greatest amateur detective, M. Valmont, is called in to help the police smash a counterfeiting gang who are expertly forging coins with real silver.
M. Valmont Charles Gray
Lord Semptam George Howe
Insp. Hale Barry Linehan

Director: Peter Duguid
Designer: Fred Pusey

The Sensible Action of Lieutenant Holst

w Michael Meyer   *(Palle Rosenkrantz)*
Copenhagen policeman Lieutenant Holst becomes involved in an international situation when a Russian Countess claims her husband is plotting her death.
Lt Holst John Thaw
Maria Wolkinski Catherine Schell
Dimitri Wolkinski Philip Madoc

Director: Jonathan Alwyn
Designer: David Marshall

The Superfluous Finger

w Julian Bond   *(Jacques Futrelle)*
Professor Van Dusen must find the answer to why eminent surgeon Prescott cut off the perfectly healthy finger of a beautiful young woman.
Van Dusen Douglas Wilmer
Prescott Laurence Payne
Miss Rossmore/Mrs Morey Veronica Strong

Director: Derek Bennett
Designer: David Marshall

Anonymous Letters

w Anthony Steven   *(Baldwin Groller)*
Who is the writer of a series of vile, anonymous letters received by Countess Nadja? Detective Dabogert Trostler seeks the solution.
Trostler Ronald Lewis
Countess Nicola Pagett
Frankenburg Francis de Wolff

Director: Dennis Vance
Designer: Allan Cameron

The Moabite Cipher

w Reginald Collin   *(R. Austin Freeman)*
When a Russian Grand Duke makes a secret
visit to London and anarchists try to
assassinate him, detective Dr Thorndyke
sets out to find out why.
Dr Thorndyke Barrie Ingham
Dr Jervis Peter Sallis
Alfred Barton Julian Glover

Director: Reginald Collin
Designer: David Marshall

The Secret of the Foxhunter

w Gerald Kelsey   *(William Le Queux)*
Detective William Drew of the Foreign
Office finds himself with the odds stacked
firmly against him when he investigates an
unusual crime.
William Drew Derek Jacobi
Colonel Davidoff Peter Arne
Marquess of Macclesfield Richard Pearson

Director: Graham Evans
Designer: Norman Garwood

(Episode title and credits unknown)

The Looting of the Specie Room

w Ian Kennedy Martin   *(C. J.
Cunliffe-Hyne)*
When a fortune in gold bullion disappears
from the strongroom of R. M. S. *Oceanic*, a
ship which is trying to establish a new
record time for crossing the Atlantic, the
ship's purser, amateur detective Mr
Horrocks, investigates.

Horrocks Ronald Fraser
First Officer Stephen Yardley
Sir Edward Markham Edward Dentith

Director: Jonathan Alwyn
Designer: Peter Le Page

The Mystery of the Amber Beads

w Owen Holder   *(Fergus Hume)*
Who murdered Mrs Arryford? Det. Sgt
Grubber believes he has the culprit, but
amateur sleuth Hagar puts her gypsy
intuition to work — and shatters Grubber's
dreams.
Hagar Sara Kestelman
DS Grubber Joss Ackland
Vark Philip Locke

Director: Don Leaver
Designer: Roger Allan

THE RIVALS OF SHERLOCK HOLMES
Producers: Robert Love and Jonathan Alwyn
(Season 1)
Reginald Collin and Jonathan Alwyn
(Season 2)
Executive producers: Lloyd Shirley(Season 1)
Kim Mills (Season 2)
Music by: Bob Sharples
Story editors: George Markstein (Season 1)
Harry Moore (Season 2)
A Thames Television Production
26 colour 60-minute episodes
20 September – 9 December 1971
29 January – 16 April 1973
(USA: PBS 1975/1976
13 episodes)

RIVIERA POLICE

Take four rugged policemen (guaranteed to please the mums);
add lots of leggy, near-naked girls in revealing bikinis (to please
the dads); throw in a sprinkling of intrigue and crime set against
a backdrop of the sun-drenched French Riviera; and you had all
the ingredients for a hit television series . . . or so the producers
thought.

   In reality this series proved that sunshine, boobs and tinsel
(however glossy the package), did not a series make.

REGULAR CAST

Inspector Legrand **Brian Spink**   *Lt Col Sorel* **Frank Lieberman**
Supt Hunter **Geoffrey Frederick**   *Supt Johnson* **Noel Trevarthen**
(Note: The only time that all four men were seen working together
was in the first story)

Who Can Catch a Falling Star?

w Brian Clemens and Jordan Lawrence
When someone kills a rising star during the
Cannes Film Festival, the Riviera Police
find themselves racing against time to
discover why. Unless they discover the
motive for killing, death will strike again.
Tony Lorenz Anthony Valentine
Joan Mayer Katherine Blake
Eric Vitch Alan Gifford

Director: Ian Fordyce

That Kind of Girl

w David Weir
Murder intrudes into the gay atmosphere of
the Nice Flower Festival and Superintendent
Hunter and his team find themselves
looking for a dangerous killer among the
exotic blooms.
Jeremiah Canlon John Le Mesurier
Jean Howard Veronica Lang
Bill Fleming Bill Nagy

Director: Bill Turner

The Lucky One Was the Snake

w Donald and Derek Ford
Colonel Sorel finds himself looking for a
sniper who has killed once and will do so
again unless he is found. But the Riviera
offers many vantage points to a man who is
looking to stay hidden.
Lisa Nadja Regin
Marguerite Wanda Ventham
Baghoulle Harold Innocent

Director: Christopher Hodson

But the Company She Keeps

w Anthony Skene
The squad keeps a watchful eye on a girl
they believe to be in danger. Her friends
have a dubious past and she is unaware that
the mysterious stranger she's befriended is
hiding a dark secret.
Tomasso William Abey
Inge April Wilding
Helen Philippa Gail

Director: Ronald Marriott

Duet for Two Guns

w Patrick Alexander
Has Harry Borden achieved the impossible?
The squad are certain that he is behind two
Riviera murders – but Harry is residing in a
prison cell in England! Nevertheless,
someone is seeking revenge on his behalf –
and the squad must discover who.
Marianne Pamela Greer
Jack Roy Marsden
Luc La Sale John Turner

Director: Ian Fordyce

A Shot in the Dark . . . and Two in the Midday Sun

w Max Marquis
Johnson and Hunter find themselves the
prey of an assassin who is determined to kill
a beautiful young film starlet, in Cannes for
a shoot. Somewhere amid the cameras and
floodlights a killer hides.
Sheila Ward June Thorburn
Larry Bryant Paul Maxwell
Joyce Perelli Jennifer Jayne

Director: Marc Miller

Take it Sideways and Pray

w Patrick Alexander
When a death from his past becomes an
obstacle to his chances of competing in the
Monaco Grand Prix, Lew Scarsdale decides
to hedge his bets by ridding himself of his
burden. But doing so brings him under the
scrutiny of Supt Johnson.

Lew Scarsdale John Meillon
Jenny Jill Curzon
Jack Dysart David Burke

Director: Richard Doubleday

There Comes a Point

w Max Marquis
When a wealthy man treats everyone with
contempt, there comes a point when
someone will crack. The problem facing the
Riviera team is: who will crack first? They
or the elusive opponent?
Dimitri Smith David Bower
Hector Skowas Patrick Mower
Comtesse Pauline Letts

Director: Ian Fordyce

Past Indefinite — Future Imperfect

w Anthony Skene
Aware that archaeologists Lady Cataret and
her son David are overly fascinated by the
past, the Riviera team expect trouble. It
arrives sooner than they expected in the
shape of Karl — a very clever conman.
Lady Cataret Peggy Thorpe-Bates
David Cataret Gary Bond
Karl Peter Tory

Director: Bill Turner

There's Something Moving in the Water

w Donald and Derek Ford
A girl on the beach, one step away from
danger. A man who knows a secret he
cannot share. A death from the past believed
forgotten. Three ingredients in a puzzle that
tax the Riviera team to the hilt.
Martine Bouchet Edina Ronay
Ereole Mark Kingston
Eva Marceau Pamela Brown

Director: Christopher Hodson

Girl on a Plate

w David Gordon
A beautiful model provides the best chance
of finding a murderer before he tries to kill
again. But should the Riviera team gamble
with her life to unmask the killer? That's
the dilemma facing Supt Hunter.
Liz Reboe Stephanie Randell
Raglan-Smith Basil Dignam
Debbie Raglan-Smith Helen Lindsay

Director: Christopher Hodson

Bubbles Through a Looking Glass

w Donald and Derek Ford
Bubbles and Katya have a very clever
cabaret act, but when murder enters the
footlights it is down to Superintendent
Johnson and his team to rehearse their
moves with slick precision.
Bubbles Jacqueline Ellis
Katya Lisa Madron
Anton Irvick George Pravda

Director: Richard Doubleday

A Rainbow Has Two Ends

w Donald and Derek Ford
Within days of his departure from Nice,
Superintendent Hunter finds that two
identical cars provide him with enough
thrills and intrigue to last a lifetime. It also
leads him into a merry chase with the
criminal fraternity.
Marceau Erica Rodgers
Gerrard Frederick Jaeger
Keppler Michael Beint

Director: Ian Fordyce

RIVIERA POLICE
Producer: Jordan Lawrence
Title music by: Laurie Johnson
Story editor: Jordan Lawrence
A Rediffusion Network Production
13 monochrome 60-minute episodes
2 August – 27 October 1965
(USA: Syndicated 1965)

ROBIN OF SHERWOOD

In the beginning there was Richard Greene as the dashing hero of Sherwood. Almost a quarter of a century later, a new and totally different kind of Robin Hood appeared on our screens to a fanfare of trumpets and the declaration: 'In the days of the Lion spawned of the Devil's Brood, the Hooded Man shall come to the forest. There he will meet Herne the Hunter, Lord of the Trees, and be his son and do his bidding. The powers of Light and Darkness shall be strong within him. And the guilty shall tremble.' The 'Hooded Man' of course, was Robin Hood – but a totally different Robin from the one we'd grown used to. Gone was the familiar Lincoln green; gone were the fairytale heroics portrayed so splendidly by Richard Greene. In their place we had Robin of Loxley, a man persuaded by Herne (an elemental woodland spirit who materialised as a stag or a 'man') that his true destiny was to lead his band of followers to free all men from the insidious Norman treachery.

Furthermore, black magic and sorcery was rife in the stories (the powers of Herne and his mystical sword Albion). Black magic! Sorcery! What, you may ask, had all this to do with the legend of Robin Hood? In a word, everything – provided the legend was told with flair and panache – which it well and truly was. The series' creator, Richard Carpenter, turned the legend upside down and made an all-too-familiar tale into riveting viewing.

REGULAR CAST

Robin of Loxley **Michael Praed**   *Robin of Huntingdon* **Jason Connery**
Little John **Clive Mantle**   *Will Scarlet* **Ray Winstone**   *Maid Marion* **Judy Trott**
Much **Peter Llewellyn**   *Friar Tuck* **Phil Rose**   *Nasir* **Mark Ryan**
Sheriff of Nottingham **Nicholas Grace**   *Guy of Gisburne* **Robert Addie**
Herne the Hunter **John Aberini**

Season One

*4 colour 60-minute episodes and
1 double-length introductory story*

Robin Hood and the Sorcerer

w Richard Carpenter
(Double-length intro. story)
Imprisoned in Nottingham Castle by Sir Guy of Gisburne, Robin of Loxley sets out on his crusade against the Sheriff's villainy. Along the way he encounters the evil Baron de Belleme, a Satanist from whom Robin will eventually rescue the lovely Lady Marion – and the Silver Arrow: 'Herne's arrow. A cult object. A symbol of magic bearing the inscription which can only be deciphered by Baron Belleme – or, Herne's son, Robin i' th' Hood!'
Baron Belleme **Anthony Valentine**
Abbot Hugo **Philip Jackson**
Ailric **Wayne Michaels**

Director: **Ian Sharp**
Designer: **John Biggs**

The Witch of Elsden

w Paul Carpenter

When Abbot Hugo and his brother, the Sheriff, persecute a young girl and her husband and accuse them of witchcraft, Robin and his men set out to set right the Sheriff's villainy. But with Herne's help, it is Marion who saves the day.

Jennet Angharad Rees
Gregory David Goodlamb
Thomas Martin West

Director: Ian Sharp
Designer: John Biggs

Seven Poor Knights from Acre

w Richard Carpenter

Led by the fanatical Reynald de Villaret, the Knights Templar, a group of warrior monks feared throughout Europe, wreak a vengeance on Robin and his men, whom they believe are responsible for stealing their sacred emblem.

De Villaret Yves Beneyton
Von Erlichshausen Duncan Preston
Siward Simon Rouse

Director: Ian Sharp
Designer: John Biggs

Alan A'Dale

w Richard Carpenter

Alan A'Dale rides into Sherwood seeking Robin's help. His beloved Mildred is being forced to marry the Sheriff of Nottingham, and Alan swears to kill him – but Robin has another way to sting his enemy.

Alan A'Dale Peter Hutchinson
Mildred Stephanie Tague
Martin Martin West

Director: Ian Sharp
Designer: John Biggs

The King's Fool

w Richard Carpenter

When Robin rescues a strange knight from ambush, he earns both the gratitude of King Richard of England and the anger of his men, who suspect the King and Sir Guy of Gisburne of treachery – with good cause: Richard plans to have Robin killed!

King Richard John Rhys Davies
Mercadier Doc O'Brien
Abbot Hugo Philip Jackson

Director: Ian Sharp
Designer: John Biggs

Season Two

7 colour 60-minute episodes

The Prophecy

w Richard Carpenter

Who is the strange hooded prisoner being held in Nottingham Castle by Prince John? Herne prophesies the death of King Richard and tells Robin, 'One close to you.' But the outlaw cannot realise the impact the prisoner will have on them all – especially Marion.

De Leon John Nettles
Prince John Philip Davies
Sir Richard George Baker

Director: Robert Young
Designer: John Biggs

The Children of Israel

w Richard Carpenter

When the Sheriff uses the precedent of the Jewish massacre in York to stir up a riot to avoid paying money he owes to Jewish moneylender, Joshua de Talmont, he finds himself not only facing Robin Hood – but the sinister powers of the Cabala, a book of ancient wisdom.

De Talmont David de Keyser
Ester de Talmont Amy Rosenthal
Samuel de Talmont Adam Rosenthal

Director: Alex Kirby
Designer: John Biggs

Lord of the Trees

w Richard Carpenter

In the Sheriff's absence Gisburne hires a band of ruthless Flemish mercenaries to finish off Robin Hood. As it is the time of 'The Blessing', no blood must be spilled – so the outlaw relies on Herne's magic to destroy his enemies.

De Nivelle Oliver Tobias
Guillaume Patrick Gordon
Abbot Hugo Philip Jackson

Director: James Allen
Designer: John Biggs

The Enchantment

w Richard Carpenter
When Lilith, an evil enchantress, bewitches
Robin and persuades him to steal Herne's
Silver Arrow, so that she can raise a deadly
enemy from the grave, the outlaws seek
Herne's help to free their leader.
Lilith Gemma Craven
Baron Belleme Anthony Valentine
Edward Jeremy Bulloch

Director: James Allen
Designer: John Biggs

The Swords of Wayland (Part 1)

w Richard Carpenter
Having left Sherwood to defend a distant
village from the Hounds of Lucifer – eerily
clad horsemen who terrorise the
neighbourhood – Robin and his men find
themselves up against a devilish enemy led
by the servants of Morgwyn of Ravenscar's
powerful coven.

The Swords of Wayland (Part 2)

The coven's purpose is to find the seven
swords of Wayland to use for a ritual which
will invoke Lucifer – the devil. Herne has
entrusted Albion, one of the seven swords,
to Robin. It eventually falls into Morgwyn's
hands – and Robin finds himself alone and
locked in combat with the forces of
darkness.
Morgwyn Rula Lenska
Earl Godwin Anthony Steel
Adam Norman Bowler

Director: Robert Young
Designer: John Biggs

The Greatest Enemy

w Richard Carpenter
Threatened by Prince John with loss of
office should he fail to dispose of Robin

Hood, the Sheriff sets up a successful
ambush. Only Robin, Marion and Much
escape. Pursued by hounds and men-at-
arms, Robin pays the greatest sacrifice – and
Robin i' th' Hood is no more.
   The outlaws pay their final respects to
their dead leader – and are joined by a
hooded figure . . .
Edward Jeremy Bulloch
Matthew Robbie Bulloch
Giscard Robert Daws

Director: Robert Young
Designer: John Biggs

Season Three
13 colour 60-minute episodes

Herne's Son (Part 1)

w Richard Carpenter
Robin of Loxley is dead. The Merry Men
have scattered and Marion, having been
pardoned by the King, has returned to
Leaford. But a new hooded man arrives in
the area, Robert of Huntingdon who, after a
struggle with his conscience, finally accepts
his destiny and sets out to regroup the
outlaws.

Herne's Son (Part 2)

Reunited with the outlaws, Robin sets out
to rescue Marion and her father from Clun
Castle, where Lord Owen is determined to
take Marion for his bride – but the Sheriff
and Gisburne are hot on their heels.
Gulnar Richard O'Brien
Lord Owen Oliver Cotton
Sir Richard George Baker

Director: Robert Young
Designer: John Biggs

The Power of Albion

w Richard Carpenter
When Robin is badly wounded in a raid the
outlaws send for Marion, but she is arrested
by the Sheriff on her return from Sherwood.
Wounded or not, Robin must enter
Nottingham alone and attempt to save both
Marion and Albion.

Sir Richard George Baker
Edward Jeremy Bulloch
Oliver Max Faulkner

Director: Gerry Mill
Designer: John Biggs

The Inheritance

w Anthony Horowitz

When Agrivaine, the guardian of a priceless treasure, foresees his own death in the Tarot cards, his daughter Isadora seeks Robin's help to deal with Raven, a one-eyed thief who threatens to pillage the secret guarded by her father.

Agrivaine Cyril Cusack
Isadora Cathryn Harrison
Raven Derrick O'Connor

Director: Ben Bolt
Designer: John Biggs

The Cross of St Ciricus

w Richard Carpenter

After a lucrative robbery, Much and Scarlet make their way to Croxten Abbey to give their plunder to the church. En route, they come across Lady Gisburne, mother of Sir Gisburne, who, believing she is going to die, tells Tuck a very unusual story.

Lady Margaret Dorothy Tutin
Abbot Martin Brendan Price
Monk David Sivier

Director: Dennis Abbey
Designer: Ken Sharp

The Sheriff of Nottingham

w Anthony Horowitz

Tired of having his taxes stolen, King John decides to replace the Sheriff. His replacement, Philip Mark (known as the Butcher of Lincoln), and his Saracen sidekick, Sarak, immediately become another thorn in Robin's side.

Philip Mark Lewis Collins
Sarak Valentine Pelka
Edward Jeremy Bullock

Director: Christopher King
Designer: Ken Sharp

Cromm Cruac

w Anthony Horowitz

Miles away from Sherwood, the outlaws accept the hospitality of a kindly carter. Before long, they find themselves reacquainting themselves with their old enemy Gulnar, the evil Druid from Clun Castle.

Gulnar Richard O'Brien
Tom the Miller Ian Redford
Reeve David Plimmer

Director: Gerry Mill
Designer: John Biggs

The Betrayal

w Andrew McCullock and John Flanagan

When the Sheriff himself visits Nottingham to collect his taxes, he brings with him Roger de Carnac, a ruthless man who has devised a way to rid him of Robin Hood forever – but Robin has plans of his own and Carnac is frustrated.

De Carnac Matt Frewer
King John Philip Davies
Tom the Villager Ian Redford

Director: James Allen
Designer: John Biggs

Adam Bell

w Anthony Horowitz

In return for his nephew, held in Sherwood by Adam Bell, an ageing outlaw, the Sheriff takes Much hostage and threatens to hang him. Only Robin can save the situation – providing Bell allows him to do so.

Adam Bell Bryan Marshall
Moth Leo Dolan
Martin Charlie Condou

Director: Gerry Mill
Designer: John Biggs

The Pretender

w Anthony Horowitz

Bedridden by a dog bite, the hapless Sheriff watches in disgust as Gisburne gives free rein to his power. The powerful Duke of Gloucester is plotting against the King, and Robin finds his troubles compounded by Arthur – a newcomer who wishes to join the outlaws.

Arthur Reece Dinsdale
Queen Hadwisa Patricia Hodge
Duke of Gloucester Russell Enoch

Director: Robert Young
Designer: John Biggs

Rutterkin

w Richard Carpenter

Little John's elopement with Meg of
Wickham is halted by a surprise visit to
Sherwood of Robin's uncle, Lord Edgar
who, unknown to Robin, is plotting against
his father. But how is Mad Mab, the pig
lady, connected to the affair?
Lord Edgar Ian Ogilvy
Mad Mab Annabelle Lee
Earl of Huntingdon Michael Craig

Director: Gerry Mill
Designer: Ken Sharp

Time of the Wolf (Part 1)

w Richard Carpenter

When King John plunders Wickham village
to feed his army, Robin, unwilling to let his
friends starve, leads a raid on the Sheriff's
larder. While the outlaws are away from the
village, Gulnar, Robin's old enemy, returns
and takes the villagers of Wickham prisoner
to the wolfmen's lair at Grimton Abbey.

Time of the Wolf (Part 2)

Captured by Gisburne and the wolfmen,
Robin must find a way to escape and
prevent Gulnar from releasing his latest evil
creation upon the world. Believing he is all-
powerful, Gulnar makes his move – but
Herne stands hidden in the shadows.
Gulnar Richard O'Brien
Grendal James Coombes
Edward Jeremy Bulloch

Director: Sid Robertson
Designer: Ken Sharp

ROBIN OF SHERWOOD
Created by: Richard Carpenter
Producers: Paul Knight (Season 1 and 2)
Paul Knight and Esta Charkham (Season 3)
Executive producer: Patrick Dromgoole
Title and incidental music by: Clannad
*An HTV Production in association with
Goldcrest Films and Television*
26 colour 60-minute episodes
(First two episodes transmitted as one story)
28 April – 26 May 1984
9 March – 13 April 1985
5 April – 28 June 1986

RUMPOLE OF THE BAILEY

The delightful courtroom antics of barrister Horace Rumpole,
mainstay of the Old Bailey and the darling of the criminal
fraternity, an advocate whose pleas could sway the toughest of
juries.

Rumpole's unsurpassed knowledge of blood and typewriters
and his penchant for reciting poetry from the *Oxford Book of
English Verse* had made him a legend amongst his colleagues.
With his love of cigars, his fondness for a 'bottle of plonk' at
Chateau Fleet Street (Pomeroy's Wine Bar) and his habit of
calling his judge 'old darling', his legal skullduggery knew no
bounds. Happiness and Horace Rumpole walked hand in hand –
his one vexation in life being the incessant nagging of his wife
Hilda ('She who must be obeyed').

John Mortimer's classic creation brought brilliantly to life by
actor Leo McKern – a truly inspired piece of casting.

REGULAR CAST

Horace Rumpole **Leo McKern**   Erskine-Brown **Julian Curry**
Phyllida Trant/Erskine-Brown **Patricia Hodge**
Guthrie Featherstone **Peter Bowles**   George Frobisher **Moray Watson**
Uncle Tom **Richard Murdoch**
Hilda Rumpole **Peggy Thorpe Bates** (Seasons 1 – 3)
Marion Mathie (Season 4)   Henry (Clerk of Chambers) **Jonathan Coy**
Diane (Clerk of Chambers) **Maureen Derbyshire**
Fiona Allways **Rosalyn Landor** (Season 3)
Marigold Featherstone **Joanna Van Gyseghem**

Season One

6 colour 60-minute episodes

Rumpole and the Younger Generation

w John Mortimer

Rumpole's first love is justice. He's happiest defending criminals at the Old Bailey. But she who must be obeyed wants him to succeed her father as Head of Chambers. Will Rumpole fulfil her wishes? Or devote his activities to defending Jim Timson?
Jim Timson **Keith Jayne**
Fred Timson **Peter Childs**
Mr Justice Everglade **Ralph Michael**

Director: **Herbert Wise**
Designer: **David Marshall/Mike Hall**

Rumpole and the Alternative Society

w John Mortimer

Rumpole finds himself defending Kathy Trelawny, a young girl accused of handling £10,000 worth of cannabis resin. Contrary to his expectations, he finds himself impressed by the hippie commune in which his client lives.
Kathy **Jane Asher**
Bobby Dogherty **Liz Fraser**
Sam Dogherty **Peter Jeffrey**

Director: **Herbert Wise**
Designer: **David Marshall/ Mike Hall**

Rumpole and the Honourable Member

w John Mortimer

When Rumpole finds himself defending Ken Aspen MP, a man charged with the rape of Bridget Evans, one of his party workers, he finds little comfort when his battle continues out of court with his son's fiancée – an ardent exponent of Women's Lib.
Ken Aspen **Anton Rodgers**
Bridget Evans **Elizabeth Romilly**
Erica **Deborah Fallender**

Director: **Graham Evans**
Designer: **Mike Hall/David Marshall**

Rumpole and the Married Lady

w John Mortimer

Hard up for work, Rumpole takes on a divorce case – and finds himself embattled on all sides. Joined on the case by newcomer to Chambers Phyllida Trant, their most fearsome opponent turns out to be Norman, child of the divorcing pair – and Hilda suspects he's having an affair!
Phyllida Trant **Patricia Hodge** (Intro.)
Norman Thripp **Matthew Ryan**
Mr Thripp **Clifford Parrish**

Director: **Graham Evans**
Designer: **Mike Hall/ David Marshall**

Rumpole and the Learned Friends

w John Mortimer

Rumpole defends safe-breaker Charlie Wheeler, accused of blowing the safe at the Dartford Post Office. His ferocious attack on the police arouses the ire of Judge Bullingham – and Rumpole's legal career seems doomed.
Charlie Wheeler **Ken Jones**
Judge Bullingham **Bill Fraser**
DS Dickerson **Malcolm Storry**

Director: **Graham Evans**
Designer: **Mike Hall/David Marshall**

Rumpole and the Heavy Brigade

w John Mortimer

As Rumpole finds out, taking on the defence of Peter Delgardo, the youngest of the disagreeable Delgardo brothers, leads him into conflict with Judge Prestcold – who seems more interested in Rumpole's appearance than the case itself.
Peter Delgardo Stewart Harwood
Basil Delgardo Derek Newark
Judge Prestcold Mark Dignam

Director: Herbert Wise
Designer: David Marshall/Mike Hall

Season Two
6 colour 60-minute episodes

Rumpole and the Man of God

w John Mortimer

Rumpole finds himself appearing before an unsympathetic judge when he defends an elderly, absent-minded vicar on a shoplifting charge, brought by store-detective Alfred Batt.
Rev. Skinner Derek Farr
Alfred Batt Don McKillop
Judge Bullingham Bill Fraser

Director: Brian Farnham
Designer: Philip Blowers

Rumpole and the Case of Identity

w John Mortimer

At the Old Bailey, defending Anstey, who is accused of attacking O'Neill, the manager of an off-licence, Rumpole finds his defence complicated when Freddie, the man who supplied Anstey's alibi, changes his story when called by the prosecution.
Dave Anstey Martin Fisk
O'Neill Chris Gannon
Freddie Albright Tony Caunter

Director: Derek Bennett
Designer: Bill Palmer/Alan Craig

Rumpole and the Show Folk

w John Mortimer

When Maggie Hartley, the leading lady of a repertory company, sacks her leading counsel and asks Rumpole to represent her

on a murder charge, the barrister is flattered. But he soon finds himself apprehensive as they await the jury's verdict.
Maggie Hartley Eleanor Bron
Mr Croft Harry Markham
Daniel Derwent John Wells

Director: Peter Hammond
Designer: Mike Hall

Rumpole and the Fascist Beast

w John Mortimer

Defending a known fascist, Captain Rex Parkin, on a charge under the Race Relations Act, Rumpole uses his own defence methods – and receives a surprise reaction from his Pakistani pupil, barrister Latif Khan.
Captain Parkin Robert Lang
Latif Khan Lyndham Gregory
Judge Jamieson Paul Curran

Director: Robert Knights
Designer: Bill Palmer

Rumpole and the Course of True Love

w John Mortimer

Supported by his old friend George Frobisher, now on the bench, Rumpole is asked to defend school-teacher Ronald Ransome, who is charged with unlawful carnal knowledge of one of his pupils, 15-year-old Francesca Capstick. Meanwhile, Erskine-Brown tries to convince Phyllida Trant that marriage will not affect her career.
Ronald Ransome Nigel Havers
Francesca Capstick Kate Dorning
Mr Justice Vosper Donald Eccles

Director: Brian Farnham
Designer: Philip Blowers

Rumpole and the Age for Retirement

w John Mortimer

Rumpole is defending Percy Timson on a charge of possessing a stolen religious art work estimated to be worth half a million pounds. Rumpole always handles the Timson family defence, but he is saddened to learn that the family have conspired to

get rid of the elderly Percy – and not amused to discover that his own family have plans for his retirement!
Percy Timson **George Hilsdon**
Cyril Timson **Frank Coda**
Noreen Timson **Julia McCarthy**

Director: **Donald McWhinnie**
Designer: **Bill Palmer**

Rumpole's Return

w John Mortimer
(A 120-minute Special)
Rumpole is supposed to be enjoying his well-earned retirement in the Florida sunshine. But he is not content to ripen like an orange and a surprise letter from a lady barrister tempts him back to Chambers to take command of a 'juicy Blood Case' – and yet another crack at his sworn enemy, Judge Bullingham.
Hubert Simpson **Albert Welling**
Professor Blowfield **Dick Sterling**
Judge Bullingham **Bill Fraser**

Director: **John Glenister**
Designer: **Philip Blowers**

Season Three
6 colour 60-minute episodes

Rumpole and the Genuine Article

w John Mortimer
Rumpole defends Harold Brittling, an artist accused of forgery, who seems anxious to tease the art connoisseurs, even at the risk of imprisonment. Rumpole must decide whether the painting *Nancy at Dieppe* by the late Septimus Cragg, sold at an auction for £38,000, is a forgery.
Harold Brittling **Emlyn Williams**
Nancy **Sylvia Coleridge**
DI Tebbit **Malcolm Mudie**

Director: **Robert Knights**
Designer: **Bill Palmer**

Rumpole and the Golden Thread

w John Mortimer
Rumpole flies to the new African state of Neranga to defend David Mazenze, charged with the murder of Bishop Kareele. Neranga is deeply divided by the Apu and Matatu tribes, and Rumpole suspects the tribal system may have little to do with justice.
David Mazenze **Olu Jacobs**
Grace Mazenze **Carmen Munro**
Dr Mabile **Tommy Eytle**

Director: **Donald McWhinnie**
Designer: **Bill Palmer**

Rumpole and the Old Boy Net

w John Mortimer
Rumpole defends an unlikely, respectable couple, charged with blackmail and running a brothel – and obtaining money by threats from Mr X, a senior Foreign Office official. To help his brief, Rumpole engages the help of Phyllida Trant's pupil, Fiona Allways.
Napier Lee **Michael Denison**
Lorraine Lee **Dulcie Gray**
Fiona Allways **Rosalyn Landor (Intro.)**

Director: **Tony Smith**
Designer: **Bill Palmer**

Rumpole and the Female of the Species

w John Mortimer
Rumpole uses all his guile, a supergrass and his own colleagues to tackle two cases. The first is to defend Tony Timson against a charge of armed robbery. The second is to help young barrister Fiona Allways secure a place in Chambers.
Tony Timson **Ray Brooks**
Mr Bernard **Denis Lill**
Samuel Ballard QC **Peter Blythe**

Director: **Donald McWhinnie**
Designer: **Bill Palmer**

Rumpole and the Sporting Life

w John Mortimer
Rumpole is persuaded by Fiona Allways to defend her sister, Jennifer, on trial for the murder of her husband. He despairs when he learns that the presiding judge is Mr Justice Twyburne, well-known for favouring the death penalty.
Jennifer Postern **Joanna David**
Mr Justice Twyburne **Ronald Culver**
Jonathan Postern **Andrew Burt**

Director: **Bill Hays**
Designer: **Bill Palmer**

Rumpole and the Last Resort

w John Mortimer

His bank manager is unimpressed by outstanding fees owed to Rumpole, and pressure makes it imperative for Rumpole to collect some of his debts. An adjournment of his present case – defending Frank Armstrong on fraud charges – would help, but his attempts to bring that about are repeatedly thwarted by Judge Bullingham. And what of the £3,000 Rumpole is owed by solicitor Perivale Blythe?

Frank Armstrong Michael Melia
Perivale Blythe Terence Rigby
Judge Bullingham Bill Fraser

Director: Stuart Burge
Designer: Bill Palmer

Season Four

6 colour 60-minute episodes

Rumpole and the Old Old Story

w John Mortimer

Following a Scales of Justice dinner, Rumpole, a little the worse for drink, makes a hasty decision – one which incurs the wrath of she who must be obeyed, and tests his friendship with colleagues Phyllida and Claude Erskine-Brown to the limit.

Captain Gleason David Waller
Daphne Jelena Budimir
Mr Justice Gwent-Evans Maurice Denham

Director: Roger Bamford
Designer: Bill Palmer

Rumpole and the Blind Tasting

w John Mortimer

Defending yet another member of the Timson family, Rumpole finds himself being given a hard time by the doom-laden Judge Graves. No wonder the prospect of a wine-tasting with Claude Erskine-Brown seems appealing – but even that brings unwanted troubles.

Hugh Timson George Innes
Hetty Timson Leslie Nunnerley
Judge Graves Robin Bailey

Director: Roger Bamford
Designer: Bill Palmer

Rumpole and the Official Secret

w John Mortimer

Rumpole finds himself surrounded by secrecy. Claude Erskine-Brown is conducting some duplicity, she who must be obeyed is being evasive about an Irishman, and the Ministry of Defence overreacts to a leak about the number of biscuits consumed by its staff!

Tim Warboys Guy Henry
Attorney General Donald Pickering
Lord Chief Justice Paul Daneman

Director: Rodney Bennett
Designer: Bill Palmer/Ian Russell

Rumpole and the Judge's Elbow

w John Mortimer

Due to appear in a massage parlour case before his old head of chambers, Guthrie Featherstone QC – who appears extremely reluctant to try the case – Rumpole finds troubles elsewhere when a new man in Chambers gets under his skin.

Charles Hearthstoke Nicholas Gecks
Mar Addison David Allister
Mrs Addison Hazel McBride

Director: Donald McWhinnie
Designer: Bill Palmer/Ian Russell

Rumpole and the Bright Seraphim

w John Mortimer

Rumpole finds great delight in accepting a court martial in Germany. Trooper Danny Boyne is charged with murdering his Sergeant, a bully disliked by everyone – but when Rumpole gets to the truth of the affair he finds himself cold-shouldered by the defending officer.

Danny Boyne Leonard O'Malley
Captain Ransom Dominic Jephcott
Lt Col Undershaft Neil Stacey

Director: Martyn Friend
Designer: Bill Palmer/Ian Russell

Rumpole's Last Case

w John Mortimer

While defending yet another petty villain of the Timson family before his arch-enemy

Judge Bullingham, Rumpole finds the temptation to escape from it all too strong to resist. Pinning all his hopes on a four-horse accumulator, he decides to indulge himself in some plain speaking to the 'Mad Bull', as he embarks on what is positively his *last* case! But is it?

Den Timson **Ron Pember**
Cyril Timson **Michael Robbins**
Judge Bullingham **Bill Fraser**

Director: **Rodney Bennett**
Designer: **Bill Palmer/Ian Russell**

RUMPOLE OF THE BAILEY
Created by: John Mortimer
Producers: Irene Shubik (Season 1)
Jacqueline Davis (Remaining Episodes)
Executive producer: Lloyd Shirley
Music by: Joseph Horowitz
A Thames Television Network Production
24 colour 60-minute episodes
and 1 Christmas Special
3 April – 15 May 1978
29 May – 26 June 1979
30 December 1980
11 October – 15 November 1983
19 January – 23 February 1987

SAILOR OF FORTUNE

The adventures of Grant Mitchell, Captain of the American motor freighter *The Shipwreck*. An adventurer who, though desperate to keep his nose out of other people's affairs and earn his living carrying legal cargo, continued to find himself and his crew mixed up in villainy in all corners of the world.

REGULAR CAST

Grant Mitchell **Lorne Greene**   *Sean* **Jack MacGowan**
Seamus **Rupert Davies**   *Johnny* **Paul Carpenter**

Tangier
Port Jeopardy
It Started in Paris
Crete Story
The Counterfeit Cigars
The Desert Hostages
The Final Bargain
The Kings' Four Wives
The Deserted Yacht
The Dead Paratrooper
Stranger in Danger
Desert Tomb
The Eastern Lighthouse

The Crescent and the Star*
The Desert Bus
Ship on the Reef
Diamond Chips
The Lost Portrait
Aircraft in the Desert
Death at Sunset
Castle for Sale
Hearse at High Noon
Million Dollar Tree
Case for Murder
Cargo Dynamite
The Golden Head

SAILOR OF FORTUNE
Producer: Michael Sadler
Associate producer: Ted Holliday
Writer: Lindsay Galloway
26 monochrome 30-minute episodes
Filmed at Elstree Studios
30 November 1955 – 14 May 1956
(USA: Syndicated 1957)

* This story featured one of the first appearances by an up-and-coming actor named **Sean Connery**.

THE SAINT

The adventures of Simon Templar, aka the Saint, a modern-day Robin Hood who raised hell with his adversaries, rescued damsels in distress with a twinkle in his eye, and found himself involved in hair-raising adventures that took him all over the world.

Known as the Saint, because of his initials, S. T., (and because he always helped those in need), Templar's zest for adventure lead him into many dangerous situations from which he always emerged triumphant – usually with a pretty girl at his side. A man with impeccable taste, a connoisseur of fine food and wine, and an appreciative eye for the best things in life, women found his handsome looks and suave charm irresistible.

Wherever he travelled, trouble and the Saint were seldom far apart. One adventure would find him helping a lady friend escape from the clutches of a cruel blackmail attempt; another thwarting an ingenious scheme to pull off the crime of the century – more often than not right under the nose of his hapless Scotland Yard adversary, the peppermint-chewing Chief Inspector Claud Eustace Teal (a man jokingly regarded by Templar as 'Scotland Yard's finest').

The series contained more than its share of fisticuffs and for the first 71 adventures at least stuck closely to the stories of Templar's creator, Leslie Charteris, which were adapted for the series. Thereafter the plots got more extreme – some say downright foolish (?) – but with world sales estimated to have passed the £370-million mark, the production company (not to mention Roger Moore, who owns the rights to the colour series) must be well satisfied with the end result.

(As I write this, a new series of The Saint is currently in production in the USA (See also *Return of The Saint*).

REGULAR CAST

Simon Templar **Roger Moore**   *CI Teal* **Ivor Dean** (**Campbell Singer**, **Wensley Pithey**, and **Norman Pitt** appeared as *Teal* in three first-season stories)

Season One

17 monochrome 60-minute episodes

(Note I have been unable to verify that this and the following season entries are correct. However, based on material from other sources, it is believed that the first 39 episodes constituted seasons one and two, in the following order.)

The Talented Husband

w Jack Sanders

Was the death of playwright John Clarron's wife an accident or murder? Together with Adrienne, a glamorous insurance agent, Simon Templar delves into Clarron's background – and turns up a few surprises.

Adrienne Halberd Shirley Eaton
John Clarron Derek Farr
Madge Clarron Patricia Roc

*Director:*Michael Truman

The Latin Touch

w Gerald Kelsey and Dick Sharples
Going to the rescue of an American girl who is being overcharged by a taxi-driver in Rome, Simon soon finds himself involved in an intriguing kidnapping case – and uncovers a few guilty secrets along the way.
Sue Inverest Suzan Farmer
Hudson Inverest Alexander Knox
Marco Warren Mitchell

*Director:*John Gilling

The Careful Terrorist

w Gerald Kelsey and Dick Sharples
When Simon's journalist friend Lester Boyd decides to run an exposé of a crooked union boss, and is murdered before he can submit his story, the Saint decides to continue the crusade – but doing so places his life in danger.
Herman David Kossoff
Grendel Peter Dyneley
Insp. Fernack Allan Gifford

Director: John Ainsworth

The Covetous Headman

w John Roddick
The Saint tests the theory that wearing a St Christopher medallion protects one from harm. For Valerie North, a girl he meets during a flight to Paris, the opposite proves true, and Simon finds himself up to his neck in danger and intrigue.
Valerie North Barbara Shelley
Insp. Quercy Eugene Deckers
Olivant George Pastell

Director: Michael Truman

The Loaded Tourist

w Richard Harris
Witnessing a murder leads to the Saint becoming involved with an emigré family – and joining in the hunt for a briefcase

containing valuable papers which the family can ill-afford to lose.
Helen Ravenna Barbara Bates
Fillipo Ravenna Edward Evans
Oscar Kleinhaus Guy Deghy

Director: Jeremy Summers

The Pearls of Peace

w Richard Harris
When Simon invests money in his friend's quest to find gems, it isn't long before both men find themselves facing a dangerous enemy. Simon's intervention proves costly – and his friend Brad discovers pearls of wisdom.
Brad Ryan Bob Kanter
Joss Henry Erica Rogers
Consuelo Dina Paisner

Director: David Greene

The Arrow of God

w Julian Bond
Simon finds danger in the most unlikely surroundings – murder and mayhem between a number of hotel guests explode into his holiday break in Nassau.
Pauline Stone Honor Blackman
Herbert Wexall Ronald Leigh-Hunt
John Herrick Tony Wright

Director: John Paddy Carstairs

The Element of Doubt

w Norman Borisoff
Carlton Rood is a brilliant but corrupt attorney. He wins acquittals for his clients by any means open to him. Nothing, it seems, can halt his criminal activities – until a brush with the law sets the Saint on his heels.
Carlton Rood David Bauer
Insp. Fernack Alan Gifford
Joe Sholto Bill Nagy

Director: John Ainsworth

The Golden Journey

w Lewis Davidson
She is beautiful, warm-hearted and generous – but has been spoilt by doting parents. Her

name is Belinda and a chance encounter provides the Saint with the opportunity to show the girl that there are other things in life besides wealth.
Belinda Erica Rogers
Woodcutter Paul Whitsun-Jones
Joan West Stella Bonheur

Director: Robert S. Baker

The Effete Angler

w Norman Borisoff
When Simon takes a fishing holiday in Miami and discovers a beautiful 'mermaid' casting her magic over a ship-owner, he finds himself swimming in dangerous waters – and netting a bigger catch than he expected.
Gloria Shirley Eaton
Uckrose George Pravda
Supt. Marsh Jack Gwillim

Director: Anthony Bushell

The Man Who Was Lucky

w John Gilling
With the help of two lovely girls, Simon deals with a protection gang who are threatening a bookmaker. But his involvement in the affair brings him to the attention of Inspector Claude Eustace Teal – a policeman with whom Simon will share many adventures.
Lucky Joe Luckner Eddie Byrne
Cora Delphi Lawrence
Insp. Teal Campbell Singer

Director: John Gilling

The Charitable Countess

w Gerald Kelsey and Dick Sharples
Simon meets a Countess who can't count very well: someone is using her to feather their own nests at her expense – with money meant for a charity. Their chance meeting paves the way for Simon to trim the gang's feathers and prove that charity begins at home.
Countess Patricia Donahue
Aldo Petri Nigel Davenport
Marco de Cesar Warren Mitchell

Director: Jeremy Summers

The Fellow Traveller

w Harry H. Junkin
'Get Maria . . . go to the Blue Goose' – words spoken to Simon by a dying man lead the Saint into putting his life on the line to expose a killer. The Blue Goose is owned by the beautiful Maria – and she wants Simon dead!
Maria Dawn Addams
Nick Vastenti Neil McCallum
Marsh Ray Austin

Director: Peter Yates

Starring the Saint

w Harry H. Junkin
When Simon agrees to star as the Saint in a new film, it isn't long before someone rewrites the scenario with scenes of Simon's death. But why should anyone wish to kill their leading star? The answer leads Simon into danger beneath the floodlights.
Byron Ufferlitz Ronald Radd
David Brown Ivor Dean
Insp. Teal Wensley Pithey

Director: James Hill

Judith

w Leonard Grahame
A quiet drive in the country turns into a headlong chase to stop a cunningly conceived fraud attempt taking place. Simon is accused of trespassing, and the accusation leads to an exciting adventure in the Swiss Alps.
Judith Julie Christie
Burt Northwade David Bauer
Helena Northwade Margot Johns

Director: Robert Lynn

Teresa

w John Kruse
When Simon becomes involved with a beautiful woman trying to solve the disappearance of her husband, he finds himself being chased by Mexican bandits – and discovers that life under the big top is not as it first appears.

Teresa Lana Morris
Casemegas Eric Pohlmann
Borata Marne Maitland

Director: Roy Ward Baker

The Elusive Ellshaw

w Harry H. Junkin   (From a story by John Kruse)
A cashier's strange behaviour before her death leads Simon to suspect foul play. Before he's done, he will have thwarted an assassination attempt, unearthed the woman's 'dead' husband -- and caused much annoyance to a gang of cut-throats.
Anne Ripwell Angela Browne
Sir John Ripwell Richard Vernon
Insp. Teal Norman Pitt

Director: John Moxey

Season Two

22 monochrome 60-minute episodes

Marcia

w John Kruse   (From a story by Harry H. Junkin)
After her face is disfigured in an acid attack, international film starlet Marcia Landon commits suicide. Her death presents a convenient opportunity for Claire Avery to step into the dead star's shoes – but the Saint steps into trouble when Claire is threatened with the same fate.
Claire Avery Samantha Eggar
Johnny Desmond Johnny Briggs
Insp. Carlton Philip Stone

Director: John Krish

The Work of Art

w Harry H. Junkin
The Saint's springtime sojourn in Paris with the bewitching Juliette leads to drama when her brother, André, is suspected of murdering his partner to gain control of their fashion concern.
Juliette Yolande Turner
André Alex Scott
Major Qunitana Martin Benson

Director: Peter Yates

Iris

w Bill Strutton
The Saint becomes involved in the schemes of a racketeer and his wife to frame a man for blackmail. The 'man' marked down to be the hapless recipient of bad news is Simon himself – so he plays out enough rope to hang his adversaries.
Rick Lansing David Bauer
Iris Lansing Barbara Murray
Insp. Teal Ivor Dean (Intro.)

Director: John Gilling

The King of the Beggars

w John Gilling
When several attempts are made on the life of a beautiful Italian actress, the Saint dons a beggar's disguise to get to the bottom of the villainy – and the gang behind the attacks are soon begging for mercy.
Dolores Marcello Maxine Audley
Joe Catelli Oliver Reed
Marco Warren Mitchell

Director: John Gilling

The Rough Diamonds

w Bill Strutton
A consignment of industrial diamonds is hijacked on arrival in England. Two security guards are murdered – and someone is out to lay the blame at the Saint's door. Inspector Teal of Scotland Yard refuses to believe Simon's alibi – so the Saint sets out to throw a halo around the real culprits.
Uttershaw Douglas Wilmer
Ourley George A. Cooper
Insp. Teal Ivor Dean

Director: Peter Yates

The Saint Plays with Fire

w John Kruse
What connects the death of a journalist to a dark and isolated country house? Simon intends to find out, even if it means taking on the powerful force behind a new Nazi party – a man who has signed the Saint's death warrant.

Kane Luker Joseph Furst
Lady Valerie Justine Lord
Insp. Teal Ivor Dean

*Director:*Robert S. Baker

The Well-meaning Mayor

w Robert Stewart
Following up the death of a councillor, the
Saint discovers corruption and treachery
permeating through to the very heart of
local government. One alone bears no
investigation – the Mayor – but who is
pulling his strings?
Sam Purdell Leslie Sands
Alice Purdell Mary Kenton
Molly Mandy Miller

Director: Jeremy Summers

The Sporting Chance

w John Kruse
In Canada on a fishing holiday, the Saint
uncovers a plot to bring a German scientist
back to the East – against his best interests.
So Simon goes fishing for the villains – and
hooks a major prize by way of a result.
Netchideff Derren Nesbitt
Prof. Mueller Gerald Heinz
Pavan Geoffrey Quigley

Director: Jeremy Summers

The Bunco Artists

w Lewis Davidson
When two confidence tricksters divert the
funds they received for the restoration of the
village church into their own pockets, the
Saint steps in and plays a confidence trick of
his own – one which benefits the church
twofold.
Richard Eade Peter Dyneley
Jean Yarmouth Justine Lord
Sophie Yarmouth Mary Merrall

Director: Peter Yates

The Benevolent Burglary

w Larry Forrester
Vascoe is an arrogant millionaire who is
used to getting his own way. But when
Simon bets him that his 'impregnable'
Riviera home will be burgled within four
days – and it appears that the Saint will win
the stake of £5,000 – Vascoe employs tactics
unbecoming to a gentleman.
Eliot Vascoe John Barrie
Meryl Vascoe Suzanne Neve
Bill Fulton Gary Cockrell

Director: Jeremy Summers

The Wonderful War

w John Graeme
When greed, murder and intrigue follow
the discovery of oil in the Middle East state
of Sayeda, the Saint wages his own kind of
war on behalf of the deposed ruler's son
Karim, who suspects his father's advisers of
plotting to assassinate him.
The Imam Ferdy Mayne
Karim Louis Raynor
Harry Shannet Alfred Burke

Director: Robert S. Baker

The Noble Sportsman

w John Graeme
When her husband Lord Yearley starts to
receive threats to his life, Lady Anne seeks
Simon's help to find out why anyone should
want to kill him. The Saint uncovers a web
of intrigue which reaches back into her
husband's past.
Lady Anne Sylvia Syms
Lord Yearley Anthony Quayle
Rose Yearley Jane Asher

Director: Peter Yates

The Romantic Matron

w Larry Forrester
Trouble is seldom far away from Simon
Templar, but even the Saint is surprised
when a beautiful girl bursts into his Buenos
Aires hotel bedroom and beseeches him to
help her. From that moment Simon's life
hangs from a thread.
Beryl Carrington Ann Gillis
Raymond Venino John Carson
Police Inspector Patrick Troughton

Director: John Paddy Carstairs

Luella

w John Kruse and Harry H. Junkin
When Simon bumps into his old friend Bill
Harvey, he finds himself painting the town
red as Harvey sallies into one bar after
another. But Simon soon tires of the game –
when he finds himself the victim of
blackmail attempts.
Doris Suzanne Lloyd
Bill Harvey David Hedison
Luella Susan Lloyd

Director: Roy Baker

The Lawless Lady

w Harry H. Junkin
To avenge a murder, Simon joins forces with
the glamorous Countess Audrey Marova –
one of the most astute crooks in London.
Their combined efforts result in a team of
modern-day pirates biting the dust – before
Simon sets out to reform his companion.
Audrey Dawn Addams
Hilloran Julian Glover
Insp. Teal Ivor Dean

Director: Jeremy Summers

The Good Medicine

w Norman Borisoff
When Simon meets the elegant and lovely
Denise Dumont, the woman behind the
Dumont beauty combine, he discovers the
scent of something nasty hiding behind the
facade of the woman's loving husband.
Denise Dumont Barbara Murray
Philipe Anthony Newlands
David Stern Bill Nagy

Director: Roy Baker

The Invisible Millionaire

w Kenneth Hayles
When strange things start to happen after a
millionaire and his assistant are reported
killed in a car crash, Simon's suspicions lead
him to unravel the unusual affair of a man
who continues spending his money from the
grave.
Rosemary Chase Katherine Blake
Dr Quintus Michael Goodliffe
Jim Chase Nigel Stock

Director: Jeremy Summers

The High Fence

w Paddy Manning O'Brine
A dinner date with glamorous actress
Gabrielle leads the Saint to a murder
investigation and a grim hunt for one of
London's most notorious master-criminals –
an old enemy of Simon's and one who swore
to kill him should they ever meet again.
Insp. Pryor James Villiers
Gabby Suzanne Lloyd
Insp. Teal Ivor Dean

Director: James Hill

Sophia

w Robert Stewart
On holiday in a Greek village, Simon takes
time out from his sightseeing to settle
accounts with an Americanised crook who is
threatening the peace of the inhabitants
with his reign of bully-boy tactics.
Sophia Imogen Hassall
Aristides Oliver Reed
Niko Peter Kriss

Director: Roger Moore

The Gentle Ladies

w John Graeme
They are three gentle ladies – not so young,
but not too old. What awful secret do they
suspect will fall upon them when a
blackmailer enters their lives? Simon
Templar determines to find out.
Florence Warshed Avice Landon
Ida Warshed Renee Houston
Violet Warshed Barbara Mullen

Director: Jeremy Summers

The Ever-loving Spouse

w Norman Borisoff
Convention delegate Otis Q. Fennick is
alone in his room when a near-naked girl
bursts in . . . followed by a photographer.
Grounds for blackmail? Then why should
the Saint suspect that murder is afoot?
Liane Fennick Jeanne Moody
Brent Kingman Paul Carpenter
Vern Dalton David Bauer

Director: Ernest Morris

The Saint Sees It Through

w Ian Kennedy Martin

The Saint is asked to assist the police in the breaking of an international art-smuggling ring, when a valuable Raphael miniature, stolen in Moscow, is discovered in the New York locker of Lili, a friend of Simon's.

Lili Margrit Saad
Dr Zellerman Joseph Furst
Police Captain Carl Duering

Director: Robert S. Baker

Season Three

32 monochrome 60-minute episodes

The Miracle Tea Party

w Paddy Manning O'Brine

When a pretty young nurse visits London and a packet of tea is slipped into her bag, and then a man who has been following her is murdered, Simon Templar finds himself involved in a tense adventure with danger at every turn.

Hattie Fabia Drake
Geraldine McLeod Nanette Newman
Dr Sandburg Conrad Phillips

Director: Roger Moore

Lida

w Michael Cramoy

Wealthy Lida Verity falls victim to the smooth-talking nightclub blackmailer Maurice Kerr. Her sister, Joan, is alarmed at their relationship so she is delighted when her old friend Simon Templar arrives on the scene.

Lida Verity Jeanne Moody
Joan Erica Rogers
Maurice Kerr Peter Bowles

Director: Leslie Norman

Jeannine

w Harry H. Junkin

When Simon visits Paris at the same time as Madame Chen, and their paths cross, the Saint is off and running into a new adventure to find a valuable pearl necklace which has been stolen from the girl.

Jeannine Roger Sylvia Syms
Madame Chen Jacqui Chan
Insp. Quercy Manning Wilson

Director: John Moxey

The Scorpion

w Paul Erickson

Hiding somewhere in the background of unexplained happenings, blackmail and murder in which Simon finds himself involved, there hides a mysterious mastermind known only as The Scorpion. Who is he? Unless Simon unmasks the villain, a young girl faces certain death.

Karen Bates Catherine Woodville
Patsy Butler Nyree Dawn Porter
Insp. Teal Ivor Dean

Director: Roy Baker

The Revolution Racket

w Harry H. Junkin

Suspicious that an astute South American policeman is combining duty with personal gain, Simon dupes the man into showing his true colours by laying the seeds of doubt in the policeman's mind.

Carlos Xavier Eric Pohlmann
Pablo Enriquez Peter Arne
Doris Suzanne Lloyd

Director: Pat Jackson

The Saint Steps In

w John Kruse

The Saint becomes involved in big business to break apart the highly explosive relationship between a tycoon's daughter and the daughter of a scientist who is out to seek revenge for her father's failure to win a large contract.

Hobart Quennel Geoffrey Keen
Andrea Quennel Justine Lloyd
Madeline Gray Annette Andre

Director: John Gilling

The Loving Brothers

w John Graeme

Simon becomes involved with an old Australian prospector who believes he's

struck it rich by discovering a silver mine.
He needs finance to work the dig, but his
two wealthy sons refuse to cough up – until
Simon tries a little gentle persuasion.
Pop Kinsall Reg Lye
Willie Kinsall Ray Barrett
Wally Kinsall Ed Devereaux

Director: Leslie Norman

The Man Who Liked Toys

w Basil Dawson
When he tries to investigate the shady
dealings of a toy-loving business executive
whom he suspects of bribery and corruption,
Simon finds out that toy soldiers can
sometimes win battles all on their own.
Well, not quite, they sometimes require the
help of the Saint.
John Hammel John Paul
George Fowler Maurice Kaufmann
Insp. Teal Ivor Dean

Director: John Gilling

The Death Penalty

w Ian Stuart Black
Holidaying in the South of France would be
a breeze for anyone else, but when you're
the Saint and you give a lift to a young girl,
you can expect trouble to follow. It does,
and Templar finds himself sorting out a vice
ring – and a witness to murder.
Laura Stride Wanda Ventham
Abdul Soman Paul Stassino
Galbraith Brewster Mason

Director: Jeremy Summers

The Imprudent Politician

w Norman Hudis
When a politician allows himself to become
involved with a scheming girl and betrays
secrets to make a killing on the stock
market, he is asking for trouble. When the
trouble arrives in the shape of blackmail,
the man turns to the Saint for help.
Christopher Waites Anthony Bate
Denise Grant Justine Lord
Colin Philips Michael Gough

Director: John Moxey

The Hijackers

w Paul Erickson
In Munich to visit an old friend, the Saint
meets a beautiful Fraulein and finds himself
plunged headlong into an audacious scheme
to rob the American army of high-powered
weapons.
Mathilde Baum Ingrid Schoeller
Ed Jopley Neil McCallum
Hans Lasser Walter Gotell

Director: David Eady

The Unkind Philanthropist

w Marcus Demian
A girl with a boy's name can lead to
misunderstandings. The Saint takes
advantage of this fact to repay a cruel and
uncaring father for the selfish way he has
been treating his step-children.
Elmer Quire Charles Farrell
Juan Gamma David Graham
Tristan Brown Sarah Brackett

Director: Jeremy Summers

The Damsel in Distress

w Paul Erickson
The owner of Templar's favourite restaurant
is distraught . . . his daughter is pregnant,
but has no husband. Her betrothed has
absconded with a lot of money, so Simon
plays matchmaker to restore the status quo.
Alessandro Naccaro Richard Wyler
Barbara Astral Catherine Woodville
Insp. Teal Ivor Dean

Director: Peter Yates

The Contract

w Terry Nation
Eight years after robbing an American
airbase in England, the thief returns to his
old haunts to recover the money he secreted
away. The Saint's evidence put him away –
and he's out for revenge.
Dunstan Dick Haymes
Farburg Robert Hutton
Insp. Teal Ivor Dean

Director: Roger Moore

The Set-up

w Paddy Manning O'Brine

When Simon finds his life threatened, a beautiful film starlet uses her acting talent to lead his unseen adversary into the open so that he can foil an ingenious plot to kill him – and lay the blame on someone else.

Oonagh O'Grady Penelope Horner
Jack Laurie Edward Underdown
Insp. Teal Ivor Dean

Director: Roy Baker

The Rhine Maiden

w Brian Degas

Quick action by the Saint saves the life of a pretty girl and plunges him into an intriguing mystery from which he barely escapes with his halo intact.

Julia Harrison Stephanie Randall
Charles Voyson Nigel Davenport
Haus Anthony Booth

Director: James Hill

The Inescapable Word

w Terry Nation

While on a grouse-shooting holiday in the Scottish highlands, Simon finds himself confronted by some weird happenings surrounding the staff who work at a top-secret government research laboratory.

Majorie North Ann Bell
Jock Ingram James Maxwell
Ivor North Maurice Hedley

Director: Roy Baker

The Sign of the Claw

w Terry Nation

The Saint finds himself involved in an anti-terrorist campaign in Southeast Asia. He has been invited there by a girl, but upon arrival she is nowhere to be found. Concerned for her safety, Simon delves deeper – and finds himself a terrorist prisoner.

Jean Morland Suzan Farmer
Don Morland Peter Copley
Tawau Bert Kwouk

Director: Leslie Norman

The Golden Frog

w Michael Cramoy

No one could be more gallant towards the fair sex than the Saint. But when an attractive girl uses Simon Templar to score a point with her rival, Simon decides to teach the girl a sharp lesson.

Alice Jacqueline Ellis
Nestor Hugh McDermott
Quintana Alan Tilvern

Director: John Moxey

The Frightened Innkeeper

w Norman Hudis

In response to an intriguing SOS from his friend Martin, the Saint travels to Cornwall. His arrival there appears to cause consternation to the local innkeeper, and Martin is nowhere to be found.

Martin Jeffroll Michael Gwynn
Julia Jeffroll Susanne Neve
Tom Kane Percy Herbert

Director: Roy Baker

Sibao

w Terry Nation

When the Saint meets the beautiful Sibao in a Haitian bar, he suddenly finds himself involved in the shadowy world of native superstition and voodoo practice – with himself and the girl as the sacrificial lambs.

Sibao Jeanne Roland
Theron Netlord John Carson
Malon Christopher Carlos

Director: Peter Yates

The Crime of the Century

w Terry Nation

When the Saint impersonates a tough, greying American safebreaker to foil a crime, he is amused to find that he is working side by side with his old Scotland Yard adversary Chief Inspector Claude Eustace Teal.

Bernhard Raxel Andre Morell
Betty Tregarth Sarah Lawson
Insp. Teal Ivor Dean

Director: John Gilling

The Happy Suicide

w Brian Degas

Ziggy Zaglan enjoys the standing ovation he
receives nightly from the crowds gathered to
watch his television chat show. But Simon
finds that sinister mischief lurks behind
Ziggy's smiling face.
Ziggy Zaglan John Bluthal
Lois Norroy Jane Merrow
Ralph Damian William Sylvester

Director: Robert Tronson

The Chequered Flag

w Norman Hudis

The Saint finds himself helping a friend to
discover what lies behind a long spell of bad
'luck' that has dogged a former racing-
driver. He comes to the grim decision that
one of the man's competitors is playing the
game by his own sordid rules.
Oscar Newly Eddie Byrne
Mandy Ellington Justine Lord
Beau Ellington Edward de Souza

Director: Barry Norman

The Abductors

w Brian Degas
(From a story by Harry H. Junkin)
An English girl wins a prize of a weekend in
Paris but finds it very dull – until she
bumps into The Saint. Within minutes, the
couple find themselves pursued by a gang of
crooks and Simon finds himself
investigating a kidnap plot.
Madeline Annette Andre
Brian Quell Robert Urquhart
Jones Dudley Foster

Director: Jeremy Summers

The Crooked Ring

w Harry H. Junkin
Simon becomes involved in bribery and
corruption in the fight game when he is
asked to help a young boxer, Steve Nelson,
whose life has been threatened unless he
follows orders and takes a 'dive' in his next
contest.

Doc Spangler Walter Brown
Steve Nelson Tony Wright
The Angel Nosher Powell

Director: Leslie Norman

The Smart Detective

w Michael Cramoy

When a private detective boasts that his
security precautions at a jewel exhibition are
foolproof, Somon becomes suspicious and
decides to find out if the building is really
as secure as it seems.
Peter Corrio Brian Worth
Janice Dixon Anne Lawson
Insp. Teal Ivor Dean

Director: John Moxey

The Persistent Parasites

w Norman Hudis

When the Saint is invited to join Waldo his
millionaire friend on an island off the South
of France, believing that he's in for a
pleasant weekend sojourn, he accepts – but
the weekend ends in tragedy.
Waldo Cec Linder
Vera Jan Holden
Wilma Ann Gillis

Director: Robert Tronson

The Man Who Could Not Die

w Terry Nation

The Saint goes underground in an attempt
to save a friend who has been tricked into
going pot-holing with a dangerous man – a
man who has already killed once, and looks
set to do so again, unless Simon can stop
him.
Miles Hallin Patrick Allen
Nigel Perry Robin Phillips
Insp. Teal Ivor Dean

Director: Roger Moore

The Saint Bids Diamonds

w Norman Hudis

Alarmed that a friend is facing bankruptcy
because his most valuable asset, a famous
diamond, has been stolen, Simon
impersonates a diamond-cutter in an
attempt to track down the jewel thieves.

Abdul Graner George Murcell
Christine Graner Eunice Gayson
Madame Calliope Jean St Clair

Director: Leslie Norman

The Spanish Cow

w Paul Erickson
The Saint becomes involved with the lovely widow of an assassinated South American politician who believes that the men who killed her husband will not rest until she, too, is dead. Simon's dilemma: is the woman telling the truth?
Consuela Flores Vivienne Ventura
Gilberto Gary Raymond
Col. Latignant Arnold Diamond

Director: John Gilling

The Old Treasure Story

w Ronald Duncan
An old seafaring friend of Simon's leads him into a strange treasure hunt that takes them from Cornwall to the West Indies. Simon's suspicions that they are on a wild goose chase are confirmed when someone tries to kill them.
Duncan Rawl Jack Hedley
Jack Forrest Robert Hutton
April Erica Rogers

Director: Roger Moore

Season Four
30 colour 60-minute episodes

Queen's Ransom

w Leigh Vance
The Saint moves into regal circles. He comes to the aid of Queen Adana, whose husband is the deposed ruler of a Middle Eastern country. But Simon's problems are compounded by the woman herself, when she insists on having her own way.
Queen Adana Dawn Addams
King Fallouda George Pastell
Georges Stanley Meadows

Director: Roy Baker

The House on Dragon's Rock

w John Kruse
What is the secret of the mysterious rambling old house in the Welsh mountains which is being used as a research laboratory? Holidaying in Wales, Simon tries to crack its secret – and comes face to face with a diabolical enemy.
Dr Sardon Anthony Bate
Carmen Annette Andre
Dr Davis Mervyn Johns

Director: Roger Moore

(Note: In some areas, this episode carried a warning: 'Unsuitable for children and people of a nervous disposition'. In others it was banned altogether – until repeat transmissions.)

The Russian Prisoner

w Harry H. Junkin
A beautiful girl and a Russian professor combine to make the Saint's holiday in Switzerland one of the most memorable of his career. Someone is out to return the scientist to his homeland – until the Saint intervenes.
Prof. Jorovitch Joseph Furst
Irma Jorovitch Penelope Horner
Insp. Kleinhaus Guy Deghy

Director: John Moxey

The Reluctant Revolution

w John Stanton
Simon stumbles into the activities of a girl he finds carrying a gun and determined to kill a man. He sets out to find out why – and ends up organising a revolution to overthrow a ruthless president.
Diane Jennie Linden
Victor Lawrence Barry Morse
President Alvarez Peter Illing

Director: Leslie Norman

The Helpful Pirate

w Roy Russell
Few people are able to resist the attraction of money for nothing, but when it is wrapped up in the guise of hidden treasure which is providing a profitable racket for confidence trickster Kolben, the Saint steps in to see fair play.

Kolben Paul Maxwell
Eva Erika Remberg
Roskin Vladek Sheybal

Director: Roy Baker

The Convenient Monster

w Michael Cramoy
When the Saint encounters a monster
mystery in Scotland – none other than the
Loch Ness Monster itself – he must decide if
'Nessie' is behind a series of macabre
killings, or is it the work of human hands?
Ann Clanraith Suzan Farmer
Noel Bastion Laurence Payne
Willie Fulton Mackay

Director: Leslie Norman

The Angel's Eye

w Paul Erickson
Why should a respected Dutch jeweller lie
about a valuable stone which the Saint
knows he has been given for cutting? When
the man refuses to acknowledge receiving
the diamond, Simon determines to find out
why.
Tom Upwater Liam Richmond
Mabel Jane Merrow
Malone T. P. McKenna

Director: Leslie Norman

Interlude in Venice

w Paddy Manning O'Brine
Simon finds out that the sun doesn't always
shine in Italy – and there is always a warm
welcome when you're the Saint and hot on
the trail of a gang of racketeers, who intend
to seek revenge.
Helen Lois Maxwell
Foots Fortunati William Sylvester
Cathy Quin O'Hara

Director: Leslie Norman

Locate and Destroy

w John Stanton
In South America to visit a friend, Simon
finds himself the unwilling prey of a gang of
Israeli patriots who are searching for a
former Nazi prisoner-of-war officer, who

they believe to be alive and living in a local
village.
Coleman John Barrie
Maria Francesca Annis
Karsh Victor Beaumont

Director: Leslie Norman

The Better Mousetrap

w Leigh Vance
Simon combines romance with acute
observation when he decides to expose the
woman behind a series of audacious jewel
thefts in the South of France – but by
becoming involved, he finds himself arrested
and charged as the real thief.
Natalie Sheridan Alexandra Stewart
Alphonse Ronnie Barker
Milo Gambodi Lisa Daniely

Director: Gordon Flemyng

Little Girl Lost

w D. R. Mutten
When Simon visits Ireland and meets with
Mildred, a young girl who claims to be
Hitler's daughter, he finds himself dancing
a merry Irish jig to escape from the clutches
of a ruthless gang of Irish patriots.
Mildred June Ritchie
Brendhan Cullen Noel Purcell
Mullins Shay Gorman

Director: Roy Baker

The Paper Chase

w Michael Cramoy
(From a story by Harry H. Junkin)
Persuaded to follow a defecting Civil
Servant who has been tricked into
smuggling secret papers into East Germany,
Simon finds himself playing the part of a
British agent to save the man's life.
Colonel Probst Niall McGinnis
Hanya Penelope Horner
Mets Gordon Costelow

Director: Leslie Norman

Flight Plan

w Alfred Shaughnessy
When he spots a nun wearing high-heeled
shoes whilst collecting for charity at a

London railway station, Simon's interest is aroused and he is soon plunged into an exciting cross-London chase to thwart the schemes of a clever gang of criminals.
Mike William Gaunt
Diana Fiona Lewis
Nadya Imogen Hassell

Director: Roy Baker

Escape Route

w Michael Winder
The Saint finds himself behind bars, staring at the delighted features of Claude Eustace Teal – but his sentence is part of a police plan to smash a major international escape organisation.
Colonel Roberts John Gregson
John Wood Donald Sutherland
Insp. Teal Ivor Dean

Director: Roger Moore

The Persistent Patriots

w Michael Pertwee
Having rescued Liskard from death, Simon discovers that the man's enemies will stop at nothing to get their man. Liskard, it appears, is more vulnerable than most – he has political as well as personal enemies.
Jack Liskard Edward Woodward
Mary Ford Jan Waters
Anne Liskard Judy Parfitt

Director: Roy Baker

The Fast Women

w Leigh Vance
The Saint finds himself caught in the crossfire between two unscrupulous women who are rivals on the motor-racing circuit and rivals in love as well. Simon's intervention pleases neither woman – and he's soon in trouble again.
Cynthia Quillen Jan Holden
Teresa Montesino Kate O'Mara
Godfrey Quillen John Carson

Director: Leslie Norman

The Death Game

w John Kruse
A remarkable modern-day death cult has spread among students throughout the world. But when Simon finds himself marked down as the latest victim – and the threatened events become the real thing – he turns his attention to preventing further deaths.
Jenny Turner Angela Douglas
Vogler George Murcell
Insp. Teal Ivor Dean

Director: Leslie Norman

The Art Collectors

w Michael Pertwee
Paris, and a damsel in distress. A combination which leads the Saint into meeting a girl who is selling her family's art treasures – before someone tries to steal them. Disbelieving her, Simon digs deeper to get at the truth.
Natasha Ann Bell
Serge Peter Bowles
Lucille Nadja Regin

Director: Roy Baker

To Kill a Saint

w Michael Winder
It's the most unusual assignment he's ever undertaken – Simon is hired to disguise himself as a gangster and kill . . . the Saint! Determined to find out who is behind the scheme, Simon arranges his own death.
Paul Verrier Peter Dyneley
Annette Annette Andre
André Francis Matthews

Director: Robert Asher

The Counterfeit Countess

w Philip Broadley
A plane crash sets the Saint on the trail of a counterfeiting gang, which takes him from London to Switzerland. While there he develops an interest in a wine of a very unusual vintage.
Nadine/Evette Kate O'Mara
Alson Philip Madoc
Insp. Teal Ivor Dean

Director: Leslie Norman

The Man Who Liked Lions

w Douglas Enefer
When Simon's journalist friend is murdered while on the biggest story of his life, the

Saint decides to put a stop to the antics of a modern-day Caesar – a man who refuses to accept that the glory of Rome is over.

Tiberio Peter Wyngarde
Claudia Suzanne Lloyd
Franco Michael Wynne

Director: Jeremy Summers

Simon and Delilah

w C. Scott Forbes

A temperamental film star is kidnapped. Is it a publicity stunt or something more sinister? On a visit to Rome, the Saint finds himself involved with the petty bickerings of a film production team – one of whom is a killer.

Roberto Vittorini Ronald Radd
Beth Lois Maxwell
Serenia Suzanne Lloyd

Director: Roy Baker

Island of Chance

w John Stanton

Murder is unpleasant at the best of times, but when the gaiety of a West Indian holiday turns into a macabre murder enquiry, Simon finds himself dancing to the rhythm of a calypso death march.

Marla Clayton Sue Lloyd
Dr Krayford David Bauer
Venderfelt Alex Scott

Director: Leslie Norman

The Gadget Lovers

w John Kruse

When he finds himself involved in a strange death campaign – the organised assassination of British intelligence agents – Simon dons the identity of a Russian Secret Police Chief to track down the people responsible.

Smolenko Mary Peach
Igor Glyn Edwards
Colonel Wing Bert Kwouk

Director: Jim O'Connolly

A Double in Diamonds

w Donald and Derek Ford

Why should wealthy Lord Gillingham wish to purchase a copy of his fabulous family diamond necklace? Intrigued, the Saint attends a fashion show – and ends up preventing a robbery.

Lord Gillingham Cecil Parker
Pierre Anton Rodgers
Insp. Teal Ivor Dean

Director: John Gilling

The Power Artist

w John Kruse

Finding himself dropped outside a Chelsea studio instead of his own apartment by a taxi-driver, who instructs him to go to the top floor, a mystified Simon climbs the staircase – and finds himself framed for murder.

Cassie Pauline Munro
Volgar George Murcell
Insp. Teal Ivor Dean

Director: Leslie Norman

When Spring is Sprung

w Michael Pertwee

The combination of the French Riviera and an attractive girl lands the Saint in the unexpected position of being asked to rescue her father, a Russian spy who is being held against his will.

Joanne Dell Toby Robins
Marie Spring Ann Lynn
Insp. Teal Ivor Dean

Director: Jim O'Connolly

The Gadic Collection

w Philip Broadley

After finding a girl participating in a robbery in an Istanbul museum, the Saint soon finds the taste of Turkish delight a little hard to swallow. Someone is out to silence her – and Simon soon finds himself in the gunman's sights.

Diya Georgia Brown
Turin Peter Wyngarde
Sukan Michael Ripper

Director: Freddie Francis

The Best Laid Schemes

w Joseph Morhain and Sandford Wolfe

Who is the victim of a drowning tragedy? The Saint meets with more than he

bargained for when he sets out to prove that the 'dead' man is still alive. But why would anyone wish to convince his family that he's the victim of murder?
Arlene Sylvia Syms
Dr Ormesby Paul Daneman
Diana Gabrielle Drake

Director: John Moxey

Invitation to Danger

w Terry Nation
When a daring attempt is made to frame him, Simon finds himself surrounded by suspicion and intrigue – and smack in the middle of an international secrets-for-sale drama. But is the cool blonde really a British secret agent – or his true enemy?
Reb Denning Shirley Eaton
Brett Sunley Robert Hutton
Falconi Julian Glover

Director: Roger Moore

Season Five
17 colour 60-minute episodes

Legacy for the Saint

w Michael Winder
Ed Brown is a retired gangster with a sense of humour – which includes getting his four greatest enemies at one another's throats. Simon helped to put him in jail the last time and intends to repeat the favour – providing Brown allows him to live.
Ed Brown Reginald Marsh
Charlie Lewis Alan MacNaughton
Insp. Teal Ivor Dean

Director: Roy Baker

The Desperate Diplomat

w Terry Nation
When diplomat Jason Douglas disappears with a million dollars of aid destined for an African country, Simon finds himself pleading his old friend's innocence to a less-than-interested Claude Eustace Teal.
Jason Douglas John Robinson
Sarah Douglas Suzan Farmer
Insp. Teal Ivor Dean

Director: Ray Austin

The Organisation Man

w Donald James
When the Saint signs on as a mercenary and finds that things are none too healthy on the health farm where he's being trained, he decides to find out the real function of the establishment. Is it a school for murder?
Jonathan Roper Tony Britton
Kate Barnaby Caroline Mortimer
Major Carter Mark Dignam

Director: Monte Norman

The Double Take

w John Kruse
Which man is which? That's the problem facing Simon when a business tycoon claims he is being impersonated by a perfect double who intends to grind his business empire into obscurity.
Eugene Patroclos Gregoire Aslan
Annabel II Kate O'Mara
Annabel I Denise Buckley

Director: Leslie Norman

The Time to Die

w Terry Nation
The Saint finds himself playing a deadly game of cat and mouse with a would-be killer. Simon's dilemma is twofold: why should anyone want to put a dent in his halo, and who is the man known only as 'The Avenger'?
Mary Brent Suzanne Lloyd
Steven Lyall Maurice Good
Charlie Mason Terence Rigby

Director: Robert Tronson

The Master Plan

w Harry H. Junkin
When he discovers a plan to turn Britain and America into a dumping ground for some dangerous drugs, Simon sets out to crush the diabolical drugs-smuggling organisation at its source – a small island off the China coast.
Ford Chrandel John Turner
Jean Lane Lyn Ashley
Cheng Burt Kwouk

Director: Leslie Norman

The Scales of Justice

w Robert Holmes

When four directors of a large business combine die in mysterious circumstances, Simon finds himself investigating a fiendishly clever murder market – and racing against time to save the life of a fifth director.

Gilbert Kirby Andrew Keir
Anne Kirby Jean Marsh
Lamberton John Barron

Director: Robert Asher

The Fiction Makers (Part 1)

w John Kruse

When he is mistaken for the author of several way-out thrillers, the world of fiction comes vividly to life for the Saint – as does the real 'Amos Klein', a beautiful young woman with a more-than-vivid imagination.

The Fiction Makers (Part 2)

Simon finds himself abducted with a girl who has been using the nom-de-plume Amos Klein. But why? Before he discovers the answer to that question, Simon and the girl share several hair-raising adventures.

'Amos Klein' Sylvia Syms
Warlock Kenneth J. Warren
Galaxy Justine Lord

Director: Roy Baker

The People Importers

w Donald James

The Saint investigates a racket in which illegal immigrants are being smuggled into Britain to serve as slave-labour in various Mafia-run establishments. His involvement leads him to personal tragedy – and the head of the enterprise.

Bonner Neil Hallett
Laura Susan Travers
Slater Gary Miller

Director: Ray Austin

Where the Money Is

w Terry Nation

When a film producer's daughter disappears and he suspects that she has been kidnapped, then an unusual ransom demand arrives in the form of scenes cut from a film, the man seeks Simon's help in obtaining his daughter's release.

Ben Kersh Kenneth J. Warren
Jenny Kersh Judy Morton
Jean Latoure Sandor Eles

Director: Roger Moore

Vendetta for the Saint (Part 1)

w John Kruse and Harry H. Junkin

Suspecting that a man named Destamio is tied up with the Mafia, Simon attempts to prove it, but all he receives for his pains are threats to his life – which make him more determined than ever to reveal the truth.

Vendetta for the Saint (Part 2)

Continuing his investigations into Destamio's background, Simon discovers that the present Mafia head is dying. Suspecting that Destamio is plotting to take his place, the Saint decides to face his enemy.

Destamio Ian Hendry
Gina Rosemary Dexter
Lily Aimi Macdonald

Director: Jim O'Connolly

The Ex-king of Diamonds

w John Kruse

Simon finds himself mixed up with drama on the French Riviera when he meets an ex-king who cheats at cards, and a beautiful young girl with an infallible system for winning at the casino tables.

Flambeau Ronald Radd
Janine Flambeau Isla Blair
Red Houston Stuart Damon

Director: Alvin Rakoff

The Man Who Gambled with Life

w Harry H. Junkin   (From a story by Michael Cramoy)

The Saint has led a long and adventurous life. But now he's been chosen as the subject for an experiment which entails being frozen to death and later being brought back to life. Will he give the scientists the cold shoulder?

Longman Clifford Evans
Vanessa Veronica Carlson
Stella Jayne Sofiano

Director: Freddie Francis

The Portrait of Brenda

w Harry H. Junkin

Gurus, pop singers and disc jockeys combine to set the Saint spinning at 45rpm when he finds himself involved in a large-scale swindle involving a fake guru and a group of music-loving innocents.

Diane Huntley Anna Carteret
Guru Marne Maitland
Insp. Teal Ivor Dean

Director: John Gilling

The World Beater

w Donald James

With a beautiful blonde by his side the Saint mops up the mysterious events surrounding a series of deaths among drivers at a car rally meeting – and finds himself steering around dangerous bends.

Kay Patricia Haines
Justin Pritchard John Ronane
Harold Laker George A. Cooper

Director: Leslie Norman

THE SAINT
Monochrome
Producers: Robert S. Baker and
Monty Norman
An ATV Production for New World/ITC Ltd
Filmed at Associated British Picture Corp.
(Elstree)
4 October 1962 – 19 March 1964
8 October 1964 – 11 March 1965
1 July –26 August 1965
71 monochrome 60-minute episodes

Colour
Producer: Robert S. Baker
Music by: Edwin Astley (Throughout)
Script supervisor: Harry H. Junkin
(Throughout)
A Bamore Production for ITC
Filmed on location and at Elstree Studios
30 September 1966 – 2 June 1967
22 September 1968 – 9 February 1969
47 colour 60-minute episodes
(USA: Syndicated 1963 – 1966
NBC May – September 1967
February – September 1968
April – September 1969
114 episodes)

THE SANDBAGGERS

The exploits of the Special Intelligence Force (SIF), a team of undercover agents nicknamed the Sandbaggers. Men and women of the highest calibre who were trained to carry out the dirty and dangerous jobs whenever Britain's security was threatened. Men like Neil Burnside, head of the department, a single-minded man with a heart of granite who believed in the end totally justifying the means – but who would sacrifice his soul to protect his team of agents. Burnside alone carried the awesome responsibility of taking decisions that could send a Sandbagger into the field – always with their lives at great risk. The danger was real, the threat to their lives horrifying, but Burnside had learned the hard way that intelligence work demanded patience – and courage. If he couldn't alleviate the risks taken by his team, he'd come up with ways to cut down the odds in their favour with computer-like determination.

Riveting stuff – and quite simply the best thing around at that time.

REGULAR CAST

Neil Burnside **Roy Marsden** (Seasons 1 and 2)   *Willie Caine* **Ray Lonnen**   *Laura Dickens* **Diane Keen** (Season 1)   *Karen Milner* **Jana Sheldon**   *Diane Lawler* **Elizabeth Bennett**   *'C' (His Chief of Staff)* **Richard Vernon**   **Dennis Burgess** (Season 3)   *Sir Geoffrey* **Alan MacNaughton**   *Jeff Ross* **Bob Sherman**   *Matthew Peele* **Jerome Willis**   *Mike Wallace* **Michael Cashman**

Season One

7 colour 60-minute episodes

First Principles

w Ian Macintosh

When a Norwegian spy plane goes down in Russian-occupied territory, they ask their NATO allies, the British Government, to help retrieve it – and its secrets. Burnside's department gets the job, and he sends in a Sandbagger.
Neil Burnisde Roy Marsden (Intro.)
C Richard Vernon (Intro.)
Willie Caine Ray Lonnen (Intro.)

Director: Michael Ferguson
Designer: Roger Andrews

A Proper Function of Government

w Ian Macintosh

Though Burnside accepts that his new position carries a heavy responsibility, his mood turns to rancour when Sir Geoffrey decides to test his loyalties by blocking his application for further Sandbagger staff.
Sam Brian Osborne
Stan Michael O'Hagan
Sir Geoffrey Alan MacNaughton

Director: Michael Ferguson
Designer: Roger Andrews

Is Your Journey Really Necessary?

w Ian Macintosh

It's one thing for Burnside, SIF Director of Operations, to break the rules by mounting a covert operation without approval – but

quite another to be caught doing so. Can Burnside emerge from the encounter without loss of face?
Alan Denson Steven Grives
Jake Landy David Glyder
Sally Graham Brenda Cavenish

Director: Derek Bennett
Designer: Roger Andrews

The Most Suitable Person

w Ian Mackintosh

With only one Sandbagger left to him, Burnside faces a crisis: it appears that the unit is about to accept the first ever woman Sandbagger to its depleted ranks – Laura Dickens, the only trainee left.
Laura Dickens Diane Keen (Intro.)
Peele Jerome Willis (Intro.)
Jeff Ross Bob Sherman (Intro.)

Director: David Reynolds
Designer: Roger Andrews

Always Glad to Help

w Ian Mackintosh

A succession of bitter clashes with Peele and a Sandbagger who wants to leave the unit makes life tough for Burnside – but not quite tough enough to overlook the backlog of work that is piling up arond him.
Hamad Peter Miles
Intelligence Chief Terence Longden
Intelligence Director Gerald James

Director: David Reynolds
Designer: Roger Andrews

A Feasible Solution

w Ian Mackintosh

While Willie Caine faces danger in Ceylon, Burnside faces a testing time in London where he is 'put on the carpet' to face the facts. However, the unit controller has other things on his mind – can it be that he's fallen for Sandbagger Two?

Colby Donald Churchill
Milton Barkley Johnson
Jill Ferris Sarah Bullen

Director: Michael Ferguson
Designer: Roger Andrews

Special Relationship

w Ian Mackintosh

There is always the danger of a clash between professional and personal priorities, but Burnside must face the unenviable decision of whether to send the girl he loves into what is almost certain death.

Mittag Brian Ashley
Baumel Alan Downer
Paul Cyril Varley

Director: Michael Ferguson
Designer: Roger Andrews

Season Two
6 colour 60-minute episodes

At All Costs

w Ian Mackintosh

Last winter, in Berlin, Sandbagger Two had bled to death in no-man's land. Burnside had ordered her assassination. Today, in London, exactly one year later, SIF receives a priority signal from behind the Iron Curtain. For Burnside, the nightmare begins again.

Karen Milner Jane Sheldon (Intro.)
Mike Wallace Michael Cashman (Intro.)
Edward Tyler Peter Laird

Director: Michael Ferguson
Designer: Jeremy Bear

Enough of Ghosts

w Ian Mackintosh

When Government Under-Secretary Sir Geoffrey Wellingham goes missing while travelling to Brussels, and Burnside has to make a split-second decision, the Sandbagger unit is threatened as never before. Something's got to give – but will it be Burnside?

Lady Wellingham Edith Macarthur
Nigel Elliott Donald Pelmear
Albrecht Jurgen Anderson

Director: Peter Cregreen
Designer: Jeremy Bear

Decision by Committee

w Ian Mackintosh

An aircraft is hijacked 30 minutes after it leaves Britain. The danger is real, the threat horrifying. Can Burnside prevent the destruction of the aircraft and its passengers – two of whom are Sandbaggers Caine and Milner?

Kadim David Freedman
Stewardess Marta Gillot
CGS David Beale

Director: Michael Ferguson
Designer: Jeremy Bear

A Question of Loyalty

w Ian Mackintosh

In a world where survival is often bought with experience, Mike Wallace still has a lot to learn. That's Burnside's dilemma when informed that Wallace, working behind the Iron Curtain, is in need of assistance.

Wheatley Patrick Godfrey
Maddison Charles Hodgson
Gary Shearburn Philip Blaine

Director: Michael Ferguson
Designer: Roger Andrews

It Couldn't Happen Here

w Ian Mackintosh

Two unconnected events, more than 4,000 miles apart, force SIS chief Neil Burnside to take a desperate decision – and Willie Caine to risk his life trying to protect a man determined to walk the thin line between life and death.

Senator O'Shea **Weston Garvin**
Mary Herron **Daphne Anderson**
Briscoe **Don Fellows**

Director: **Peter Cregeen**
Designer: **Roger Andrews**

Operation Kingmaker

w Ian Mackintosh
'C' has died and must be replaced. The most likely candidate is a man with a long-standing grudge against Burnside. Diane Lawler, Burnside's personal assistant, hands in her notice. It's a black day indeed for the Controller.
'C' **Dennis Burgess (Intro.)**
Tyler **Peter Laird**
Marianne Straker **Sue Holderness (Intro.)**

Director: **Alan Grint**
Designer: **Peter Caldwell**

Season Three

7 colour 60-minute episodes

All in a Good Cause

w Ian Mackintosh
Hearing the the Director of Intelligence is investigating the wife of Sandbagger Jeff Ross, Burnside, already in conflict with his new boss, has to bear the agony of watching his team endure a game of cat-and-mouse with an enemy they can see – but not identify.
Jenny Ross **Gale Gladstone**
D'Arcy **John Steiner**
Edward Tyler **Peter Laird**

Director: **Peter Cregeen**
Designer: **Jeremy Bear**

To Hell with Justice

w Ian Mackintosh
When Edward Tyler, the Director of Intelligence, a man with a headful of priceless information, flies to Malta for a much-needed rest and he is met by a young SIF officer and a beautiful girl, Burnside suspects something afoot.
Len Shepherd **John Aiken**
Margarete Muller **Glynis Barber**
Tinsdale **Mark Eden**

Director: **Peter Cregeen**
Designer: **Jeremy Bear**

Unusual Approach

w Ian Mackintosh
Knowing that Burnside can't stand holidays, C decides to send him on one and leave Willie Caine in charge of the unit. But where does the holiday begin and the mind-searching end? Is Burnside being manipulated?
Philip Skinner **David Horovitch**
Christina Stratos **Brigitte Kahn**
ASPO **Terry Pearson**

Director: **David Cunliffe**
Designer: **Mary Rea**

My Name is Anna Wiseman

w Gidley Wheeler
An extraordinary document handed to Burnside in a London playground rapidly involves the SIF controller in a devious double-game with his own superiors and requires him to send Sandbagger Wallace on a dangerous mission.
Anna Wiseman **Carol Gillies**
Steve Rogerson **Anthony Schaeffer**
ASPO **Terry Pearson**

Director: **Michael Ferguson**
Designer: **Jeremy Bear**

Sometimes We Play Dirty Too

w Arden Winch
Businessman and scientist Robert Banks was one of the best sources the Joint Intelligence Bureau had. Was his death in Czechoslovakia an accident or cold-blooded killing? SIF man Burnside is determined to seek out the answer.
Nadina **Susan Kodicek**
Valas **Milos Kirek**
Robert Banks **Derek Godfrey**

Director: **Peter Cregeen**
Designer: **Jeremy Bear**

Who Needs Enemies

w Gidley Wheeler
Burnside must go! It appears that everybody wants to bring the iron man down to size – if not get rid of him completely. Even the loyalty of his Sandbaggers is evaporating. Why?

Dalgetty David Robb
Dr O'Toole Harry Webster
Pearson John Eastham

Director: Peter Cregeen
Designer: Jeremy Bear

Len Shepherd John Aiken
Yuri Filatov Frank Moorey
Sarkisiyan Larry Hooderoff

Director: Peter Cregeen
Designer: Jeremy Bear

Opposite Numbers

w Ian Mackintosh
The Sandbaggers team are called in to
handle the security arrangements for the
Third Strategic Arms Limitation Talks
being held in Malta. It calls for men of the
highest calibre – men like SIF controller
Neil Burnside.

THE SANDBAGGERS
Created by: Ian Mackintosh
Producer: Michael Ferguson
Executive producer: David Cunliffe
Music by: Roy Budd
A Yorkshire Television Network Production
20 colour 60-minute episodes
18 September – 30 October 1978
28 January – 3 March 1980
9 June – 21 July 1980

SAPPHIRE AND STEEL

'All irregularities will be handled by the forces controlling each
dimension. Transuranic heavy elements may not be used where
there is life. Medium atomic weights are available: Gold! Lead!
Copper! Jet! Diamond! Radium! Sapphire, Silver and Steel . . .
Sapphire and Steel have been assigned!' those words, spoken by a
God-like voice, introduced us to one of the most unusual fantasy
programmes ever to appear on television – the time-hopping
adventures of Sapphire and Steel, two 'time detectives' who
materialised out of nowhere to repair breaks in the fabric of time
and do battle with the dark forces which had crept into our world
through the broken time corridor. Exactly what they were doing,
or where they came from was never made clear (although hints
were made that they were elements, working for a superior race
of elementals). What we knew (or were told by the Sapphire
character in the first story) was that: 'Time is a corridor. It
surrounds all things. You can't see it – only sometimes . . . and
that's when it is dangerous. You cannot enter into time but, once
in a while, Time itself can try to enter into the Present – break
in, burst through, to take things . . . take people. Sometimes,
the present becomes weakened – like fabric. And when there is
pressure upon the fabric, Time reaches in.'

That's where Sapphire and Steel came in. It was their job to
restore the rip in time and restore the equilibrium – two time
agents sent to discover what had crept through the time-warp
and use their special talents to destroy the alien entity and repair
time itself.

Totally original in concept and execution. A pure delight.

(Note: the entire series carried no individual story titles or episode identification numbers. For easy reference, I've clubbed together each story under one compact entry.)

REGULAR CAST

Sapphire Joanna Lumley   *Steel* David McCallum   *Silver* David Collings

Season One

14 colour 30-minute episodes

Adventure One   *(A 6-part story)*

Young Robert Jardine is doing his homework. His parents are reading nursery rhymes to his younger sister, Helen. Suddenly, the clock stops ticking. Robert races upstairs to find his sister alone – their parents have vanished! Enter Sapphire and Steel to take on the challenge of the invader through time who has whisked away their parents. The battle begins and Sapphire finds herself trapped in an old painting where Roundhead soldiers are trying to kill her. Steel tries to save her by reducing his body temperature, but he fails and calls for the assistance of Lead.

Together they finally overcome their enemy, reunite the children with their parents and restore the rip in time.
Robert Steven O'Shea
Helen Tamasin Bridge
Lead Val Pringle

Director: Shaun O'Riordan
Designer: Stanley Mills

Adventure Two   *(An 8-part story)*

Station-owner and psychic expert George Tully is convinced his railway station is haunted. He's right, but he has no idea by what. In fact it's a being that creates havoc with the balance of time and Sapphire and Steel are caught up in its struggle for vengeance. Together with Tully they begin their search and Steel attempts to identify their opponent – a ghostly figure, dressed in the uniform of a World War I soldier.

Steel's attempts to defeat the spectre almost result in Sapphire losing her life, but Tully finally makes contact with the dead man and unleashes a new and frightening force – a duplicate of Sapphire, which is every bit as malevolent as its creator. The tension mounts as Steel is forced to negotiate with the dead for the lives of his partners and himself.
Tully Gerald James
Spectre (Pearce) Tom Kelly
Pilot David Cann

Director: Shaun O'Riordan (Eps 1, 3, 7)
David Foster (Eps 2, 4, 5, 6, 8)
Designer: Stanley Mills

Season Two

10 colour 30-minute episodes

Adventure Three   *(A 6-part story)*

A modern block of flats holds the secret of a strange mystery. It has an extra penthouse that no one can see. It's invisible and it is occupied by two time travellers from the future. Sapphire and Steel are aware of its occupants, but cannot hear or see them. They are certain, however, that the strange couple have brought a strange creation with them – something that snatches Sapphire away when she tries to contact the strangers. Joined by Silver, who tells Steel that unless they close the time source, the whole of Earth is in danger, they attempt to rescue Sapphire from the creature, but it releases Sapphire unharmed and escapes into time.
Silver David Collings
Rothwyn Catherine Hall
Changeling Russell Wooton

Director: Shaun O'Riordan
Designer: Stanley Mills

Adventure Four   *(A 4-part story)*

Discovering that something new has broken through the time corridor, Sapphire and Steel have their first encounter with the

'shape', a being which can slip in and out of any photograph and take refuge in its time zone – taking with it humans, who are then trapped forever in in the photograph. If they allow the shape to continue its work, it will tear apart the slender fabric of time itself. So the two agents are forced to enter a photograph to fight their enemy in its own environment.
Shapes Philip Bird/Bob Horney
Liz Alyson Spiro
Ruth Shelagh Stephenson

Director: David Foster
Designer: Stanley Mills

Season Three
6 colour 30-minute episodes

Adventure Five *(A 6-part story)*

When Lord Mullrine celebrates 50 years of business in a partnership he set up with his late friend Dr McDee, and Sapphire and Steel attend as two of the party guests, Sapphire immediately senses that the place is subject to a time tear. But she is unable to pinpoint its source – until Mullrine's partner graces the party with an unexpected visit and his arrival is greeted with murder. The entire surroundings revert to a 1930s setting and the 'death' of Dr McDee begins all over again.
Lord Mullrine Davy Kaye
Dr McDee Stephen Macdonald
Lady Mullrine Patience Collier

Director: Don Houghton (Eps 1,3,4)
Anthony Read (Eps 2,5, 6)
Designer: Sue Chases

Season Four
4 colour 30-minute episodes

Adventure Six *(A 4-part story)*

Sapphire and Steel find themselves at a present-day service station where the only travellers are from the past – 1948. Hearing a man approach, they hide, but only a shadow arrives. Joined by Silver, they attempt to solve the strange mystery of the people from the past – only to discover that they themselves must play their part in the scenario in which they have been cast as the principal players. The die is cast, the executioners assembled and the time agents must face their destiny – to be imprisoned forever in a window in the sky and drift endlessly through space and time!
Man Edward de Souza
Woman Johanna Kirby
Silver David Collings

Director: David Foster
Designer: Stanley Mills

SAPPHIRE AND STEEL
Created and written by: P. J. Hammond
Producer: Shaun O'Riordan
Executive producer: David Reid
Music by: Cyril Ornadel
An ATV Network Production
for ITC World-Wide Distribution
34 colour 30-minute episodes
10 July – 22 November 1979
6 January – 5 February 1981
11 – 26 August 1981
19 – 31 August 1982

THE SCARLET PIMPERNEL

The central figure of this costume piece was Baroness Orczy's classic hero, Sir Percy Blakeney – aka The Scarlet Pimpernel – a man of great wealth who adopted the disguise of the mysterious freedom fighter whenever oppression and villainy reared its head in the days when George III ruled England. For no personal gain, Blakeney risked his life to protect the innocent from the cruel and sadistic Chauvelin — an enemy determined to see the Pimpernel's head gracing the guillotine's blade. One of the earliest television costume dramas, viewers had the time of their lived trying to penetrate the astonishing variety of disguises adopted by actor Marius Goring, who would appear as a 60–year old duchess one minute, only to reappear moments later as a barrow boy or foppish lord.

REGULAR CAST

Sir Percy/The Scarlet Pimpernel Marius Goring *Chauvelin* Stanley van Beers *Sir Andrew* Patrick Troughton *Prince Regent* Alexander Gauge *The Countess* Lucie Mannteim

The Hostage

w Ralph Gilbert Bettinson

The Scarlet Pimpernel must rescue the Baroness Suzanne de Fleury and her son from Chauvelin's clutches — a task which must be achieved without revealing his alterego of Sir Percy Blakeney.
Suzanne de Fleury Yvonne Furneaux
Lord Anthony Robert Shaw
Lord Richard Anthony Newlands

Director: Michael McCarthy

Sir Percy's Wager

w Joel Murcott and R. S. Bettinson

Outwardly foppish and simple, Sir Percy is always ready to make a wager. However, betting on the outcome of the Pimpernel's latest escapade can be dangerous — and almost cost him his freedom.
Lord Richard Anthony Newlands
Bibot Cyril Shapps
Lady Arabella Joanna Duncan

Director: Dennis Vance

Lady in Distress

w Ralph Gilbert Bettinson

Chauvelin uses the Pimpernel's strong sense of chivalry to bait a trap with the beautiful Cecile as the prize. Informed that Madame Guillotine awaits her pretty neck, Sir Percy makes plans to rescue her.
Cecile Ingeborg Wells
Durand Harold Young
Citizen Alfie Bass

Director: Dennis Vance

The Elusive Chauvelin

w Ralph Gilbert Bettinson

It's his strangest mission yet. The pimpernel must rescue a young man accused of being the Pimpernel — and discover whether Chauvelin was behind the plot to plant the false avenger in France.
Harding Gordon Whiting
Louis Christopher Lee
Christine Thea Gregory

Director : Dennis Vance

Something Remembered

w Joel Murcott and R. G. Bettinson

Answering an appeal from the Comtesse de Fleury to bring her brother Jacques to safety from France, the Pimpernel finds his activities brought to a standstill when the lad refuses to leave his sweetheart.
Melanie de Monsants Maureen Connell
Jacques William Franklyn
Blind man Esme Percy

Director: David Macdonald

The Sword of Justice

w Ralph Gilbert Bettison

Hearing that the Scarlet Pimpernel is being impersonated in France by an Englishman who is robbing and murdering French aristocrats, Sir Percy, believing that his enemy Chauvelin is behind the scheme, sets a trap to catch the impostor.

Count Latour Ian Fleming
Sir Thomas Brian Wilde
Biggs Dennis Shaw

Director : Dennis Vance

Thanksgiving day

w Michael Hogan
Why should an American who desperately needs the Pimpernel's help challenge him to a duel to the death? Sir Percy must find a way of protecting his second identity and protecting the man at the same time.
Rawlingson Phil Brown
Adams William Abbey
Myra Rawlingson Ginger Hall

Director: David Macdonald

Sir Andrew's Fate

w Ralph Gilbert Bettinson
How can a wax effigy of the Pimpernel lead his enemy Chauvelin to the original? As Sir Percy finds to his cost, his reputation of being elusive is put under severe test when he faces this latest threat to his existence.
Collette Duclos Balbina
Madame Tussaud Susan Richmond
Chauvelin's agent Ivor Dean

Director: Wolf Rilla

The Ambassador's Lady

w Joel Murcott and R. G. Bettinson
Lord Richard Hasting's eye for a pretty girl places himself and Sir Percy in the spotlight – and right under Chauvelin's nose. Will the gossip prove to be their undoing, or can the Pimpernel save the day?
Renée Fleury Simone Lovell
Jacques Fleury William Franklyn
Chico Robert Cawdron

Director: David Macdonald

The Christmas Present

w Ralph Gilbert Bettinson

It's Christmas. But Sir Percy has no time for festivities, he's busy helping a group of children escape from Chauvelin's clutches. To keep the children amused during their flight, Sir Percy tells them a story.

Mrs Burton Sybil Arundale
Jean Paul Chris Toyne
Antoinette Lesley Dudley

Director : David Macdonald

The Flower Woman

w Marius Goring
The Comtesse de la Vallire, who has long been Chauvelin's spy at the English court, has a change of heart and joins Sir Percy. Or does she? Can Sir Percy really trust the woman with his secret?
Lady Arabella Joanna Duncan
Assassin Michael Hitchman
Sergeant Peter Halliday

Director: David Macdonald

The Imaginary Invalid

w John Moore
Hearing that the daughter of Rothstein, an old enemy, is being held ransom by Chauvelin and the ransom demand is high, Sir Percy sets out to see that the ransom is never paid – at least, not to Chauvelin's coffers.
Dr Dufay John Laurie
Rothstein Milton Rosmer
Rachelle Jean Aubrey

Director: David Macdonald

The Princess

w Ralph Gilbert Bettinson
Having rescued her neck from the guillotine, why should Sir Percy be so glib when introduced to the latest Lady at Court, the Marquise de Manton? At the time of her rescue she was a servant girl, but now she is a court favourite. How?
Marquise de Manton Rachel Gurney
Gisette Susan Lyall Grant
Sergeant Julian Somers

Director: David Macdonald

Antoine and Antoinette

w Diane Morgan & Angus McPhail
Finding themselves spending their honeymoon in a rat–infested prison cell, Antoine and Antoinette pray for

deliverance. It arrives in the shape of the Scarlet Pimpernel – who sets out to teach Chauvelin a lesson.

Antoine Eric Lindsay
Antoinette Greta Watson
Elise Gillian Town

Director: David Macdonald

Winged Madonna

w Joel Murcott and R. G. Bettinson
The Abbey of Nanterre has been plundered by Chauvelin and its monks lie dead. Hearing this, Sir Percy decides to set the hand of Pimpernel on his enemy's shoulders – and force Chauveling to say his prayers.

Madeleine Renée Goddard
Delong Nicholas Bruce
Jean Jimmy Ray

Director: Wolf Rilla

Gentlemen of the Road

w Ralph Gilbert Bettinson
When Sir Percy notices a beautiful woman showing an unusual interest in the Prince Regent's affairs and is unconvinced by her reply to his questions, he decides that it's time for the Pimpernel to show his true colours.

Madame Melanie Maureen Connell
Rachell Jean Aubrey
Latour Conrad Phillips

Director: David Macdonald

The Farmer's Boy

w John Moore
By giving one of Sir Percy's agents false information, Chauvelin hopes to lure the man he suspects of being the Pimpernel into the open. He achieves his aim – but is astonished when a 'simple–minded' farmer's boy arrives at court.

Jeanette Elvi Hale
André Roger Delgado
Elbeuf Michael Ripper

Director: David Macdonald

A Tale of Two Pigtails

w Angus McPhail and Diana Morgan
Why has Chauvelin returned to England to spend some time at the Court of the Prince Regent? Sir Percy must discover the purpose of his visit – the Pimpernel's life could depend on the outcome.

Princess Melanie Maureen Connell
Alice Sybil Wise
Attendant Peter O'Toole

Director: David Macdonald

THE SCARLET PIMPERNEL
Producers: Dennis Vance, David Macdonald and Marius Goring
Executive producer: David Macdonald
Music by: Sidney Torch
*A Towers of London Production
for ITC Ltd*
18 monochrome 30 minute episodes
24 February – 22 June 1956

USA: Syndicated 1954

THE SECRET SERVICE

Gerry Anderson's seldom-seen series about a far-from-ordinary, dotty, slightly-deaf village priest, who had a remarkable electronic device hidden in a book left in his care by a parishioner which could miniaturise his gardener Matthew – or any object – to one third its original size.

But why would a vicar wish to do such a thing? Answer: he wasn't a vicar at all, but a Secret Service agent working for BISHOP (British Intelligence Secret Headquarters, Operation

Priest), who kept in contact with other BISHOP operatives via a radio device in his hearing aid, and carried the miniature Matthew around in a specially designed briefcase!

At the time a new departure for the master of Supermarionation (Anderson elected to combine puppets with real-life actor Stanley Unwin), the series failed to attract good ratings and only 13 episodes were produced.

REGULAR CAST
Father Unwin Stanley Unwin
CHARACTER VOICES
Father Unwin Stanley Unwin *Matthew* Keith Alexander
Mrs Appleby Sylvia Anderson *The Bishop* Jeremy Wilkin

A Case for the Bishop

w Gerry and Sylvia Anderson
The theft of the XK20 mini-computer threatens the exports of the Healy Automation Company. Discovering that the device is to be smuggled out of Britain by the Ambassador Dreisenburg in a diplomatic pouch, The Bishop contacts Father Unwin who places a miniaturised Matthew aboard the Ambassador's aircraft.
Director: Alan Perry

A Question of Miracles

w Donald James
Why should new desalination plants explode after only 250 hours of operation? The Bishop asks Father Unwin to find out if sabotage is the answer – and to save another plant which is nearing the 250 zero deadline.
Director: Leo Eaton

To Catch a Spy

w Tony Barwick
When top spy Grey is sprung from prison in a daring helicopter raid, Father Unwin sends Matthew to check out the home of Sir Humphrey Burton – the man suspected of being behind the breakout.
Director: Brian Heard

The Feathered Spies

w Tony Barwick
Aerial photographs of a new fighter plane are being sold on the international espionage market. The Bishop asks Father Unwin to find out how the photographs were taken and the priest becomes a pigeon fancier – to avert a bomb threat.
Director: Peter Anderson

Last Train to Bufflers Halt

w Tony Barwick
After one attempt to hijack a gold shipment fails, Father Unwin is assigned to accompany the gold shipment during a train journey. It isn't long before he and the train crew are hijacked – leaving a miniaturised Matthew to rout the hijackers.
Director: Alan Perry

A Hole in One

w Shane Rimmer
When a satellite's orbit is tampered with by someone with inside information, Father Unwin is assigned to keep an eye on General Brompton, the only man who had access to the information. Unwin joins him on the golf course – and learns the secret of the 15th hole.
Director: Brian Heard

Recall to Service

w Pat Dunlop
Father Unwin is asked to attend the NATO demonstration of the Army's latest tank which has suffered control failures to its on-board computer. It soon becomes clear that the tank is going to attack the lookout post – but fortunately Matthew is secreted inside it.
Director: Peter Anderson

Errand of Mercy

w Tony Barwick

Confined to bed by illness, Father Unwin falls asleep and dreams that he and Matthew are flying to Africa in Gabriel, his Model T-Ford to deliver urgent medical supplies. His dream continues unabated – and ends up with him fending off a rocket attack.

Director: Leo Eaton

The Deadly Whisper

w Donald James

While Father Unwin is away visiting friends, Matthew discovers that Professor Soames and his daughter are being held hostage by saboteurs who plan to use the scientist's sonic rifle to shoot down a new test aircraft.

Director: Leo Eaton

The Cure

w Pat Dunlop

Father Unwin follows notorious agent Sakov to the Klam Health Centre. His mission: to head off a sabotage attempt by Sakov on a car being used to test a new fuel. Matthew is hidden in the car, but Father Unwin, trapped by Sakov at the Klam Centre, cannot warn him of the impending attack.

Director: Leo Eaton

School for Spies

w Donald James

When several priests are seen at a series of sabotage operations, Father Unwin unearths a group of mercenaries posing as clergy. Hearing that they need a new explosives expert, he knocks out the man summoned and takes his place.

Director: Ken Turner

May-day, May-day

w Bob Keston

Assigned to safeguard the welfare of an Arab King after several attempts have been made on his life, Father Unwin and Matthew usher the Arab aboard a plane to New York, content that all is well. It's not. The crew have been gassed – and the priest will have to land the plane himself.

Director: Alan Perry

More Haste – Less Speed

w Tony Barwick

Hoping that Mullins, a counterfeiter released from jail, will lead them to where he has hidden his printing plates, the Bishop asks Father Unwin to follow the man. All they find are a bunch of thieves – each determined to reach the plates before anyone else.

Director: Ken Turner

THE SECRET SERVICE
Series format created by: Gerry and Sylvia Anderson
Producer: David Lane
Executive producer: Reg Hill
Music by: Barry Gray
(Theme tune sung by: Mike Sammes Singers)
Visual effects director: Derek Meddings
Script editor: Tony Barwick
An ITC Entertainments/Century 21 TV Production
13 colour 30-minute episodes
21 September – 14 December 1969

THE SENTIMENTAL AGENT

The series that gave us the opportunity to catch up on the further adventures of Carlos Varela, the devil-may-care import-export agent with a nose for trouble first seen in *Man of the World* (see entry under that name).

Now based in London, the impeccably dressed, cigar-smoking hero would jet off to some dangerous adventure that would tax his wit, ingenuity and charm, and place him at the centre of dangerous situations which would require him to rescue a fair maiden's honour. (One of the more notable damsels in distress being the then comparatively unknown Diana Rigg.)

Passable thrills for viewers who like their heroes to have charm – but little acting ability.

REGULAR CAST
Carlos Varela Carlos Thompson   *Chin* Burt Kwouk   *Bill Randle* John Turner

All That Jazz
w Julian Bond
When Varela undertakes responsibility for a jazz group making its debut in England, he soon finds himself with more problems than he bargained for and it isn't long before the band are serenading a group of spies to save the life of a musician.
Major Nelson Anthony Bushell
Stirink Peter Arne
Chin Burt Kwouk (Intro.)

Director: Charles Frend

The Beneficiary
w Julian Bond
Finding himself in trouble in Greece, Jarrell, a wartime colleague of Varela's, sends his ex-comrade a prearranged distress signal: a campaign ribbon and a torn half of a document – the two items that spell 'danger'.
Jarrell Michael Godfrey
Anna Lubna Aziz
Klaus Derek Francis

Director: John Paddy Carstairs

Express Delivery
w Lindsay Hardy
When Varela promises to help a young Polish girl escape across the border, he finds himself involved in more than a simple escape attempt. It appears that the girl has witnessed a crime – and someone wants to silence her.
Katrina Ann Bell
Major Patrick Magee
Priest Donald Morley

Director: Charles Frend

Never Play Cards with Strangers
w Julian Bond
Hearing that some passengers have been fleeced of their savings while on a cruise booked through his agency, Varela decides to give the cardsharps a taste of their own medicine by settling the score personally.
Colonel Dewer Jack Melford
Mrs Carter Clemence Bettany
Mamie Bessie Love

Director: John Paddy Carstairs

May the Saints Preserve Us
w Patrick Campbell
It's an unusual job – shipping an ancient Irish castle to America for a wealthy Texan heiress, but when there's money to be made Varela doesn't stop to think. Perhaps he should have done so – someone doesn't approve of the deal.
Sylvester O'Toole Brian Phelan
Sgt Dooley Godfrey Quigley
Sheila Carol Cleveland

Director: Charles Frend

Meet My Son, Henry
w Lindsay Hardy
Varela finds himself involved with the mysterious disappearance of top-secret flight plans from a Space Development Centre. At the request of a millionaire, he embarks on an intriguing escapade to recover the plans.
Bill Randall John Turner
Henry Peabody Sr John Philips
Darrin Glyn Edwards

Director: John Paddy Carstairs

A Little Sweetness and Light

w Tudor Gates

Informed that his business representative has been killed in a motoring accident, Varela flies to the Greek island of Athos to investigate the man's death – and why his trade figures with the island have suddenly decreased.

Petrides Patrick Allen
Melina Zena Marshall
Ridou Patrick Newell

Director: Harold French

The Height of Fashion

w Peter and Betty Lambda

Varela moves in fashion circles and discovers that anything can be sold as the latest vogue – provided you sell your product with panache and style. Yes, anything – including horse blankets!

Jackie Sue Lloyd
Victor Frey Dennis Price
Pugh Warren Mitchell

Director: Charles Frend

A Very Desirable Plot

w Brian Clemens

It must be a con trick. Someone is selling off worthless plots of land in the Bahamas to unsuspecting holidaymakers. Varela sends his representative along to report on the situation.

Colonel Wilde William Mervyn
Lamont Paul Maxwell
Franey Diana Rigg

Director: Harry Booth

Finishing School

w Peter and Betty Lambda

When a young girl goes missing from an exclusive ladies' finishing school, everyone suspects she has been kidnapped. Varela thinks otherwise and at the headmistress's request he sends Bill Randall to investigate.

Lady Graffham Helen Cherry
Philipa Susan Clark
Betsy Ann Annette Andre

Director: Harold French

The Scroll of Islam

w Jack Davies

Varela is intrigued when Professor Fletcher approaches him and requests his help in obtaining photographs of a relic which could prove more important than the Dead Sea Scrolls.

Fletcher Alan Gifford
Shaw William Sylvester
Sheikh Patrick Troughton

Director: John Paddy Carstairs

Not Quite Fully Covered

w Leslie Harris and Roger East

Assigned to transport a consignment of rare furniture which has been smuggled out of Gregoria to England, Bill Randall soon finds himself involved in the shadier side of the antiques business.

Yanni Keith Baxter
Nikki Imogen Hassall
Truman Jones Reginald Beckworth

Director: Charles Frend

A Box of Tricks

w Ian Stuart Black

Why won't the Palabria people receive an £11 million gift to their country? Bill Randall is sent to investigate – and finds himself playing the role of an African witch-doctor to encourage them to do so.

Mateo Gary Raymond
Count de Ricci Ferdy Mayne
Souza Walter Gotell

Director: Harold French

THE SENTIMENTAL AGENT
Producer: Harry Fine
Music by: Ivor Slaney
Script supervisor: Ian Stuart Black
An ATV Production
13 monochrome 60-minute episodes
28 September – 27 December 1963
(USA: Syndicated 1962)

SERGEANT CORK

Set in Victorian times, this sharply-observed whodunnit series depicted the origin and development of Scotland Yard's CID division as seen through the casebook of Sergeant Cork, a policeman who set out to prove that his 'modern' scientific methods of detection could work – despite the opposition of his superiors who viewed his ideal as 'futuristic claptrap'.

A determined man who wished to break the red tape that dogged the CID in its infancy, Cork waged a one-man war with his superiors to prove that science could – and would – play a major part in bringing criminals to justice.

Helping the sergeant to gain recognition for his ideas was Detective Sergeant Bob Marriott, a mentally-alert young policeman who, though not fully understanding Cork's methods, nevertheless developed a keen interest in what his colleague was trying to achieve.

Both men found themselves at loggerheads with their superior Detective Joseph Bird, a man who dismissed Cork's theories whenever the opportunity to do so presented itself – which was frequently in a head-to-head confrontation with Superintendent Billy Nelson, a man who admired and respected Cork and was prepared to back him to the hilt.

Midway through the series Cork and Marriott found a further ally when Bird was transferred to another division and replaced by Superintendent Rodway, a quick-witted detective who took notice of Cork's views and ideas and was well-placed to give him the help he required to pursue his 'modern' methods of detection.

REGULAR CAST

Sergeant Cork **John Barrie**   *Bob Marriott* **William Gaunt**
Det. Bird **Arnold Diamond**   *Supt Nelson* **John Richmond**
Supt Rodway **Charles Morgan**

SERGEANT CORK
Created by: Ted Willis
Producer: Jack Williams
Writers: Ted Willis, Bill McIllwraithe,
Richard Harris, Julian Bond, Bill Craig,
Michael Pertwee,
Alan Prior, Malcolm Hulke, Bruce Stewart
Directors: Quentin Lawrence, Phil Dale,
Dennis Vance, Josephine Douglas, Bill
Stewart, Ian Fordyce
An ATV Network Production
65 monochrome 60-minute episodes
9 June 1963 – 26 March 1968

9 June 1963 – 26 March 1968

SEXTON BLAKE

The adventures of Sexton Blake, a detective who, like Sherlock Holmes before him, also operated from Baker Street and shared the title 'The Great Detective'. That is where the similarity ended – unless one considers that, like Holmes, Blake too was sometimes called upon by Scotland Yard to assist them with their inquiries. (For Inspector Lestrade substitute Police Inspectors Evans, Cardish or Davies.)

Set in the late twenties, the series depicted how Blake, an inveterate cigar smoker, would drive the Grey Panther (his gleaming white Rolls Royce), his two assistants, 'Tinker' (real name Edward Clark) and Pedro, his bloodhound, into all kinds of intriguing mysteries which the detective had to solve.

Made for children. Junior whodunnits on a grand scale.

REGULAR CAST

Sexton Blake **Laurence Payne**   *Tinker* **Roger Foss**   *Pedro* **Himself**
Mrs Bardell (Blake's Housekeeper) **Dorothea Phillips**
Insp. Cutts **Ernest Clark**   *Insp. Van Steen* **Leonard Sachs**
Insp. 'Taff' Evans **Meredith Edwards**   *Insp. Cardish* **Eric Lander**
Insp. Davies **Charles Morgan**

SEXTON BLAKE
Producer: Ronald Marriott
Directors: Adrian Cooper, Peter Croft, Ian Fordyce, Michael Currer-Briggs, Peter Moffatt,
Nicholas Ferguson
Writers: Peter Ling, Max Oberman, David Edwards, Roy Russell, Ivor Jay
An Associated Rediffusion Production
32 colour 30-minute episodes
25 September 1967 – 24 July 1968
A Thames Television Production
28 colour 30-minute episodes
14 November 1968 – 13 January 1971

SHADOW SQUAD

In its day, this twice-weekly detective series picked up viewing figures of over 12 million that today would have seen it placed number one in the ratings. It was hugely popular and made household names of Peter Williams and George Moon.

Each story, told in two 30-minute parts which made up one complete adventure, depicted the adventures of Vic Steele, a former member of the Flying Squad who had resigned from the force so that he could pursue crime without being hampered by the restrictions placed on a policeman.

Sharing his adventures were Ginger Smart, a likeable Cockney, and Mrs Moggs, a cleaning lady who appeared to spend more time helping Ginger sift through clues than dusting the office.

Steele called the agency *Shadow Squad* to attract clients, and the two men would take on anything from murder mysteries to searching for someone's lost pet – providing it satisfied their taste for the unusual.

Three months (and 26 episodes) into the series, Vic Steele disappeared from the scene and a new face was at the helm, ex-Scotland Yard Detective Inspector, Don Carter. (No explanation was ever given as to why the changeover took place, but the producers explained Steele's departure by having him summoned to Australia on a security assignment of 'indefinite duration' – he never returned.)

With the appearance of Carter, the series grew in popularity and lasted for two years – a total of 175 episodes. (The story introducing Don Carter being a 3-parter, and the final 9 stories being one complete adventure each week of 30-minutes duration.)

It did, however, end on a high note. The final story, *Swan Song*, had Don and Ginger investigating a murder in a television studio which, after the dénouement, was revealed to be the actual Granada studio in which the production had been made. A handshake, and the two men walked off the set forever. (And all this thirty years before *Moonlighting*!)

Though nothing further was seen of Don Carter, Ginger Moon reappeared a few weeks later in *Skyport*, a series about policing a major airport. It failed to click with the audience and disappeared after a short run.

CAST

Vic Steele **Rex Garner** *Don Carter* **Peter Williams**
Ginger Smart **George Moon** *Mrs Moggs* **Kathleen Boutall**

SHADOW SQUAD

Producer: Barry Baker
Directors: Bill Hitchcock, Jean Hamilton, James Ormerod, Herbert Wise, David Main, Michael Scott, Max Morgan Witts, Robert Tronson
Writers: Barry Baker, Peter Yeldham, Julian Bond, H. V. Kershaw, Tony Warren, John Whitney, Geoffrey Bellman

An Associated Rediffusion Network Production (Episodes 1 – 26)
A Granada Television Network Production (Remainder)
175 monochrome 30-minute episodes
17 June – 23 September 1957
26 September 1957 – 24 June 1959

SIR FRANCIS DRAKE

The sea-faring adventures of Sir Francis Drake, sailor, explorer, adventurer and confidant of Queen Elizabeth I. The man who repelled the invading Spanish Armada and was appointed Admiral of the Queen's Navy.

Aboard the pride of the fleet, the *Golden Hind*, Drake led his adventurous Elizabethan crew into many exciting exploits and Drake's fame spread before him. A lone wolf, and expert swordsman, Drake took his orders directly from the Queen and defended her throne and the shores of England against the warring invaders.

High-spirited adventures that found favour with an audience seeking thrills.

REGULAR CAST

Sir Francis Drake **Terence Morgan**   Queen Elizabeth I **Jean Kent**
Trevelyan **Patrick McLoughlin**   John **Michael Crawford**
Mendoza **Roger Delgado**   Don Pedro **Alex Scott**

The Prisoner

w Ian Stuart Black

Sir Francis Drake sails into the life of the haughty but beautiful Countess Inez, a Spanish aristocrat whose life he saves. In return she attempts to sink the *Golden Hind* with all hands!

Countess Inez **Natasha Parry**
Roberto **Warren Mitchell**
Don Antonio **Clifford Elkin**

Director: **Peter Maxwell**

The Lost Colony of Virginia

w Larry Forrester

Hearing that a colony of English settlers in Virginia are badly in need of provisions, and face disaster unless they receive aid, Drake and his crew ignore the threat of Don Pedro's fleet to help them.

Jenny **Olive McFarland**
Tom Brewster **Barry Foster**
Governor **John Welsh**

Director: **David Greene**

Mary, Queen of Scots

w Lindsay Galloway

Drake foils a plot by Mendoza to dupe Queen Elizabeth into signing the death warrant of Mary, Queen of Scotland. But trouble awaits his return to England and Drake finds himself occupying a prison cell.

Queen Mary **Noelle Middleton**
Thomas Philips **Harvey Hall**
Walsingham **Richard Warner**

Director: **David Greene**

Doctor Dee

w Doreen Montgomery

Having seen success in the Queen's horoscope, Doctor Dee, Elizabeth's alchemist, advises Drake that the time is favourable to attack a Spanish fleet carrying fabulous wealth. He does so – and finds himself under heavy fire.

Doctor Dee **Raymond Huntley**
Munro **Ewan Roberts**
Gazio **Patrick Troughton**

Director: **Clive Donner**

Bold Enterprise

w John Roddick

Financed by a wealthy merchant banker, Drake sails to the West Indies to raid one of Spain's treasure-filled gold vaults. No sooner has he set to sea, his ship comes under Spanish fire.

Munro Ewan Roberts
Laura Patricia Dainton
Governor Michael Peake

Directors: Anthony Bushell and Harry Booth

The English Dragon

w Ian Stuart Black

When Queen Elizabeth's favourite ward of court falls deeply in love with a French Countess, it sets in operation a series of events which almost cost Drake his life – and culminates with the Spanish invasion almost succeeding.

Lord Oakshoot David McCallum
The Countess Delphi Lawrence
Grenville Howard Lang

Director: Clive Donner

Escape

w David Greene

After escaping from his enemy by jumping overboard, Drake struggles ashore to find he's landed on Spanish territory. Dragged from the sea by two soldiers, he is taken before a sadistic Governor.

Governor Barry Morse
Withers Charles Heslop
Estaban Brian Bedford

Director: David Greene

Boy Jack

w Cedric Wells and Ian Stuart Black

Queen Elizabeth's godson John Harrington finds himself on a mission to Spain in the company of Sir Francis Drake. While there, he proves to the Captain that he has more courage and character than his colleague gave him credit for.

Boy Jack Michael Anderson
Ambassador Clive Morton
Munro Ewan Roberts

Director: Clive Donner

The Garrison

w Ian Stuart Black

When he fails to deliver fresh supplies to an English garrison, Drake and his crew are accused of cowardice and treason and sent for trial. Only one man can prove their innocence – but he's been captured by the Spaniards.

Sir Miles Laurence Naismith
Captain Williams Patrick Wymark
Bosun Peter Richmond

Director: David Greene

Visit to Spain

w Doreen Montgomery

Alarmed that Queen Elizabeth has promised the hand of Anne to an heir of the Spanish throne, Drake finds himself risking his position with Elizabeth to save the girl from a loveless marriage.

Anne Catherine Woodville
King Philip Zia Mohyeddin
Wentham Bryan Coleman

Director: Terry Bishop

The Flame-thrower

w Doreen Montgomery

Sir Martin has invented a powerful weapon – one which Drake believes could win the war, but should only be used for peaceful purposes. Count Julio thinks otherwise – and sets out to steal the invention for the Spaniards.

Count Julio William Lucas
Sir Martin Neil McCallum
Lambert William Peacock

Directors: Clive Donner and Harry Booth

The Governor's Revenge

w John Baines

Whilst buying provisions at a Spanish port, Drake finds that the Governor's brother died in a sea battle with the *Golden Hind*. To take his revenge, the Governor traps Drake's crew – and sentences them to death.

Governor Roy Purcell
Hawkins Ronald Leigh-Hunt
Dona Inez Marie Burke

Director: Clive Donner

The Slaves of Spain

w Ian Stuart Black

Dropping anchor off the isle of Tobago, Drake finds the islanders have been enslaved by the Spaniards to help build a garrison which would overlook British shipping lanes and give the enemy the upper hand.

Yana Nanette Newman
Almighty Jones Michael Ripper
Carrett Marshall Jones

Directors: Anthony Bushell and Harry Booth

The Doughty Plot

w Margaret Irwin and David Greene

It's a sea-going captain's nightmare. Drake must face the terrible ordeal of having to decide the fate of one of his crew who has been found guilty of mutiny. The law specifies hanging – but Drake believes his friend innocent.

Tom Doughty Anthony Bushell
Vicary Frederick Jaeger
Brewer Victor Maddern

Director: David Greene

King of America

w Ian Stuart Black

When Drake's nephew, John, sets off with a crewman who states that he's off to the New World and will proclaim himself King of America, neither man has reckoned with the Spanish, the weather – or Drake's temper.

Stutely Kieron Moore
Flavel Andrew Keir
Celia Susan Hampshire

Director: David Greene

The Irish Pirate

w David Giltinian

Ordered by the Queen to capture the Lord O'Neil, a rebellious Irish earl, Drake finds himself totally unprepared for the events which follow: O'Neil has plans of his own – ones which don't include Sir Francis Drake.

Lord O'Neil Liam Gaffneg
Grace O'Malley Espeth March
The Abbot Gordon Phillott

Director: Peter Graham Scott

Beggars of the Sea

w Ian Stuart Black

Despite the Queen's command that no ships should interfere with a special Spanish cargo, Dutch freedom-fighters, 'The Beggars of the Sea', ignore her words – and enable Drake to help himself to another victory.

Count Julio William Lucas
Alva Gerard Heinz
Riccardo Robert Rietty

Director: Terry Bishop

Drake on Trial

w Tudor Gates

Graveney, a ruthless pirate bearing a strong resemblance to Drake, decides to plunder English shipping and leave Drake to take the blame – but his lookalike knows no bounds when seeking revenge on his enemy.

Gazio Patrick Troughton
Graveney Terence Morgan
Governor Arnold Diamond

Director: John Lamont

The Bridge

w Brian Clemens

When Drake sets out to rescue a Portuguese hero held by the Spanish, he finds his attempts to do so frustrated by the reluctance of the man to be saved. Why should this be? Drake is astonished when he finds the answer.

Maria Zena Marshall
Gazio Patrick Troughton
De Vazim Dennis Edwards

Director: Terry Bishop

Johnnie Factotum

w John Keir Cross

On his way home after a successful mission against the Spanish, Drake hears word that a gang of cut-throats intend to deprive him of the booty he has stolen in battle.

Forewarned is forearmed, and the thieves receive an unwelcome surprise.

Johnnie Factotum Philip Guard
The Dark Lady Katherine Blake
Lord Marmont Laurence Davidson

Director: Peter Graham Scott

Mission to Paris

w Lindsay Galloway
The Queen hands Drake the delicate task of visiting Paris to discover why a young French woman, who promised to visit her, has not done so – although Elizabeth has received notice of her arrival in England.
De Medici Pamela Brown
Aleneon Leon Peters
Navarre Patrick Allen

Director: David Greene

The Reluctant Duchess

w Gordon Wellesley and Paul Tabori
Whilst trying to persuade the ruler of a small European state, threatened by a Spanish invasion, to leave the country, Drake finds himself having to use all his guile to escape from his enemy.
Joos Ferdy Mayne
Duchess Mary Merrall
Duke Basil Dignam

Director: Terry Bishop

The Gypsies

w John Baines
When Drake and his crew rescue four people from an abandoned boat and take them aboard his ship, the dark clouds of defeat loom large on the horizon. The people are gypsies – and are being hunted by Don Pedro.
Sara Sarah Branch
Pastora Eileen Way
Will Martin Glyn Edwards

Director: John Lamont

Court Intrigue

w Hugh Ross Williamson
The Spanish hatch a cunning plot to keep Drake on English soil until a Spanish treasure ship deposits its cargo safely in Seville – but the scheme misfires and Drake and his crew attack the ship at sea.
Ambassador John Arnatt
Sir Christopher Bernard Archard
Munro Ewan Roberts

Director: Terry Bishop

Gentlemen of Spain

w John Keir Cross
When Barbary pirates attack Wales and capture a kinsman of Queen Elizabeth's, she instructs Drake to rescue the prisoner and return him to court unharmed. But the captain makes alternative arrangements to save the prisoner.
Don Miguel Nigel Davenport
Hassan Bey Paul Stassino
Ulrich Ali Marne Maitland

Director: John Lamont

The Fountain of Youth

w Ian Stuart Black
Has the Queen been duped? Drake believes so as he sets out to find an Indian well in Florida. Legend has it that its waters possess magical qualities which prevent the ageing process. The Queen is determined to find it – but Drake has other ideas.
Sir Henry Reginald Beckwith
Little Dove Catherine Woodville
Black Eagle Endre Muller

Director: Terry Bishop

SIR FRANCIS DRAKE
Producer: Anthony Bushell
Associate producer: Harry Fine
An ABC/ATV Joint Network Production
26 monochrome 30-minute episodes
12 November 1961 – 29 April 1962
(USA: NBC June – September 1962
23 episodes)

SMUGGLER

Another rousing swashbuckler from the prolific pen of Richard Carpenter, which depicted the escapades of ex-naval officer turned smuggler Jack Vincent, a reckless loner, who lived by his wits, his skill with the blade and his seamanship.

Set in 1802, this was family viewing at its very best.
(See THE ADVENTURER)

REGULAR CAST

Jack Vincent Oliver Tobias   *Sarah Morton* Lesley Dunlop
Honesty Evans Hwyel Williams Ellis   *Captain Konig* Peter Capell
Silas Kemble George Murcell   *Jacob* Michael O'Hagan

The Right Price (Part 1)

w Richard Carpenter

The mysterious newcomer Vincent attracts the unwelcome attention of the Kemble Gang, a bunch of notorious brigands who control the locality. Vincent finds himself captured – and staked out to die on the treacherous Gull Beach.

The Right Price (Part 2)

Having escaped from the Kemble Gang's clutches, Honesty makes a desperate bid to save Vincent's life. He must be quick – the tide is entering Gull Beach and Vincent faces a watery death.
Naylor Bill Robinson
William Kemble Simon Rouse
Benjamin Edward Palmer

Director: Dennis Abey
Designer: Ken Jones

Forced Run

w Bob Baker

When Vincent decides to make a smuggling run to France for brandy and claret, but finds a stowaway on board – who puts both himself and his cargo at risk – the smuggler must make an on-the-spot decision.
Ginette Marianne Borgo
Roach John Hallam
Marcel Yves Beneyton

Director: Jim Goddard
Designer: Ken Jones

The Respectable Traitor (Part 1)

w John Kane

Sarah's grandfather, Walter Konig, is accused of being a French spy. Suspecting that the Kembles are behind the accusations, Sarah begs Vincent to help – but Jack has other things to occupy his mind. Revenue man Marwood is after his blood.

The Respectable Traitor (Part 2)

Discovering that the Kembles are in league with a French spy – whose identity is known to him – Vincent sets out to prove Konig's innocence by facing the villains in their own stronghold.
Francis Marwood Morman Bowler
Captain Armstrong Murray Mayne
Giles Sawney Alan Ford

Director: Charles Crichton
Designer: Ken Jones

Press Gang

w Richard Carpenter

When Honesty Evans is forced into taking a navy commission by a press gang, Vincent has to find a way of freeing him – without breaking the law. He does so, by a cleverly executed plan.
Scott-Ponsonby Robert Addie
Higgins Ronald Forfar
Jenkins Aaron Shirley

Director: Jim Goddard
Designer: Ken Jones

In at the Death

w John Kane

Little knowing that revenue officer Taggart has laid a trap for him, Vincent sets out to help an old smuggler, Rummy Culbert, pull off one last result before he retires. Can Vincent outwit his adversary?

Rummy Culbert Arthur English
Nan Avril Angers
Taggart Barry Jackson

Director: Dennis Abey
Designer: Ken Jones

Missing Princess

w John Kane
When Honesty takes an interest in Sophia, a spoilt young girl staying with Sarah, it culminates with both himself and Vincent being captured by two of Jack's old enemies seeking revenge.
Sophia Tina Umlauf
Morgan Eric Deacon
Cade Paul Humpolez

Director: Dennis Abey
Designer: Ken Jones

Hogshead

w Richard Carpenter
A barrel of rum is washed ashore from a ship cast up on the reef. Honesty finds it and takes it to Jack. Vincent makes plans to recover the remaining cargo – but other people are interested.
Dick Cross John Junkin
Lt Phillips David Troughton
Stanton Morgan Shepherd

Director: Jim Goddard
Designer: Ken Jones

The Felon

w Richard Carpenter
It's a task fraught with danger. Shipwrecked convicts are holding Sarah and her grandfather prisoner. Jack must engineer a plan to rescue them – one which could cost him his own life in exchange for their freedom.
Dick Waller Nick Brimble
Ned Waller Jan Brimble
Johns Sebastian Abineri

Director: Dennis Abey
Designer: Ken Jones

An Eye for an Eye

w John Kane
When two sailors from Vincent's past appear seeking their revenge, Jack finds himself faced with accusations that he alone can prove untrue – but will his friends believe his story?
Agate Ian Hendry
Dutchie Gernot Duda
Stanton Morgan Shepherd

Director: Charles Crichton
Designer: Ken Jones

Straw Man (Part 1)

w Richard Carpenter
When Vincent rescues revenue officer Arrow from an attack by cut-throats, but a second attempt on Arrow's life proves successful and the man is killed in mysterious circumstances, Jack finds himself accused of murdering the man.

Straw Man (Part 2)

The evidence against Jack is that his knife was found at the scene of Arrow's death, but Vincent denies all knowledge of the crime – not that it matters to the dead man's friends: they have arranged for Jack to be shot while 'attempting to escape'!
Sir Paul Fisher Horst Janson
Lt Col Ward Jon Laurimore
Arrow Hugh Frazer

Director: Jim Goddard
Designer: Ken Jones

SMUGGLER
Producers: Paul Knight and Sidney Cole
Executive producer: Patrick Dromgoole
Music by: Dennis King
A Gatetarn Production
An HTV Network Presentation
13 colour 30-minute episodes
5 April – 19 July 1981

SPACE 1999

Gerry Anderson's third outing into the live-action field, a science fiction opus distinguished by two formats.

Format one showed how Commander John Koenig arrived at Moonbase Alpha to supervise a deep-space-probe experiment, only to find himself and the Alphans marooned in space when a freak nuclear accident blasted the moon from its orbit and into a space-time warp light years away from Earth (thereby allowing the scriptwriters to dish up abysmal adventures which had Koenig and his people encountering alien life forms during their endless drift through space and, on several occasions, time).

Year Two (as the second season was known) found the Alphans stationed underground in a gigantic space complex that rivalled the sets of *Star Trek*, but the adventures remained the same – further (ludicrous) encounters of the alien kind.

Neither series managed to impress – although the programme found acclaim in the USA.

REGULAR CAST

John Koenig **Martin Landau**   *Dr Helena Russell* **Barbara Bain**
Prof. Bergman **Barry Morse**   *Alan Carter* **Nick Tate**
Tony Verdeschi **Tony Anholt**   *Maya* **Catherine Schell**
Sandra Beines **Zienia Merton**   *Yasko* **Yasuko Magazumi**

Season One
24 colour 60-minute episodes

Breakaway

w George Bellak
When John Koenig arrives at Moonbase Alpha to supervise a deep-space-probe project, and radiation plague hits the Moonbase crew, Koenig has no idea that within hours of his arrival a chain reaction will blast the Moon – and its occupants – into the far reaches of outer space.
John Koenig **Martin Landau**
Helena Russell **Barbara Bain**
Commissioner Simmonds **Roy Dotrice**

Director: Lee H. Katzin

Force of Life

w Johnny Byrne
Technician Zoref becomes infused with an all-consuming need for heat. The people he touches freeze on contact and he is pulling life-giving energy from the Moonbase generators. Koenig must destroy him – before Alpha itself is destroyed.
Anton Zoref **Ian McShane**
Eva Zoref **Gay Hamilton**
Dominick **John Hamill**

Director: David Tomblin

Collision Course

w Anthony Terpiloff
Should he allow the moon to collide with Astheria? That's the dilemma facing Koenig. He wants to use explosives to blast the moon out of the rogue planet's path, but Arra, Astheria's Queen, asks him to do nothing.
Arra **Margaret Leighton**

Director: Ray Austin

War Games

w Christopher Penfold

Attacked by a fleet of mysterious warships, with 129 dead and its life-support system smashed, Moonbase Alpha is no longer habitable. Joined by Dr Russell, Koenig pleads with the aliens for mercy but receives death in return.

Alien man Anthony Valentine
Alien woman Isla Blair

Director: Charles Crichton

Death's Other Dominion

w Anthony Terpiloff

The Moonbase Alpha personnel discover Ultima Thule, a planet of ice. There are no signs of life but someone has left a message inviting Koenig and his people to share this 'paradise' with Earthmen who have lived for over 800 years!

Rowland Brian Blessed
Jack Truner John Shrapnel
Freda Mary Miller

Director: Charles Crichton

Voyager's Return

w Johnny Byrne

Alpha catches up with a space-probe launched from Earth years before the Moon was shot into space. The ship is out of control and could kill millions of lives if left to roam the galaxy. Koenig wants to destroy it – Dr Russell has other ideas.

Dr Linden Jeremy Kemp
Aarchon Alex Scott
Haines Barry Stokes

Director: Bob Kellett

Alpha Child

w Christopher Penfold

The first birth on Alpha – a young male, who adopts the name Jarak and quickly develops from a five-year-old child into an adult – plunges Koenig into further danger. Aliens are after the newborn's secret – and threaten to annihilate Alpha to get it.

Jarak Julian Glover
Cynthia Cyd Hayman
Jackie Wayne Brooks

Director: Ray Austin

Dragon's Domain

w Christopher Penfold

Nobody believes Tony Cellini's story of a graveyard for spaceships, guarded by a terrible monster – until frightening events overtake Moonbase Alpha and Koenig and Dr Russell almost meet their deaths.

Cellini Gianni Garko
Commissioner Dixon Douglas Wilmer
Gina Barbara Kellerman

Director: Charles Crichton

Mission of the Darians

w Johnny Byrne

A spaceship which has been broadcasting its distress signal for over 800 years is discovered by Moonbase, who send a mission to help any survivors aboard. But a shock awaits them – the ship's occupants have been kept alive by cannibalism!

Kara Joan Collins
High Priest Aubrey Morris
Neman Denis Burgess

Director: Ray Austin

Black Sun

w David Weir

When Moonbase Alpha is under threat of being drawn into a 'black sun' and there appears to be little hope of averting the crisis, Koenig banks on Dr Bergman's force field for salvation.

Ryan Paul Jones
Smithy Jon Laurimore

Director: Lee Katzin

Guardian of Piri

w Christopher Penfold

Lured by false computer information, the Alphans land on Piri. To their joy, they find a seductive woman who can apparently satisfy their every whim – but Koenig alone sees through her magic and fights to free his people from her influence.

Guardian of Piri Catherine Schell
Irving Michael Culver

Director: Charles Crichton

End of Eternity

w Johnny Byrne

Koenig finds himself risking his life to destroy an injured humanoid, which is doomed to spend eternity on a rock floating in space. Released by the Alphans, the creature is now hungry to inflict pain and destruction upon his saviours.
Balor Peter Bowles
Baxter Jim Smilie

Director: Ray Austin

Matter of Life and Death

w Art Wallace

When Dr Russell's husband mysteriously appears after years spent drifting in space, and warns the Alphans that his planet is composed of anti-matter, his warning arrives too late to save several of Koenig's team from being destroyed.
Lee Russell Richard Johnson
Parks Stuart Damon

Director: Charles Crichton

Earthbound

w Anthony Terpiloff

When an alien spaceship crashlands on Alpha, Commissioner Simmonds, who was visiting moonbase when it was blasted out of orbit, sees a chance to return to Earth – providing its captain, Zandor, allows him to do so.
Commissioner Simmonds Roy Dotrice
Zandor Christopher Lee

Director: Charles Crichton

The Full Circle

w Jesse Lasky Jr and Pat Silver

When two Alpha cruisers get caught in a time warp, the crews find they are hunting themselves in an age before they were born. Koenig nearly loses his life and, little realising that he is hunting his friends, Carter sets out to destroy the 'primitives'.
Spearman Oliver Cotton

Director: Bob Kellett

Another Time Another Place

w Johnny Byrne

Alpha finds itself and its occupants duplicated by a strange space phenomenon, and Koenig is surprised to see Earth again. But it is a duplicate earth, with an identical moon – and the Alphans meet themselves!
Regina Judy Geeson

Director: David Tomblin

The Last Sunset

w Christopher Penfold

The Alphans prepare for Operation Exodus. A new planet, Ariel-Alpha, has been discovered which closely resembles Earth and offers hope of a new life – but their dreams fade when they discover a new alien force.

Director: Charles Crichton

The Infernal Machine

w Anthony Terpiloff and Elizabeth Barrows

Koenig and Dr Russell meet the Companion, an old man who built a computerised spaceship and programmed his own personality into its computers. He is now the computer's slave – and he wants the Earthlings to remain as its human companions until they die!
Companion Leo McKern

Director: David Tomblin

Ring Around the Moon

w Edward Di Lorenzo

Moonbase Alpha comes under threat from the Tritons, an alien race who plan to attack Earth. To gather information for their invasion, they begin killing off Koenig's people – and beam Dr Russell aboard their ship.
Ted Clifford Max Faulkner

Director: Ray Austin

Missing Link

w Edward Di Lorenzo

A scientist from the planet Zenno takes Koenig prisoner to study him as a

representative of ancient Earth. His daughter, Vana, falls in love with the Earthman – and Koenig finds himself bewitched by her charms.
Raan Peter Cushing
Vana Joanna Dunham

Director: Ray Austin

Space Brain

w Christopher Penfold
Two Alphan astronauts are sent to investigate a strange organism in space. Their Eagle is destroyed and the alien being takes possession of crew-member Kelly's mind. Meanwhile Koenig and his team are threatened with total extinction.
Kelly Shane Rimmer
Melita Carla Romanelli
Wayland Derek Anders

Director: Charles Crichton

The Troubled Spirit

w Johnny Byrne
When Koenig refuses to allow Mateo to continue with his experiments (he has been trying to communicate with plants), and the man dies, within hours a strange spirit materialises to avenge his death – which has yet to occur!
Mateo Giancarlo Prette
Laura Adams Hilary Dwyer
Dr Warren Anthony Nicholls

Director: Ray Austin

The Testament of Arkadia

w Johnny Byrne
Koenig finds himself trying to save Moonbase Alpha from the power of Arkadia, a planet that once sustained life but is now barren. His attempts to do so are hampered by two Alphans – who wish to start a new civilisation on the planet.
Ferro Orso Maria Guerrini
Anna Lisa Harrow

Director: David Tomblin

The Last Enemy

w Bob Kellett
Finding itself in the middle of an interplanetary war between two hostile planets, Koenig must try to negotiate a ceasefire so that Dione, a commander from one of the planets who has crash-landed on Alpha, can return home – but her enemies refuse to concede defeat.
Dione Caroline Mortimer
Theia Maxine Audley
Talos Kevin Stoney

Director: Bob Kellett

Season Two
24 colour 60-minute episodes

The Metamorph

w Johnny Byrne
When two of his crew are captured by Mentor, an evil alien from the planet Psychon, Koenig and Dr Russell lead a rescue mission to save them. They too become captives – but are helped to escape by Maya, Mentor's daughter.
Maya Catherine Schell (Intro.)
Mentor Brian Blessed
Annette Anouska Hempel

Director: Charles Crichton

The Exiles

w Donald James
Two innocent-looking young aliens, rescued by Koenig's team, wreak disaster and havoc on Moonbase when they take over Alpha and abduct Tony and Dr Russell – whom they transport to their home planet.
Cantar Peter Duncan
Zova Stacy Dorning
Mirella Margaret Inglis

Director: Ray Austin

Journey to Where

w Donald James
When Alpha receives a radio message from the USA (!), Koenig, Dr Russell and Alan Carter become involved in a strange journey through time and they end up back on Earth in the year 1339 – during the scourge of the Black Death.
Dr Logan Freddie Jones
Carla Isla Blair
MacDonald Roger Bizley

Director: Tom Clegg

One Moment of Humanity

w Tony Barwick

Dr Russell and Tony Verdeschi are taken captive by Zamara, a beautiful female alien who wishes them to give her the secret of emotion. She is the leader of a species of androids and she wants to make them human.

Zamara Billie Whitelaw
Zarl Leigh Lawson
Number Eight Geoffrey Bayldon

Director: Charles Crichton

Brian the Brain

w Jack Ronder

An all-powerful robot, originally created on Earth, kidnaps Koenig and Dr Russell and takes them to a distant planet. Tony and Maya mount a rescue mission − not knowing that they're placing Koenig's life in danger.

Captain Michael Bernard Cribbins

Director: Kevin Connor

New Adam, New Eve

w Terence Feely

Magus, a space being who believes himself to be 'God', offers the Alphans the opportunity to begin a new Garden of Eden − by matching Koenig and Maya as the new Adam and Eve.

Magus Guy Rolfe

Director: Val Guest

The Mark of Archanon

w Lew Schwartz

Alan Carter and crewman Johnson find a man-made metal coffin. Dr Russell revives its two occupants, Pasc and his son, Etrec, with disastrous results. A deadly disease affects Pasc which threatens to infect the whole of Moonbase.

Pasc John Standing
Etrec Michael Gallagher

Director: Charles Crichton

The Rules of Luton

w Charles Woodgrove

When Koenig and Maya land their Eagle on a lush green planet, within minutes they find themselves transported to another planet where they are forced to fight three hideous aliens.

Alien 1 David Jackson
Alien 2 Godfrey James
Alien 3 Roy Marsden

Director: Val Guest

All That Glisters

w Keith Miles

A planet possessed by living rocks, beings that can communicate, move and fire death-bringing rays. That's the situation that Tony Verdeschi and Dr Russell find themselves facing when they land on a planet to search for mineral specimens.

Reilly Patrick Mower

Director: Ray Austin

Seeds of Destruction

w John Goldsmith

Jewel-like asteroids seem to be causing a power-loss on Alpha. Koenig and Alan Carter fly to an asteroid to investigate − and Koenig finds himself facing a duplicate of himself, which returns to Alpha in his place!

Director: Kevin Connor

The Taybor

w Thomas Keyes

Taybor, an insterstellar slave-trader, lands on Alpha bearing the 'gift' of a jump-drive device that could take Koenig's people back to Earth. There's just one catch − he wants Maya as payment!

Taybor Willoughby Goddard

Director: Bob Brooks

The A B Chrysalis

w Tony Barwick

A planet sending energy beams into space is causing serious damage to Alpha − which

finds itself being drawn into a collision course with the planet. Koenig leads a team to investigate — and discovers a species of horrifying alien monsters.
A Ina Skriver
B Sarah Douglas

Director: Val Guest

A Matter of Balance

w Pip and Jane Baker
Whilst exploring an apparently lifeless planet, the Alphans find an ancient temple, but its guardian allows only crew-woman Shermeen to enter. She meets Vindrus, the keeper of the temple — who has plans to enslave the Alphans.
Shermeen Lynne Frederick
Vindrus Stuart Wilson

Director: Charles Crichton

Space Warp

w Charles Woodgrove
When Alpha slips through a space warp and is thrown 500 miles off its course — Tony Verdeschi and Alan Carter, returning from a mission in an Eagle, are left behind. Meanwhile, a strange fever begins to affect the Alphans.

Director: Peter Medak

The Beta Cloud

w Charles Woodgrove
Koenig's people are attacked by a huge terrifying space creature which appears impervious to the Alphans' laser blasts. The creature seems unstoppable — unless Maya can transform herself into a deadly virus.

Director: Robert Lynn

The Lambda Factor

w Terence Dicks
With Koenig suffering from terrible nightmares and Alpha affected by a series of strange incidents, Dr Russell investigates a gas cloud which has turned Carolyn Powell into a superhuman being.
Carolyn Powell Deborah Fallander
Mark Saunders Jess Conrad

Director: Charles Crichton

The Bringers of Wonder (Part 1)

w Terence Feely
When a spaceship from Earth lands on Moonbase Alpha and its pilot, Tony Verdeschi's brother Guido, steps out to greet the Alphans, it appears that the Alphans have finally won their battle to return home. Then why is Koenig ordering the newcomers to be destroyed?!

The Bringers of Wonder (Part 2)

Being treated by an experimental Brain Impulse Machine, Koenig appears to be the only Alphan who sees the strangers as aliens. Is he alone suffering from hallucinations — or will Maya learn the truth and rescue her comrades?
Guido Stuuart Damon
Dr Shaw Patrick Westwood

Director: Tom Clegg

The Seance Spectre

w Donald James
Sighting a giant planet on a direct collision course with Alpha, Koenig and Maya take off in Eagle One to examine the planet. Unknown to them, a group of dissident Alphans have sabotaged their spaceship — and Eagle One crashes.
Sanderson Ken Hutchison
Eva Carolyn Seymour

Director: Peter Medak

Dorzac

w Pip and Jane Baker
When a spaceship carrying Sahala, a pretty young alien, requests permission to land on Alpha, it plunges Maya into a battle of wits with Dorzac, a dangerous criminal from her own planet.
Dorzac Lee Montague
Sahala Jill Townsend

Director: Charles Crichton

Devil's Moon

w Michael Winder
Koenig is captured and held prisoner by three alien catwomen, who carry electrical

whips with which to overpower their enemies. He is told that the only way to win his freedom is through an ordeal called 'The Hunt'.
Catwoman Hildegard Neil

Director: Tom Clegg

Return of the Dorcons

w Johnny Byrne

A Dorcon battle-cruiser attacks Moonbase Alpha, and the Dorcon leader Varda demands that Koenig hands over Maya. Aware that they intend to use her as a guinea pig, Koenig refuses – and the Dorcons invade Alpha.
Varda Ann Firbank
Archon Patrick Troughton
Malik Gerry Sundquist

Director: Charles Crichton

The Immunity Syndrome

w Johnny Byrne

Koenig leads a reconnaisance team to investigate an Earth-type planet. Landing on its surface the group separate. Moments later Koenig and Alan Carter find Tony Verdeschi nearly dead. They try to take him back to Alpha – but their Eagle crash-lands back on the planet's surface.

Zoran Nadine Sawalha
Travis Karl Held
Joe Ron Boyd

Director: Tom Clegg

Catacombs of the Moon

w Anthony Terpiloff

Laying explosive charges in an underground cavern, Crewman Osgood begins to receive strange visions of doom. The Alpha sensors detect a strange heat surge, Osgood goes insane and Koenig is left to face the terrible force which has caused the mystery.
Osgood James Laurenson
Michelle Osgood Pamela Stephenson

Director: Robert Lynn

SPACE 1999
Producers: Sylvia Anderson (Season One)
Fred Frieberger (Season Two)
Executive producer: Gerry Anderson
Music by: Barry Gray
Special effects: Brian Johnson
An ITC Production
48 colour 60-minute episodes
4 September 1975 – 19 February 1976
4 September 1976 – 1 May 1977
(USA Syndicated 1975)

SPACE PATROL

The adventures of Captain Larry Dart of Space Patrol – men from Earth, Mars and Venus who banded together as the United Galactic Guardians of Peace.

The 'star' of this forgotten puppet series was Space Captain Larry Dart, the commander of Galasphere 347, Space Patrol's main space vehicle who, together with Husky the Martian and Slim the Venusian, patrolled the solar system in search of adventure.

CHARACTER VOICES

Captain Larry Dart Dick Vosburgh   *Husky/Slim* Ronnie Stevens
Colonel Raeburn Murray Cash   *Professor Haggerty* Ronnie Stevens
Female voices Libby Morris

Season One
26 monochrome 15-minute episodes

The Swamps of Jupiter

When a team of scientists exploring Jupiter fail to report in, Colonel Raeburn sends Captain Larry Dart and his crew to find out why. Landing on the planet, they are told by a friendly native that the scientists were killed by Martians.

The Dark Planet

Professor Haggerty, an Irish scientist with a touch of genius (and madness) who works with his daughter Cassiopeia, discovers a new breed of plant which has the ability to walk and talk.

The Shrinking Spaceman

Larry Dart and his crew are sent to inspect a sonar beam transmitter, stationed on an asteroid of Pallas, which has ceased to function. As they land on the asteroid, radiation emitted by the beacon causes Husky to shrink.

The Fires of Mercury

When Professor Haggerty's new invention, a machine which can translate the language of ants, is found to change infra-red rays into radio waves, it spells trouble for Captain Dart and his crew.

The Slaves of Neptune

There is further trouble afoot for Captain Dart when Husky adopts a large, noisy Martian parrot, Gabbladictum, as his pet.

The Robot Revolution

Granted two weeks leave, Slim goes home to Venus while Larry and Husky visit an Atlantic underwater farm run by Jim Barratt. Scarcely have they arrived, when an undersea eruption plunges them into a new adventure.

The Cloud of Death

When the sky grows dark and alien invaders hide inside the mists waiting to attack an isolated city, Captain Dart and the crew of the Galasphere 347 find themselves in a deadly game of cat and mouse with the enemy.

The Rings of Saturn

When Dart encounters a Saturnian ship in space and is taken to the planet's surface to meet its leader, a reptilian, his adventure ends with the Saturnians becoming members of the United Galactic Organisation.

The Forgers

Because Captain Dart and his crew are on leave, Colonel Raeburn must investigate the glut of forged banknotes flooding the world's currency markets, alone.

Time Watch (aka Time Stands Still)

Professor Haggerty invents a time watch which will speed up Dart's reactions 60 times and make him invisible, so that he is able to defeat the threats of Martian Zota who is holding Mars ransom.

The Human Fish

Larry, Slim and Husky are sent to investigate reports that a breed of fish on the planet Venus is rapidly developing human characteristics and starting to attack fishermen.

The Talking Bell

Out hunting, Colonel Raeburn and Professor Haggerty trap a strange bell-like creature with one leg and it isn't long before the Space Patrol crew discover that the creature also talks – and becomes an unwanted nuisance.

The Wandering Asteroid

When the Space Patrol Martian observatory locates a huge comet that has pulled an asteroid out of its orbit, Larry, Slim and Husky are sent on a mission to destroy it before it can collide with inhabited worlds.

The Glowing Eggs of Titan

The President of Mars contacts Colonel Raeburn and explains that his world is facing a crisis. The electricity supplies of Mars are running low. The crew of Galasphere 347 are sent to investigate.

The Planet of Thought

It's a day to celebrate. Colonel Raeburn is expecting a visit from Tyro, leader of the Neptunians, who wishes to discuss terms for joining the United Galactic Organisation.

The Invisible Martian (aka Husky Becomes Invisible)

When Professor Zeifer of the Martian observatory invents a machine for measuring the distance between the stars, Husky finds the machine has other, unforeseen properties – its rays make him invisible.

Message from a Star

Continuing with his experiments, Professor Zeifer picks up some strange sounds from Alpha Centauri. Soon a space creature from another galaxy arrives and shows Larry how to modify the Galasphere to enable it to fly back to his star system.

The Miracle Tree of Saturn

Earth is being attacked by a mysterious fungus which is destroying all food and plant life. The only things that can stop it are the leaves from the Miracle Tree of Saturn. Larry and his crew are sent to collect some – with a stowaway on board.

Mystery on the Moon

Space headquarters is shaken by an explosion – the third such explosion within a month. Larry, Husky and Slim are sent to the Moon to discover the unknown source of the catastrophe.

Planet of Light

Heading back to Earth from a mission, Larry and his crew are surprised when a strange spaceship appears on their flight path – and even more surprised when two light filaments appear from it and ask to board the Galasphere.

The Buried Space Ship

It's crisis time on Mars again. Colonel Raeburn is notified by the President of the planet that the drought situation on Mars is worsening. Captain Dart and his crew are sent to help.

The Invisible Invasion

Larry Dart and his team find themselves facing their most unusual adventure yet – an invasion by unseen attackers. But how does one combat an enemy who is invisible?

The Walking Lake of Jupiter

Informed by scientists from the planet Jupiter that they have discovered a strange lake that moves, Colonel Raeburn sends the Galasphere 347 to investigate the water mass.

Explosion of the Sun

Earth is in danger of burning up from a tremendous heatwave caused by an enormous explosion on the sun's surface. What can the Space Patrol do to rectify the situation?

Volcanoes of Venus

When Maria, Colonel Raeburn's absent-minded Venusian secretary, finally remembers that she has something important to tell her chief about a strange virus that is paralysing her home planet, Captain Dart must act with the utmost urgency to alleviate disaster.

The New Planet

When Galasphere 347 goes off course and heads into deep space, Captain Dart and his crew enter an adventure in which they discover a new planet beyond Pluto which is populated by Earth-type giants.

Season Two
13 monochrome 15-minute episodes

The Unknown Asteroid

Informed that space pirates have plundered another cargo ship, Colonel Raeburn sends Captain Dart to track them to their hideout – an asteroid deep in space.

The Evil Eye of Venus

Captain Dart and his gallant crew set off on another adventure to save Earth from destruction.

Secret Formula

Flying home after a mission, Larry and his team are faced with disaster when Husky finds himself unable to break free from a steel cobweb on an alien planet desert.

The Telepathic Robot

Professor Haggerty's latest invention, 'Busy Lizzie', a robot who obeys its controller through brain impulses, soon finds a mind of its own – and begins to cause mischief.

The Deadly Whirlwind

Captain Dart and his crew are given the task of spraying a chemical formula over the Martian vegetation, to stop a dust virus destroying Martian supplies.

The Jitter Waves

Colonel Raeburn assigns the Space Patrol team to discover what is behind the latest threat to Earth – the Earth's surface is being shaken by an unknown force.

Sands of Death

The hapless president of Mars has more problems. This time he informs Colonel Raeburn that the leader of the opposition party on the planet intends to use nerve gas to take control.

The Hairy Men of Mars

Forced to land Galasphere 347 in the unexplored equatorial jungle of Mars, Captain Dart and his crew find the Martian equivalent of the missing link.

The Grass of Saturn

A new leader, unsympathetic to the UGO, assumes power on Saturn and threatens to conquer Earth by planting a Saturnian species of grass there. Colonel Raeburn has other ideas.

Force Field X

Extreme heat forces Colonel Raeburn to send Larry and his crew into the outer reaches of the stratosphere with a probe machine to seek the reason.

The Water Bomb

Is there no end to his problems? This time the President of Mars, three-quarters of which is desert, asks Colonel Raeburn to urge Professor Haggerty to speed up his work to discover a device to make Mars fertile.

Destruction by Sound

Professor Zeifer has invented a new machine which can transmit a person from Earth to Mars in 30 seconds – Captain Dart is the first guinea pig.

The Shrinking Gas of Jupiter

Galasphere crewman Slim becomes even slimmer when on a visit to Jupiter he encounters a weird gas which causes him to shrink.

SPACE PATROL
Created and written by: Roberta Leigh
Producers: Roberta Leigh and Arthur Provis
Director: Frank Goulding
Modelwork: Derek Freeborn
Special effects and animation: Bill Palmer, Brian Stevens, Bert Walker
A National Interest Picture Production/ Wonderama Productions Ltd
39 monochrome 15-minute episodes
7 April 1963 – 8 February 1964
3 July 1966 – 28 July 1968

SPECIAL BRANCH

A series that introduced a new breed of copper to British television, Inspector Jordan of the Special Branch, a trendy, well-dressed policeman with an eye for the ladies. He worked directly under his chief, Superintendent Eden, the man assigned the task of running Scotland Yard's SB division, a team of spy-hunters whose duties led them into situations that threatened national security – little-known heroes whose job was to protect VIPs under a cloak of secrecy.

After two seasons (produced on videotape) had proved successful, the show was revamped and recast. Jordan had disappeared, as had Supt Eden (and Detective Superintendent Inman, the man who replaced him mid-way through the first season).

Starring this time around was Detective Chief Inspector Alan Craven and, after two stories, Detective Chief Inspector Tom Haggerty. Also introduced were Detective Sergeant North and Commander Nicols – both of whom were replaced for the fourth season by Commander Fletcher, and Strand, a high-powered, toffee-nosed civil servant, whose main objective appeared to be that of keeping the detectives on their toes – and the department's running costs low.

Notable for being the first filmed series produced by Euston Films.

REGULAR CAST

Videotaped series
Insp. Jordan **Derren Nesbitt**   *Supt Eden* (Eps 1 – 7) **Wensley Pithey**
Det. Supt Inman (Ep 8 onwards) **Fulton Mackay**
Filmed series
Det. Chf Insp. Craven **George Sewell**   *Det. Chf Insp. Haggerty* **Patrick Mower**
DS North **Roger Rowland**   *Commander Nicols* **Richard Butler**
Commander Fletcher **Frederick Jaeger**   *Strand* **Paul Eddington**

Season One

13 colour 60-minute episodes
(Episodes marked with an asterisk
transmitted in b/w)

Troika*

w George Markstein
Troika – the codename for a top secret
security net thrown around hostile agents.
But has the net been broken? That's the
challenge facing Superintendent Eden's
department as he endeavours to plug a
security leak.
Supt Eden **Wensley Pithey** (Intro.)
Insp. Jordan **Derren Nesbitt** (Intro.)
Det. Chf Insp. Harris **Anthony Sagar** (Intro.)

Director: **Dennis Vance**

The Promised Land*

w Trevor Preston
For many immigrants England holds the
status of the Promised Land, but as Eden
and his team discover when investigating a
shipload of immigrants deposited at the
docks who are then left to fend for
themselves, the milk and honey turns to
bread and water.
Vousden **Windsor Davies**
Dr Bukht **Uska Joshi**
Rushner **Geoffrey Bayldon**

Director: **Dennis Vance**
Designer: **Roger Allen**

A Date with Leonides*

w C. Scott Forbes
A teenager's vow of vengeance leads to
Inspector Jordan interrupting a wedding
and Superintendent Eden accepting a parcel
that contains death. Before the day is over
both men have cause for concern.

Leonides **Damien Thomas**
Katerina **Tamara Hinchco**
Mr Snell **Robert Webber**

Director: **Dennis Vance**
Designer: **Peter Le Page**

The Kazmirov Affair

w Emanuel Litvinoff
Informed that the manuscript of a Russian
author's novel which has been smuggled
into Britain is a forgery and could discredit
the Government, Inspector Jordan goes
against orders and investigates the claim.
Prof. Croucher **Edward Burnham**
Peter Brovnik **John Bailey**
Douglas Lifford **Gerald Sim**

Director: **Mike Vardy**
Designer: **Fred Pusey**

A New Face*

w Tom Brennand and Roy Bottomley
If they are to save a man from being killed,
Superintendent Eden's team must put a
name to a face photographed in a crowd.
One of the faces belongs to the intended
victim, the other the man intending to kill
him – but which is which?
Peter Harris **Andrew Bradford**
Mrs Harris **Doreen Mantle**
Det. Chf Insp. Harris **Anthony Sagar**

Director: **Peter Duguid**
Designer: **Neville Green**

You Don't Exist*

w Anthony Skene
When Barbara Cartwright is stopped by
customs officials at London airport and told
that, because England doesn't recognise the
Rhodesian Government, she cannot stay in

Rumpole of the Bailey (Leo McKern).

(Above and right) The Saint
Roger Moore as Simon
Templar.

The Sandbaggers Left to right, Willie Caine, Neil Burnside and Mike Wallace.

Sapphire and Steel (Joanna Lumley and David McCallum).

The Scarlet Pimpernel Marius Goring as Sir Percy Blackeney.

Shadow Squad

Special Branch Insp. Jordan and Det. Supt Inman.

Special Branch Det. Chf Insps. Craven and Haggerty.

Strangers (Above) Unit 23, (Below) The Inner City Squad.

The Sweeney In the story 'Hearts & Minds', two of England's most popular comedians, Morecambe and Wise, starred alongside the crime fighters.

The Top Secret Life of Edgar Briggs

Van Der Valk (Barry Foster).

Virgin of the Secret Service Capt. Robert Virgin and Mrs Virginia Cortez.

Worzel Gummidge

Young Sherlock Holmes

The XYY Man William 'Spider' Scott was played by Stephen Yardley.

this country, the Special Branch are called in – and one of Eden's coppers falls in love.
Barbara Cartwright Mel Martin
Hippie woman Pamela Miles
Hippie man Harry Meacher

Director: Dennis Vance
Designer: Peter Le Page

The Children of Delight*

w Adele Rose
Is there something sinister going on behind the facade of 'The Children of Delight' – a group of hippies who have arrived on Eden's patch. Detective Sergeants Webb and Gifford go undercover to investigate.
DS Webb Wendy Rutter
DS Gifford Sheila Fearn
Charles Moxon Morris Perry

Director: Peter Duguid
Designer: Stan Woodward

Reliable Sources*

w Tom Brennand and Roy Bottomley
Superintendent Eden is on the spot. The Security Commission has met to consider the leak that tipped a spy during the Troika affair. The detective is cleared – but told that he cannot continue his role as Special Branch controller!
Supt Eden Wensley Pithey (Exit)
Deputy Commander David Garth
Clive Bradbury Tony Britton

Director: Dennis Vance
Designer: David Marshall

Short Change

w George Markstein
The Troika affair refuses to go away. It appears that the 'other side' wish to exchange a spy, but Detective Superintendent Inman, the department's new controller, thinks they are up to no good – and he wants results. Fast!
Det. Supt Inman Fulton Mackay (Intro.)
Christine Morris Sandra Bryant
Charlie Brewer Maurice Good

Director: William G. Stewart
Designer: Fred Pusey

Exit a Diplomat

w George Markstein
When a member of a foreign embassy is caught shoplifting in London, but tries to hide her status by willingly accepting arrest, Superintendent Inman takes an interest in her employers.
Mira Kobylnova Barbara Leigh-Hunt
Jan Kobylnova George Pravda
Colonel Donald Bissett

Director: Voytek
Designer: Colin Andrews

Care of Her Majesty

w Robert Banks Stewart
When Jordan arrives at an overseas British Embassy to investigate the theft of £10,000 from its strongroom, his heavy-handed methods create immediate friction with the Ambassador and his team of officials.
Colonel Dysart Lindsay Campbell
Sir Percy Challis Geoffrey Lumsden
Sarah Landring Hilary Dwyer

Director: Jonathan Alwyn
Designer: Roger Allen

Visitor from Moscow

w Paul Wheeler
When a KGB officer is sent to London to coordinate security measures with the SB team for the forthcoming visit of a Russian VIP, Inman instructs Jordan to help him – with disastrous results.
Karamov Alan Browning
Mary Pearce Helena Ross
Peter Watson Jack Shepherd

Director: Dennis Vance
Designer: Peter Le Page

Time Bomb

w David Gordon
Sent to investigate the death of the son of a pro-British oil sheikh in a bomb plot, Superintendent Inman finds a hotbed of intrigue and a dangerous international situation about to explode in his face.

Sheikh Abhil Harold Kasket
Omar Ben Abhil Galmaan Peer
Beryl Gilliam Hawser

Director: Voytek
Designer: Colin Andrews

(Note: A story entitled 'Smokescreen' was transmitted as the second story in some regions. Beyond the title and the writer (George Markstein), I have been unable to confirm any other production details.)

Season Two
13 colour 60-minute episodes

Inside

w Trevor Preston
Jordan finds himself in Wormwood Scrubs. What's he up to? No one is saying – least of all Supt Inman, who believes that time is running out in a situation that could place his department in danger.
Scace Constantin de Goguel
Gillard Michael Goodliffe
Falk Kenneth Watson

Director: Guy Verney
Designer: Fred Pusey

Dinner Date

w George Markstein
Jordan flies to Frankfurt to escort a British subject, Selby, back to England. Selby had disappeared three years earlier in East Germany and the British Government are anxious to learn what he's been up to – but the Russian KGB hide in the shadows.
Selby John Rolfe
Pohl Frederick Jaeger
Bauer John Bailey

Director: William G. Stewart
Designer: Neville Green

Depart in Peace

w Alan Falconer
A retired Special Branch officer has promised to give evidence against a former terrorist, but refuses to do so when called. Moxon and Inman decide to find out why the man changed his mind.

Moxon Morris Perry (Intro.)
Edward Kirk David Langton
Mary Kirk Pauline Letts

Director: Mike Vardy
Designer: Mike Hall

Miss International

w Tom Brennand and Roy Bottomley
What appeared to be a straightforward case – protecting the wife of a foreign VIP, who has entered a beauty competition in the cause of female emancipation for her own country – turns into a nightmare situation for Insp. Jordan.
Frida Gemal Jasmina Hilton
Nina Saretna Yutte Stensgard
Miss Amsterdam Rona Bower

Director: James Goddard
Designer: Neville Green

Warrant for a Phoenix

w Stewart Farrar
An accusation of theft against a highly respected Greek historian sets the Special Branch team a problem. Interpol have requested his extradition from England – but Inman isn't satisfied with the facts of the case.
Emile Kuzatos Paul Stassino
Proudie Clifford Rose
Loukia Kuzatos Monica Vassilion

Director: Jim Goddard
Designer: David Marshall

The Pleasure of Your Company

w George Markstein
Inman meets the CIA's new man in London. Jordan meets an old friend from Moscow. All perfectly legal – until the two men are seen together at regular intervals and the Special Branch team become involved in international politics.
Lester Swift Bruce Boa
Ed Potter Daniel Moynihan
Anatoli Golovin Peter Arne

Director: William G. Stewart
Designer: Colin Andrews

Not to Be Trusted

w George Markstein

Is an eminent scientist, on loan to a top-secret research establishment, a security risk? That's the question facing Inman and his team. The research establishment is suddenly prone to 'leaks'. Has the man been got at?

Sir Hugh Lodge Ronald Russell
Dr Clifford William Lucas
Karin Aria Marson

Director: Guy Verney
Designer: Peter Le Page

Borderline Case

w Lewis Greifer

While a member of the SB team keeps watch on Karl Peter's flat, Inman and his team scan through his charge sheet. They believe he will attempt to incite London dockworkers into taking industrial action against their employers.

Karl Peters Richard Durden
Insp. Williams Richard Davies
Hoffman Leon Rissek

Director: Tom Clegg
Designer: Mike Hall

Love from Doris

w C. Scott Forbes

When military security intercepts letters written to a lonely serviceman by his foreign 'penpal' Rita, which contain casual references to secret information, Supt Inman sends DS Jordan to investigate.

Major Carter John Woodnutt
Lisa Georgina Hale
Drysdale Kevin Stoney

Director: John Russell
Designer: Colin Andrews

Sorry is Just a Word

w Michael Chapman

When a Czech au-pair goes missing in London and her father is one of the most powerful men in the country, Inman and Jordan must find out what's happened to her. But their enquiries lead to a dead end.

Karolina Gabrielle Drake
DS Jarvis James Cossins
DS Pritchard Colin Rix

Director: James Goddard
Designer: Mike Hall

Error of Judgement

w Peter Hill

When Inman discovers that 'The Guardians' are taking a more-than-usual interest in a group of pro-germ-warfare people and finds that their leader is a pretty girl, he decides to send Jordan along to question her.

Angela Ballie Miranda Connell
Colonel Harkstead Basil Dignam
Sgt Edwards Michael Lynch

Director: Guy Verney
Designer: Nigel Green

Reported Missing

w Louis Marks

An attractive Russian ballerina from a visiting ballet company goes missing. Jordan has doubts about the report's authenticity, but Inman goes out on a limb to champion the girl's cause — with disastrous results.

Lynda Tamarov Nicola Pagett
Sheila Franklyn Sheila Ruskin
Ilena Petrova Rachel Herbert

Director: Dennis Vance
Designer: Mike Hall

Fool's Mate

w George Markstein

When Britain's top code and cypher breaker is forced to mingle with Communist players during a chess tournament, Inman goes along to keep an eye on him. Moxon, meanwhile, is playing a dangerous game of his own: the pawn being Jordan.

Christopher Haddon Simon Lack
Christine Morris Sandra Bryant
Deputy Commander David Garth

Director: Dennis Vance
Designer: Peter Le Page

Season Three
13 colour 60-minute episodes

A Copper Called Craven

w Roger Marshall

A new beginning and a new threat to the
Special Branch team. Detective Chief
Inspector Alan Craven occupies his desk for
the first time – and immediately comes
under suspicion of taking bribes.
Craven George Sewell (Intro.)
DS North Roger Rowland (Intro.)
Commander Nicols Richard Butler (Intro.)

Director: William Brayne

Round the Clock

w Tom Brennand and Roy Bottomley

Joined by his old adversary Inspector Tom
Haggerty, who has been transferred from
Scotland Yard, Craven sets out to seek a
known villain whom he believes is plotting
a crime. Haggerty thinks otherwise: he
believes the man is dead.
Pam Sloane Sheila Scott-Wilkinson (Intro.)
Chf Supt Knight Richard Leech
Frank Perry Sinclair

Director: Mike Vardy

Inquisition

w Trevor Preston

Brought in by Craven on fraud charges,
Yearsley astonishes everyone by admitting
the crime – then accuses Craven of
persecuting him. Sgt North sees a way to
clear his boss – but can he do so before
Craven makes a blunder?
Yearsley Clifford Rose
Shepherd Alan Downer
Manning Keith Anderson

Director: Mike Vardy

Assault

w Tom Brennand and Roy Bottomley

Every city has its muggers, thugs who run
wild through the streets. London proves no
exception, but this is mugging with a
difference – one that brings the Special
Branch team onto the streets.

Townsend Richard Vernon
Mr Haggerty Robert Keegan
Bernard Philips John Plume

Director: Douglas Camfield

Polonaise

w Alan Scott and Chris Bryant

A Polish cargo and passenger ship steams
towards London. Its captain, Wedniki,
receives a radio-telegram informing him
that he is going to be killed on arrival.
Craven and Haggerty move in to protect
Wedniki – but are they themselves safe
from harm?
Wedniki Richard Warner
Scabrienski Andre Morell
Embassy official Milos Kirek

Director: Mike Vardy

Red Herring

w Peter Hill

Craven and North join forces with bomb-
disposal expert Captain Dwyer to find a
group of terrorists who have been planting
bombs all over London – and who threaten
to kill more people unless their demands are
met.
Captain Dwyer Norman Jones
Borotchek Leon Eagles
Sarah Diane Quick

Director: Mike Vardy

Death by Drowning

w John Kershaw

Haggerty and Craven must sift through the
clues to decide if the body of a young girl
found floating in the Thames was the result
of murder or suicide. Their enquiries
unearth more than they expected.
Chf Supt Knight Richard Leech
Mrs Dolland Gwen Watford
Wolfram Arto Morris

Director: Dennis Vance

All the King's Men

w Trevor Preston

Craven and North find themselves facing a
dangerous opponent. Sumner, an

emotionally unbalanced man, is threatening to blow up a block of flats near to the Houses of Parliament. He has already taken a young girl as hostage and Craven must free her – without tipping the man over the edge of his emotional limit.

Sumner Geoffrey Bayldon
Mrs Sumner Ursula Howells
Webb Brian Haines

Director: Dennis Vance

Threat

w Tom Brennand and Roy Bottomley
When British-born Hollywood film star Sue Arden arrives in London, and receives a tip-off from the FBI that she may be a target for a murder attempt, the Special Branch team are assigned to protect her.

Sue Arden Stephanie Beacham
Hon. James Bancroft Jack Hedley
McCall Frank Barrie

Director: William Brayne

The Other Man

w Roger Marshall
Acting on a tip-off from another Special Branch man, Craven and North find themselves investigating Dr Lovett, a man suspected of passing information to the enemy. But is the man really a traitor? Are the policemen on the right track?

Dr Lovett Roger Hume
Sarah Lovett Annette Crosbie
Denning John Arnatt

Director: Dennis Vance

You Won't Remember Me

w Anthony Skene
It's an unusual assignment: Craven is ordered to keep an eye on a young couple who are engaged to be married. But why has he been asked to do so? What are the couple up to that requires 24-hour surveillance?

David Michael Latimer
Clare Mary Maude
Sergeant Neal Arden

Director: John Robbins

Hostage

w John Kershaw
Craven and Haggerty are faced with the task of finding a diplomat's kidnapped daughter before the deadline for payment expires and the man carries out his threat to kill the girl..

Muller Michael Gambon
Frau Muller Ann Lynn
Hilda Muller Karen Stark

Director: David Wickes

Blueprint for Murder

w Peter Hill and Ian Black
It's the kind of job the Special Branch are trained for, protecting visiting foreign diplomats during their stay in London. But this time Craven and Haggerty will need all their experience to come away unharmed.

Coatzee Kenneth J. Warren
Graham Alex Scott
Wildebrand Arne Gordon

Director: William Brayne

Season Four

13 colour 60-minute episodes

Double Exposure

w Michael J. Bird
Craven and Haggerty investigate a handsome, successful photographer who takes intimate pictures of the famous. Their assignment: to discover if the man is a patriot – or a threat to national security.

Cmndr Fletcher Frederick Jaeger (Intro.)
Strand Paul Eddington (Intro.)
Steven Gill Stuart Wilson

Director: Don Leaver

Catherine the Great

w John Brason
Informed that Rehfuss, a dangerous assassin, has slipped into the country, Craven is ordered to bring him in. A difficult task: the policeman has no idea what he looks like – or the name of his intended victim.

Rehfuss Tony Beckley
Helga Jacqueline Pearce
DS Isobel Ross Claire Nielson

Director: Douglas Camfield

Jailbait

w Michael Chapman

Craven and Haggerty must find out who organised a jail break which allowed a dangerous traitor to escape. Was it the criminal underworld? Or the spy's foreign friends? A man's life depends on them reaching an answer quickly.

Palliser Paul Shelley
Horniman Barry Keegan
Finch Stephen Grief

Director: William Brayne

Stand and Deliver

w Michael J. Bird

The Special Branch team face an explosive situation when they are asked to find the thieves who stole a top-secret weapon fitted with a new laser device. The weapon is unstable – and could blow up at any time.

Leonard Gosling Ronald Radd
Frank Gosling Dennis Waterman
Jean Gosling Stephanie Turner

Director: Tom Clegg

Something About a Soldier

w Michael J. Bird

When two children run riot in the luggage department at London Airport and cause a mix-up with passengers' baggage, it inadvertently results in the discovery of a sinister secret – which leads Craven to investigate two army officers.

Sgt Crocker Godfrey James
Major Hallett Garfield Morgan
Lydia Rula Lenska

Director: William Brayne

Rendezvous

w Tony Williamson

Craven is put in charge of security for a vital debriefing exercise being held at a derelict mental institution. He has difficulty deciding which of the group is mad – the interrogator, the KGB agent, or the woman being interrogated.

Nadya Chelnov Cyd Hayman
Sir Gerald Geoffrey Chater
Colonel Lang Anthony Nicholls

Director: Terry Green

Sounds Sinister

w David Butler

It's blackmail with a difference. Key public figures are having their dirty linen washed in public by a pirate radio station. Craven and Haggerty tune into the people behind the scheme and DS Ross becomes a DJ.

Philip Weston John Carson
DS Isobel Ross Claire Nielson
Maxie Levinston Stanley Meadows

Director: Terry Green

Entente Cordiale

w John Kershaw

Craven's personal problems intrude into his police activities. Opening his door to a midnight caller, he finds his ex-wife, Claudia. Within hours Craven finds himself suspected of being connected with his wife's terrorist activities.

Claudia Dora Reisser
Jean Paul George Murcell
Le Fevre Al Mancini

Director: William Brayne

Date of Birth

w Lewis Greifer

A spy is killed in Canada and Craven must find out what connection he had with a young au-pair working in London. A girl he apparently never met, but whose welfare the dead man had watched from afar.

Commander Glover Richard Beale
DS Mary Holmes Susan Jameson
Odette Guttman Mia Nardi

Director: Don Leaver

Intercept

w Ian Kennedy Martin

The Special Branch team face a quandry. Why should Morales, a foreign VIP whose help is vital to Britain, turn out to be as dubious as the thugs who relieve him of a fortune in diamonds? Craven is given the job of finding out.

Morales Walter Gotell
Hodges Maxwell Shaw
Paddy Regan Patrick Duggan

Director: William Brayne

Alien

w Ray Jenkins

Gunter Hellman, a student revolutionary, is allowed into Britain with his wife Gisela to continue his studies. The condition of his entry permit states that he must not engage in political activities. Suspecting that he has, Craven and Haggerty pay him a call.
Hellman **Damien Thomas**
Gisela **Ann Firbank**
Professor Denny **Patrick Troughton**

Director: **Douglas Camfield**

Diversion

w Peter J. Hammond

Why has Strand suddenly begun a relationship with a lady colleague and started to drink heavily? Has the pressure finally caught up with him? Or is he playing a solo game to unmask a villain.
Beth Summers **Nicolette McKenzie**
Lister **John Cairney**
Tim Summers **Denis Lil**

Director: **William Brayne**

Downwind of Angels

w Peter Hill

The media carries the news: 'Murder at Maison Igor's.' Craven and his team must use their own approach to get a line on an unseen gunman now stalking the London streets intent on further killings.

Igor **Peter Bowles**
DS Holmes **Susan Jameson**
Fountain **Peter Blythe**

Director: **Tom Clegg**

SPECIAL BRANCH
Season One and Two
Producers: Reginald Collin (Eps 1 – 7)
Robert Love (Remainder)
Series editor: George Markstein
Story editor: Maggie Allen
26 colour 60-minute episodes

Season Three
Producer: Geoffrey Gilbert
Executive producer: Lloyd Shirley
Music by: Robert Earley
Script editor: Ian Black
13 colour 60-minute episodes

Season Four
Producer: Ted Childs
Executive producers: Lloyd Shirley and George Taylor
Music by: Robert Earley
Script editor: Ian Black
13 colour 60-minute episodes
A Thames Television Network Production
52 colour 60-minuite episodes
17 September – 17 December 1969
11 August – 4 November 1970
4 April – 4 July 1973
14 February – 9 May 1974
(USA: Season Four syndicated 1976)

SPYDER'S WEB

'Who is the Spyder and for which side does it weave?' That was the intriguing question which complemented the titles for this unusual one-off espionage series created by writer Roy Clark.

The answer was: no one knew – or at least the Spyder wasn't an individual. Well, that isn't quite right, 'he' was – but 'he' was never addressed as Spyder throughout the entire series. In fact 'Spyder' was Charlotte Dean, Clive Hawkesworth or Wallis Ackroyd, depending on which one of the three was working on a case. (Confused? You were meant to be – that's how the series was presented, with lots of twists, red-herrings and a genuine feel for the off-beat.)

The 'web' of the title referred to a mysterious government organisation that was totally unknown to anyone but its 'agents', the three people mentioned above, who handled problems outside the province of official organisations (Scotland Yard, MI5 and others).

The series' premise was that those who weave an international web of espionage often got caught up in the sinister traps of their enemies – therefore Spyder's Web, a team of unusual agents who spun enough 'rope' to hang their enemies.

Played mainly for laughs, it delivered the goods.

REGULAR CAST

Charlotte 'Lottie' Dean **Patricia Cutts**   Clive Hawkesworth **Anthony Ainley**
Wallis Ackroyd **Veronica Carlson**
Albert Mason (Lottie's butler) **Roger Lloyd Pack**

Spyder Secures a Main Strand

w **Roy Clarke**
After a British agent fleeing across a Communist border is picked up by a car, and shot, the Web weaves its way into the hunt for a traitor. A reshuffle of British security is called for and Charlotte accepts the challenge.
Chief **John Savident**
'One' **Oliver Ford-Davies**
'Two' **Derek Chinnery**

Director: **Dennis Vance**

The Executioners

w **Alfred Shaughnessy**
When three people, each in the forefront of the permissive society, are killed, Lottie sets out to expose the executioners by deciding to make herself an irresistible target as the lady behind the bluest film ever made.
Lord Rashmore **Andre Morell**
Peter Fairchild **Richard Kay**
Judge **Donald Layne-Smith**

Director: **Roy Ward Baker**

Romance on Wheels

w **Roy Clark**
Romance on Wheels Ltd is a package tour operator with a difference – its customers fall in love then disappear without trace! Believing that a foreign power is behind the operation, Clive and Lottie board a coach for a not-so-romantic adventure.
Grovnik **Peter Sallis**
Mrs Dewhurst **Helen Lindsay**
Parker **Anthony Sagar**

Director: **James Gatward**

The Hafiz Affair

w **Roy Clark**
Lottie and Hawkesworth set off to find out why an African leader appears to have vanished off the face of the earth, just weeks before his country gains its independence.
General Limbo **Rudolph Walker**
Freddy Hafiz **Earl Cameron**
Diwani **Horace James**

Director: **Dorothy Denham**

Life at a Price

w **Frank Driscoll**
Web is asked to investigate a nursing home that can 'arrange' almost anything. Lottie plays mother to her 'daughter', while Clive dons his 'doctor' hat to unearth a clever murder plot.
Dr Hatchington **Cyril Shaps**
Ambassador **Harold Kasket**
Bodyguard **Sean Lynch**

Director: **Dennis Vance**

Emergency Exit

w David Ellis

Have the 'other side' found a new escape route for agents? To test her theory that they have, Lottie feeds an agent into the enemy's pipeline, then sits back to see what comes out the other end.

Ratznik Kenneth Griffith
Kalashnikov Barry Linehan
Felton Jon Laurimore

Director: David Wickes

Red Admiral

w Alan Hackney

When a government computer coughs up a printout that points to Admiral Manders being a pacifist, Lottie and Clive decide to investigate the Admiral's activities in the field. Just to be sure, they take a camera – and a gun.

Admiral Manders John Barron
Mrs Manders Joan Peart
Michael Manders David Firth

Director: John Cooper

Ladies and Dolls

w Alfred Shaughnessy

The mysterious organisation finds another way to give Lottie her orders – a talking mynah bird, whose little story leads Lottie and Clive into the world of underground art, life size puppets, and international intrigue.

Dr Dolek Mark Eden
Dr Karvony Otto Diamant
Grolik David Nettheim

Director: Dennis Vance

Things That Go Bang in the Night

w Marc Brandel

Why should the family of a blown-up inventor go to so much trouble to discover his final secret weapon? Lottie and Clive find themselves mixing in the shady affairs of a family who seek to make a million by selling off secrets to the 'other side'.

Tom Woffington Daniel Moynihan
Ava Woffington Anne Jameson
Dr Long Mark Heath

Director: Ian Fordyce

An Almost Modern Man

w Roy Clarke

Lottie and Clive find themselves up to their necks in a mystery that involves voodoo, political leaders on the make and an ingenious plot to set civilisation back 1,000 years.

President Baras Mike Pratt
Eva Leila Goldoni
Dominic Peter Birrel

Director: Dennis Vance

Nobody's Strawberry Fool

w Robert Holmes

When a British Secret Service agent, dead since 1941 and preserved in a glacier, finally breaks the ice, many people – including Spyder – lay claim to the body. Lottie is instructed to ensure that Spyder wins the race.

Pyke Allan Cuthbertson
Chief John Savident
Mrs Gibbs Joan Haythorne

Director: John Cooper

The Prevalence of Skeletons

w Marc Brandel

A gadget nicknamed Herbert which prematurely ages both documents and humans, and produces instant skeletons, takes the interest of the Web. Lottie and Clive are assigned to ensure the safety of Whitehall VIPs.

Peter Toney Ferdy Mayne
Sir Nigel Pilgrim Richard Warner
Heather/Val/Julie Lois Baxter

Director: Ian Fordyce

Rev Counter

w Roy Clarke

It can't be happening? Can it? Lottie and Clive find themselves face to face with a very unusual 'villain' – a vicar who is providing spiritual guidance to a gang of freedom-fighters in a mad, mad, mini-war in . . . Hampshire!

Newbold Joe Gladwin
Leader Sean Lynch
Edwards Kenneth J. Warren

Director: Dorothy Denham

SPYDER'S WEB
Created by: Richard Harris
Producer: Dennis Vance
An ATV Network Production
13 colour 60-minute episodes
22 February – 14 April 1972

STRANGERS

The return of Detective Sergeant George Bulman and Detective Constable Derek Willis, last seen in the superb thriller series *The XYY Man* (see entry under that title). This time, they found themselves working side-by-side with a new recruit, Detective Constable Linda Doran, as part of a new four-sided team known as Unit 23 – three officers seconded to the North of England to infiltrate areas of crime where local detectives might have been recognised. Visiting policemen – the strangers. Helping Bulman to run the unit was Detective Sergeant Singer, a local policeman with 15 years' experience under his belt.

This line-up continued unchanged until WDC Doran left the ranks and was replaced by WDC Frances Bennett in the penultimate episode of season two.

With the arrival of the third season, the format had undergone a change. The team were now under the direct command of newcomer Detective Chief Superintendent Lambie, a no-nonsense policeman who had brought the team together to form the Inner City Squad – a team of dedicated trouble-shooters whose brief was to solve crimes nationwide. Willis had gained promotion to Detective Sergeant, and it was during this season that Bulman first met William Dugdale, a university man who was somehow connected with the British Secret Service, and a man with whom Bulman would share many further adventures.

That's how things remained until, at the beginning of season four, Bulman himself was promoted to Detective Chief Inspector.

However, though we'd seen the last of the Inner City Squad, we hadn't seen the last of George Bulman. Five years later, the tough, uncompromising detective would return for a new series of adventures (see entry under *Bulman*).

REGULAR CAST

Det. Sgt George Bulman Don Henderson   *Det. Sgt Willis* Dennis Blanch
Det. Sgt Singer John Ronane   *Det. Chf Supt Lambie* Mark McManus
WDC Doran Frances Tomelty   *WDC Bennett* Fiona Mollison
William Dugdale Thorley Walters

Season One

7 colour 60-minute episodes

The Paradise Set

w Murray Smith

Day one. Willis is working on a diamond robbery. Bulman and Doran are trying to track villains who are systematically beating up nightclub hostesses. The two enquiries lead in one direction and the CID team find themselves working together on the same problem.

DS Bulman Don Henderson (Intro.)
DC Willis Dennis Blanch (Intro.)
DS Singer John Ronane (Intro.)
WDC Doran Frances Tomelty (Intro.)

Director: Carol Wilkes
Designer: Mike Grimes

Duty Roster

w Ivor Marshall

Bulman and Willis find themselves investigating the theft of a mailbag from a postman. A straightforward case? Not when their enquiries point to something fishy afoot.

Det. Insp. Rainbow David Hargreaves (Intro.)
Bill Robinson Jackie Shinn
Crookes William Maxwell

Director: Oliver Horsbrugh
Designer: Chris Wilkinson

Silver Lining

w Steve Wakelam

Assigned to investigate a betting racket, Bulman takes a job in a betting shop, while WDC Doran finds employment with a professional gambler. It isn't long before the detectives discover a link to the horse-racing world.

Jack Slater Hywel Bennett
Glenys Annette Ekblom
Jimmy Paul Duncan

Director: Bill Gilmour
Designer: Colin Rees

Accidental Death

w Brian Finch

WDC Linda Doran working as a journalist! DC Derek Willis helping out at a coroner's office! It's all part of an investigation to find out whether the death of a newspaper man was an accident or murder.

Harker William Russell
Cassandra Harker Briony McRoberts
Harrison Reginald Marsh

Director: Philip Draycott
Designer: Alan Price

Briscoe

w Leslie Duxbury

Is a uniformed police sergeant, suspected of being crooked, really guilty? Bulman poses as a copper on the beat to find out what has led the sergeant to be suspected of being 'dirty' — but finds that an ordinary policeman's lot is not a happy one.

Sgt Briscoe Michael Byrne
Insp. Veevers Michael Turner
Torchy David Neilson

Director: Brian Mills
Designer: Margaret Coombes

Right and Wrong

w C. P. Taylor

Convinced that a local politician is taking bribes, but frustrated that his enquiries have brought no results, DS Singer assigns Willis and Doran to pose as newly-weds and move into the house opposite.

Roy Stevens David Dakar
Council chairman Roger Rowland
Audrey Stevens Anne Reid

Director: John Bruce
Designer: Chris Wilkinson

Paying Guests

w Leslie Duxbury

When a petty crook finds a hoard of hot money and begins to receive unwanted attention from the villains who stole it, Bulman finds himself moving in with the man's family to protect him.

Grafton Parker John Tordoff
Mrs Parker Amanda Barrie
Sgt Briscoe Michael Byrne

Director: Quentin Lawrence
Designer: Colin Rees

Season Two
5 colour 60-minute episodes

The Wheeler Dealers

w Murray Smith

The squad find themselves investigating some odd occurences at the local docks and attempting to discover what links Britain, Ireland and Holland. They follow a trail that leads them to a disued brickworks and the answer – bicycles!
Dr Slater Anne Kristen
WPC West Jo Beadle
Det. Insp. Deacon Neil Johnson

Director: Carol Wilks
Designer: Michael Grimes

Call of the Wild

w Leslie Duxbury

When Bulman successfully infiltrates a gang of villains, it isn't long before he finds himself on the run from the police – and desperately in need of the assistance of his undercover colleagues.
WDC Doran France Tomelty (Last)
Det. White Paul Copely
DS Foster Bob Mason

Director: Baz Taylor
Designer: Chris Wilkinson

Clever Dick

w Brian Finch

When counterfeit Deutschmarks flood Germany and the CID officers try to establish a connection in England, they find themselves facing violent and ruthless opposition from a gang with murder on their minds.
Lennie Brooks John Duttine
Hirsch Gunnar Moller
Barker Geoffrey Chater

Director: Quentin Lawrence
Designer: David Batley

Friends in High Places

w Murray Smith

When a successful businessman begins to receive blackmail threats, the squad expect a straightforward case. They discover more than they bargained for and learn that people in high places prove to be bad losers.
Sir Harry Adams Anthony Steele
Effingham Freddie Jones
DC Bennett Fiona Mollison (Intro.)

Director: Bill Gilmour
Designer: Colin Rees

Marriages, Deaths and Births

w Murray Smith

Bulman's dedication to duty is such that he tries to arrest Carmos, a pyschopathic killer, during his wedding. The squad must use all their ingenuity to extricate him from the villain's clutches – Bulman is wounded and in danger of dying.
Nick Carmos Ben Cross
Aristole Carmos Bill Fraser
Chief Insp. Rainbow David Hargreaves (Last)

Director: Charles Sturridge
Designer: David Buxton

Season Three
7 colour 60-minute episodes

Retribution

w Murray Smith

Assigned to the new Inner City Squad, Bulman and the newly-promoted Detective Sergeant Willis find themselves involved in their first case – tracking down a gang of sophisticated villains who are running an arms-for-sale racket in London.
Det. Chf Supt Lambie Mark McManus (Intro.)
Det. Insp. Casey Bruce Bold (Intro.)
Cressida Lacey Sarah Neville

Director: Carol Wilks
Designer: Tim Wilding

You Can't Win 'Em All

w Murray Smith

Detective Sergeant Bulman and Willis are assigned to a case involving widespread fraud of major banks. Their investigations eventually lead them to Oxford and a clash with Dugdale – a man who will share several adventures with Bulman.

Bill Dugdale Thorley Walters (Intro.)
Sophy Sabina Franklin
Harry Jerome Adam Bareham

Director: Bill Gilmour
Designer: Tim Wilding

Armed and Dangerous

w Murray Smith
Assigned to bring a villain to London for
questioning, Bulman and Willis find their
routine escort duty turns dangerous when
the man's partners in crime, fearing he
might grass on them, decide to eliminate
him.
Det. Insp Casey Bruce Bould (Last)
Eddie Verity Keith Buckley
Jean Rutter Rachel Davies

Director: William Brayne
Designer: Chris Truelove

Racing Certainty

w Murray Smith
Bulman and Willis find themselves working
undercover to track down a gang who are
hedging their bets by ensuring that the odds
are in their favour when they bet on a
racehorse meeting at Newmarket.
Harry Degas Barrie Houghton
John Rutter Maurice Colbourne
Lucy Degas Karen Mayo Chandler

Director: Ken Grieve
Designer: Tim Wilding

Clowns Don't Cry

w Murray Smith
When one of Bulman's criminal contacts is
beaten up for no apparent reason, the
detective and his colleague Willis find that
danger lies beneath the big top of a circus
that chooses its locations very carefully
indeed.
Bill Dugdale Thorley Walters
The Prince Boris Isarov
Rashinski Zr Sieciechowicz

Director: William Brayne
Director: Chris Truelove

Tom Thumb and Other Stories

w Murray Smith
Bulman finds himself working undercover in
Liverpool's dockland to crack a drug-
smuggling ring. He soon discovers that
with a fortune at stake the organisation
behind the ring will stop at nothing to
protect their interests.
Smee Robert Oates
O'Dowd John O'Toole
Malone James Coyle

Director: Lawrence Moody
Designer: Tim Wilding

No Orchids for Missing Blandisch

w Murray Smith
Through a police informer, Det. Sgts
Bulman and Willis follow a trail which
begins on the fringes of the criminal
underworld, but progresses via arms-dealing
to a sordid murder mystery.
Blandisch Ray McAnally
Chf Supt Hislop Ralph Lawton
Willie Bruce Kenneth Cranham

Director: Bill Gilmour
Designer: Chris Truelove

Season Four
6 colour 60-minute episodes

The Moscow Subway Murders

w Murray Smith
Bulman, now promoted to Detective Chief
Inspector, isn't too happy with his new job.
He feels he's becoming office-bound – but
he's soon caught up in a string of murders
which present him with some intriguing
facts.
Bill Dugdale Thorley Walters
Pushkin George Pravda
Razanov Eugene Lapinski

Director: William Brayne
Designer: Stephen Fineren

The Loneliness of the Long Distance Copper

w Murray Smith
Why should an escaped convict leave a trail
of clues to his whereabouts which will

ensure that his recapture is only handled by
the Inner City Squad? Bulman suspects
revenge. Is he right?
Anderson Frederick Treves
Jackson Roy Barraclough
Loco Parmini Trevor Thomas

Director: Tristan De Vere
Designer: Colin Pocock

A Dear Green Place

w Edward Boyd
A routine assignment for the Inner City
Squad – escorting a prisoner from Glasgow
to London – turns into something altogether
different when the man escapes and leads his
escorts on a merry cross-country chase.
Bill Dugdale Thorley Walters
Willie Mauchlin James Copeland
DS Galbraith James Cosmo

Director: Bill Gilmour
Designer: James Weatherup

Stand and Deliver

w Murray Smith
A modern-day highwayman holds up a
tourist coach and sets in motion a chain of
surprising events which call for the
specialised services of Bulman, Willis and
Singer – the Inner City Squad.
Frisco Michael Deeks
DI Forsythe Gregory Fisher
Luke Simon Dutton

Director: Tristan De Vere
Designer: Colin Pocock

The Flowers of Edinburgh

w Edward Boyd
Having arrested a man carrying what they
believe to be an incriminating roll of film,
Bulman and Willis find themselves visiting
Edinburgh to root out a gang that specialise
in political blackmail of a very nasty variety.
Bill Dugdale Thorley Walters
Brendan Matthew Francis
Morton Fulton Mackay

Director: Jonathan Wright-Miller
Designer: Christopher George

Soldiers of Misfortune

w Murray Smith
An argument between a group of
mercenaries over a valuable piece of defence
equipment leads the Inner City Squad,
headed by George Bulman, to settle their
differences by cornering them as they set
about their devious business.
Bill Dugdale Thorley Walters
Lynch Anthony Booth
Reid Michael Goldie

Director: William Brayne
Designer: Tim Farmer

Season Five

7 colour 60-minute episodes

A Much Underestimated Man

w Murray Smith
Bulman and Willis are assigned to trail an
experienced hitman and discover the
identity of his next target. But what if the
man gives them the slip and manages to
make his next hit? Who will carry the can?
Ewan Walters Edward Peel
DI O'Rourke Paul McDowell
Helena Russell Pamela Salem

Director: Ken Grieve
Designer: Christopher George

A Swift and Evil Rozzer

w Murray Smith
When a group of prominent businessmen
decide to choose crime as a short cut to
riches, the Inner City Squad gets on their
trail when they kidnap a prominent
politician.
Nick Paget-Lombardi Edward De Souza
Sophy Paget-Lombardi Catherine Schell
Perill Geoffrey Bateman

Director: William Brayne
Designer: Alan Price

The Tender Trap

w Bruce Crowther
Bulman and Willis investigate a successful
land-developer whom they believe to be
guilty of criminal activity – and find

themselves unearthing a great deal more than at first met the eye.
Richard/Leonard Barkham Simon Williams
Philip Franklin Bernard Gallagher
Albert Canfield Nigel Stock

Director: Ben Bolt
Designer: James Weatherup

The Lost Chord

w Murray Smith
When several extremist politicians die in mysterious circumstances, Bulman and Willis find themselves doing a tour of duty in the grounds of a Cambridge college – on bicycles!
Bill Dugdale Thorley Walters
Prof. Whittingham Michael Gough
Sir Geoffrey Richard Vernon

Director: Bill Gilmour
Designer: David Batley

A Free Weekend in the Country

w Bruce Crowther
The Inner City Squad find themselves taking part in a weekend seminar on urban terrorism, and getting to grips with a problem first hand. Before the convention is through, they'll have learned a thing or two about themselves.
Det. Chf Supt Miller Kenneth Cope
Det. Supt Gray Fred Pearson
DS Shepherd John Buick

Director: Bill Gilmour
Designer: Tim Farmer

Charlie's Brother's Birthday

w Murray Smith   *(A 2-part story)*
When some coffins are stolen but no one informs the police, the Inner City Squad

find themselves going undercover in a jazz club to expose an international smuggling ring.
Sonny Boy Saltz Lol Coxhill
Peter Smollett Colm Meaney
Gail Merrian Suzanne Danielle

Director: Roger Tucker
Designer: David Buxton

With These Gloves You Can Pass Through Mirrors

w Murray Smith   *(Part 2 of above)*
Peter Mollett – known as the Sandman – acted as an agent smuggling stolen art treasures, often in coffins. A rival gang headed by Gail Merrian, Finbar Malone and Brendan O'Halloran hope to cash in on his lucrative trade – but the Inner City Squad are also interested.

Bulman retires to a life of ease with his ladyfriend – leaving his gloves behind!
O'Halloran Patrick Mower
Finbar Malone Daragh O'Malley
Bill Dugdale Thorley Walters

Director: William Brayne
Designer: Tim Farmer

STRANGERS
Producer: Richard Everitt
Music by: Mike Moran
A Granada Television Network Production
32 colour 60-minute episodes
5 June – 17 July 1978
9 January – 6 February 1979
14 October – 25 November 1980
25 September – 30 October 1981
8 September – 20 October 1982

THE STRANGE REPORT

The unusual cases solved by ex-police criminologist, Adam Strange, a man who investigated cases that had baffled the best minds of Scotland Yard. Crimes of such complexity that the powers that be only turned to him when they had exhausted all other avenues of detection open to them. Crimes of the 'impossible' variety, which the criminologist solved with monotonous regularity – although that isn't to say that the programme itself was boring. Far from it. It was in fact one of the best of its genre and gave the viewer a seldom repeated opportunity to watch the multi-talented Anthony Quayle going through his paces, with tongue firmly in cheek.

Strange himself had developed his talent for solving crime while working at the Home Office, but was now retired and able to pursue his 'hobby' without the restrictions placed on him by his former job. One moment he'd be bringing his specialised talent to bear on a uniquely-executed crime, the next he'd be speeding through the London streets in his somewhat unusual transport – a black, unlicensed London taxi.

Never far away was Hamlyn Gynt, his young assistant, who shared a lab with Strange at his London home, and Evelyn McLean, who lived next door to the criminologist and sometimes helped him in his work.

Splendid stuff.

REGULAR CAST

Adam Strange Anthony Quayle   *Hamlyn Gynt* Kas Garas
Evelyn McLean Anneke Wills
Semi Regulars
Chf Supt Cavanagh Gerald Sim   *Prof. Marks* Charles Lloyd Pack

Report No: 0649. Skeleton: Let Sleeping Dogs Lie

w Brian Degas and Tudor Gates
When the skeleton of a man found on a London bomb site is discovered to have been killed not by bombs but a bullet, Adam Strange is asked to roll back the years to trace what he was up to 30 years earlier!
Elleston Eric Portman
James Hugh Burden
Clinton Tom Adams

Director: Peter Medak

Report No: 2641. Hostage: 'If You Won't Learn, Die!'

w John Kruse
The Chinese Chargé D'Affaires is kidnapped in London and held as hostage for the release of a man held in Peking. When the Chinese threaten to retaliate, Strange is called in to ease the situation.
Blake Kenneth Haig
Sung Lee Eric Young
Chf Supt Cavanagh Gerlad Sim

Director: Charles Crichton

Report No: 0846. Lonely Hearts: Who Killed Cupid?

w Roger Parkes
What's so special about Leonard Grey that leads the police to arrest him for the murder of the boss of a Lonely Hearts Club? With the help of Ham and Evelyn, Adam Strange unearths what appears to be a case with political implications.
Leonard Grey Donald Douglas
Jack White John Bennett
Prof. Marks Charles Lloyd Pack

Director: Peter Duffell

Report No: 8319. Grenade: What Price Change?

w Bill Strutton

To air their views, two opposing factions at Radcliffe University are planning various activities to stop defence research taking place at the establishment. Because the campus is outside their jurisdiction, the police ask Adam Strange to look into the affair.

Ferdy Walker Anthony Corlan
Bob Tremayne Jeremy Bulloch
Arthur Peters Bernard Lee

Director: Charles Crichton

Report No: 3906. Covergirls: Last Year's Model

w Terence Maples

When fear enters the fashion world, Adam finds himself involved in the affairs of a fashion designer whose latest creations have been stolen and who is now being threatened unless she pulls out of the parade.

Maddeline Lisa Daniely
Cricket Elaine Taylor
Bruce Richard Vanstone

Director: Peter Duffell

Report No: 3424. Epidemic: A Most Curious Crime

w Don Brinkley

Adam finds himself facing a man who turns blood into gold — by smuggling illegal immigrants into the country and making vast profits from their misery. With Ham's help, he teaches the rogue a lesson.

Morrison Peter Vaughan
Ameen Saeed Jaffrey
Zeba Zienia Merton

Director: Daniel Petrie

Report No: 2475. Revenge: When a Man Hates

w Martin Hall

When an ex-convict vows to carry out his threat to kill those who put him inside — one of whom was Adam Strange — the criminologist finds himself involved in a race against time to discover the man's hiding place.

Paul Webber Gerald Flood
Carol Webber Sylvia Syms
George Holliday Leo Genn

Director: Charles Crichton

Report No: 1021. Shrapnel: The Wish in the Dream

w Jan Read

A piece of shrapnel in a dead man's body reveals an unexpected twist in an eternal triangle that reaches out of the past. Called in to attend the autopsy, Adam Strange finds himself personally involved.

Mary Hanson Rosemary Leach
James Hanson Julian Glover
Inspector Jenner John Thaw

Director: Brian Smedley-Ashton

Report No: 8944. Hand: A Matter of Witchcraft

w Edward De Blasio

Adam and Ham find themselves immersed in the chilling world of witchcraft when a beautiful young office secretary is murdered in brutal circumstances. Murder is one thing but as Adam finds out — the black-magic variety is difficult to solve.

Miss Dalton Renee Asherson
Insp. Graves Keith Barron
Mrs Brearley Helen Lindsay

Director: Peter Duffell

Report No: 1553. Racist: a Most Dangerous Proposal

w Arthur Dales

Trouble and heartbreak is a foregone conclusion when the ideals of a father and daughter clash. He is the leader of an anti-black organisation, she is strong in her belief for racial equality. But no one expected the result to be murder, least of all Adam Strange.

Crowley Guy Doleman
Jill Jane Merrow
Sir George Davis Griffith Jones

Director: Peter Duffell

Report No: 7931. Sniper: When Is Your Cousin Not?

w Nicholas Palmer

Student demonstrations in an East European country, and murder, involve Adam Strange in a search for truth as well as a killer. Back in London, Ham comes up with a startling piece of evidence.
Marisha Lelia Goldini
Kulik Vladek Sheybal
Savi Martin Shaw

Director: Peter Medak

Report No: 4821. X-Ray: Who Weeps for the Doctor?

w Roger Parks

Has anyone the right to help a man take his own life even though death is threatening to close in at any day? That's the dilemma facing Adam Strange when he finds himself in a human tragedy.
Miss Collingford Ann Firbank
Peggy Gale Trisha Mortimer
Doctor Hornsey John Laurie

Director: Charles Crichton

Report No: 2493. Kidnap: 'Whose Pretty Girl Are You?'

w Don Brinkley

When a beauty queen is 'kidnapped', Adam must find out whether the event has been organised as a publicity stunt or is for real? If it's the latter, he has barely 24 hours to find the girl.
Otis Dean David Bauer
Toby Ian Ogilvy
Jennifer Dean Sally Geeson

Director: Daniel Petrie

Report No: 4407. Heart: No choice for the Doctor

w Edward de Blasio

The police are baffled. A famous heart surgeon has been kidnapped but no ransom note is delivered nor is anything heard from his abductors. Adam Strange is called in – and uncovers a most unusual reason for the man's disappearance.
Doctor Saunders Robert Hardy
Segarus Kenneth Griffith
Mrs Saunders Barbara Murray

Director: Robert Asher

Report No: 4977. Swindle: Square Root of Evil

w Leigh Vance

When a Bank of England company responsible for printing genuine bank notes are duped into carrying out a massive order for a gang of swindlers, Adam Strange and his assistant Ham discover that greed lurks within.
Nils Paavo Derren Nesbitt
Klaus Frei Anton Diffring
Jago Patrick Connell

Director: Brian Smedley-Aston

Report No: 5055. Cult: Murder Shrieks Out

w Morris Farhi

When a pop singer is electrocuted during a charity pop performance, Adam Strange becomes involved in the twilight world of a charity-collecting religious sect. Suspecting that the death was no accident, he asks Ham to infiltrate the group.
Lars Ray McAnally
Newcombe John Ronane
Moran Ed Bishop

Director: Charles Crichton

THE STRANGE REPORT
Producer: Robert Berger
Executive producer: Norman Felton
Music by: Roger Webb
An Arena Production for ITC Ltd
16 colour 60-minute episodes
21 September 1968 – 28 December 1969
(USA: NBC. January – September 1971)

STINGRAY

'Stand by for action! Anything can happen in the next half hour!' Those words, spoken by Commander Shore (a character in the series), introduced us to Gerry Anderson's latest puppet creation, Captain Troy Tempest, Phones and the green-haired Marina, members of the World Aquanaut Security Patrol (WASP) and the crew of Stingray, a super-submarine equipped with an atomic engine, 16 Sting missiles and the ability to leap in and out of the sea 'salmon fashion'. A deadly killer-sub whose mission was to protect earthlings in the year 2000 from any sort of undersea dangers.

Troy Tempest (described in the original press release as the 'dynamic hero, a strikingly handsome, fearless, conscientious man') captained the team. Assisting him was George Sheridan, nicknamed Phones, because he operated the ship's hydrophones (short-range sonar equipment).

The third (unofficial) member of the crew was Marina, the young daughter of Aphony, Emperor of the peaceful undersea kingdom of Pacifica, a huge shell city on the bed of the Pacific ocean.

In command of Marineville (an undersea city based somewhere off the North American coast, which served as WASP headquarters) was Commander Shore. Crippled during a mission (he relied on a hover chair for mobility), Shore had set up and run the WASP team for five years.

Other characters were: Shore's daughter, Atlanta; Sub-Lieutenant Fisher; and the inevitable pet, Oink, Marina's seal cub.

Their enemies were: Titan, the tyrannical ruler of Titanica, who had vowed to destroy the WASPS; and the Aquaphibians, a monstrous ocean race who obeyed Titan and attacked Marineville in their mechanical fish (Terror Fish, which fired missiles from their gaping 'mouths').

Notable for being the first British TV series to be made in colour — although the series has always been transmitted in monochrome in England.

CHARACTER VOICES

Troy Tempest **Don Mason**   *Phones* **Robert Easton**   *Atlanta* **Lois Maxwell**
Commander Shore **Ray Barrett**   *Titan/SL Fisher* **Ray Barrett**   *X20* **Robert Easton**
Marina **Non-speaking**

Stingray

w Gerry and Sylvia Anderson

Investigating the destruction of a World Navy sub, Captain Troy Tempest and Phones come under attack from an enemy submarine in the form of a giant fish. They are taken prisoner and sent to the undersea kingdom of Titanica

Director: Alan Pattillo

Plant of Doom

w David Elliott

Enraged when Stingray escapes, Titan has Surface agent X20 deliver a deadly plant to Marina's father, who then gives it to his daughter – who is suspected of being a spy.

Director: Alan Fennell

Sea of Oil

w Dennis Spooner

When Atlanta is captured by an undersea race while Stingray is investigating the collapse of an oil rig, and her kidnappers plant a bomb aboard Stingray, the girl finds herself racing against time to contact Troy before the bomb explodes.

Director: John Kelly

Hostages of the Deep

w Alan Fennell

When Admiral Carson and his wife are taken prisoner by Gadus, Stingray is sent to secure their release but Marina, attempting a rescue, is captured – leaving Troy and Phones to rescue her before she is killed by a giant swordfish.

Director: Desmond Saunders

Treasure Down Below

w Dennis Spooner

Following a treasure map obtained by Phones, the crew of Stingray meet two underwater pirates who are over 300 years old. Troy and Phones are captured and when they refuse to agree to the pirates' terms, an undersea battle breaks out.

Director: Alan Pattillo

The Big Gun

w Alan Fennell

After destroying an underwater gunship, Stingray pursues a second ship into an undersea tunnel and discovers Solarstar, the refuge of the gunships – but the water pressure threatens to crush Stingray and Troy turns to Marina for help.

Director: David Elliott

The Golden Sea

w Dennis Spooner

Titan plans to trap Stingray during its regular visits to a group of scientists who are mining the sea bed for gold. His weapon is to be a giant killer swordfish – but Troy Tempest turns the tables once again.

Director: John Kelly

The Ghost Ship

w Alan Fennell

When Commander Shore and Phones are taken prisoner by Idotee, who is based on a sunken Spanish galleon, Shore orders Troy to launch missiles against Idotee, but Tempest attempts a rescue bid – and sends the enemy into fits of laughter.

Director: Desmond Saunders

Countdown

w Dennis Spooner

Disguised as a professor who can make mute people speak, agent X20 convinces Troy and Phones to hand Marina over to him. He then ties her up and leaves her beside a time bomb – set to explode when Troy attempts a rescue bid.

Director: Alan Pattillo

Ghost of the Sea

w Alan Fennell

During a flashback sequence, the viewer is told how Commander Shore was crippled during a sea battle with the enemy. He was saved by a mysterious stranger whom he never saw again – until Troy repays the Commander's debt by rescuing the stranger.

Director: David Elliott

Emergency Marineville

w Alan Fennell

Having tracked down the launching site of missiles aimed at Marineville, Troy and his crew are captured. Marina is tortured in an attempt to get her to betray the coded

signal that would destroy Marineville's interceptor missiles.
Director: John Kelly

Subterranean Sea

w Alan Fennell

Stingray's crew probe the ocean depths and discover a deep shaft that leads to a desert plateau, but before they can leave, a wall of water turns the desert into an underground sea. Will they be able to escape?
Director: Desmond Saunders

The Loch Ness Monster

w Dennis Spooner

When Admiral Denver finds himself the prey of the Loch Ness monster, Troy and his crew investigate. But the creature attacks as they enter the Loch and Stingray launches a missile at the monster – only to discover that it is a fake, designed to attract tourists.
Director: Alan Pattillo

The Invaders

w Dennis Spooner

When aliens set up a trap at a weather station and the Stingray crew are captured – then unknowingly give away vital Marineville secrets – Troy Tempest finds himself fighting a lone battle to stop an alien invasion.
Director: David Elliott

Secret of the Giant Oyster

w Alan Fennell

Two amateur divers trick Troy and his crew into helping them obtain a priceless pearl from a giant oyster. Marina is worried about a legend that says bad luck will befall anyone who steals the pearls – and Troy suddenly finds himself in danger.
Director: John Kelly

Raptures of the Deep

w Alan Fennell

Racing to the rescue of two madcap treasure-hunters, Troy runs out of air and dreams that he is the ruler of an undersea castle with Atlanta and a talking Marina at his side. But the Aquaphibians attack and the castle falls to ruins – as he wakes up.
Director: Desmond Sanders

Stand by for Action

w Dennis Spooner

Marineville as the location for a film and everyone playing themselves – except Troy Tempest, who is replaced by a handsome actor to whom Atlanta and Marina are attracted. Is it another dream? And why does the film director resemble agent X20?
Director: Alan Pattillo

The Disappearing Ships

w Alan Fennell

Searching for three freighter ships that were to be blown up, Troy and his crew discover a strange ship's graveyard inhabited by Nomads – who have no idea that the ships they live in are about to explode.
Director: David Elliott

Man from the Navy

w Alan Fennell

Troy becomes involved with a Naval Captain who has come to Marineville to demonstrate a new missile, little knowing that agent X20 had replaced the missile heads with real explosives. When the Captain is accused of treason, Troy must prove him innocent.
Director: John Kelly

Marineville Traitor

w Alan Fennell

When a vital piece of equipment is stolen from Marineville and Commander Shore is accused of being a traitor, Troy finds himself having to arrest his friend and place him in the brig.
Director: Desmond Saunders

Tom Thumb Tempest

w Alan Fennell

Troy and the crew of Stingray find themselves shrunken to Tom Thumb size and trapped in a fishtank. They discover that Titan is hatching a plot to overthrow Marineville and Stingray cannot stop him – until Troy awakens from his dream.
Director: Alan Pattillo

Pink Ice

w Alan Fennell

When it is reported that pink ice is falling all over the world, Stingray investigates, but becomes trapped in a block of frozen flesh-coloured water. Troy calls for the ice to be bombed – but will Stingray escape damage?
Director: David Elliott

The Master Plan

w Alan Fennell

It looks like the end for Troy Tempest. Poisoned by Titan, who wants Marina returned to him before he gives Troy the antidote, will Troy and Phones be able to overcome this latest threat?
Director: John Kelly

Star of the East

w Alan Fennell

Blaming Marineville for the revolt in his country, El Hudat is ordered from the city. But he takes Marina with him against her will and Troy and Phones try to rescue her before the deposed leader can cause her harm.
Director: Desmond Saunders

An Echo of Danger

w Dennis Spooner

Disguised as a psychiatrist, X20 finds a way to discredit Phones, who fails to report a distress signal from Stingray. But one of Troy's crew finds a way to restore the status quo – and save Phone's honour.
Director: Alan Pattillo

Invisible Enemy

w Alan Fennell

Returning to Marineville from a rescue mission with a man in a comatose state, Troy reports to Commander Shore. Meanwhile the patient recovers and places everyone in the city in an hypnotic trance. Can Troy save the day before an attack is launched?
Director: David Elliott

Deep Heat

w Alan Fennell

Investigating the disappearance of a robot probe, Stingray finds itself drawn to the bottom of the ocean where two survivors from a doomed city attempt to steal the vehicle to use it in their escape attempt.
Director: John Kelly

In Search of the Tajmanon

w Dennis Spooner

Assigned to help Professor Graham find the missing temple of Tajmanon, which was submerged when a dam was built in Africa, Troy and his crew encounter danger and intrigue at the bottom of the sea.
Director: Desmond Saunders

Titan Goes Pop

w Alan Fennell

Believing that he has captured a VIP visiting Marineville, X20 takes his prisoner to Titan. But the man turns out to be Duke Dexter – a pop singer, whose 'weird music' lies heavy on Titan's ears.
Director: Alan Pattillo

Set Sail for Danger

w Dennis Spooner

When Commander Shore accepts a challenge that his agents cannot take the rigours of an old-time sailing vessel, Phones and Lt Fisher find themselves all at sea when a storm overturns their boat.
Director: David Elliott

Tune of Danger

w Alan Fennell

When a jazz group visits Marineville everyone expects the evening to go with a bang – but not the kind that threatens to explode in their faces when X20 plants a bomb in a bass player's fiddle.
Director: John Kelly

Rescue from the Skies

w Dennis Spooner

During his training to become an aquanaut, Lt Fisher takes command of Stingray. His assignment involves target practice on a

Terrorfish, but X20 has attached a limpet-bomb to Stingray's hull and Troy must attempt to remove it.
Director: Desmond Saunders

The Cool Caveman

w Alan Fennell
Troy's dream that he and Phones are pitted against a race of underwater cavemen who plunder the cargo of a vessel carrying radioactive fuel, gives him the idea of wearing a caveman's outfit at Marineville's fancy-dress ball.
Director: Alan Pattillo

A Nut for Marineville

w Gerry and Sylvia Anderson
Professor Burgoyne, a man developing a new super-missile needed to destroy an indestructible craft heading towards Marineville, is presumed dead when his lab is destroyed by flames. Things look bleak for WASP headquarters.
Director: David Elliott

Trapped in the Depths

w Alan Fennell
When Atlanta is taken prisoner by Cordo, the ruler of a race of underwater people, Stingray is sent to rescue her. But Cordo lures Troy and Phones into a duplicate Stingray while his men steal the real one – and set off to destroy Marineville.
Director: John Kelly

Eastern Eclipse

w Alan Fennell
El Hudat returns to wreak havoc on Marineville, by substituting his twin brother for himself and escaping from his cell. But Stingray is soon hot on his trail and Commander Shore has to make a double-sided decision.
Director: Desmond Saunders

A Christmas to Remember

w Dennis Spooner
In an attempt to brighten up the Christmas festivities for the orphaned son of an aquanaut, Troy asks the boy to join his Stingray crew and reenact a famous battle. Unknown to either of them, Phones has been hypnotised to lead them into a trap.
Director: Alan Pattillo

The Lighthouse Dwellers

w Alan Fennell
When disaster strikes a pilot approaching a new airfield and his ship crashes because a lighthouse beacon flashes on, then off again, confusing the pilot, it isn't long before Stingray is sent to investigate.
Director: David Elliott

Aquanaut of the Year

w Gerry and Sylvia Anderson
Having received the 'Aquanaut of the Year' award, Troy finds himself the subject of 'This Is Your Life'. His most exciting adventures are relived before his eyes – but it's the question from the host-master that worries him: Are you and Atlanta more than 'good friends'?
Director: Alan Pattillo

STINGRAY
Producer: Gerry Anderson
Associate producer: Reg Hill
Music by: Barry Gray
(Title vocal by: Gary Miller)
Special effects: Derek Meddings
An A. P. Films Production in association with ATV for ITC Worldwide Distribution
39 colour 30-minute episodes
6 October 1964 – 30 June 1965
(USA: Syndicated 1965)

STRYKER OF SCOTLAND YARD

The investigations of Chief Inspector Robert Stryker of Scotland Yard, a staid, but capable police officer who investigated cases in which innocent people had become involved in the machinations of master criminals.

A passable who-dunnit-and-why crime series notable only for the strong performance from Welsh actor, Clifford Evans.

REGULAR CAST

Insp. Stryker Clifford Evans   *Sgt Hawker* George Woodbridge

Production credits unknown
39 monochrome 30-minute episodes
2 November 1961 – to various dates
until 1963
(USA: NBC 1957)

SUPER CAR

Gerry Anderson's third outing into Supermarionation puppet land (or fourth, if one counts *The Adventures of Twizzle*) and his first encounter with the realms of science-fiction.

The 'star' of the series was Supercar, a vehicle which could travel on land, underwater, or through the skies. With eight rockets that retracted like wings, Supercar could travel anywhere, from cities to the dense jungles of Earth, to the limits of outer space – a wonder vehicle, the supercar of the future.

At its controls was Mike Mercury, Supercar's test pilot. Sharing his adventures were Professor Popkiss and his assistant Doctor Beaker, co-inventors of the wonder car, who spent much of their time fussing over their invention while trying to devise new components for it.

Rounding up the team were Jimmy Gibson, a ten-year-old boy who, together with his pet monkey Mitch, often joined Mike on his missions against the villain of the piece, Masterspy, a rogue who had set his mind on stealing the fabulous machine in order to use it for his own foul schemes. During most stories the villain shared the limelight with his worm-like assistant, Zarin.

CHARACTER VOICES

Mike Mercury **Graydon Gould**   *Professor Popkiss* **George Murcell**
Jimmy Gibson **Sylvia Anderson**   *Doctor Beaker* **David Graham**
Mitch **David Graham**   *Masterspy* **George Murcell**   *Zarin* **David Graham**

Season One
26 monochrome 30-minute episodes

(All scripts by Reg Hill, Gerry and Sylvia Anderson, and Hugh and Martin Woodhouse. All stories directed by Barry Gray.)

Rescue

Mike Mercury uses Supercar's Clear-Vu device to rescue brothers Bill and Jimmy Gibson when their aeroplane crashes into the sea and their life raft becomes enveloped in thick dense fog.

Amazonian Adventure

Mitch the Monkey falls ill and Mike and his team take off to find a cure – a plant which grows only in a remote South American jungle. They find themselves captured by a tribe of headhunters and Mike uses Supercar to conjure up a little 'white magic'.

Talisman of Sargon

In disguise, Masterspy tricks Dr Beaker into revealing the entrance of the Tomb of Sargon, which holds the Talisman of Sargon, a jewel reputed to have magic powers. Mike and Supercar must save the day.

False Alarm

Determined to steal Supercar, Masterspy and Zarin send out a phoney distress call. Mike sets out to rescue them but is overcome and drugged and the villains steal the vehicle – only to be given the ride of their lives when Mitch out-manoeuvres them.

What Goes Up

Beaker and Popkiss are helping a USAF colonel to test-drive a new rocket fuel when things go wrong and the balloon carrying the fuel flies away. Mike must risk his own life to detonate the balloon at close range – a very risky mission.

Keep It Cool

Transporting a new experimental Supercar fuel across the desert, Bill Gibson and Beaker come under attack by Masterspy. Realising that the fuel will explode when it reaches above freezing point, Mike sets out to avert disaster.

Grounded

Chasing after two villains who have stolen Beaker's printed circuits for Supercar, Mike crashes as a result of sabotage. However, the vehicle is still useful as a car so, for the very first time, Mike continues the journey by road.

Jungle Hazard

Little realising that Felicity, the girl from whom he's trying to take an estate in Malaya, is the cousin of Dr Beaker, Masterspy plans his next devious scheme. Enter Mike Mercury and Supercar to save the day – and Felicity's life.

High Tension

Masterspy tries again to steal Supercar by kidnapping Dr Beaker. But Mike retaliates by using Supercar's remote control device to rescue his friend – and give Masterspy a very nasty shock.

A Little Art

Not realising that a painting he's purchased contains a visual clue to the location of a forger's counterfeit plates, Beaker is angry when the art-dealer steals back the artwork. But all is not lost – as Mike discovers.

Ice Fall

On a trip to the mountains, Beaker finds himself in trouble when he sets out to find some ice-falls in a deep underground cavern. Encased in an ice avalanche, he shivers in anticipation as Mike attempts to release him via Supercar's engines.

Island Incident

Asked to help the deposed leader of Pelota to regain power, Mike and his friends, finding themselves under fire, manage to negotiate an underwater escape route to expose the man's evil brother as a criminal.

The Tracking of Masterspy

Posing as a reporter, Masterspy tricks Mike into giving him information about Supercar. He then steals the plans to the vehicle – or so he believes. In reality he has stolen a tracking device and Mike is soon on his tail.

The Phantom Piper

Mike and his team travel to Scotland to help a woman solve the mystery of the Phantom Piper. They uncover a clever scheme to dupe the woman out of a fortune in buried treasure.

Deep Seven

To see how far it can dive underwater, Mike plunges Supercar into the ocean and descends to 400 feet. Suddenly the cockpit begins to leak and the engines stop working. Worse still, the vehicle becomes entangled in a mine cable and threatens to explode! Can Mike and his machine be saved?

Pirate Blunder

Black Morgan, a pirate, holds up ships and plunders their cargo. Mike sets out to stop him, but Morgan holds the aces – he has hostages and he will torpedo them if Mike interferes with his plans. Mike, however, has a trump card.

Flight of Fancy

Jimmy dreams that he and Mitch fly off in Supercar to rescue a Princess from the evil Hertz and Marzak. As a reward, Jimmy and Mitch are knighted by the King – then Jimmy wakes up.

Hostage

On holiday in Ireland, Dr Beaker finds himself in a kidnapping plot staged by two villains, who take a girl hostage and force Beaker to send for Mike and his Supercar – who spring a surprise on the villains with a baseball bat.

The Sunken Temple

Whilst helping a Professor to excavate an underwater cavern, Mike and Dr Beaker find a safe containing stolen loot – but Professor Terman becomes trapped beneath a statue on the seabed and Mike finds himself using Supercar to save him.

Trapped in the Depths

Hearing that an American officer and an Australian scientist are trapped in a bathyscaphe at the bottom of the sea and are under attack by giant fish, Mike dives into the ocean and uses Supercar's ultrasonic gun to rescue them.

Crash Landing

When Supercar and its team crashlands in the jungle, it isn't long before Mitch discovers a new playmate – a female monkey – and Mike and his team find themselves lumbered with an extra passenger.

The Dragon of Ho Meng

Forced down by a terrible typhoon, Mike, Jimmy and Mitch come face to face with Ho Meng and his daughter Lotus Blossom, who look upon Supercar as a dragon. When the girl is kidnapped, Mike shows Ho Meng Supercar's full capabilities.

The Lost City

Professor Watson, a deranged scientist, plans to destroy Washington DC with a guided missile from his hideout beneath a lost city. Assigned to stop him, Mike and Dr Beaker are captured – but Supercar itself saves the day.

The Magic Carpet

Sent to deliver some urgent medical supplies to Prince Hassan, Mike and his friends find themselves thrown into prison by Alif Bey, who wants the prince to die so that he can seize power. But Mitch escapes and enables the team to reach Supercar.

The White Line

The Supercar team are called in by Scotland Yard to help solve a series of bank and armoured car robberies carried out by two Chicago gangsters. Dr Beaker is sent out with the next armoured car delivery – and finds himself captured.

Supercar: Take One

When Dr Beaker plays around with his new toy, a movie camera, and his exposed film gets mixed up with some film shot by spies, Mike and his team find themselves flying to New York to face the spies on their own ground.

Season Two
13 monochrome 30-minute episodes

The Runaway Train

Dr Beaker and Professor Popkiss find their journey aboard a new atomic train interrupted by the unwelcome entrance of Masterspy and Zarin, who have sabotaged the train. When all seems lost, Mike enters the scene with Supercar.

Precious Cargo

Professor Popkiss, requiring a special wine for a dish he's preparing, visits wine-merchant Laval – an event which leads Mike and his friends into the problems of Zizi, a young girl.

Operation Superstork

When Mitch accidentally releases the guide rope of a new balloon being tested by Dr Beaker, sending Mike, Beaker and Jimmy off into danger, Mike finds himself parachuting to Earth to fetch Supercar to rescue them.

Hijack

It appears that Masterspy and Zarin haven't learnt their lesson. This time they try to hijack an airliner, but Mike takes off in Supercar to teach them that they shouldn't build sky-high plans.

Calling Charlie Queen

When Professor Karloff plans to take over America by miniaturising its citizens and Mike and Dr Beaker find themselves cut down to size, with the help of Karloff's miniaturised assistant, they give the Professor a taste of his own medicine.

Space for Mitch

Mitch the Monkey finds himself in trouble again, this time as the unwilling pilot of a rocket that he fires off into orbit. Mike takes Supercar to rescue him and teaches the pet some monkey business of his own.

The Sky's the Limit

Their efforts to steal Supercar know no bounds: Masterspy and Zarin devise a new scheme – they attempt to buy the vehicle using phoney money. When this fails, they employ two villains to steal the machine, but all four are in for a surprise – Supercar has 'vanished'!

70-B-Lo

Popkiss needs a blood transfusion. But his blood is a rare type and the nearest compatible donor, Professor Karlinsky, is trapped on the Arctic wasteland. Mike and Supercar fly off to rescue him.

Atomic Witch Hunt

The Supercar team set out to discover who has planted atomic bombs all over the United States. They soon discover the culprit, a villainous Sheriff, but find themselves captured – leaving Mitch to save the day.

Jailbreak

Using a helicopter, Red James attempts to free his friend Joe Anna from prison. Piloting the helicopter at gunpoint is Sam Weston, who is forced to take the two criminals to Black Rock – where Mike and Supercar are ordered to fly them to Mexico.

The Day Time Stood Still

Mike shares his birthday with his friends. Suddenly time itself is frozen: Mike's friends

are motionless and a stranger from another planet presents Mike with a belt that will allow him to fly into the sky. What a present. But before Mike can use it, he wakes up. It was all a dream.

Transatlantic Cable

Masterspy is tapping into a transatlantic cable from his hideout under the sea. The Supercar team discover his hiding place and Mike uses the vehicle's latest device – a huge drill – to pour cold water on his enemy's scheme.

King Kool

When Mitch is tricked by King Kool, a famous TV gorilla jazz-drummer, and is locked in a cage, Mike and his friends find themselves up to their necks in monkey business of the most devious variety.

SUPERCAR
Producer: Gerry Anderson
Music by: Barry Gray
Special effects: Derek Meddings
An A. P. Films Production
for ITC Worldwide Distribution
39 monochrome 30-minute episodes
14 September 1961 – 7 June 1962
(USA: Syndicated 1962)

THE SWEENEY

A rough, tough, kick-'em-in-the-teeth crime series which picked up where the pilot story *Regan* left off, with Detective Inspector Jack Regan and Detective Sergeant George Carter continuing to make life difficult for villains – two gangbusters from the Sweeney (underworld slang for the Flying Squad).

Regan, a tough, resourceful detective, had spent 14 years in the force before being transferred to the Flying Squad. A total professional, a 24-hours-a-day policeman, his philosophy was 'Don't bother me with forms and procedures, let me get out there and nick villains.' He swore a lot, drank to excess – but always got his man (even if it meant bending the rules to do so).

His subordinate, DS Carter, a young cockney who could just as easily have ended up on the side of the opposition (until a concerned school-teacher instilled in him notions of public service), admired Regan and enjoyed working with him, although he'd sometimes argue with his partner over his methods of approach and style of working. Both men were not averse to thumping the odd villain if they thought it would help their cause, and both believed that to catch a crook you need to think like him, so both spent a lot of time socialising with villains – a situation that frequently brought both men a reprimand from Chief Inspector Frank Haskins, the man given the tough job of keeping Regan in line, of ensuring that he didn't go too far to get results.

Disregarding the overuse of bad language, the series had top-drawer appeal and fulfilled its initial promise.

REGULAR CAST

DI Jack Regan John Thaw   *DS George Carter* Dennis Waterman
CI Frank Haskins Garfield Morgan

Season One

13 colour 60-minute episodes

Ringer

w Trevor Preston
Girlfriends can be trouble, as Det. Insp. Regan finds out when he loses his girlfriend's car – and jeopardises an important police operation.
Brooker Ian Hendry
Kemble Brian Blessed
Jenny Jill Townsend

Director: Terry Green

Jackpot

w Tony Marsh
With £30,000 missing and suspicion of theft hanging over DI Jack Regan and his squad, Jack must ask himself if his boys are as guilty as the villains they've arrested?
Biggleswade Ed Devereaux
Morrison Morgan Shepherd
Chf Supt Maynon Morris Perry

Director: Tom Clegg

Thin Ice

w Troy Kennedy Martin
Regan becomes an animal lover to stave off the escape route of Bishop, a criminal who has pulled off a 'stroke' against the Flying Squad.
Bishop Alfred Marks
Pringle Peter Jeffrey
Chf Supt. Maynon Morris Perry

Director: Tom Clegg

Queen's Pawn

w Ranald Graham
When three top villains walk out of court free men after a year of hard work by the Squad, it's enough to test the mettle of any copper. Regan doesn't like it – and he's angrier than most.
Lyon Tony Selby
Bernard Stone Julian Glover
Chf Supt Maynon Morris Perry

Director: Viktors Ritelis

Jigsaw

w Tudaor Gates
With the odds stacked against him, can Regan overcome the opposition of his

superiors, an MP and even his own men, to obtain a conviction?
Eddie Del Henney
Fat Eric Ken Parry
Alison Carter Stephanie Turner

Director: William Brayne

Night Out

w Troy Kennedy Martin
Why should a headline-hunting police colleague invite Regan to spend a night out with the boys? Regan's suspicions lead him to uncover far more than he at first imagined.
Grant T. P. McKenna
Iris Long Mitzi Rogers
Jellineck David Hargreaves

Director: David Wickes

The Placer

w Trevor Preston
To find the link in a series of long-distance lorry hijacks, Regan hits the road posing as a lorry driver.
Harry Poole Stanley Meadows
Andrew Barkis Tony Steedman
Sergeant Kent Carl Rigg

Director: Ted Childs

Cover Story

w Ranald Graham
Journalist Sandy Williams has the knack of predicting crimes before they happen. How does she do it? The answer surprises even tough copper Jack Regan.
Sandy Williams Prunella Gee
Maureen Whittle Bernadette Milnes
Justin Michael McStay

Director: Douglas Camfield

Golden Boy

w Martin Hall
Why should a man help a group of thieves export millions in gold? Regan finds a man with something to hide – something hidden deep in his past.

Conway John Nolan
Deller Dudley Sutton
Potter Colin Campbell

Director: Tom Clegg

Stoppo Driver

w Allan Prior
When a gang require a get-away driver, who better than a highly-trained policeman to ensure a clean escape route? Regan finds crime on his doorstep.
Cooney Billy Murray
Greg Wolfe Morris
Sara Nicola Pagett

Director: Terry Green

Big Spender

w Alan Prior
Too much money and no idea how to spend it. Regan meets a wealthy man with crime on his mind and helps to solve his problem – by putting him aside.
Wardle Warren Mitchell
Stella Catherine Schell
Charley Smith Julian Holloway

Director: Viktors Ritelis

Contact Breaker

w Robert Banks Stewart
Once a crook, always a crook. That's what his colleagues are saying. But Regan believes the man was framed. Believing is one thing – but can he prove it?
Danny Keever Warren Clarke
Brenda Coral Atkins
Mark Tony Anholt

Director: William Brayne

Abduction

w Trevor Preston
When Mrs Kate Regan discovers that her daughter Susie is missing, her panic leads to terror – and her estranged husband Jack finds himself on the wrong end of a gun.
Kate Regan Janet Key
Brenda Wanda Ventham
Miss Mayhew Naomi Chance

Director: Tom Clegg

Season Two
13 colour 60-minute episodes

Chalk and Cheese

w Trevor Preston
When a series of violent robberies threaten
to turn Regan's patch into a battleground,
Regan and Carter find themselves
broadening their horizons to crack a gang of
thieves.
Caroline Lesley Ann Down
Garret Paul Jones
Pop Garret David Lodge

Director: Terry Green

Faces

w Murray Smith
A series of bank robberies leads to Regan
and Carter matching the faces of villains to
people in high places, as they have to decide
who are the guilty, the innocent – and the
dangerous.
Tober Colin Welland
Jake Keith Buckley
The German Barry Stanton

Director: William Brayne

Supersnout

w Ranald Graham
Why should his boss Det. Chf Insp. Quirk
know all the finer details of a robbery when
Regan himself can't get his 'snouts' to talk?
Has someone put the frighteners on them?
Det. Chf Insp. Quirk Bill Maynard
Kretchmar Vernon Dobtcheff
Dantziz Carl Duering

Director: Tom Clegg

Big Brother

w Trevor Preston
When a villain accuses Regan of using
unreasonable force to extract a confession
from him, Det. Chf Insp. Haskins must use
all his guile to save the department and
Regan's reputation.
Lee Michael Robbins
Phil Deacon Maurice Roeves
Andy Deacon David Dixon

Director: Tom Clegg

Hit and Run

w Roger Marshall
Hit and run – but by accident or design?
Regan and Carter find themselves drawn
into a personal tragedy that affects their
relationship.
Crofts Patrick Troughton
Fowler Gary Waldhorn
Judy Shelia Ruskin

Director: Mike Vardy

Trap

w Ray Jenkins
It's natural for a mother to love her son –
even though he's a thug. So when Regan
and Carter refuse to share a mother's
emotions, they find themselves out in the
cold.
Mrs Riley Elizabeth Begley
Noel Riley Kenneth Colley
Manny Bellow Sydney Tafler

Director: Jim Goddard

Golden Fleece

w Roger Marshall
When two young Australian tearaways end
up on Regan's patch with dreams of making
a million, Regan and Carter find themselves
faced with an outbreak of violence.
Colin Patrick Mower
Ray George Layton
Judy Cheryl Kennedy

Director: David Wickes

Poppy

w Trevor Preston
Suspecting that a professional has stolen half
a million pounds – and got away with it –
Regan and Carter are somewhat surprised
when the man blows his cover by trying a
repeat performance on their patch!
Lubett James Booth
Brett John Rhys-Davies
Mrs Lubett Veronica Lang

Director: Tom Clegg

Stay Lucky, Eh?

w Trevor Preston

Has Jack Regan gone soft? It appears that his partner has been taken in by money and the good life. DS Carter thinks not – Det. Chf Insp. Haskins thinks otherwise.

Kirby Peter Vaughan
Jenner Alun Armstrong
Tyson Paul Moriarty

Director: Douglas Camfield

Trojan Bus

w Roger Marshall

Colin and Ray, the two Aussie layabouts who gave Regan and Carter so much trouble, have dared to return to England. What's more, they're at it again on Regan's patch . . . they wouldn't dare pull a stroke – would they?

Colin Patrick Mower
Ray George Layton
Nancy Lynda Bellingham

Director: Ted Childs

I Want the Man

w Ray Jenkins

Who is the head man behind a series of brilliantly organised crimes? Regan wants his name – even if it means fishing in dangerous waters and casting a minnow to net a shark.

Frankie Little Roy Kinnear
Maynard Michael Coles
Popeye Russell Hunter

Director: Tom Clegg

Country Boy

w Andrew Wilson

Can a country boy gain Regan's confidence and fit into his squad? More to the point, once in can he remain there knowing that Regan is a hard task-master.

David Keel Robert Swan
Kathy Peters Christine Shaw
Peters Shaun Curry

Director: Jim Goddard

Thou Shalt Not Kill

w Ranald Graham

It's a commandment that Regan will not allow to be broken, 'Thou shalt not kill.' But how are his squad to ensure people's safety in a deadly situation – unless they can protect themselves?

Barry Monk Ronald Lacey
Jimmy Wands Dean Harris
Ass. Commissioner Barrie Cookson

Director: Douglas Camfield

Season Three

13 colour 60-minute episodes

Selected Target

w Troy Kennedy Martin

When a prison quarrel appears to involve the 'Target Criminal' – a man Regan is keeping a close watch on – it leads Regan and Carter into a tough, and deadly case.

Kibber Lee Montague
Oates Ronald Fraser
Mrs Smedley Maureen Lipman

Director: Tom Clegg

In from the Cold

w Tony Hoare

When a policeman is crippled by a vicious criminal and Regan feels responsible, it's little wonder that Regan has 'something special' planned when he meets the gunman again.

Daniels John Alkin
Mason Johnny Shannon
Medhurst Anthony Heaton

Director: Terry Green

Visiting Firemen

w Troy Kennedy Martin

When they arrange to meet a Turkish police officer in a nightclub, Regan and Carter find themselves in an explosive situation – and Regan becomes a song and dance man.

Chf Supt. Maynon Morris Perry
Shebbeq Nadim Savalha
Beemax Frederick Treves

Director: Tom Clegg

Tomorrow Man

w Andrew Wilson
Regan and Carter try to thwart the
machinations of a computer expert who has
programmed a computer for revenge. The
man bears a grudge – and Regan is in the
firing line.
Grey John Hurt
Longfield George Cole
Burnham Peter Bayliss

Director: David Wickes

Taste of Fear

w Roger Marshall
When the Shaw family is viciously attacked
by a couple of army deserters, Regan, Carter
and new recruit, Hargreaves, try to flush
them out. But will the newcomer have what
it takes at the showdown?
Hargreaves Norman Eshley
Tug Wilson Arthur English
Eileen Shaw Lesley Dunlop

Director: David Wickes

Bad Apple

w Roger Marshall
Regan finds himself working as a barman to
discover the truth behind allegations that
two detectives have been arranging lenient
bail in exchange for a cut of robbery
proceeds.
Huke John Lyons
Perraut Norman Jones
Letts Colin Rix

Director: Douglas Camfield

May

w Trevor Preston
Young Davey Holmes stands accused of a
crime – but has the evidence been planted
to dupe the police into believing he's
guilty? Regan and Carter intend to find out.
Davy Holmes Karl Howman
Cree Brian Gwaspari
May Marjorie Yates

Director: Tom Clegg

Sweet Smell of Sucession

w Peter Hill
Regan and Carter stand on the sideline as
Joe Castle, one of London's biggest villains,
is laid to rest. But even they are surprised
when a wreath presents them with an
unusual problem.
Peter Castle Hywel Bennett
Miss Baker Sue Lloyd
Arthur Castle Peter Dyneley

Director: William Brayne

Down to You, Brother

w Richard Harris
When thieves fall out, who knows what
surprises they have in store? Regan and
Carter find themselves more than casual
observers when a crisis threatens to explode
in their faces.
Meadows Derek Francis
Owen Terence Budd
Holder Kenny Lynch

Director: Chris Menaul

Payoff

w P. J. Hammond
Is Eddie Glass really dead? Or is he alive
and well, and living in London? Regan
prays that the former is true – otherwise
Carter's relationship with Eddie's old flame
will bring him some unwelcome trouble.
Drake Dave King
Shirley Glass Geraldine James
Killick Ken Kitson

Director: Douglas Camfield

Loving Arms

w Robert Wales
Regan and Carter must find the source of
illegal guns being sold to young children
before further lives are lost. One man has
already died – killed by a ten-year-old!
Ward Roy Sone
Blakeney Alan David
Fred Booth Clifford Kershaw

Director: Tom Clegg

Lady Luck

w Ranald Graham

Regan's morale and that of his men has reached its lowest ebb. Things must change – mustn't they? But if so – which way?
Marcia Moira Redmond
Edmunds Norman Rodway
Colonel Rosier James Cossins

Director: Mike Vardy

On the Run

w Roger Marshall

It's bad enough that Tim Cook, a man convicted of armed robbery, has been sprung from jail – but knowing that he's after the man who put him there sends shivers down Carter's spine. That man was Regan.
Tim Cook George Sweeney
Pinder Brendan Price
Uncle John Sharp

Director: David Wickes

Season Four

14 colour 60-minute episodes

Messenger of the Gods

w Trevor Preston

Wedding plans and an investigation into a mercury robbery, two separate events that draw Regan and Carter into a new adventure – with a unhappy finale.
Mrs Rix Diana Dors
Linda Rix Dawn Perllman
Uncle Billy James Ottaway

Director: Terry Green

Hard Men

w Troy Kennedy Martin

Chasing around London after a gang of tough villains, Regan and Carter find their progress hampered by Strathclyde policeman DS Freeth – a man who works strictly by his own methods.
DS Freeth James Cosmo
Jellyneck James Warrior
Ross Stewart Pearson

Director: Graham Baker

Drag Act

w Ted Childs

When £75,000 worth of brandy is snatched by thieves who switch a container on an articulated lorry, Regan is called in – and Carter falls in love.
Julie Kingdom Katherine Fahy
Mike Seton Albert Welling
Mason Patrick Malahide

Director: Tom Clegg

Trust Red

w Richard Harris

It's a fact of life. Old age comes to everyone. But when Regan's slow reactions in a crisis almost end with him losing his life it takes Carter some time to get his partner to admit that he's getting long in the tooth.
Daniels John Alkin
Con Nigel Humphries
Maurice Anthony O'Donnell

Director: Douglas Camfield

Nightmare

w Ranald Graham

Is Regan in danger of losing his life? Who is after him and why? For Regan it's a nightmare situation – for his girlfriend it spells danger.
Farrell Paul Antrim
Hay J. D. Devlin
Flynn Tony Rohr

Director: David Wickes

Money, Money, Money

w Trevor Preston

When a reformed criminal friend of Regan's wins the pools, and then loses his life in mysterious circumstances, it's only natural that Regan wants to find out why.
Eddie Monk Edward Judd
Wally Hough Glynn Owen
Dave Leeford Michael Culver

Director: Sid Robertson

Bait

w Trevor Preston

Vic Tolman is a nasty piece of work, a villain who makes his living from grinding those below him into the dust. Regan intends to put an end to his game – but can he?

Vic Tolman George Sewell
Joan Barbara Ewing
Lennie Edward Peel

Director: Sid Robertson

The Bigger They Are

w Tony Hoare

How far will people with a dubious past go to protect their new-found wealth and prominence? All the way – as Jack Regan discovers.

Gold Colin Jeavons
Sharon Jenny Runacre
Grey Donald Burton

Director: Mike Vardy

Feet of Clay

w Roger Marshall

Albert Ember, an ex-informer, and his wife Margot are worried. Their son is missing. Fearing the worst, Regan and Carter make enquiries – and the clues point to abduction.

Alan Ember Joss Ackland
Margot Ember Thelma Whitely
Commander Watson Geoffrey Palmer

Director: Chris Burt

One of Your Own

w Tony Hoare

When DS Carter poses as a villain to unmask a gang, but finds himself in a vicious situation, it is down to his partner Jack Regan to attempt a rescue bid.

Fleet Michael Elphick
Daniels John Alkin
Morris Neil Hallett

Director: Chris Menaul

Hearts and Minds

w Donald Churchill and Ted Childs

Members of a Marxist Revolutionary Front, a beautiful girl and an eminent research scientist provide an intriguing puzzle for Regan – but not so intriguing as the antics of two comedians and a dummy called Charlie.

Bellcourt Edward De Souza
Busby Edward Hardwicke
Hildegard Caroline Blakiston
Special guest stars Morecambe and Wise

Director: Mike Vardy

Latin Lady

w Ted Childs

Why should Jack Regan take up with Chrissie Delgardo, the girlfriend of a villain he's recently put behind bars – and is the girl all she seems to be?

Christobel Meg Davies
Knox Stuart Wilson
Delacroix Donald Morley

Director: Peter Smith

Victims

w Roger Marshall

Haskins's wife Doreen has been acting strangely. She buys the wrong size shirts for her husband, cuts holes in a newspaper, and hugs a doll close to her. What's behind it?

Doreen Haskins Sheila Reed
Eve Fisher Lynda Marchal
Jimmy Park Peter Wright

Director: Ben Bolt

Jack or Knave

w Ted Childs

Has Jack Regan finally reached the end of his tether with his superiors? Like it or not, he finds himself in deadly serious trouble when Haskins reopens old wounds.

Canning Barrie Ingham
Harries Richard Griffiths
Gloria Jo Warne

Director: Tom Clegg

THE SWEENEY
Created by: Ian Kennedy Martin
Producer: Ted Childs
Executive producers: Lloyds Shirley and
George Taylor
Associated producer: Mary Morgan
Title music by: Harry South
*A Euston Films Production for Thames
Television*
52 colour 60-minute episodes
Networked
2 January – 27 March 1975
1 September – 24 November 1975
6 September – 20 December 1976
7 September – 28 December 1978
(USA: Syndicated 1976)

SWORD OF FREEDOM

The adventures of Marco del Monte, a freedom-loving painter who wielded a sword as well as his paintbrush to defend the weak and needy people of Florence in their fight for liberty against the cruel and despotic rule of the banking house of Medici, rulers of Florence in the Renaissance period of the 15th century.

Helping him in his struggle were Angelica, a reformed pickpocket who had become his model, and Sandro, his burly friend. Together they outwitted the wicked Duke de Medici and his corrupt sister, Francesca.

REGULAR CAST

Marco de Monte Edmund Purdom   *Angelica* Adrienne Corri
Sandro Rowland Bartrop   *Duke de Medici* Martin Benson
Francesca Monica Stevenson

Francesca
The Suspects
The Sicilian
Portrait in Emerald Green
Forgery in Red Chalk
Vespucci
The Woman in the Picture
Caterina
The Duke
The Eye of the Artist
The Bracelet
The Hero
The Value of Paper
Choice of Weapons

Pagan Venus
The Princess
The School
The Ambassador
The Lion and the Mouse
Angelica's Past
Cristina
Strange Intruder
The Primavera
The Marionettes
Vendetta
Serenade in Red
Chart of Gold
A Game of Chance

Marriage of Convenience
The Bell
The Tower
The Ship
The Besieged Duchess

The Reluctant Duke
Who is Felicia?
Violetta
The Assassin
Adrianna
  Alexandro

SWORD OF FREEDOM
Producer: Sidney Cole
Executive producer Hannah Weinstein
Writers: Samuel B. West, Leighton
Reynolds, George Baxt,
Robert Westerby, William Templeton
Directors: Terence Fisher, Terry Bishop,
Bernard Knowles,
Peter Maxwell, Anthony Squire

A Sapphire Films Production for ITC
Filmed at Walton Studios
39 monochrome 30-minute episodes
21 February 1959 – 14 March 1961
(USA: Syndicated 1957)

TAGGART

The investigations of Detective Chief Inspector Jim Taggart, a cynical, footsore, Glasgow CID officer, and his assistant, Detective Sergeant Peter Livingstone, two policemen who found themselves called in to solve crimes of a tough, grisly and sometimes macabre nature, in the sprawling district of Glasgow.

A new face was added to the roster in the final story, Detective Constable Alan Jardine, a young recruit taken under Taggart's wing.

A classic of the genre.

REGULAR CAST

DCI Jim Taggart Mark McManus   *DS Peter Livingstone* Neil Duncan
Supt McVitie Iain Anders   *Supt Murray* Tony Watson
DC Alan Jardine James Macpherson   *Jean Taggart* Harriet Buchan
Alison Taggart Geraldine Alexander   *Dr Andrews* Robert Robinson

Killer

w Glenn Chandler   *(A 3-part story)*
CI Taggart and DS Livingstone are called to the scene of a murder – a young woman found strangled. Taggart believes he can wrap up the case within hours, but as the days slip by, and the strangler claims another victim, the detectives realise that they are up against a compulsive killer –

and time is against them as the killer claims a third life.
Patricia Patterson Anne Kidd
Michael Boyd Gerard Kelly
Liz Boyd Linda Muchan
Charlie Patterson Roy Hanlon

Director: Laurence Moody
Designer: Marius Der Werff

Dead Ringer

w Glenn Chandler *(A 3-part story)*
When the remains of a dismembered body
are found in a Glasgow cellar, Taggart and
Livingstone find themselves sifting through
clues to discover a murderer. Balfour, a man
recently released from prison after being
cleared of killing his wife, is their main
suspect – until his baby nephew is
kidnapped and Taggart finds himself on the
carpet accused of mishandling the case.
David Balfour Alexander Morton
Ronnie MacIsaac Jake D'Arcy
Josephine Pebbles Colette O'Neil
Bill Lynch J. D. Devlin

Director: Laurence Moody
Designer: Marius Der Werff

Murder in Season

w Glenn Chandler *(A 3-part story)*
When opera-singer Eleanor Samson
attempts a reconciliation with her husband
John, and Samson's 'girlfriend' is burned to
death shortly afterwards, Eleanor finds
herself accused of murder. Called in to
investigate the killing, Taggart and
Livingstone discover that Eleanor's father
witnessed the fire but refuses to say more.
With two further murders in quick
succession, the detectives find themselves
racing against the clock to prevent a fourth.
Eleanor Samson Isla Blair
Keith Brennan Ronnie Letham
Graeme Samson Danny Hignett
Olive McQueen Dorothy Paul

Director: Peter Barber-Fleming
Designer: Marius Der Werff

Knife Edge

w Glenn Chandler *(A 3-part story)*
With the discovery of a severed female leg
found in a layby, detectives Taggart and
Livingstone find themselves investigating a
grisly case. When a third skilfully
amputated female leg is found on a golf
course, Taggart finds himself searching the
Glaswegian underworld for clues to the
killer's identity.

DS Forfar Stuart Hepburn
Fred Swann Andrew McCulloch
George Bryce Alex Norton
Judy Morris Siobhan Redmond

Director: Haldane Duncan
Designer: Marius Der Werff

Death Call

w Glenn Chandler *(A 3-part story)*
When Eva Russell, the glamorous wife of
wealthy Scottish landowner Robert Russell,
is found dead in a remote loch, and then
Russell himself disappears, Taggart and
Livingstone find themselves investigating a
trio of murders – and trying to make sense
of Russell's dying words, 'the boys'.
DS Forfar Stuart Hepburn
Tony Meacher Dawn Grainger
Sandy Russell Michael Carter
Stephen Hendry James McKenna

Director: Haldane Duncan
Designer: Marius Der Werff

The Killing Philosophy

w Glenn Chandler *(A 3-part story)*
When a masked man carrying a crossbow
enters the homes of several lonely
housewives, ransacks their larders for food,
and then leaves the women in a state of
horror, Det. Chf Insp. Taggart, DS
Livingstone and DC Jardine find themselves
in a race against the clock to prevent further
break-ins by the mysterious bowman – but
their prey eludes them and before long they
are investigating a series of vicious murders.
DC Jardine James Macpherson (Intro.)
Kevin Redman Rod Culbertson
Kim Redman Sheila Grier
Patrick Clark Philip Dupuy

Director: Haldane Duncan
Designer: Marius Der Werff

Funeral Rites

w Glen Chandler
A charred corpse, the confession of a man
determined to kill his wife and a missing
teenager lead Taggart and Jardine into a
baffling case that appears to have black

magic connections. While Taggart attempts to solve the puzzle of a dead man's fingerprints found on a murder weapon, DS Jardine finds himself working undercover in a hippy community. Tommy Campbell has witnessed a murder, but deaf and dumb, he is unable to help the detectives.

Colin Davidson **Paul Young**
Maggie Davidson **Annette Crosbie**
Tommy Campbell **Vincent Friell**
Roger Freedman **Nic d'Avirro**

Director: **Alan Macmillan**
Designer: **Geoff Nixon**

TAGGART
Created by: Glenn Chandler
Producer: Robert Love
Music by: Mike Moran
Title song sung by: Maggie Bell
A Scottish Television Network Production
21 colour 60-minute episodes
6 – 20 September 1983
2 – 16 July 1985
23 July – 6 August 1985
24 February – 10 March 1985
2 – 16 September 1986
15 – 29 April 1987
9 – 23 September 1987

TARGET LUNA

The programme that introduced Professor Wedgwood and his family of space adventurers (see *Pathfinders* entry).

A cheaply-made, but nevertheless interesting science-fiction oater, straight from the pages of a boy's comic book. (Most of the time the sets were in danger of falling over, and the acting was, unintentionally, way over-the-top.)

REGULAR CAST

Professor Wedgwood **David Markham**   *Mrs Wedgwood* **Annette Kerr**
Valerie Wedgwood **Sylvia Davies**   *Jimmy Wedgwood* **Michael Hammond**
Geoffrey Wedgwood **Michael Craze**   *Mr Henderson* **Frank Finlay**
Dr Stevens **Robert Stuart**   *Flt Lt Williams* **William Ingram**

Target Luna

w **Malcolm Hulke and Eric Paice**
(A 6-part serial)
Having successfully sent a man into outer space, Professor Wedgwood invites his children to join him at his rocket station for their Easter holidays. They find an even more daring experiment is in preparation – the first manned rocket to the moon.

When the pilot falls ill, Jimmy Wedgwood is given the opportunity of taking his place, but an electrical storm cuts his radio contact with Earth as he circles the moon – and the rocket's heating system is in danger of breaking down (leaving the boy to freeze to death). Did Jimmy escape? Of course he did. But not before his rocket had been bombarded by cosmic particles and the real pilot (now recovered from his illness) had talked him down to a safe landing.

The Rocket Station
Countdown
The Strange Illness
Storm in Space
Solar Flare
The Falling Star

Director: **Adrian Brown**
Designer: **David Gillespie**

TARGET LUNA
Producer: Sidney Newman
An ABC Television Network Presentation
6 monochrome 30-minute episodes
24 April – 29 May 1960

TERRAHAWKS

Thirteen years after Gerry Anderson amazed the viewers with his marvellous Supermarionation process, the puppet-master returned with a new technique dubbed Supermacromation (the use of puppets controlled without strings – glove puppets). The programme: Terrahawks. The format: the exploits of five gallant heroes whose mission was to save Earth from the evil (and ugly) Zelda, an android from the planet Guk who, together with her equally evil (and ugly) son Yung Star, and her (hideous) twin sister Cy Star, set out to make life difficult for Earth by trying to conquer the planet with her cube-shaped robots – only to be thwarted time and again by the Terrahawks: Dr Tiger Ninestein, a clone with nine lives; Mary Falconer, pilot of the team's spacecraft, the Battlehawk; Kate Kestrel, a pop-singer turned heroine; Hawkeye, an American; and Lt Hiro, the 'brains' of the outfit.

Aiding the 'human' heroes with a team of circular robots called Zeroids, who were commanded (on Earth) by Sergeant Major Zero, and (in Space) by Space Sergeant 101, pilot of the Zeroid spaceship, Spacehawk.

By far and away the least enjoyable of the Anderson programmes (unless you're between the ages six to ten).

CHARACTER VOICES
Windsor Davies, Denise Bryer, Jeremy Hitcher, Anne Ridler, Ben Stevens

Season One
13 colour 30-minute episodes

Expect the Unexpected (Part 1)

w Gerry Anderson
The year: 2020. The Terrahawks Organisation is mounted and they are ready to defend Earth against hostilities. When an energy source is picked up heading for Earth, Lt Hiro and his robot Zeroids blast off – but fail to destroy it . . .

Expect the Unexpected (Part 2)

w Gerry Anderson
The Hawkwing and Battlehawk are launched to investigate, but Ninestein is captured by Zelda, who uses him as a hostage in a bid to escape – but Hiro frees Tiger.
Director: Alan Pattillo

Thunder Roar

w Tony Barwick

When Zelda releases one of her allies, Lord Sram, from suspended animation and sends him to Earth, Sram is shot down by Kate Kestrel. But the alien survives the crash – and makes life very uncomfortable for Tiger Ninestein.

Director: Alan Pattillo

Happy Madeday

w Tony Barwick

Master of disguise, Mold, a faceless alien, is sent to Earth by Zelda. He crash-lands in the Arctic and takes the form of Lt Hiro, to sabotage Earth's defences and allow Zelda to invade the planet.

Director: Tony Lenny

The Ugliest Monster of All

w Tony Barwick

When Spacehawk picks up an unmanned and unharmed space capsule, then finds it contains Yuri, a cuddly space bear, Mary Falconer and Kate Kestrel adopt Yuri as their pet – but the bear is really Zelda's agent.

Director: Tony Lenny

Close Call

w Tony Barwick

Journalist Mark Darrol threatens to expose the Terrahawks. Zelda contacts him and puts him aboard a ship taking food to the Terrahawks' base. But Tiger Ninestein has his own methods of writing off this latest threat.

Director: Desmond Saunders

The Gun

w Tony Barwick

When an AS4 titanium ore carrier is drawn off course and Zelda places her cube robots on board, the Terrahawks find themselves up to their necks in trouble when the robots transform into a huge space gun and threaten a new dam.

Director: Tony Bell

Gunfight at Oaky's Corral

w Tony Barwick

Sergeant Major Zero and the Battlehawk destroy five of Zelda's cube robots in the wild west county of Bad Water. But one cube survives and Zelda uses it to take over hill-billy Sam Oaky – and plan a shoot-out with Tiger at high noon.

Director: Tony Bell

Thunder Path

w Tony Barwick

Zelda tries again. This time she sends a second Lord Sram to Earth and the alien manages to sabotage the Overlander in a valley. He boards it and sets out on a collision course with a fuel refinery.

Director: Tony Lenny

From Her to Infinity

w Tony Barwick

Alpha Probe, first launched in 1999, returns to Earth and the Terrahawks are assigned to bring it to their base, where the Zeroids begin to work on it, unaware that Zelda has secreted one of her cube robots on board – with a gravity bomb.

Director: Alan Pattillo

Mind Monster

w Tony Barwick

When Lt Hiro and Kate pick up a glass cabinet of mist and take it back to Hawknest, Mary finds herself confronting Sra, Hawkeye meets Moid, and Tiger finds himself menaced by the Sporilla.

Director: Tony Bell

A Christmas Miracle

w Tony Barwick

It's Christmas Eve, but neither Ninestein or Zelda have time for festivities. Both are busy planning their strategies for their battle on the moon. On Christmas Day, their battle begins in earnest.

Director: Tony Lenny

To Catch a Tiger

w Tony Barwick

While they are searching for gold on Mars, two crewmen from a space transporter find themselves Zelda's prisoners. She holds them hostage until Ninestein agrees to come to her headquarters – to be executed by Moid.

Director: Tony Lenny

Season Two

13 colour 60-minute episodes

Operation SAS

w Tony Barwick
When Yung Star seizes his chance to fly to Earth, Zelda makes him take Yuri the Space Bear along with him. Later, Kate is captured and Ninestein decides that it will take an SAS-type operation to rescue her.
Director: Tony Lenny

Ten Top Pop

w Tony Barwick
Zelda is up to her tricks again. This time she plans to gain control of her destiny by launching another assault against her enemies. But as usual, the Terrahawks exit from the adventure victorious.
Director: Tony Bell

Play It Again, Sram

w Tony Barwick
After Kate Kestrel wins the World Song Contest, Ninestein receives an unexpected challenge from Zelda – who sends the mighty Sram to destroy the Terrahawks and their entire operation.
Director: Tony Bell

The Ultimate Menace

w Tony Barwick
Why should the Terrahawks team be sent to Mars – the base for Zelda's operations? Tiger is baffled by his assignment. Until Zelda plays her trump card – and the Terrahawks are once again pitted in battle against her cube robots.
Director: Tony Lenny

Midnight Blue

w Tony Barwick
When Spacehawk fires at a Zeaf but it escapes, Hawkwing is assigned to pursue the alien. Suddenly the Zeaf becomes miniaturised. Has Hawkwing chased her too far and become trapped in orbit?
Director: Tony Lenny

My Kingdom for a Zeaf

w Tony Barwick
Richard III and Yung Star in the 21st century? What is going on? Ninestein and his team must find out soon. The scenario spells death for one of the Terrahawks team.
Director: Tony Lenny

Zero's Finest Hour

w Tony Barwick
By using the Overlander, the supply line to Hawknest, Zelda hopes to gain a victory over her enemies. But why has she delivered a pretty bunch of flowers to the Terrahawks team? Is she seeking a truce?
Director: Tony Bell

Cold Finger

w Tony Barwick
Zelda has a new ally, Cold Finger. Together they plot to destroy Earth by bombing it with millions of tons of ice. Will her plan succeed? Or can the Terrahawks pump holes in Zelda's murderous scheme?
Director: Tony Bell

Unseen Menace

w Tony Barwick
Moid (the Master of Infinite Disguise) has perfected an impersonation that is guaranteed to destroy Ninestein and his friends. He travels to Earth as an invisible man to wreak havoc with the Terrahawks.
Director: Tony Bell

Space Giant

w Tony Barwick
When two space miners capture a baby Sporilla and decide to smuggle it back to Earth, the Terrahawks will soon have their work cut out defending their base against Zelda's latest plot to destroy them.
Director: Tony Lenny

Cry UFO

w Tony Barwick
Stewed Apple is disturbed when he sees a close-encounter-type spaceship. But Tiger and the Terrahawks discover that it belongs to Zelda and blow it up – ending yet another attempt to defeat them.
Director: Tony Bell

The Midas Touch

w Trevor Lansdown and Tony Barwick
The world's gold reserves, stored at Fort
Knox, attract the attention of Zelda and her
friends. Realising that it would cause
economic disaster if she could destroy it, she
sends the monstrous Knell to Earth.
Director: Alan Pattillo

Ma's Monsters

w Tony Barwick
Aware of the fact that the Terrahawks have
overcome everything she has thrown at
them, Zelda decides to mount another
attempt to defeat her enemies – but this
time she has a powerful surprise in store.
Director: Tony Bell

Season Three

13 colour 30-minute episodes

Two for the Price of One

w Tony Barwick
When they plan an attack on Zelda's
Martian base, the Terrahawks are in for a
big surprise. They discover that Cy Star is
about to produce a baby. Tiger decides the
time is ripe to change the situation.
Director: Tony Lenny

First Strike

w Tony Barwick
Against Tiger's better judgement, the
military send a giant space carrier on a first-
strike mission against Zelda's base on Mars.
It isn't long before the Terrahawks are
needed to straighten out the mess.
Director: Tony Lenny

Terrabomb

w Tony Barwick
When a Zeaf crash-lands on Earth,
Battletank is sent out to destroy it. But
then Zelda announces that she has planted a
bomb at Hawknest and the Terrahawks face
a race against time to find and defuse it.
Director: Tony Bell

Space Cyclops

w Tony Barwick
An alien meteorite lands on the moon and a
giant Cyclops begins to form from the
wreckage – yet another of Zelda's monsters.
The Zeroids attack, but the Cyclops appears
unbeatable – until SM Zero has an idea.
Director: Tony Lenny

Doppelganger

w Tony Barwick
When two statues – one of Yung Star and
the other of Cy Star – appear in a museum,
the Terrahawks investigate. But the statues
suddenly begin to move – and Mary
Falconer finds her life in danger.
Director: Tony Lenny

Child's Play

w Tony Barwick
It's attack time. Zelda plants a giant bomb
under the Trans-American pipeline, while
her friend Birlgoy produces a super-
explosive guaranteed to take care of the
Terrahawks.
Director: Tony Bell

Jolly Roger One

w Tony Barwick
When a space pirate joins forces with Zelda
to attack the Terrahawks, and his pirate
spaceship fights a winning battle with
Spacehawk, it appears that Zelda has finally
defeated her enemy. But has she?
Director: Tony Lenny

Runaway

w Tony Barwick
Has Zelda finally discovered the location of
Hawknest? When the station comes under
attack it seems as though she has. Is this the
end of the Terrahawks? Can Tiger and his
crew survive?
Director: Tony Bell

Space Samurai

w Tony Barwick
Tamura, a space samurai and commander of
a powerful battle cruiser, insists that Zelda
and Ninestein patch up their vendetta.
Prepared for the worst, Tiger agrees –
knowing that Zelda cannot be trusted.
Director: Desmond Saunders

Time Warp

w Tony Barwick

Using Lord Tempo's powers, Zelda tries to introduce a time warp into Hawknest. But Mary's mind proves too strong and rejects the attempt – so Zelda decides to try the same ruse on SM Zero . . . with hilarious results.

Director: Tony Bell

Operation Zero

w Tony Barwick

When SM Zero is admitted to hospital for an operation and comes round to find that Zelda has infiltrated Hawknest and Ninestein now speaks with Yung Star's voice, the Zeroid believes he's losing his mind.

Director: Tony Lenny

The Sporilla

w Tony Barwick

A visit to the distant moon Callisto is an unpleasant experience for Tiger and his crew. They find themselves faced by a fearsome Sporilla – one of Zelda's most terrifying monsters.

Director: Tony Bell

Gold

w Tony Barwick

While the Zeroids are exploring a crater on a meteorite they believe may contain gold, Zelda sits back and smiles. The 'golden nugget' they find is secretly a bomb – planted there for just such an occasion.

Director: Desmond Saunders

TERRAHAWKS
Created by: Gerry Anderson
Producers: Gerry Anderson and Christopher Burr
Associate producer: Bob Bell
Music by: Richard Harvey
(Additional music by: Gerry Anderson and Christopher Burr)
Special effects by: Stephen Begg
An Anderson-Burr Pictures/LWT Production
39 colour 30-minute episodes
8 October – 31 December 1983
23 September – 30 December 1984
3 May – 26 July 1986

THUNDERBIRDS

The rescue operations of International Rescue (IR), five fabulous life-saving machines operated by five fabulous heroes whose brief was to undertake rescue missions of every type, in any situation.

Based on a mountain-top fortress somewhere in the Pacific, the five *Thunderbirds* soared off to avert disaster and save the lives of people trapped in unusual predicaments with a blend of panache and determination that wouldn't have gone amiss in the control room of Captain Kirk's USS *Enterprise*.

Head of the operation was ex-astronaut Jeff Tracey and his five sons, each of whom had been named after the first five American astronauts in space.

There was Scott, pilot of Thunderbird I, a sleek craft capable of speeds in excess of 7,000 mph; Virgil, pilot of Thunderbird II, a freighter used for carrying the rescue equipment; Alan, who controlled Thunderbird III, a machine capable of flying into the outer reaches of space; Gordon, co-pilot of Thunderbird II, who also took over the controls of Thunderbird IV (a submersible, which was used in underwater rescue missions); and John, the controller of Thunderbird V, the team's space satellite.

Rounding up the team were 'Brains' the scientific genius who invented the vehicles, and Lady Penelope, the organisation's upper-crust heroine, who was driven to her missions in her shocking-pink Rolls Royce (Reg. No: FAB 1) by her off-beat Cockney chauffeur and manservant Parker.

The villain of the piece was the Hood, a ruthless, dome-headed space-age villain who had taken a liking to the Thunderbirds and laid plans to steal them.

Without doubt, the best-loved of all the Gerry Anderson 'Supermarionation' series. Each adventure was a small-screen epic and the series (rightly) earned itself a niche in television history. (It also spawned two full-length feature films: *Thunderbirds Are Go* (1966) and *Thunderbird Six* (1968).)

CHARACTER VOICES

Jeff Tracey Peter Dyneley   *Scott Tracey* Shane Rimmer
Virgil Tracey David Holliday   *Alan Tracey* Matt Zimmerman
Gordon Tracey David Graham   *John Tracey* Ray Barrett
Lady Penelope Sylvia Anderson   *Brains* David Graham
Parker David Graham   *The Hood* Ray Barrett
Tin Tin/Grandma Christine Finn

Season One
26 colour 60-minute episodes

Trapped in the Sky (Pilot Story)

w Gerry and Sylvia Anderson
International Rescue set out on their first mission – to save the atomic airliner Fireflash from destruction. The Hood has planted a bomb in its landing gear and the superplane's passengers will be exposed to atomic radiation unless IR can avert disaster.
Director: Alan Pattillo

Pit of Peril

w Alan Fennell
When Sidewinder, a US Army walking fortress, slips from its rails and crashes into an underground pit of fire and US Army helicopters are unable to retrieve the vehicle, IR are called in to rescue the crew trapped in Sidewinder's control room.
Director: Desmond Saunders

The Perils of Penelope

w Alan Pattillo
Assisting Sir Jeremy Hodge in his attempts to find the missing Professor Borender, a man who has discovered how to turn water into rocket fuel, Lady Penelope finds herself taken hostage by the evil Dr Godber.
Directors: Alan Pattillo and Desmond Saunders

Terror in New York City

w Alan Fennell
When TV reporter Ned Cook decides to take secret film of the Thunderbird's team during their rescue missions, Thunderbird II is accidentally shot down, and plans to move the Empire State building end in a state of collapse, IR are soon on the scene.
Directors: David Lane and David Elliott

Edge of Impact

w Donald Robertson
Paid by General Bron to destroy the new British Red Arrow fighter-plane, the Hood

is delighted when the plane crashes, but soon has cause for remorse when Red Arrow II hits a television relay tower, trapping two men in its pressurised cabin.
Director: Desmond Saunders

Day of Disaster

w Dennis Spooner
Lady Penelope and Brains, watching the Mars Probe rocket being taken to its launch site across the Arlington Bridge, find themselves involved in another IR rescue mission when the bridge collapses and the rocket becomes trapped in the river bed.
Director: David Elliott

30 Minutes after Noon

w Alan Fennell
Another tense mission for IR. This time they have to rescue Prescott, a man with a bomb locked securely to his wrist before he and Southern, a British agent, are destroyed in an office building.
Director: David Elliott

Desperate Intruder

w Donald Robertson
Having joined the eccentric Professor Blakely on his mission to discover treasure in the underwater temple of Lake Anasta, Brains and Tin Tin are taken prisoner by the Hood – who buries Brains in the desert sand.
Director: David Lane

End of the Road

w Dennis Spooner
Determined to complete the building of a mountain road before the storm season breaks, Eddie Houseman finds himself trapped when his truck-load of explosives is blown onto a cliff-ledge. Gray, boss of the construction team, calls in IR.
Director: David Lane

The Uninvited

w Alan Fennell
Shot down over the Sahara Desert by mysterious fighter planes, Scott lands Thunderbird I and meets two archaeologists who have found the lost tomb of

Khamandides. Sometime later, all three men are captured by Zombites – the creatures who shot down Thunderbird I.
Director: Desmond Saunders

Sun Probe

w Alan Fennell
Informed that three solarnauts from the Sun Probe project have accidentally left their orbit and are on course for the Sun, IR launch Thunderbirds II and III to attempt to fire Sun Probe's rockets by remote control.
Director: David Lane

Operation Crash Dive

w Martin Crump
Thunderbird IV is sent to rescue two crewmen trapped on board Fireflash, which has crashed into the sea. Meanwhile, suspecting sabotage, Scott tracks the next flight in Thunderbird I – and the saboteurs strike again.
Director: Desmond Saunders

Vault of Death

w Dennis Spooner
A bank clerk finds himself trapped inside a new impregnable bank vault. The man will die of suffocation unless Lord Seton, the only man in England with a key to the vault, is located. Parker finds himself involved in a drama of his own making.
Director: David Elliott

The Mighty Atom

w Dennis Spooner
The Hood plans to gain the secrets of a new atomic power station in the Sahara. To do so, he steals a robotic mouse – the Mighty Atom – and then sets fire to the plant so that IR will arrive to avert an atomic explosion.
Director: David Lane

City of Fire

w Alan Fennell
When a car accident in one of its parking areas causes the Thompson Tower shopping complex to catch fire, Scott and Virgil use

the Mole to burrow into the inferno to rescue some people trapped amid the flames.
Director: David Elliott

The Imposters

w Dennis Spooner

Someone is impersonating IR, so Jeff shuts down operations. IR agent Jeremiah Tuttle gets a lead to the impostors, but Jeff is forced to resume operations when an American astronaut is lost in space and only Thunderbird III can rescue him.
Director: Desmond Saunders

The Man From MI5

w Alan Fennell

Asked by Bob Bondson of MI5 to help him retrieve plans for a secret atomic weapon which have been stolen, Lady Penelope agrees. Posing as model Gayle Williams, she is kidnapped – and left in a boathouse tied to a bomb!
Director: David Lane

Cry Wolf

w Dennis Spooner

When two young Australian boys accidentally call out IR while playing a game of 'rescues' and the boys are then taken prisoner by the Hood, who plans to steal satellite photos from their father, their latest distress call convinces Jeff that it's just another hoax.
Director: David Elliott

Danger at Ocean Deep

w Donald Robertson

When Ocean Pioneer I explodes after launching and Brains discovers that a cargo of liquid alsterene will explode when in contact with OD60, a chemical liquid dumped in the same region as that being used for Pioneer II's maiden voyage, IR find their services in great demand.
Director: Desmond Saunders

Move and You're Dead

w Alan Pattillo

After winning the Parola Sands motor race in Brains's new car, Alan falls foul of rival driver Victor Gomez, who traps Alan and

Grandma on a bridge with an ultrasonic bomb that will detonate if they move. Enter IR to save the day.
Director: Alan Pattillo

The Duchess Assignment

w Martin Crump

On holiday in France, Lady Penelope observes crooks swindling a Duchess out of her wealth at a casino, but is unable to stop their getaway. She contacts IR, and her friends retrieve the situation.
Director: David Elliott

Brink of Disaster

w Alan Fennell

Approached by crooked businessman Grafton, who wants her to finance a Trans-American monorail, Lady Penelope alerts Jeff – and inadvertently places his life in danger when part of the monorail track collapses, leaving Jeff and Tin Tin in danger.
Director: David Lane

Attack of the Alligators!

w Alan Pattillo

When Dr Orchard develops Thuramine, a plant extract to enlarge animals and end famine, but his boatman Culp tries to steal some and flushes it into a creek, the IR team soon find themselves called out to avert the threat of giant alligators.
Director: David Lane

Martian Invasion

w Alan Fennell

Posing as a film financier, the Hood traps two actors in a flooded cave while they are making a Martian invasion film. Using his hypnotic powers, he has Kyrano disable Thunderbird I's automatic camera detector so that he can film the rescue attempt.
Director: David Elliott

The Chan-Chan

w Alan Pattillo

Every time that the Cass Carnaby Five do a live performance of their 'Dangerous Game' act, their fighter planes are destroyed. Disguised as Wanda L'Amour, Lady

Penelope travels to Paradise Peak in Switzerland to investigate.
Director: Alan Pattillo

Security Hazard

w Alan Pattillo
Returning from a mission in England, Thunderbirds I and II find they have an unwanted guest on board – a young boy called Chip, who has stowed away in Pod I. While awaiting their next mission, the Tracey brothers tell Chip about some of their missions.
Director: Desmond Saunders

Season Two

6 colour 60-minute episodes

Atlantic Inferno

w Alan Fennell
Having persuaded Jeff to take a holiday, Scott is in charge when a World Navy submarine test-missile ignites a gas pocket, which threatens a Seascape rig and the lives of its crew. Against his father's wishes, Scott mobilises IR.
Director: Desmond Saunders

Path of Destruction

w Donald Robertson
When Crablogger One, an atomic tree-feller and pulp processor, goes on the rampage after its crew fall foul of food-poisoning, and the machine threatens to crush the San Martino dam atomic-reactor, IR receive an urgent distress call.
Director: David Elliott

Alias Mr Hackenbacker

w Alan Pattillo
Brains, alias Hiram K. Hackenbacker, places a new secret safety-device on board the Skythrust aircraft, on which Lady Penelope is holding a fashion show with designer Francois Lemaire. Skythrust is hijacked by a gang seeking Lemaire's new fabric design.
Director: Desmond Saunders

Lord Parker's 'Oliday

w Tony Barwick
Parker comes into his own. When a solar energy-plant goes haywire after a storm causes its solar dish to collapse and focus the sun's rays on the town below, 'Lord' Parker and Bruno distract the town's inhabitants by playing bingo.
Director: Brian Burgess

Richochet

w Tony Barwick
The Telesat 4 rocket from Sentinel Base goes rogue and IR have to designate a sector for its destruction – not knowing that the place they choose is occupied by DJ Rick O'Shea, a space pirate who runs an unlicensed TV station.
Director: Brian Burgess

Give or Take a Million

w Alan Pattillo
Nicky, a child from Coralville children's hospital arrives at Tracey Island to spend Christmas with IR. The boy and the Traceys find themselves spending Christmas 2026 in a story of high adventure.
Director: Desmond Saunders

THUNDERBIRDS
Producers: Gerry Anderson (Season One)
Reg Hill (Season Two)
Associate producers: Reg Hill (Season One)
John Read (Season Two)
Executive producers: Gerry Anderson (Season Two)
Music by: Barry Gray
Script editor: Alan Pattillo (Season One)
Special effects director: Derek Meddings
An ITC Entertainment/APF TV Production in association with ATV
(APF not involved in Season Two)
32 colour 60-minute episodes
30 September 1965 – 31 March 1966
3, 4 October – 26, 27 December 1966
(Season Two stories screened in two parts)
(USA: Syndicated 1968)

THE TOMORROW PEOPLE

The exploits of *The Tomorrow People*, a group of youngsters who possessed the ability to travel through time and space ('jaunting') and the powers of extra-sensory perception (ESP) and telekinesis.

Created by Roger Price (who described the team as Homo Superiors – the next stage of human evolution), the series spanned five years of cleverly devised stories which depicted how the team saved the human race from all manner of alien invaders by using their remarkable abilities for the good of mankind.

Sadly, though the programme started out as an intelligent attempt to combine science-fiction and adventure in a package that would attract younger viewers, midway through its third season it developed into grade B juvenile antics and went quickly downhill.

REGULAR CAST

John **Nicholas Young**   *Stephen* (Seasons 1 – 4) **Peter Vaughan-Clarke**
Carol (Season 1) **Sammie Winmill**   *Kenny* (Season 1) **Stephen Salmon**
Elizabeth (Seasons 2 – 8) **Hazel Adare**   *Tyso* (Seasons 3 and 4) **Dean Lawrence**
Mike (Seasons 4 – 8) **Mike Holloway**   *Hsui Tai* (Seasons 7 and 8) **Misako Koba**
Voice of Tim **Philip Gilbert**
Professor Cawston (Seasons 2 and 3) **Brian Stanion**

Season One

13 colour 30-minute episodes

The Slaves of Jedikiah

w Brian Finch and Roger Price
(A 5-part story)
Stephen, a young schoolboy, learns that he is a 'Tomorrow Person'. Helped by John, Carol and Kenny, they overcome the threat of Jedikiah, an alien, shape-changing robot, and Stephen sets off for further adventures with his new friends.
Jedikiah **Francis de Wolff**
Ginge **Michael Standing**
Cyclops **Robert Bridges**
Lefty **Derek Crewe**

Director: **Paul Bernard**
Designer: **Harry Clark**

The Medusa Strain

w Brian Finch and Roger Price
(A 4-part story)
Stephen, now a fully-fledged Tomorrow Person, finds himself facing the evil Jedikiah

again, this time in the company of Rabowski, a space pirate who has captured Peter, a Guardian of Time, whose powers the aliens intend to use to wreak havoc on Earth.
Jedikiah **Roger Bizley**
Peter **Richard Speight**
Rabowski **Roger Booth**
Android **Dave Prowse**

Director: **Roger Price**
Designer: **Harry Clark**

The Vanishing Earth

w Brian Finch and Roger Price
(A 4-part story)
A new adventure, a new enemy – Spidron, an alien who has the power to destroy Earth by causing volcanoes to erupt and earthquakes to devastate land masses. The Tomorrow People face their greatest challenge yet – but will their combined powers prove strong enough to avert worldwide disaster and the death of the human race?

Carol Sammie Winmill (Exit)
Steen Kevin Storey
Spidron John Woodnutt
Kenny Stephen Salmon (Exit)

Director: Paul Bernard
Designer: Harry Clark

Season Two
13 colour 30-minute episodes

The Blue and the Green

w Roger Price   *(A 5-part story)*
Elizabeth, a young schoolgirl, becomes
involved in an outbreak of riots in schools
all over the country and faces the threat of
the strange paintings that mysteriously
change their scenes and cast an evil spell
over anyone near them. The girl meets John
and Stephen and learns that she is a
Tomorrow Person. With their help, she
solves the mystery of the stranger called
Robert.
Elizabeth Hazel Adare (Intro.)
Grandfather Nigel Pegram
Robert Jason Kemp
Chris Christopher Chittell

Director: Roger Price
Designer: Michael Minas

A Rift in Time

w Roger Price   *(A 4-part story)*
When Tomorrow People John and Stephen
share a simultaneous dream about Peter, the
young Guardian of Time they met during
the Medusa Strain affair, and discover that
the boy has been captured by Zennon, a
renegade Time Guardian, with the aid of a
time disc made by TIM, they follow Peter
to the 21st century – and into an adventure
in which they almost lose their powers
forever!
Peter Richard Speight
Gaius Stanley Lebor
Zennon Stephen Jack
Professor Cawston Brian Stanion (Intro.)

Director: Darrol Blake
Designer: Michael Minas

The Doomsday Men

w Roger Price   *(A 4-part story)*
The Tomorrow People meet the Doomsday
Men, a race of beings devoted to preserving

war. Stephen is sent to a school where the
pupils include Douglas McLelland, the
grandson of 'Iron Mac', leader of the
Doomsday men. His mission, to bring
Douglas to the Tomorrow People's
laboratory, where the team will attempt to
convince him that war is brutal. But when
Stephen and Douglas 'jaunt' back to the lab
they find themselves face to face with Iron
Mac and his war adviser, Major Longford.
Iron Mac Lindsay Campbell
Douglas William Relton
Major Longford Derek Murcott
Lee Wan Eric Young

Director: Roger Price
Designer: Michael Minas

Season Three
13 colour 30-minute episodes

Secret Weapon

w Roger Price   *(A 4-part story)*
An adventure which starts with a new
Tomorrow Person, Tyso, asking for help. It
transpires that Tyso is being held against his
will by Colonel Masters and his assistant
Miss Conway – a woman who has the ability
to read minds. Using her powers, she
attempts to learn the Tomorrow People's
secrets – until John 'jaunts' in to interfere
with her plans . . . and almost pays with
his life.
Tyso Dean Lawrence (Intro.)
Miss Conway Anne Curthoys
Colonel Masters Trevor Bannister
Professor Cawston Bryan Stanton

Director: Stan Woodward
Designer: Philip Blowers

Worlds Away

w Roger Price   *(A 3-part story)*
Heeding a request from Timus Nosta, who
begs them to free the people of the planet
Peerie from the dreadful Khultan, a strange
creature who is terrorising the Vesh – that
planet's Tomorrow People – and hunting
them down to be burned by the Veshtakers,
the Homo Superiors find themselves racing
against time to defeat their enemy. The
burnings begin at noon.

Timus **Philip Gilbert**
Veshtaker **Barry Linehan**
Lenda **Lydia Lisle**
Arkron **Keith Chegwin**

Director: **Dennis Kirkland**
Designer: **Philip Blowers**

A Man for Emily

w **Roger Price** *(A 3-part story)*
Jaunting into space to inspect a spaceship
which has entered Earth's orbit, John and
Elizabeth find the ship occupied by an alien
family consisting of the Momma and her
children, their alien servant Elmer and the
spoilt Emily. Within moments, they find
themselves involved in the affairs of Elmer,
who escapes to Earth and wreaks havoc,
landing in jail and refusing to return to the
ship to continue his role as Emily's
'companion', whereby Momma decides that
John must take Elmer's place as Emily's
'Man-Boy'.
Emily **Sandra Dickinson**
The Momma **Margaret Burton**
Elmer **Peter Davidson**
Mr Greenhead **Bill Dean**

Director: **Stan Woodward**
Designer: **Philip Blowers**

The Revenge of Jedikiah

w **Roger Price** *(A 3-part story)*
Released from imprisonment in the Khultan
pyramid, Jedikiah sets out to take revenge
on the Tomorrow People. Within hours he
takes Stephen's form and enters a research
establishment; he shoots Colonel Masters
and takes on the form of Miss Masters,
luring John and Elizabeth into a trap. Tim
begs Timus for galactic aid, and Timus
gives it – but is killed by Jedikiah – and
Stephen and Tyso are forced to take their
enemy to their lab to confront TIM.
Jedikiah **Francis de Wolff**
Professor Cawston **Bryan Stanion**
Timus **Philip Gilbert**
Evergreen **Denise Cooke**

Director: **Vic Hughes**
Designer: **Philip Blowers**

Season Four
7 colour 30-minute episodes

One Law

w **Roger Price** *(A 3-part story)*
Unaware that he is really a Tomorrow
Person, young Mike Bell decides to use his
special gift of being able to open locks with
his mind to rob banks and get rich, but he
falls into the hands of Lord Dunning, an
unscrupulous man who forces him to
cooperate in his plans to steal a fortune in
gold. Stephen, rescued by John and
Elizabeth, finally learns his true destiny and
the Tomorrow People increase their ranks.
Mike **Mike Holoway** (Intro.)
O'Reilly **Patrick McAlinney**
Lord Dunning **Harold Kasket**
Inspector Burke **Tim Barrett**

Director: **Leon Thau**
Designer: **Peter Elliot**

Into the Unknown

w **John Watkins** *(A 4-part story)*
As Mike is composing a pop song in the
lab, a message from outer space flashes on
screen – a distress signal that takes the
Tomorrow People on a journey to the Pluto
Five region of the Solar System to try to
help a stricken spaceship. They find
themselves trapped and helpless as the ship
plunges deeper and deeper into a black hole
– their only chance of survival depending on
Tim.
Tyso **Dean Lawrence** (Exit)
Tiraiyaan **Geoffrey Bayldon**
Stephen **Peter Vaughan Clarke** (Exit)
Vaktaan **Brian Coburn**

Director: **Roger Price**
Designer: **Peter Elliot**

Season Five
6 colour 30-minute episodes

The Dirtiest Business

w **Roger Price** *(A 2-part story)*
The Tomorrow People become involved in
the espionage business when they are asked
to free Pavla, a young girl agent, from the
SIS and KGB. Will they be able to rescue

her from Major Turner's brainwashing machine and prevent the enemy triggering off their secret X-delta device?
Pavla Anulka Dubinska
KGB Man Jan Murzynowski
Major Turner Vivien Heilbron
Senior KGB Man Gabor Vernon

Director: Vic Hughes
Designer: David Richens

A Much Needed Holiday

w Roger Price   *(A 2-part story)*
When they unearth valuable treasures during their archaeological survey on the planet Gallia, the Tomorrow People find themselves involved with two runaway slaves who have escaped from a diamond mine – and are being hunted by the fearsome Kleptons.
Gremlon Anthony Garner
Trog David Corti
Trig Guy Humphries
Timus Philip Gilbert

Director: Richard Mervyn
Designer: David Richens

The Heart of Sogguth

w Roger Price   *(A 2-part story)*
When the Head of Ethnic Studies at a university offers to manage Mike's pop group, the young Tomorrow Person finds himself playing a drum tattoo that could raise the forces of evil and bring about the destruction of the Universe. Meanwhile, John and Elizabeth come face to face with a force that can rule their minds.
Jake Roddy Maude-Roxby
Derek Derek Pascoe
Mike Harding James Smilie
Bill Bill Rice

Director: Vic Hughes
Designer: David Richens

Season Six
6 colour 30-minute episodes

The Lost Gods

w Roger Price   *(A 2-part story)*
When Mike tries flying solo in a hang glider, he receives a telepathic message from a remote religious sect in the Far East – and the Tomorrow People suddenly find themselves plunged into a new adventure in which ancient spirits are called from the dead to witness the rebirth of a god – with the Tomorrow People as human sacrifices in a ceremony of fire!
Hsui Tai Misako Kobo (Intro.)
Matsu Tan Burt Kwouk
Sage Robert Lee

Director: Peter Webb
Designer: David Richens

Hitler's Last Secret

w Roger Price   *(A 2-part story)*
What connection is there between the Tomorrow People and a young boy wearing a Nazi uniform, killed in a road accident in a remote town in Germany? The team face a race against time to find the answer – before their telepathic powers are snuffed out when they come face to face with the most diabolical enemy they have ever faced . . . the return of the Third Reich.
Hitler Michael Sheard
Blitz Ray Burdis
Professor Friedl Richard Warner
Brandt Nicholas Hurst

Director: Leon Thau
Designer: Allan Cameron

The Thargon Menace

w Roger Price   *(A 2-part story)*
When a terrifying weapon – the Ripper Ray, powerful enough to destroy an entire planet – falls into the hands of General Papa Minn, a deranged alien despot who has landed on Earth and threatens to destroy all human life unless the government accedes to his demands, the Tomorrow People are called in to avert world disaster.
General Papa Minn Olu Jacobs
Flyn Michael Audreson
Sula Jackie Cowper
Major Marcos Eric Roberts

Director: Peter Yolland
Designer: Martyn Herbert

Season Seven

6 colour 30-minute episodes

Castle of Fear

w Roger Price   *(A 2-part story)*
The most unusual adventure yet for the
Tomorrow People: they dream of the Loch
Ness Monster, 'meet' Frankenstein's creation
(plus a ghost and a gorilla) and end up
fighting a battle between the Redcoats and
the Highlanders. What is going on? Who is
controlling their thoughts?
Andrew Forbes Nigel Rhodes (Intro.)
McDuff Bill Gavin
Bruce Forbes Dominic Allan
Dr Mayer Jennifer Watts

Director: Vic Hughes
Designer: Gordon Toms

Achilles Heel

w Roger Price   *(A 2-part story)*
With only 10 minutes left in which they
can prevent the destruction of an entire
galaxy, the Tomorrow People are powerless
to help – they have been stripped of their
powers by two mysterious alien visitors to
Earth.
Yagon Hilary Minster
Bruce Dominic Allan
Glip Stanley Bates
Cantor Christian Rodska

Director: Vic Hughes
Designer: Gordon Toms

Living Skins

w Roger Price   *(A 2-part story)*
When John and Elizabeth go shopping at a
fashionable boutique, they bring back more
than they bargained for and the Tomorrow
People must overcome the latest threat to
Earth by giving a unique and priceless gift
to the Homo Sapiens – one that saves all life
on Earth.

Wilton Ralph Lawford
Young girl Judith Fielding
Guard Dave Carter

Director: Stan Woodward
Designer: Gordon Toms

Season Eight

4 colour 30-minute episodes

War of the Empires

w Roger Price   *(A 4-part story)*
Concerned that the war raging between the
Thargons and Sorsons is moving closer to
Earth, the Tomorrow People request the
help of the Galactic Empire to keep Earth
out of the conflict – but they refuse. The
following day the Sorson leader, General
Vishishnou, lands on Earth and makes a
pact with the President of the USA, and
John, Mike and Hsui Tai are imprisoned
and stripped of their telepathic powers
–leaving John and Elizabeth to face the
mighty Thargon battle fleet.
Vishishnou Richard Bartlett
Thargon Leader Percy Herbert
USA President John F. Parker
Thargon officer Anthony Stafford

Director: Vic Hughes
Designer: John Plant

THE TOMORROW PEOPLE
Created by Roger Price
Producers: Ruth Boswell (Seasons 1 – 3)
Roger Price (Seasons 1 and 4)
Vic Hughes (Seasons 5 – 8)
Music by: Dudley Simpson and
Brian Hodson
A Thames Television Network Production
68 colour 30-minute episodes
30 April - 30 July 1973
4 February – 6 May 1974
26 February – 21 May 1975
28 January – 10 March 1976
28 February – 4 April 1977
15 May – 26 June 1978
9 October – 13 November 1978
29 January – 19 February 1979

Top Secret

The adventures of Peter Dallas, a British Intelligence agent living in Buenos Aires, who was granted a year's leave of absence to join Argentine 'businessman' Miguel Garetta in his fight against the kind of villainy that the official law enforcement agencies could not – or would not – get involved with. (Though his true position was never fully explained, enough hints were given in the stories to persuade viewers that Garetta himself held some high-powered connection with the British Secret Service.)

Dallas, one of the toughest, meanest (but most-likeable) secret agents ever to grace the television screen, would travel across the South American pampas pitting his wits and experience against villains and foreign agents. Aided by Garetta's young nephew Mike, the two men faced danger-fraught assignments which, more often than not, ended in some of the toughest action scenes ever seen in a British television series.

The series made a star of William Franklyn and spawned a worldwide smash hit record, *Sucu Sucu* (Several years later, Franklyn became the voice behind the Schweppes 'Sch-you-know-who' ad.)

Regular Cast

Peter Dallas **William Franklyn**   *Miguel Garetta* **Patrick Cargill**
Mike **Alan Rothwell**

Season One
13 monochrome 60-minute episodes

Destination Buenos Aires

w **Rex Berry**
Arriving in Buenos Aires to accept his first assignment from Miguel Garetta, agent Peter Dallas finds that the enemy, a formidable crime organisation, is waiting for him – with a bullet with his name on it.
Rauch **Honor Blackman**
Salinus **George Rose**
Wilson **Joseph O'Connor**

Director: **Ian Fordyce**

Death on Wheels

w **John Kruse**
Assigned to shadow a foreign president visiting Buenos Aires, Dallas finds himself given 24 hours to track down a deadly assassin who has been commissioned to kill the visitor.
Pereira **Edgar Wreford**
Casamegas **Basil Dignam**
Molina **William Devlin**

Director: **Ian Fordyce**

The Dead Village

w **John Kruse**
Dallas and Mike begin their search for a top British agent who has disappeared while visiting a remote South American village – a place they find deserted. What sinister plot is afoot? The men barely escape with their lives trying to find out.
Kapulka **Kenneth J. Warren**
Commandante **Manning Wilson**
Maria **Maureen Pryor**

Director: **Mark Lawton**

Merchant of Death

w Roger Marshall

Garetta's attempts to involve Dallas in his fight to destroy a powerful drug-smuggling combine almost result in the agent losing his life. His boss 'forgets' to tell Dallas that his cover is blown and the enemy are aware of his every move.

Reinhardt Alan Gifford
Gilda Delphi Lawrence
Becker David Bauer

Director: John Frankau

The Inca Dove

w Bill Strutton

Dallas is assigned to wreak havoc among the troops of a ruthless dictator who threatens to put his newly-acquired kingdom under military rule. Dallas's task, to overcome the despot – by any means he deems necessary.

President Valentine Dyall
Cuyu Frederick Piper
Anita Collette Wilde

Director: Ian Fordyce

Stranger in Cantabria

w Richard Lucas

Who is the mysterious stranger who has sent a message to Dallas asking him to meet him at a secret rendezvous? What is his mission? Dallas has no option but to follow the stranger's request – his life depends upon getting the answer.

Pinerollo Robert Rietty
Mary Fielding Hazel Court
Armas Guy Deghy

Director: Jonathan Alwyn

Vendetta

w John Warwick

A murder has been announced in the local press. Garetta assigns Dallas to unmask the would-be assassin before he can commit the deed. But neither Garetta nor his agent realise that Dallas himself is the intended victim.

Leon Mantez Kevin Stoney
Jose Chambi Carl Bernard
Victor Chambi Paul Eddington

Director: Mark Lawton

The Disappearing Trick

w Roger Marshall

It's a tough mission. Dallas must find Diaz, a man branded as a traitor by a South American government. Garetta can prove the man innocent – but Diaz has disappeared into thin air. Where does Dallas begin his search?

Diaz Robert James
Luis Derek Waring
Mariana Vivienne Drummond

Director: Ian Fordyce

After the Fair

w Bill Strutton and Roger Marshall

Why should anyone wish to kill Halifax, recently arrived in Buenos Aires? The man seems harmless enough, but if someone is out to destroy him he must have something to hide. Dallas is assigned to find the answer.

Halifax Cameron Hall
Hernandez Bernard Archard
Jacquetta Delena Kidd

Director: John Frankau

X

w William Franklyn

Is the man found exhausted and drifting in mid-ocean one of Garetta's agents? He claims to be, so Dallas is handed the task of proving his theory that 'X' is really an impostor in the pay of Garetta's enemies.

X Alfred Burke
Bossman John Glen
Domici William Peacock

Director: Jonathan Alwyn

The Men from Yesterday

w Larry Forrester

Foreign agents believe that Wolf Eberhardt is a war criminal. Garetta is assigned to prove his innocence before the enemy get their man. But Dallas, assigned to prevent Eberhardt leaving the country, loses his man en route to Buenos Aires.

Leader Peter Vaughan
Diana Honor Blackman
Eberhardt Dennis McCarthy

Director: Ian Fordyce

Shakedown at Saramino

w Robert Stewart

Should his enemies ever find him, death will be swift for Hugo Valdes. When it appears that someone has discovered his hiding place, Garetta and Dallas have less than 12 hours to save Valdes's life.

Hugo Valdes Clifford Evans
Dai Morgan Glyn Owen
Tod Macoll Stratford Johns

Director: John Frankau

Festival of Fear

w John Warwick

An appeal for help from an old friend takes Garetta and Dallas to Brazil – and leads them into a manhunt for a dangerous secret which could, if disclosed, upset the balance of power between two rival gangs.

Lambetta Edwin Richfield
Carol Miranda Connel
Inspector Matson John Glyn-Jones

Director: Mark Lawton

Season Two

13 monochrome 60-minute episodes

The Little One Is Dangerous

w Robert Stewart

One of Garetta's agents is a traitor. Three of his team have been betrayed and lost their lives and Dallas must find the fourth agent before he too meets his death. But where should Dallas begin? Whom can he trust?

Ventura Hugh Burden
Connie Ann Castle
Hendrickson John Lee

Director: John Frankau

Threat from the Past

w Jordan Lawrence

Dallas must reach a former double-agent, now in hiding, before an enemy spy-ring gets to him first. It's a race against time. The enemy know Dallas, but the agent has no idea what or whom he's up against.

Tina Frieda Knorr
Colonel Santos Mark J. Roberts
Filipah Gary Hope

Director: Ian Fordyce

The Man from Carataz

w Lewis Davidson

Assigned to recover a highly-secret document from Don Enrique Broca, before his enemies reach him first and put the document up for sale to a foreign power, Dallas finds himself running a gauntlet of hostile guns.

Broca John Wentworth
Commandante Harry Walker
Major Grio Gerald Flood

Director: Christopher Hodson

The Burning Question

w Alan Prior

When a series of mysterious fires devastate a dock, Dallas is assigned to find the person responsible. He uncovers a firebug who is as dangerous as the flames he ignites – and finds himself trapped in a blazing warehouse.

Juarez Seymour Green
Manuel Cortez Arthur Hewlett
Juanita Jasmine Dee

Director: Peter Moffatt

The Death of Stefano

w Peter Yeldham

Dallas, searching for a vicious killer, finds himself the next target on the assassin's hit-list. With himself as a target, how much time does he have left to track down his unknown enemy?

Gomez Arthur White
Pedro Philip Madoc
Elsa Laurie Lee

Director: Christopher Hodson

The Second Man

w Peter Bryan

As a direct result of General Cuesta's request for help, Garetta cables Dallas to return to Buenos Aires – little knowing that it is a summons to death for his colleague.

General Cuesta Robert Sansom
Marcia Adrienne Posta
Doctor Philip Stone

Director: Ian Fordyce

Maggie

w Cedric Wells
When the San Felix Government requests Garetta's help to forstall a student uprising, Dallas finds himself facing sudden death among the student fraternity. Sinister forces are at work and the agent must find the people behind them.
Maggie Joyce Carey
Cardonna Donald Eccles
Fernando Paul Martin

Director: Peter Moffatt

The Eagle of San Gualo

w Alan Prior
In order to stop the friendly State of San Gualo falling into the hands of rebel forces, Dallas and Mike must unmask the identity of the traitor known only as 'The Eagle'.
Major Moreno Manning Wilson
Captain Felipe Geoffrey Palmer
Carimella Yvonne Romain

Director: Bill Turner

Vengeance at La Vina

w Don Matthews
It's the most dangerous assignment Dallas has undertaken: he must try to locate the whereabouts of a cattle-rustler – perhaps a killer – in the vast South American pampas and bring him to justice.
Stannard William Devlin
Lopez Ken Wynne
Elena Penelope Horner

Director: Geoffrey Hughes

The Life Stealers

w Larry Forrester
When a consignment of urgently needed drugs fails to reach Buenos Aires, Dallas, watched by an unknown enemy, must find the hijackers of what appears to be an impossible theft.
Galdos Gerald Flood
Colonel Robeldo Olaf Pooley
Captain Gonzales Hedger Wallace

Director: Christopher Hodson

Dangerous Project

w Thomas Clarke
Assigned to protect millionaire Harry Grant, Dallas learns that two unscrupulous people want him dead. There could be more. If so, when will they make their move and what kind of reception will Dallas get?
Harry Grant Alan Gifford
Lyn Grant Sandra Dorne
Philip Ryan Paul Maxwell

Director: Adrian Brown

Dance for Spies

w Angus Cooper
Suspicious that at least one member of a visiting ballet company may be working for the enemy, Dallas, playing a hunch, is given just 48 hours to prove his claim. After that time the dance company will fly home – with secret information.
Mikov John Bennett
Solnikov Charles Kay
Gorki Richard Burell

Director: Raymond Menmuir

Escape to Danger

w Patrick Cargill and Ian Shand
The order is given: 'Get rid of Garetta and Dallas.' By whom, no one knows, but the two men must find out, even if it means fighting a powerful and relentless enemy – one which has ordered them to be shot on sight!
Magella Bruce Barnabe
Informer Philip Madoc
Chita Diana King

Director: Adrian Brown

TOP SECRET
Producer: Jordan Lawrence
Music by: Laurie Johnson
(*Sucu-Sucu* theme by Laurie Johnson)
An Associated Rediffusion Network Production
26 monochrome 30-minute episodes
11 August – 10 November 1961
9 May – 20 July 1962
(USA: Syndicated 1961
13 episodes)

THE TOP SECRET LIFE OF EDGAR BRIGGS

The misadventures of Edgar Briggs, personal assistant to the Commander of the British Secret Intelligence Service (SIS) – and the most inept spy ever to grace the corridors of Whitehall!

Handed a file of classified information, Briggs would wreak havoc with the department's filing system (or accidentally run the paperwork through a shredder). Assigned to help his colleagues stake out a busy British Railways station he would destroy their carefully laid plans by finding himself aboard a nonstop train to Brighton.

Briggs was a walking disaster. A mistake. A bumbling idiot who had been transferred to his position by an error of paperwork (probably his own). Yet somehow, he always managed to get the right results and achieve the impossible by becoming the department's top counter-espionage agent.

REGULAR CAST

Edgar Briggs **David Jason**   *The Commander* **Noel Coleman**
Buxton **Michael Stainton**   *Jennifer Briggs* **Barbara Angell**
Spencer **Mark Eden**   *Cathy* **Elizabeth Councel**

A Dinner Date with Death

w Bernard McKenna and Richard Laing
Informed by Buxton that the 'other side' are plotting to kill the Commander, Briggs goes undercover as a restaurant waiter and ends up saving the Commander's life – but not before he lands himself, and a gun, in the soup.
Director: Bryan Izzard

The Defector

w Bernard McKenna and Richard Laing
Having tracked to a heliport two Russian agents suspected of organising escape routes to Moscow for agents on the run, Briggs accidentally switches on the airport's Tannoy system – and broadcasts his plans to capture them!
Director: Bryan Izzard

The Leak

w Bernard McKenna and Richard Laing
While attending a cocktail party with his wife, Briggs saves the day by handing a roll of 'classified' film to an enemy contact – the man believes he's getting film of a secret missile base but Briggs accidentally hands over his holiday film!
Director: Bryan Izzard

The Escape Route

w Bernard McKenna and Richard Laing
Assigned to discover who is behind an escape route, Briggs finds himself swimming in muddy water but nevertheless stumbles across the ringleader – and accidently rounds up the gang single-handed.
Director: Bryan Izzard

The Traitor

w Bernard McKenna and Richard Laing
Suspecting that Edwards, a clerk in the Documents Section, is responsible for betraying the department's agents to the enemy, Briggs exposes a network of traitors – by mistakenly arresting two 'innocent' men!
Director: Bryan Izzard

The Abduction

w Bernard McKenna and Richard Laing
When the Commander is abducted and
Briggs is left to engineer his escape, the
agent does so, but not until he has bumbled
his way through another mission and driven
the abductor's getaway car – and the
Commander – to safety.
Director: Bryan Izzard

The Exchange

w Bernard McKenna and Richard Laing
Busy redecorating his home, Briggs stops
his DIY activities to oversee an exchange of
spies between SIS and the East Germans and
finds himself face to face with enemy agents
– with only a paintbrush in his gun holster!
Director: Bryan Izzard

The Courier

w David Jason
Suspecting that a member of the
International Symphony Orchestra, a
pianist, has devised a clever scheme to
smuggle secret information to the KGB,
Briggs thwarts the man's plans – but not
before he finds himself singing in a radio
broadcast!
Director: Bryan Izzard

The KGB

w Bernard McKenna and Richard Laing
Assigned to organise the defection of a top
Russian nuclear scientist, Briggs, heavily
disguised, collects the woman in his car.
Taking a 'short cut' to evade his pursuers,
he gets lost in a multi-storey car park!
Director: Bryan Izzard

The Drawing

w Bernard McKenna and Richard Laing
Informed that someone at the Naval Section
is selling vital missile drawings to the
enemy, Briggs enters into a game of roulette
with the suspect and discovers that the
secret information has been incorporated
into the design of a £5 note – one which
Briggs hands over to the croupier as a tip!
Director: Bryan Izzard

The President

w Bernard McKenna and Richard Laing
When assassination attempts are made on
the life of a visiting president, our hero is
put in charge of security. A mistake: before
the day is through Briggs will pursue the
enemy in a bread van – and leave three
security cars crippled in a ditch!
Director: Bryan Izzard

The Appointment

w Bernard McKenna and Richard Laing
Given the task of training new recruit
Maxwell, Briggs teaches the man the tricks
of self-defence and marksmanship – but
forgets to load Maxwell's gun. A fortunate
move – Maxwell is a traitor and Briggs finds
himself looking down the wrong end of the
barrel.
Director: Bryan Izzard

The Contact

w Bernard McKenna and Richard Laing
Assigned to observe a meeting between an
SIS man and his enemy-contact and take
photographic evidence, Briggs causes chaos
at Victoria Station by hiding on a train –
and is carried off non-stop to Brighton!
Director: Bruce Gowers

THE TOP SECRET LIFE OF EDGAR
BRIGGS
Created by Bernard McKenna and
Richard Laing
Producer: Humphrey Barclay
A London Weekend Network Production
13 colour 30-minute episodes
15 September – 20 December 1974

UFO

Puppet-master Gerry Anderson's first outing into the live-action field, a series that portrayed the activities of the Secret Headquarters, Alien Defence Organisation (SHADO), a group of scientists and military personnel who were brought together in the mid-eighties to defend Earth from the threat of invasion by aliens from another world. The series' opening episode introduced the viewer to SHADO's multi-faceted defence systems: Control, the operational HQ of SHADO command, a vast computer-orientated complex situated hundreds of feet below a bogus film studio; Moonbase, the organisation's moon defence arm from which Interceptor jets would zoom into outer space to repel the enemy UFOs whenever the Earth-orbiting Space Intruder Detector (TIM) sighted alien spacecraft heading towards Earth; Skydiver, an atomic submarine from which Sky One, a jet-fighter, could be launched into the stratosphere (or repel the invaders in an undersea environment). The aliens themselves were green-skinned beings whose intention was to travel to Earth to capture humans and use their vital internal organs as spare parts to keep themselves alive.

A fast-paced, spectacular series complete with A1 special effects. The programme was given a raw deal by the ITV network, who obviously felt that the series' content was too provocative for 'family' viewing and hid it away in a late-night transmission spot. But you can't keep a good thing down and the series is now regarded as one of the best of its genre.

REGULAR CAST
CONTROL
Commander Ed Straker Ed Bishop   *Colonel Alec Freeman* George Sewell
Colonel Paul Foster Michael Billington
Colonel Virginia Lake Wanda Ventham   *Dr Jackson* Vladek Sheybal
MOONBASE
Lt Gay Ellis Gabrielle Drake   *John Harrington* Antonia Ellis
Nina Barry Dolores Mantez
SHADO PERSONNEL
Captain Carlin Peter Gordeno   *Lt Mark Bradley* Harry Baird
General Henderson Grant Taylor   *Skydiver navigator* Jeremy Wilkin

Identified

w Gerry and Sylvia Anderson, Tony Barwick
SHADO engages in its first battle with the enemy. Sky One cripples an alien ship which crash-lands in a lake. Straker's team capture its pilot, a strange blue-skinned humanoid – and the grim secret behind the aliens' plans are revealed.
Seagull co-pilot Shane Rimmer
Minister Basil Dignam
Lew Waterman Gary Myers

Director: Gerry Anderson

Exposed

w Tony Barwick

When an experimental plane being fight-tested by Paul Foster and his co-pilot is attacked and shot down by a UFO and the co-pilot loses his life, events lead Foster to a face to face confrontation with Ed Straker – and the start of a new career.

Paul Foster Michael Billington (Intro.)
Jackson Vladek Sheybal (Intro.)
Kofax Robin Bailey

Director: David Lane

The Cat with Ten Lives

w David Tomblin

When Jim Regan, a SHADO interceptor pilot, is captured by the aliens, taken aboard a UFO, and put through a grim medical test, the events bring sinister drama for the pilot and his wife – and deadly trouble for Ed Straker.

Regan Alexis Kanner
Jean Regan Geraldine Moffatt
Miss Holland Lois Maxwell

Director: David Tomblin

Conflict

w Ruric Powell

Convinced that the aliens have hidden a satellite among the flying debris of space which is being used to knock out his re-entry craft, Straker requests to have the space junk cleared, but General Henderson opposes his plea – and Foster disobeys orders to prove his chief's theory.

Maddox Drewe Henley
Spaceship pilot Gerard Norman
Spaceship navigator Alan Tucker

Director: Ken Turner

A Question of Priorities

w Tony Barwick

When Straker's son is knocked down by a car and the plane carrying the drug that can save his life is threatened because of a communications breakdown, the SHADO commander finds himself having to choose between his duty to his son and his duty to protect Earth.

Mary Suzanne Neve
John Barnaby Shaw
Mrs O'Connor Mary Merrall

Director: David Lane

E.S.P.

w Alan Fennell

A UFO evades SHADO interceptors and crash-lands on Earth close to the house of a man named Croxley, and Straker and Freeman find themselves facing death when Croxley is taken over by an alien – and given the power to read minds.

Croxley John Stratton
Stella Croxley Deborah Stanford
Doctor Ward Douglas Wilmer

Director: Ken Turner

Kill Straker!

w Donald James

Straker takes a split-second decision when a lunar module captained by Paul Foster and Frank Craig is attacked by a UFO. The vehicle manages to land safely – but Craig immediately attempts to kill Straker.

Craig David Sumner
Lt Ford Keith Alexander
Astronaut Harry Baird

Director: Alan Perry

Sub-smash

w Alan Fennell

When a UFO sinks a freighter and Straker realises that the alien vessels can travel underwater, he and Nina Barry join Skydiver One in a search for the UFO. But Skydiver is hit during an attack – leaving Straker and his team trapped.

Captain Waterman Gary Myers
Lt Chin Anthony Chinn
Lt Lewis Paul Maxwell

Director: David Lane

Destruction

w Dennis Spooner

Faced with an information blackout, when a Navy ship shoots down a UFO but refuses to allow Straker and Colonel Lake to investigate the alien vessel – the matter, he is told, is secret – Straker is determined to seek the truth.

Admiral Sherringham Edwin Richfield
Sarah Bosanquet Stephanie Beacham
Navy Captain Philip Madoc

Director: Ken Turner

The Square Triangle

w Alan Pattillo

When Straker deliberately allows a UFO to land in England, in the hope of capturing the craft and its pilot, he has no idea that he will soon become involved in a murderous love triangle and the death of an alien.

Cass Fowler Patrick Mower
Liz Newton Adrienne Corri
Alien Anthony Chinn

Director: David Lane

Close-up

w Tony Barwick

SHADO wait for the results of their latest experiment: a new electron telescope fitted to a tracking probe, which will allow them to photograph the alien's home planet and track a UFO to its origin in space.

Doctor Kelly Neil Hallett
Doctor Young James Beckett
Masters John Kelly

Director: Alan Perry

The Psychobombs

w Tony Barwick

When three average people are taken over by the aliens and are given superhuman strength in order to seek out and destroy the SHADO organisation, Straker's team face danger and death.

Linda Deborah Grant
Mason Mike Pratt
Clark David Collings

Director: Jeremy Summers

Survival

w Tony Barwick

The aliens land a UFO on the moon under the cover of a meteorite storm and an alien

blasts his way through the leisure dome, killing Bill Grant, Foster's close friend. Foster leads the mission to find the intruder – but finds himself marooned, far from Moonbase.

Alien Gito Santana
Tina Duval Suzan Farmer
Rescue pilot Ray Armstrong

Director: Alan Perry

Mindbender

w Tony Barwick

Why should two members of an interceptor crew suddenly go beserk and try to kill their colleagues, whom they believe to be their enemies? Straker must find the answer before the aliens take over Moonbase.

Beaver James Charles Tingwell
Dale Craig Hunter
Howard Byrne Stuart Damon

Director: Ken Turner

Flight Path

w Ian Scott Stewart

Forced into supplying secret data from SID – the Space Intruder Detector – because of his devotion to his wife who is being held hostage by the aliens, Moonbase operative Roper brings danger into Straker's life.

Paul Roper George Cole
Carol Roper Sonia Fox
Dawson Keith Grenville

Director: Ken Turner

The Man Who Came Back

w Terence Feely

The return of Craig Collings, a spacecraft pilot who was presumed dead and has been missing for two months, spells trouble for Straker and a shock for his girlfriend, when his reappearance portends danger to the SHADO organisation.

Craig Collings Derren Nesbitt
Miss Holland Lois Maxwell
Colonel Grey Gary Redmond

Director: David Lane

The Dalotek Affair

w Ruric Powell

The sudden failure of all radio and video equipment on Moonbase alarms Foster, who suspects that there is a fault in the geological scanner at the nearby research base run by the Dalotek company. He closes down the scanner – but the breakdown continues.

Tanner Clinton Greyn
Jane Carson Tracy Reed
Mitchell David Weston

Director: Alan Perry

Timelash

w Terence Feely

When Straker and Colonel Lake are attacked by a UFO, the SHADO commander finds himself fighting an unbeatable enemy. Time stands still and SHADO headquarters is locked in a time barrier – from which there is no escape.

Turner Patrick Allen
Miss England Norma Ronald
Casting agent Ron Pember

Director: Cyril Frankel

Ordeal

w Tony Barwick

When Paul Foster gets drunk the night before entering a SHADO health-farm and falls asleep in the sauna, then wakes up to find aliens raiding the establishment and Straker ordering a UFO to be shot down, the SHADO member finds further troubles before his nightmare ends.

Sylvia Graham Quinn O'Hara
Joe Franklin David Healy
Astronaut Mark Hawkins

Director: Ken Turner

Court Martial

w Tony Barwick

It's a clash between Straker's loyalty and Foster's courage. Paul Foster stands accused of being responsible for a security leak and he is sentenced to death. Straker refuses to accept his guilt, and sets out to prove his innocence.

Webb Jack Hedley
Diane Pippa Steele
Mason Neil McCallum

Director: Ron Appleton

Reflections in the Water

w David Tomblin

It's a nightmare situation for the team of Straker and Freeman. To investigate reports of 'flying fish', the two men take Skydiver deep into the sea – and find themselves in a strange world in which they come face to face with their doubles.

Skipper Conrad Phillips
Skydiver Captain David Warbeck
Lt Anderson James Cosmo

Director: David Tomblin

Computer Affair

w Tony Barwick

The death of an astronaut has strange implications for Straker and his SHADO operatives when the Moonbase team are recalled to Earth to give evidence against a computer which suggests that 'love' was responsible for the man's death.

Ken Matthews Michael Mundell
Doctor Murray Peter Burton
Lt Bradley Harry Baird

Director: David Lane

Confetti Check A-O.K.

w Tony Barwick

The birth of a child to one of the female SHADO operatives causes Straker to think back to his own marriage. In the early seventies he was already involved in the creation of SHADO – and the work cost him the love of his wife.

Mary Suzanne Neve
CIA man Shane Rimmer
Porter Frank Tregear

Director: David Lane

The Sound of Silence

w David Lane and Bob Bell

When SHADO track a UFO heading towards Earth and it lands near the home of

international showjumper Russel Stone, who then disappears, Paul Foster believes that the alien responsible has taken refuge in a nearby lake.
Stone Michael Jayston
Anne Stone Susan Jameson
Alien Gito Santana

Director: David Lane

The Responsibility Seat

w Tony Barwick
Left in charge of SHADO headquarters, Colonel Freeman takes command when three alien spacecraft are detected heading for the moon. Straker, meanwhile, is busy on a wild goose chase.
Jo Fraser Jane Merrow
Film director Ralph Bell
Stuntman Royston Rowe

Director: Alan Perry

The Long Sleep

w David Tomblin
When a young girl, Cathy Ross, regains consciousness after being in a coma for 10 years, Straker becomes personally involved in the case. The girl had muttered something about a UFO before her long sleep – and Straker wishes to learn more.
Catherine Tessa Wyatt
Tim Christian Roberts
Bomb disposal expert Christopher Robbie

Director: Jeremy Summers

UFO
Created by: Gerry and Sylvia Anderson
Producer: Reg Hill
Executive producer: Gerry Anderson
Music by: Barry Gray
Special effects: Derek Meddings
An ATV/ITC Entertainments/Century 21 Television Production
26 colour 60-minute episodes
16 September 1970 – 15 March 1973
(USA: Syndicated 1972)

UNDERMIND

Odd in both content and episode duration (the complete series ran to only 11 stories), this unusual 'mind-bender' series depicted how Drewe Heriot and his wife Anne set out to discover what had made their brother-in-law Detective Sergeant Frank Heriot, a hard-working, conscientious policeman, throw up his job and begin to act strangely. As they delved deeper into Frank's strange actions, they discovered that people from all walks of life had suddenly become victims of the unseen threat – an unknown menace that had struck at respectable members of the community and led them into acts of scandal and violence against their loved ones.

When it arrived, the dénouement – that a secret organisation was attempting to undermine public confidence in the British Government and the institutions that formed its backbone, by a mind-bending process – was somewhat less than satisfactory, but while it ran, the programme was gripping stuff.

REGULAR CAST

Drewe Heriot **Jeremy Wilkin**   Anne Heriot **Rosemary Nicols**
Frank Heriot **Jeremy Kemp**   Prof. Randolph **Dennis Quilley**

Onset of Fear

w Robert Banks Stewart

Why has Detective Sergeant Frank Heriot, a family man with no problems, suddenly begun to act strangely? When his brother Drewe and his brother's wife Anne unexpectedly arrive from Australia, the couple find themselves plunged into a deadly web of menace. Concerned about Frank's sanity, Drewe decides to make some enquiries into his brother's activities.
Dr Polson Paul Maxwell
Police Insp. Frank Mills
Police Sergeant Alec Clunes

Director: Bill Bain

Flowers of Havoc

w Robert Banks Stewart   *(From a story by Jon Manchip White)*
Drewe Heriot begins his search for clues to explain his brother's odd behaviour – but places both his own life and that of his wife Anne in danger.
Prof. Randolph Dennis Quilley (Intro.)
Charles Ogilvie Glynn Edwards
Rev. Anderson Michael Gough

Director: Peter Potter

The New Dimension

w David Whittaker

Are they one step nearer to discovering their unknown enemy, or just a few paces from danger? Drewe and Anne find further clues to the nightmare situation that is threatening to ruin the lives of their friends.
Smith Garfield Morgan
Fenway Patrick Allen
Marianne Gordon Judy Parfitt

Director: Bill Bain

Death in England

w Hugh Leonard

Why should respectable Army wives suddenly become involved in scandal? And what is behind the note Drewe has received that threatens his life? Two further pieces of the jigsaw puzzle – but can Drewe complete the full picture?
Sir Geoffrey Savage Robert James
Captain Morrell Mark Burns
Rumbold Terence Lodge

Director: Peter Potter

Too Many Enemies

w Robert Banks Stewart

Who is the mystery man in the hospital bed, being attended by an equally inquisitive surgeon? Drewe and Anne are in attendance and overhear a terrible revelation – one that places their lives at risk.
Dr Hepworth Tenniel Evans
Tubby Chambers Dave King
Dr Burath Leslie Nunnery

Director: Peter Daws

Intent to Destroy

w John Kruse

Drewe becomes involved in the mystery of a man who tries to kill a national television celebrity during a live programme – and then commits suicide before millions of viewers.
Ursula Smythe Jan Holden
Victor Liberton Peter Barkworth
TV celebrity Eamonn Andrews

Director: Bill Bain

Song of Death

w Bill Strutton

The coroners' inquests point to death by natural causes, but Drewe and Anne know differently. Can they prove it before they find themselves immersed in a spiral of madness?
John Rossleigh Jeremy Burnham
Dr Christian David Bauer
Dr Spring John Wentworth

Director: Laurence Bourne

Puppets of Evil

w Max Sterling

When evil masquerades as innocence and stalks a sunny English garden, Drewe and Anne unearth another clue to the unknown threat which is affecting the community. They also find death – and an ally.

Benton Derek Nimmo
Kate Orkney Katherine Blake
Cyrus Benton Norman Tyrell

Director: Patrick Dromgoole

Test for the Future

w David Whittaker

The outcome of the deliberations by two violent men offers serious consequences for the whole country: Britain's future is being rehearsed – and Drewe and Anne find themselves marked down as victims.

Kennedy Barrie Ingham
Lodge Dudley Jones
Davies Murray Taylor

Director: Laurence Bourne

Waves of Sound

w Robert Holmes

Drewe and Anne Heriot find themselves racing against time to thwart the evil plans of their mysterious enemy. When all seems lost, a voice from the past tips the scales in their favour – but can they prevent the final onslaught?

Sir Geoffrey Tillinger John Barron
James George Moon
Dr Whittaker Ruth Dunning

Director: Raymond Menmuir

End Signal

w Robert Holmes

The list of names is finally complete and the picture becomes clearer. But who is the mysterious figure in the background? And is the threat really over?

Thallon George Baker
Killick Barry Warren
Reynolds Richard Owens

Director: Peter Potter

UNDERMIND
Producer: Michael Chapman
Script consultant: Robert Banks Stewart
An ABC Weekend Television Network Production
11 monochrome 60-minute episodes
8 May – 17 July 1965

VAN DER VALK

Based on the books by Nicholas Freeling, this Amsterdam-based detective series depicted the exploits of Dutch detective Van Der Valk.

Notable for spawning 'Eye Level', a number one hit record for the Simon Park Orchestra, which topped the charts on 29 September 1973 and stayed at that position for four weeks.

REGULAR CAST

Van Der Valk Barry Foster   *Arlette* Susan Travers (Seasons 1 and 2)
Arlette Joanna Dunham (Season 3)
Kroon Michael Latimer   *Samson* Nigel Stock

Season One
6 colour 60-minute episodes

One Herring's Not Enough

w Michael Chapman

Dutch detective Van Der Valk investigates a baffling murder mystery in which an innocent man confesses to murder and a phone call from a stranger adds confusion to what is an already confusing case.
Kroon Michael Latimer (Intro.)
Arlette Susan Travers (Intro.)
Brigadier Mertens Alain Haines

Director: Dennis Vance
Designer: David Marshall

Destroying Angel

w Michael Chapman

Two seemingly unconnected incidents: a car crash in France 20 years ago and a case of suspected murder by poisoning in a sleazy Amsterdam boarding house give Van Der Valk cause for concern when he has to find the connecting link.
Dr Jagermann James Cairncross
Yvonne Patricia Quinn
Mulder Walter Brown

Director: Graham Evans
Designer: Peter Le Page

Blue Notes

w Geoffrey Gilbert

When a world famous violinist arrives in Amsterdam and is greeted by death threats and a dried-up bunch of flowers, Van Der Valk finds himself trying to solve the mystery. His investigations are hampered when the man refuses to help the police.
Jan Servas Edgar Wreford
Westermann Peter Pratt
Djiker Julian Somers

Director: Mark Miller
Designer: David Marshall

Elected Silence

w Geoffrey Gilbert

The Dutch detective finds himself investigating the intriguing case behind a death threat to a pop group. Somewhere in Amsterdam lurks someone with murder on his mind – Van Der Valk must find the would-be assassin before he can carry out his threat.
Brigadier Mertens Alain Haines
Samson Martin Wlydeck
Harkemer Michael Sheard

Director: Douglas Camfield
Designer: Tony Borer

Thicker Than Water

w Geoffrey Gilbert

When a body wrapped in a shroud is dredged from a canal, Van Der Valk finds himself investigating a murder with a difference – and the telephone line between The Hague and London provides him with a vital clue to the killer's identity.
Dr Roest Michael Lees
Peter Hackforth Richard Smith
Hilda Ruysbroek Joyce Heron

Director: David Wickes
Designer: Roger Allan

The Adventurer

w Michael Chapman

A hunch tells Van Der Valk that for someone bad news is just around the corner, and the detective is proved right when a young man dies in a rush-hour accident. The detective's dilemma: was it an accident or murder?
Wolf Gebhardt Paul Eddington
Paul Moen Harold Goldblatt
Peter Jamal Nigel Anthony

Director: Peter Duguid
Designer: Bernard Spencer

Season Two
7 colour 60-minute episodes

A Death by the Sea

w Philip Broadley

Van Der Valk investigates the death by drowning of a prominent Dutch businessman. What appears to be a case of suicide takes on dramatic overtones when a second girl is found dead in similar circumstances.

Van Teeseling Patrick Allen
Halsbeck Sydney Tafler (Intro.)
Lucienne Joanna Dunham

Director: Don Leaver
Designer: Neville Green/Mike Hall

A Man of No Importance

w Arden Wynch

When the body of a man wearing only
pyjama bottoms is discovered on a canal
barge, the Dutch detective must find out
how it got there, and overcome the
reluctance of his superiors, who decide they
don't want him to continue on the case.
Why?
Grenech Ian Fairburn
Yvonne Karin Fernald
Kemeling Kevin Stone

Director: Douglas Camfield
Designer: Neville Green/Mike Hall

A Rose for Mr Reinhart

w Peter Yeldham

When his wife Arlette says that she believes
that Karen Seger, a woman she and the
children sometimes meet in the park, may
be in great danger, Van Der Valk, after a
busy day, pays her no heed – until events
prove Arlette right and murder occurs.
Karen Seger Carolyn Courage
Reinhart Arne Gordon
Van Houten Denis Lil

Director: Mike Vardy
Designer: Neville Green/Mike Hall

A Dangerous Point of View

w Jeremy Paul

Van Der Valk investigates the death by
stabbing of a man in a flat that does not
belong to him. But who could have known
that the man would be there? Was the
man's death caused by an intruder – or a
cleverly planned murder?
Zondag John Quarmby
Mrs Hackman Pamela Duncan
Mrs Zondag Sally Sanders

Director: James Goddard
Designer: Neville Green/Mike Hall

Season for Love

w Philip Broadley

When rich American Margo Roslin seeks
Van Der Valk's help to find Ko Brinkman, a
young man missing in Amsterdam, the
detective finds himself involved in one of
the most intriguing cases he has ever
investigated.
Margo Lisa Daniely
Huismann John Bailey
Bekker Ronald Leigh-Hunt

Director: Mike Vardy
Designer: Neville Green/Mike Hall

Rich Man, Poor Man

w David Butler

Why should a man insist on taking the
responsibility for a factory accident in which
a worker has died, when Van Der Valk is
certain that someone else was responsible?
Finding the answer leads the detective into
dangerous waters.
Leo David Webb
Mulder Christopher Benjamin
Peko Kovacic Keith Buckley

Director: Douglas Camfield
Designer: Neville Green/Mike Hall

The Rainbow Ends Here

w Philip Broadley

Van Der Valk finds himself facing a moral
problem over a kidnapping: the victim has a
tycoon brother who regards the payment of
ransom as a deal between himself and the
kidnappers – no police involvement. Should
the detective stand aside and allow the man
to continue?
Ernest Christopher Timothy
Judith Stolle Lalla Ward
Evert Stolle Donald Burton

Director: Graham Evans
Designer: Neville Green/Mike Hall

Season Three

12 colour 60-minute episodes

Enemy

w Paul Wheeler

When Van Der Valk and his wife Arlette
receive death threats, the detective finds

himself looking for a mysterious hidden enemy who could strike at any second.
Hanson Jim Norton
Tahlen Donald Gee
Marken Brian Gwaspari

Director: Mike Vardy

Accidental

w Ted Childs
When Rokin, the Chief Prosecutor in an international scandal over charges of corruption in high places, disappears, Van Der Valk must find out if the man has been bought off by the villains of the piece.
Rokin William Russell
Mrs Rokin Hildegard Neil
Father Bosch Patrick Troughton

Director: Tom Clegg

The Runt

w Leslie Sands
When a young thief admired by Van Der Valk suddenly becomes wealthy and appears to have connections in high places, the Dutch detective must find out how the miracle occurred — without treading on too many toes.
Albert de Vink Richard Pasco
Kurt Maurice O'Connell
Jan Ken Kitson

Director: Mike Vardy

Wolf

w Philip Broadley
When the body of a young German is discovered murdered in his bed and the apartment is littered with clues, Van Der Valk must ask himself if there is one clue too many? Has the killer left a deliberate trail to his identity?
Paul Sam Dastor
Magda Lorna Heilbron
Ressel John Price

Director: Mike Vardy

Man of Iron

w Michael Chapman
When one of Van Der Valk's close friends suffers a series of apparently pointless and petty thefts, the Dutch detective takes investigative action — and uncovers a murder and a confusion of identities.
Paul Philip Sager
Doff Michael Da Costa
Pastor Weavers Morris Perry

Director: William Brayne

Everybody Does It

w Philip Broadley
When Arlette finds it difficult to resist the temptation to buy a cheap — but dubious — bargain, her poor judgement lands her husband up to his neck in trouble with a crime syndicate.
Nick Scholtz Maurice Colbourne
Ehrlich John Standing
Marijka Suzy Kendall

Director: Ben Bolt

Face Value

w Robert Wales
A dead painter and a valuable collection of pictures lead Van Der Valk to take a look behind the scenes into the world of art forgery. He finds more than he's bargained for when someone makes an attempt on his life.
Roberts Denis Lil
De Groote Clifford Rose
Piet Gobel Ian Lowe

Director: Mike Vardy

Dead on Arrival

w Patrick O'Brien
When a Dutch clairvoyant, adept at solving crimes for the police, is requested to visit England to help in an eight-year-old murder inquiry, Van Der Valk is staggered when the man foresees startling revelations.
Johnny Palmer Bob Hoskins
Millie Sanger Pamela Salem
James Michael Culver

Director: Ted Childs

The Professor

w Roger Marshall
Two spoiled adolescent children hunting for new kicks add up to trouble for Van Der

Valk when a burglary takes place and the detective is given some insight into the not-so-innocent background of their wealthy parents.
Boersma Ian Hendry
Mrs Visser Lisa Daniely
Treesje Phoebe Nicholls

Director: Tom Clegg

In Hazard

w Paul Wheeler
When a beautiful women tells him a story he finds hard to believe, the Dutch detective finds himself with two choices – to play a hunch, or to adopt the orthodox procedure and let the case take its own course.
Margit Jan Harvey
Wim Michael Petrovitch
Johannes Jon Croft

Director: William Brayne

Gold Plated Delinquents

w Roger Marshall
Two spoiled adolescent children hunting for new kicks add up to trouble for Van Der Valk when a burglary takes place and the detective is given some insight into the not so innocent background of their wealthy parents.
Boersma Ian Hendry
Mrs Visser Lisa Daniely
Treesje Phoebe Nicholls

Director: Tom Clegg

Diane

w Philip Broadley
When a woman tries to bury her past, but it overtakes her in Amsterdam, Van Der Valk finds himself being drawn into some strange – and dangerous – incidents that neither he nor the girl find beneficial to their health.
Diane Jane Merrow
Jean William Ellis
Ranieri Alexander Davion

Director: Mike Vardy

VAN DER VALK
Originally created by: Nicholas Freeling
Producers: Michael Chapman (Season 1)
Robert Love (Season 2)
Geoffrey Gilbert (Season 3)
Associate producers: Geoffrey Gilbert (Season 1)
Chris Burt and Mary Morgan (Season 3)
Executive producer: Lloyd Shirley (Seasons 1 to 3)
George Taylor (Season 3)
Seasons One and Two produced by Thames Television
Season Three by Euston Films Ltd
On location in Amsterdam and at Teddington Studios
Networked
25 colour 60-minute episodes
13 September – 18 October 1972
29 August – 10 October 1973
5 September – 21 November 1977

VIRGIN OF THE SECRET SERVICE

The blood and thunder exploits of Captain Robert Virgin of the British Secret Service, a courageous soldier of fortune and Britain's top secret agent during the Northwest Indian Frontier campaign of the 1900s.

A man of incredible bravery who would have laid down his life to protect Britain's honour (and was frequently asked to do so by his superior, Colonel Shaw-Camberley), Virgin fought his way through his adventures with a stiff upper lip and considerable panache. Using the sword, the knife, or his fists (he was highly proficient with all three), he blazed his way across the frontier protecting the honour of his regiment and saving his beautiful (though thoroughly emancipated) Edwardian lady assistant, Mrs Virginia Cortez, from the dastardly overtures of their adversaries, the diabolically evil Karl Von Brauner and his equally evil (and deranged) aide, Klaus Striebeck, both of whom shared an intense hatred for the upright and intrepid hero, and forced him to face unspeakable tortures whenever he fell into their hands.

REGULAR CAST

Captain Robert Virgin Clinton Greyn
Mrs Virginia Cortez Veronica Strong
Doublett (Virgin's batman) John Cater   *Von Brauner* Alexander Dore
Klaus Striebeck Peter Swannick   *Colonel Shaw-Camberley* Noel Coleman

Dark Deeds on the Northwest Frontier

w Nicholas Palmer
Together with Doublett, Captain Virgin travels by balloon to the Northwest Frontier. His mission: to save India for the Empire – and outwit the diabolical plans of his old adversary, the thoroughly evil Karl Von Brauner.
Theodor Green Cyril Luckham
Princess Katerina Patience Collier
Poll Green Margo Andrew

Director: Paul Bernard

Russian Roundabout

w Basil Dawson
During a mission to St Petersburg, Virgin finds a Prince who dreams of becoming Emperor of India. In a mission filled with intrigue and mystery, the agent puts paid to the man's dreams and once again foils Von Brauner's aspirations to greatness.
Prince Rouvaloff Michael Coles
Countess Kolinsky Gabrielle Drake
Count Kolinsky Desmond Llewellyn

Director: John Sichel

Entente Cordiale

w Betty Lambda
When the Entente Cordiale is threatened by von Brauner's attempts to have the Duke of Albany killed when he visits the opera, Virgin and Mrs Cortez, impersonating the Duke and his wife, find themselves held prisoner by a group of Chinese white slave traders.
Duke of Albany Frederick Peisley
Prince Frederick Rober Crewson
Cigarette Katherine Schofield

Director: Paul Bernard

The Great Ring of Akba

w Ted Willis
Captain Virgin travels to Arabia alone, to meet a cruel usurper face to face – and finds himself held prisoner by Von Brauner and Klaus Striebeck, who put him through their 'ordeal by animal': a deep pit filled with venomous reptiles.
Omar Hassin John Collin
Akba governor John Horsley
Abu Mark Colleano

Director: Paul Bernard

The Amazons

w Basil Dawson
Virgin, Doublett and Mrs Cortez arrive in Brazil and find themselves caught up in a plot to seize Inca gold. Lurking in the background are their enemies Brauner and Striebeck – who have a few nasty surprises in store for the trio.

Manuel Sean Lynch
Dermot O'Rourke John Webb
Atahualpa Tom Kempinski

Director: Robert D. Cardona

The Rajah and the Suffragette

w Anthony Steven and Vincent Tilsley
When Virgin learns of a dastardly plot to
entomb a British regiment in the valley of
Sindra-Lal, he enters a Rajah's school of love
to rescue a missing suffragette and save the
honour of his regiment.
Rajah Rodney Bewes
Hon. Maud La Motte Jennie Linden
Vizier Roger Delgado

Director: John Sichel

Persuasion of a Million Drops

w Ted Willis
A man who dreams of making the whole
world a province of China by using a new
and terrifying invention places Virgin's life
at stake when he subjects our hero to the
horrific Chinese torture of a thousand drips
of water on the head.
Chu Chen Yu Norman Scace
Professor Lemaire Michael Lees
Mrs Cherry White Marji Lawrence

Director: Robert D. Cardona

Pride of Assassins

w Anthony Steven
Virgin is assigned to hunt down the
brilliant French marksman Bobo le Mec,
who has been hired to assassinate the King
of Croatia. To do so, Virgin infiltrates Le
Mec's school for killers – but his cover is
blown and he is taken prisoner.
Bobo le Mec Eugene Deckers
Domino George Innes
Gandolfio Tommy Godfrey

Director: Paul Bernard

Across the Silver Pass of Gusri Song

w Ted Willis
Caught in a web of prophecy while
searching for a missing comrade, Virgin
finds himself imprisoned in a cage above a
red-hot cauldron of fire. His only hope of

escape is Doublett – but he, too, has been
captured and subjected to torture.
Shung Si Georgina Hale
Yuente Edward Brayshaw
The Oracle Ewen Solon

Director: Josephine Douglas

The Pyramid Plot

w Basil Dawson
Who is behind the disappearance of seven
British officers in Cairo? Virgin and his
team are stumped – until the beautiful Lady
Clea Merrion offers to help them. But can
she be trusted – or do her true loyalties lie
elsewhere?
Lady Merrion Lisa Daniely
Major Zaki Peter Birrel
Lord Merrion William Kendal

Director: Robert D. Cardona

A Fate Worse Than Death

w Stuart Douglas
When Von Brauner and Striebeck's latest
scheme threatens the very heart of British
rule in India, Captain Virgin and his friends
expose their arch-enemies' diabolical plans
with a clever scheme of their own.
Pell Oscar Quitak
Stikow Sean Lynch
Vlakon Michael Wynne

Director: Henrich Hirsch

The Professor Goes West

w Nicholas Palmer
Attempting to engineer the release of an
Englishman being held prisoner in deepest
Texas, Captain Virgin comes face to face
with Big Jack, the fastest gun in the West –
and is ordered to prepare for a gunfight at
dawn.
Big Jack David Bauer
Jesse Al Mancini
Professor Whitestone Carlton Hobbs

Director: Robert D. Cardona

Wings over Glencraig

w John Roberts
In a desperate bid to save the world from a
new and terrifying invention, Captain
Virgin and his friends travel to Scotland to

take on the greatest assignment they have yet faced – the threat of Lord Glencraig.
Lord of Glencraig John Grieve
Prince Luigi Ian White
Taro Milton Reid

Director: Robert D. Cardona

VIRGIN OF THE SECRET SERVICE
Created by: Ted Willis
Produced by: Josephine Douglas
Theme music by: Larry Adler
An ATV Network Production
13 colour 60-minute episodes
28 March – 20 June 1968

WHITE HUNTER

By far and away the best of the heroics-in-the-jungle oaters produced in the late fifties, this lively series of African Adventures (based on the real life exploits of John A. Hunter, 'the surest and fastest shot in Africa') took little time to establish itself as a viewers' favourite – mainly due to some exciting scripts and the sincere approach of its subject material.

REGULAR CAST
John Hunter Rhodes Reason

Dead Man's Tale	Operation Transfer
The Valley of the Dead	The Stepfathers
Big Bwana Brady	The Long Knife
Gun Duel	The Plague
One Fatal Weakness	Deadfall
Let My People Go	The No-account
Day of Reckoning	The Lonely Place
The Treasure of Tipu Tib	Marked Man
The Lion's Paw	The Fugitive
Rogue Man	Run to Earth
Web of Death	Out of the Wind
The Trophy	The Prisoner
The Jackals	Forest of the Night
A Moment of Truth	The Squire of the Serengeti
Inside Story	The General
Pegasus	Voodoo Wedding
Killer Leopard	Sister My Spouse
Decision	This Hungry Hell
No Survivors	Girl Hunt
Second Dealer	

WHITE HUNTER
Producer: Norman Williams
Music by: Philip Green
Story editor: Don Mullally
An ITP Independent Production Ltd
Filmed on location in Africa and at Twickenham Studios

39 monochrome 30-minute episodes
17 September 1958 – 17 October 1960
(USA: Syndicated 1958)

WIDOWS

The story of four women, three of whom found their lives changed when their criminal husbands were killed by explosives they intended to use to blast their way into a security van which were accidentally detonated when their getaway van crashed into another vehicle during the hold-up attempt, and a fourth girl whose husband had died from a drugs overdose.

Having been handed the key to her late husband Harry's bank safety deposit box and found detailed plans for further robberies planned by him, Dolly Rawlins faced demands from her husband's rivals, the Fisher Brothers, to sell the documents to them. Instead, she called in Shirley Miller and Linda Perelli, the two other widows, and suggested that they pull off the next job planned by Harry themselves. Realising that her late husband's plans called for four people, Dolly added Bella O'Reilly, a friend of Linda's, to the roster.

Watched from the sidelines by Resnick, the policeman investigating the attempted security van hold-up, and under the noses of the Fisher Brothers, the women managed to pull off the job successfully – but that's when their troubles really began.

Invigorating stuff. The first story paved the way for a second six-parter which found similar acclaim.

REGULAR CAST

Dolly Rawlins **Ann Mitchell**   *Linda Perelli* **Maureen O'Farrell**
Shirley Miller **Fiona Hendley**   *Bella O'Reilly* **Eva Mottley** (First story)
Bella O'Reilly **Debbie Bishop** (Second story)   *Harry Rawlins* **Maurice O'Connell**

Series One: The Adventure Begins

w Lynda La Plante   *(A 6-part story)*
Dolly Rawlins, Linda Perelli and Shirley Miller share one thing in common – their husbands, members of a gang who were robbing security vans, were all killed during their last raid.

Inviting Linda and Shirley to join her, Dolly decides to carry out the next robbery planned by her late husband Harry. Having recruited Bella O'Reilly, a stripper and prostitute whose husband died of a drugs overdose, the four women proceed with their plan to rob a security van and make their escape to South America – unaware that the police (and a dark figure in the background) are keeping a close watch on their activities.

The women successfully pull off the heist, but now face the daunting task of getting their suitcases stuffed with money through the customs at Rio.
Det. Insp. Resnick **David Calder**
Harry Rawlins **Maurice O'Connell**
(Intro. ep. 3)
Det. Sgt Fuller **Paul Jesson**
Eddie Rawlins **Stanley Meadows**

Director: **Ian Toynton**

Series Two: The Adventure Ends

w Lynda La Plante   *(A 6-part story)*
Six weeks after pulling off the security van raid, Dolly and her friends are looking forward to a life of ease and luxury in Rio. But Dolly's husband Harry isn't dead and he

arrives in Rio to force Linda Perelli to tell him where the girls have hidden the money.

In a desperate attempt to save their ill-gotten fortune, the girls return to London and offer Harry a share of their loot to get him off their backs — only to discover that Rawlins is planning another robbery. If they can find out the details of Harry's plans, they may be able to set a trap to have him caught and put away — but things don't quite work out, and Shirley falls victim to their own trap.

Vic Morgan **Stephen Yardley**
Det. Insp. Fuller **Paul Jesson**
Mickey Tesco **Andrew Kazamia**
Det. Insp. Frinton **Jim Carter**

Director: **Paul Annett**

WIDOWS
Created by: Lynda La Plante
Producers: Linda Agran (Season 1)
Irving Teitelbaum (Season 2)
Executive producers: Verity Lambert
(Season 1)
Linda Agran and Johnny Goodman
(Season 2)
A Thames Television Network Production
12 colour 60-minute episodes
16 March – 20 April 1983
3 April – 8 May 1985

WILDE ALLIANCE

From the pen of Ian Mackintosh (the man who gave us *The Sandbaggers*), and Yorkshire Television (the company who produced *The Main Chance*), the series centred on the lives of detective fiction writer Rupert Wilde and his wife Amy, a couple who often found themselves involved in real-life mysteries which were every bit as compelling and unusual as those dreamed up by Rupert for his books.

REGULAR CAST

Rupert Wilde **John Stride**   *Amy Wilde* **Julia Foster**
Christopher Bridgewater **John Lee**   *Bailey* **Patrick Newell**

Question of Research
Flower Power
Too Much, Too Often
Things That Go Bump
The Private Army of Colonel Stone
Danny Boy
Well Enough Alone
Express from Rome
A Game for Two Players
Time and Again
Affray in Amsterdam
A Suspicion of Sudden Death
Some Trust in Chariots

WILDE ALLIANCE
Producer: Ian Mackintosh
Executive producer: David Cunliffe
Writers: Ian Mackintosh, Philip Broadley,
Anthony Skene, Jacques Gillies,
John Bowen
Directors: Derek Bennett, Bob Hird, Marc
Miller, David Reynolds, Matthew
Robinson, Leonard Lewis
A Yorkshire Television Network Production
13 colour 60-minute episodes
17 January – 11 April 1978

WOLF TO THE SLAUGHTER

Based on the Inspector Wexford novels by Ruth Rendell, this 4-part murder mystery introduced viewers to the latest in a long line of television sleuth stories adapted from the printed page.

A somewhat old-fashioned, Shakespeare-quoting country copper obsessed by his weight, Wexford found himself investigating a baffling case – a murder, without a body.

REGULAR CAST

Det. Chf Insp. Wexford   George Baker
Det. Insp. Burden   Christopher Ravenscroft
Det. Con. Drayto   Robert Reynolds

Episode 1

w Clive Exton

When Detective Chief Inspector Wexford receives an anonymous letter informing him that 'a girl named Ann has been killed by a small, dark young man named Geoff Smith', he little realizes that his investigation will turn out to be among the most baffling of his career.
Monkey Matthews Russell Hunter
Rupert Margolis Nicholas Gecks
Ruby Branch Carmel McSharry

Director: John Davies
Designer: Christine Ruscoe

Episode 2

w Clive Exton

Who is Ann? Who is Geoff Smith? Who sent the anonymous letter? Inspector Wexford and his team appear nowhere nearer solving the mystery. Perhaps if they found the missing girl's body things would become clearer. But where to begin?
Linda Grover Kim Thompson
Mrs Kirkpatrick Stephanie Fayerman
Mr Kirkpatrick Christopher Ellison

Director: John Davies
Designer: Christine Ruscoe

Episode 3

w Clive Exton

A gold lighter is found and provides a vital clue to the girl's disappearance. Its inscription reads 'For the girl who lights up my life', but which girl? And where is the body?
Mr Scatcherd Raymond Francis
Mrs Penistan Jean Heywood
Mrs Anstey Mitzi Rogers

Director: John Davies
Designer: Christine Ruscoe

Episode 4

w Clive Exton

Wexford and his colleagues now know the identity of Anita Margolis's killer, but there is a problem – he died some 18 months before the murder! Are the detectives investigations at a halt?
Russell Cawthorne Donald Hewlett
Mrs Cawthorne Hal Dyer
Richard Fairfax Marc Sinden

Director: John Davies
Designer: Christine Ruscoe

WOLF TO THE SLAUGHTER
Based on characters created by: Ruth Rendell
Producer: John Davies
Executive Producer: Graham Benson
A TVS Network Production
4 colour 60-minute episodes
2 – 23 August 1987

WORZEL GUMMIDGE

The hilarious adventures of Worzel Gummidge, a walking, talking scarecrow who got up to all kinds of mischievous antics in the company of his equally exotic friends, Aunt Sally, an animated fairground doll, and The Crowman, Worzel's creator.

Adapted from the books of Barbara Euphan Todd by Keith Waterhouse and Willis Hall, this popular children's series (a hit with children and grown-ups alike) was one of television's most successful creations. The character proved so popular that when the series was cancelled after a four-year run, a new set of stories (financed and produced in New Zealand) were filmed for transmission in 1987. (The pilot story for this, *Worzel Gummidge Down Under*, rounds off this entry.)

REGULAR CAST

Worzel Gummidge **Jon Pertwee**   *Aunt Sally* **Una Stubbs**
The Crowman **Geoffrey Bayldon**   *John* **Jeremy Austin**   *Sue* **Charlotte Coleman**
Mr Peters **Mike Berry**   *Mrs Braithwaite* **Megs Jenkins**
Mr Braithwaite **Norman Bird**   *Dolly Clothes-Peg* **Lorraine Chase**
Mrs Bloomsbury-Barton **Joan Sims**   *Mr Shepherd* **Michael Ripper**
Colonel Bloodstock **Thorley Walters**

Season One
7 colour 30-minute episodes

Worzel's Washing Day

w Keith Waterhouse and Willis Hall
Worzel meets young John and Sue Peters when they move to the country with their father. It isn't long before they discover that their turnip-headed friend has a very mischievous nature.
Director: James Hill

A Home Fit for Scarecrows

w Keith Waterhouse and Willis Hall
When Worzel decides to set up home and large amounts of domestic items suddenly disappear from houses in the village, the law investigates.
Mr Shepherd Michael Ripper (Intro.)
PC Parsons Norman Mitchell (Intro.)

Director: James Hill

Aunt Sally

w Keith Waterhouse and Willis Hall
Enter Aunt Sally, a fairground doll whom Worzel has worshipped from afar – but who has no intention of becoming the scarecrow's regular girlfriend.
Aunt Sally Una Stubbs (Intro.)
Mrs Bloomsbury-Barton Joan Sims (Intro.)

Director: James Hill

The Crowman

w Keith Waterhouse and Willis Hall
When Worzel falls headlong in love with a female scarecrow in the next field and asks the Crowman to create a new head for him to impress her, our hero finds that good looks bring unexpected results.
Director: James Hill

A Little Learning

w Keith Waterhouse and Willis Hall
Calamity strikes the village community. Worzel loses one of his turnip heads – the one which makes him clever.
Director: James Hill

Worzel Pays a Visit

w Keith Waterhouse and Willis Hall
John and Sue find themselves involved in
another of Worzel's outlandish adventures –
this time with hilarious results.
Director: James Hill

The Scarecrow Hop

w Keith Waterhouse and Willis Hall
When Worzel and Aunt Sally decide to go
to the village dance and Aunt Sally is
repossessed by her creator, Mr Shepherd,
Worzell's marriage plans go up in smoke.
Director: James Hill

Season Two

8 colour 30-minute episodes

Worzel and the Saucy Nancy

w Keith Waterhouse and Willis Hall
When Worzel falls for Saucy Nancy, the
figurehead on a galleon, and Aunt Sally
arrives unexpectedly, our hero expects
trouble – and gets it.
Saucy Nancy Barbara Windsor

Director: James Hill

Worzel's Nephew

w Keith Waterhouse and Willis Hall
Worzel's delight at meeting Pickles, his
young Cockney nephew, is short-lived when
the youngster proves to be more than a
match for his uncle.
Pickles Wayne Norman

Director: James Hill

A Fishy Tale

w Keith Waterhouse and Willis Hall
When Worzel decides to take up fishing, he
catches more than he bargained for – to the
cost of his fellow anglers and Mrs
Bloomsbury-Barton.
Director: James Hill

The Trial of Worzel Gummidge

w Keith Waterhouse and Willis Hall
When Mr Braithwaite decides to buy an
electronic scarecrow and Worzel tries to

prove his worth as a crow-scarer, it leads to
disaster – and a trial before his fellow
scarecrows.
Sgt Beetroot Bill Maynard (Intro.)

Director: James Hill

Very Good, Worzel

w Keith Waterhouse and Willis Hall
When Mrs Bloomsbury-Barton throws a
party to impress her neighbour Lady
Partington and her 'butler' and 'parlour
maid' turn out to be Worzel and Aunt
Sally, disaster is guaranteed.
Director: James Hill

Worzel in the Limelight

w Keith Waterhouse and Willis Hall
It's a talent contest with a difference.
Worzel and Aunt Sally take part and once
again disaster ensues – but this time with a
difference.
Director: James Hill

Fire Drill

w Keith Waterhouse and Willis Hall
When Mrs Bloomsbury-Barton plans a
village bonfire – with Worzel as the perfect
guy – John and Sue must think of a way to
rescue their turnip-headed friend.
Dafthead Frank Marlborough (Intro.)

Director: James Hill

The Scarecrow Wedding

w Keith Waterhouse and Willis Hall
When Aunt Sally finally agrees to marry
Worzel and make him 'the 'appiest
scarecrow this side of Foggy Bottom', all the
scarecrows gather to celebrate the wedding –
but Saucy Nancy's arrival heralds mischief.
Saucy Nancy Barbara Windsor
Pickles Wayne Norman
Cobber Gummidge Alex Scott
Sgt Beetroot Bill Maynard

Director: James Hill

Season Three

8 colour 30-minute episodes

Moving On

w Keith Waterhouse and Willis Hall
When Worzel's girlfriend Aunt Sally
decides to leave Scatterbrook Farm and join

a travelling funfair, Worzel sets off in hot pursuit of his sweetheart.
Director: James Hill

Dolly Clothes-Peg

w Keith Waterhouse and Willis Hall
Jealousy rears its head when Worzel meets a dressmaker's dummy called Dolly Clothes-Peg and Aunt Sally is smitten by the fairground's strongman.
Dolly Clothes-Peg Lorraine Chase (Intro.)
Strongman David Lodge

Director: James Hill

A Fair Old Pullover

w Keith Waterhouse and Willis Hall
When Worzel goes shopping for new clothes and finds himself as the showpiece for a department store window, his antics attract more than just customers.
Director: James Hill

Worzel the Brave

w Keith Waterhouse and Willis Hall
When hot-tempered Colonel Bloodstock calls Worzel a coward, the scarecrow sets out to prove his worth — with highly amusing results.
Colonel Bloodstock Thorley Walters (Intro.)

Director: James Hill

Worzel's Wager

w Keith Waterhouse and Willis Hall
When Worzel decides to prove that Ratter, the Crowman's dog, can outrun other whippets, by entering Ratter in a race, the odds are stacked against our hero.
Bookmaker Jimmy Jewel

Director: James Hill

The Return of Dafthead

w Keith Waterhouse and Willis Hall
When Dafthead, the scarecrow Worzel made to avoid being used as a bonfire guy, reappears and takes over Worzel's position in Ten Acre field, our hero challenges his creation to a duel.

Dafthead Frank Marlborough

Director: James Hill

Captain Worzel

w Keith Waterhouse and Willis Hall
When Worzel and Aunt Sally join Mr Shepherd on a boating holiday and Aunt Sally's old rival Saucy Nancy turns up, Worzel finds himself in stormy waters.
Saucy Nancy Barbara Windsor

Director: James Hill

Choir Practice

w Keith Waterhouse and Willis Hall
Worzel and Aunt Sally join the church choir and Worzel's furry friends find the Harvest Festival offerings to their liking.
Director: James Hill

A Cup o' Tea an' a Slice o' Cake

w Keith Waterhouse and Willis Hall
(A 60-minute special)
Worzel's Christmas adventure finds him helping 'Santy Claus' find his way back to the North Pole. Along the way our hero encounters Saucy Nancy and her crew of pirates, becomes involved in a duel with rival scarecrow Bogle McNeep and ends his adventures at the Scarecrow Ball.
Colonel Bloodstock Thorley Walters (Last)
Sgt Beetroot Bill Maynard (Last)
Saucy Nancy Barbara Windsor (Last)
Pickles Wayne Norman (Last)
Bogle McNeep Billy Connolly

Director: James Hill

Season Four
7 colour 30-minute episodes

Muvvers' Day

w Keith Waterhouse and Willis Hall
When Worzel decides that he too needs a mother, the Crowman has his work cut out appeasing his turnip-headed creation.
Sarah Pigswill Beryl Reid

Director: James Hill

The Return of Dolly Clothes-Peg

w Keith Waterhouse and Willis Hall
When Dolly Clothes-Peg bakes Worzel a special cake but Aunt Sally grabs it, Worzel finds himself having to decide whom he wants as his wife – Dolly or Sally.
Dolly Clothes-Peg Lorraine Chase (Last)

Director: James Hill

The Jumbly Sale

w Keith Waterhouse and Willis Hall
Worzel decides he needs a new suit. Where better to find it than at the 'Jumbly Sale' – but will Aunt Sally like the 'new' Worzel?
Director: James Hill

Worzel in Revolt

w Keith Waterhouse and Willis Hall
When Aunt Sally appears to be totally dominating our hero, the Crowman tells Worzel to assert himself. He does so – with disastrous results.

Director: James Hill

Will the Real Aunt Sally . . . ?

w Keith Waterhouse and Willis Hall
When Worzel sees two Aunt Sallies – so alike he can't tell the difference between them – Scatterfield Farm becomes the scene of some hilarious antics.
Aunt Sally II Connie Booth

Director: James Hill

The Golden Hind

w Keith Waterhouse and Willis Hall
When Worzel meets Jolly Jack, a nautical figurehead, and Aunt Sally begins to display a decided preference for the newcomer's charms, our hero decides to play his trump card.

Jolly Jack Bernard Cribbins

Director: James Hill

Worzel's Birthday

w Keith Waterhouse and Willis Hall
Just when it appears that Worzel's friends have forgotten his birthday, our hero is delighted to be asked to two birthday parties in his honour.
Director: James Hill

Worzel Gummidge Down Under

w Keith Waterhouse and Willis Hall
(A 90-minute pilot episode)
The first of Worzel's adventures down under finds our hero heading for New Zealand in pursuit of his beloved Aunt Sally, who has been sold to a museum. Along the way he meets the King of the Scarecrows (and his terrifying band of 'zombie' followers) and the evil scarecrow-maker – who kidnaps Aunt Sally, leaving Worzel to put on his brave head to find and rescue her.

Director: James Hill

WORZEL GUMMIDGE
Producer: James Hill
Executive producer: Lewis Rudd
Associate producer: David Pick
Music by: Dennis King
A Southern Television Production
30 colour 30-minute episodes and 60-minute special
25 February – 8 April 1979
6 January – 24 February 1980
1 November – 20 December 1980
27 December 1980
12 June – 31 July 1981

WORZEL GUMMIDGE DOWN UNDER
Not yet transmitted

THE XYY MAN

The adventures of William 'Spider' Scott, a reformed cat-burglar, whose talents were used for clandestine activities by British Intelligence.

Unlike most people, Scott had one too many of those sex

chromosomes that make up each male cell in the body – a genetic fault in his make-up that made him a natural criminal. (Normal people have an exact balance of chromosomes, 23 'x' and 23 'y', but Spider had an extra 'y', which made him of above average height and tended to make him predisposed to crimes against property rather than violence.) It was this talent that led Fairfax – a mysterious figure connected with British Intelligence – to seek him out and hand him a proposition that would appeal to Spider's sense of adventure: £15,000 to be deposited in a Swiss bank account, if Spider could break into a foreign embassy and steal a metal box, then hand it over to Fairfax's representative. (The money would only be paid for a successful mission. Should Spider be caught, Fairfax could offer him no protection from the law.)

Making his debut in this series was Police Sergeant George Bulman – but a vastly different Bulman from the character who would later be seen in *Strangers* and *Bulman* (see entries elsewhere). The Bulman of this series was a violent rule-bender who pursued a confession and conviction with crass disregard for legal rights – a far cry from the quirky, glove-wearing, sympathetic character he later became.

REGULAR CAST

Spider Scott **Stephen Yardley**   *Maggie Parsons* **Vivienne McKee**
Sgt Bulman **Don Henderson**   *DC Willis* **Dennis Blanch**
Fairfax **Mark Dignam** replaced by *Laidlaw* **William Squire**

Season One
3 colour 60-minute episodes

Episode One: The Proposition

w Ivor Marshall   *(A 3-part story)*
Released from prison, cat burglar Spider Scott vows to go straight. But Fairfax of British Intelligence has other plans for Spider's talents – and Police Sergeant Bulman stands in the shadows, waiting to pounce should Spider make an illegal move.
Maggie Parsons **Vivienne McKee** (Intro.)
Fairfax **Mark Dignam** (Intro.)
Sgt Bulman **Don Henderson** (Intro.)
DC Willis **Dennis Blanch** (Intro.)

Episode Two: The Execution

w Ivor Marshall
Having successfully broken into the 'impregnable' building for Fairfax, Spider finds himself on the run from foreign agents who are eager to learn where he has hidden a valuable photograph which could be used to bring down the British Government.
Li Tshien **Eric Young**
Superintendent Cummings **Alan Rowe**
Ray Lynch **Paul Freeman**

Episode Three: The Resolution

w Ivor Marshall
Playing a lone hand, Spider takes on Fairfax at his own game. But offering to sell Li Tshien the photograph could cost Spider his life: British Intelligence, the CIA and the Chinese all seek the incriminating photograph – and are prepared to kill to obtain it!
Jomo Ibbon **Don Warrington**
Groot **Peter Birrel**
Brian **Ron Boyd**

Director: **Ken Grieve**
Designer: **Chris Wilkinson**

Season Two

10 colour 60-minute episodes

Friends and Enemies

w Tim Aspinall   *(A 3-part story)*
Having bought a half-share in a small
executive aircraft charter company, Spider is
surprised when one of his first customers is
an acquaintance from his criminal days. He
considers it coincidence – until one of his
friends turns up dead in the Thames.
Laidlaw William Squire (Intro.)
Penny Fiona Curzon (Intro.)
Reisen Brian Croucher (Intro.)
Don Stevens Oliver Maguire (Intro.)

The Missing Civil Servant

What connection does Reisen have with
American crime? And has Spider's old
adversary really changed his spots? Spider
thinks not, but Reisen has a forceful way of
asking for favours – and should the reformed
cat burglar refuse to help, he too could lose
his life.
Warren Johnny Shannon
Dodson Arnold Diamond
Rod Barkley Johnson

The Big Bang

w Tim Aspinall
Pressured into helping some criminals get a
man out of the country by using his aircraft,
Spider decides to play along, thinking it
will help him find his friend's killer. He
doesn't know that he's being set up as a
decoy for a large – and deadly –
international operation.
Bob Stephen Davey
Norah Pamela Cundell
Tony James Coyle

Director: Ken Grieve
Designer: Chris Wilkinson

At the Bottom of the River

w Tim Aspinall
Having settled accounts with his best
friend's killer, Spider finds himself
implicated in robbery and murder, with
Laidlaw and the newly-promoted Detective

Sergeant Bulman after his blood. Will the
XYY factor come to Spider's aid?
Laidlaw William Squire (Exit)
Reisen Brian Croucher (Exit)
Penny Fiona Curzon (Exit)

Director: Ken Grieve
Designer: Chris Wilkinson

When We Were Very Greedy

w Murray Smith   *(A 2-part story)*
Asked to serve on a committee investigating
prison conditions, Spider agrees to do so –
but is asked to resign by the committee
chairman. Intrigued, Spider decides to
break into the man's office building – and is
caught by the police as he leaves.
Peter Thresher Ronald Lewis
Cindy Thresher Jennifer Lonsdale
Fairfax Mark Dignam (Return)

Now We Are Dead

w Murray Smith
Convinced that the police received a tip-off,
Spider decides to strike up an acquaintance
with Thresher's daughter in the hope of
finding the solution – but within hours
several attempts are made on his life.
Tom Moody Glyn Houston
Lord Brasenose Anthony Benson
Roberts Derrick O'Connor

Director: Carol Wiles
Designer: Jack Robinson

Whisper Who Dares

w Murray Smith
When Spider finds his girlfriend threatened
by a man who has organised several
murders, the cat burglar finally runs the
man to ground – in a confrontation that
could lead to either man losing his life.
Damien Alan Gaunt
Tom Moody Glyn Houston
Brooks Barry Andrews

Director: Carol Wiles
Designer: Jack Robinson

Law and Order

w Edward Boyd   *(A 3-part story)*
Under threat of a murder charge, Spider
finds himself coerced back to prison to do an

'inside job' for Fairfax. His assignment is to spring one of the prisoners – a task which goes smoothly and leads Spider into an international conspiracy.

Norden Peter Marinker
Dero Norman Jones
Fairfax Mark Dignam (Last)

The Detrimental Robot

w Edward Boyd

Having made good their escape, Spider and his friend find themselves on the run from the police – and some very dangerous men. During their flight, his fellow traveller disappears and Spider finds himself face to face with his pursuers.

Det. Sgt King Ray Mort
Det. Insp. Pearson John Price
Torliss Christopher Jenkinson

THE XYY MAN
Created by: Kenneth Royce
Producer: Richard Everitt
A Granada Television Network Production
13 colour 60-minute episodes
3 – 17 July 1976
27 June – 29 August 1977

A View to a Death

w Edward Boyd

Hearing that Spider is being held, Maggie discovers where he is and goes to him. To her surprise, Spider is released. The reason soon becomes clear: Spider is asked to risk his life again – this time to capture an enemy agent.

Lucy Mahler Sarah Bullen
Jacob Mahler Tony Jay
David Wiseman Garrick Hagon

Director: Alan Grint
Designer: Chris Wilkinson

YOUNG SHERLOCK
The Mystery of the Manor House

Notable for being Granada producer Michael Cox's first association with a Sherlock Holmes television series (on this occasion Cox was Executive Producer), this children's drama series, based on the life of the famous Baker Street detective when he was a schoolboy, preceded Steven Spielberg's *Young Sherlock Holmes and the Pyramid of Fear* by four years.

REGULAR CAST
Sherlock Guy Henry

The Young Master

w Gerald Frow   *(A 60-minute story)*
Young schoolboy Sherlock Holmes sets out on an adventure that will involve him in the mystery of the Manor House.

Mrs Turnbull June Barry
Mrs Cunliffe Jane Lowe
Natty Dan Davy Kaye

Director: Nicholas Ferguson
Designer: Margaret Coombs

The Gipsy Calls Again

w Gerald Frow
With Natty Dan dead, Sherlock, convinced
of foul play, is determined to find his killer
and discover the identity of 'Old Mo',
mentioned by Dan in his last message.
Colonel Turnbull Donald Douglas
Aunt Rachel Heather Chasen
Uncle Gideon John Fraser

Director: Nicholas Ferguson
Designer: Margaret Coombs

The Riddle of the Dummies

w Gerald Frow
Helped by Tom Hudson, Sherlock unravels
the mystery of 'Ol Mo'. Hours later,
Sherlock and John Whitney are witnesses to
a strange event.
Tom Hudson Robert Grange
John Whitney Tim Brierley
Doctor Sowerbutts David Ryder-Futcher

Director: Nicholas Ferguson
Designer: Margaret Coombs

A Singular Thorn

w Gerald Frow
Having solved the mystery of the rose
thorn, Sherlock decides to pursue his
investigation to its logical conclusion.
Charity Eva Griffith
Jasper Moran Christopher Villiers
The Munchi Stefan Kalipha

Director: Nicholas Ferguson
Designer: Margaret Coombs

The Woman in Black

w Gerald Frow
Events at the Manor House take a strange
turn and Sherlock and John Whitney
witness a remarkable experiment by their
enemies.

Ranjeet Lewis Fiander
Sgt Grimshaw Tom Chatto
Albert Bates Brian Orrell

Director: Nicholas Ferguson
Designer: Margaret Coombs

The Glasscutter's Hand

w Gerald Frow
Outmanoeuvred at every turn, Sherlock and
John Whitney find their lives in great peril
in their attempts to bring their enemies to
justice.

Director: Nicholas Ferguson
Designer: Margaret Coombs

The Unexpected Visitors

w Gerald Frow
One step away from solving the mystery,
Sherlock finds the tables turned when his
Aunt Rachel receives some unexpected
visitors.
Captain Cholmondeley Andrew Johns
Newbugs Ian McCurrach
William Creasley Michael Irwin

Director: Nicholas Ferguson
Designer: Margaret Coombs

The Eye of the Peacock

w Gerald Frow
Having solved the Manor House mystery,
Sherlock finds himself receiving the thanks
of a very important person, H. M. Queen
Victoria.
Queen Victoria Marina McConnell
Charlotte Zuleika Robson

Director: Nicholas Ferguson
Designer: Margaret Coombs

YOUNG SHERLOCK
Producer: Pieter Rogers
Executive producer: Michael Cox
A Granada Television Network Production
8 colour episodes
(1 60-minute and 7 30-minute episodes)
31 October – 19 December 1982

ZODIAC

A light-hearted thriller series that observed what might happen if a policeman, David Gradley (the sceptic), and an astrologer, Esther Jones (the practitioner), combined forces to use stargazing as an alternative to forensics to catch crooks.

REGULAR CAST

David Gradley **Anton Rodgers**   *Esther Jones* **Anouska Hempel**

Death of a Crab

w Roger Marshall

Astrology is strictly for the birds. That's the emphatic view of policeman David Gradley – until he meets beautiful, young astrologist Esther Jones, and his ideas get knocked for six. If only Bradley had read his horoscope one fateful Sunday, his whole future might have been different . . .

Parker **Peter Childs**
Aikman **John Rhys-Davies**
Mrs Letts **Frances Cuka**

Director: **Raymond Menmuir**
Designer: **Bill Palmer**

The Cool Aquarian

w Roger Marshall

If Cathy Selby had read her horoscope that fateful Thursday, she might never have been kidnapped . . .

Cathy Selby **Deborah Fairfax**
Mark Braun **George Baker**
George Sutton **Bill Maynard**

Director: **Don Leaver**
Designer: **David Ferris**

The Strength of the Gemini

w Philip Broadley

If Paul Deering had read his horoscope that Thursday, his lucrative, smooth-talking career might not have ended so abruptly . . .

Paul Deering **Norman Eshley**
Elizabeth Clarmont **Jenny Handley**
Toby **Charles Lloyd Pack**

Director: **James Ferman**
Designer: **Peter Le Page**

Saturn's Rewards

w Pat Hoddinott

If Martin Seacombe had read his horoscope that day, a murder might never have been committed . . .

Martin Seacombe **Ian Ogilvy**
Susan Meade **Dinah Sheridan**
Richard Meade **Peter Vaughan**

Director: **Don Leaver**
Designer: **Philip Blowers**

Sting, Sting, Scorpio!

w Roger Marshall

If Peggy had read her horoscope that morning, the Brighton Hotel robber might never have been caught . . .

Peggy **Susie Blake**
Madame Lavengro **Anne Dyson**
Brian Godfrey **Robert Powell**

Director: **Piers Haggard**
Designer: **Peter Le Page**

The Horns of the Moon

w Peter Yeldham

If only Tony Weston had read his horoscope, his father might not have caught a chill; a will might never have been signed; and Tony wouldn't be facing a murder charge . . .

Tony Weston **Peter Egan**
General Weston **Peter Jones**
Julie Prentiss **Michele Dotrice**

Director: **Joe McGrath**
Designer: **Neville Green**

ZODIAC
Created by Jackie Davis and Roger Marshall
Producer: Jacqueline Davis
Executive producer: Kim Mills
Script editor: Roger Marshall
A *Thames Television Network Production*
6 colour 60-minute episodes
25 February – 1 April 1974

THE ZOO GANG

The exploits of four World War II French Resistance fighters who found themselves reunited 30 years later to fight crime and intrigue in Europe. Four service veterans who re-formed to use their resources, guile and experience to become modern-day Robin Hoods who stole from criminals and distributed the spoils of their 'crimes' to the needy.

Organiser of the team was Captain Tommy Devon, codename the Elephant, who ran a small jewellery business on the French Riviera. Lending his electronics expertise to the gang's cause was former American secret agent Stephen Halliday, codename the Fox, now a New York business executive. Madame Manouche Roget, codename the Leopard (and widow of Claude Roget, 'The Wolf', who was a member of the Resistance until his death at the hands of the Gestapo, and whose death the gang had sworn to avenge) ran a bar in Nice. An expert with explosives, her safe-cracking talents were put to good use by Tommy and Co. Rounding up the quartet was ex-Canadian Air Force Lieutenant Alec Marlowe, codename the Tiger, whose wizardry with mechanics kept the show on the road.

Appearing in most episodes was French policeman Lt George Roget, Mamouche's son. Despite suspecting that his mother and her friends were up to 'something' (he recognised old 'Zoo Gang' tricks as those spoken about by his mother), he ignored their activities and allowed them to pull off jobs without reporting his suspicions to his superior.

Star-studded though it was, the series failed to live up to expectations. The enterprise folded after 6 stories.

REGULAR CAST

Tommy Devon John Mills   *Stephen Halliday* Brian Keith
Manouche Roget Lilli Palmer   *Alec Marlowe* Barry Morse
Lt Georges Roget Michael Petrovitch
Jill Burton (Tommy's niece) Seretta Wilson

Revenge Postdated

w Reginald Rose

The Gestapo had dubbed them 'The Zoo Gang' because of their French Resistance-adopted animal names. They had been betrayed to the Nazis and found themselves imprisoned and tortured. Thirty years later Tommy Devon recognises the man entering his shop as Maurice Boucher, the Nazi who had him arrested and tortured. Tommy contacts his Resistance comrades and they plan their revenge. The Zoo Gang are back in business.

Boucher Walter Gotell
Calvin Smith Henry McCarthy
Harry Crane Gordon Tanner

Director: Sidney Hayers

Mindless Murder

w Howard Dimsdale

Three apparently motiveless murders on the French Riviera lead the Zoo Gang to uncover an extortion racket. But in order to expose the ringleaders and protect the lives of two famous film stars, Manouche must set herself up as the killers' next target.

Lynn Martin Ingrid Pitt
Anthony Martin Clinton Greyn
Jean Alex Scott

Director: Johnny Hough

African Misfire

w Peter Yeldham

When a deposed African president's art collection is stolen on its way to an auction in France, the Zoo Gang make plans to recover it. Their interest is a matter of principle: the proceeds of the sale were earmarked for African famine relief – or so they're led to believe.

Jacques Picard Kieron Moore
General Naganda Nathan Dambuza
Jombote Earl Cameron

Director: Sidney Hayers

The Counterfeit Trap

w John Kruse

It's a daring plan: to steal forged money to pay for smuggled gold. That's their intention, but playing two ends against the middle is a game fraught with danger – as Alec Marlowe discovers to his cost.

Judge Gautier Peter Cushing
Brigitte Gautier Jacqueline Pearce
Paul Sabot Philip Madoc

Director: Johnny Hough

The Lion Hunt

w Sean Graham

The arrest by the French of El Leon, a Latin American revolutionary viewed as a hero by most of the world, proves to be an embarrassment to the French Government. The media are demanding his release, but to accede to their wishes could spark off an international incident. Solution: call in the Zoo Gang – but is it that simple?

Dupont Leo Genn
Pedro Roger Delgado
De Broux Ferdy Mayne

Director: Sidney Hayers

The Twisted Cross

w William Fairchild

Informed that Schroeder, a Nazi officer, has received – and concealed – a Nazi fortune in gold, the Zoo Gang set out to recoup the treasure and use the proceeds from its sale to help those more needy than themselves.

Schroeder Bernard Kay
Helene Schroeder Ann Lynn
Andre Tim Hardy

Director: Johnny Hough

THE ZOO GANG
Based on a novel by Paul Gallico
Producer: Herbert Hirshman
Music by: Ken Thorne
(Zoo Gang Theme by Paul and
Linda McCartney)
*An ATV Television Network Production
for distribution by ITC*
6 colour 60-minute episodes
5 April – 10 May 1974
(USA: NBC July – August 1975)